WORLD REPORT

2020

EVENTS OF 2019

Printed in the United States of America

ISBN-13: 978-1-64421-005-5

Cover photo: *Protesters in Hong Kong, June 5, 2019.*
© 2019 Chris McGrath/Getty Images

Back cover photo: *Claudio Jose da Silva, the coordinator of the "Forest Guardians" of Caru Indigenous Territory, Maranhao State, at the bank of the Pindare River in June 2018. The Guardians are Tenetehara Indigenous people who patrol the land to detect illegal logging and report it to the authorities.*
© 2018 Brent Stirton/Getty Images for Human Rights Watch

Cover and book design by Rafael Jiménez

www.hrw.org

Human Rights Watch defends the rights of people worldwide.

We scrupulously investigate abuses, expose facts widely, and pressure those with power to respect rights and secure justice.

Human Rights Watch is an independent, international organization that works as part of a vibrant movement to uphold human dignity and advance the cause of human rights for all.

Human Rights Watch began in 1978 with the founding of its Europe and Central Asia division (then known as Helsinki Watch). Today it also includes divisions covering Africa, the Americas, Asia, Europe and Central Asia, the Middle East and North Africa, and the United States. There are thematic divisions or programs on arms; business and human rights; children's rights; crisis and conflict; disability rights; the environment and human rights; international justice; lesbian, gay, bisexual, and transgender rights; refugee rights; and women's rights.

The organization maintains offices in Amman, Amsterdam, Beirut, Berlin, Bishkek, Brussels, Chicago, Geneva, Goma, Hong Kong, Johannesburg, Kiev, Kinshasa, London, Los Angeles, Miami, Moscow, Nairobi, New York, Paris, San Francisco, São Paulo, Seoul, Silicon Valley, Stockholm, Sydney, Tokyo, Toronto, Tunis, Washington DC, and Zurich, and field presences in more than 50 other locations globally.

Human Rights Watch is an independent, nongovernmental organization, supported by contributions from private individuals and foundations worldwide. It accepts no government funds, directly or indirectly.

HUMAN RIGHTS WATCH

Table of Contents

Foreword

World Report 2020 is Human Rights Watch's 30th annual review of human rights practices around the globe. It summarizes key human rights issues in more than 100 countries and territories worldwide, drawing on events from late 2018 through November 2019.

In his keynote essay, Human Rights Watch Executive Director Kenneth Roth examines the increasingly dire threat to the global system for protecting human rights posed by the Chinese government under President Xi Jinping. Deepening and increasingly sophisticated domestic repression show that China's leaders view human rights at home as an existential threat. That, in turn, has led Beijing to see international laws and institutions for the defense of human rights as an existential threat.

As a result, Chinese authorities seek to censor criticism of China overseas, mute attention to human rights in its global engagements, and weaken global rights mechanisms. At stake is a system of governance built on the belief that every person's dignity deserves respect—that regardless of official interests, limits exist on what states can do to people.

Noting that global institutions are built in part "on the belief that every person's dignity deserves respect, that regardless of the official interests at stake, there are limits to what states can do to people," Roth concludes that China is not simply a new and emerging power finding its place, but a country that poses an existential threat to the international human rights system.

The rest of the volume consists of individual country entries, each of which identifies significant human rights abuses, examines the freedom of local human rights defenders to conduct their work, and surveys the response of key international actors, such as the United Nations, European Union, African Union, United States, China, and various regional and international organizations and institutions.

The book reflects extensive investigative work that Human Rights Watch staff undertook in 2019, usually in close partnership with human rights activists and groups in the country in question. It also reflects the work of our advocacy team, which monitors policy developments and strives to persuade governments and international institutions to curb abuses and promote human rights. Human Rights Watch publications, issued throughout the year, contain more detailed accounts of many of the issues addressed in the brief summaries in this volume. They can be found on the Human Rights Watch website, www.hrw.org.

As in past years, this report does not include a chapter on every country where Human Rights Watch works, nor does it discuss every issue of importance. The absence of a country or issue often simply reflects staffing or resource limitations and should not be taken as commentary on the significance of the problem. There are many serious human rights violations that Human Rights Watch simply lacks the capacity to address.

The factors we considered in determining the focus of our work in 2019 (and hence the content of this volume) include the number of people affected and the severity of abuse, access to the country and the availability of information about it, the susceptibility of abusive forces to influence, and the importance of addressing certain thematic concerns and of reinforcing the work of local rights organizations.

The World Report does not have separate chapters addressing our thematic work but instead incorporates such material directly into the country entries. Please consult the Human Rights Watch website for more detailed treatment of our work on children's rights; women's rights; arms and military issues; business and human rights; health and human rights; disability rights; the environment and human rights; international justice; terrorism and counterterrorism; refugees and displaced people; and lesbian, gay, bisexual, and transgender people's rights; and for information about our international film festivals.

The book was edited by Danielle Haas, senior editor at Human Rights Watch, with assistance from Naimah Hakim, Program associate. Grace Choi, director of publications and information design, oversaw production of visual elements and layout.

[illegible]

[illegible]

[illegible]

[illegible]

[illegible]

China's Global Threat to Human Rights

By Kenneth Roth, *Executive Director, Human Rights Watch*

> ***It doesn't matter where I am, or what passport I hold.***
> ***[Chinese authorities] will terrorize me anywhere,***
> ***and I have no way to fight that.***
>
> —UYGHUR MUSLIM WITH EUROPEAN CITIZENSHIP, WASHINGTON, SEPTEMBER 2019

China's government sees human rights as an existential threat. Its reaction could pose an existential threat to the rights of people worldwide.

At home, the Chinese Communist Party, worried that permitting political freedom would jeopardize its grasp on power, has constructed an Orwellian high-tech surveillance state and a sophisticated internet censorship system to monitor and suppress public criticism. Abroad, it uses its growing economic clout to silence critics and to carry out the most intense attack on the global system for enforcing human rights since that system began to emerge in the mid-20th century.

Beijing was long focused on building a "Great Firewall" to prevent the people of China from being exposed to any criticism of the government from abroad. Now the government is increasingly attacking the critics themselves, whether they represent a foreign government, are part of an overseas company or university, or join real or virtual avenues of public protest.

No other government is simultaneously detaining a million members of an ethnic minority for forced indoctrination and attacking anyone who dares to challenge its repression. And while other governments commit serious human rights violations, no other government flexes its political muscles with such vigor and determination to undermine the international human rights standards and institutions that could hold it to account.

If not challenged, Beijing's actions portend a dystopian future in which no one is beyond the reach of Chinese censors, and an international human rights system so weakened that it no longer serves as a check on government repression.

To be sure, the Chinese government and Communist Party are not today's only threats to human rights, as the Human Rights Watch World Report shows. In many armed conflicts, such as in Syria and Yemen, warring parties blatantly disregard the international rules designed to spare civilians the hazards of war, from the ban on chemical weapons to the prohibition against bombing hospitals.

Elsewhere, autocratic populists gain office by demonizing minorities, and then retain power by attacking the checks and balances on their rule, such as independent journalists, judges, and activists. Some leaders, such as US President Donald Trump, Indian Prime Minister Narendra Modi, and Brazilian President Jair Bolsonaro, bridle at the same body of international human rights law that China undermines, galvanizing their publics by shadow boxing with the "globalists" who dare suggest that governments everywhere should be bound by the same standards.

Several governments that in their foreign policies once could be depended upon to defend human rights at least some of the time have largely abandoned the cause. Others, faced with their own domestic challenges, mount a haphazard defense.

Yet even against this disturbing backdrop, the Chinese government stands out for the reach and influence of its anti-rights efforts. The result for the human rights cause is a "perfect storm"—a powerful centralized state, a coterie of like-minded rulers, a void of leadership among countries that might have stood for human rights, and a disappointing collection of democracies willing to sell the rope that is strangling the system of rights that they purport to uphold.

Beijing's Rationale

The motivation for Beijing's attack on rights stems from the fragility of rule by repression rather than popular consent. Despite decades of impressive economic growth in China, driven by hundreds of millions of people finally emancipated to lift themselves out of poverty, the Chinese Communist Party is running scared of its own people.

Outwardly confident about its success in representing people across the country, the Chinese Communist Party is worried about the consequences of unfettered popular debate and political organization, and thus afraid to subject itself to popular scrutiny.

As a result, Beijing faces the uneasy task of managing a huge and complex economy without the public input and debate that political freedom allows. Knowing that in the absence of elections, the party's legitimacy depends largely on a growing economy, Chinese leaders worry that slowing economic growth will increase demands from the public for more say in how it is governed. The government's nationalist campaigns to promote the "China dream," and its trumpeting of debatable anti-corruption efforts, do not change this underlying reality.

The consequence under President Xi Jinping is China's most pervasive and brutal oppression in decades. What modest opening had existed briefly in recent years for people to express themselves on matters of public concern has been decisively closed. Civic groups have been shut down. Independent journalism is no more. Online conversation has been curtailed and replaced with orchestrated sycophancy. Ethnic and religious minorities face severe persecution. Small steps toward the rule of law have been replaced by the Communist Party's traditional rule by law. Hong Kong's limited freedoms, under "one country, two systems," are being severely challenged.

Xi has emerged as the most powerful leader of China since Mao Zedong, building a shameless cult of personality, removing presidential term limits, promoting "Xi Jinping thought," and advancing grandiose visions for a powerful, yet autocratic, nation. To ensure that it can continue to prioritize its own power over the needs and desires of the people of China, the Communist Party has mounted a determined assault on the political freedoms that might show the public to be anything but acquiescent to its rule.

The Unconstrained Surveillance State

More than any other government, Beijing has made technology central to its repression. A nightmarish system has already been built in Xinjiang, the northwestern region that is home both to some 13 million Muslims—Uyghurs, Kazakhs, and other Turkic minorities—and to the most intrusive public monitoring system the world has ever known. The Chinese Communist Party has long sought to monitor people for any sign of dissent, but the combination of growing economic means and technical capacity has led to an unprecedented regime of mass surveillance.

The ostensible purpose is to avoid recurrence of a handful of violent incidents several years ago by alleged separatists, but the venture far surpasses any perceptible security threat. One million officials and party cadre have been mobilized as uninvited "guests" to regularly "visit" and stay in the homes of some of these Muslim families to monitor them. Their job is to scrutinize and report "problems" such as people who pray or show other signs of active adherence to the Islamic faith, who contact family members abroad, or who display anything less than absolute fealty to the Communist Party.

This in-person surveillance is just the tip of the iceberg, the analog prelude to the digital show. Without regard to the internationally recognized right to privacy, the Chinese government has deployed video cameras throughout the region, combined them with facial-recognition technology, deployed mobile-phone apps to input data from officials' observations as well as electronic checkpoints, and processed the resulting information through big-data analysis.

Data it collects are used to determine who is detained for "re-education." In the largest case of arbitrary detention in decades, one million or more Turkic Muslims have been deprived of their freedom, placed in an indefinite detention of forced indoctrination. The detentions have created countless "orphans"—children whose parents are in custody—who are now held in schools and state-run orphanages where they, too, are subjected to indoctrination. Children in regular Xinjiang schools may face similar ideological training.

The apparent aim is to strip Muslims of any adherence to their faith, ethnicity, or independent political views. Detainees' ability to recapture their freedom depends on persuading their jailers that they are Mandarin-speaking, Islam-free worshipers of Xi and the Communist Party. This brazen endeavor reflects a totalitarian impulse to reengineer people's thinking until they accept the supremacy of party rule.

The Chinese government is building similar systems of surveillance and behavior engineering throughout the country. Most notable is the "social credit system," which the government vows will punish bad behavior, such as jaywalking and failure to pay court fees, and reward good conduct. People's "trustworthiness"—as assessed by the government—determines their access to desirable social goods, such as the right to live in an attractive city, send one's children to a private school, or travel by plane or high-speed train. For the time being, political criteria are not included in this system, but it would take little to add them.

Ominously, the surveillance state is exportable. Few governments have the capacity to deploy the human resources that China has devoted to Xinjiang, but the technology is becoming off-the-shelf, attractive to governments with weak privacy protections such as Kyrgyzstan, the Philippines, and Zimbabwe. Chinese companies are not the only ones selling these abusive systems—others include companies from Germany, Israel, and the United Kingdom—but China's affordable packages make them attractive to governments that want to emulate its surveillance model.

China's Template for Prosperous Dictatorship

Many autocrats look with envy at China's seductive mix of successful economic development, rapid modernization, and a seemingly firm grip on political power. Far from being spurned as a global pariah, the Chinese government is courted the world over, its unelected president receiving red-carpet treatment wherever he goes, and the country hosting prestigious events, such as the 2022 Winter Olympics. The aim is to portray China as open, welcoming, and powerful, even as it descends into ever more ruthless autocratic rule.

The conventional wisdom once held that as China grew economically, it would build a middle class that would demand its rights. That led to the convenient fiction that there was no need to press Beijing about its repression; it was sufficient to trade with it.

Few today believe that self-serving rationale, but most governments have found new ways to justify the status quo. They continue to prioritize economic opportunities in China but without the pretense of a strategy for improving respect for the rights of the people there.

In fact, the Chinese Communist Party has shown that economic growth can reinforce a dictatorship by giving it the means to enforce its rule—to spend what it takes to maintain power, from the legions of security officials it employs to the censorship regime it maintains and the pervasive surveillance state it constructs. Those vast resources buttressing autocratic rule negate the ability of people across China to have any say in how they are governed.

These developments are music to the ears of the world's dictators. Their rule, they would have us believe with China in mind, can also lead to prosperity without the nettlesome intervention of free debate or contested elections. Never mind that the history of unaccountable governments is littered with economic devastation.

For every Lee Kwan Yew, the late Singaporean leader who is often mentioned by proponents of autocratic rule, there are many more—Robert Mugabe of Zimbabwe, Nicolas Maduro of Venezuela, Abdel Fattah al-Sisi of Egypt, Omar al-Bashir of Sudan, or Teodoro Obiang Nguema Mbasogo of Equatorial Guinea—who led their country to ruin. Unaccountable governments tend to put their own interests above their people's. They prioritize their power, their families, and their cronies. The frequent result is neglect, stagnation, and persistent poverty, if not hyperinflation, public health crises, and economic debacle.

Even in China, an unaccountable system of government allows no voice to those left out of China's growing economy. Officials boast of the country's economic progress, but they censor information about its widening income inequality, discriminatory access to public benefits, selective corruption prosecutions, and the one in five children left behind in rural areas as their parents seek work in other parts of the country. They hide the forced demolitions and displacements, the injuries and deaths that accompany some of the country's massive infrastructure projects, and the permanent disabilities resulting from unsafe and unregulated food and drugs. They even deliberately underestimate the number of people with disabilities.

Moreover, one need not go back far in China's history to encounter the enormous human toll of unaccountable government. The same Chinese Communist Party that today proclaims a Chinese miracle only recently imposed the devastation of the Cultural Revolution and the Great Leap Forward, with deaths numbering in the tens of millions.

China's Campaign Against Global Norms

To avoid global backlash for crushing human rights at home, the Chinese government is trying to undermine the international institutions that are designed to protect them. Chinese authorities have long pushed back against foreign concern for human rights as an infringement on its sovereignty, but these efforts were comparatively modest. Now China intimidates other governments, insisting that they applaud it in international forums and join its attacks on the international human rights system.

Beijing seems to be methodically building a network of cheerleader states that depend on its aid or business. Those who cross it risk retaliation, such as the threats to Sweden after an independent Swedish group gave an award to a Hong Kong-based publisher (and Swedish citizen) whom the Chinese government had arrested and forcibly disappeared after he printed books critical of the Chinese government.

Beijing's approach puts it at odds with the very purpose of international human rights. Where others see people facing persecution whose rights need defending, China's rulers see a potential precedent of rights enforcement that could return to haunt them. Using its voice, its influence, and sometimes its Security Council veto, the Chinese government seeks to block United Nations measures to protect some of the world's most persecuted people, turning its back on the Syrian civilians facing indiscriminate airstrikes by Russian and Syrian planes; the Rohingya Muslims ethnically cleansed from their homes by the Myanmar army's murder, rape and arson; Yemeni civilians under bombardment and blockade by the Saudi-led coalition; and the Venezuelan people suffering economic devastation due to the corrupt mismanagement of Nicolas Maduro. In all of these cases, Beijing would rather leave the victims to their fate than generate a model of defending rights that might boomerang on its own repressive rule.

Beijing's methods often have a certain subtlety. The Chinese government adopts international human rights treaties but then tries to reinterpret them or to undermine their enforcement. It has become skilled at appearing to cooperate with UN reviews of its rights record while sparing no effort to thwart honest discussion. It prevents domestic critics from traveling abroad, denies key international experts access to the country, organizes its allies—many of them notoriously repressive themselves—to sing its praises, and often presents blatantly dishonest information.

Even when it comes to economic rights, Beijing wants no independent assessment of its progress because that would require examining not its preferred indicator—the growth in gross domestic product—but measures such as how the least favored in China are faring, including persecuted minorities and those left behind in rural areas. And it certainly wants no independent evaluation of civil and political rights, because respect for them would create a system of accountability—to civic activists, independent journalists, political parties, independent judges, and free and fair elections—that it is determined to avoid.

The Enablers

Although China is the driving force behind this global assault on human rights, it has willing accomplices. They include a collection of dictators, autocrats, and monarchs who themselves have an abiding interesting in undermining the human rights system that might hold them to account. They also include governments, as well as companies and even academic institutions, that are ostensibly committed to human rights but prioritize access to China's wealth.

To make matters worse, several countries that once often could have been counted on to defend human rights have been missing in action. US President Trump has been more interested in embracing friendly autocrats than defending the human rights standards that they flout. The European Union, diverted by Brexit, obstructed by nationalist member states, and divided over migration, has found it difficult to adopt a strong common voice on human rights. Even as people have taken to the streets for human rights, democracy, and the rule of law in Algeria, Sudan, Lebanon, Iraq, Bolivia, Russia, and Hong Kong in an impressive wave of global protests, democratic governments have often responded with lukewarm and selective support. This inconsistency makes it easier for China to claim that concerns expressed about its human rights record are a matter of politics rather than principle.

There have been rare exceptions to this acquiescence to China's oppression. In July, at the UN Human Rights Council, 25 governments joined together for the first time in such numbers to express concern about the extraordinary crackdown in Xinjiang. Remarkably, fearing the wrath of the Chinese government, none was willing to read the statement aloud to the council, as is customary. Instead, finding safety in numbers, the group simply submitted the joint statement in writing. That changed in October at the UN General Assembly when the United Kingdom read aloud a parallel statement from a similar coalition of governments, but the initial hesitation shows the great reluctance of even the most committed countries to challenge China frontally. This fear underpins the impunity that China has come to enjoy in international circles despite the sweeping nature of its abuses.

Other governments were all too happy to embrace Beijing. In response to these two instances of collective criticism, the Chinese government organized its own joint statements of support, which shamelessly applauded its "counter-terrorism and de-radicalization measures in Xinjiang" that have led to a "stronger sense of happiness, fulfillment, and security." Up to 54 governments signed on, including such notorious human rights violators as Russia, Syria, North Korea, Myanmar, Belarus, Venezuela, and Saudi Arabia. This gallery of repressive governments may have little credibility, yet their sheer numbers illustrate the uphill battle faced by the few countries willing to confront China on human rights.

One would have hoped that the Organization of Islamic Cooperation (OIC)—the group of 57 mostly Muslim-majority nations—would come to the defense of the persecuted Muslims of Xinjiang, as they did for the Rohingya Muslims ethnically cleansed by the Myanmar military. Instead, the OIC issued a fawning panegyric, commending China for "providing care to its Muslim citizens." Pakistan—despite its role as OIC coordinator and its corresponding responsibility to speak out against abuses faced by Muslims—has championed such efforts.

Notably, however, OIC members Turkey and Albania have supported the call for an independent UN assessment in Xinjiang, while Qatar withdrew from China's counterstatement. In total, about half of the OIC member states declined to sign on to China's attempts to whitewash its record in Xinjiang—an important first step, but hardly sufficient in the face of such massive abuses.

OIC members and other states disinclined to challenge Beijing also participated in the propaganda tours of Xinjiang that the Chinese government organized to address criticism of its detention of Muslims. Mounting a Great Wall of Disinformation, Chinese authorities absurdly claimed that this mass deprivation of liberty was an exercise in "vocational training." They then arranged for delegations of diplomats and journalists to visit some of those in "training." What little opportunity there was to speak freely with the Muslim inmates quickly punctured the cover story. The staged exhibition was often so preposterous as to be self-refuting, as when a group of inmates was forced to sing, in English, the children's song "If you're happy and you know it, clap your hands!"

The point of these show tours was not to be convincing; it was to give governments an excuse not to criticize Beijing. They were a fig leaf to hide behind, an alibi for indifference.

World leaders who visited China, including those who see themselves as human rights champions, have not performed significantly better. For example, French President Emanuel Macron visited China in November 2019 but made no public mention of human rights. Visiting leaders have typically excused such public silence by insisting that they raise human rights with Chinese officials in private discussions. But little if any evidence exists that this behind-the-scenes approach does any good.

Quiet diplomacy alone does nothing to shame a government that seeks acceptance as a legitimate and respected member of the international community. Instead, the photo-ops of smiling officials combined with the public silence on human rights signal to the world—and, most important, the people of China, who are the ultimate agents of change—that the VIP visitor is indifferent to Beijing's repression.

The Elements of China's Power

Chinese authorities orchestrate their attacks on human rights criticism in part through the centralized deployment of their economic clout. No Chinese business can afford to ignore the dictates of the Communist Party, so when word comes down to punish a country for its criticism of Beijing—for example, by not purchasing its goods—the company has no choice but to comply. The result is that any non-Chinese government or company seeking to do business with China, if it publicly opposes Beijing's repression, faces not a series of individual Chinese companies' decisions about how to respond but a single central command, with access to the entire Chinese market—16 percent of the world economy—at stake. For example, after the Houston Rockets general manager irked the Chinese government by tweeting his support for Hong Kong's pro-democracy protesters, all of the National Basketball Association's 11 official Chinese business partners—including a travel website, a milk producer, and a fast-food chain—suspended ties with the league.

The Trump administration is one government that has been willing to stand up to China, best evidenced by its October 2019 imposition of sanctions on the Xinjiang Public Security Bureau and eight Chinese technology companies for their complicity in human rights violations. But strong rhetoric from US officials condemning human rights violations in China is often undercut by Trump's praise of Xi Jinping and other friendly autocrats, such as Russia's Vladimir Putin, Turkey's Recep Tayyip Erdoğan, Egypt's Abdel Fattah al-Sisi, and Saudi Arabia's Mohammad bin Salman, not to mention the Trump administration's own rights-violating domestic policies such as its cruel and illegal forced separation of children from their parents at the US-Mexican border.

This inconsistency makes it easier for Beijing to discount Washington's human rights criticisms. Moreover, the Trump administration's misguided withdrawal from the UN Human Rights Council because of concerns for Israel has paved the way for the Chinese government to exert greater influence over this central institution for the defense of rights.

An important instrument of China's influence has been Xi's "Belt and Road Initiative" (BRI)—a trillion-dollar infrastructure and investment program that facilitates Chinese access to markets and natural resources across 70 countries. Aided by the frequent absence of alternative investors, the BRI has secured the Chinese government considerable good will among developing countries, even though Beijing has been able to foist many of the costs onto the countries that it purports to help.

China's methods of operation often have the effect of bolstering authoritarianism in "beneficiary" countries. BRI projects—known for their "no strings" loans—largely ignore human rights and environmental standards. They allow little if any input from people who might be harmed. Some are negotiated in backroom deals that are prone to corruption. At times they benefit and entrench ruling elites while burying the people of the country under mountains of debt.

Some BRI projects are notorious: Sri Lanka's Hambantota port, which China repossessed for 99 years when debt repayment became impossible, or the loan to build Kenya's Mombasa-Nairobi railroad, which the government is trying to repay by forcing cargo transporters to use it despite cheaper alternatives. Some governments—including those of Bangladesh, Malaysia, Myanmar, Pakistan, and Sierra Leone—have begun backing away from BRI projects because they do not look economically sensible. In most cases, the struggling debtor is eager to stay in Beijing's good graces.

So rather than really being "no strings," BRI loans effectively impose a separate set of political conditions requiring support for China's anti-rights agenda. That ensures at best silence, at worst applause, in the face of China's domestic repression, as well as assistance to Beijing as it undermines international human rights institutions.

Pakistani Prime Minister Imran Khan, for example, whose government is a major BRI recipient, said nothing about his fellow Muslims in Xinjiang as he visited Beijing, while his diplomats offered over-the-top praise for "China's efforts in providing care to its Muslim citizens." Similarly, Cameroon delivered fawning statements of praise for China shortly after Beijing forgave millions in debt: referencing Xinjiang, it lauded Beijing for "fully protect[ing] the exercise of lawful rights of ethnic minority populations" including "normal religious activities and beliefs."

China's development banks, such as the China Development Bank and the Ex-Im Bank of China, have a growing global reach but lack critical human rights safeguards. The China-founded Asian Infrastructure Investment Bank is not much better. Its policies call for transparency and accountability in the projects it finances and include social and environmental standards, but do not require the bank to identify and address human rights risks. Among the bank's 74 members are many governments that claim to respect rights: much of the European Union including France, Germany, the Netherlands, Sweden, and the United Kingdom, along with Canada, Australia, and New Zealand.

Subversion of the United Nations

> ***We thought this institution could protect our rights when the government violates them. But it is no different.***
>
> –A CHINESE HUMAN RIGHTS DEFENDER ABOUT THE UN, GENEVA, JUNE 2016

The Chinese government, allergic to foreign pressure about its domestic human rights problems, does not think twice about twisting arms to protect its image in international forums. Because a central purpose of the United Nations is to promote universal human rights, the UN has been a key target. The pressure has been felt all the way to the top. UN Secretary-General Antonio Guterres has been unwilling to publicly demand an end to China's mass detention of Turkic Muslims, while heaping praise on Beijing's economic prowess and the BRI.

At the UN Human Rights Council, China routinely opposes virtually every human rights initiative that criticizes a particular country unless it is watered down enough to secure that government's consent. In recent years, China has opposed resolutions condemning human rights violations in Myanmar, Syria, Iran, the Philippines, Burundi, Venezuela, Nicaragua, Yemen, Eritrea, and Belarus. China also seeks to distort the international rights framework by suggesting that economic progress should precede the need to respect rights and by urging "win-win cooperation" (subsequently renamed "mutually beneficial cooperation"), which frames rights as a question of voluntary cooperation rather than legal obligation.

When China's human rights record came up for a routine review in 2018 and 2019 at the Human Rights Council, Chinese officials threatened critical delegations while encouraging allies to heap praise. Beijing also flooded the speakers list reserved for civil society organizations with government-sponsored groups tasked with lauding its record. Meanwhile, its diplomats gave blatantly false information to the reviewing body, threatened delegations with consequences if they attended a panel discussion of abuses in Xinjiang, and sought to prevent an independent group focused on Xinjiang from speaking at the council. To top it off, Chinese authorities mounted a large photo display outside UN meeting rooms depicting Uyghurs as happy and grateful to them.

At UN headquarters in New York, a major Chinese government priority has been to avoid discussion of its conduct in Xinjiang. Often working in tandem with Russia, China also has taken an increasingly regressive approach to any action on human rights in the Security Council, where it has veto power. For example, Beijing has been clear that it will not tolerate pressure on Myanmar, despite a UN fact-finding mission's conclusion that Myanmar's top military leaders should be investigated and prosecuted for genocide. Along with Russia, China opposed—though unsuccessfully—the Security Council even discussing Venezuela's humanitarian crisis. In September, as 3 million civilians faced indiscriminate bombing by Russian and Syrian jets, China joined Russia to veto a Security Council demand for a truce.

Global Censorship

> ***We self-police ourselves.... Everybody [who participates in the student salon] is scared. Just this fear, I think creating the fear, it actually works.***
>
> —UNIVERSITY STUDENT, VANCOUVER, JUNE 2018

In addition to longstanding practices such as censoring access to foreign media, limiting funding from overseas sources to domestic civil society groups, and denying visas to scholars and others, Beijing has taken full advantage of the corporate quest for profit to extend its censorship to critics abroad. In recent years, a disturbing parade of companies have given in to Beijing for their perceived offenses or for criticism of China by their employees.

Hong Kong-based Cathay Pacific airlines threatened to fire employees in Hong Kong who supported or participated in the 2019 pro-democracy protests there. Volkswagen's chief executive, Herbert Diess, told the BBC he was "not aware" of reports about detention camps holding thousands of Muslims in Xinjiang, even though Volkswagen has had a plant there since 2012. Marriott fired a social media manager for "liking" a tweet praising the company for calling Tibet a country, and vowed "to ensure errors like this don't happen again." The accounting giant PwC disowned a statement published in a Hong Kong newspaper supporting the pro-democracy protests said to have been placed by employees of the Big Four accounting firms. Hollywood is increasingly censoring its films for Beijing's sensibilities, such as the digital removal of a Taiwan flag from Tom Cruise's bomber jacket in the recent sequel to the 1986 movie "Top Gun."

This list is telling. First, it demonstrates how small and insignificant the perceived slights are that incur the wrath of various voices in China. Even though the Great Firewall prevents most people in China from learning of criticism abroad, and even though the Chinese Communist Party devotes enormous resources to censoring social media at home and spreading its propaganda there, powerful actors in China still bristle at foreign criticism. With that sensitivity in mind, companies seeking to do business with China often silence themselves and their employees even without an edict from Beijing.

Second, it shows that Chinese censorship is becoming a global threat. It is bad enough for companies to abide by censorship restrictions when operating inside

China. It is much worse to impose that censorship on their employees and customers around the world. One can no longer pretend that China's suppression of independent voices stops at its borders.

Free-speech problems are also cropping up at universities worldwide. The goal of maintaining the flow of students from China, who often pay full tuition, can easily become an excuse for universities to avoid uncomfortable subjects. In Australia, Canada, the United Kingdom, and the United States, some pro-Beijing students have sought to shut down campus discussions about human rights abuses in Hong Kong, Xinjiang, or Tibet. In other cases, students from China who want to join campus debates on ideas that would be taboo at home feel they cannot for fear of being reported to Chinese authorities. Universities have done little publicly in such cases to assert the rights of free speech.

That tendency is only compounded by Beijing's deliberate effort to enlist Chinese citizens abroad to propagate its views and to monitor each other and report any criticism of Xi Jinping's rule. For example, staff at the Chinese embassy in Washington met with and praised a group of students for censuring a Chinese student at the University of Maryland for criticizing the Chinese government in a commencement speech.

Chinese authorities also routinely threaten relatives in China of dissidents abroad to silence their criticisms. A technology consultant in Vancouver said: "If I criticize the [Chinese Communist Party] publicly, my parents' retirement benefits, their health insurance benefits could all be taken away." A Toronto-based journalist for a Chinese-language newspaper whose parents in China were harassed for her work said, "I don't feel there is free speech here. I can't report freely."

Censorship is also a threat as Chinese technology extends overseas. WeChat, a social-media platform combined with a messaging app widely used by Chinese people at home and abroad, censors political messages and suspends users' accounts on political grounds even if they are based outside China.

Rising to the Challenge

An extraordinary threat requires a commensurate response—and much still can be done to defend human rights worldwide from Beijing's frontal attack. Despite the Chinese government's power and hostility to human rights, its ascent as a global threat to rights is not unstoppable. Rising to this challenge demands a radical break from the dominant complacency and business-as-usual approach. It calls for an unprecedented response from those who still believe in a world order in which human rights matter.

Governments, companies, universities, international institutions, and others should stand with those in and from China who are struggling to secure their rights. As a first principle, no one should equate the Chinese government with the people of China. That blames an entire people for the abuses of a government that they had no say in choosing. Instead, governments should support critical voices in China and publicly insist that, in the absence of genuine elections, Beijing does not represent the people there.

Just as governments have stopped promoting the convenient fiction that trade alone promotes human rights in China, so they should abandon the reassuring-but-false view that quiet diplomacy suffices. The question to ask of dignitaries visiting Beijing who claim to discuss China's human rights record is whether the people of China—the main engine of change—can hear them. Do those people feel emboldened or disillusioned by the visit? Do they hear a voice of sympathy and concern or see only a photo-op at the signing of more commercial contracts? By regularly and publicly calling out Beijing for its repression, governments should raise the cost of that abuse while emboldening the victims.

The Chinese model of repressive economic growth can be refuted by highlighting the risks of unaccountable rule, from the millions left behind in China to the devastation caused by the likes of Mugabe of Zimbabwe or Maduro of Venezuela. Calling attention to how dictators around the world claim to serve their people while in fact serving themselves accomplishes much the same purpose.

Governments and international financial institutions should offer compelling, rights-respecting alternatives to China's "no strings" loans and development aid. They should leverage their membership in such organizations as the Asian

Infrastructure Investment Bank to push for the highest human rights standards in development rather than to enable a global race to the bottom.

Governments committed to human rights should be sensitive to the double standards of "China exceptionalism" that can creep into their conduct and enable Beijing to get away with abuses for which poorer and less powerful governments would be challenged. If they seek to hold Myanmar officials accountable for their abusive treatment of Muslims, why not Chinese officials? If they are attentive to Saudi or Russian efforts to buy legitimacy, why not similar Chinese efforts? If they encourage debates about human rights violations by Israel, Egypt, Saudi Arabia, or Venezuela, why not by China? They rightly challenged the Trump administration's appalling separation of children from their parents on the US-Mexico border, so why not also challenge the Chinese government's separation of children from their parents in Xinjiang?

Governments should deliberately counter China's divide-and-conquer strategy for securing silence about its oppression. If every government alone faces a choice between seeking Chinese economic opportunities and speaking out against Chinese repression, many will opt for silence. But if governments band together to address China's flouting of human rights, the power balance shifts. For example, if the Organization of Islamic Cooperation were to protest against the Chinese government's repression of Turkic Muslims in Xinjiang, Beijing would need to retaliate against 57 countries. The Chinese economy cannot take on the whole world.

By the same token, companies and universities should draft and promote codes of conduct for dealing with China. Strong common standards would make it more difficult for Beijing to ostracize those who stand up for basic rights and freedoms. These standards would also make matters of principle a more important element of the institutions' public images. Consumers would be better placed to insist that these institutions not succumb to Chinese censorship as the price to obtain Chinese business, and that they should never benefit from or contribute to Chinese abuses. Governments should tightly regulate the technology that empowers China's mass surveillance and repression—and bolster privacy protections to check the spread of such surveillance systems.

Universities in particular should provide a space where students and scholars from China can learn about and criticize the Chinese government without fear of being monitored or reported. And they should never tolerate Beijing curtailing the academic freedom of any of their students or scholars.

Beyond issuing statements, governments that are committed to human rights should redouble cross-regional outreach efforts with a view to presenting a resolution at the UN Human Rights Council establishing a fact-finding mission, so the world can know what is happening in Xinjiang. These states should also force a discussion of Xinjiang at the UN Security Council so Chinese officials understand that they will have to answer for their actions.

More fundamentally, UN member states and senior officials should defend the United Nations as an independent voice on human rights. For example, until a UN fact-finding mission is created, reporting by the UN high commissioner for human rights as well as the Human Rights Council's experts is crucial. If China succeeds in leaving the UN toothless on human rights, all will suffer.

Governments committed to human rights should also stop treating China as a respectable partner. The red-carpet treatment for Chinese officials should be conditioned on real progress on human rights. A state visit should come with a public demand to give UN investigators independent access to Xinjiang. Chinese officials should be made to feel that they will never gain the respectability they crave so long as they persecute their people.

At a more targeted level, Chinese officials directly involved in the mass detention of Uyghurs should become persona non grata. Their foreign bank accounts should be frozen. They should fear prosecution for their crimes. And the Chinese companies that build and help run the detention camps in Xinjiang, and any company that exploits the labor of prisoners or provides the surveillance infrastructure and big data processing, should be exposed and pressured to stop.

Finally, the world should recognize that Xi Jinping's lofty rhetoric about establishing a "community of shared future for mankind" is really a threat—a vision of rights worldwide as defined and tolerated by Beijing. It is time to acknowledge that the Chinese government seeks to repudiate and reshape an international human rights system built on the belief that every person's dignity deserves respect—that regardless of the official interests at stake, limits exist on what states can do to people.

Unless we want to return to an era in which people are pawns to be manipulated or discarded according to the whims of their overlords, the Chinese government's attack on the international human rights system must be resisted. Now is the time to take a stand. Decades of progress on human rights are at stake.

HUMAN
RIGHTS
WATCH
AFGHANISTAN:
LITTLE HELP FOR
CONFLICT-LINKED TRAUMA
Government, Donors Should Expand Mental Health Programs

WORLD REPORT
2020

COUNTRIES

Algeria

Algeria in 2019 experienced the largest and most sustained anti-government demonstrations since gaining independence in 1962. Beginning February 22, Algerians flooded the streets every Friday in the capital Algiers and elsewhere, first to protest the re-election bid of their four-term president, Abdelaziz Bouteflika, who has appeared publicly only rarely since suffering a debilitating stroke in 2013; then, after his resignation on April 2, to demand a transition to more democratic governance.

After Bouteflika's resignation, Senate President Abdelkader Bensalah became acting president while Gen. Ahmed Gaid Salah, the army chief of staff and deputy defense minister, wielded effective power. Gaid Salah set a new presidential election for July 4, later postponed until December 12.

In response to continuing protests, authorities dispersed peaceful demonstrations, arbitrarily detained protesters, blocked meetings organized by political and human rights groups, and imprisoned critics.

Freedom of Assembly

While large anti-government street protests occurred weekly, police forces deployed massively in the capital's downtown streets and squares and at checkpoints, effectively limiting the number of people who could reach the marches, and then tightly controlling those who did. Authorities arrested hundreds of peaceful protesters, releasing most without charge after a few hours but prosecuting and imprisoning dozens.

Authorities arrested and charged 86 persons between June and October according to the National Committee of the Release of Detainees. All were accused of "harming the integrity of the national territory," including for carrying the flag symbolizing the country's Kabyle, or Berber, population. This charge can result in a sentence of up to 10 years in prison, under penal code Article 79. As of October, six had been tried and acquitted, one was freed pending trial, and 79 remained in prison awaiting trial.

Freedom of Speech

On February 7, human rights activist Hadj Ghermoul, 37, was sentenced to six months in prison for "offending a state institution" after he posted a picture of himself carrying a sign near the northwestern city of Mascara expressing opposition to a fifth mandate for President Bouteflika. Local authorities said he was arrested while drunk and insulting police forces.

On July 9, a first instance court near Algiers sentenced Mouaffak Serdouk, a 40-year-old supporter of Algeria's football team, to a year in prison for "publicly displaying a paper that can harm the national interest." He had stood near a stadium in Cairo where the Algerian team was playing, carrying a sign demanding the departure of those who hold power in Algeria, before being deported to Algeria, where he was prosecuted and sentenced.

On June 30, police arrested 87-year-old Lakhdar Bouregaa, a prominent veteran of Algeria's independence war, at his home in Algiers. The arrest came four days after he said at a public meeting, later broadcast on YouTube, that Algeria's army is a collection of "militias." An investigative judge opened an investigation for "weakening the morale of the army," a charge that could lead to a prison sentence of up to 10 years.

On September 11, authorities arrested Karim Tabbou, spokesperson of the Democratic and Social Union (UDS) opposition party, in front of his house in Douira, and charged him with "participating in undermining the morale of the army" after he publicly criticized Gaid Salah. Authorities released Tabbou on September 25, then rearrested him the next morning. On October 2, an investigating judge in Algiers opened an investigation based on him "inciting violence" and "harming national unity by publishing statements and videos on social media." If convicted, he faces prison and a deprivation of his civil rights, including the right to run for office.

On September 25, a military court in Blida sentenced Louisa Hanoune, leader of the Labour Party, to 15 years in prison for "harming the authority of the army" and "conspiracy against the authority of the state." She was prosecuted alongside Said Bouteflika, the ex-president's brother, and Gen. Mohamed "Tewfik" Mediene, former head of Algeria's most powerful intelligence service. International human rights standard prohibits the trial of civilians before military courts.

Authorities charged Salah Dabouz, a former president of the Algerian League for the Defense of Human Rights (LADDH), with "insulting" the judiciary for Facebook posts in which he criticized the prosecution of members of the Mozabite ethnic minority. Dabouz was provisionally released on April 7 but required to report three times a week to authorities in Ghardaia, 600 kilometers from his home in Algiers. Authorities lifted this reporting requirement on July 24. He was awaiting trial at time of writing. On September 9, an unknown man attacked him with a knife in Ghardaia, injuring him on both arms.

Kamaleddine Fekhar, a leading activist for the rights of the Mozabite minority in Algeria, died May 28 after a prolonged hunger strike in prison. Authorities had arrested Fekhar on March 31 and placed him in pretrial detention for "undermining" state institutions. Fekhar had completed an earlier sentence for charges that included violence against state officials, incitement to violence, hatred and discrimination, distributing material harmful to the national interest, and defamation of state institutions, following ethnic clashes between Mozabites and Arabs in and around Ghardaia between 2013 and 2015.

Freedom of Religion

The Algerian penal code punishes with three to five years in prison and/or a fine whoever "offends the Prophet and God's messengers, denigrates the dogma or precepts of Islam by whatever means." Authorities have used this article to sentence members of the tiny Ahmadiyya community, which practices a version of Islam different from the officially recognized dogma.

A 2006 ordinance discriminates against non-Muslims by subjecting them to constraints that do not apply to Muslims. Collective worship by non-Muslims can only be organized by government-licensed religious organizations in designated places. The Protestant Church of Algeria said that in the year ending in October 2019, authorities had shuttered nine of their churches because they lacked permission or were not suited to receive the public.

Migrants

Since at least December 2016, Algeria has rounded up and summarily expelled en masse thousands of Sub-Saharan migrants, including women and children.

Algerian authorities reportedly expelled almost 5,000 people during the first half of 2019, most of them Nigerian.

Women's Rights and Sexual Orientation

While Algeria's 2015 law on domestic violence criminalized some forms of domestic violence, it contained loopholes that allow convictions to be dropped or sentences reduced if victims pardoned their perpetrators. The law also did not set out any further measures to prevent abuse or protect survivors. Article 326 of the penal code allows a person who abducts a minor to escape prosecution if he marries his victim.

Algeria's Family Code allows men to have a unilateral divorce without explanation but requires women to apply to courts for a divorce on specified grounds.

Same-sex relations are punishable under article 338 of the penal code by up to two years in prison.

Measures against International Human Rights Organizations and Media

Authorities deported a Human Rights Watch official, Ahmed Benchemsi, on August 19. They held Benchemsi's passports for 10 days after arresting him on August 9 near a demonstration in Algiers and holding him for 10 hours. They confiscated his cellphone and laptop computer, which they returned when deporting him. Benchemsi was visiting Algeria to observe human rights conditions.

Authorities expelled several international journalists covering protests. Tarek Amara, a Reuters journalist and Tunisian national, was expelled on March 31, after being detained for reporting on a March 29 protest against Bouteflika. Aymeric Vincenot, AFP bureau chief, was forced to leave the country on April 9, after authorities declined to renew his accreditation.

Polisario-Run Sahrawi Refugee Camps

The Polisario Front government-in-exile that administers the camps in Algeria's southern desert for refugees from Western Sahara detained three critics on suspicion of treason, acts of aggression against the Sahrawi State, and incitement to disobedience and slander, apparently over Facebook posts they published and private messages they exchanged on social media apps. Activists Moulay Abba Bouzid and Fadel Mohamed Breica, and Mahmoud Zeidan, a journalist, were arrested between June 17 and 19. They spent five months in custody, during which they alleged harsh conditions of interrogation, including torture threats and coercion, to confess. The men were acquitted of all charges and freed on November 11.

Key International Actors

On October 2, authorities deported French parliamentarian Mathilde Panot and three other French citizens after they had come to Bejaia to express their support with protesters. Authorities denounced "foreign interference and an attack against Algerian sovereignty."

On September 13, Marie Arena, chair of the European Parliament's Subcommittee on Human Rights, denounced "arbitrary arrests" and demanded the release of "political prisoners" in Algeria. On September 30, the European Union issued a statement highlighting "the importance of guaranteeing freedom of speech and assembly" to Algerians, but failing to denounce the wave of arrests and the crackdown on dissent in general.

Angola

In 2019, Angola made some progress in respecting the rights to freedom of expression and peaceful assembly, allowing several protests and marches to take place across the country. But the crackdown on peaceful protesters and activists in the oil-rich enclave of Cabinda and the diamond-rich Lunda Norte continued. In January, parliament approved a new law that limits the right to freedom of religion, leading to the closure of thousands of places of worship. Same-sex conduct was decriminalized in January, following the approval, by parliament, of the new penal code.

Crackdown on Cabinda Activists

Crackdown on peaceful protesters and activists in the Cabinda enclave continued in 2019. Between January 28 and February 1, 2019, police arrested 63 Cabinda pro-independence activists ahead of an announced protest to celebrate the anniversary of the signing of the 1885 treaty that gave Cabinda the status of a protectorate of former colonial power Portugal. Many of the activists were members of the Movimento Independista de Cabinda (Independence Movement of Cabinda), a peaceful separatist group that wants independence or autonomy from Angola.

In March, police arrested 10 more activists who had gathered in a square in Cabinda city, to demand the release of fellow activists. Also in March, after visiting the province, members of the main opposition party, the National Union for the Total Independence of Angola (UNITA), accused Cabinda authorities of intimidating and repressing residents of the province.

Human Rights Abuses in Lunda Norte

Authorities violated the rights of residents and artisanal miners in Lunda Norte province. In April, police fired live bullets killing a boy and injuring three people, during a protest that took place after an artisanal miner was shot dead by an alleged private security agent in one of the diamond mines in Calonda. In March, Angola's leading human rights group, Associacao Justica, Paz e Democracia (AJPD) and community leaders accused authorities of arbitrarily limiting the movements of people in areas near the diamond fields, forcing local residents to abandon their farms for lack of access to their land. In some cases, according to community leaders, private security forces guarding the diamond mines beat and ill-treated residents who were caught trespassing in the diamond fields. In February, police killed a community leader, when a group of Capenda Camulenda residents were protesting against the concession of farming land to a diamond company.

Right to Peaceful Assembly

Despite some progress in respecting the rights to freedom of expression and peaceful assembly, the Angolan police intimidated and arbitrarily arrested activists for planning protests. In September, police arrested 23 people in Luena city during a peaceful protest against the administration of the governor of the Moxico province, ahead of a visit of President Joao Lourenco.

In May, police jailed activist Hitler "Samussuku" Tshikonde for 72 hours without charge or access to a lawyer. He was informed that that he was under investigation for allegedly "insulting the president" in a video that he had posted on social media.

In July, police detained seven people who were peacefully protesting against lack of water supply in Benguela province.

In August, police used tear gas and dogs to disperse a group that had gathered without authorization in front of the Parliament building to demand that next year's municipal elections take place in every Angolan city.

Housing Rights

Hundreds of families who were forcibly evicted from their houses without the necessary procedural guarantees, or the provision of alternative housing or adequate compensation, continued to await resettlement. In August, some residents of an informal settlement of "Areia Branca" in Luanda, told Human Rights Watch that they were living in dangerous conditions and subject to infectious diseases after they were illegally evicted in 2013 by a company contracted by the office of Luanda's governor to modernize the city. Over 400 families were set to be relocated to another neighborhood following the demolitions. Human Rights Watch confirmed that new houses were allocated to only 18 families, but without tittle deed or any other documents giving them ownership of the properties.

Sexual Orientation and Gender Identity

In January, Angola decriminalized same-sex conduct, after repealing the "vices against nature" provision in its law, widely interpreted to be a ban on homosexual conduct. The government also prohibited discrimination against people based on sexual orientation. Anyone refusing to employ or provide services to individuals based on their sexual orientation may face up to two years' imprisonment.

The changes came as Angola's parliament adopted its first new penal code since gaining independence from Portugal in 1975. While there have been no known prosecutions under the old penal code, such provisions curtail the rights and freedoms of lesbian, gay, bisexual, and transgender (LGBT) people, subjecting their intimate lives to unwarranted scrutiny.

Landmine Accidents

Almost 17 years after the end of Angola's civil war, landmines and other explosive remnants of war continued to kill and maim people, especially children. In June, five children were seriously injured by a landmine while hunting near Balombo, Benguela province. A month earlier, nine children aged 3 to 11 were injured after they detonated a landmine as they lighted a fire to warm themselves in the compound of their home in Cuito, Bie province.

In September, Britain's Prince Harry visited the country as part of a tour of southern Africa. In Angola, hhe witnessed the work of the HALO Trust demining project in Huambo province, where his late mother Princess Diana was photographed in 1997 walking into a minefield as part of her efforts to generate concern to clear landmines from Angola. According to the government, at least 1,220 areas of Angola are still contaminated by landmines, against 2,700 in 2007. The most affected provinces are Cuando Cubango, Moxico, Cuanza Sul and Bie.

Freedom of Religion

A new law that limits the right to freedom of religion was approved by parliament in January. The Law on Freedom of Religion, Belief and Worship stipulates that religious groups must have at least 100,000 members to be officially recognized. In May, the government announced that as part of Rescue Operation, which aimed at restoring state authority by instituting order in worship, on the roads, and over illegal migrations, among others, over 2,000 churches and places of worship had been closed.

A Muslim community leader told media that 39 mosques have been closed in Lunda Norte, and more than 10,000 Muslims forced to cross the border to the Democratic Republic of Congo to hold Ramadan in May. Islam is not an authorized religion in Angola, and mosques are not allowed to operate in most parts of the country. In January, the minister of culture told parliament that the government was monitoring Islam linked groups in the country and would soon make an official decision about the religious group.

Key International Actors

In 2009, Angola took over the leadership of two important defense roles in regional bodies, the Southern African Development Community (SADC) Defense Inspection and the African Union Peace and Security Council. Both bodies are tasked with promoting security, peace and stability. Their mandate also includes conflict prevention and undertaking peace-building missions in member states.

In August 2019, Angola mediated a summit that culminated with the leaders of Uganda and Rwanda agreeing to reopen the border between the two countries, ending months of tensions that raised fears of armed hostilities.

Also in August, United States Secretary of State Michael Pompeo welcomed the reforms President João Lourenço has implemented since taking office in 2017. In March, the US deputy assistant secretary in the Bureau of Democracy, Human Rights and Labor, Scott Busby, pledged to support the government to enhance mechanisms of accountability for human rights abuses.

In October, the European Union welcomed Angola's ratification of three international human rights treaties: the Second Optional Protocol to the International Covenant on Civil and Political Rights, aiming at the abolition of the death penalty, the Convention against Torture and Other Cruel Inhuman or Degrading Treatment or Punishment, and the Convention on the Elimination of All Forms of Racial Discrimination.

Argentina

Longstanding human rights problems in Argentina include police abuse, poor prison conditions, and endemic violence against women. Restrictions on abortion and difficulty accessing reproductive services remain serious concerns, as are impunity for the 1994 bombing of the AMIA Jewish center in Buenos Aires and delays in appointing permanent judges.

Argentina continues to make significant progress protecting lesbian, gay, bisexual, and transgender (LGBT) rights and prosecuting officials for abuses committed during the country's last military dictatorship (1976-1983), although trials have been delayed.

In October, Alberto Fernández was elected president of Argentina. He took office in December.

Confronting Past Abuses

Pardons and amnesty laws shielding former officials implicated in the dictatorship's crimes were annulled by the Supreme Court and federal judges in the early 2000s. As of March 2019, the Attorney General's Office reported 3,161 people charged, 901 convicted, and 142 acquitted. Of 611 cases alleging crimes against humanity, judges had issued rulings in 221.

As of September 2019, 130 people illegally taken from their parents as children during the dictatorship had been identified and many were reunited with their families.

The large number of victims, suspects, and cases makes it difficult for prosecutors and judges to bring those responsible to justice while respecting their due process rights. Argentine law allows judges to send inmates age 70 and older to serve their time under house arrest. The Attorney General's Office reported in March that 650 pretrial detainees and convicted prisoners were under house arrest.

Prison Conditions and Abuses by Security Forces

A 2018 United Nations report found that prisons and jails are so crowded that some pretrial detainees are being held in police stations. Prison guards have taken "disobedient" detainees to isolation cells without following established sanction procedures. Security forces have detained children and subjected them to abuse.

The National Penitentiary Office, tasked with supervising federal prisons and protecting detainees' rights, reported 558 alleged cases of torture or ill-treatment in federal prisons in 2018 and 232 cases from January through June 2019.

Official statistics show that more than half of the 14,400 detainees in federal prisons have not been convicted of a crime but are awaiting trial.

Security forces occasionally employ excessive force. In December 2018, the Argentine Security Ministry approved a resolution regarding the use of firearms by members of federal security forces that grants federal agents overly broad discretion to use firearms.

Freedom of Expression

In June, a federal court in Buenos Aires summoned Daniel Santoro, an investigative journalist from Clarin newspaper, to appear before the court regarding his alleged participation in a scheme to extort people by threatening them with negative news coverage. The court had requested and obtained "details of all calls received or made" on Santoro's phone from January 2016 to April 2019, undermining his right to protect sources. In September, a judge ordered the destruction of the document containing Santoro's phone records, alleging it violated his privacy, according to Clarin. The case remained pending at time of writing.

In April 2017, the Argentine government committed to reforming the criminal code to narrow the definition of "sedition," but had yet to present a new definition at time of writing.

Upon taking office, former President Mauricio Macri adopted a "temporary" set of decrees to "regulate" media and create a "temporary" agency to implement new rules. The agency reports to the Modernization Ministry, compromising its ability to act independently from government interests. In 2016, the government said it was drafting a communications law that it claimed would respect free speech. As of November 2019, though, no comprehensive media law had been adopted by Congress, and the "temporary" agency had issued rulings regulating media.

A 2016 law created a national agency to ensure public access to government information. The agency is also charged with protecting personal data. As of July, individuals had filed 6,785 information requests. Authorities responded to most requests within a month, but as of November, citizens had filed 524 appeals before the agency, in most cases after authorities failed to respond to the original requests.

Some provinces and municipalities still lack freedom of information laws, undermining transparency at those levels of government.

Judicial Independence

In March, the government asked the Judiciary Council to investigate Judge Alejo Ramos Padilla, arguing he had carried out an investigation in a "political and journalistic way" and had "failed to comply with his duties regarding impartiality and secrecy." The judge had testified before a Congressional commission about an investigation into allegations that intelligence agents had carried out illegal operations. The bulk of the information cited by the judge had already been disclosed online through the official website of the judicial branch.

The delayed appointment of permanent judges by the Judiciary Council has led to temporary appointments of judges who lack security of tenure, which the Supreme Court ruled in 2015 undermines judicial independence. As of October, 460 judgeships remained vacant.

Impunity for the AMIA Bombing

Twenty-four years after the 1994 bombing of the Argentine Israelite Mutual Association (AMIA) in Buenos Aires that killed 85 people and injured more than 300, allegedly at the hands of Iranian suspects, no one has been convicted of the crime. In March 2018, an appeals court upheld a decision ordering the pretrial detention of former President Cristina Fernández de Kirchner for allegedly participating in a conspiracy with Iranian officials to undermine investigation of the bombing. It has not been implemented because she had parliamentary immunity as a senator, and is currently Argentina's vice president.

Alberto Nisman, a prosecutor in charge of investigating the bombing, was found dead in his home in January 2015 with a single gunshot wound to the head and a pistol matching the wound beside him. In June 2018, an appeals court held Nisman's death appeared to be a murder.

In February, a court acquitted former President Carlos Menem of alleged interference in the initial investigation into the bombing, but convicted a former head of intelligence and a judge of interfering. An appeal of the acquittal was pending in September 2019.

Indigenous Rights

Indigenous people in Argentina generally face obstacles in accessing justice, land, education, health care, and basic services. Argentina continues to fail at implementing existing laws to protect indigenous peoples' right to free, prior, and informed consent to government decisions that may affect their rights—a right provided for in international law.

In November 2017, Congress approved a law extending the deadline for completing a survey of indigenous lands to 2021. The survey is being conducted, but slowly.

Women and Girls' Rights

Abortion is illegal in Argentina, except in cases of rape or when the life or health of the woman is at risk. But even in such cases, women and girls are sometimes subject to criminal prosecution for seeking abortions and have trouble accessing reproductive services, such as contraception and voluntary sterilization.

In May, a coalition of legislators, activists, and organizations under the umbrella "National Campaign for Legal and Free Abortion" presented to Congress their proposed bill to decriminalize abortion completely during the first 14 weeks of pregnancy and, after that period, to allow women and girls to end pregnancies when they are the result of rape, when the life or health of the woman or girl is at risk, or when the fetus suffers from severe conditions not compatible with life outside the womb. Congress had approved a similar bill in 2018, but the Senate rejected it.

Despite a 2009 law setting forth comprehensive measures to prevent and punish violence against women, the unpunished killing of women remains a serious concern. The National Registry of Femicides, administered by the Supreme Court, reported 278 femicides—the murder of women based on their gender—but only 7 convictions, in 2018.

Sexual Orientation and Gender Identity

In 2010, Argentina became the first Latin American country to legalize same-sex marriage. The Civil Marriage Law allows same-sex couples to enter civil marriages and affords them the same legal marital protections as different-sex couples. Since 2010 more than 20,000 same-sex couples have married nationwide.

Key International Actors and Foreign Policy

In April, Argentina, along with Brazil, Colombia, and Paraguay, signed a declaration proposed by Chile that called on the Inter-American human rights system bodies to take into consideration the "political, economic, and social realities" of each country in its decisions, which would undermine the agencies' work.

In March, after an in-country visit, the UN Working Group of Experts on People of African Descent expressed concern regarding the "invisibility" of and "structural discrimination" against Afro-Argentines. The working group reported it had received information on cases of arbitrary arrest and abuse against street sellers of African origin.

During the Macri administration, Argentina was an active member of the Lima Group, a coalition of governments that monitors and speaks out about Venezuela's poor human rights record and has called for the release of its political prisoners. In June, Argentina prohibited the entry to the country of more than 400 Venezuelan officials implicated in human rights abuses and corruption. The number of Venezuelans moving legally to Argentina has steadily increased since 2014, reaching more than 170,000 as of November.

During the 2019 presidential campaign, Fernández took a softer approach towards Venezuela, and suggested Argentina would withdraw from the Lima Group.

Armenia

Armenia's Prime Minister Nikol Pashinyan swept to office in 2018 after popular protests, further consolidated his power following the December 2018 snap parliamentary elections, which international observers found genuinely competitive and in line with international standards. Having secured a parliamentary majority, the government embarked on an ambitious reform agenda, including tackling corruption and reforming the economic and justice sectors. However, investigations into past violence and excessive use of force by law enforcement remained limited. Violence and discrimination based on sexual orientation and gender identity, discrimination against and segregation of people with disabilities, and domestic violence persisted.

Accountability for Law Enforcement Abuse

Armenia's police have a long record of impunity for using excessive force to break up largely peaceful protests. Authorities revived an investigation into the 2008 deadly clashes between protesters and security forces, and in June 2019, charged a high-ranking official with murdering a protester while security forces were breaking up a demonstration.

However, investigations into two episodes of excessive police force against largely peaceful demonstrators and journalists in 2016 and 2015 remained suspended. Authorities claimed they were unable to identify the alleged perpetrators.

Environment and Human Rights

In August, environmental protests against plans to restart construction on the Amulsar gold mine turned into confrontations between police and protesters after security officials barred them from demonstrating in a public park surrounding parliament. Police briefly detained six protesters on misdemeanor disobedience charges.

Related protests continued near the town of Jermuk, where local residents and environmental activists blocked the roads to the mine, opposing its construction on environmental and economic grounds.

Violence against Women

Domestic violence persisted as a serious problem. According to official data, during the first half of 2019, authorities investigated 331 criminal domestic violence cases, including 176 that were newly initiated. They brought charges in 209 cases and sent 45 cases to courts.

But in most cases, authorities do not protect women and child survivors of domestic violence, jeopardizing their lives and well-being. The 2017 family violence law requires police to urgently intervene "when there is a reasonable assumption of an immediate threat of repetition or the continuation of violence" in the family. But in practice, law enforcement bodies lack awareness and training on protection mechanisms envisaged by the law, such as protection orders, and do not adequately use them. Armenia has only one shelter for domestic violence survivors, run by a nongovernmental organization (NGO). While there are plans to open another shelter, with an overall capacity of 10 to 13 people, Armenia falls far short of the Council of Europe recommendation of one shelter space per 10,000 people.

The Coalition to Stop Violence Against Women reported that 10 women had been killed by their intimate partners in the first half of 2019. One victim, Mariam Asatryan, 30, was beaten to death by her partner in May in Ararat province. Asatryan had sought the coalition's assistance several times in 2017 and 2018, when she suffered serious injuries, including broken arms, as a result of domestic violence. According to the coalition, Asatryan had filed a complaint, but law enforcement failed to take adequate measures to protect her.

Domestic violence is neither a stand-alone felony nor an aggravating criminal circumstance in the criminal code. In October, authorities introduced amendments to domestic violence legislation, removing references to "restoring harmony in family" and reconciliation as the law's principle concepts, widening its applicability to "former and current partners," and including controlling behavior as a form of domestic violence. The amendments had not been adopted at time of writing. The Council of Europe Convention on Preventing and Combating Violence against Women and Domestic Violence (Istanbul Convention) had not been sent to parliament for ratification.

Armenia made progress in transforming some residential institutions for children into community centers and supporting family-based care. Authorities are committed to ending the institutionalization of children with disabilities and to ensuring adults in institutions can transition to live independently, with support as necessary. In April 2019, the government, in cooperation with a community group, committed to working with families to prevent placing children with disabilities in institutions. In June, authorities amended laws to facilitate foster care.

Armenia aims to have fully inclusive education by 2025, whereby children with and without disabilities study together in community schools. Despite progress, many children with disabilities remain segregated in separate special schools or classrooms, or isolated in home education. Children with disabilities in community schools do not always receive necessary support, called reasonable accommodations, for their education. Accommodations can include assistive devices like hearing aids, books in braille, audio, or other formats, or aides to assist students with behavior, self-care, or learning support.

Armenia's legislation allows for adults with psychosocial or intellectual disabilities to be deprived of legal capacity, or the right to make decisions, and does not envisage any supported decision-making mechanisms. Authorities drafted a law on the rights of people with disabilities, but at time of writing, it has not yet been introduced in parliament.

Sexual Orientation and Gender Identity

Lesbian, gay, bisexual, and transgender (LGBT) people often face harassment, discrimination, and violence. The criminal code does not recognize homophobia and transphobia as aggravating criminal circumstances. Discussions around the ratification of the Istanbul Convention descended to hateful and derogatory speech by some public officials against LGBT people, suggesting that the convention has a hidden agenda of "LGBT propaganda" and legitimizing same-sex marriage.

Fear of discrimination and public disclosure of their sexual orientation prevent many LGBT people from reporting crimes. PINK Armenia, an LGBT rights group, documented at least 17 incidents of physical attacks based on sexual orientation or gender identity from January through August 2019.

In February, Max Varzhapetyan, 24, a gay activist, was assaulted and beaten on a Yerevan street. Three men chased him, shouting profanities and homophobic slurs. The men broke his tooth and injured his mouth and nose. Police launched an investigation but had pressed no charges at time of writing.

In April, during a parliamentary hearing on human rights, a transgender activist, Lilit Martirosyan, took the floor to highlight the discrimination and violence transgender people face. A backlash followed her address, including hate speech and death threats directed at Martirosyan. Law enforcement refused to launch an investigation, citing lack of criminal intent.

Openly gay men fear for their physical security in the military, and some seek exemption from obligatory military service. An exemption, however, requires a medical conclusion finding them "psychologically or mentally unfit" to serve. The process may be accompanied by derogatory treatment by officials. For example, in January, officers at a military draft board subjected Artak Arakelyan, a 19-year-old queer activist, to abuse and discrimination, using homophobic slurs to describe him, mocking him, and threatening to out him to his parent. Officials rejected Arakelyan's request for an investigation.

The government-proposed bill on equality, intended as comprehensive anti-discrimination legislation, does not include sexual orientation and gender identity as grounds for protection from discrimination. In a September report, the Organization for Security and Co-operation recommended the government include sexual orientation and gender identity as additional protected categories. It also recommended that the government ensure that groups that have legitimate interests could bring cases on behalf of an alleged discrimination victim.

Key International Actors

In May, the United Nations special rapporteur on the rights to freedom of peaceful assembly and of association published a report on his country visit, welcoming Armenia's democratic transition and calling on the authorities to undertake profound reforms "to strengthen the judiciary, the independent investigative bodies and police."

In May, the European Union published the EU-Armenia partnership implementation report, welcoming steps to implement economic, justice sector, and political reforms, but also acknowledging the early stage of the reform process. It also highlighted the need to address discrimination against LGBT people and people with disabilities.

In his July meeting with Pashinyan, European Union Council President Donald Tusk stressed the importance of rule of law and an independent judiciary.

In April, the EU delegation and member states' embassies in Yerevan and the UN Armenia Office expressed concerns about the hate speech directed at the transgender activist, Lilit Martirosyan.

In June, the Council of Europe launched the Action Plan for Armenia 2019-2022 to support the government's efforts to "reinforce human rights, ensure justice, combat threats to the rule of law, and promote democratic governance."

In her January report, Council of Europe Commissioner for Human Rights Dunja Mijatovic called on Armenia to improve women's rights, protect vulnerable groups, and ensure accountability for past human rights abuses.

In October, the Venice Commission, a Council of Europe advisory body, issued an expert opinion countering harmful myths about the Istanbul Convention, and concluding that Armenia's ratification of the treaty would not contradict its constitution.

Australia

Australia is a vibrant multicultural democracy with robust institutions. Yet 2019 saw freedom of expression come under unprecedented pressure, with police raids on journalists and a government official, and the prosecution of a whistleblower and his lawyer for violating secrecy laws. Overly broad national security laws are open to misuse.

Six years after it introduced offshore processing of refugees and asylum seekers, the government maintains its stance that no one who arrives by boat will be resettled in Australia. In 2019, following a new law, more than 135 refugees and asylum seekers were transferred to Australia for urgent medical care.

Asylum Seekers and Refugees

At time of writing, about 600 refugees and asylum seekers remained in Papua New Guinea (PNG) and Nauru, with more than 600 resettled to the US under an Australia-US resettlement deal. Of those remaining offshore, all are adults and most have been there since 2013.

At least 12 refugees and asylum seekers have died in Australia's offshore processing system since 2013, six of them suicides. Self-harm and suicide attempts surged in PNG following the Australian election in May 2019, with media reporting dozens of attempts, and local authorities struggling to respond to the crisis.

Medical facilities in PNG and Nauru are unable to cope with the complex medical needs of asylum seekers and refugees, particularly their mental health needs. In February, Australia's parliament passed a law to facilitate transfers of refugees and asylum seekers requiring medical treatment from offshore locations to Australia. So far, 135 people have been transferred for treatment. Prior to the law, lawyers repeatedly had to take the government to court to obtain appropriate medical care for clients. In December, the government repealed the law. Those transferred to Australia remain in limbo, with no permanent visas and little support.

Australia has repeatedly rejected offers by New Zealand to take some of the refugees, with the government arguing that accepting the offer would encourage more boat arrivals as New Zealand is a "backdoor route" to Australia.

HUMAN
RIGHTS
WATCH
"Fading Away"
How Aged Care Facilities in Australia Chemically Restrain
Older People with Dementia

Indigenous Rights

Indigenous Australians are significantly over-represented in the criminal justice system, often for minor offenses like unpaid fines. Aboriginal and Torres Strait Islander people comprise 28 percent of Australia's adult prison population, but just 3 percent of the national population.

In 2017, Aboriginal woman Tanya Day died when she sustained a head injury in a police cell, after police detained her for public drunkenness. In August 2019, the Victorian state government announced it would abolish public drunkenness as a crime, and replace it with an Aboriginal-led, public health response. In November, a police officer was charged with murder in relation to the shooting of a 19-year-old indigenous man in Yuendumu, Northern Territory. In September, police shot dead a 29-year-old indigenous woman in Geraldton, Western Australia.

Aboriginal and Torres Strait Islanders issued the "Uluru Statement from the Heart" in May 2017, but their recommendations to establish a First Nations voice in the constitution and a truth and justice commission have not been implemented. In July, the minister for Indigenous Australians, Ken Wyatt, announced plans to hold a referendum in the next three years on whether to enshrine constitutional recognition of Australia's indigenous people.

Children's Rights

Incarceration disproportionately affects indigenous children: they are 26 times more likely to be detained than non-indigenous children. Across Australia, around 600 children under the age of 14 are imprisoned each year, according to the Human Rights Law Centre. Australia states and territories set the age of criminal responsibility at 10.

The Northern Territory introduced legislation to "clarify" use of force, restraints and separation of children in detention centers, contradicting recommendations of a 2017 royal commission into abuses in the juvenile justice system that said restraints should only be used in emergency situations.

In August, the ABC reported that Queensland police were detaining children as young as 10 in police cells for weeks because of overcrowding in child detention centers. In May, an indigenous boy with a cognitive disability was pinned down, stripped naked, and locked in a police holding cell for three days.

In September, the Victorian ombudsman urged an end to solitary confinement after finding an alarming number of instances of the practice in jails, including of children and young people.

Freedom of Expression

Broadly drafted national security laws have been used against lawyers, journalists, and whistleblowers. In June, police raided the home of a journalist in relation to her story on a leaked plan to expand government surveillance. The next day, police raided the ABC's Sydney headquarters over a series of stories in 2017 alleging abuses by Australian special forces in Afghanistan. The warrant authorized the police to "add, copy, delete or alter other data ... found in the course of a search."

In August, former spy "Witness K" indicated he would plead guilty while his lawyer Bernard Collaery continues to fight charges of breaching secrecy laws for exposing wrongdoing by the Australian government to obtain an advantage in trade negotiations with Timor-Leste. The hearings have been held in secret.

In July and August, tensions flared between students on university campuses when students supporting democracy in Hong Kong were confronted by aggressive counter protesters. Academics have told Human Rights Watch that students from mainland China face surveillance on Australian campuses. In August, Education Minister Dan Tehan announced the creation of a national foreign interference taskforce, following concerns about Chinese government interference on Australian university campuses.

In October, police arrested a former federal senator and dozens of activists at a climate change protest for not complying with police direction regarding a road closure. The bail conditions for arrested protesters restricted them from going to the Sydney CBD and banned them from associating with other protesters. These conditions were overturned following a legal challenge.

In response to increased environmental protests and activism, in November Prime Minister Morrison called for new laws to ban revenue damaging secondary boycotts, such as urging banks to withdraw funds from mining projects.

Cybersecurity and Surveillance

In December 2018, the Australian parliament rushed through legislation undermining encryption and cybersecurity, allowing law enforcement and security agencies to order technology companies, and even individuals, to facilitate access to encrypted data and devices. At a parliamentary review into the new legislation, concerns were raised that the new laws were being used to bypass journalist protections.

Disability Rights

In April, Prime Minister Morrison announced a royal commission into violence, abuse, neglect, and exploitation of people with disabilities which held its first hearing in November.

Over half the prison population has a physical, sensory, psychosocial (mental health) or cognitive disability. People with disabilities struggle to cope in often overcrowded prisons without adequate access to support services and are particularly at risk of neglect and abuse. In February, in Hakea prison in Perth, prisoners beat to death an Aboriginal man with a mental health condition. At least two Aboriginal men with mental health conditions committed suicide in Western Australia prisons in 2019. The May 2019 coroner's inquest into the 2015 suicide of an Aboriginal man, Mr. Jackamarra, whose full name is not used for cultural reasons, recommended that mental health staff should assess prisoners with mental health issues or past self-harm attempts when they arrive at prison.

Rights of Older People

Australia's legal and regulatory framework is inadequate to protect older people in aged care facilities from chemical restraint. Many facilities in Australia routinely give older people with dementia dangerous drugs to control their behavior.

In July, a new regulation came into effect purporting to minimize the use of physical and chemical restraints, but may in fact simply normalize the practice. A parliamentary committee investigated the regulation's compliance with Australia's human rights obligations and recommended some changes including the right to informed consent.

The Royal Commission of Inquiry into Aged Care Quality and Safety released its interim report in October, finding Australia's aged care system to be a "shocking tale of neglect." It urged the government to take immediate action in three areas, including chemical restraint.

Women's Rights

In April, the High Court upheld the constitutional validity of "safe access zones" to prohibit harassment outside abortion clinics, and in September, the New South Wales government passed legislation to decriminalize abortion. Abortion laws vary state by state, but now only the states of South Australia and Western Australia still have laws in place that restrict women's access to abortion.

Terrorism and Counterterrorism

In June, the Australian government repatriated from al-Hol camp in northeast Syria eight Australian children of parents suspected of involvement in the armed group Islamic State (ISIS). Days after the children's evacuation, the government banned alleged foreign fighters as young as 14 from returning to Australia for two years. At time of writing, approximately 66 Australian nationals, 44 of them children, remain trapped in harsh conditions in camps in northeast Syria.

Foreign Policy

While the Australian government has tended towards a foreign policy that favors a "quiet diplomacy" approach to human rights, in 2019 it was more vocal on some key human rights issues. Foreign Minister Payne said in October, that Australia should lead by speaking honestly and consistently about human rights, and that "speaking our minds does not constitute interference in another country."

However, Prime Minister Morrison has responded to questions on human rights in countries such as China and Vietnam by referring to state sovereignty, in the same way that Association of Southeast Asian Nations (ASEAN) countries and the Chinese government seek to deflect criticism of their rights records.

After initially taking a low-key approach to its membership in the UN Human Rights Council, Australia stepped up in its second year to ensure the council renewed the mandate of the special rapporteur on human rights in Eritrea, and joined a statement urging China to end arbitrary detention of about 1 million Muslims in Xinjiang. At the Council's September session, Australia led a joint statement bringing attention to human rights violations by Saudi Arabia.

Australia exports military equipment to Saudi Arabia and the United Arab Emirates, despite concerns about alleged war crimes by the Saudi-led coalition in Yemen. There is little transparency about the types or quantities of equipment sold or the end-user.

The Australian government opposes a ban on fully autonomous weapons also known as "killer robots." Australia has not signed the Safe Schools Declaration, an intergovernmental pledge by countries to protect education in times of conflict.

Key International Actors

In March, the UN High Commissioner for Human Rights critiqued Australia's treatment of refugees and asylum seekers held offshore, saying "people have been suffering for more than six years; more humane policies could, and should, be implemented." The High Commissioner also spoke at a forum hosted by the Australian Human Rights Commission in October, raising a number of issues, including barriers faced by women, indigenous persons, persons with disabilities, and migrants and refugees.

In June 2019, United Nations' experts on migrant rights, torture, health and mercenaries urged the Australian government to immediately provide healthcare to refugees on Manus Island and Nauru, and transfer those requiring urgent care to Australia.

Azerbaijan

Azerbaijan's authorities continued to maintain rigid control, severely curtailing freedoms of association, expression, and assembly. The government released over 50 human rights defenders, journalists, opposition activists, religious believers and other perceived critics imprisoned on politically motivated charges. But at least 30 others remained wrongfully imprisoned, while authorities regularly targeted its critics and other dissenting voices.

Other human rights problems persisted, including torture and ill-treatment in custody, violations of freedom of assembly, undue interference in the work of lawyers, and restrictions on media freedoms.

Prosecuting Government Critics

In March, President Ilham Aliyev pardoned over 50 imprisoned perceived critics, including journalists, bloggers, opposition political parties' activists, and others. Their convictions remained in force, and some faced travel restrictions, while others left the country fearing further politically motivated persecution.

Among those released was Bayram Mammadov, a youth opposition movement activist. But two weeks later, police arrested him following a media interview in which he said he would continue his political activism. A court sentenced him to 30 days in jail on spurious disobedience charges. Police summoned several other pardoned activists for conversations, warning them not to engage in activities critical of the government, such as demonstrations and online criticism.

In March, prominent anti-corruption blogger Mehman Huseynov was freed after fully serving a two-year prison sentence on groundless libel charges. In December 2018, two months before his term was to end, the authorities brought new, false charges, claiming Huseynov physically assaulted a guard. Authorities dropped the charges in January 2019, following local and international outcry.

In February, Mammad Ibrahim, an advisor to the opposition Azerbaijan Popular Front Party (APFP), was released. Arrested in 2016, Ibrahim fully served both his sentence on bogus hooliganism charges and an additional five-month sentence, based on a new charge that authorities pressed two days before his originally scheduled release.

Three leading APFP members, Orkhan Bakhishli, Fuad Ahmadli, and Asif Yusili, remained in prison on bogus drugs, private data misuse, and forgery charges, respectively. In June, a court reduced Bakhishli's term from six to three years.

In October, ahead of an unsanctioned rally, APFP member Pasha Umudov was arrested and sent to pretrial detention on bogus drug charges. Authorities pressed bogus misdemeanor hooliganism, public swearing, and other charges against dozens of opposition activists and other critics. In August alone, courts sentenced at least six active APFP members to fines or jail terms ranging from 10 to 60 days.

Authorities lifted travel bans against several activists and journalists, but restrictions remained in place for others due to their verdicts or, in several cases, to their status as witnesses in investigations dating to 2014. APFP chairman Ali Karimli has been banned from foreign travel since 2006, when his passport expired. Authorities have since refused to reissue it, citing bogus pretexts.

At least 17 members of Muslim Unity, an unregistered, conservative Shiite movement, remained in prison on extremism and other charges, following a 2017 verdict flawed by credible torture allegations. In July, authorities released another member, Abulfaz Bunyadov on medical grounds due to injuries he sustained during his 2015 arrest.

Freedom of Assembly

Azerbaijan effectively imposes a blanket ban on protests in the central areas of Baku and instead offers demonstrators a remote location on the outskirts of the city to for rallies. In 2019, the number of people handed administrative fines or brief jail terms for supposedly violating the country's restrictive regulations on public gatherings was several times higher than throughout 2018.

In January, about 40 people received jail terms of 10 to 30 days for demanding the release of the blogger Mehman Huseynov through sanctioned peaceful protests and social media activism.

In October, police violently broke up three unsanctioned, peaceful protests in central Baku, and arrested and beat protesters who demanded freedom for political prisoners and an end to economic injustice and violence against women. Courts sentenced dozens of protesters in pro forma hearings to fines and detentions. Police denied detainees access to lawyers of their choosing. At least 35 senior AFPF politicians received sentences of up to 60 days on bogus charges. Numerous peaceful protesters sustained injuries, including bruising, and fractures, from police beatings. While in police custody, AFPF leader Ali Karimli sustained bruises on his head, face, and neck due to police beatings. Police also beat Tofig Yabublu, another prominent opposition politician and former political prisoner and ordered him to publicly pledge to stop his political activism.

Police also made home visits to warn people who had indicated on social media that they would attend rallies. Days before one of the protests, police detained most of the protest organizers.

Intimidation of Lawyers

In 2019, the Azerbaijani Bar Association, which is seen as closely tied to the government, restored the licenses of three lawyers who work on cases involving political persecution. Their licenses had been suspended for one year following complaints filed by the prosecutor's office. But pressure continued on several other lawyers.

In February, a court approved the disbarment of Yalchin Imanov, whom the Bar Association expelled in 2017 after he publicly reported about his client's torture in prison.

Also in February, the Bar Association reprimanded Elchin Sadigov for advising his client, Yunis Safarov, about filing a torture allegation. Safarov is in custody and charged with the 2018 murder of the Ganja mayor. The reprimand followed a prosecutor's office complaint denying the torture and alleging Sadigov unlawfully tried to persuade Safarov to make an allegation. The complaint referred to a statement Safarov signed in custody about alleged pressure by Sadigov and to a confidential conversation between the two.

Freedom of Expression

All mainstream media remained under tight government control. Defamation is a criminal offense.

Journalist Seymur Hazi was released from prison in August after serving out his five-year sentence on a politically motivated hooliganism conviction.

In June, Polad Aslanov, editor of independent news websites Xeberman and Press-az, was jailed on treason charges, which he claimed were in retaliation for his criticism of public officials and his ongoing investigation into alleged corruption in the Ministry of National Security. Aslanov's lawyer said Aslanov faced government harassment in previous years in retaliation for his reporting.

In February and March, respectively, a court handed Mustafa Hajibeyli and Anar Mammadov, two journalists with small, independent news websites, five-and-a-half-year suspended sentences for their coverage of the 2018 assassination attempt on the Ganja mayor and subsequent nationwide electricity blackout. Hajibeyli edited the pro-opposition Bastainfo.com news website, which remained blocked since July 2018. Mammadov is editor-in-chief of Criminal.az. Both journalists' articles criticized the mayor's brutal rule and faulted the authorities for failing to prevent the ensuing violence.

Both were convicted on trumped-up sedition, forgery, and abuse of office charges. They remained at liberty but under foreign travel bans.

Other journalists including Afgan Mukhtarli, Ziya Asadli, Araz Guliyev, and Elchin Ismayilli, who publicly criticized the authorities, remained behind bars on bogus charges.

Harassing Critics Abroad

Authorities tried to silence exiled activists by intimidating their relatives in Azerbaijan. Security officials repeatedly interrogated relatives of activists based in Germany and France to pressure them to denounce their relatives and threatened to jail them if their relatives continued their activism.

In April, REAL TV, a private news station closely tied to the government, launched an intimidation campaign against Sevinj Osmangizi, who lives in exile and runs a popular YouTube news channel about Azerbaijan. In a series of broadcasts, REAL TV tried to blackmail her, including through illegally obtained photos and fabricated emails, into ceasing her broadcasts. It also broadcasted an illegally recorded conversation between Osmanqizi and another independent journalist.

Sexual Orientation and Gender Identity (SOGI)

On April 1, police detained around 14 people, gay men, and transgender women, claiming they engaged in illegal sex work. According to Nefes LGBT Azerbaijan Alliance, an independent group, in some cases the men were detained after being lured for dates through mobile apps. Police took at least some for unlawful, forced testing for HIV and other sexually transmitted diseases. Courts fined two for "hooliganism" and handed jail sentences of up to 15 days to another three for resisting police, then fined and released them upon appeal. No confirmed information is available regarding sanctions against the other nine.

Torture and Ill-Treatment

Authorities typically dismiss complaints of torture and other ill-treatment in custody, and the practice continued with impunity.

In February, a court sentenced three senior APFP members, Saleh Rustamov, Agil Maharramov, and Babek Hasanov, to seven, four, and three years, respectively, on illegal entrepreneurship, drug, and other charges. The charges stem from allegations that Rustamov illegally used his company's funds to support imprisoned party activists and party activities. Police arrested the men in May 2018. Authorities held Rustamov incommunicado for 17 days and denied him access to his lawyer for a month. During trial, the men testified they were tortured and pressured to confess. No effective investigations followed the allegations.

In March, law enforcement personnel repeatedly slapped and kicked Bayram Mammadov (see above), and held him for nearly 24 hours, handcuffed, legs tied, and lying on the floor. His lawyer said he had bruises. Authorities failed to conduct an effective investigation.

Also in March, 14 defendants convicted on mass rioting and other charges for the July 2018 unrest in Ganja testified in court that police had beat them repeatedly to elicit confessions and testimony. The authorities conducted a superficial investigation into the allegations before closing it. According to the defendants' lawyers, authorities claimed that the wounds and injuries that staff at the pretrial facility documented had been sustained when the men were resisting arrest.

Key International Actors

The March pardon prompted statements from the US administration and the European Union urging Baku to release others in prison on politically motivated charges.

The EU continued to negotiate a new partnership agreement with Azerbaijan to enhance political and economic ties. In April, following meetings with top Azerbaijani officials, then-EU High Representative Federica Mogherini said that she had raised concerns regarding "the limited space for civil society and human rights defenders in Azerbaijan." The statement also said that the EU intends to make human rights an essential element of its cooperation with Azerbaijan.

Following his July trip to Baku and meeting with President Aliyev, then-European Council President Donald Tusk underlined the "essential importance" the EU "attach[es] to the respect for the rule of law, human rights and fundamental freedoms" in cooperation with Azerbaijan. Tusk also met with civil society activists to hear their concerns.

In January, the European Parliament adopted a resolution on the case of Mehman Huseynov and called for the immediate and unconditional release of all political prisoners.

In September, the rapporteur for the Parliamentary Assembly of the Council of Europe on political prisoners in Azerbaijan went to Baku. She met four prisoners, civil society representatives, and others. Her report was expected by the end of 2019.

In July, Council of Europe Human Rights Commissioner Dunja Mijatovic visited Baku, where she raised concerns about arbitrary arrest and misuse of criminal law against critics and highlighted the need to release "all persons who are in detention because of the views they expressed." She also called on authorities to create better livelihood opportunities for internally displaced people.

The EU and the human rights commissioner of the Council of Europe (CoE), as well as the rapporteurs on Azerbaijan of the CoE's parliamentary assembly all issued statements expressing concern about violent dispersals of the October protests and urging effective investigations and release of all detainees.

Bahrain

The human rights situation in Bahrain remained dire in 2019. Authorities have banned all independent media from operating in the country, dissolved all opposition groups, and cracked down on critical online posts. The government executed three people in July, including two prisoners who were convicted in a mass trial marred by serious due process violations and allegations of torture.

Authorities continue to arrest, convict, and harass prominent human rights defenders, journalists, and opposition leaders. The Court of Cassation upheld unjust sentences against prominent human rights defender Nabeel Rajab and opposition leader Shaikh Ali Salman. Authorities have failed to hold officials accountable for torture and ill-treatment, and oversight mechanisms are not independent of the government.

King Hamad al-Khalifa and the courts have reinstated the citizenship of 698 individuals who had their nationality revoked on apparently trumped-up terrorism or national security charges. However, almost 300 individuals remain stripped of their Bahraini nationality.

Bahrain continued to deny access to the United Nations special procedures, including the special rapporteur on torture.

Freedom of Expression, Association, and Peaceful Assembly

On December 31, 2018, the Court of Cassation upheld a five-year sentence for Nabeel Rajab, head of the Bahrain Center for Human Rights, arising from his 2015 tweets alleging torture in Jaw Prison and criticizing Bahrain's participation in the Saudi-led military campaign in Yemen. Rajab, who has already served two years on other charges related to peaceful expression, is set to remain behind bars until 2023. He appears to have at times been subjected to treatment that may amount to arbitrary punishment, and his health has deteriorated significantly. On August 2018, the UN Working Group on Arbitrary Detention called for Nabeel Rajab's immediate release, saying his detention was not only arbitrary but also constituted "discrimination based on political or other opinion, as well as on his status as a human rights defender."

On January 28, the Court of Cassation also upheld the life sentence against Shaikh Ali Salman, leader of Al-Wifaq, Bahrain's largest but now-dissolved opposition political society. The government in November 2017 filed trumped up charges against Salman for allegedly spying for Qatar. A lower court acquitted him of these charges, but on November 4, 2018, an appeals court overturned that decision and sentenced him to life in prison.

Thirteen prominent dissidents have been serving lengthy prison terms since their arrest in 2011. They include human rights advocates Abdulhadi al-Khawaja and Abduljalil al-Singace, and Hassan Mushaima, leader of the unrecognized opposition group Al Haq, all three serving life terms.

In 2019 Bahrain widened its suppression of online and social media activity. On May 30, 2019, the Bahraini Interior Ministry declared that it will prosecute people who follow "inciting accounts" or share their posts on Twitter. The on-line platform in a June 6 post agreed with activists that such statements "post a significant risk to free expression and journalism."

No independent media operate in Bahrain. In 2017, the Information Affairs Ministry suspended *Al Wasat*, the country's only independent newspaper. Independent and foreign journalists rarely have access to Bahrain, and Human Rights Watch and other rights groups are routinely denied access. International wire services, when they cover Bahrain, do so from Dubai or elsewhere outside the country.

Death Penalty

On July 27, Bahrain executed three men, including two men, Ali al-Arab and Ahmad al-Malali, convicted of terrorism offenses. A court had sentenced them to death on January 31, 2018, in a mass trial marred by allegations of torture and serious due process violations. The Court of Cassation upheld their death sentences on May 6. Under Bahraini law, the king must ratify a death sentence before it can be carried out. He also has the power to commute it or grant a pardon.

Currently eight people in Bahraini prisons are at imminent risk of execution, having exhausted all legal remedies, according to the London-based Bahrain Institute for Rights and Democracy (BIRD).

Security Forces and Prisons

Authorities in 2019, as in years past, failed to credibly investigate and prosecute officials and police officers who allegedly committed violations, including torture. Despite numerous complaints by detainees and their family members, the Interior Ministry's Ombudsman Office and Special Investigations Unit failed to display independence from the government and did not hold prison guards and officers to account.

On August 15, prisoners in the Jaw Prison and Dry Dock Detention Center began a hunger strike to protest conditions in detention, including placement in "isolation" cells where prisoners are held with individuals with whom they do not share a common language, culture, or religion. Prisoners also demanded an end to anti-Shia religious persecution and abuse by prison guards, as well as removal of glass barriers during family visits.

The Interior Ministry's Ombudsman on August 23 claimed that the demands of the prisoners do not fall within the issues that the ombudsman is competent to consider.

On September 17, a Bahraini court rejected a motion filed by Nabeel Rajab's legal team asking that he be granted a non-custodial sentence instead of the jail term he is currently serving, invoking a 2017 law that allows courts to convert jail terms into alternative sanctions. Rajab is currently detained with nine other prisoners convicted of prostitution offenses. Hajer Mansoor and Medina Ali, two female activists at the Isa Town Prison, also applied for non-custodial sentences, but authorities rejected their motions.

On the occasion of Eid al-Adha, on August 10, King Hamad issued a royal pardon for 105 detainees, including activist Najah Yusuf. Yusuf was imprisoned and subjected to physical abuse and sexual assault after she criticized the Formula One races in Bahrain on social media in April 2017.

Arbitrary Citizenship Revocations

Courts stripped 180 persons of their citizenship for alleged offenses that include "terrorism," "national security," and "offending the country," between January and April, according to the London-based Bahrain Institute for Rights and Democracy (BIRD).

On April 20, the king reinstated the citizenship of 551 individuals who had their citizenship stripped through a court order. In July, the courts restored the nationality of another 147 individuals. However, almost 300 persons whose citizenship had been stripped in recent years remain without Bahraini nationality and in most cases stateless.

On June 27, Bahrain amended its citizenship revocation laws, restricting the power to strip nationality to the cabinet. Under the amendments, the king and the judiciary no longer have the power to unilaterally strip Bahrainis of their citizenship for national security or terrorism crimes. All known citizenship revocations since 2012 have been handed down by the courts, or by royal decree, or by order of the Interior Ministry.

Human Rights Defenders

The Court of Cassation upheld the three-year prison sentences against three relatives of prominent exiled activist Sayed Ahmed al-Wadaei on February 25. They were arrested in March 2017 and convicted in October 2017 on dubious terrorism charges that appear to have been filed as a reprisal for al-Wadaei's human rights work. The judicial process was marred by due process violations and allegations of ill-treatment and coerced confessions.

Women's Rights, Gender Identity, and Sexual Orientation

Bahraini family laws discriminate against women in the right to divorce, inherit, and transmit Bahraini nationality to their children on an equal basis to men, and deprive their children of the right to obtain citizenship on an equal basis with children of Bahraini men. Article 353 of the penal code exempts perpetrators of rape from prosecution and punishment if they marry their victims. Bahrain's parliament proposed a full repeal of that article in 2016, but the cabinet rejected the proposal. Article 334 of the penal code reduces the penalties for perpetrators of so-called honor crimes.

In December 2018, Bahrain amended its labor law to ban discrimination on the basis of sex, origin, language or creed, and sexual harassment in the workplace.

Adultery and sexual relations outside marriage are criminalized. There is no law to prohibit general discrimination on the grounds of gender identity or sexual orientation.

While domestic workers are included in the labor law, they are excluded from most of its protections, including those related to weekly rest days, a minimum wage, and limits on working hours. In 2017, Bahrain introduced a unified standard contract for domestic workers, which requires detailing the nature of the job, work and rest hours, and weekly days off. While this contract is important, it lacks the legal protection and enforcement mechanisms to ensure domestic workers have their rights respected.

Key International Actors

Bahrain continued to participate in Yemen military operations as part of the Saudi Arabia-led coalition, which is responsible for serious laws of war violations. The coalition has failed to credibly investigate potential war crimes, and coalition members, including Bahrain, have provided insufficient or no information about their role in alleged unlawful attacks.

The US maintains a major naval base in Bahrain. During a meeting with King Hamad on January 11, US Secretary of State Mike Pompeo thanked Bahrain for its strategic partnership with the United States, including counterterrorism. There were no indications that Bahrain's human rights record was part of their conversation.

On May 3, the State Department approved two major weapons sales to Bahrain for Patriot Missile Systems worth $2.5 billion and weapons to support F-16 fighter jets worth $750 million.

King Hamad met with French President Emmanuel Macron in Paris on April 30, during which Marcron urged Bahrain to establish "political dialogue that includes all components of Bahraini society," according to the president's office. Bahrain's foreign minister denied that Macron had raised this issue during the meeting.

On July 27, the European Union expressed concerns about the executions of Ali al-Arab and Ahmad al-Malali and urged Bahrain to introduce a moratorium on executions as a step towards abolition. It also criticized the Cassation Court's life sentence against Shaikh Ali Salman, calling the verdict "a further step against dissenting voices."

Bahrain has not responded to requests from UN human rights experts to visit. The government effectively cancelled the visit of the special rapporteur on torture in 2013, which it had earlier approved.

Bangladesh

Bangladesh's ruling Awami League government ignored calls during the year for an independent investigation into serious allegations of electoral fraud after the December 2018 national elections.

Impunity for abuses by security forces, including enforced disappearances and extrajudicial killings, remained pervasive. The government continued to violate international standards on freedom of speech in its crackdown on government critics.

Host to nearly 1 million Rohingya refugees from neighboring Myanmar, Bangladesh has kept its commitment under international law not to force returns. Conditions in the camps worsened, however, as the government resisted infrastructure improvements, repeatedly threatened to relocate refugees to a potentially uninhabitable island, and took steps to restrict freedom of movement and access to the internet in the camps.

In March, following strikes in which workers demanded wage hikes, at least 7,500 garment workers were dismissed from their jobs in the largest crackdown on workers in Bangladesh in years.

More women entered the workforce and the country made another step towards gender equality when the High Court removed the requirement that Muslim women in Bangladesh declare whether they are virgins on their marriage certificate.

National Election Aftermath

The national election on December 30, 2018, was characterized by abuses including attacks on opposition members, arbitrary arrests, and voter intimidation. The ruling Awami League won 96 percent of the contested parliamentary seats and Prime Minister Sheikh Hasina returned for a third consecutive term. The Election Commission rushed to call the election free and fair. Instead of investigating irregularities, Bangladesh authorities arrested journalists for their reporting.

The government ignored calls for an independent investigation into allegations of election fraud from the European Union, United Nations, United States, and United Kingdom.

Khaleda Zia, leader of the opposition Bangladesh National Party (BNP), has remained in prison for nearly two years at time of writing over longstanding corruption cases.

Freedom of Expression and Association

The silencing of critics, journalists, students, and activists did not subside even after the Awami League claimed the 2018 election. Instead, the landslide victory seemed only to embolden authorities in their crackdown.

Journalists faced pressure to self-censor or risk arrest. The Digital Security Act, passed in October 2018 to replace the often-misused Information and Communication Technology Act, included harsher provisions that have been used to penalize criticism of the government. The Bangladesh's Editors' Council, an association of newspaper editors, said that it effectively prohibits investigative journalism. But the government refused to budge despite repeated calls to bring the law in line with Bangladesh's international commitments to protect freedom of expression.

Authorities increased internet censorship. The government blocked nearly 20,000 websites in February in what was described as an "anti-pornography" sweep, but which included a number of popular blogging sites. In March, the National Telecommunication Monitoring Centre blocked access to Al Jazeera's English news website after the news agency published a report citing allegations against Prime Minister Sheikh Hasina's security advisor.

Lack of Accountability

The government continued to deny enforced disappearances, extrajudicial killings, torture and other violations by security forces including by the Rapid Action Battalion, Directorate General of Forces Intelligence (DGFI), or the police, particularly its Detective Branch. Security forces persisted with a long-standing pattern of covering up unlawful killings by claiming deaths occurred during a gun-fight or in crossfire. Hundreds were killed in alleged "crossfire" exchanges including during a drive against recreational drugs.

Refugees

Bangladesh continued to host and contribute humanitarian services to Rohingya refugees who fled ethnic cleansing by the Myanmar military since August 2017. However, conditions in the camps deteriorated as the government increased pressure on refugees to return to Myanmar. According to the United Nations High Commissioner for Refugees, many refugees require psychosocial support due to the psychological impact of conflict and difficult conditions in the camps, but mental health services are not sufficient.

In August, Bangladesh attempted for a second time to begin repatriations. Refugees refused, fearing that they would face the same violence and oppression in Myanmar that they fled.

Insisting that the camps are temporary, the Bangladesh government obstructed certain infrastructure improvements, particularly in shelter and education. The majority of the camps' population are children, yet the Bangladesh government barred agencies from providing any formal, accredited schooling. When Rohingya children, desperate for an education, acquired falsified documents to enroll in Bangladesh schools, the government cracked down, expelling the students.

In September, the government restricted refugees' access to the internet and online communications. Bangladesh made repeated threats to relocate refugees to the silt island of Bhasan Char, despite serious concerns over the island's habitability.

In November, the government announced that work had begun on building fences around the refugee camps in Cox's Bazar, a measure neither necessary nor proportional to maintain camp security and therefore in violation of international human rights law.

Labor Rights

In early 2019, over 50,000 garment workers participated in wildcat strikes protesting changes to the minimum wage. Police used excessive force to disperse the protesters, killing one worker and injuring over 50. At least 7,500 garment workers were dismissed from their jobs. Many of these workers were blacklisted from work at other factories.

The Bangladesh Accord on Fire and Building Safety, a legally binding agreement between unions and brands established in the wake of the Rana Plaza disaster to ensure factory safety, transitioned to the Readymade Sustainability Council, a national monitoring mechanism.

Indigenous Rights

Activists continued to call for the full implementation of the Peace Accord in the Chittagong Hill Tracts. Over 20 years after the peace agreement, the region remains under military occupation and indigenous rights activists face threats of arrest, enforced disappearance, and violence.

On April 9, Michael Chakma, an indigenous rights activist, disappeared on his way to Dhaka. On May 21 the High Court asked the Home Ministry to submit a report on the progress of investigation within five weeks. There had been no response at time of writing.

Women's and Girls' Rights

Protests broke out nationwide calling on the government to reform and enforce Bangladeshi laws and practices concerning sexual assault after Nusrat Jahan Rafi, 19, was burned to death after she filed a complaint of attempted rape against her madrassa teacher. Authorities failed to properly enforce laws to protect women and girls and have yet to pass legislation on sexual harassment.

Bangladesh continues to have one of the highest rates of child marriage in the world. Prime Minister Sheikh Hasina committed to end marriage for girls under 15 by 2021, but there was little meaningful progress during the year. Instead, a special provision remained in effect that allows for child marriage in "special cases," with permission of their parents and a court.

Sexual Orientation and Gender Identity

Sexual and gender minorities remained under pressure and threat following the killing of two activists in 2016. The government failed to properly enforce policies protecting rights of hijras.

Key International Actors

The Bangladesh government ignored or dismissed key recommendations, particularly with regards to credible reports of electoral fraud, crackdown on free speech, torture practices by its security forces, and increasing cases of enforced disappearances and killings.

Bangladesh participated in a review of its practices by the United Nations Committee against Torture for the first time since ratifying the Convention against Torture over 20 years ago. When the United Nations Committee against Torture pressed Bangladesh to put an end to the increasing cases of enforced disappearances by law enforcement officials and asked about torture allegations consistently documented by human rights groups, the government vehemently denied the allegations.

In March, Bangladesh welcomed the Office of the Prosecutor of the International Criminal Court (ICC) on its first mission to Bangladesh as part of a preliminary examination into alleged crimes against humanity against ethnic Rohingya from Myanmar.

After a visit to Bangladesh, European Union Special Representative for Human Rights Eamon Gilmore emphasized the importance of labor rights to bilateral EU-Bangladesh relations and in the trade relations under the "Everything but Arms" trade scheme. In September, the European Parliament commended Bangladesh's efforts hosting Rohingya refugees, and called on authorities to guarantee full and discrimination-free access to quality education for Rohingya children; lift restrictions on internet access, online communications, and freedom of movement; and ensure the security forces operating in the camps uphold all standards to protect refugees' personal security.

India failed to speak up against human rights violations in Bangladesh, including against the political opposition.

China resisted international efforts to hold the Myanmar military accountable for abuses against the Rohingya, and instead pushed for repatriation. Bangladesh accused Myanmar of failing to create conditions that would enable the safe and voluntary return of Rohingya refugees.

Belarus

In 2019, Belarus continued to harass and pressure civil society activists and independent media. Authorities denied access to journalists at government events, arbitrarily prosecuted dozens of journalists, and arrested peaceful environmental protesters.

Belarus remains the only European country to use the death penalty. Those condemned to death are executed by a shot to the head. Authorities do not inform families of the execution date or the burial place.

Death Penalty

In November 2018, authorities executed Ihar Hershankou and Siamion Berazhnou, sentenced on murder charges. In June, they executed Aliaksandr Zhylnikau. The fate of his codefendant on murder charges, Viacheslau Suharka, is unknown. According to Viasna, a leading local rights group, inmates sentenced on the same case are usually executed simultaneously.

Aliaksandr Asipovich and Viktar Paulau were sentenced to death on murder charges in January and July 2019 respectively. In October, Viktar Syargel was also sentenced to death on murder charges.

In August, Belarusian authorities and the Council of Europe (CoE) announced plans to develop a roadmap to a moratorium on capital punishment.

Freedom of Expression and Attacks on Journalists

Belarusian media law requires journalists working for media outlets registered outside Belarus to obtain accreditation from the Foreign Ministry and have an official labor contract with the accredited foreign media outlet. Freelancers find it virtually impossible to become accredited. Authorities often arbitrarily denied accreditation to journalists working for foreign media.

In May, the Foreign Ministry refused accreditation to Viktar Parfionenka and Yauhen Skrabets of Poland-based Radio Racyja. The response to Skrabets indicated his accreditation was denied because Radio Racyja had published work by non-accredited journalists.

As of January, only five media websites have been granted official registration, according to the Belarusian Association of Journalists (BAJ). Unregistered websites cannot file requests for accreditation with government institutions.

Authorities routinely blocked media access to official events. In April, journalists from TUT.by, BelaPAN agency, newspaper Belarusy I Rynok, and European Radio of Belarus (ERB) were denied accreditation to cover President Aleksandr Lukashenko's address to the National Assembly, despite both BelaPAN and ERB holding permanent accreditation to cover parliament. In May, authorities blocked journalists from attending a session in the Pershamaiki district administration on the redevelopment of a part of Minsk. In June, officials denied a Brestskaya Gazeta journalist entry to a court building due to "lack of accreditation." Some independent media and bloggers were denied access to a news conference with the administration of the Brest battery factory project, and to a meeting between the head of Brest regional government Anatol Lis and environmental protesters.

According to the Belarussian Association of Journalists, in the first nine months of 2019, authorities brought 39 cases against 18 journalists for "illegal production and distribution of mass media products." They were fined a total of approximately US$36,600.

In January, border guards at the Minsk airport denied entry to Olga Vallee, Fojo Media Institute program coordinator and a Swedish national, who traveled to Belarus at the invitation of BAJ.

BAJ reported that in mid-March 2019, police in Minsk detained two Russian journalists, Pavel Nikulin and Jan Potarsky, before their lecture at the Belarusian Press Club. Both were released three hours later without charge, but police seized their presentation materials.

In April, a court convicted an independent media editor of criminal negligence on allegations that some of her staff had been accessing the website of BelTA, the state news agency, without paying a subscription fee.

Also in April, authorities searched the offices of Belsat TV and seized computers and data storage devices following a libel complaint from a public official.

Siarhei Piatrukhin, a popular critical blogger, was repeatedly detained and fined throughout 2019 for coverage of protests against the battery plant construction near Brest. In April, he was convicted of criminal slander and libel for a series of videos he had uploaded to YouTube alleging police abuses.

Freedom of Information

In December 2018, amendments to the media law entered into effect requiring that all online media outlets keep records of and disclose to the authorities the names of people who submit comments. The amendments also provide for holding owners of registered online media criminally liable for any content on their website.

In May, President Lukashenko signed a decree blocking websites that called for "unauthorized protests" during the European Games, a large multi-sport event organized by the European Olympic Committees in Minsk in June.

In July, amendments to the criminal code articles on libel and defamation limited the definition of criminal slander and insult to speech uttered in a public space, such as in the media, a public speech, or on the internet.

Freedom of Assembly

In January, amendments to the law on mass events came into effect introducing a notification procedure for organizing public assemblies. However, in practice, sign-off is often denied, and organizers and participants are fined.

During Freedom Day on March 25, treated by many as an unofficial holiday and an alternative Belarus Independence Day, police detained 15 persons at an unauthorized opposition rally in Minsk. At least two were held in jail overnight.

Since 2018, of over 90 requests made to authorities to hold protests in Brest against the battery plant construction, only one was permitted. In April, police arrested 18 activists and fined three for their involvement in the peaceful protests. Also in April, police searched the car of activist Maisey Mazko, allegedly found cartridges and a briquette of an unknown substance, and opened a criminal case into alleged possession of ammunition. Another activist present during the search said the evidence was fabricated. Between May and August, authorities arrested and charged with administrative offenses at least 15 other activists involved in the peaceful protests in Brest.

Freedom of Association

Laws and regulations governing public associations remain restrictive, preventing rights groups or political opposition movements from operating freely. Authorities continued to deny registration to independent groups and opposition parties on arbitrary pretexts.

In July, new legislation entered into force eliminating criminal liability for participation in the activities of unregistered organizations and replacing it with an administrative fine of up to 1,225 Belarusian rubles (US$600).

Discrimination against Roma

In May 2019, approximately 100 Roma in Mahilioŭ were detained for supposed disorderly conduct during the investigation of a policeman's alleged murder. Viasna reported that the detentions were ethnicity-based and involved violence, threats, and intimidation. Police held over 50 men in custody for three days, allegedly humiliating and beating them. They released the men without charge, threatening them with re-arrest if they spoke to media.

Later, the investigation found that the policeman in question had committed suicide. The head of the president's office apologized to the Roma community; however, the interior minister refused to apologize and dismissed allegations of xenophobia. In June, a working group convened by the prosecutor general to investigate reports of police brutality found "no illegal actions or abuse of power."

People with Disabilities

In 2018, an interdepartmental working group drafted a law "On the rights of persons with disabilities and their social integration." A vote in parliament was expected before the end of the year.

Key International Actors

Belarus continued to refuse to cooperate with the United Nations special rapporteur on Belarus, Anaïs Marin, appointed in 2018. In her first report to the UN Human Rights Council (UNHRC) in May, Marin noted the "cyclical" and "systemic" nature of human rights violations. In July, UNHRC renewed her mandate for another year.

In February, the European Union prolonged its embargo on arms and on equipment that could be used for internal repression, as well as the asset freeze and travel ban against four people designated in connection with the unresolved disappearances of two opposition politicians, one businessman and one journalist in 1999 and in 2000. The EU and the CoE's Committee of Ministers and Parliamentary Assembly issued statements condemning the death sentences of Asipovich and Paulau, and the execution of Zhylnikau, calling for a moratorium on executions as a step towards abolition.

The CoE also organized a round table on capital punishment in Belarus as part of the World Congress Against the Death Penalty in Brussels. The UN Human Rights Committee also condemned the execution of Zhylnikau and called for a moratorium on capital punishment. In June, the EU and Belarus held the sixth round of their bilateral Human Rights Dialogue, at which the EU called attention to the restrictions on freedom of assembly, the lack of anti-discrimination legislation, and the use of the death penalty.

In March, the Organization for Security and Co-operation in Europe (OSCE) representative on freedom of the media made an official visit to Minsk and called on the government to protect freedom of speech and de-monopolize state-owned media. In April, he denounced the search of the offices of Belsat.

In June, the German Bundestag Committee on Human Rights and Humanitarian Aid issued a statement on human rights and the death penalty in Belarus to coincide with the European Games in Minsk.

Bolivia

Bolivian President Evo Morales resigned on November 10 following massive social protests, an Organization of American States (OAS) report detailing "clear manipulation" of the voting system during the October presidential election, and a request from the Armed Forces chief that he step down.

On November 13, Jeanine Áñez, vice president of the Senate and a political opponent of Morales, took office as interim president in a highly controversial move that the Constitutional Court endorsed.

The Morales administration created a hostile environment for human rights defenders and promoted judicial changes that pose a serious threat to the rule of law in the country. After taking office, President Áñez announced and adopted alarming measures that run counter to fundamental human rights standards, including a decree that will shield military personnel from accountability for abuses during crowd-control operations.

Violence against women, due process rights of detainees, child labor, and impunity for human rights violations are also major concerns.

Elections

In October, President Evo Morales ran for a fourth term. A majority of the Bolivian people had backed term limits in a 2016 national referendum, but Morales was allowed to run by the Constitutional Court in a 2017 ruling.

Massive protests broke after the election, which many Bolivians saw as unfair and fraudulent.

On October 25, the Supreme Electoral Tribunal (TSE) indicated that Morales won the presidency. But on November 10, the OAS presented a report detailing a "clear manipulation" of the voting system.

After the OAS report, Morales said the country would hold new elections and replace all TSE members. Later that day, the national military chief, Gen. Williams Kalima, asked Morales to resign. Morales resigned that day, saying he was being ousted in a coup. He traveled to Mexico the following day, after the Mexican government granted him asylum.

Protest-Related Violence and Abuses

As of November 17, 23 people had died and over 700 had been injured in the context of protests since the October 20 elections, according to the Inter-American Commission on Human Rights (IACHR).

On November 15, 9 people died and 122 were wounded during a demonstration in Chapare province. The United Nations High Commissioner for Human Rights said that the deaths "appear to be the result of unnecessary or disproportionate use of force by the police and army." Protesters, including Morales supporters, have also engaged in serious acts of violence.

On November 15, Áñez adopted a presidential decree deploying the military in "defense of society and public order." The decree exempts members of the armed forces from criminal responsibility when they act "in legitimate defense or state of necessity" and respect the "principles of legality, absolute necessity and proportionality" as defined under specific provisions of Bolivian law. The decree is inconsistent with international human rights standards and sends the dangerous message to soldiers in the streets that they will not be held accountable for abuses.

Judicial Independence

The Morales aministration sought to reform the Bolivian justice system, which has been plagued, for years, by corruption, delays, and political interference. But some initiatives pose a serious risk to judicial independence.

In 2017, the Magistrate's Council ruled that all judges appointed before enactment of the 2009 constitution were to be considered transitory and could be summarily removed. The council has since summarily dismissed roughly 100 judges, without providing reasons for the dismissals nor opportunity to challenge them.

In December 2017, by popular election, voters elected high court judges and members of the Magistrate's Council from closed lists created by the Plurinational Assembly, where the party of President Morales, Movement towards Socialism (MAS), holds a majority.

In 2018, the Magistrate's Council adopted a resolution granting itself broad powers to transfer judges to other cities or court circuits.

In August 2019, an opposition congresswoman released audio recordings strongly suggesting that high-level judges and members of the Magistrate's Council had exercised improper influence in the appointment of low-level judges.

Impunity for Abuses

Bolivia has prosecuted only a few of the officials responsible for human rights violations committed under authoritarian governments from 1964 through 1982, partly because the armed forces have at times refused to share information with judicial authorities about the fate of people killed or forcibly disappeared.

A "Truth Commission" that the government established in August 2017 to conduct non-judicial investigations of grave human rights abuses during that period is intended to provide information to prosecutors and judges to convict those responsible. The findings had yet to be published at time of writing. The Armed Forces have made limited progress in declassifying military files and releasing information about victims of enforced disappearance.

Due Process and Prison Conditions

Around 66 percent of all Bolivians in detention have not been convicted of a crime. Extended pretrial detention and trial delays overcrowd prisons and lead to poor and inhumane conditions. By mid-2019, more than 19,000 inmates were packed into prisons built to hold a maximum of around 5,000.

In July 2018, the UN Subcommittee on Prevention of Torture said that prison officials' "delegation of authority" to inmates, a "system of inmate self-government," and "corruption" had heightened the vulnerability of inmates to "systemic forms" of exploitation, torture, and other ill-treatment. In March 2019, eight police officers were charged with the rape, earlier in the year, of a 21-year-old Brazilian inmate at the Rurrenabaque prison in the Department of Beni, northeast of La Paz.

In May 2019, the Legislative Assembly passed a law restricting pretrial detention of men and women responsible for the care of children. At time of writing, an implementation plan and special budget to implement the law had yet to be approved.

The Attorney General's Office has repeatedly used a 2010 anti-corruption law to charge suspects with crimes alleged to have been committed before the law was enacted, violating the well-established the international principle of non-retroactive application of criminal law.

In 2018, the Legislative Assembly approved a government-sponsored amnesty law for former presidents Jorge Quiroga and Carlos Mesa. They had been charged with "anti-economic conduct"—a crime included in the 2010 law anti-corruption law–for acts committed in the early 2000s. The amnesty law requires that Quiroga and Mesa "request" the application of the amnesty. At time of writing they had not requested it, arguing that they are not guilty, and the cases against them remained pending.

On November 13, the newly appointed minister of government under Añez, Arturo Murillo, warned that the government will "go after" and incarcerate people who commit "sedition"—a vaguely defined crime that carries up to three years in prison under Bolivian law. Murillo said that the government would also "hunt down" Juan Ramón Quintana, minister of government under former President Morales, whom he described as "an animal."

Human Rights Defenders

A law and decree that President Morales signed in 2013 grants the government broad powers to dissolve civil society organizations. Under the decree, any government office may ask the Ministry of Autonomy to revoke the permit of a nongovernmental organization (NGO) if it performs activities other than those listed in its bylaws, or if its legal representative is convicted for crimes that "undermine security or public order."

The decree also allows the Legislative Assembly to request revocation of an NGO's permit in cases of "necessity or public interest." These measures give the government broad powers to shut down independent civil society groups.

Morales administration officials accused human rights groups of engaging in an international conspiracy against the government, without presenting evidence to support their claims.

On November 10, a group of men set fire to the home of Waldo Albarracín, a university dean and human rights defender. Albarracín blamed Morales supporters.

Freedom of Expression

While public debate is robust, the Morales administration periodically lashed out at journalists, accusing them, without presenting evidence, of publishing lies and politically motivated distortions. In May 2018, then President Morales tweeted that "some media outlets" receive "instructions from Washington to lie, manipulate [the truth] and misinform [the public]." The Morales government also repeatedly accused the media of participating in an international conspiracy against Bolivia and the president

In the context of the post-electoral violent protests, several news outlets and journalists were attacked or threatened. At least four outlets had to temporarily cease broadcasting.

On November 14, the newly appointed communication minister under Añez, Roxana Lizárraga, said that the government will take "pertinent actions," including "deportation," against journalists who "commit sedition."

Bolivia lacks transparent criteria for using government funds to purchase media advertisements—an important source of media revenue—and some media outlets have accused the Morales admnistration of discriminating against those who criticize government officials by withholding advertising from them.

Indigenous Rights

The 2009 constitution includes comprehensive guarantees of indigenous groups' rights to collective land titling, intercultural education, prior consultation on development projects, and protection of indigenous justice systems.

Indigenous peoples' right to free, prior, and informed consent (FPIC) regarding legislative or administrative measures that may affect them is not fully enshrined in Bolivian law. International standards call for FPIC through all stages of projects that affect indigenous peoples' rights to land and natural resources, yet one current Bolivian mining law governing indigenous land concessions limits FPIC to the exploitation phase.

Gender-Based Violence and Reproductive Rights

Women and girls in Bolivia remain at high risk of gender-based violence, despite a 2013 law that sets forth comprehensive measures to prevent and prosecute violence against women. The law created the crime of "femicide" (the killing of a woman in certain circumstances, including domestic violence) and called for the establishment of shelters for women, as well as special prosecutors and courts for gender-based crimes.

The Attorney General's Office reported 136 victims of femicide in 2018, and 82 between January and September 2019.

Under Bolivian law, abortion is not a crime when the pregnancy is due to rape or if the procedure is necessary to protect the life or health of a pregnant woman or girl. In 2017, the Plurinational Assembly passed a government-sponsored criminal reform that would have fully decriminalized abortion for girls and allowed a woman to end a pregnancy in a range of circumstances, including if her life or health is at risk; if the pregnancy is a result of rape; and if the fetus suffers from severe conditions not compatible with life outside the womb. But in response to protests, the assembly abrogated the bill in January 2018, before it took force.

Child Labor

In 2018, the Constitutional Court abrogated a provision of a 2014 law that had allowed children as young as 10 to work in activities deemed not "dangerous" or "unhealthy." Later that year, the legislature passed a law raising the working age for children and adolescents to 14 years. According to the Ministry of Labor, approximately 390,000 children work in Bolivia, often in hazardous industries, such as construction, the sugar-cane harvest, and mining.

Sexual Orientation and Gender Identity

In 2016, the Plurinational Assembly passed a bill that allows people to revise the gender listed on their identification documents without prior judicial approval. However, in 2017, the Constitutional Court ruled that such a revision of gender did not grant the right to marry a person of the same biological sex. Same-sex couples are not allowed to marry or engage in civil unions. Bolivia's 2009 constitution defines marriage as the union of a man and a woman.

In July, President Morales signed a decree abrogating a discriminatory rule that forbade homosexuals and bisexuals from becoming blood donors.

Key International Actors

On November 14, UN Secretary-General Antonio Guterres appointed Jean Arnault as his personal envoy to "offer United Nations support in efforts to find a peaceful resolution to the crisis" in Bolivia.

On November 18, the IACHR requested the government's authorization to carry out a mission to Bolivia to observe the human rights situation. The same day, the Office of the UN High Commissioner for Human Rights (OHCHR) said it would deploy a mission to the document the situation in the country.

In November, Bolivia was subject to its third UN Universal Periodic Review at the Human Rights Council.

The OHCHR mandate in Bolivia ended in December 2017, after the government did not renew the agreement for it to work in the country.

Bolivia has consistently opposed resolutions at the Organization of American States (OAS) spotlighting serious human rights abuses in Venezuela and Nicaragua.

Bosnia and Herzegovina

In 2019, Bosnia and Herzegovina (BiH) saw little improvement in protecting people's rights. The holding of its first LGBT Pride was a welcome development, even though lesbian, gay, bisexual, and transgender people continue to face discrimination and violence. The state fails in practice to protect women from gender-based violence or hold most of those responsible for it to account. A decade after provisions in the constitution were ruled discriminatory by a human rights court, they have yet to be changed. Media freedom remains compromised and the pace of war crimes prosecutions slow.

Discrimination and Intolerance

December 2019 marked 10 years since the *Sejdić-Finci* ruling by the European Court of Human Rights (ECtHR), which found that the Bosnian constitution discriminates against ethnic and religious minorities by not allowing them to run for the presidency. In the decade that followed, the ECtHR has found similar constitutional violations in three further cases, but the constitution still has not been amended.

In October, the ECtHR ruled that Bosnian authorities had discriminated against a resident of the city of Mostar on the grounds of her place of residence, by failing to hold municipal elections for 11 years because of a disagreement among its main parties about the voting system. The court ordered Bosnia to hold elections in Mostar within six months.

The 2019 World Bank study examining Roma inclusion in the Western Balkans between 2011 and 2017 found only limited progress in improving access to education, employment, health, housing, and documentation for Roma in the country. In July 2019, Bosnia joined other governments in adopting a Declaration on Roma Integration within the EU Enlargement Process, committing to improve access to services for Roma and involve them in policy formation.

The Organization for Security and Co-operation in Europe (OSCE) between January and September 2019 registered 109 incidents of hate crimes—66.67 percent involving religion or ethnicity. The failure of Bosnian authorities to record statistics on types of hate crime impede comprehensive assessment of the problem and effective response to it.

In March 2019, a Bosniak post-war returnee from Prijedor was physically and verbally attacked by someone who identified themselves as a Bosnian Serb and posted a video of the incident on social media. At time of writing, a criminal investigation was ongoing.

Asylum Seekers and Internally Displaced People

The numbers of asylum seekers and migrants coming to Bosnia increased. Between January and August 2019, the state Service for Foreigners' Affairs registered 18,071 new asylum seekers, 5,000 more than the same period last year. The most common country of origin was Pakistan, followed by Afghanistan, Bangladesh, Iraq and Syria.

In the first of half of 2019, 17,165 people indicated an intention to seek asylum. Only 426 people actually applied during the same period. According to the UN Refugee Agency, UNHCR, short application deadlines and limited state capacity to process claims hinder access to asylum procedures.

At time of writing, there was one state-managed asylum center and six temporary accommodation centers with total capacity of around 4,000 people, an improvement on 2018, but still leaving thousands unable to access shelter and basic services.

At time of writing, a program aimed at building houses for 96,421 Bosnians who remain displaced by the war in the 1990s had built 1,000 homes. Authorities said this should allow residents to relocate from 8 out of the 121 collective centers for the internally displaced that are still open. Fifty-eight percent of refugees who fled the Bosnia war in the 1990s have not returned to the country.

Accountability for War Crimes

A revised National War Crimes Processing Strategy to improve the process of allocating cases across courts has awaited approval by the Council of Ministers since February 2018, made no progress in 2019, slowing down the rate at which war crimes cases are prosecuted.

According to information provided by the OSCE, in August 2019 there were 250 war crimes cases against 512 defendants in the post-indictment phase pending before all courts in BiH.

Between January and June 2019, BiH courts rendered first instance judgments in 26 cases: 15 in the State Court, 9 in the Federation BiH (FBiH) court and 2 in the Republika Srpska (RS) court. In total, 23 of the 38 defendants were convicted. During the same period, Bosnian courts reached final judgments in 21 cases: 10 in the State Court, 9 in the FBiH court, 1 in RS court, and 1 in the Brčko court. In total, 29 of 42 defendants were convicted.

In cases involving conflict-related sexual violence, courts reached first instance judgments in 8 cases in the first half of 2019, with 8 of the total 10 defendants convicted, and final judgments in 4 cases, with 9 defendants convicted and 1 acquitted.

In March 2019, the United Nations Mechanism for International Criminal Tribunal (MICT) ruled against the appeal of Radovan Karadzic, former Bosnian Serb wartime president, confirming his 2016 conviction for genocide and other crimes and extending his initial 40-year sentence to life in prison.

In a positive move, in July 2019 BiH signed agreements with Serbia and Croatia to facilitate better cooperation in the search for missing persons from the 1990s wars.

There was less progress in coming to terms with the past. In April, the Serb member of the Bosnian Presidency Milorad Dodik called the Srebrenica genocide a myth.

Women's Rights

BiH has an established legislative framework for tackling gender-based violence and human trafficking and institutional gender equality mechanisms, including in politics. Implementation remained patchy or non-existent in 2019, according to women's rights organization Kvinna Till Kvinna, leaving women vulnerable to domestic violence and employment discrimination, and underrepresented in political life.

The state response to gender-based violence remained inadequate, despite the ratification of the Istanbul Convention on violence against women. According to Kvinna Till Kvinna, police officers do not always inform women of their rights and available support, and perpetrators are just given a warning.

A September study from the United Nations Development Program's found that women's representation in Bosnian political institutions is only half of the 40 percent legally mandated proportion.

There is currently no systematic data collection on gender-based violence across the entities. In April 2019, the Council of Europe recommended Bosnia institutions increase the quality of such data. According to an OSCE regional survey in 2019, of 2,321 women interviewed in Bosnia, 42 percent do not know what to do if they experience violence, and 37 percent are not aware of any support organizations.

According to BiH Ombudsman Office, violence against women is still under-reported and some of the reasons are fear of the perpetrator, long court proceedings, low penalties for the perpetrator, distrust in the institutions, and social stigma.

Freedom of Media

Journalists continued to face interference with their work. As of August 2019, the BiH journalists' association BH Novinari recorded 41 violations of journalists' rights, including three verbal threats, eight instances of political pressure, six physical assaults, and five death threats. Most of the cases were reported to police and at time of writing 15 were with the relevant prosecutor's office. Although the number of solved cases has not significantly increased, BH Novinari reported police were more engaged and proactive with cases than in the past, and that other relevant state institutions communicated better regarding attacks on journalists.

In January, the owner of the portal Visoko.co.ba received threats after publishing articles about nepotism. Photojournalist Adi Kebo was attacked and his camera was damaged in March by a politician. At time of writing, both cases were with the relevant prosecutor's office.

By August 2019, there were four court convictions for attacks on journalists, including a four-year sentence for Marko Čolić for the attempted murder of journalist Vladimir Kovačević in 2018.

Sexual Orientation and Gender Identity

Between January and September 2019, organization Sarajevo Open Center (SOC), an LGBTI and women's rights group, recorded 12 hate incidents against LGBTI people, three of which were physical attacks. The organization registered eight attacks in public places.

According to Foundation CURE, a feminist activist organization, the first Pride Parade, held on September 8, was a success and an important victory for LGBT rights in Bosnia. The event was well secured by police and there were no registered incidents of violence.

In a December 2018 ruling concerning the violent attack on Merlinka queer festival five years ago, the Constitutional Court of BiH found Sarajevo Canton and the Federation of Bosnia and Herzegovina guilty for failing to secure the event and properly investigate the attack.

Civil society groups identified the most pressing issues as the lack of legal family rights of same-sex couples, lack of available medical procedures for gender reassignment, and the inability to freely express their sexual orientation and gender identity without fear of violence.

Key International Actors

In January, Council of Europe Human Rights Commissioner Dunja Mijatović expressed concern over glorification of war crimes and war criminals in Bosnia.

In February, the European Parliament adopted a resolution calling on BiH to address a number of human rights concerns, including introducing a property restitution law and compensating for historically-seized property.

In a May progress report, the European Union Commission urged Bosnia to improve its legal framework to allow holding municipal elections in Mostar and to implement Sejdić Finci ruling.

In June report, the OSCE expressed concern over a sharp decline in the number of first-instance convictions for war crimes by Bosnian State Court since 2016, calling into question the quality of investigations and indictments of the Prosecutor's Office.

In August, the UN Committee Against Torture (CAT) recommended the state to pay 15,000 euros in compensation to a woman raped in the war after the perpetrator, who was initially ordered by Bosnian court to pay the victim, did not have the funds, and to establish a state fund to compensate other victims of war. The CAT also rejected the government's statute of limitations on prosecution of wartime sexual violence.

Brazil

During his first year in office, President Jair Bolsonaro has embraced an anti-rights agenda, pursuing policies that would put vulnerable populations at greater risk. The courts and Congress blocked some of those policies.

The Bolsonaro administration has put forward a bill that would allow police officers convicted of unlawful killings to avoid prison. Its environmental policies have effectively given a green light to criminal networks that engage in illegal logging in the Amazon and use intimidation and violence against Indigenous people, local residents, and environmental enforcement agents who try to defend the rainforest.

Public Security and Police Conduct

Violent deaths fell 11 percent in 2018, but high crime levels remain a problem around the country. Police abuses make fighting crime harder by discouraging communities from reporting crimes or cooperating with investigations. Those abuses contribute to a cycle of violence that undermines public security and endangers the lives of civilians and police officers alike. In 2018, 343 police officers were killed, two-thirds of them off duty.

Killings by police jumped 20 percent in 2018, reaching 6,220, state data compiled by the nonprofit Brazilian Forum on Public Security show. While some police killings are in self-defense, many others are the result of unlawful use of force. In São Paulo, killings by on-duty officers went up by 8 percent from January through September 2019. In Rio de Janeiro, police killed 1,402 people from January through September, the highest number on record for that period.

President Bolsonaro has encouraged police to kill suspects. Criminals should "die like cockroaches," he said in August. His administration sent a bill to Congress, which he said was intended for police officers, to allow judges to suspend sentences of people convicted of homicide if they acted out of "excusable fear, surprise, or intense emotion." President Bolsonaro also announced he would pardon police officers convicted of crimes if he deemed the conviction to be "unfair"

In Rio de Janeiro, the governor has encouraged police to kill armed suspects. Three days after 8-year-old Ágatha Félix was killed during a police operation in September, the governor changed a bonus scheme that had been credited with helping reduce police violence. Under the new rules, officers will no longer be rewarded when police killings drop.

In São Paulo, prosecutors sued the state government to force it to reduce killings by and of police officers, and install cameras and other technology to help investigate police misconduct.

A 2017 law moved trials of members of the armed forces accused of unlawful killings of civilians from civilian to military courts, in contravention of international norms. Less than a month after the law was enacted, eight civilians were killed during a joint civil police and army operation in Rio de Janeiro. Military prosecutors closed the case in May 2019 without having interviewed key civilian witnesses or having conducted forensic analysis of the area from where the shots were fired.

In April, army soldiers opened fire on a family travelling in a car in Rio de Janeiro, killing one man and injuring another. The military command initially said the soldiers responded to shots from criminals, but later admitted "inconsistencies" in the soldiers' statements. Police found no weapons in the car. The military itself is investigating the case.

Prison Conditions and Torture

As of October 1, more than 830,000 adults were incarcerated in Brazil, more than 40 percent of them awaiting trial, according to the National Council of Justice. The number of detainees exceeded the maximum capacity of facilities by 70 percent in June 2017, according to the latest data.

Overcrowding and understaffing make it impossible for prison authorities to maintain control within many prisons, leaving detainees vulnerable to violence and recruitment into gangs. Inmates killed 117 fellow inmates in five prisons in Amazonas and Pará in less than three months in 2019.

In August, media reported that nobody had been tried for the killings of almost 300 inmates in the past three years.

In 2018, several Supreme Court rulings and a new law mandated house arrest instead of pretrial detention for pregnant women, mothers of people with disabilities, and mothers of children under 12, except for those accused of violent crimes or of crimes against their dependents. Yet official data showed that in July 2019 more than 5,100 women entitled to house arrest, 310 of them pregnant, awaited trial behind bars.

The National Council of Justice ordered that by May 2016 all detainees should have, within 24 hours of arrest, a hearing to determine if they should be detained or set free pending trial. By September 2019, at least seven states were still not holding such "custody hearings" everywhere in their territory, according to the National Council of Justice. Without such hearings, detainees often wait months in jail to see a judge.

A 2019 study by the Institute for the Defense of the Right to Defense reported that a quarter of detainees said at their hearings that police had mistreated them.

In Pará, federal prosecutors said in September they had received evidence that a federal task force deployed by the Bolsonaro government to prisons in that state was mistreating and torturing detainees. A federal judge ordered the removal of the chief of the force.

The Bolsonaro administration initially blocked a prison visit in Ceará state by the National Mechanism to Prevent and Combat Torture, a body of experts established by law to detect torture. When the mechanism was finally able to visit, it found "evidence of widespread torture." In June, President Bolsonaro fired the experts by decree and eliminated payment for future members of the mechanism. The attorney general stated the decree violated fundamental rights and asked the Supreme Court to revoke it. In August, a federal judge suspended it temporarily.

In June, President Bolsonaro signed a bill that allows for the compulsory internment of drug users in treatment facilities without judicial authorization.

Children's Rights

Overcrowding, mistreatment, and lack of access to educational and health services remain chronic problems in detention facilities for children in conflict with the law.

In Espírito Santo state in November 2018, the National Mechanism to Prevent and Combat Torture found as many as 10 children held in juvenile-detention rooms built for one. In May 2019, the Supreme Court found severe overcrowding in four states and ordered it reduced. In June, the Piauí state committee to combat torture reported children in detention had suffered beatings and other abuses.

By June 2019, Brazil's juvenile detention facilities housed more than 21,000 children and young adults.

President Bolsonaro has tried to prevent children from accessing comprehensive sexuality education. He ordered the Health Ministry to remove from circulation a health booklet for adolescents about pregnancy and sexually-transmitted diseases because he objected to its images.

He also ordered the Ministry of Education to draft a law banning what he calls "gender ideology" in schools. The governor of São Paulo ordered the removal from public schools of 330,000 booklets that explain sexual orientation and gender identity because they promoted "gender ideology." In September, a judge determined that the booklets be returned to schools.

Sexual Orientation and Gender Identity

President Bolsonaro has made homophobic statements and sought to restrict the rights of lesbian, gay, bisexual, and transgender (LGBT) people.

President Bolsonaro said in April that Brazil must not become a "gay tourism paradise" and said in August that families are only those made of a man and a woman. In September, Brazil's Supreme Court reaffirmed that same-sex unions are families.

The Bolsonaro administration suspended public funding for four films addressing LGBT issues and the mayor of Rio de Janeiro banned a comic showing two men kissing. The Supreme Court ruled the mayor's actions illegal.

In January, Jean Wyllys, an advocate of LGBT rights who had received death threats, resigned his seat in Congress, fearing for his life. He was replaced by David Miranda, who, like Wyllys, is openly gay and has also reported receiving death threats.

Women's and Girls' Rights

Brazil made important progress in fighting domestic violence with the adoption of the 2001 "Maria da Penha" law, but implementation is lagging. Only 8 percent of municipalities had police stations specializing in violence against women and about 2 percent operated women's shelters in 2018. One million cases of domestic violence were pending before the courts in 2018, including 4,400 femicides, defined under Brazilian law as the killing of a women "on account of being persons of the female sex."

Abortion is legal in Brazil only in cases of rape, to save a woman's life, or when the fetus suffers from anencephaly, a fatal congenital brain disorder. Article 19, an NGO, contacted the hospitals the government lists as performing legal abortions in 2019, and found the majority did not, in fact, perform them.

Women and girls who have clandestine abortions not only risk injury and death but face up to three years in prison, while people convicted of performing illegal abortions face up to four years.

An outbreak of the Zika virus in 2015-2016 caused particular harm to women and girls. When a pregnant woman is infected, Zika can cause complications in fetal development, including of the brain. In September, the government established a lifelong monthly payment to low-income children affected with Zika whose families agree not to file Zika-related suits against the government.

In July, the Federal Council of Medicine published a resolution giving doctors the power to conduct procedures on pregnant women without their consent, even if no imminent risk of death exists. Federal prosecutors argued that the rule may lead to unnecessary cesarean deliveries, and to procedures not recommended by the World Health Organization when performed on a routine basis, such as episiotomy.

Freedom of Expression and Association

President Bolsonaro has repeatedly lashed out at Brazil's vibrant civil society and independent media.

In January, his administration restricted public access to government information, but Congress revoked the decree.

President Bolsonaro has verbally attacked media outlets and reporters whose coverage he did not like. Those reporters have often suffered online harassment after being singled out. In September, the Bolsonaro administration urged prosecutors to open a criminal investigation of a news site for publishing a story that laid out the World Health Organization's recommendations for safe abortion.

The Bolsonaro administration is openly hostile toward nongovernmental organizations (NGOs), particularly those defending the environment and Indigenous peoples' rights. In January, the government granted itself the power to "supervise, coordinate, monitor, and track" NGOs, but Congress revoked that power.

The Bolsonaro administration eliminated most federal councils, committees, and working groups, many of which had representatives of civil society, and reduced NGO representation in committees that were not eliminated.

Disability Rights

Thousands of people with disabilities, including children and infants, are needlessly confined in institutions, where they may face neglect and abuse, sometimes for life. At the request of a relative or an institution's director, courts can strip people with disabilities of their right to make decisions for themselves. People stripped of this right can leave institutions only with the consent of their guardians, a requirement that violates the Convention on the Rights of People with Disabilities.

Migrants, Refugees, and Asylum Seekers

Thousands of Venezuelans have crossed the border into Brazil fleeing hunger, lack of basic health care, or persecution. Government figures show that in September, more than 224,000 Venezuelans lived in Brazil, more than half of whom had requested asylum.

In June, Brazil's federal refugee agency declared "serious and widespread violation of human rights" exists in Venezuela, a legal declaration that speeds up the granting of asylum.

In July, the Bolsonaro administration issued a regulation that allows authorities to bar entry into the country or summarily deport anyone deemed "dangerous" or to have violated "the principles and objectives of the Constitution." After public criticism, in October the administration modified some of the provisions but maintained the authority to deport foreigners when it has "serious reasons" to believe they are "dangerous."

Environment and Human Rights

Criminal networks that are largely driving illegal logging in the Amazon continued to threaten and even kill Indigenous people, local residents, and public officials who defended the forest.

The Bolsonaro administration has effectively given a green light to those networks by slashing funding for and undermining the power of environmental agencies. Preliminary data show that from January through October, deforestation in the Amazon increased by more than 80 percent, compared to the same period in 2018.

The Indigenist Missionary Council (CIMI), a non-profit organization, reported 160 cases of illegal logging, land grabbing, and other infringement upon Indigenous territories from January through September. In November, Paulo Paulino Guajajara, an Indigenous forest defender, was killed, allegedly by loggers.

From January to October 3, the Bolsonaro administration approved 382 new pesticides, many of them restricted or banned as toxic in the United States and Europe. In July, the government established risk of death as the only criterion for classifying a pesticide as "extremely toxic." Human Rights Watch research shows the government does not adequately monitor pesticide exposure and pesticide residues in drinking water and food.

Military-Era Abuses

The perpetrators of human rights abuses during the 1964 to 1985 dictatorship are shielded from justice by a 1979 amnesty law that the Supreme Court upheld

HUMAN
RIGHTS
WATCH
RAINFOREST MAFIAS
How Violence and Impunity Fuel Deforestation in Brazil's Amazon

in 2010, a decision that the Inter-American Court of Human Rights ruled was a violation of Brazil's obligations under international law.

Since 2010, federal prosecutors have charged about 60 former agents of the dictatorship with killings, kidnappings, and other serious crimes. Lower courts dismissed most of the cases, citing the amnesty law or the statute of limitations. A few such cases are pending before the Supreme Court. In August, a federal court for the first time approved charges of rape against an agent of the military regime.

President Bolsonaro has praised the dictatorships in Brazil and other South American countries. Bolsonaro called a convicted torturer "a national hero." He denied that journalist Miriam Leitão was tortured by the military and that Fernando Santa Cruz, father of the president of Brazil's Bar Association, was killed by the regime, but offered no evidence.

The Bolsonaro administration packed with allies, some of whom had publicly defended the dictatorship, two commissions that examine requests of compensation for victims of the dictatorship and seek to locate the bodies of the disappeared. From January through September, the amnesty commission denied 92 percent of compensation requests.

Key International Actors

The United Nations High Commissioner for Human Rights (OHCHR), Michelle Bachelet, reportedly warned in September that "public discourse legitimizing summary executions" by police in Brazil can "entrench impunity and reinforce the message that state agents are above the law." She also criticized "a shrinking of civic and democratic space." President Bolsonaro responded to Bachelet praising the "courage" of Chile's dictatorship to fight "communists, among them her father." Alberto Bachelet was tortured and died in detention.

The UN rapporteur on extreme poverty and human rights in June labeled President Bolsonaro's promises to end demarcation of Indigenous territories and weaken environmental protections "short-sighted steps in the wrong direction."

The UN Subcommittee on Prevention of Torture called on President Bolsonaro to revoke the decree that "severely weakened" the national anti-torture mechanism, and criticized the governor of São Paulo for vetoing the creation of a state anti-torture mechanism.

Foreign Policy

The Bolsonaro administration instructed its diplomats to argue that the word "gender" means "biological sex: male or female." In July, it criticized a UN resolution on violence against women for including a reference to "sexual and reproductive health care services," declaring that the expression "has become associated with pro-abortion policies."

Burundi

Members of Burundi's ruling party's youth league, the Imbonerakure, often working with local officials, the national intelligence service (Service national de renseignement, SNR), and police carried out widespread human rights abuses throughout 2019, including extrajudicial executions, disappearances, arbitrary arrests, sexual violence, beatings, and intimidation of suspected political opponents. They often targeted real or perceived political opponents or those who refused to join the ruling party.

The humanitarian situation remained dire and by November, over 2,800 of the 7 million people who had contracted malaria died from the disease. Over 1.7 million people were food insecure, in part due to high population density and the influx of returning and new refugees.

The country's once vibrant civil society and media bore the brunt of the government's ire. In June, the government suspended one of the last remaining rights organizations, PARCEM. In October, four Iwacu journalists and their driver were arrested while travelling to Bubanza province to report on an outbreak of fighting between rebels and security forces. They were later charged with complicity in "threatening the security of the state."

A United Nations Human Rights Council-mandated Commission of Inquiry (COI) reported in September that serious violations, including crimes against humanity, continued in 2018 and 2019, mainly perpetrated by state agents and the Imbonerakure and affecting mostly rural dwellers.

Abuses by Security Forces and Ruling Party Youth

Although President Pierre Nkurunziza said he would not contest the presidential election in 2020, tensions continued to rise. Authorities lifted the suspension of some opposition parties and registered new parties, but many Burundians suspected of being political opposition supporters were killed, disappeared, arbitrarily arrested, and beaten. People who refused to join the ruling National Council for the Defense of Democracy-Forces for the Defense of Democracy (Conseil national pour la défense de la démocratie-Forces pour la défense de la démocratie, CNDD-FDD) and its youth league, donate money to it, participate in the

HUMAN
RIGHTS
WATCH
"We Let Our Children
Go Hungry to Pay"
Abuses Related to the 2020 Election Levy in Burundi

construction of its offices, or attend its rallies also reported facing beatings, fines, and arrest.

Authorities have particularly targeted members of the opposition National Congress for Freedom (Congrès national pour la liberté, CNL) party. In 2019, members of the Imbonerakure and local authorities killed, disappeared, arbitrarily arrested, and beat dozens of CNL supporters across the country. According to local media reports, several local CNDD-FDD and CNL party offices were attacked or destroyed across the country.

People were forced to contribute money to the elections scheduled for May 2020 and to the ruling party. Imbonerakure members and local authorities mainly responsible for collecting the contributions largely did so by using force and threats, often at informal roadblocks set up to verify proof of payment. Those who could not provide receipts or refused to contribute faced violent retribution and intimidation. In some cases, people reported being denied access to public services if they were unable to prove they had contributed. In some provinces, CNDD-FDD and Imbonerakure members forced people to join the construction of local CNDD-FDD offices, and threatened, beat, or detained those who refused to comply, which constitutes forced labor.

Humanitarian Situation

The humanitarian situation in Burundi, one of the world's poorest countries, was dire, with around 1.7 million people facing food insecurity, according to the UN Office for the Coordination of Humanitarian Affairs (OCHA).

Despite this, there were reports that the Imbonerakure were asking Burundians to "donate" food to them and were preventing people from accessing humanitarian food distributions. The COI report documented violations of the rights to food, health, and work.

Refugees

In November, there were approximately 326,000 Burundian refugees in Tanzania, Rwanda, Uganda, and the Democratic Republic of Congo. Between September 2017 and October 31, 2019, around 80,000 refugees returned to Burundi under the United Nations refugee agency-backed assisted voluntary repatriation program, including 78,380 who returned from Tanzania. The agency said 8,293 Burundians arrived in Tanzania between January 1 and October 31, 2019.

Tanzania and Burundi signed an August 24 agreement that said about 180,000 Burundian refugees in Tanzania were "to return to their country of origin whether voluntarily or not" by December 31. An October agreement between the Burundian and Tanzanian police to allow cross-border operations by both police forces heightened fears of arrest among refugees, local media reported.

In August, UNHCR said that conditions in Burundi were "not conducive to promote returns." In its latest report, the UN COI said that Burundians who had returned from abroad were among the main targets of human rights abuses.

Civil Society and Freedom of Media

On June 17, a government order was published suspending PARCEM, accusing the organization of tarnishing the image of the country and its leaders. Three PARCEM members sentenced in March 2018 to 10 years in prison for threatening the security of the state were acquitted upon appeal in December 2018 and released on March 21, 2019.

The 32-year sentence of human rights activist Germain Rukuki, a member of Action by Christians for the Abolition of Torture (ACAT), was confirmed on appeal in July. He was convicted of charges related to state security in April 2018. Judicial authorities told the media they had lost his file, which led to significant delays in the case. Nestor Nibitanga, an observer for the Association for the Protection of Human Rights and Detained Persons (APRODH), who was sentenced to five years for "threatening state security" in August 2018, remained in detention.

On October 1, 2018, authorities suspended the activities of foreign nongovernmental organizations (NGOs) for three months to force them to re-register, including by submitting new documentation stating the ethnicity of their Burundian employees. By March, at least 93 foreign NGOs were registered following a three-month suspension. It is not clear if the other organizations were denied registration for refusing or failing to declare the ethnicity of local staff. In May, the Supreme Court president ordered that the property of several high profile exiled Burundian human rights defenders and journalists be seized.

On March 29, the National Communication Council (CNC) announced it would extend the suspension order on the Voice of America's (VOA) and withdraw the British Broadcasting Corporation's (BBC) operating license. The CNC also forbade any journalist in Burundi from "providing information directly or indirectly that could be broadcast" by either the BBC or VOA.

Freedom of Religion

Burundian authorities increasingly sought to control churches in the country, warning religious leaders against making critical or "political" statements. On May 21, the Seventh Day Adventist Church leader, Pastor Lamec Barishinga, and his deputy were arrested and accused of "rebellion."

Sexual Orientation and Gender Identity

Burundi punishes consensual same-sex sexual relations between adults with up to two years in prison under Article 567 of the penal code. Article 29 of the Constitution of Burundi explicitly bans same-sex marriage.

Right to Education

In March, some of the seven schoolchildren arrested in Kirundo province were charged with "insulting the head of state" for allegedly scribbling on the president's photo in their schoolbooks. The incident triggered a global social media campaign that eventually led to their release, although five of the seven were expelled indefinitely.

Several students reported being prevented from attending school for failing to make a contribution toward the 2020 elections. According to the COI report, some students affiliated with the opposition were harassed and threatened by students and teachers who are members of the ruling party.

Key International Actors

In February, the facilitator of the Inter-Burundi dialogue, Benjamin Mkapa, presented his final report to the Summit of Heads of State of the East African Community. At a June UN Security Council Meeting, Smaïl Chergui, African Union commissioner for peace and security said "there is no alternative to intra-Burundi dialogue."

Burundi refused to cooperate with any international and regional human rights mechanism. In February, the Office of the United Nations High Commissioner in Burundi was forced to close down at the insistence of the government. The COI on Burundi was not given access to the country, despite repeated requests. In September, the Human Rights Council renewed the COI's mandate for another year.

According to UN diplomats, the government threatened to cut ties with UN special envoy Michel Kafando in May, forcing the UN Security Council to postpone a scheduled meeting on Burundi. In October, Special Envoy Kafando resigned after two-and-a-half years into the role. Russia, China and Equatorial Guinea publicly called for Burundi to be removed from the council's agenda.

The International Criminal Court (ICC) continued investigations into crimes committed in Burundi since 2015. The European Union's 2016 suspension of direct budgetary support to the government under article 96 of the Cotonou Agreement remained in place.

Cambodia

Respect for human rights in Cambodia deteriorated in 2019, following national elections the previous year in which Prime Minister Hun Sen and the ruling Cambodian People's Party (CPP) secured all 125 National Assembly seats after the CPP-controlled Supreme Court dissolved the main opposition party, effectively creating one-party rule. The number of political prisoners also increased, with key opposition figures either in detention or having fled the country to avoid arrest. Authorities criminalize involvement with the main opposition party, the Cambodia National Rescue Party (CNRP); 107 out of 118 senior CNRP politicians remained banned from engaging in politics for five years.

In mid-November 2019, the government held around 90 people in pretrial detention or prison on politically motivated convictions. While Hun Sen sought royal pardons for 16 political prisoners after the 2018 elections to deflect international criticism, targeting of peaceful dissent continued in 2019, and other human rights defenders and political opposition activists were tried and imprisoned in 2019.

The European Union (EU) launched a review procedure for suspension of the "Everything But Arms" (EBA) trade preferences granted to Cambodia based on the latter's non-compliance with international human rights treaties and core International Labour Organization conventions. At risk is Cambodia's tariff-free access into the European Union market of certain exported goods, such as garments. The EU's decision should be final by February 2020.

Attacks on Human Rights Defenders

A series of new repressive laws or amendments to existing laws—including amendments to the Law on Political Parties, the Law on Non-Governmental Organizations, the Law on Trade Unions and a lese majeste clause in the penal code—severely restrict rights to freedom of expression, peaceful assembly, and association.

In December 2018, a court convicted six prominent union leaders on baseless charges of initiating intentional violence and causing damage, handing them suspended prison sentences of between eight months and four-and-a-half years

HUMAN
RIGHTS
WATCH
“What Hell Feels Like”
Acid Violence in Cambodia

and a collective 35 million Cambodian riels (US$8,600) compensation payment to civil parties. An appeals court overturned the convictions in May 2019, just ahead of the arrival of an EU fact-finding mission related to the EBA review.

In December 2018, Thai authorities forcibly returned Cambodian dissident Rath Rott Mony to Cambodia. Authorities then prosecuted him for his role in a Russia Times documentary "My Mother Sold Me," which describes Cambodian girls forced by their mothers into sexual exploitation. In July, the court convicted Mony of "incitement to discriminate" and sentenced him to two years in prison.

Since the introduction of a lese majeste crime in 2018, three people have been convicted and imprisoned under the law; a fourth person was being held in pre-trial detention at time of writing. All the cases involved people expressing critical opinions of the government and the king on Facebook, or sharing other people's Facebook posts.

In July 2019, authorities detained two youth activists, Kong Raya and Soung Neakpoan, for participating in a commemoration ceremony on the third anniversary of the murder of prominent political commentator Kem Ley in Phnom Penh. In November, the Supreme Court denied Raya bail. Authorities charged both with "incitement to commit a felony." They arrested seven people for commemorating the anniversary; and disrupted or canceled commemorations around the country.

On January 20, 2019, soldiers arrested land activist Sum Moeun in Preah Vihear and detained him at the Kulen Promtep Wildlife Sanctuary Headquarters. Authorities could not account for his whereabouts the next morning. Two months later, he reappeared out of hiding after having escaped the Sanctuary, waiting to receive assurances that he will not be re-arrested. Fourteen other villagers, including his son, were arrested and charged with illegal clearing of state forest land; the charges against four were dropped and the ten others were released on bail between June and July, their charges are pending. While Moeun had not been re-arrested, a trial against him started in October based on same charges as the fourteen.

Attacks on Political Opposition

On January 6, 2019, an amendment to the Law on Political Parties gave Prime Minister Hun Sen unfettered discretion to decide which of the initial 118 banned senior CNRP members could regain their political rights. The amendments provide that political rights can be restored only if the individual first submits a request to Hun Sen or Interior Minister Sar Kheng, which is then passed on to the king. Less than a dozen banned CNRP members have made such a request; the rest have refuse to submit to what they maintain is a politicized and arbitrary process.

On November 10, 2019, the investigating judge decided to lift CNRP leader Kem Sokha's restrictive judicial supervision, amounting to house arrest, upon the condition that he refrain from political activities and from travelling abroad and be cooperative in his continuing investigation into bogus treason charges. Kem Sokha had been in arbitrary detention for over two years. If convicted of treason, he faces up to 30 years in prison.

On March 12, 2019, a court issued arrest warrants on charges of "conspiring to commit treason" and "incitement to commit felony" for eight leading members of the CNRP who had left Cambodia ahead of the July 2018 election—Sam Rainsy, Mu Sochua, Ou Chanrith, Eng Chhai Eang, Men Sothavarin, Long Ry, Tob Van Chan, and Ho Vann. On September 26, a Phnom Penh court charged them.

Between January and May 2019, Cambodian authorities issued over 147 arbitrary court and police summonses against CNRP members or supporters. Summonses seen by human rights groups lack legal specifics, containing only vague references to allegations that the person summoned may have violated the Supreme Court ruling dissolving the CNRP. Between August and November, authorities arrested and detained over 60 opposition members and supporters based on different spurious charges and charged over 100. On August 16, acting and exiled CNRP leader, Sam Rainsy announced his return to Cambodia on November 9; however, based on a number of restrictive measures adopted by Hun Sen, including the closure of land border crossings and arrest warrants sent to ASEAN governments, CNRP leadership was prevented from entering the country—a blatant violation of their human rights.

On January 16, 2019, police arrested Kong Meas, a banned CNRP member, after he posted on Facebook that the EU was planning to impose a tariff on Cambodian rice. On October 18, the Phnom Penh court convicted him of incitement to commit a felony and sentenced him to 18 months in prison.

On April 18, 2019, Tith Rorn, a CNRP activist and the son of a former CNRP commune council member in Kampong Cham province, died in police custody. His body had visible bruises, suggesting he was beaten. Police had arrested him on April 15 in connection with a 13-year-old assault charge, even though the statute of limitations for the offense had expired. Cambodian authorities claim Tith Rorn fell in the bathroom of his jail cell, but failed to seriously investigate.

Freedom of Media

The Cambodian government continued in 2019 to significantly curtail media freedom. While Voice of Democracy and Voice of America have conducted independent English and Khmer online reporting in 2019, previously existing local independent newspapers and radio outlets remained shut or sold to owners with ties to the government. Social media networks also continued to face surveillance and intervention by the government, reinforced by the adoption of a decree titled "Publication Controls of Website and Social Media Processing via Internet" in 2018, which allows for interference with online media and government censorship.

Cambodian authorities proceeded in 2019 with the politically motivated prosecution of two Radio Free Asia (RFA) journalists, Yeang Sothearin and Uon Chhin. The journalists were arrested on November 14, 2017, on fabricated espionage charges for reporting for RFA after the government forcibly shuttered RFA's Cambodia office. Upon determining that sufficient evidence was lacking for a conviction, the judge of the Phnom Penh court decided on October 3 to send the case back to the investigating judge for re-investigation.

On January 11, 2019, Hun Sen announced the resubmission to the National Assembly of a cybersecurity bill and a "fake news" law, raising concerns about additional restrictions on free expression and expanded surveillance against civil society groups, the political opposition, and independent media. While such laws have not been adopted yet, intimidating threats by the Cambodian authorities of all communication being surveilled has left Cambodians fearful and cautious.

Key International Actors

China is Cambodia's largest foreign investor and has close political and security cooperation with Phnom Penh. In mid-2019, the US government claimed to have documents showing Hun Sen agreed to give China access to Ream naval base on the Gulf of Thailand, which Cambodia and China deny.

In January 2019, China pledged 4 billion yuan (US$588 million) in aid to Cambodia from 2019 to 2021. In mid-2019, China bolstered its loans with an additional 10 agreements, following a "Belt and Road" Initiative Forum in Beijing.

Japan remained silent on Cambodia's deteriorating human rights situation, as it competed with China for influence in Cambodia with large amounts of development aid and investment. In September, Japan helped shepherd a UN Human Rights Council resolution on Cambodia that was just as weak as its 2017 predecessor, failing to put meaningful pressure on Cambodia to improve its human rights record.

In 2019, the United States upheld a suspension on aid to Cambodia government agencies. In July 2019, the US House of Representatives passed the "Cambodia Democracy Act of 2019," which seeks to sanction Cambodia's top officials implicated in abuses. At time of writing, the Office of the US Trade Representative was also considering stripping Cambodia of trade privileges under the Generalized System of Preferences (GSP) because of labor rights violations.

At its Universal Periodic Review (UPR) at the UN Human Rights Council in 2019, Cambodia accepted 173 UPR recommendations, but rejected key recommendations on civil and political rights.

Cameroon

Armed groups and government forces committed widespread human rights abuses across Cameroon throughout 2019. Freedoms of expression, association, and assembly continued to be curtailed after President Paul Biya, 86, won his seventh term in October 2018, in elections marred by low voter turnout and allegations of fraud. The government denied a Human Rights Watch researcher entry to the country in April.

The Islamist armed group Boko Haram carried out over 100 attacks in the Far North region since January 2019 killing more than 100 civilians. The conflict between government forces and Boko Haram has killed thousands of Cameroonians and displaced over 270,000 since 2014, leading to the rise of self-defense vigilante groups.

In Anglophone regions, violence intensified as government forces conducted large-scale security operations and armed separatists carried out increasingly sophisticated attacks. Over 3,000 civilians and hundreds of security forces personnel have been killed in the Anglophone regions since 2016, when the crisis started. The unrest in these regions led to the displacement of over half-a-million people. In August, 10 leaders of a separatist group, the Ambazonia Interim Government, were sentenced to life by a military court, following a trial that raised concerns of due process and violations of fair trial rights.

Government forces and armed separatists have killed, violently assaulted, or kidnapped people with disabilities as they struggled to flee attacks, or because they were left behind.

Cameroonian authorities cracked down on the political opposition, violently broke up peaceful protests, and arrested hundreds of opposition party leaders, members, and supporters.

The Anglophone Crisis

Cameroon's Anglophone regions have been engulfed in crisis since late 2016, when English-speaking lawyers, students, and teachers began protesting what they saw as their under-representation in, and cultural marginalization by, the central government.

The response of government security forces has included killing civilians, torching villages, and using torture and incommunicado detention. Armed separatists have also killed, tortured, and kidnapped dozens of civilians, including teachers, students, and government officials.

On September 10, amid increasing violence and following sustained international pressure, President Biya called for a "national dialogue," a series of nationwide discussions aimed at addressing the Anglophone crisis. The dialogue ended with the adoption of a special status for the two Anglophone regions and the release of hundreds of political prisoners, including Maurice Kamto, leader of the opposition Cameroon Renaissance Movement (MRC), and other people arrested in connection with the unrest in the North-West and South-West regions.

Killings, Destruction of Property, Torture by Government Forces

Responding to increasing attacks by armed separatist groups, security forces killed scores of people, burned hundreds of homes and other property in villages and cities across the North-West and South-West regions, and tortured suspected separatists in detention.

On February 6, security forces, including soldiers of the Rapid Intervention Battalion (BIR), stormed the market in Bole Bakundu village, South-West region, killing up to 10 men.

On April 4, Cameroonian soldiers, gendarmes, and BIR members carried out a deadly attack on the North-West region village of Meluf, killing five civilian males, including one with a mental disability, and wounding one woman. The forces also forcibly entered at least 80 homes in Meluf, looted some, and burned down seven.

On May 15, Air Force and BIR soldiers attacked Mankon, Bamenda, North-West region, burning over 70 homes and killing a man. On July 10, Air Force soldiers went back to Mankon and killed two men.

On September 24, BIR soldiers attacked a UNESCO World Heritage site, the Royal Palace in Bafut, shot and wounded one man, and looted the palace museum, taking several precious artifacts.

During the year, there was widespread use of incommunicado detention and torture of people suspected of ties to armed separatist groups at the State Defense Secretariat (Secrétariat d'Etat à la défense, SED) prison in Yaoundé. Gendarmes and other security personnel at the SED used torture, including severe beatings and near-drowning, as well as other ill-treatment to force suspects to confess to crimes, or to humiliate and punish them.

While the government maintained it did not tolerate crimes committed by security forces, it failed to demonstrate progress in investigating and punishing them.

Kidnappings, Torture, Occupation of Schools by Armed Separatists

Armed separatist groups have killed, tortured, assaulted, and kidnapped dozens of people, including students, teachers, clergy, and administrative and traditional authorities.

On February 16, a group of armed separatists abducted 170 students, mostly girls under 18, a teacher, and two guards from a boarding school in Kumbo, North-West region. They were all released the following day amid rumors of ransoms being paid. The school remained closed at time of writing.

Human Rights Watch authenticated a video showing armed separatists in mid-May torturing a man in an abandoned school in Bali village, North-West region. The school has been closed since mid-2017 due to violence and the separatists' enforced boycott of education. Armed separatists have used schools as bases, deploying fighters and weapons and holding people hostage in and near them.

On June 18, separatists kidnapped at least 40 people, including women and children, beat and robbed them in Bafut, North-West region. They were released the following day.

On June 28, armed separatists beat and kidnapped John Fru Ndi, a well-known Cameroonian politician, from his home in Bamenda, North-West region. Three days before, armed separatists abducted and released another high-profile figure, Cornelius Fontem Esua, the archbishop of Bamenda.

Crackdown on Political Opposition

Since elections in October 2018, the government has increased its crackdown on political opposition. Cameroon security forces have used excessive and indiscriminate force to stop demonstrations organized by the members and supporters of the MRC, Cameroon's main opposition party.

In January, MRC leader Maurice Kamto and some of his closest allies were arrested with another 200 MRC members and supporters after they held countrywide protests. A trial started in August, as they remained in detention on politically motivated charges.

On April 5, the Ministry of the Territorial Administration issued a press release banning a week of demonstrations planned by the MRC, accusing the party of destabilizing the country.

Between June 1 and 2, at least 350 MRC members and supporters, including its vice president, were arrested across the country after they tried to hold demonstrations.

On September 25, gendarmes arrested Abdul Karim Ali, an outspoken Anglophone activist and political analyst, in Yaoundé. Abdul Karim was detained at SED and denied access to a lawyer for five days. He was released on November 1.

In November, authorities banned three MRC meetings in the cities of Ebolowa, Yaoundé, and Douala. Defying the meeting ban, hundreds of MRC supporters gathered in the capital, Yaoundé, on November 2 before anti-riot police violently dispersed them. Police severely beat and injured at least 10 demonstrators. Thirty-three MRC members and supporters were arrested but released the same day.

Sexual Orientation and Gender Identity

Cameroon's penal code punishes "sexual relations between persons of the same sex" with up to five years in prison, and its cybercrimes law punishes "whoever uses electronic communication devices to make sexual advances toward a person of the same sex" with up to two years in prison. Police and gendarmes continued to arrest and harass people they believe to be lesbian, gay, bisexual, or transgender (LGBT). Humanity First Cameroun and Alternatives-

Cameroun, two nongovernmental organizations (NGOs) working on LBGTI issues, reported that 60 people were arrested on the basis of their sexual orientation or gender identity in 2018, while over 200 were subjected to physical violence.

Justice and Accountability

In a March letter to Human Rights Watch, government officials said that about 30 cases were pending before the Military Courts in Bamenda and Buea for crimes committed by security forces, including torture, destruction of property, violation of orders, and theft. Officials added that, while investigations were conducted, information about them are confidential. However, the visible lack of accountability appears to have fueled abuses, including killings, destruction of property, and torture.

The trial of seven soldiers allegedly caught on video carrying out the 2015 execution of two women and two children in the Far North region started in August, however hearings have been delayed several times, including following a request by defense lawyers to hold the trial behind closed doors.

In May, authorities announced an investigation into the burning of at least 70 homes allegedly carried out by security forces in Mankon, Bamenda on May, 15, as well as the establishment of a commission of inquiry to evaluate the material damage and property destroyed. The commission was due to submit its report by May 24, but authorities have made no information about the findings public.

On April 12 in what appears to be an attempt to curb reports of abuse by its security forces, the government denied a Human Rights Watch researcher access to the country. Despite several attempts to obtain explanations, Human Rights Watch had yet to receive any clarification from the government as to the basis for its decision to block access.

Key International Actors

France, the United States, the United Kingdom, and Germany are Cameroon's principal partners, primarily in the context of operations to counter Boko Haram in the country's Far North region. Both France and the US provide Cameroon with significant military and security assistance and training.

In February, the US announced the scaling back of its security assistance to Cameroon following credible allegations that the Cameroonian military carried out human rights violations. In July, Germany also announced the end of its military cooperation with Cameroon. In October, the US announced to cut Cameroon trade privileges enshrined in the African Growth and Opportunity Act (AGOA) over rights abuses.

The international community has become increasingly aware of the serious crimes in the Anglophone regions, despite Cameroonian government efforts to prevent coverage and documentation of violations. The United National high commissioner for human rights visited Cameroon in May, expressed concerns over allegations of serious human rights violations and urged the government to conduct transparent investigations. A fact-finding mission by her office took place in September.

The US, UK, and France publicly raised concerns on the situation in the Anglophone regions and the restrictions on basic rights and freedoms. In March, the UK, on behalf of 38 members of the Human Rights Council, expressed its deep concern about the deteriorating human rights situation in Anglophone regions, and called on Cameroon to engage fully with the UN Office of the High Commissioner for Human Rights. On April 4, the European Union Parliament passed a resolution expressing concerns over abuses committed in the North-West and South-West regions of the country, and called on President Biya to release opposition party leader Kamto and all other detainees held on politically motivated charges.

In May, the UN Security Council convened an informal meeting on the humanitarian situation in Cameroon, amid resistance from the Cameroonian government and the council's three African members.

Canada

Canada is a diverse, multi-cultural democracy that enjoys a global reputation as a defender of human rights and a strong record on core civil and political rights protections guaranteed by the Canadian Charter of Rights and Freedoms. The government of Prime Minister Justin Trudeau has made notable efforts to advance human rights in Canada. The Trudeau government has been a vocal advocate for a pluralistic society that respects the rights of immigrants, people with disabilities, lesbian, gay, bisexual, and transgender (LGBT) people, and other minorities.

Despite these efforts, Canada continues to struggle to address longstanding human rights challenges, including wide-ranging abuses against Indigenous peoples, the continued confinement of immigration detainees in jails, and a prison law that does not rule out prolonged solitary confinement. Canada also grapples with serious human rights issues relating to the overseas operations of Canadian extractive companies, and persistent exports of military equipment to countries with a record of human rights violations.

Indigenous Rights

There remain considerable challenges to undoing decades of structural and systemic discrimination against Indigenous people in Canada. While Canada officially removed its objector status to the United Nations Declaration on the Rights of Indigenous Peoples (UNDRIP) in 2016 and vowed to implement UNDRIP in accordance with the Canadian Constitution, a private member's bill to ensure that Canadian laws are in harmony with UNDRIP failed to pass in the Senate in June.

Inadequate access to clean, safe drinking water continues to pose a major public health concern in many Indigenous communities—and continues to impede efforts to advance Indigenous rights in Canada, one of the world's most water-rich countries. The government has committed to end all drinking water advisories on First Nations reserves by 2021. As of September, 56 First Nations communities across Canada remained subject to such long-term water advisories, which alert communities when their water is not safe to drink.

THE HUMAN RIGHT TO WATER
A Guide for First Nations Communities and Advocates
HUMAN
RIGHTS
WATCH

In September, the Canadian Human Rights Tribunal found that the federal government willfully and recklessly discriminated against Indigenous children living on reserves by failing to provide funding for child and family services. The Trudeau government filed an application seeking a judicial review of the ruling in October.

In January 2019, the United Nations Human Rights Committee found that Canada, through the long-controversial Indian Act, was still discriminating against First Nations women and their descendants. In August, the Trudeau government announced that First Nations women would be treated equally under the Indian Act, enabling them to retain their Indigenous status if they marry non-Indigenous men.

Violence against Indigenous Women

In June, the National Inquiry into Missing and Murdered Indigenous Women and Girls—launched by the government in 2016 to address endemic levels of violence against Indigenous women and girls—released its final report. The inquiry made 231 recommendations and concluded that acts of violence against Indigenous women and girls amount to "genocide." Prime Minister Trudeau vowed that the government will develop a national action plan to "turn the inquiry's calls to justice into real, meaningful, Indigenous-led action."

Immigration Detention

Canada's federal government and the Canada Border Services Agency (CBSA) has shown willingness to reform the immigration detention system. However, despite guidelines requiring that children be held in immigration detention only in "extremely limited circumstances" or as a "last resort" under Canada's immigration law, children are still detained in immigration detention in Canada. In 2018-19, 118 children were detained or housed in a detention center. While fewer children were held overall compared to 2017-18, the average time they spent in detention facilities rose.

Despite the introduction of a National Immigration Detention Framework that aims to reduce the use of jails and improve detention conditions, Canada continues to confine many immigration detainees in jails. According to the CBSA, 7,212 immigration detainees were detained in holding centers in 2018-19, up from 6,609 the previous year.

Solitary Confinement

In June, the British Columbia Court of Appeal confirmed that the practice of prolonged solitary confinement is unconstitutional and a violation of prisoners' rights. The federal government is currently appealing a similar decision in Ontario, which also struck down Canada's previous solitary confinement laws as unconstitutional. While the federal government has updated its prison law, it has been criticized for failing to eliminate the possibility of prolonged solitary confinement.

Corporate Accountability

Canada is home to two-third of the world's mining companies and its dominant position creates an opportunity to take the lead in addressing human rights challenges in the extractives sector. However, no Canadian law provides a mechanism to allow authorities to exercise meaningful scrutiny and oversight of the human rights impact of Canadian extractive companies operating overseas.

In January, the Supreme Court of Canada heard a civil suit against Canadian firm Nevsun Resources, involving alleged gross human rights abuses, including slavery, torture, and forced labor, at an Eritrean mine. It is expected to be a precedent-setting decision on whether Canadian courts can hold Canadian corporations accountable for human rights violations committed abroad.

Since 2011, Human Rights Watch has urged the Canadian government to establish an ombudsperson's office with a mandate to independently investigate and publicly report on human rights abuses involving Canadian extractive companies and hold responsible parties accountable. The Trudeau government has backpedaled on its previous commitment to create such an office.

Instead, in April, the government announced the establishment of the Canadian Ombudsperson for Responsible Enterprise (CORE), an advisory post, with few investigative powers and limited capacity to hold corporations accountable. This position is not independent, but rather reports as an advisor to the minister of international trade diversification.

The Canadian Parliament is exploring options for a modern slavery law. Following a private member's bill and ongoing government consultation, an all-party parliamentary group announced in April a draft Transparency In Supply Chains Act (TSCA), which seeks to impose obligations, including a legal duty of care, on Canadian businesses to actively take steps to prevent the use of modern slavery in their overseas supply chains.

Religious Freedom

In June 2019, the Canadian province of Quebec passed Bill 21 banning certain categories of public employee from wearing religious symbols at work. Teachers, judges, police officers, among other civil servants, are prohibited from wearing symbols of their faith (including hijabs, kippahs, and turbans) in the workplace. The controversial law also prohibits anyone with religious face coverings from receiving government services, including healthcare and public transit. In enacting the ban, Quebec preemptively invoked the exceptional "notwithstanding" clause, which allows provincial or federal authorities to temporarily override some of the guarantees of the Charter of Rights and Freedoms, making it difficult to overturn the law in the courts.

In May, three United Nations special rapporteurs warned that the law is "likely to undermine the freedom of conscience, religion and equality of citizens."

Disability Rights

After years of activism by disability rights advocates, Canada passed the Accessible Canada Act in June 2019. The act, which seeks to make Canada barrier-free by 2040, requires federally regulated sectors—including banking and telecommunications—to comply with forthcoming accessibility regulations in employment, programs and service delivery, buildings and public spaces, and transportation that operate across provincial or federal borders. The act does not apply to provincially regulated sectors, although Ontario, Manitoba, and Nova Scotia have implemented accessibility legislation. British Columbia has committed to implement accessibility legislation.

Key International Actors

In May, the UN special rapporteur on hazardous substances, Baskut Tuncak, visited Canada to evaluate the federal government's progress on managing toxic materials and their effect on human rights. The rapporteur found that Indigenous people are disproportionately affected by toxic waste and expressed disappointment at the failure of both the province of Ontario and the federal government to address the health consequences of mercury contamination in the First Nation community of Grassy Narrows.

Foreign Policy

Canada, as a member of the Lima Group—together with states from Latin America—has consistently pressed Venezuelan authorities to address the ongoing political, humanitarian, human rights, and economic crisis in the country. In response to human rights violations by the government of Nicolás Maduro, Canada imposed several rounds of targeted sanctions and temporarily suspended its diplomatic operations in Caracas. In April, Canada imposed sanctions on 43 more individuals, bringing the total to 113 Venezuelan officials subject to Canadian sanctions.

In June, Canada announced sanctions against Nicaragua for its systematic human rights violations. The measures include asset freezes and travel bans on nine Nicaraguan government officials. Then-Foreign Minister Chrystia Freeland said that the Nicaraguan government must be "held accountable" and must end the current crisis through "real dialogue with opposition groups."

In September, the Canadian government acceded to the international Arms Trade Treaty and faced increasing pressure from a coalition of civil society organizations to end its $15-billion arms contract with Saudi Arabia and release the findings of its 2018 review of military export permits to the kingdom. Canada has yet to suspend existing arms sales to the Saudi-led coalition despite policy guidelines urging close control over exports of military equipment to countries with a record of human rights violations.

In June, 34 senators and more than 100 human-rights organizations and advocates sent a joint letter to then Foreign Minister Freeland urging Canada to take more international action to hold Myanmar accountable for the genocide of the

Rohingya people by initiating proceedings before the International Court of Justice (ICJ) for breaching the UN convention against genocide.

At the June session of the UN Human Rights Council, Canada joined 24 other governments in urging China to end its mass arbitrary detentions and other violations against Muslims in Xinjiang region. The joint statement also called on China to cooperate with the UN high commissioner for human rights and UN experts to allow unfettered access to the region.

In 2019, Canada also co-presented with other states resolutions on Venezuela, Nicaragua, Yemen, and Sri Lanka at the UN Human Rights Council.

HUMAN
RIGHTS
WATCH
CENTRAL AFRICAN REPUBLIC:
NEW COURT SHOULD STEP UP EFFORT
Donors, Government Should Increase Support

Central African Republic

A Political Agreement for Peace and Reconciliation was signed between the government of the Central African Republic and 14 armed groups in Bangui in February. As part of the agreement, a new government was formed, with several members of armed groups appointed to senior positions, including rebel leaders against whom there is credible evidence of responsibility for atrocities in recent years. The deal was the sixth signed since the crisis started in late 2012 and represents the greatest effort by both international and national actors to include all relevant parties to date.

Despite the peace deal, armed groups committed serious human rights abuses against civilians country-wide in 2019, with more than 70 percent of the country remaining under their control. Fighting between predominantly Muslim Seleka rebels, anti-balaka militias, and other armed groups forced thousands to flee their homes as fighters killed civilians and looted and burned properties. The most serious incident occurred on May 21, when fighters of rebel group Return, Reclamation, Rehabilitation, or 3R, killed 46 civilians in coordinated attacks in Ouham-Pendé province.

Tensions escalated in Bangui when representatives of a political platform known as E Zingo Biani), comprising of leaders from civil society organizations and opposition parties, criticized the government for appointing leaders of armed groups to key official positions. Between April and June, the platform made several calls for demonstrations, which authorities prohibited. During one demonstration, which had been banned, members of the Central Office for the Repression of Banditry violently assaulted and arrested two French journalists and a Central African political opponent.

In August and September, two rebel leaders, Mahamat al-Khatim, head of the Patriotic Movement for the Central African Republic (MPC), and 3R commander, Sidiki Abass, resigned from their government positions.

Some local courts rendered convictions of armed group leaders implicated in serious crimes, and seven investigations were pending before the Special Criminal Court (SCC), a new war crimes court based in Bangui staffed by national and international judges and prosecutors and operating with substantial UN assistance. The SCC remained underfunded.

The International Criminal Court (ICC) continued its second investigation of crimes committed in the country related to the current conflict, which started in late 2012. In September, the ICC held hearings on whether to confirm charges against two suspects associated with the anti-balaka militias, Patrice-Edouard Ngaïssona and Alfred Yékatom.

Attacks on Civilians

In January, fighting broke out between UN peacekeepers and fighters from the Union for Peace in the Central African Republic (UPC), when UPC fighters killed two policemen in Bambari ahead of a visit by the country's president. The fighting resulted in a UN attack on a large UPC base at Bokolobo, 60 kilometers south of Bambari, and left several people dead and wounded.

In April, UPC also attacked several villages between Kouango and Mobaye, in Ouaka and Basse-Kotto provinces, leading to the displacement of at least several thousand civilians.

Clashes between UPC members and self-defense groups at Zangba, Basse-Kotto province, between April 17 and 23, left dozens dead.

On April 28, violence erupted in Amo village in Kemo province, when a local militia attacked members of the minority Peuhl community, killing seven people, including two children and forcing scores of civilians to flee the area. The attack was in response to a Peuhl attack on a local resident the same day.

The most serious incident since the signing of the peace agreement occurred on May 21 when fighters from the armed group 3R killed at least 46 civilians in three attacks in the villages of Bohong, Koundjili, and Lemouna, in Ouham Pendé province. The 3R commander, Gen. Sidiki Abass (also known as Bi Sidi Souleymane), was appointed military adviser to the prime minister in March by presidential decree, but resigned from the post in September. 3R also looted properties in Bohong. On May 24, Abass handed three men whom he claimed were responsible for the killings in Koundjili and Lemouna to local authorities and MINUSCA. The men were detained in Bangui awaiting trial. In August, the Special Criminal Court took over the file of serious crimes committed in Lemouna, Kounjili, and Bohong from the national Attorney General's Office.

Violence erupted in the capital Bangui in July, when clashes between traders and self-defense groups in PK5 neighborhood killed at least 11 civilians.

Attacks on Humanitarian Workers

Following the signing of the peace deal, humanitarian actors were able to operate more freely and safely across the country, as well as to deliver assistance to previously inaccessible areas. However, the operating environment for humanitarians remained challenging and the Central African Republic continues to be one of the most dangerous countries in the world for humanitarian actors. According to the United Nations, there were 244 incidents directly affecting humanitarian personnel or property from January to October, leading to at least 3 deaths.

In June, former Seleka fighters and 3R combatants attacked a local nongovernmental organization (NGO) vehicle transporting eight staff in Pougol village, Ouham-Pendé province. The assailants threatened and beat the humanitarian workers, looted their belongings, and stole the vehicle.

Refugees and Internally Displaced Persons

In some areas, there were reports of spontaneous voluntary returns of internally displaced persons; however, fighting and attacks by armed groups continued to force tens of thousands of people to flee their homes throughout 2019. Fighting between the Popular Front for the Renaissance of the Central African Republic (FPRC) and the Movement of Central African Liberators for Justice (MLCJ) in Birao in September caused the displacement of around 14,000 civilians.

The total number of internally displaced persons in the country, based on UN figures, reached over 600,000, and the total number of refugees was 600,000. Conditions for internally displaced people and refugees, most of whom stay in camps, remained harsh, with little to no access to humanitarian assistance.

About 2.6 million people, out of a population of 4.6 million, needed humanitarian assistance, but the humanitarian response plan remained underfunded, with a budget gap of around US$206 million in September.

Regional and International Forces

The UN peacekeeping mission, MINUSCA, deployed 10,833 military peacekeepers and 2,050 police across many parts of the country.

Under Chapter VII of the UN Charter, the mission is authorized to take all necessary means to protect the civilian population from threat of physical violence and to "implement a mission-wide protection strategy."

In September, the UN Security Council adopted a resolution easing the UN arms embargo and extending a modified sanctions regime against the Central African Republic through January 2020. The resolution outlined details on the types of weapons and lethal equipment permitted pursuant to previous resolutions. In addition, it decided that the supplying member state is primarily responsible for notifying the Central African Republic Sanctions Committee responsible for overseeing sanctions imposed by the UN Security Council at least 20 days in advance of delivery of any supplies. Russia continued training and re-arming the national army.

In September, the UN Human Rights Council decided to continue the mandate of the Independent Expert on the Central African Republic for another year.

Justice for War Crimes and Crimes Against Humanity

Rendering justice for serious crimes continued to be a key challenge in 2019.

After a slow start since the SCC was established in 2015, the court's special prosecutor opened four investigations from 22 priority cases he identified, and the judges conducted investigations into three cases, which were transferred from the ordinary courts. The special prosecutor also examined 27 complaints that individuals submitted to the SCC.

The level of court staff overseeing investigations is limited, and additional prosecutors and judges are needed. The court needs programs that do not yet exist in the country's domestic system, including witness and victim protection and support, legal assistance for accused and victims, and outreach to affected communities. Ensuring adequate security for court premises, staff, and witnesses and victims remained one of the most significant challenges during the year, as much of the country remained under the control of armed groups.

As of July 10, the court had a funding gap of approximately US$1 million for 2019 operations, and no funds pledged for future years, anticipated to cost approximately $12.4 million annually.

The Office of the Prosecutor at the ICC continued its second investigation into the situation in the Central African Republic, into alleged war crimes and crimes against humanity committed in the country since 2012. The ICC combined proceedings against Alfred Yékatom, known as "Rambhot," and Patrice-Edouard Ngaïssona began in September. Central African Republic authorities surrendered Yékatom, an anti-balaka leader, to ICC custody in November 2018. Ngaïssona, also an anti-balaka leader, was transferred to ICC custody in January, after he was arrested in France in December 2018. A decision on whether to confirm the charges against Ngaïssona and Yékatom was expected by the ICC judges in early 2020.

Chile

Chile's national police (Carabineros) used excessive force in responding to massive demonstrations, some of them violent, that started in October and continued at time of writing. Thousands of people were injured, including more than 220 with serious eye injuries after police shot them with anti-riot shotguns. Many of those arrested reported serious abuses in detention, including brutal beatings and sexual abuse. While the government took some positive steps, including adopting a protocol on the use of force and deploying 250 specialists to instruct crowd control units on compliance with human rights standards, at time of writing it had yet to undertake other reforms to help prevent police misconduct and strengthen oversight.

Chile faces other important human rights challenges. Women encounter significant barriers to abortion in situations where abortion is allowed by law. Proposals to recognize same-sex marriage remain at an impasse. Tightened visa regulations on Venezuelans could in practice make it impossible for many to enter Chile. And overcrowding and inhumane conditions persist in many prisons.

Chile made human rights progress in some areas in 2019. Congress passed a gender identity law that allows individuals to change their name and gender in the civil registry, and a law outlawing public sexual harassment. Chile also took steps to hold accountable former police and military officers for abuses during Augusto Pinochet's dictatorship.

Abuses by Security Forces during Protests

Massive protests over public services and inequality broke out across Chile in October. While most demonstrators were peaceful, some groups attacked police with rocks, looted, and burned public and private property. Almost 2,000 officers were injured from October 18 to November 20.

Police responded using excessive force against demonstrators and bystanders, whether they were engaged in violence or not. Medical services treated more than 11,000 people injured from October 18 to November 22, including more than 220 people who suffered eye injuries, most hit by pellets police fired from anti-riot shotguns. At time of writing, police had suspended the use of those shotguns while experts analyzed the pellets' composition.

The police also detained more than 15,000 people from October 18 to November 21 and ill-treated some of them. The National Human Rights Institute filed 442 complaints concerning inhumane treatment, torture, sexual abuse, and other crimes. Human Rights Watch collected credible testimony that police forced detainees, especially women and girls, to undress and squat fully naked, a practice banned by police protocols. We also documented brutal beatings and rape in detention. Prosecutors are investigating at least five killings supposedly caused by security forces in the context of demonstrations.

Confronting Past Abuses

Chilean courts continue to prosecute former police and military officers responsible for human rights abuses during Augusto Pinochet's dictatorship from 1973 to 1990.

In December 2018, a Chilean judge convicted 53 former agents of the Chilean secret police (DINA) for the kidnapping, torture, and enforced disappearance of seven communist leaders in 1976, and the murder of former Communist Party leader, Victor Diaz, in 1977.

In January 2019, a Chilean judge convicted six men, including one security agent, four doctors, and a driver, for poisoning to death the former president of Chile, Eduardo Frei Montalva, in 1982.

In March, a Chilean judge convicted 11 ex-military officers for burning alive 19-year-old photographer Rodrigo Rojas in 1986.

Chile maintains a 50-year veil of secrecy over testimony by victims before the National Commission on Political Prison and Torture from November 2003 to May 2004. The testimony revealed places of detention and torture methods used by the dictatorship and identified former political prisoners and torture victims. The Bachelet administration (2014-2018) submitted a bill to lift the secrecy order in 2017, which generated heated debate between those who believe revealing the testimony would violate victims' rights to privacy, and those who believe revealing it is necessary to fully punish the guilty and bring justice to victims.

In December 2018, a commission of the House of Representatives approved a bill that would punish anyone who "justifies," "approves" of, or "denies" human rights violations committed during the dictatorship with up to 3 years in prison. The bill, which violates freedom of speech provisions of international human rights law, remained pending at time of writing.

Women's Rights

Chile's 28-year total ban on abortion came to an end in 2017 when the Constitutional Court upheld a new law decriminalizing abortion in three circumstances: when the pregnancy is the result of rape, the life of the pregnant woman is at risk, or the fetus is unviable. Although passage of the law signaled progress for reproductive rights in Chile, significant barriers to access remain even for legally permissible abortions.

The law in its current form allows doctors and private institutions to refuse to provide abortions on moral grounds. Of 1,148 specialist medical doctors working in public hospitals, over 50 percent object to providing abortions after rape, 28.5 percent when the fetus is unviable, and 20.5 percent when the life of the pregnant woman is at risk, according to a report issued by the Chilean Ministry of Health in June.

In April, Chile outlawed public sexual harassment, making acts including verbal assaults, groping, stalking, and obscene public indecency punishable by fines and even jail time.

Indigenous Rights

Chilean courts continue to prosecute Mapuche land-rights activists under the country's counterterrorism law for violence and destruction of property during protests. The law has faced criticism for its overly broad definition of terrorism and insufficient due process guarantees. Both the Bachelet and Piñera administrations proposed modifications to update the law and clarify its scope. A bill amending the counterterrorism law remained pending in the Senate at time of writing.

In November 2018, Camilo Catrillanca, a 24-year-old Mapuche activist, was shot dead by police. The killing sparked widespread outrage and became a symbol of police brutality. Police said Catrillanca was killed in a shootout and that the incident had not been recorded. But in December 2018, videos surfaced that showed Catrillanca was unarmed when he was shot in the back. President Piñera removed the head of the police force, Gen. Hermes Soto. At time of writing, eight individuals, including seven ex-police and one lawyer accused of helping to conceal evidence, were on trial for their role in the killing.

Sexual Orientation and Gender Identity

In August, Chile's gender identity law, promulgated by President Piñera in November 2018, passed its final stage of approval and is due to go into full effect by early 2020. The law allows transgender individuals over 14 years of age to legally change their name and gender in the civil registry, with no requirement for surgery or change in physical appearance. The passage of the law marks an important step forward for the trans community in Chile, but work remains to be done to guarantee the rights of married couples, who under the current law are required to divorce before accessing their right to a legal gender change.

The Bachelet administration's bill to legalize same-sex marriage and allow same-sex couples to adopt children and pursue other reproductive options, submitted in August 2017, remains pending in the Senate. In September, the Chilean government removed language promoting equal marriage from its Human Rights Plan.

Refugees and Migrants' Rights

In August, Chile's Senate agreed unanimously to consider an immigration reform bill to further regulate and systematize the immigration process to address the growing migrant population. Immigration laws have not been updated since 1975.

In August, the United Nations Refugee Agency estimated that around 400,000 Venezuelan migrants had entered Chile since 2016, making it the third highest recipient of Venezuelan refugees and migrants after Colombia and Peru. While Chile has made efforts to welcome Venezuelans, rules for obtaining visas, in practice, make it hard for some Venezuelans to take refuge. In June, Chile changed its rules to require Venezuelans entering on tourism grounds to obtain a visa before they arrive at the border. The tourist visa, valid for 90 days, is available at all Chilean consulates, but to obtain it, Venezuelans must present a passport issued after 2013 and pay US$50.

Chile also made available at all consulates a one-year "democratic responsibility visa"; the visa previously had been available only in Caracas. While increased access to the democratic responsibility visa may help some Venezuelans, it still carries a cost of US$30 and requires some form of valid documentation. Obtaining either visa may prove an insurmountable obstacle for the thousands fleeing without money or proper identification documents.

Children's Rights

The Piñera administration has taken several concrete steps to overhaul the historically flawed National Service for Minors (SENAME), including passing a law to double government subsidies for 200 residences that house and care for foster children, establishing the first specialized residence to care for children with psychosocial disabilities, and taking steps to move children out of traditional SENAME centers and into residences with increased personalized care and resources. SENAME had been the subject of scrutiny for several years due to reports of abuse, ill-treatment, and death in its centers.

In July, the Piñera administration passed a law that removes the statute of limitations from sex crimes against children, following an increase in allegations of abuse by members of the Catholic Church. At time of writing, Chilean prosecutors were investigating more than 200 such cases.

Prison Conditions

A report released in April by the National Human Rights Institute (INDH) showed that 19 of the 40 state-run prisons in Chile were above capacity in 2016 and 2017, 24 lacked sufficient access to bathrooms and drinking water, and many had problems with sanitation, mold, pests, air circulation, and heating. Furthermore, 50 percent of men and 35 percent of women did not have access to individual beds. The INDH has filed dozens of lawsuits on behalf of inmates living in undignified and unhealthy conditions.

Key International Actors

As a member of the United Nations Human Rights Council (HRC), Chile supported UN efforts in 2019 to scrutinize human rights violations in Nicaragua, Syria, Sri Lanka, Myanmar, North Korea, South Sudan, Belarus, Eritrea, Iran, Ukraine, and the Occupied Palestinian Territory. Yet in July it abstained in a resolution putting a spotlight on abuses in Philippines.

Chile has served since 2018 as the co-chair of the Organization of American States (OAS) Permanent Council Working Group on Nicaragua. In August, Chile supported a resolution to appoint a commission to monitor Nicaragua's ongoing human rights crisis and compliance with the Inter-American Democratic Charter.

Chile has also supported resolutions before both the UN and the OAS condemning abuses in Venezuela.

China

The Chinese Communist Party (CCP) in 2019 marked the 70th anniversary of its rule by deepening repression. Under President Xi Jinping's leadership, the one-party Chinese government tightened its grip over sectors of society it found threatening, such as the internet, activists, and nongovernmental organizations. It strengthened ideological control, particularly in higher education, among religious and ethnic minorities, and within the bureaucracy. It devoted massive resources to new technologies for social control, adding artificial intelligence, biometrics, and big data to its arsenal to monitor and shape the minds and behaviors of 1.4 billion people. Government censorship now extends far beyond its borders; its mix of typically financial incentives and intimidation are manipulating discourse about China around the world.

Thirteen million Uyghur and other Turkic Muslims in Xinjiang are suffering particularly harsh repression. The government's "Strike Hard Campaign against Violent Extremism" has entailed mass arbitrary detention, surveillance, indoctrination, and the destruction of the region's cultural and religious heritage. Credible estimates indicate that about 1 million Turkic Muslims are being indefinitely held in "political education" camps, where they are forced to disavow their identity and become loyal government subjects. Others have been prosecuted and sent to prison, and some have received lengthy and even death sentences for crimes that violate fundamental rights, "splitism" or "subversion."

In a year in which the CCP was especially keen to maintain a veneer of stability, Hong Kong, a special administrative region of China that enjoys limited—but eroding—freedoms, exploded with open defiance. Beginning in June, at least 2 million people in a city of 7 million filled the streets to demand greater freedoms.

The protests, sparked by the Hong Kong government's introduction of legal amendments that would have allowed extraditions to China, have evolved into a city-wide resistance movement against CCP rule.

A number of governments and international institutions issued public condemnations of China's most egregious human rights violations, but few took concrete actions, such as imposing sanctions or export controls.

Xinjiang

The extraordinarily repressive Strike Hard Campaign, launched in 2014, continued unabated against the Turkic Muslim population. To counter mounting international concern about the crackdown, Chinese authorities organized multiple, highly controlled trips for selected journalists and diplomats—including from the United Nations—to Xinjiang. In March, Xinjiang authorities announced that they had arrested nearly 13,000 "terrorists" in the region since 2014, and on July 30, publicly stated that "most" held in Xinjiang's "political education" camps had "returned to society"; neither claim was substantiated with credible evidence.

Several media reports in 2019 revealed that some people who had been "released" were assigned to factories against their will, where they were given wages far below the legal minimum and prohibited from leaving.

Xinjiang authorities also continued to remove children whose parents were detained or in exile and hold them in state-run "child welfare" institutions and boarding schools without parental consent or access.

The Chinese government continues to deny independent observers—including UN human rights experts—unfettered access to the region, which makes verifying information, particularly concerning detainees, very difficult.

Authorities' use of technologies for mass surveillance and social control has been unprecedented, especially in a region where people cannot challenge such intrusions. The Integrated Joint Operations Platform, a computer program central to Xinjiang's mass surveillance systems, keeps tabs on many facets of people's lives, including their movements and electricity use, and alerts authorities when it detects irregularities. Even tourists to the region—including non-Chinese citizens—are required to download a phone app that secretly monitors them.

International scrutiny of foreign academics and companies operating in the region has increased. One company, the US-based Thermo Fisher Scientific, which supplied DNA sequencers to Xinjiang police when authorities were indiscriminately collecting DNA from residents, announced in February that it would "cease all sales and servicing of our human identification technology" in Xinjiang.

Hong Kong

On January 23, the Hong Kong government introduced a bill that would criminalize "insults" to the Chinese national anthem. On February 12, the Hong Kong Security Bureau proposed changes to two laws that would enable criminal suspects in the city to be extradited to the Chinese authorities—which have a track record of torturing suspects and subjecting them to unfair trials—while removing public oversight over the process.

In April, a Hong Kong district court convicted nine leaders of the 2014 nonviolent pro-democracy "Umbrella Movement" on public nuisance charges. Legal scholar Benny Tai and retired professor Chan Kin-man were each handed 16-month prison terms.

On June 9, anger over the proposed extradition amendments and deteriorating freedoms prompted 1 million people to protest, according to organizers. On June 12, tens of thousands gathered around Hong Kong's legislature, the Legislative Council (LegCo), to press the government to drop the amendments. In response, Hong Kong police moved to disperse the protesters, firing teargas, beanbag rounds, and rubber bullets. Hong Kong's Chief Executive Carrie Lam condemned the protest, calling it "a riot." Although Lam later suspended the amendments, her long refusal to formally withdraw them or condemn police brutality, and her designation of the June 12 protest as "riot" led to a record-breaking march with an estimated 2 million demonstrators on June 16. On July 1, some broke into LegCo, painting slogans on some chamber walls. Protests spread across the city, and continued at time of writing.

Although most protesters acted peacefully, Hong Kong police dispersed them with excessive force, including by beating those subdued on the ground. Suspected gang, or "triad," members also repeatedly attacked protesters and pro-democracy lawmakers, leading to public accusations that police responded inadequately to violence against protesters. Some protesters used violence, throwing Molotov cocktails at police, setting roadblocks on fire; and in a number of cases attacked people they accused of being pro-Beijing infiltrators, including setting one person on fire.

Police increasingly restricted freedom of assembly by denying applications for protests.

On September 4, Lam formally withdrew the amendments, and on September 26 she staged a "dialogue" with some members of the public. But the unrest continued as the government would not meet most of the protesters' central demands, including implementing genuine universal suffrage—a right promised in Hong Kong's functional constitution—and launching an independent investigation into police abuses.

Tibet

Authorities in Tibetan areas continue to severely restrict religious freedom, speech, movement, and assembly, and fail to redress popular concerns about mining and land grabs by local officials, which often involve intimidation and unlawful use of force by security forces. In 2019, officials further intensified surveillance of online and phone communication.

Authorities in Tibetan areas have also stepped up use of a nationwide anti-crime campaign to encourage people to denounce members of their communities on the slightest suspicion of sympathy for the exiled Dalai Lama or opposition to the government. Two cases publicized by the Qinghai authorities in 2019, involving local opposition to land acquisition by the government, demonstrate that Tibetans are being prosecuted under the campaign for defense of their economic and cultural rights.

From May to July 2019, the authorities expelled thousands of Buddhist monks and nuns from the Yachen Gar monastery in Sichuan, and their dwellings demolished. Those without residence status in Sichuan were deported to their home provinces, where they were reportedly detained for reeducation. Meanwhile, Tibetan Autonomous Region leaders called for an intensification of "Sinicization" policies to "strengthen the management of monasteries," subjecting monastic populations to "legal" exams to test their competence in political reeducation, and requiring senior religious figures to endorse state policies on the selection of the next Dalai Lama.

In the Ngawa Tibetan region of Sichuan, two more young men set themselves on fire in protest against the Chinese government, in November and December 2018. Since March 2009, 155 Tibetans have self-immolated.

Human Rights Defenders

In July, dissident Ji Sizun, 69, died in state custody. Two months after being released from prison, Ji succumbed to unknown illnesses, guarded by police in a hospital in Fujian province. He had reportedly been ill-treated while serving a four-and-a-half-year sentence on fabricated charges of "gathering a crowd to disrupt public order" and "picking quarrels." Consistent with a number of other cases in recent years of prominent human rights defenders dying in or soon after release from detention, authorities have not held anyone accountable for wrongdoing.

Courts handed down lengthy prison terms to prominent human rights activists after sham proceedings. In January, a court in Tianjin sentenced human rights lawyer Wang Quanzhang to four-and-a-half years in prison for "subversion." In the same month, a court in Hubei province sentenced Liu Feiyue, a veteran activist and founder of the human rights news website Minsheng Guancha, to five years in prison for "inciting subversion."

In April, a Sichuan court sentenced activist Chen Bing to three-and-a-half years for commemorating the 1989 Tiananmen Massacre. In July, a court in Sichuan province handed down a 12-year sentence to Huang Qi, a prominent activist and founder of human rights website 64 Tianwang, on "leaking state secrets" charges. Huang, detained since November 2016, suffers from several serious health conditions for which he has not been given adequate treatment.

More human rights defenders were detained in 2019. As part of an ongoing nationwide crackdown on labor activism that began in July 2018, Shenzhou police in January and March detained Yang Zhengjun, Ke Chengbing, and Wei Zhili, editors of the workers' rights news website New Generation, accusing them of "picking quarrels." In June, Guangdong police detained labor activist Ling Haobo on unknown charges. In August, Hunan authorities detained Cheng Yuan, Liu Dazhi, and Wu Gejianxiong, staff members of the anti-discrimination group Changsha Funeng, on "subversion" charges.

Police across the country detained activists and citizens? who showed support for the pro-democracy protests in Hong Kong. In June, Beijing police detained activist Quan Shixin for "picking quarrels." In September, Guangzhou authorities detained Lai Rifu after he shared a protest song on social media. In October

Guangzhou authorities detained Sophia Huang Xueqin, a journalist who has written extensively about China's #MeToo movement and about the protests in Hong Kong.

Aside from detentions and enforced disappearances, authorities continue to subject human rights activists and lawyers and their families to house arrest, harassment, surveillance, and travel bans. In April, Beijing authorities blocked lawyer Chen Jiangang from leaving China to take part in a fellowship program in the United States. Sichuan police harassed the octogenarian mother of imprisoned activist Huang Qi, in an apparent attempt to prevent her from speaking out. Police forcibly disappeared her mother by placing her under incommunicado house arrest for days, and sending government agents to live in her home. Beijing authorities pressured schools in the city to expel or deny admission to the 6-year-old son of imprisoned lawyer Wang Quanzhang.

Freedom of Expression

Authorities continued a national crackdown on users of Twitter—already blocked in China—that started in November 2018. Authorities detained or summoned hundreds of Twitter users, forcing them to delete "sensitive" tweets or close their accounts. Meanwhile, the government launched a disinformation campaign on Twitter and Facebook that frames Hong Kong's protesters as violent and extreme, prompting the platforms to suspend hundreds of accounts originating in China.

Authorities further restricted the internet in China. In March, censors removed social media accounts of Ma Liang, a clickbait blogger who commanded an audience of more than 16 million. Ma was accused by state media of circulating false information. In June, China's internet regulator shut down the financial news aggregator wallstreetcn.com, and ordered Q Daily, a news site known for its stories on social issues, to stop updating content for at least three months.

The government also tightened its ideological grip over universities and schools. In a March speech, President Xi called for educators to fend off "false ideas and thoughts" when teaching ideologies and politics courses. In March, Tsinghua University suspended prominent law professor Xu Zhangrun and placed him under investigation after he published a series of essays that warned of deepening repression under President Xi.

HUMAN
RIGHTS
WATCH
CHINA'S ALGORITHMS
OF REPRESSION
Reverse Engineering a Xinjiang Police Mass Surveillance App

The effect of Chinese government censorship continues to reach beyond the Chinese borders. WeChat, China's popular messaging platform used by more than a billion Chinese-speakers at home and abroad, is subject to the usual Chinese censorship applied to all domestic social media. Dissent artist Ai Weiwei's involvement with the Hollywood film "Berlin, I Love You" was cut after investors, distributors, and other partners raised concerns about the artist's political sensitivity in China. In an episode of "The Good Fight," American broadcaster CBS censored an animated short that depicted a host of references to topics that have been censored on the Chinese internet. CBS said it was concerned with risks of its shows and movies being blocked in China and the safety of its employees in China.

Mass Surveillance

The government's use of mass surveillance technologies is on the rise. Police, security agencies, and public and private entities targeted their use at vulnerable communities. In 2019, media reports revealed that a Hangzhou school had installed cameras to monitor students' facial expressions and attentiveness, while a Nanjing company had required sanitation workers to wear GPS watches to monitor their efficiency.

Chinese technology companies, particularly Huawei but also artificial intelligence companies such as Cloudwalk, were under intense scrutiny for their ties to the Chinese government and their cooperation with foreign technology counterparts. As they expand worldwide, offering affordable equipment and services to governments and companies, there are concerns that they are enabling the proliferation of mass surveillance. In July, a media report found that US technology companies had collaborated with a Chinese company, Semptian, in developing microprocessors that enable computers to analyze vast amounts of data more efficiently, and that Semptian had used them to enhance mass surveillance and censorship for Chinese security agencies.

China does not have a unified privacy or data protection law. Although the government shows growing interest in regulating private companies' collection of consumer data, such regulations are limited to the commercial sphere.

Freedom of Religion

The government restricts religious practice to five officially recognized religions in officially approved premises. Authorities retain control over religious bodies' personnel appointments, publications, finances, and seminary applications. The government classifies many religious groups outside its control as "evil cults," and subjects members to police harassment, torture, arbitrary detention, and imprisonment.

In December 2018, police detained the pastor and scores of members of Early Rain Covenant Church, an independent Protestant church in the southwestern city of Chengdu. Most were released days or months later. Pastor Wang Yi, a prominent member of China's Christian community and a former legal scholar, remains in police custody and has been charged with "inciting subversion."

In a speech in March, Xu Xiaohong, the official who oversees state-sanctioned Christian churches, called on churches to purge Western influence and to further "Sinicize" the religion. In September, a state-sanctioned church in Henan province was ordered to replace the Ten Commandments with quotes by President Xi.

In its continuing campaign to crack down on Islamic traditions, authorities in Gansu, Ningxia, and other Hui Muslim areas demolished domes on mosques and banned the public use of Arabic script.

A CCP notice banning retired Tibetan government employees from performing kora, the practice of circumambulating a sacred site, appears to have been issued in early August 2019.

Women's and Girls' Rights

As the country's sex ratio imbalance has made it difficult for many men to find wives, "bride" trafficking from neighboring countries to China appears to have increased from Cambodia, Laos, Myanmar, North Korea, and Pakistan. Many women and girls are deceived through false promises of employment into travelling to China, only to be sold to Chinese families as brides and held in sexual slavery, often for years. In April, a Pakistani television station gained entry to what it said was a "matchmaking center" in Lahore where six women and girls, two only 13 years old, were held awaiting transit to China as brides.

In July, Wang Zhenhua, a prominent businessman and philanthropist, was detained by the police as they investigated a child molestation incident that injured a 9-year-old girl. Government censors initially blocked online discussions and media reporting of the case, leading to an online uproar. Also in July, a court in Chengdu ruled in a case of alleged sexual harassment in favor of the plaintiff, marking the first ruling since the #MeToo movement gathered momentum in China.

Sexual Orientation and Gender Identity

China decriminalized homosexuality in 1997, but it still lacks laws protecting people from discrimination on the basis of sexual orientation or gender identity, and same-sex partnership is not legal. In March, during the UN Human Rights Council's Universal Periodic Review, China accepted recommendations to adopt legislation prohibiting discrimination based on sexual orientation and gender identity in education and employment. However, a National People's Congress spokesperson said in August that the government would not consider marriage equality.

In January, the Guangzhou government banned two lesbian, gay, bisexual, and transgender rights organizations, including a student-led group at the University of Guangzhou. In March, government censors cut scenes depicting homosexuality from the Oscar-winning movie "Bohemian Rhapsody."

Refugees and Asylum Seekers

China continued to detain and forcibly return hundreds, and perhaps thousands, of North Korean refugees, thus violating its obligations as a party to the 1951 Refugee Convention. The government refused to consider fleeing North Koreans as refugees, even though those returned have long been persecuted. Human Rights Watch considers North Koreans in China as refugees sur place, meaning their arrival in China put them at risk if returned.

Key International Actors

A number of governments and parliaments have publicly expressed grave concerns about the situation in Xinjiang and other serious human rights violations by the Chinese government, and continue to seek to monitor trials and assist human rights defenders. The US Congress and European Parliament issued resolutions and considered legislation on issues including Hong Kong, Tibet, and Xinjiang, yet few governments were willing to impose tougher responses, such as sanctions or export controls, to press Beijing to change its policies.

In June, Germany granted refugee status to two activists from Hong Kong.

In March, the European Commission announced a review of its relations with China, defining the country also as a "systemic rival promoting alternative models of governance." The European Union regularly raised human rights concerns in its Human Rights Council statements, in the EU-China human rights dialogue, and in occasional statements throughout the year. However, no human rights concerns were publicly raised by EU leaders during the 21st EU-China Summit, held in Brussels in April.

The US repeatedly rhetorically condemned China's human rights violations, yet these comments were weakened by President Trump's complimentary commentary of President Xi. In October, the US placed the Xinjiang Public Security Bureau and its subsidiary agencies, the quasi-military entity in Xinjian known as the bingtuan, and eight Chinese technology firms on the Department of Commerce's "entities list," effectively blocking them from doing business with US companies, in response to their role in repression in Xinjiang. At around the same time, the US State Department announced it would withhold visas from Chinese government officials found to be culpable in Xinjiang abuses.

In July, 25 governments signed a letter to the UN Human Rights Council president, echoing the high commissioner's call for an independent investigation in the Xinjiang region. China promptly organized a competing letter, signed by 50 governments, praising China's regional approach to "counter-terrorism," and noting that people in Xinjiang "enjoy a stronger sense of happiness." Yet throughout the year the Organization of Islamic Cooperation (OIC) did not condemn abuses against Turkic Muslims in Xinjiang—while sharply criticizing abuses against Muslims elsewhere—and instead praised China's treatment of Muslims.

Foreign Policy

In April, China hosted the second Belt and Road Forum in Beijing. The "Belt and Road Initiative" (BRI), announced in 2013, is China's trillion-dollar infrastructure and investment program stretching across some 70 countries. During the forum, President Xi pledged to work with other countries to foster environment-friendly development, yet some of the BRI projects have been criticized for lack of transparency, disregard of community concerns, and threats of environmental degradation.

In February, thousands of people in Kachin State in Myanmar marched to protest a proposed China-financed mega-dam project. In March, the state-owned Bank of China said it would evaluate the funding commitment to a hydropower plant in Indonesia.

In late 2018, Chinese authorities detained two Canadians, Michael Kovrig and Michael Spavor, in what is widely viewed as an act of retaliation against Canada for the arrest of Meng Wanzhou, an executive at the Chinese tech giant Huawei.

In August, Beijing formally arrested writer and China-born Australian citizen Yang Hengjun on espionage charges, seven months after he was detained in southern China.

Chinese authorities continued to try to restrict academic freedom abroad. In February, the Chinese consulate in Toronto told students at McMaster University to notify the consulate of the academics present at an event on repression in Xinjiang. At a number of universities in Australia in August, pro-Beijing students attempted to forcibly silence other students demonstrating peacefully in support of Hong Kong's democracy movement; similar incidents have been reported across Europe, New Zealand, and the United States. Few universities have responded with robust defenses of all students' and scholars' right to academic freedom.

HUMAN
RIGHTS
WATCH
THE WAR IN CATATUMBO
Abuses by Armed Groups Against Civilians including
Venezuelan Exiles in Northeastern Colombia

Colombia

The 52-year armed conflict between the Revolutionary Armed Forces of Colombia (FARC) and the government officially ended with a peace accord in 2016. Despite an initial overall decline, conflict-related violence has taken new forms and serious abuses continue.

In 2019, civilians in affected parts of the country suffered serious abuses at the hands of National Liberation Army (ELN) guerrillas, FARC dissidents, and paramilitary successor groups. Human rights defenders, journalists, indigenous and Afro-Colombian leaders, and other community activists have faced death threats and violence. The government has taken insufficient steps to protect them. Violence associated with the conflicts has forcibly displaced more than 8.1 million Colombians since 1985.

In 2017, the Colombian government initiated formal peace talks with the ELN. But in January 2019, shortly after the ELN exploded a car bomb at a police academy in Bogotá, the government of President Iván Duque ended the peace talks.

Impunity for past abuses, barriers to land restitution for displaced people, limits on reproductive rights, and extreme poverty and isolation faced by indigenous communities remain important human rights concerns in Colombia.

Guerrillas and FARC Dissidents

In June 2017, the United Nations political mission in Colombia verified that FARC guerrillas who accepted the peace agreement with the government had handed over their weapons to the mission. The demobilized guerrilla group later announced it was forming a political party, the Revolutionary Alternative Force of the Common People.

But a minority of dissident guerrilla fighters rejected the terms of the peace agreement, refused to disarm, and continue to commit abuses. Other FARC fighters disarmed initially but then joined or created new groups, partly in reaction to inadequate reintegration programs. As of May, the military estimated that FARC dissident groups had more than 2,300 members.

In the eastern province of Arauca, on the border with Venezuela, a FARC dissident group has committed violations of the laws of war and other serious human rights abuses against civilians including those who defy the group's "rules." Abuses include murder, sexual violence, child recruitment, kidnappings, and forced labor. In some cases, fighters from this group have taken victims across the border to Venezuela.

In September, Karina García Sierra, who was running to be mayor of Suárez, Cauca, was attacked and killed. Authorities blamed a FARC dissident group.

The ELN continued in 2019 to commit war crimes and other serious abuses against civilians, including killings, forced displacement, and child recruitment. Its fighting with the Popular Army of Liberation (EPL)—a hold-out from a rival guerrilla group that demobilized in the 1990s—forced over 3,500 people to leave their houses in Catatumbo, a region in the northeast, between January and the end of July 2019.

In the Chocó province, on the country's west coast, fighting between the ELN and the Gaitanist Self-Defense Forces of Colombia (AGC)—a group that emerged from the paramilitaries. Fears of landmines, threats by armed groups, and getting caught in the crossfire have limited the ability of nearly 2,800 people in Chocó to leave their communities, a situation known as "confinement." In already poor communities, confinement often undermines access to food.

In January, a car bomb detonated at a police academy in Bogotá, killing 22 cadets and injuring over 60 others. Days later, the ELN claimed responsibility, saying they had acted "within the laws of war."

Paramilitaries and Successors

Between 2003 and 2006, right-wing paramilitary organizations with close ties to security forces and politicians underwent a deeply flawed government demobilization process in which many members remained active and reorganized into new groups. These successor groups continue to commit violations of the laws of war and serious human rights abuses, including killings, disappearances, and rape.

Fighting between the AGC and a FARC dissident group caused 2,200 people to flee their homes in the Córdoba province, in northern Colombia, between March and April 2019.

Implementation of the Justice and Peace Law of 2005, which offers reduced sentences to demobilized paramilitary members who confess their crimes, has been slow. Of more than 30,000 paramilitary troops who demobilized, 4,000 have sought to exchange a confession for a lighter sentence. As of March 2018, 215 had been sentenced.

Santiago Uribe, brother of former President Alvaro Uribe, was on trial, at time of writing, on charges of murder and conspiracy for his alleged role in the paramilitary group "The 12 Apostles" in the 1990s.

The Supreme Court summoned former President Uribe to appear in court in October to answer allegations that he tampered with witnesses who implicated him in paramilitary atrocities in the 1990s.

Violations by Public Security Forces

From 2002 through 2008, army brigades across Colombia routinely executed civilians in what are known as "false positive" killings. Under pressure from superiors to show "positive" results and boost body counts in their war against guerrillas, soldiers and officers abducted victims or lured them to remote locations under false pretenses—such as promises of work—shot them dead, placed weapons on their bodies, and reported them as enemy combatants killed in action. The number of allegations of unlawful killings by security forces has fallen sharply since 2009, though credible reports of some new cases continue to emerge.

As of September 2019, the Attorney General's Office had opened over 2,000 investigations on alleged unlawful killings by army personnel from 2002 through 2008, and had achieved over 900 convictions in cases against more than 1,600 mid- and low-level soldiers, including convictions against the same individual in various cases. As of February 2019, 55 members of the Armed Forces had testified about their roles in false positives before the Special Jurisdiction for Peace, a transitional justice mechanism created by the peace agreement with the FARC.

Authorities have largely failed, however, to prosecute senior army officers involved in the killings and instead have promoted many of them through the military ranks. As of September 2019, cases against 29 army generals under investigation for false-positive killings had seen scant progress.

In December 2018, President Duque named Gen. Nicacio de Jesús Martínez Espinel as head of the army, despite credible evidence linking him to false positives.

The army apologized for the April 29 killing by one of its soldiers of Dimar Torres, a former FARC fighter, in Catatumbo, in northeast Colombia. A sergeant was charged with the murder, while a colonel was accused of cover up.

In 2019, the *New York Times, Semana* magazine, and Human Rights Watch published documents showing that in 2019 the army reinstated military policies resembling those that led to the "false positives." The bulk of the new policies remained in force at time of writing.

In November, Defense Minister Guillermo Botero resigned as he was facing an impeachment process in Congress.

Violence Against Community Activists

Indigenous, Afro-Colombian, and other community activists continue to be targeted with threats and attacks. The Office of the UN High Commissioner for Human Rights (OHCHR) documented the killings of 41 human rights defenders between January and late July 2019.

In March, a group of young men broke into the home of Argemiro López, a community activist who promoted the substitution of coca for food crops in La Guayacana, in the southwestern municipality of Tumaco. They shot and killed López and injured his wife.

Most such killings have occurred in areas where illegal economic activities, such as drug production and trafficking, are common. These include Cauca and Nariño provinces in the south; Catatumbo, in the northeast, on the border with Venezuela; and the Bajo Cauca and southern Córdoba regions in the northwest.

In August, the Attorney General's Office said it had issued arrest warrants against at least one alleged perpetrator in 58 percent of the cases reported by the OHCHR since January 2016 in which human rights defenders have been murdered. The office said it had obtained convictions against 62 perpetrators. Authorities have made much less progress in prosecuting people who ordered murders against community leaders.

The National Protection Unit—a national body charged with protecting people at risk— has granted individual protection measures to hundreds of human rights defenders, providing cellphones, bulletproof vests, and bodyguards. Such measures are provided in response to threats, but many community leaders killed had not reported threats or requested protection.

In April 2018, the government signed a decree creating collective protection programs for communities and rights groups at risk. It had not been implemented at time of writing.

An action plan introduced in November 2018 to protect community leaders has not led to any evident results.

Peace Negotiations and Accountability

The peace agreement between the Colombian government and the FARC provided for the creation of a "Special Jurisdiction for Peace" to try those responsible for gross human rights violations and violations of international humanitarian law committed during the conflict. FARC guerrillas and members of the armed forces responsible for crimes against humanity and serious war crimes who fully cooperate with the new jurisdiction and confess their crimes are subject to as many as eight years of "effective restrictions on freedoms and rights," but no prison time.

At time of writing, Special Jurisdiction magistrates had prioritized seven situations for analysis: kidnappings committed by the FARC; false-positive killings; army and FARC abuses against Afro-Colombian and indigenous people in three municipalities in Nariño province, in the south; FARC and army abuses committed in the Urabá region, in the north; FARC and army abuses committed in the northern part of Cauca province; government abuses against members of the Patriotic Union, a political party created by the FARC in the 1980s; and recruitment and use of children by the FARC.

During 2019, the Special Jurisdiction opened investigations to determine whether four former FARC commanders had failed to fulfill their responsibilities under the peace accord, including reincorporating former guerrilla fighters into society and testifying before the Special Jurisdiction. In April, the Special Jurisdiction issued a warrant for arrest of one of them, alias "El Paisa," ruling his failure to testify before the Special Jurisdiction was unjustified.

The whereabouts of all four, including the group's top peace negotiator, alias "Iván Márquez" and alias "Jesús Santrich," who the US is seeking to have extradited to the US on drug charges, remained unknown at time of writing. In August, these four former FARC commanders, along with about 20 other former mid-level FARC commanders, announced that they were taking up arms again in response to what they called a "betrayal by the state of the peace accord."

In March, the Constitutional Court ruled unconstitutional a 2018 law containing a provision that suspended, unless defendants requested otherwise, Special Jurisdiction prosecutions of armed forces soldiers until the government created a "special and differentiated process" for them.

Internal Displacement and Land Restitution

Conflict-related violence has displaced more than 8.1 million Colombians, out of a population of 49 million, since 1985, government figures reveal. Around 33,000 people were displaced between January and the end of July 2019.

The government's implementation of land restitution under the 2011 Victims' Law continues to move slowly. The law was enacted to restore millions of hectares of land that were left behind by or stolen from internally displaced Colombians during the conflict. As of July, the courts had issued rulings in only 10,400 of more than 116,000 claims filed.

In August, a Democratic Center senator introduced a bill that would limit land restitution in cases where the land was stolen and since sold.

Migration from Venezuela

Colombia has received by far the largest number of Venezuelan exiles fleeing the human rights and humanitarian crisis in Venezuela. More than 1.4 million people moved from Venezuela to Colombia between March 2017 and August 2019.

In July 2017, the Colombian government created a special permit that allows Venezuelan citizens who enter the country legally but overstay their visas to regularize their status and obtain work permits and access to basic public services.

As of July, nearly 600,000 Venezuelans had obtained the permit. Many still remain with irregular status. In August, the Colombian government passed a regulation allowing more than 24,000 Venezuelan children born to undocumented Venezuelan immigrants to claim Colombian nationality.

Women's and Girls' Rights

Gender-based violence, including by armed groups, is widespread in Colombia. Lack of training and poor implementation of treatment protocols impede timely access to medical services and create obstacles for women and girls seeking post-violence care and justice. Perpetrators of violent, gender-based crimes are rarely held accountable.

In the southwestern municipality of Tumaco, where sexual violence, including by armed groups, is pervasive, women face an array of obstacles in ensuring protection and accountability.

Abortion in Colombia is legal only when the life or health of the woman or girl is at risk, the pregnancy is the result of rape, or the fetus suffers conditions incompatible with life outside the womb.

Sexual Orientation and Gender Identity

In recent years, authorities have taken several steps to recognize the rights of lesbian, gay, bisexual, and transgender (LGBT) people. In 2015, the Justice Ministry issued a decree allowing people to revise the gender noted on their identification documents without prior judicial approval. Also that year, the Constitutional Court ruled that Colombians cannot be barred from adopting a child because of their sexual orientation. In 2016, the court upheld the right of same-sex couples to marry.

Indigenous Rights

Indigenous people in Colombia suffer disproportionate levels of poverty that greatly impede their ability to exercise their social and economic rights. From January through mid-August 2019, at least 21 children under age five—the majority of them belonging to Wayuu indigenous communities—died in the province of La Guajira of causes associated with malnutrition and limited access to drinking safe water. In August 2019, Colombia's inspector general said that the government had not taken coordinated action to address the crisis.

Key International Actors

The United States remains the most influential foreign actor in Colombia. The US House of Representatives approved at least US$457 million for Colombia in June; the bill was pending in the Senate at time of writing. A portion of US military aid is subject to human rights conditions, but the US Department of State has not seriously enforced them.

In April, US senators Patrick Leahy, Chris Van Hollen, and Benjamin L. Cardin sent a letter to President Duque expressing their concern with the appointment of officers to senior positions in the army, despite credible information that they were linked to "false positives."

The Office of the Prosecutor (OTP) of the International Criminal Court continues to monitor Colombian investigations of crimes that may fall within the court's jurisdiction.

In 2016, at the request of the government of then-President Juan Manuel Santos, the UN Security Council established a political mission in Colombia to monitor and verify implementation of the FARC peace accord. In July 2019, President Duque asked the Security Council to extend the mandate of the UN mission for another year.

The Office of the UN High Commissioner for Human Rights (OHCHR) continues to play a key role in defending and promoting human rights in Colombia. In October, the government and high commissioner renegotiated the agreement establishing an OHCHR office in Colombia and extended its mandate for three more years.

The Colombian government continues to support regional efforts to address the human rights crisis in Venezuela, including by leading efforts of the Lima Group, a coalition of governments in the region that is monitoring Venezuela's crisis.

Côte d'Ivoire

Côte d'Ivoire's continued strong economic growth in 2019 led to some improvements in social and economic rights. The government, however, failed to tackle the root causes of past political violence, notably entrenched impunity, a politicized judiciary, and longstanding political and ethnic tensions.

The International Criminal Court (ICC)'s January 2019 acquittal of former President Laurent Gbagbo and his youth minister and militia leader Charles Blé Goudé, and the halting of domestic prosecutions, further entrenched impunity for crimes committed after the 2010-11 elections, which left thousands dead.

Divisive political rhetoric, residual tensions from the 2018 local elections, and recurring disputes over access to land led to an increase in intercommunal tensions. At least 14 people died and dozens were injured during clashes between communities in Béoumi, in northern Côte d'Ivoire, on May 15 and 16.

A flurry of law reforms led to some improvements in the legal protection of human rights. The government passed laws that defined torture as a stand-alone crime and introduced measures that could reduce reliance on pretrial detention and improve marriage equality. Some provisions of the new laws, however, could be used to restrict freedom of assembly and expression. The arrest of several opposition or civil society figures for organizing anti-government protests raised concerns of a closing of civic space ahead of the 2020 presidential elections.

Accountability for Past Crimes

An ICC trial chamber on January 15 acquitted Gbagbo and Blé Goudé of crimes against humanity after an almost three-year trial, ending the case before the defense was even required to present evidence. In its written decision on July 16, the two-judge majority strongly criticized the weakness of the prosecution evidence.

The ICC prosecutor appealed the acquittals on September 16, asking judges to declare a mistrial. At time of writing, Gbagbo and Blé Goudé were on conditional release, in Belgium and the Netherlands respectively.

The ICC continued its investigations into crimes committed by pro-Ouattara forces during the post-election crisis, but has yet to issue arrest warrants. President Alassane Ouattara has said that no further suspects will be transferred to The Hague.

In the year after President Ouattara's August 2018 amnesty for crimes committed during the 2010-11 post-election violence, there was little progress in domestic investigations by the Special Investigative and Examination Cell. The cell, established in 2011, had in previous years charged more than two dozen senior military officers and political leaders with crimes against humanity or war crimes.

The Ivorian government stated in February that the amnesty law does not preclude Ivorian judges from investigating the worst crimes committed during the crisis, noting that it does not apply to individuals who are "members of the military and armed groups." On November 6, Ivorian judges confirmed charges against Blé Goudé in Côte d'Ivoire for alleged crimes during the 2010-11 post-election crisis, including murder, rape, and torture. Other than the Blé Goudé's case, however, the Special Cell has frozen its investigations, making it unlikely that alleged perpetrators will ever face trial.

On April 4, three human rights groups, two Ivorian and one international, filed a Supreme Court complaint contesting President Ouattara's authority to issue the amnesty, arguing that it violated Côte d'Ivoire international human rights treaty obligations. At time of writing, the case had not yet been decided.

Neither Côte d'Ivoire's Special Cell nor the ICC have investigated crimes committed during election-related violence in 2000, or the 2002-2003 armed conflict. A government reparations program continued to give victims of the 2002-2011 conflicts financial payments, medical treatment, and other forms of assistance.

Judiciary and Detention Conditions

The justice system lacks independence and judges regularly experience pressure from the executive. Judges report that the risk of interference is greatest in political cases, but can occur in any civil or criminal trial.

Prison conditions and overcrowding remained a problem. For example, Abidjan's central prison in October housed 7,100 in a facility designed for 1,500, with 2,500 in pretrial detention. Despite some efforts to rehabilitate prisons, detainees still lack adequate access to medical care and inmates suffer extortion by prison guards and fellow inmates.

On December 21, 2018, the National Assembly adopted a new Code of Criminal Procedure that replaced the Cour d'Assises, a criminal court that sat only periodically, with permanent criminal courts able to try the most serious offenses. Magistrates said that, with adequate staffing, this could reduce the backlog of criminal cases awaiting trial. The new law could also introduce time limits on pretrial detention and, if properly implemented, would offer sentencing alternatives to prison, such as probation or community service.

Security Force Abuses and Security Sector Reform

Much needed efforts continued to professionalize the army and improve discipline in the security forces, both through training and the reform of army leadership.

Several former "comzones," powerful military commanders implicated in serious human rights abuses from 2002 to 2011, were demoted in March. However, some of them remain in positions of authority within the armed forces.

Security forces opened fire on protesters demonstrating against the arrest of an opposition politician in Bouaké on October 3, killing one person and injuring several others.

Members of the security forces continued to engage in racketeering and extortion, particularly at checkpoints on secondary roads. Online activist Soro Tangboho was arrested in November 2018 for live streaming police officers whom, he claimed, were extorting money from motorists. He was convicted on June 7 for public order offenses; his initial one-year sentence was increased to two after a July 31 appeal. Members of the army, police, or gendarmerie were rarely punished for corruption and other more serious offenses.

Election Framework

The National Assembly and Senate in July and August enacted reforms to modify the composition of the election commission, as required by a 2016 judgment by the African Court on Human and Peoples' Rights. Opposition and some civil society organizations strongly criticized the reforms, arguing that the government's role in nominating members of the commission means it will still be subject to executive influence. Two of the largest opposition parties in September refused to nominate members of the commission.

Freedom of Assembly and Expression

The government in several instances prohibited opposition rallies, and on multiple occasions police or gendarmes arrested and briefly detained opposition politicians and civil society activists who organized anti-government demonstrations.

On June 26, President Ouattara promulgated a new criminal code that makes the organization of an "undeclared or prohibited" demonstration punishable by one to three years' imprisonment and a financial penalty. International human rights standards require that protest organizers should not be sanctioned for merely failing to notify authorities in advance.

The new criminal code also creates vague offenses, punishable by imprisonment, which threaten freedom of speech, including offenses for "sharing false news where that results or could result in" disturbance to public order and "causing offense to the president or vice-president."

Opposition parliamentarian Alain Lobognon was sentenced to a year's imprisonment on January 29, reduced to a six-month suspended sentence on appeal, for disclosing "fake news" after alleging on social media that police were planning to imprison an opposition mayor whom the government had accused of corruption.

Land Reform and Instability in the West

A rural land agency, established in 2016 finally began to implement programs to speed up implementation of a 1998 land law designed to reduce conflicts over land by registering customary land rights and issuing legal titles. The vast majority of rural land, however, remained unregistered.

Côte d'Ivoire in July 2019 adopted a new forestry code that signals a renewed effort to protect and rehabilitate the country's protected forests, which have been devastated by cocoa farming. Past government-led forestry reclamation efforts left thousands of evicted farmers' families without access to adequate food, water, or shelter.

Women and Girl's Rights

The legislature in July passed new laws on marriage and inheritance that establish co-ownership of martial property. The laws also give a widow the right to one- quarter of the husband's estate, with the remaining three-quarters going to the children. Under the old law, widows often received nothing. The law confirmed the age of consent for marriage as 18, but child marriage is still common.

The new criminal code creates a presumption of consent to sex between married couples, which could prevent victims of marital rape from pursuing successful prosecutions. It also criminalizes abortion except where necessary to protect the life of the mother or for victims of rape.

Sexual Orientation and Gender Identity

Consensual sexual relations between consenting individuals of the same sex are not criminalized in Côte d'Ivoire. The new criminal code removed references to acts between members of the same sex as an aggravating factor in cases of public indecency. However, the new marriage law defines marriage as between a man and a woman, and incidents of discrimination against lesbian, gay, bisexual, and transgender (LGBT) persons—including physical assaults—are common.

Key International Actors

France, the US, and the EU remained major donors, including in the justice and security sector, although Côte d'Ivoire has increasingly strong economic ties with China.

Côte d'Ivoire completed a two-year term as a member of the United Nations Security Council in December 2019.

Cuba

The Cuban government continues to repress and punish dissent and public criticism. The number of short-term arbitrary arrests of human rights defenders, independent journalists, and others was lower in 2019 than in 2018, but remained high, with more than 1,800 arbitrary detentions reported through August. The government continues to use other repressive tactics against critics, including beatings, public shaming, travel restrictions, and termination of employment.

In February, a new Constitution of the Republic of Cuba was approved in a referendum, which entered into force in April. Prior to the referendum, authorities repressed activists opposing its adoption, including through raids and short detentions, and blocked several news sites seen as critical of the regime.

On October 10, Miguel Díaz-Canel was confirmed as president of Cuba with 96.76 percent of votes of National Assembly members.

Arbitrary Detention and Short-Term Imprisonment

The Cuban government continues to employ arbitrary detention to harass and intimidate critics, independent activists, political opponents, and others. The number of arbitrary short-term detentions, which increased dramatically between 2010 and 2016—from a monthly average of 172 incidents to 827—started to drop in 2017, according to the Cuban Commission for Human Rights and National Reconciliation, an independent human rights group that the government considers illegal. The number of reports of arbitrary detentions continued to drop in 2019, with 1,818 from January through August, a decrease of 10 percent compared to the 2,024 reports during the same period in 2018.

Security officers rarely present arrest orders to justify detaining critics. In some cases, detainees are released after receiving official warnings, which prosecutors can use in subsequent criminal trials to show a pattern of "delinquent" behavior.

Detention is often used to prevent people from participating in peaceful marches or meetings to discuss politics. Detainees are often beaten, threatened, and held incommunicado for hours or days. Police or state security agents routinely harass, rough up, and detain members of the Ladies in White (Damas de

Blanco)—a group founded by the wives, mothers, and daughters of political prisoners—before or after they attend Sunday mass.

In September, in an effort to prevent a demonstration organized by the Cuban Patriotic Union, authorities detained over 90 activists and protestors and raided the union's headquarters, media reported. The protest supported the Ladies in White and other persecuted groups, and rejected the 2017 Political Dialogue and Cooperation Agreement between the Cuban government and the European Union. It coincided with a high level European delegation visit to Cuba.

Freedom of Expression

The government controls virtually all media outlets in Cuba and restricts access to outside information. According to the Committee to Protect Journalists (CPJ), an independent organization that promotes press freedom worldwide, Cuba has the "most restricted climate for the press in the Americas."

A small number of independent journalists and bloggers manage to write articles for websites or blogs, or publish tweets. The government routinely blocks access within Cuba to these websites. In February, before the referendum on the new constitution, it blocked several news sites seen as critical of the regime, including 14ymedio, Tremenda Nota, Cibercuba, Diario de Cuba and Cubanet. Since then, it has continued to block other websites.

Only a fraction of Cubans can read independent websites and blogs because of the high cost of, and limited access to, the internet. In 2017, Cuba announced it would gradually extend home internet services. In July 2019, the government issued new regulations allowing for the creation of private wired and Wi-Fi internet networks in homes and businesses and to import routers and other equipment.

Independent journalists who publish information considered critical of the government are routinely subject to harassment, violence, smear campaigns, travel restrictions, raids on their homes and offices, confiscation of their working materials, and arbitrary arrests. The journalists are held incommunicado, as are artists and academics who demand greater freedoms.

In April, police agents detained Roberto de Jesús Quiñones, an independent journalist who publishes on the news site CubaNet, outside the Guantánamo Municipal Tribunal when he was covering a trial. They beat him while transporting him to the police station. Authorities released him five days later but initiated criminal proceedings against him. According to a local free speech group, in August a municipal court sentenced Quiñones to a year in prison on charges of "resistance" and, for failing to pay a fine imposed upon his release in April, "disobedience." He was detained on September 11 and transferred to the Guantánamo Provincial Prison, where he was serving his one-year prison sentence at time of writing.

In July, Decree-Law 370/2018 on the "informatization of society" entered into force, making it illegal for Cubans to host their websites from a server in a foreign country, "other than as a mirror or replica of the main site on servers located in national territory." Though the scope of the rule remains unclear, it could affect most Cuban critical independent news sites and blogs, which are purposely hosted abroad. It also prohibits the dissemination of information "contrary to the social interest, morals, good manners and integrity of people." Violations can lead to fines and confiscation of equipment.

In April, Decree 349, establishing broad and vague restrictions on artistic expression, entered into force. Under it, people cannot "provide artistic services" in public or private spaces without prior approval from the Ministry of Culture. Those who hire or make payments to people for artistic services without authorization are subject to sanctions, as are the artists. Sanctions include fines, confiscation of materials, cancellation of artistic events, and revocation of licenses. Local independent artists have protested the decree, both before and after it entered force. Three were detained in December 2018 when attempting to join protests, media reported.

Political Prisoners

According to the Cuban Commission for Human Rights and National Reconciliation, as of October, Cuba was holding 109 political prisoners. The government denies independent human rights groups access to its prisons. The groups believe that additional political prisoners, whose cases they have been unable to document, remain locked up.

Cubans who criticize the government continue to face the threat of criminal prosecution. They do not benefit from due process guarantees, such as the right to fair and public hearings by a competent and impartial tribunal. In practice, courts are subordinate to the executive and legislative branches.

In December 2018, activist Hugo Damián Prieto Blanco, of the Orlando Zapata Civic Action Front, was sentenced to a year in prison for the crime of "pre-delinquent social dangerousness." Under the Penal Code, a person can be considered in a "dangerous state" when found to have a "special proclivity" to commit crimes—even before any have been committed—"due to conduct in clear contradiction to the norms of the socialist morals." Zapata had been arrested in November 2018 when participating in a protest. In April, his sentence was suspended and he was released.

In May, after more than two years in prison, Dr. Eduardo Cardet Concepción, leader of the Christian Liberation Movement, was released with limits on his movement and activities. Cardet, a supporter of the "One Cuban, One Vote" campaign, had been sentenced to three years in prison in March 2017. During his imprisonment, he was held in solitary confinement and denied visits and contact with family members, even by phone. Authorities argued that family visits were not "contributing to his re-education."

In October, José Daniel Ferrer, opposition leader and founder of the Patriotic Union of Cuba (UNPACU), the largest and most active pro-democracy group in Cuba, was detained at his home by police forces. He has not been informed of any charges against him and has not been brought before a judge. He remained in detention at time of writing.

That same month, Armando Sosa Fortuny, the oldest political prisoner in Cuba, died from health complications at a hospital in Camague, where he was transferred from prison last August. Sosa had served 26 of a 30-year sentence issued in 1993 for illegal entry to Cuba and "other acts against the security of the state." Sosa, a well-known dissenter, spent 43 of his 76 years imprisoned in Cuba.

Travel Restrictions

Since reforms in 2003, many people who had previously been denied permission to travel have been able to do so, including human rights defenders and independent bloggers. The travel reforms, however, gave the government broad discretionary power to restrict the right to travel on grounds of "defense and national security" or "other reasons of public interest," and authorities have continued to selectively deny exit to people who express dissent without due process.

The government restricts the movement of citizens within Cuba through a 1997 law known as Decree 217, designed to limit migration from other provinces to Havana. The decree has been used to harass dissidents and prevent people from traveling to Havana to attend meetings.

In May 2019, journalist Luz Escobar, of the independent website 14yMedio, was barred from traveling to Miami. In August, she was barred from traveling to Argentina, and journalist Javier Valdés from the publication Convivencia, from traveling to Spain. Agents informed them only that they were not authorized to travel. Also in August, evangelical pastor Adrián del Sol was barred from traveling to Trinidad and Tobago, where he was scheduled to participate in an event on religious persecution.

Prison Conditions

Prisons are overcrowded. Prisoners are forced to work 12-hour days and are punished if they do not meet production quotas, according to former political prisoners. Inmates have no effective complaint mechanism to seek redress for abuses. Those who criticize the government or engage in hunger strikes and other forms of protest often endure extended solitary confinement, beatings, restriction of family visits, and denial of medical care.

While the government allowed select members of the foreign press to conduct controlled visits to a handful of prisons in 2013, it continues to deny international human rights groups and independent Cuban organizations access to its prisons.

Labor Rights

Despite updating its Labor Code in 2014, Cuba continues to violate conventions of the International Labour Organization that it ratified, regarding freedom of association and collective bargaining. While Cuban law technically allows the formation of independent unions, in practice Cuba only permits one confederation of state-controlled unions, the Workers' Central Union of Cuba.

Human Rights Defenders

The Cuban government still refuses to recognize human rights monitoring as a legitimate activity and denies legal status to local human rights groups. Government authorities have harassed, assaulted, and imprisoned human rights defenders who attempt to document abuses. In July, Ricardo Fernández Izaguirre, a rights defender and journalist, was detained after leaving the Ladies in White headquarters in Havana, where he had been documenting violations of freedom of religion. He was released after nine days in prison.

Sexual Orientation and Gender Identity

Following public protest, the Cuban government decided to remove language from the draft of the new constitution approved in February 2018 that would have redefined marriage to include same-sex couples. However, transitory disposition No. 11 of the constitution mandates that within two years after approval, a new Family Code will be submitted to popular referendum "in which the manner in which to construct marriage must be included."

In May, security forces cracked down on a protest in Havana promoting lesbian, gay, bisexual, ad transgender (LGBT) rights and detained several activists, media reported. The protest, which was not authorized, was organized after the government announced that it had canceled Cuba's 2019 Gay Pride parade.

Key International Actors

In November 2017, the US government reinstated restrictions on Americans' right to travel to Cuba and to do business with any entity tied to the Cuban military, or to Cuban security or intelligence services. In March 2019, the Trump administration opened up a month-long window in which US citizens could sue dozens of Cuban companies blacklisted by the US administration.

In June, the US administration imposed new restrictions on US citizens traveling to Cuba, banning cruise ship stops and group educational trips. The US Treasury Secretary said the restrictions are a result of Cuba continuing to "play a destabilizing role in the Western Hemisphere, providing a communist foothold in the region and propping up US adversaries in places like Venezuela and Nicaragua by fomenting instability, undermining the rule of law, and suppressing democratic processes."

In March, the Inter-American Commission on Human Rights reiterated a request to the Cuban government to be allowed to visit the country to monitor the human rights situation.

In September, the European Union's foreign policy chief, Frederica Mogherini, visited Cuba to co-chair the second EU-Cuba Joint Council which discussed EU-Cuban relations, in particular in the EU-Cuba political dialogues as well as political and trade cooperation.

Cuba's term as a member of the United Nations Human Rights Council expired at the end of 2019. During its time on the council, Cuba regularly voted to prevent scrutiny of human rights violations, opposing resolutions addressing abuses in countries including Venezuela, Syria, Myanmar, Belarus, Burundi, Iran, and the Philippines.

Democratic Republic of Congo

Felix Tshisekedi was sworn in as president on January 24, 2019, following long-delayed and disputed national elections, marred by widespread irregularities, voter suppression, violence, and interference from armed groups. More than a million Congolese were unable to vote in the presidential election because voting in three areas was postponed to March 2019, officially because of security and concerns over an Ebola outbreak in the east.

At his swearing in, Tshisekedi said his administration would "guarantee to each citizen the respect of the exercise of their fundamental rights" and to end all forms of discrimination, promising that his government would prioritize "an effective and determined fight against corruption ... impunity, bad governance, and tribalism." His administration released most political prisoners and activists detained during the country's protracted political crisis, and those living in exile were allowed to return home. In March, Tshisekedi removed Kalev Mutondo as director of the National Intelligence Agency, where he was a principal architect of former President Joseph Kabila's administration's drive to repress dissent.

Many other senior security force officers, with long histories of involvement in serious human rights abuses, remained in their posts. Members of Kabila's political coalition maintained a majority in parliament, as well as about two-thirds of the posts in the new government.

Some of the most acute violence in the country in recent years took place in Yumbi, western Congo, in mid-December 2018 when at least 535 people were killed. Most of the victims were ethnic Banunu, killed by ethnic Batende. In eastern Congo, numerous armed groups, and in some cases government security forces, attacked civilians, killing and wounding many. The humanitarian situation remained alarming, with 4.5 million people internally displaced, and more than 890,000 people from Congo were registered as refugees and asylum seekers.

Presidential Elections

Tshisekedi's victory over opposition candidate Martin Fayulu in the December 30, 2018 elections was disputed by an independent observation mission from

HUMAN
RIGHTS
WATCH
A DIRTY INVESTMENT
European Development Banks' Link to Abuses
in the Democratic Republic of Congo's Palm Oil Industry

the Catholic Church. Leaked data from the state-controlled electoral commission (Commission électorale nationale indépendante, CENI) and data gathered by the church showed that Fayulu won about 60 percent of the vote.

Fayulu's supporters from an array of opposition political parties protested in many cities across Congo. Security forces often responded to protests, some violent, with excessive, including unnecessary, lethal force. Security forces killed at least 10 people and injured dozens during protests after provisional results were announced on January 10. At least 28 people suffered gunshot wounds in Kikwit, Kananga, Goma, and Kisangani when security forces dispersed demonstrators.

On the day after the elections, the government shut down internet and text messaging throughout the country, restricting independent reporting and information-sharing. The internet was restored on January 19.

Freedom of Expression and Peaceful Assembly

There has been a significant decline in political repression since Tshisekedi came to power. Many political prisoners and activists detained in previous years were freed, while activists and politicians in exile were allowed to return. However, some peaceful demonstrators continued to be arbitrarily detained or beaten by security forces.

On June 30, Congo's independence day, police fired live ammunition, killing one person, during opposition protests in Goma against corruption and election fraud.

In July, security forces evicted thousands of illegal miners from a copper and cobalt mine in Kolwezi, Lualaba province, sparking protests outside the governor's office and looting of shops.

Attacks on Civilians by Armed Groups and Government Forces

More than 130 armed groups were active in eastern Congo's North Kivu and South Kivu provinces, attacking civilians. The groups included the largely Rwandan Democratic Forces for the Liberation of Rwanda (FDLR) and allied Congolese Nyatura groups, the largely Ugandan Allied Democratic Forces (ADF), the Nduma Defense of Congo-Renové (NDC-R), the Mazembe and Yakatumba Mai Mai groups, and several Burundian armed groups. Many of their commanders have been implicated in war crimes, including ethnic massacres, rape, forced recruitment of children, and pillage.

According to the Kivu Security Tracker, which documents violence in eastern Congo, assailants, including state security forces, killed at least 720 civilians and abducted or kidnapped for ransom more than 1,275 others in North Kivu and South Kivu in 2019. Beni territory, North Kivu province, remained an epicenter of violence, with about 253 civilians killed in more than 100 attacks by various armed groups, including the ADF. At least 257 civilians were kidnapped in Rutshuru territory, North Kivu province, often by armed groups.

The Fizi and Uvira highlands in South Kivu saw fighting between the mainly ethnic Banyamulenge Ngumino armed group and allied self-defense groups, and Mai Mai groups, comprising fighters from the Bafuliro, Banyindu, and Babembe communities, with civilians often caught in the middle. Clashes between armed groups in the South Kivu highlands surged in February, displacing an estimated 200,000 people over the following months.

In early June, violence resurfaced in parts of northeastern Congo's Ituri province, where armed assailants launched deadly attacks on villages, killing over 200 civilians and displacing an estimated 300,000 people. At least 28 displaced people were killed in Ituri in September.

Justice and Accountability

In July, a three-judge panel at the International Criminal Court (ICC) unanimously found the rebel leader and former army general Bosco Ntaganda guilty of 13 counts of war crimes and 5 counts of crimes against humanity committed in Ituri in 2002 and 2003. The charges included murder and attempted murder, rape, sexual slavery, attacking civilians, pillaging, displacement of civilians, attacking protected objects, and recruiting and using child soldiers. The judges found that Ntaganda and others agreed on a common plan to attack and drive the ethnic Lendu population out of Ituri through the commission of crimes. In November, the ICC sentenced him to 30 years in prison.

Troops under Ntaganda's command also committed ethnic massacres, killings, rape, torture, and recruitment of child soldiers in the Kivus, including when Ntaganda commanded troops in the Rwandan-backed National Congress for the Defense of the People (CNDP) and M23 armed groups, and while he served as a general in the Congolese army. His trial at the ICC only dealt with crimes related to the Ituri conflict.

The Congolese army announced on September 18 that its forces killed Sylvestre Mudacumura, the FDLR's military commander, and some of his lieutenants. Mudacumura had been wanted by the ICC since 2012 for nine counts of war crimes.

The Congolese trial, which started in June 2017, into the murders of United Nations investigators Michael Sharp and Zaida Catalán and the disappearance of the four Congolese who accompanied them in March 2017 in the central Kasai region was ongoing at time of writing.

In February, a military court in Goma found Marcel Habarugira, a former Congolese army soldier turned warlord, guilty of the war crimes of rape and use of child soldiers committed while leading a faction of an armed group known as Nyatura ("hit hard" in Kinyarwanda). Habarugira received a 15-year prison sentence. His group, which received arms and training from Congolese army officers, carried out many atrocities in 2012.

A trial against Congolese security force members arrested for allegedly using excessive force to quash a protest in Kamanyola, eastern Congo, in September 2017, during which 38 Burundian asylum seekers were killed, and more than 100 others wounded, started on June 28 and was ongoing at time of writing. Six members of the security forces faced charges of murder and attempted murder before a military court in Bukavu, South Kivu province.

The trial of Nduma Defense of Congo (NDC) militia leader Ntabo Ntaberi Sheka, who surrendered to the UN peacekeeping mission in Congo (MONUSCO), began on November 27, 2018 and was ongoing at time of writing. Sheka was implicated in numerous atrocities in eastern Congo, and he had been sought on a Congolese arrest warrant since 2011 for alleged crimes against humanity, including mass rape.

On June 7, Congolese authorities issued an arrest warrant against warlord Guidon Shimary Mwissa, Sheka's former deputy and the leader of Nduma Defense of Congo-Rénové (NDC-R) armed group, which has been responsible for widespread attacks on civilians in North Kivu. He is wanted for "participation in an insurrectional movement," "war crimes by child recruitment," and "crimes against humanity by rape." Despite these allegations, NDC-R continued to collaborate with the Congolese army in the area the group controls, which is larger than that of any other armed group in Congo. Human Rights Watch was unaware of any attempt by Congolese authorities or UN peacekeepers to arrest Guidon. He was sanctioned in 2018 by the UN Security Council and the United States.

Congo's military justice officials investigated the December 2018 Yumbi killings—in which at least 535 people were killed—and arrested dozens of suspected assailants and instigators. A trial was yet to start at time of writing.

Key International Actors

In February, the US State Department imposed visa restrictions on three electoral commission senior officials, the then-president of the national assembly, and the president of the Constitutional Court, accusing them of corruption and obstructing the presidential election. In March, the US Department of the Treasury's Office of Foreign Assets Control (OFAC) imposed financial sanctions on the same three electoral commission officials.

In May, justice ministers attending the International Conference on the Great Lakes Region meeting in Kenya said that greater efforts were needed to "uphold human rights, promote justice, and eradicate impunity." To achieve these goals, they approved a series of specific recommendations.

In March, the Security Council unanimously adopted a resolution extending the mandate of MONUSCO for nine months and called for an independent strategic review of the mission.

Ecuador

President Lenín Moreno has implemented policy changes aimed at repairing damage suffered by democratic institutions during former President Rafael Correa's decade in power. The changes have fostered a climate of open debate, but structural changes are still needed.

On October 3, 2019, protests erupted after President Moreno signed a decree establishing austerity measures that eliminated fuel subsidies. Taxi and bus drivers, student groups, and thousands of indigenous people took to the streets in response, resulting in days of unrest. Some demonstrators engaged in serious acts of violence. In response, the government declared a national state of emergency, suspending the rights to freedom of assembly and association and later restricting the right to freedom of movement throughout the country. Some security forces allegedly used excessive force. The state of emergency was lifted by President Moreno on October 13. According to the Ombudsman's Office, 10 people died in the context of the protests.

Ecuador faces chronic human rights challenges, including weak institutions, poor prison conditions, laws that give authorities broad powers to limit judicial independence, violence against women, far-reaching restrictions on women's and girls' access to reproductive health care, and disregard for indigenous rights.

Massive Venezuelan immigration is posing urgent challenges. President Moreno has responded with measures that effectively restrict Venezuelans' ability to seek legal permits to stay.

Freedom of Expression

President Moreno has taken steps to restore freedom of expression, which was severely damaged under former President Correa. With President Moreno's support, the National Assembly in 2018 amended a 2013 communications law that had given the government broad powers to limit free speech. Legislators eliminated the Superintendency of Information and Communication (SUPERCOM), a regulatory body that had been used to harass and sanction independent media outlets. But the amended law includes problematic provisions such as one treating "communications" as a "public service" and one giving anyone who can show that media published inaccurate or damaging content about them an unrestricted right to a published correction and an opportunity to respond.

In 2018, three Ecuadoreans investigating violence along the Ecuador-Colombia border for *El Comercio* newspaper were abducted by Colombian guerrillas, their bodies subsequently found in Colombia. In 2018, an Inter-American Commission on Human Rights (IACHR) investigative support team reported "no satisfactory progress" on the case by Ecuador's Attorney General's Office. In November, the IACHR president announced that the final IACHR report on the case would be presented by the end of the year.

Judicial Independence

Corruption, inefficiency, and political interference have plagued Ecuador's judiciary for years. During the Correa administration, high-level officials and Judiciary Council members interfered in cases that touched on government interests, and in the appointment and removal of judges.

Under President Moreno, a transition Council of Citizen Participation (CCP), appointed after a popular referendum in 2017, removed Judiciary Council members they determined to have created a system favoring government interests. The transition CCP was tasked with evaluating the performance of key state institutions and authorities and was empowered to replace them.

During its review of the Constitutional Court, the transition CCP removed all of the existing justices and left their positions vacant for several months. In early 2019, following a rigorous selection process provided for in Ecuadorean law, a permanent Constitutional Court was appointed.

In May, the permanent CCP, elected by popular vote, announced that it would review the performance and appointment of the new Constitutional Court justices. In response, the National Assembly removed four permanent CCP members from office, accusing them of exceeding their powers. In July, the CCP reversed its decision.

In January, the transition CCP appointed permanent Judiciary Council members. The permanent Judiciary Council then announced it would review the performance of National Court justices. The justices objected, but the review continued at time of writing.

The legal framework that allowed for political interference in the judiciary under President Correa remains in place. Ecuador's Organic Code on Judicial Function allows the Judiciary Council to suspend or remove justice officials, including judges, for acting with "criminal intent, evident negligence or inexcusable error." This broad rule, used to suspend or remove 145 judges between January 2013 and August 2017, exposes judges to political pressure and undermines judicial independence. From January through August 2019, 19 judges were removed for "inexcusable errors," after a higher court ruled they had made serious mistakes. At time of writing, the Constitutional Court was evaluating the rule's constitutionality.

Rights of Indigenous Peoples

Constitutionally, indigenous peoples have a collective right to "free prior informed consultation" regarding development of nonrenewable resources located on their lands and that could affect them environmentally or culturally. This constitutional requirement differs from the international standard calling for indigenous peoples' free, prior, and informed consent to all measures affecting them, including projects affecting their ancestral lands. For years, indigenous peoples have been saying they are not being duly consulted regarding exploitation of their ancestral lands.

In April, a Pastaza court invalidated the Ecuadorean government's 2012 consultation with the Waorani people before the auctioning of lands to oil companies. The court halted operations after finding that Ecuador had not complied with the constitutional duty to obtain free, prior and informed consultation from the Waorani.

In September, an appeals court in Pastaza Province ruled in favor of the Kichwa people's complaint that authorities had disregarded their constitutional right to prior consultation on a hydroelectric project in the Ecuadorean Amazon.

Prison Conditions

Overcrowding, poor conditions, and violence inside prisons are longstanding problems. In May, President Moreno declared a state of emergency to "protect the rights of people deprived of liberty." The decree suspended certain prisoners' rights, including freedom of association and information, and provided for the police and armed forces to coordinate efforts and assign personnel to prisons.

A gunfight among inmates of the Litoral prison in Guayaquil, in May, resulted in six prisoners' deaths. The ombudsman blamed "overcrowding and the inexistence of a government security policy."

Accountability for Past Abuses

A truth commission created by the Correa administration to investigate government abuses from 1984 to 2008 documented gross human rights violations against 456 victims, including 68 extrajudicial executions and 17 disappearances. A special prosecutorial unit created in 2010 has initiated judicial procedures in fewer than 15 cases. Final rulings have been rendered in only two. The remaining cases appear stalled.

Women's and Girls' Rights

The right to seek an abortion is limited to instances in which a woman's health or life is at risk, or the pregnancy results from rape of someone with a psychosocial disability. For illegal abortions, prison sentences range up to two years. Fear of prosecution drives some women and girls to have illegal, unsafe abortions and impedes access to services for survivors of sexual violence. In September, the National Assembly rejected a proposal to decriminalize abortion in cases of rape.

A 2012 government survey revealed high rates of gender-based violence, with an estimated 1 in 4 women facing sexual violence in the course of a lifetime. A high rate of rape of adolescent girls is of particular concern. Approximately 2,000 girls under 14 give birth in Ecuador each year. All are considered pregnancies from rape, because 14 is the age of sexual consent.

From January 2014 through August 2019, the government recorded 343 femicides, with 141 convictions; 32 were committed in 2019. Ecuador's criminal code defines femicide as the exercise of power relations resulting in the death of a woman for "being a woman."

Sexual Violence against Children

From January 2014 until June 2018, Ecuador's Ministry of Education received 4,111 complaints of sexual violence against students; 1,837 were school-related. It also re-opened 734 complaints that the ministry had archived or the State Prosecutor's Office had suspended.

Since 2017, the government has taken important steps toward tackling school-related gender-based violence, launching public information campaigns, training programs, and a database to document all cases of sexual violence in schools.

In a February 2018 referendum, voters overwhelmingly supported a proposal to remove a constitutional statute of limitations for sexual offenses against children under 12 and adolescents aged 12 to 18. At time of writing, the government had not presented legislation to enact the change.

Sexual Orientation and Gender Identity

The constitution defines marriage as "between a man and a woman," but the Constitutional Court ruled in June in favor of same-sex marriage, citing international law and constitutional provisions protecting against discrimination. In July, the Civil Registry registered the first same-sex wedding.

Labor Rights

In February, the Ministry of Labor shut down Furukawa Plantaciones, which had produced manila hemp, whose fiber is used for a variety of paper products. The ombudsman had documented labor exploitation and grave human rights violations against mostly Afro-Ecuadorean ("afrodescendientes") families who lived on site and had worked for the company for decades. In April, the ombudsman issued a follow-up report emphasizing omissions by state institutions, including failure to investigate and sanction possible criminal conduct.

Refugees

Ecuador has been receiving a huge influx of Venezuelan exiles, many passing through to other countries. The United Nations High Commissioner for Refugees reported that, as of November, 385,042 Venezuelan migrants and refugees were living in Ecuador.

In January, in response to a Venezuelan man's murder of a young pregnant woman in the northern city of Ibarra, Ecuador announced new requirements for Venezuelans to enter. These included certified background checks for criminal records and official Venezuelan ID cards. A series of xenophobic violent attacks and harassment against Venezuelans followed.

Although the Constitutional Court temporarily suspended the entry requirements while it evaluated them, the government in August announced a two-year humanitarian temporary residence visa for Venezuelans that includes requirements that in practice make it difficult for Venezuelans to apply.

Key International Actors

President Moreno continues to rebuild relations with the Inter-American human rights system. In November, the IACHR held public and private sessions in Quito.

In April, Ecuador terminated the asylum it had granted to Wikileaks founder Julian Assange in 2012 and invited British police to apprehend him at its embassy in London. Assange's asylum was predicated on the risk of being extradited to the US for publishing classified documents leaked by Chelsea Manning; the US asked the UK to extradite Assange shortly after he was in British custody. Following Assange's arrest, Ecuador allowed the US to search the embassy apartment and confiscate documents, digital files, and devices they found. Spain's National Court is investigating the private security firm retained by Ecuador for hiding microphones and cameras throughout the apartment, including the toilet where Assange tried to hold private conversations with his attorneys. Ecuador gave as reasons for withdrawing asylum his deportment in the embassy and his publication of politically embarrassing materials.

In September, the UN special rapporteur on the right to health visited Ecuador. The special rapporteur noted that women and girls, children and adolescents, members of LGBTI communities, people living with HIV/AIDS, and people on the move still face specific challenges in realizing their right to health, and stated that “violence against women and girls is endemic in Ecuador.”

The Moreno administration has continued to raise concerns about ongoing human rights abuses in Venezuela. In April, President Moreno urged a “speedy transition in Venezuela that will lead to general elections as soon as possible, and guarantee the human rights of all.”

By invitation of the Ecuadorean government, delegations from the IACHR and the Office of the UN High Commissioner for Human Rights visited the country in late October to look into allegations of human rights violations in the government response to the October protests. Their final reports were pending at time of writing.

HUMAN
RIGHTS
WATCH
"If You Are Afraid for Your Lives, Leave Sinai!"
Egyptian Security Forces and ISIS-Affiliate Abuses in North Sinai

Egypt

The Egyptian government in 2019 passed constitutional amendments that were approved in an unfair referendum in April. The amendments consolidate authoritarian rule, undermine the judiciary's dwindling independence, and expand the military's power to intervene in political life. Security forces led by the military continue to brutalize civilians in North Sinai in its conflict with Sinai Province, an armed group affiliated with the extremist group Islamic State (ISIS). The army and pro-government militias carried out serious abuses, including demolishing homes and arbitrarily arresting, torturing, and extrajudicially executing residents. ISIS militants also committed horrific violations, including kidnappings, torture, and killings of residents and detained security force members.

Under the guise of fighting terrorism, Egyptian authorities showed utter disregard for the rule of law. Since April 2017, President Abdel Fattah al-Sisi has maintained a nation-wide state of emergency that gives security forces unchecked powers. Security forces used torture and enforced disappearances systematically against dissidents from all backgrounds. Egypt's use of mass trials and the death penalty has mounted since 2013, including death sentences against children and death sentences issued in military trials.

In August, President al-Sisi approved a new law that maintains most of the drastic restrictions imposed on nongovernmental organizations (NGOs). Despite several government promises to lift restrictions, the law merely removes prison penalties but maintains severe restrictions that make it impossible for NGOs to work freely and independently.

The government failed to follow through on promises it had made to protect women and religious minorities. A law criminalizing domestic violence did not gain traction in parliament, and Christians still face discrimination and obstacles when it comes to building new churches.

Security Forces Abuses

The police and National Security Agency routinely carry out systematic enforced disappearances and torture with impunity. Torture practices have also affected well-known activists such as Alaa Abdel Fattah and Israa Abdel Fattah. Authorities keep thousands of prisoners in abysmal conditions, where overcrowding and insufficient medical care have been systematic and may have contributed to the deteriorating health and deaths of scores of detainees. Former President Mohamed Morsy, whom the army forcibly removed in 2013, died on June 17 in a Cairo court room following six years of lack of medical care and near-absolute isolation in prison. In November, two United Nations experts said that such conditions "may have directly led" to his death and "may be placing the health and lives of thousands more prisoners at severe risk." Authorities did not conduct any independent investigation into his death.

Sinai Conflict

Egyptian security forces, mainly the army, as well as ISIS-affiliated militants, committed serious and widespread abuses in North Sinai, some of which amount to war crimes, since the conflict escalated in late 2013. Human Rights Watch documented several indiscriminate and possibly unlawful air and ground attacks by security forces. Human Rights Watch also documented 50 cases of arbitrary arrests, of whom 39 were likely forcibly disappeared; at least 14 have been missing for three or four years. Both sides carried out extrajudicial killings. Since 2014, Human Rights Watch has documented 20 extrajudicial killings of residents by government forces.

The army has arrested and forcibly disappeared children as young as 12. An army spokesman acknowledged some child detentions, justifying them as part of the army's counterterrorism operations.

Those detained and disappeared are usually held in one of three main army bases in North Sinai: Camp al-Zohor in Sheikh Zuwayed, Battalion 101 Base in al-Arish, and al-Galaa Military Base in the neighboring Ismailya governorate. These are unofficial detention sites lacking judicial oversight. Detainees often face ill-treatment, abuse, and sometimes torture.

Between January 2014 and June 2018, 3,076 alleged militants and 1,266 military and police members were killed in Sinai hostilities. Egyptian authorities have not released statistics on civilian casualties, and often included civilians in militant death counts, making it difficult to ascertain what proportion of civilians make up these figures.

The Washington-based Tahrir Institute for Middle East Policy estimated that authorities arrested at least 12,000 Sinai residents between July 2013 and December 2018, though the government has only acknowledged about 7,300 in its official statements.

Egypt's military has forcibly evicted roughly 100,000 North Sinai residents, or one-fifth of North Sinai's population, and destroyed thousands of homes since 2014. Human Rights Watch documented demolitions of at least 3,600 homes and commercial buildings by the army between January and May 2018 alone. These demolitions are carried out without any judicial oversight or independent recourse mechanism.

With a state of emergency and long curfew hours imposed uninterruptedly in Sinai since late 2014, restrictions on movement, also justified under the rhetoric of counterterrorism, led to severe shortages of food and other essential items for months during 2018.

Sinai Province militants have kidnapped, tortured, and extrajudicially executed civilians, routinely targeting those they perceive to be pro-government. Sinai Province runs detention sites where civilians are held and interrogated.

Fair Trials, Due Process, and the Death Penalty

Constitutional amendments approved in an unfair referendum in April 2019 extended al-Sisi's current term from four to six years, allow him to run for one additional term, and name him the head of the Supreme Council for Judicial Bodies and Authorities. This council will supervise and be able to intervene in the judiciary's affairs, including appointments and promotions. The amendments also give the president the power to appoint the chief justice of the Supreme Constitutional Court, the head and members of the Commissioners' Authority, and Egypt's public prosecutor, among other positions.

Civilian and military courts sentenced hundreds of individuals to death in 2019, often in mass trials in cases that stem from alleged political violence or planned violence. According to the Egyptian Front for Human Rights, as of June authorities executed at least 15 prisoners in three cases on political grounds. Military and civilian courts of appeal upheld at least 32 death sentences, raising the number on death row to 74, the majority of whom were charged with political violence. In February, nine UN experts condemned the "arbitrary executions" of nine of those executed "on the basis of evidence allegedly obtained under torture," following "what appears to be seriously flawed trials."

Freedom of Assembly

President al-Sisi continued to warn against anti-government protests and gatherings. Authorities rounded up more than 4,400 people in a mass arrest campaign following rare anti-government protests on September 20. Those arrested include well-known figures, such as political science professors Hazem Hosni and Hassan Nafaa, as well as journalist and politician Khaled Dawood and human rights lawyer Mohamed al-Baker.

Over 160 activists or perceived dissidents were arrested or prosecuted by authorities for voicing criticism before the constitutional referendum in April. In June, authorities arrested and searched the homes of scores of activists and accused them of joining, aiding, or funding a "terrorist" group. The case, known as the "Hope Coalition" case, involves activists who were allegedly planning a new political coalition to contest the 2020 elections. Detainees include well-known leftist activists Ziad al-Elaimy and Hossam Mo'nis. Authorities unfairly banned 83 defendants in the case from travel and froze their assets.

Freedom of Association

The new NGO Law, which parliament passed in July and al-Sisi approved in August, prohibits NGOs from conducting field research, surveys, or opinion polls without government approval. The law also prohibits cooperating with foreign organizations or experts, or participating in any "political" activities or activities perceived to undermine "national security."

NGOs face fines up to one million Egyptian pounds (US$60,000) for sending or receiving funds without government approval or for operating without a license. Organizations refusing to provide information about their activities can expect fines of half-a-million Egyptian pounds (US$30,000). The new law permits daily monitoring of NGO activities by government or security officials.

The government did not include any critical human rights groups in the consultations around drafting the new law, and the final draft was kept secret until it was passed by the parliament.

In December 2018, an Egyptian criminal court acquitted all 43 defendants in the retrial of the 2011 foreign organizations case in which they had been sentenced to between 1 and 5 years in prison. The court said that the charges "contradict democratic values and the country's obligations under international law." The case involved staffers from four American organizations and one German. Despite the ruling, authorities continued to impose travel bans and asset freezes of at least 31 leading Egyptian human rights activists in the protracted investigations in Case 173 of 2011, known as the "foreign funding" case. One of these activists, lawyer Gamal Eid, was physically attacked in October by armed men in circumstances that indicated government involvement.

In June, the International Labour Organization placed Egypt on its list of countries that abuse workers and do not respect their right to organize and unionize. Egypt was on this list 5 times in the last 15 years and was removed only briefly in 2018.

Freedom of Expression

Egyptian authorities severely punish peaceful criticism against the government and routinely silence journalists, bloggers, and social media users. Since 2017, authorities have blocked an estimated 600 news and political and human rights websites, as well as social media sites and secure communications apps, without judicial authorization. More news and political websites were blocked before the constitutional referendum in April.

The Supreme Council for Media Regulation, a government entity established pursuant to the abusive new 2018 media law to monitor and control media, issued in March and September two sets of by-laws that impose drastic restrictions and disproportionate penalties without judicial oversight for any media outlet, including websites and social media pages, that do not abide by the council's rules. Under these rules, which among other things prohibit "insulting state institutions," "generalization," and "harming state interests," the council has censored newspapers, websites and tv shows.

Egypt was among the top three worst jailers of journalists in the world, with roughly 30 journalists behind bars, many charged with "spreading false news."

Freedom of Belief and Religion

Christians, the largest religious minority in Egypt, continued to face systematic discrimination on societal and institutional levels. The government recognizes only Islam, Christianity and Judaism as official religions. Minorities such as Baha`is and nonbelievers face discriminatory obstacles in obtaining IDs and vital documents, such as marriage and death certificates.

Discriminatory laws continue to impede building and renovating non-Sunni Muslim houses of worship. Egypt's 2016 discriminatory church-building law has achieved little in removing obstacles and sectarian violence around building churches. According to pro-government newspapers, of about 6,000 churches and service buildings that lack legal recognition, only 1,027 were given conditional permits as of July, three years after passage of the law.

Terrorist attacks against Christians continued. In January, two days before Christmas celebrations, a bomb outside a Coptic church in Nasr City killed a policeman.

Violence against Women, Girls, and LGBT People

Egypt continued to stall on a law that would tackle domestic violence. UN Women group, which works for women's empowerment, estimated that almost a third of Egyptian women experienced intimate partner physical or sexual violence in their lifetime. Despite the 2016 penal code amendments criminalizing female genital mutilation (FGM), prosecutions of perpetrators remained rare and FGM remains widely practiced throughout the country, with an estimated four out of five genital mutilations performed by doctors in professional medical environments.

Authorities prosecuted and banned from leaving the country leading women's rights activists, including Mozn Hassan, head of Nazra for Feminist Studies and Azza Soliman, head of the Centre for Egyptian Women's Legal Assistance. Egypt continued to repress lesbian, gay, bisexual, and transgender (LGBT) rights, in recent years prosecuting dozens of people based on their sexual orientation or gender identity.

Authorities continued to subject people accused of homosexual conduct to forced anal examinations, which are cruel and degrading and can rise to the level of torture. In March, Malak al-Kashef, a transgender woman, was arrested from her home and accused of "joining a terrorist group." She spent four months in pretrial detention in a male prison where she was sexually harassed and abused before being provisionally released in July. Hossam Ahmed, a transgender man, was also arrested in March and ordered detained on terrorism accusations.

In January, a TV anchor was sentenced to one year in prison for interviewing a gay man on television. Egypt censored gay-themed scenes from the film Bohemian Rhapsody, starring Egyptian-American actor Rami Malek.

Key International Actors

US President Donald Trump met with al-Sisi on three separate occasions in 2019: in the White House in April, on the sidelines of the G7 summit in August in France, and at the UN General Assembly in September. Trump did not at any point publicly raise human rights concerns, instead praising al-Sisi's "fantastic job" in Egypt.

In a September meeting with al-Sisi, UK Prime Minister Boris Johnson chose to highlight economic ties but made no mention of the mass arrests that preceded the meeting.

In January, French President Emmanuel Macron criticized human rights abuses in a Cairo press conference after meeting al-Sisi. However, France remained one of the main suppliers of weapons and surveillance technology to Egypt. In late 2018, Italian authorities named several Egyptian police and National Security Agency officers as involved in the kidnapping and murder of Italian PhD student Giulio Regeni in 2016, but Egypt failed to investigate or prosecute anyone.

In April and May, Egypt hosted the 64th Ordinary Session of the African Commission on Human and Peoples' Rights (ACHPR), the African Union's top rights body, in an oppressive atmosphere. About 70 participants did not manage to get visas on time. Two female participants were sexually assaulted by registration officials in Sharm al-Sheikh, and others reported physical surveillance.

In October, the European Parliament adopted a strong resolution condemning abuses in Egypt and North Sinai, the third such resolution in less than two years, but the European Union failed to adopt concrete measures in response.

UN High Commissioner for Human Rights Michelle Bachelet and several UN experts have repeatedly condemned abuses in Egypt. In November, during the Universal Periodic Review at the UN Human Rights Council in Geneva, Egypt received strong criticism and scores of recommendations from countries from every region. However, the states at the council have failed to introduce a collective statement of concern despite the worsening crisis in Egypt since March 2014.

El Salvador

El Salvador has among the world's highest homicide rates. Gangs exercise territorial control over specific neighborhoods and extort residents throughout the country. They forcibly recruit children and subject women, girls, and lesbian, gay, bisexual, and transgender (LGBT) individuals to sexual abuse. Gangs kill, disappear, rape, or displace those who resist. These conditions have resulted in internal and cross-border displacement.

Security forces remain largely ineffective in protecting the population from such violence. They also have been implicated in serious human rights violations, including extrajudicial executions, sexual assaults, other acts of torture and other ill-treatment, and enforced disappearances. Impunity for such violations remains the norm.

Girls and women accused of having abortions have been imprisoned for homicide and aggravated homicide. LGBT individuals face discrimination and violence with no effective state protection.

Accountability and Justice

The trial continued against former military commanders accused in the 1981 El Mozote massacre, where soldiers committed mass rapes and killed 978 civilians, including 553 children.

Investigations reached hearings in only 14 of 48 cases involving 116 extrajudicial killings committed from 2014 to 2018 that the Salvadoran Ombudsperson for the Defense of Human Rights (PDDH) examined. Two resulted in convictions.

While in office, former Presidents Antonio Saca (2004-2009) and Mauricio Funes (2009-2014) used a "secret item" fund as one of several sources to embezzle hundreds of millions. In January 2019 the Attorney General's Office (FGR) added a corruption charge to its case against Funes. Outgoing President Sanchez Cerén (2014-2019) and President Nayib Bukele, who took office in June 2019, have also spent money from this fund, but no evidence linking these actions to corruption had emerged as of September.

Abuses by Security Forces

President Bukele continued the military's role in public security operations, despite a 1992 peace accord stipulation against it. Media outlets widely reported that President Bukele's choice for national police director has been investigated for threats and links to drug trafficking and groups that have engaged in assassinations.

The Central American University Human Rights Institute received seven reports of elite police units burning victims. In March, in a sugarcane field, agents of the National Civil Police's Tactical Operation Section allegedly beat and strangled a blindfolded, handcuffed youth whom they suspected of gang membership or hiding weapons or drugs, and set fire to the field where they left him unconscious. Victims or witnesses of eight arbitrary arrests in two incidents in 2019 and late 2018 told Human Rights Watch of beatings at police barracks and threatened criminal charges for "illicit association," a vaguely defined offense used to prosecute those suspected of gang membership.

In August, the Lethal Force Monitor, a collaborative investigation by researchers in five Latin American countries, reported that Salvadoran police and soldiers killed 1,626 people from 2010 through 2017. Authorities claimed that more than 90 percent of the victims were gang members and that nearly all were killed in "confrontations" or "shootouts."

Also in August, the PDDH reported that it had examined killings of 28 boys, 7 women, and 81 men and found few resulted from confrontations. In 70 percent of cases, witnesses said victims were unarmed. In 37 percent, witnesses said they saw police move the body or place or hide evidence. In 30 percent, the body showed signs of torture, including sexual assault.

Prison and Police Barracks

As of October 2019, the country's jails, juvenile and youth facilities, and adult prisons held 45,439 people in custody, more than twice the official capacity, according to the online database World Prison Brief.

In June, President Bukele extended to all prisons a "state of emergency" that the previous government had instituted in seven prisons in August 2018. He ordered 24-hour block confinement and, for the first time since 2004, mixed gang populations across prisons. Until then, each gang had been separated from others to avoid clashes. In September, he declared an end to the state of emergency, but it is unclear whether the policy was lifted in all prisons.

The Legal Medicine Institute registered 14 murders in police barracks and prisons in 2018. Several officials and inmates told Human Rights Watch of additional deaths in custody, which they attributed to extreme heat and tuberculosis. Two inmates told Human Rights Watch that officials provided inadequate food, hygiene products, and medicine, and beat them and used pepper spray during searches.

Gangs

Approximately 60,000 gang members operate in at least 247 of the country's 262 municipalities, according to media sources. They enforce their territories' borders and extort and gather intelligence on residents and those transiting, particularly around public transport, schools, and markets.

Numerous security and elected officials have collaborated with gangs in criminal operations, media report, and all political parties have negotiated with them on daily operations, campaigns, and voting. A truce lasted from 2012-14 between the national government, 11 municipal governments, and the two largest gangs.

In 2016, the Legislative Assembly modified a counterterrorism statute to classify gangs as terrorist organizations. The law imposes prison sentences of up to 15 years on anyone who "solicits, demands, offers, promotes, formulates, negotiates, convenes or enters into a non-persecution agreement" with gangs.

Disappearances, Abductions, and Missing Persons

In 2018, the FGR registered 3,664 victims of disappearance, abductions, and unexplained missing person cases, including 1,218 women and at least 24 boys and 29 girls. The 2018 figures included suspected abductions by criminal gangs and other cases in which people have gone missing in unexplained circumstances. Since 2010, the police have registered over 10,800 such cases. Because very few cases are investigated, knowledge of perpetrators is limited.

Women's Sexual and Reproductive Rights

Since 1998, abortion has been illegal under all circumstances. Providers and those who assist face prison sentences of six months to 12 years.

Dozens of girls and women, mostly from high-poverty areas, were prosecuted in the past two decades for what lawyers and activists say were obstetric emergencies. In some cases, the courts accepted as evidence a questionable autopsy procedure known as the floating lung test to forensically support the claim that a fetus was delivered alive.

As of September, at least 16 women suspected of having abortions remained imprisoned on charges of manslaughter, homicide, or aggravated homicide. In March, a court commuted three women's sentences as "disproportionate and immoral," given that their families need them economically.

In August, the FGR tried Evelyn Hernandez a second time, in violation of due process, for aggravated homicide for a stillbirth in 2016 following her rape at age 17. The court found insufficient evidence to convict. In September, the FGR announced it would appeal the ruling. In the last decade, 40 other women have been freed after having sentences commuted or being found non-guilty.

Sexual Orientation and Gender Identity

LGBT individuals remain targets of homophobic and transphobic violence by police, gangs, and others.

In January, Camila Díaz Cordova, a transgender woman deported from the United States, was beaten to death. In July, the FGR charged three policemen with her kidnapping and aggravated homicide.

Although El Salvador introduced hate crimes into its penal code in September 2015, Honduran authorities told Human Rights Watch that to date, only two cases have been prosecuted as hate crimes. Human Rights Watch is not aware of any bias-related murders of known LGBT individuals that have resulted in conviction.

In January 2019, a judge in Zacatecoluca ruled in favor of a transgender woman seeking to change her name and gender marker on her identity document.

Attacks on Journalists

Journalists reporting on abuses of power or living in gang-controlled neighborhoods remain targets of death threats. Fake stories have circulated under the bylines of journalists who were not the authors, the Association of Journalists of El Salvador reported.

Throughout his election campaign, President Bukele accused media, including El Faro and Revista Factum, which have received journalism's highest prizes in El Salvador, of lacking objectivity. The presidential press office barred their reporters from a September press conference.

In 2019, police prevented press from covering a veteran's protest, from visiting homicide scenes, and from the presidential election and inauguration. Police threatened journalists who resisted orders to turn over equipment or to erase photos. Four journalists told Human Rights Watch that, since June, police have required presidential press office approval before discussing details of homicides.

Displacement

Large numbers of people in El Salvador are internally displaced by criminal violence, extortion, and other threats. One study estimated the number of displaced in 2017 to be nearly 300,000.

In 2018, Salvadorans had 101,000 pending asylum applications in the US, the most of any nationality. Approximately 129,500 had applications pending in other countries.

Salvadoran press reported at least 11 people murdered after deportation back to El Salvador in 2019.

Key International Actors

In fiscal year 2019, the US disbursed over $62 million in bilateral aid to El Salvador.

In July, the FGR began collaborating with Canada and the United Nations Office on Drugs and Crime to improve its response to disappearances by creating a special FGR unit, working with police to consolidate collection of statistics, and urging the addition of "disappearance" and "aggravated disappearance" to the criminal code.

In September, President Bukele requested support from the UN and the Organization of American States to investigate and prosecute corruption.

Equatorial Guinea

The world's longest serving leader, President Teodoro Obiang Nguema Mbasogo of Equatorial Guinea marked his 40th year in power in August. As in previous years, corruption and repression of civil and political rights continued unabated.

The vast majority of Equatorial Guinea citizens continued to be denied their economic and social rights, including access to health care and primary education, despite the country's vast oil revenues, which benefit the political elite. In September, the government began negotiations for a $700 million loan request from the International Monetary Fund (IMF) despite boasting Africa's third highest per capita income.

In June, against the backdrop of repression of civil society, the government reaffirmed its desire to join the Extractive Industries Transparency Initiative (EITI), a requirement of the IMF as a precondition for a loan. EITI requires transparency around oil, gas, and mining revenue and activities and respect for civil society. In July, authorities ordered the dissolution of the Center for Development Studies and Initiatives (CEID), the country's leading civic group and a former civil society representative in the EITI steering committee. CEID's vice president continued to face harassment.

In May, a court convicted 112 people for participating in a December 2017 coup attempt. Representatives of the American Bar Association who observed the trial reported serious due process violations, including confessions obtained through torture and severe restrictions on defense lawyers.

Several countries pursued several corruption allegations against powerful government officials. In December 2019, Equatorial Guinea's two-year term as a member of the United Nations Security Council ended.

In 2019, Equatorial Guinea endorsed the Safe Schools Declaration, an international commitment to protect education during armed conflict.

Economic and Social Rights

With approximately 1 million people, Equatorial Guinea, is among the region's top oil producers. Yet it has failed to provide crucial public services to large segments of its population, lagging behind regional averages in health and education indicators. Based on available data, the country has among the world's worst vaccination rates and one of highest rates of school-aged children out of school.

In June, the president's son and minister of mines reaffirmed the government's commitment to reapply to EITI, an initiative from which it was expelled in 2010, in part due to its failure to guarantee an "enabling environment" for civil society to fully participate in EITI's implementation. The IMF has made submitting an application to EITI, as well as other governance-related requirements, a precondition for obtaining a loan.

The EITI steering committee, made up of government officials, industry representatives, and civil society, met several times in 2019. Several civil society representatives said retaliation against government critics created an environment of intimidation that prevented them from freely expressing their views within the committee.

Freedom of Expression and Due Process

The few private media outlets in the country are largely owned by people close to Obiang. Freedoms of association and of assembly are severely curtailed, and the government imposes restrictive conditions on the registration and operation of nongovernmental organizations (NGOs). Some of the few local activists who work on human rights-related issues faced intimidation, harassment, and reprisals.

On February 25, police arrested Joaquin Elo Ayeto, a member of a political opposition party and founder of a youth organization. A judge ordered him held in preventative detention, where he remained at time of writing. Ayeto told his lawyer that during the interrogation, police phoned someone who recounted hearing him making remarks critical of government spending, which appears to be the basis of his detention. He also showed his lawyers marks on his body from alleged police torture.

On March 15, police prevented Alfredo Okenve, a prominent human rights activist and vice president of CEID, from boarding a plane and seized his passport and phone. Okenve was supposed to receive a Franco-German human rights award at the French embassy that day, but tried to leave the country after learning that the police were looking to arrest him. Police returned him to his home and stationed a guard outside to prevent him from leaving for several days. This incident was the latest government effort to silence him. In October 2018, four assailants, apparently undercover security officers, brutally beat him; a year earlier, in April 2017, authorities arbitrarily detained him for two weeks.

In July, authorities formally ordered the dissolution of CEID. The government previously ordered it to suspend its activities in 2016 following comments made at a youth group it organized that were critical of the government.

Political Repression

The ruling Democratic Party (PDGE) has a virtual monopoly over political life. It holds all but one seat in the 170-member bicameral parliament, and the courts regularly intervene to ban or harass political opposition groups and their members. Under the constitution, the president is the first magistrate and has absolute power to appoint and dismiss judges.

On March 22, the Bata Provincial Court began a mass trial of approximately 130 people accused of participating in a December 2017 coup attempt. Many of the defendants had been held for more than a year without access to lawyers or relatives. The American Bar Association's Center for Human Rights monitored and observed the trial. Juan Mendez, the former United Nations special rapporteur on torture, prepared a preliminary report documenting a litany of abuses.

The prosecution offered little or no evidence to support its case against most of the defendants, all of whom were charged with identical offenses; in some cases, it presented confessions that defendants testified in court were obtained under torture. The court, which included two military judges appointed mid-trial by President Obiang, placed severe restrictions on the defense, including prohibiting them from presenting evidence of torture and curtailing lawyers' access to clients.

On May 31, the eight-judge panel convicted 112 defendants, handing down sentences ranging from 3 to 97 years, with 25 defendants receiving sentences of more than 70 years.

Key International Actors

The international community, including the African Union, largely remained silent regarding these abuses. Several countries, including Switzerland, took legal measures to pursue corruption investigations into the country's leaders or began the process of repatriating stolen assets.

On February 7, Swiss prosecutors closed an investigation into Teodorin Nguema, the vice president who is also the president's eldest son, for corruption after he agreed to forfeit 25 cars worth approximately $25 million and pay $1.5 million to cover the cost of the investigation. In exchange, Swiss government relinquished a yacht worth $120 million it had seized. Swiss authorities had attempted to seize a second yacht, worth $130 million, but it was removed from its jurisdiction before authorities were able to do so.

The Swiss investigation was one of many into Nguema for corruption, money-laundering, and embezzlement. In October 2017, a French court convicted him in absentia of laundering tens of millions of dollars in France and seized his assets. He has appealed the case. In May, the French senate debated a bill that would require the government to repatriate corrupt assets it seizes as a first step to ensuring these funds are returned to the people of Equatorial Guinea.

In 2014, the United States Department of Justice settled a separate corruption case against Nguema after he agreed to forfeit $30 million to US authorities that would be repatriated for the benefit of Equatoguineans. The US is expected to determine which charities will receive the funds.

The corruption case before a Spanish court implicating several senior Equatoguinean government officials is expected to get to trial in 2020. The complaint alleged that the officials purchased homes in Spain through a private company that a US senate investigation revealed had received $26.5 million in government funds at around the time of the purchases.

Eritrea

For two decades, President Isaias Afewerki of Eritrea used the absence of peace with Ethiopia to justify authoritarianism. The July 2018 peace agreement between the two countries, which ended Eritrea's diplomatic isolation, have not, as hoped, ushered in an era of respect for human rights in one of the world's most repressive nations.

The government continued to conscript Eritreans indefinitely into the military or civil service for low pay, with no say in their profession or work location, and often under abusive conditions. The government continued to detain scores of Eritreans without trial, in extremely punitive conditions, and often incommunicado. There is no evidence that the habeas corpus provisions of the new penal code have been implemented.

There was no opening up of civil society space during the year. Independent media outlets inside Eritrea have been shut down since 2001. The government has not scheduled elections or implemented the 1997 constitution guaranteeing civil rights and including limits on executive power. The government nationalized religious schools and closed Catholic health facilities.

Eritrea's election as a member of the United Nations Human Rights Council (HRC) beginning in January has not led to greater respect of international standards or engagement with the HRC's procedures. Instead, Eritrea continues to deny access to the special rapporteur for Eritrea and all other human rights monitors. Despite strenuous opposition by Eritrea, the special rapporteur's mandate was renewed in July.

Eritrea's abuses, especially indefinite national service, continue to drive thousands of Eritreans into exile, many of them children. By the end of 2018, 507,300 Eritreans had fled, according to the United Nations High Commissioner for Refugees (UNHCR), about 10 percent of the population.

Indefinite Military Service and Forced Labor

Most men and unmarried women are forced into open-ended service for the government despite a government decree limiting service to 18 months. After military training, some conscripts are assigned to military duties, but according to

HUMAN
RIGHTS
WATCH
"They Are Making Us into Slaves, Not Educating Us"
How Indefinite Conscription Restricts Young People's Rights, Access to Education in Eritrea

the government, over 80 percent are assigned jobs in the civil service or at government agricultural or construction projects. Some conscripts have been forced to work on projects developing infrastructure for foreign mining companies.

Conscripts are subject to inhuman and degrading punishment, including torture, without recourse. Although the government has increased gross pay for certain national service conscripts since 2015, deductions and currency controls make conscript salaries inadequate to meet living costs, much less support a family. Conscientious objection is not recognized and punished. The procedures resulting in discharge from national service are incoherent and opaque.

Legally, conscription begins at 18, but children are among those caught during roundups ("giffas") in urban areas and sent directly into military service.

Right to Education

Secondary school students, some aged 16 or 17, are forced to undergo their final school-year, Grade 12, in an abusive military camp, Sawa, where they undergo mandatory military training, are under military command, and take their final school examinations before being assigned to civilian or military duties. Despite calls for reform, in August the government again conscripted the latest batch of students into national service.

At Sawa, military officials subject students to inhumane and degrading punishment. Girls and women students risk sexual harassment and exploitation. On weekends, students are assigned to forced labor at a nearby government farm.

Despite government commitments to reforming the education sector, the government relies on national service conscripts to teach in schools across the country. Conscripts have little to no choice in their assignment and no end to their deployment in sight. Absenteeism is rampant and the education system suffers.

Freedom of Religion

The government continued to "recognize" only four religious denominations as legitimate: Sunni Islam, Eritrean Orthodox, Roman Catholic, and Evangelical (Lutheran) churches.

Eritreans affiliated with "unrecognized" faiths risk raids on their homes, imprisonment, and torture; release requires written renunciation of religious affiliation. In 2019, as in previous years, there were reports of raids in Keren and Asmara.

Jehovah's Witnesses have been especially victimized since 1991 when they refused to participate in the referendum on independence. Fifty-two reportedly remain in prolonged detention at the Mai Serwa prison, including three arrested in 1994 because of their conscientious objections to military service.

The government further restricted activities of the four religions it recognized. In September, it seized control of seven religion-affiliated schools—Catholic, Islamic, and Lutheran. In June, the government confiscated all Catholic health clinics, and expelled patients receiving treatment and resident nuns. The UN special rapporteur on Eritrea expressed concern that their seizure "will negatively impact the right to health of the affected populations, in particular, those in remote rural areas." The crackdown came after the country's Catholic bishops released a pastoral letter obliquely calling for justice and reform from the government, and raising alarm about the ongoing exodus from the country.

The government has run the Eritrean Orthodox Church, the nation's largest religious institution, since it deposed its patriarch, Abune Antonios, in 2007 and placed him under house arrest. In July, media reported that five of the church's six bishops voted to expel the Abune from the church, accusing him of heresy after he released a video complaining that the church was being led by a government-appointed layman. The expulsion letter threatens punishment for mentioning his name. Five priests were reportedly arrested in June for supporting Antonios.

Unlawful, Abusive Detentions

Eritreans are subject to arrest and incarceration for long periods, without trial or opportunity to appeal. Imprisonment is frequent in vastly overcrowded cells or in shipping containers. Ill-treatment is common, including torture.

The former finance minister and critic of the president, Berhane Abrehe, remains in incommunicado detention since September 2018. His wife, Almaz Habtemariam, arrested earlier in 2018, was released in August.

Many detainees, including government officials and journalists arrested in 2001 after they questioned Isaias's leadership, are held incommunicado in places unknown to family members. Ciham Ali Abdu, daughter of a former information minister, has been held in incommunicado detention for six years since her arrest at age 15.

Some families only hear of the fate of their imprisoned relatives when the prisoners' bodies are returned to them. The body of an executive committee member of the Al Diaa school, whose proposed government takeover sparked protests, was returned shortly after his death in January.

The judicial system, partly staffed by national service conscripts subject to military control, has no independence. No public defense lawyers exist.

Freedom of Speech, Expression, and Association

Independent press has not been tolerated inside Eritrea since 2001. The Committee to Protect Journalists found that Eritrea was the world's most censored country and the sub-Saharan African country with the highest number of journalists behind bars. Internet cafes are monitored and, in May, media reported that the government briefly shut down the internet altogether.

No opposition political parties are allowed. Labor unions are also banned, except those controlled by the government, as are gatherings of more than three people. There are no independent nongovernmental organizations. Same-sex relations are prohibited.

Leaving the country without permission is illegal and individuals trying to flee risk being shot, killed, or arrested. For a time after the border to Ethiopia opened in 2018, the government did not restrict departures. At the end of 2018 and again in April 2019, however, the government unilaterally closed several border crossings and reinstated the exit permit requirements. After the Eritrea-Ethiopia border opened, the number of fleeing Eritreans, especially unaccompanied children and women, increased. Hundreds were reported to flee daily in early 2019. Among those fleeing in 2019 were five members of Eritrea's youth soccer team participating in a regional tournament in Uganda.

Key International Actors

Despite the 2018 rapprochement between Eritrea and Ethiopia, the disputed border has not been demarcated and Ethiopia has not withdrawn from Badme, the village that triggered the 1998 war.

Tensions with Djibouti remain unresolved because Djibouti claims that Eritrea has not accounted for prisoners of war captured in a 2008 border dispute. In 2019, Djibouti requested binding international arbitration; the request remained pending at time of writing.

The International Monetary Fund said Eritrea's macro-economic conditions remained "dire." Eritrea was identified in a 2019 survey as one of only three countries that place "extreme constraints" on humanitarian assistance to citizens from international organizations.

Except for a massive 50 percent Australian company-owned potash development project scheduled to begin operations in two to three years, Chinese firms have acquired all mineral mining rights. All mining firms must use government construction firms, staffed largely with conscript labor.

The European Union initiated what it dubbed a dual track approach to Eritrea, with its development arm focusing on job creation activities, and its political arm reportedly raising human rights issues. In February, under its Trust Fund for Africa aimed at stemming migration, the EU provided EUR€20 million (US$22 million) to support the procurement of equipment on a road building project on which it acknowledges national service labor, i.e., forced labor, may be used. In April, a Dutch NGO filed a summons calling on the EU to halt the project or risk further legal challenges.

The EU held two rounds of political dialogue with Eritrea under article 8 of the "Cotonou Agreement," one in November, the other in March.

Eswatini (formerly Swaziland)

In 2019, Eswatini remained an absolute monarchy ruled by King Mswati III, who has led the country since 1986, with a 1973 decree banning opposition political parties. Despite the adoption of the 2005 constitution which guarantees basic rights, and the country's international human rights commitments, the government has not reviewed the decree or changed the law to allow the formation, registration, and participation of political parties in elections.

In a move significant for women's rights, the Eswatini High Court ruled on August 30 that the common law doctrine of marital power (giving a husband the ultimate decision-making power over his wife and the matrimonial property) is unconstitutional as it discriminates against women and denies their constitutional right to equality. The progressive ruling builds on Eswatini's ongoing law reform process, aimed at promoting and protecting women's and girls' rights that included the passing of the Sexual Offences and Domestic Violence Act of 2018, which provides a framework to curb sexual and gender-based violence in the country.

Freedom of Association and Assembly

The various legislative improvements on freedom of association and assembly contained in the new Public Order Act of 2017, which imposes restrictions on the government's power to limit freedoms of assembly and association, were not fully tested in practice in 2019 as restrictions on freedom of association and assembly continued.

In August, Eswatini public servants who are part of the Swaziland National Association of Teachers (SNAT), the Swaziland National Association of Government Accounting Personnel (SNAGAP), and the National Public Services and Allied Workers Union (NAPSAWU) began mobilizing for a nationwide strike to demand an increase in wages. The police did not disrupt the nationwide mobilization campaigns, but fired teargas and water cannons to disperse thousands of protesting government workers on September 23. The new Police Service Act of 2018 limits police powers to prevent gatherings as it requires only a "notice of gathering" to be submitted to the relevant local authority, unlike the previous 1963 law that required the police to issue a license to permit public gatherings.

Although Eswatini signed the African Charter on Democracy, Elections and Governance in January 2018, the government did not take steps to ratify or implement the Charter.

Rule of Law and Freedom of Media

King Mswati holds supreme executive power over the parliament and judiciary by virtue of a 1973 State of Emergency decree. The country's courts have upheld the legality of the decree, contrary to the 2005 constitution, which provides for three separate organs of government—the executive, legislature, and judiciary. The prime minister theoretically holds executive authority, but in reality, King Mswati exercises supreme executive power and also controls the judiciary. The 2005 constitution provides for equality before the law but also elevates the king above the law.

In 2019, Reporters Without Borders ranked Eswatini as 147 out of 180 countries on media freedom. Eswatini's low ranking in media freedom is partly because journalists are constrained from working freely in the absolute monarchy and courts are not permitted to prosecute representatives of the monarchy.

Women and Girls' Rights

The Eswatini High Court ruling in August 2019 that the common-law doctrine of marital power is unconstitutional added to existing reforms to end discrimination against women and uphold their constitutional rights to equality. The court also struck down sections of the Marriage Act that subjected African women to customary marital power, perpetuating the violation of their rights contrary to constitutional provisions.

Progressive legislative reforms initiated in 2018 to further the promotion and protection of women and girls' rights included amendments to the 1964 Marriage Act, prohibiting child marriage, and the passing of the Sexual Offences and Domestic Violence Act of 2018, which provides the framework to curb sexual and gender-based violence in the country.

The under-representation of women in leadership and decision-making positions in both public and private sectors continued during 2019 despite the existence of the 2018 Election of Women Act, designed to fulfill the constitutional requirement for quotas for the representation of women and marginalized groups in parliament.

Eswatini has committed itself to a number of regional and international instruments to promote gender equality, including the Convention for the Elimination of All Forms of Discrimination Against Women (CEDAW), which Eswatini ratified without reservation, and the Southern African Development Community (SADC) Declaration on Gender and Development. Article 20 of the Eswatini Constitution provides for equality before the law and non-discrimination, but does not prevent discrimination on the grounds of sex, language, sexual orientation and gender identity. Eswatini's dual legal system where both Roman Dutch common law and Eswatini customary law operate side by side has resulted in conflicts leading to numerous violations of women and girl's rights over the years.

Under Eswatini law, mothers are not permitted to confer their citizenship to

their children under the same conditions as fathers. Eswatini's Constitution stipulates that any child born inside or outside Eswatini prior to 2005 to at least one Eswatini parent acquires Eswatini citizenship by descent. However, children born after 2005 only acquire Eswatini citizenship from their fathers, unless the child was born out of wedlock and has not been claimed by the father in accordance with customary law.

According to a 2018 national study, 48 percent of girls and women between the ages of 13 to 24 reported having experienced some form of sexual violence, with 1 in 3 girls experiencing some form of sexual violence before the age of 18. In a country with the highest HIV/AIDS prevalence in the world, sexual and gender-based violence is one of the key contributors of new HIV infections.

Sexual Orientation and Gender Identity

A colonial-era law criminalizes "sodomy," with an unspecified sentence. In spite of this law, lesbian, gay, bisexual, and transgender (LGBT) activists successfully held the second ever "Eswatini Pride" event in June 2019, with hundreds marching in the streets of Mbabane in support of LGBT equality.

Key International Actors

Eswatini's new prime minister, Mandvulo Dlamini, attended the SADC annual summit in Tanzania on August 17 and 18. SADC leaders congratulated Eswatini on holding peaceful and successful elections in September 2018. They did not raise concerns about the human rights conditions in Eswatini or press authorities to allow opposition political parties to operate in the country.

In June, representatives of local rights groups met in Geneva with Dubravka Šimonovic, the United Nations special rapporteur on violence against women, its causes and consequences. The representatives called on the special rapporteur to monitor Eswatini's implementation of the Sexual Offences and Domestic Violence Act, and to monitor and encourage the enactment of laws which strengthen women's access to land and marital property and reduce their risk of gender-based violence.

Ethiopia

Human rights reforms implemented by Prime Minister Abiy Ahmed during his first year in office were threatened in 2019 by communal, including ethnic, conflict and breakdowns in law and order.

The June 22 assassinations of several high-level government officials, which the government linked to an alleged coup attempt in the Amhara region—as well as political unrest and communal violence in the capital, Addis Ababa, and Oromia following an incident with a popular Oromo activist and media owner, Jawar Mohammed—highlighted increasing tensions ahead of Ethiopia's scheduled 2020 national elections.

In June, the parliament voted to postpone an already overdue but highly contentious national census, despite the importance of the exercise ahead of the 2020 elections.

Institutional reforms, notably around judicial independence and concrete measures to ensure truth, reconciliation, and accountability—all of which are key to dealing with heightened political and ethnic tensions—were limited.

Freedom of Expression and Association

The Sidama ethnic group submitted a request on July 18, 2018, to the federal government to hold a referendum to secede from the Southern Nations, Nationalities and Peoples' Region (SNNPR). The Sidama are the largest and the first among a number of ethnic groups in SNNPR to make such a request.

The federal government failed to organize a vote within the constitutionally stipulated one-year limit. Violence on July 18 in Awassa, capital of SNNPR, between protesters demanding a vote and security forces, followed by reported violence against non-Sidama residents of the region, resulted in the deaths of 53 people according to a zonal police official, the displacement of hundreds, and significant property damage. The SNNPR region was then placed under federal security control. In August, the National Electoral Board of Ethiopia (NEBE) said it would organize a referendum on November 13, which was later delayed to November 20.

Protests that broke out in Addis Ababa on October 23, following allegations by Jawar Mohammed that the government was removing his security detail, and then spread to many parts of the Oromia region, were met on occasion by excessive use of lethal force by the security forces, notably in Ambo town. The protests devolved rapidly into communal violence in several towns. The government said the unrest resulted in 86 deaths, 10 the result of "confrontations" with security forces.

In February, the government approved the Organization of Civil Societies Proclamation and repealed the notorious 2009 Charities and Societies Proclamation, which had decimated independent human rights reporting. The new law lifts its predecessor's 10 percent foreign funding limit. Concerns with the law remain, including limitations on foreign lobbying.

The government rewrote the country's restrictive 2009 Anti-Terrorism Proclamation (ATP); the new draft was under review in Parliament at time of writing. However, following the alleged coup plot in June, dozens of ethnic Amharas, including journalists, were held under the ATP's remand provisions. At time of writing, 13 detainees were still held on pre-charge detention, under an obscure procedure that allows for indefinite pre-charge detention after the four months allowed under the ATP had elapsed. Twelve are members of the political opposition, seven of whom are members of the National Movement of Amhara (NAMA), an ethno-nationalist opposition party, and five are members of an Amhara activist cultural movement.

On February 23, 2019, Oromia regional police temporarily detained two journalists working for the private Mereja TV on the outskirts of Addis Ababa, while reporting on the government's demolition of homes and allegations of forced displacement. Upon release, they were attacked by a group of young men, and one was beaten with sticks in plain view of police. No one was arrested in relation to the assault.

On July 18, security forces arrested employees and board members of the Sidama Media Network (SMN) and shut down the station in Awassa following protests over the government's failure to organize a referendum, according to media reports. Workers were allowed back into the office on July 23, but those arrested were detained for weeks without charge.

The government responded to growing hate speech on social media, especially Facebook, by producing a hate speech bill in April. Shortly after the communal violence in late October, the Council of Ministers approved a draft. Earlier drafts included vague definitions of hate speech, which, if not more narrowly defined to specifically address incitement to violence, discrimination, or illegality, may end up stifling legitimate expressions of dissent.

The government continued the practice of shutting down the internet. Following the alleged June 22 coup attempt , the prime minister sought to justify a country-wide internet shutdown, which was only completely restored on July 2, by telling media that the internet was "neither air nor water." Earlier in June, the government shut down the internet for a week without explanation.

Arbitrary Detention, Impunity for Past Abuses

In September, Maekelawi, the police station in the heart of Addis Ababa that for years had been infamous for abuse and repression, was opened for the first time to the public after its closure last year.

While there have been fewer reports of arbitrary arrests overall, there have been ongoing reports of abusive arrests of alleged Oromo Liberation Front (OLF) members and their alleged sympathizers in areas of Oromia where there has been fighting between suspected members of the previously banned OLF and the military.

Beyond the arrests of some high-level officials in November 2018, there has been little progress on accountability for past abuses. A national reconciliation commission was set up in December 2018 but it has an unclear mandate. In Ethiopia's Somali region, some of those who ran the region's notorious Jail Ogaden, where torture, rape and death were common, have been sentenced for abuses committed under their command; public information on these trials was lacking.

Conflict-Related Internal Displacement

Longstanding grievances over access to land and complex questions of identity and demarcation of internal borders on occasion led to abuses, including open conflict between ethnic groups, killings, and large-scale internal displacement.

The number of people internally displaced by conflict remained high; according to the International Organization for Migration, 1.6 million people were internally displaced as of July, 66.4 percent due to conflict. The Internal Displacement Monitoring Center reported that ethnic clashes in Oromia, Amhara, Somali, and SNNPR regions led to 522,000 new displacements in the first half of 2019.

Between March and May, the government returned approximately 1.5 million internally displaced people to their home areas, many still unsafe, including by restricting delivery of humanitarian assistance and demolishing camps in areas of displacement. Those that returned often faced secondary displacement due to ongoing insecurity and a lack of humanitarian assistance in areas of return.

The International Committee of the Red Cross, invited back to the Somali region for the first time in 11 years, distributed emergency relief assistance in conjunction with the Ethiopian Red Cross to people affected by communal violence.

Complex and politically charged issues surrounding the management of the ongoing expansion of Addis Ababa, and clarification of constitutional provisions around Oromia's "special interest" remain unanswered and a growing source of tension. These tensions increased in February when the Oromia regional government announced its plans to demolish 12,000 homes "built illegally" on the outskirts of Addis.

Key International Actors

Ethiopia continued to enjoy strong support from foreign donors and most of its regional neighbors, due to its role as host of the African Union, its contributions to United Nations peacekeeping and regional negotiations, regional counterterrorism efforts, and migration partnerships with Western countries.

In October, Prime Minister Abiy was awarded the Nobel Peace Prize for his efforts to achieve "peace and international cooperation," as a result of the peace agreement signed with Eritrea; yet many of the trickier issues around the agreement remain unsettled, including the border demarcation between the two countries.

Following the ouster of Sudan's President Omar al-Bashir in April and a breakdown in talks between military and civilian parties, the prime minister led efforts to mediate an agreement for a transitional government together with the African Union. However, tensions with Egypt over use of the Nile flared.

In October 2019, the European Union dispersed €7 million (US$7.8 million) of a €10 million (US$10 million) electoral support package. At time of writing, no plans for international election monitoring were in place.

In its 2019 Universal Periodic Review, Ethiopia committed to reviewing outstanding requests from special procedures on an individual basis and has since responded favorably to several, marking the first authorized visits of mandate holders since 2006. The UN special rapporteur on freedom of expression was due to visit Ethiopia in December. A request by the special rapporteur on torture was pending.

Over 100,000 Ethiopians have been deported from Saudi Arabia, many with no belongings and no money for food, transportation, or shelter. Neither the government nor the international community have earmarked adequate assistance to provide deportees medical care to help them deal with injuries or psychological trauma resulting from abuses faced in Yemen and in Saudi Arabia, shelter them, or aid them to return and reintegrate in their home villages.

European Union

The European Union acted in defense of human rights values in response to efforts by some EU governments to undermine democratic institutions inside their countries. Despite mixed fortunes at the polls, radical right populists continued to shape much of the debate around migration, as EU institutions and governments pursued migration policies that too often exposed people to violence and abuse and denied them access to asylum, especially by keeping them outside EU borders.

Migration and Asylum

Just under 101,000 people had arrived at EU borders in 2019 by mid-November, the majority by sea. EU governments remained focused on sealing borders including through reported unlawful pushbacks from EU borders including Croatia, Greece, Hungary, Romania, Poland, and Spain.

Sharp declines in boat arrivals from Morocco and Libya appeared linked to intensified migration cooperation by EU institutions and member states, despite concerns about treatment of migrants and asylum seekers in both countries.

An increase in boats reaching Greek islands underscored the lack of a functioning system for fair sharing of responsibility among EU members, and the ongoing failure of Greece to protect the rights of asylum seekers on its territory, including through pushbacks. The increase also drew attention to the 2016 EU migration control deal with Turkey, with Turkey's president again seeking to use the threat of a greater number of arrivals in the EU as a form of political leverage.

There were numerous stand-offs at sea, as Italy and Malta refused to allow nongovernmental organization (NGO) and merchant ships to disembark people rescued in the Mediterranean. Despite a change in government in Italy and several high-level EU summits, no progress was made towards the adoption of a predictable disembarkation agreement and relocation mechanism.

In March the EU's anti-smuggling mission Operation Sophia halted naval patrols in the Mediterranean that had rescued thousands, relying instead on aerial surveillance, with concerns that EU planes privileged providing information to the Libyan Coast Guard to enable interceptions and returns to Libya rather than broadcasting information about boats in distress, including to nearby rescue NGO ships. In October, the European Parliament narrowly rejected a resolution to improve search and rescue in the Mediterranean. The United Nations refugee agency UNHCR estimated that 1,098 people had died or gone missing in the Mediterranean by mid-November.

By mid-November, 12,680 people had reached Italy and Malta by sea, and 8,155 had been intercepted by the Libyan Coast Guard and taken back to automatic arbitrary detention amid worsening conditions as hostilities rage in and around Tripoli (see Libya chapter for more information).

As EU governments prioritized border control and outsourcing of responsibility for migrants and asylum seekers to other countries, they made limited progress on expanding safe and legal channels for migrants to enter the EU. The European Commission announced in September that EU countries had fulfilled 64 percent of the pledge to resettle 50,000 refugees in 2018-2019, a fraction of global needs.

Proposed reforms to EU asylum laws were not finalized before the May European elections.

At this writing, it remained unclear how the new European Parliament and Commission would take forward the package of reforms, including the most controversial issues relating to sharing of responsibility for processing asylum claims.

The charges in Italy and public vilification of Carola Rackete, captain of a Sea Watch rescue ship, exemplified the worrying trend of criminalizing humanitarian assistance to migrants and asylum seekers. Individuals faced charges related to assistance they provided to migrants and asylum seekers in several EU countries in 2019, including Belgium, France, Germany, Greece, as well as Italy.

Discrimination and Intolerance

In May's European Parliament elections, populist and Eurosceptic parties increased their vote share—securing about 25 percent of Parliament's seats compared to roughly 20 percent in the last election—but fell short of predictions in pre-election polls. Many mainstream parties that aligned with the anti-Muslim and anti-refugee agenda of the extreme right lost ground in the elections.

Racist intolerance, xenophobic, Islamophobic, and anti-Semitic sentiment and violence were still prevalent across the EU. Muslims, including women who wear the veil, continue to experience widespread hostility and intolerance in EU countries.

Anti-Semitism appeared to be on the rise. In a July report the EU's Fundamental Rights Agency (FRA) found that 44 percent of young Jewish Europeans experienced anti-Semitic harassment. Eighty percent of young victims did not report harassment to the police or any other authority, while 45 percent chose not to wear, carry or display distinguishable Jewish items in public because of concerns about their safety.

Ten years since the United Nations Convention on the Rights of Persons with Disabilities (CRPD) entered into force, persons with disabilities still lack sufficient protection against discrimination in many parts of the European Union.

At time of writing, seven member states and the EU had yet to ratify the Istanbul Convention, a Council of Europe (CoE) treaty on combatting and preventing violence against women.

The majority of EU member states still require transgender people to obtain a "mental health" diagnosis to change their legal gender—a stigmatizing and discriminatory requirement. In February, the European Parliament passed a resolution calling on EU member states to ban medically unnecessary "normalizing" surgeries on intersex children—a discriminatory practice that Malta has banned and Portugal has taken some steps to regulate.

Roma continue to be one of the most marginalized communities in Europe with Roma girls and women being particularly vulnerable to exclusion and discrimination, according to the EU Fundamental Rights Agency.

Rule of Law

EU institutions maintained scrutiny of the conduct by EU governments that threaten the rule of law and human rights, including through enforcement action in the EU Court of Justice, and discussed new mechanisms to hold EU governments to account for such breaches.

There was modest progress in proceedings against Poland and Hungary under article 7, the political sanctions mechanism of the EU treaty for addressing such threats, triggered in December 2017 on Poland and in September 2018 on Hungary.

The European Commission used its legal enforcement powers against Hungary and Poland during the year. It launched a new procedure against Poland in April over its moves to discipline judges and referred to the EU court of Justice in October. It July, it brought proceedings against Hungary for denying food to asylum seekers trapped at the border and referred Hungary to the EU Court of Justice for a 2018 law criminalizing the provision of aid to asylum seekers.

In June, the EU Court of Justice ruled that a 2018 law in Poland forcing judges out of the Supreme Court violated EU law. In November, the EU Court ruled that Poland's law on ordinary courts is contrary to EU law and affects judicial independence.

Three cases before the EU Court of Justice against Hungary were pending at time of writing. They concern three 2017 laws: forcing the Central European University out of Budapest; requiring civil society organizations that receive foreign funding to register as such or face sanctions; and an asylum law that allows for automatic detention of asylum seekers in transit zones and their summary removal to the Serbian border.

EU ministers held several debates on the laws undermining Poland's judiciary in February, April and September. In September, EU ministers held their first hearing with the government of Hungary, one year after the European Parliament activated article 7.

In April, the European Parliament adopted a resolution on the rule of law and fight against corruption in the EU, flagging specifically the constitutional debates and the lack of protection for journalists in Slovakia and in Malta. In April, the European Parliament also held a debate on the rule of law in Romania.

In July, the European Commission released its proposals to strengthen protections for the rule of law inside the EU. Proposals included an annual report on rule of law in EU countries to assist early detection of problems, a new peer review mechanism for EU governments, and a more strategic use of existing enforcement mechanisms, such as the EU Court of Justice.

Discussions continued on a proposal to tie access to EU funds in the next EU budget cycle to respect for the rule of law. In July, the then President-elect of the

European Commission, Ursula von der Leyen said, that she "stand[s] by the proposal to make the rule of law an integral part" of the next EU budget.

At time of writing, several people were charged over the murders of Daphne Caruana Galizia in Malta in 2017 and of Ján Kuciak in Slovakia in 2018, but the two cases remain unresolved. In September, Malta announced the establishment of an independent inquiry into the murder of Caruana Galizia. In April, Lyra McKee, shot during riots in Londonderry in Northern Ireland, became the fourth journalist killed in the EU in less than two years; to date, no one had been charged for her killing.

Counterterrorism

The mistreatment and fate of an estimated 1,200 Western European citizens held in Northeast Syria and Iraq as Islamic State (ISIS) suspects or their family members, most without charge, remained a major concern during the year.

European countries faced calls from the Office of the UN High Commissioner for Human Rights (OHCHR), Human Rights Watch and civil society groups to ensure the repatriation of ISIS suspects and their family members, and to take steps to avoid their exposure to the death penalty, torture, and unfair trials in Iraq.

During the year, countries including France, Sweden, Denmark, the Netherlands, and Germany brought home a small number of children each from Syria or Iraq. Italy repatriated one suspected fighter.

Following an October offensive into northeast Syria by Turkish armed forces, concerns for ISIS suspects and family members in the custody of Kurdish-led forces increased.

Some governments such as Denmark, the UK, and the Netherlands stripped citizenship from nationals believed to be in Iraq or Syria whom they suspected of having joined ISIS or other extremist armed groups. In March, the German government also announced plans to strip citizenship from dual nationals suspected of joining terrorist groups. The French government drew criticism for failing to protect 11 citizens sentenced to death by Iraqi courts following rushed proceedings in which there allegations of confessions obtained through torture in some cases.

Concerns remained about the impact on freedom of expression of EU legislative efforts to take down online content deemed to be of a "terrorist" nature. The Fundamental Rights Agency found in February that the definitions of proscribed content in a 2018 EU directive was too wide; the definition was subsequently narrowed by the European Parliament. The law had yet to be adopted at time of writing.

There was no discernable progress in 2019 towards accountability for involvement by EU governments in the CIA's post-September 11, 2001, torture and secret detention program.

Croatia

According to Croatian Ministry of Interior, in the first eight months of 2019, 11,813 new migrants and asylum seekers were recorded, mainly from Afghanistan, Pakistan, and Turkey, an increase of more than 8,600 compared to the same period in 2018. In the same period 974 people claimed asylum and authorities approved 71 asylum requests, including 13 from 2018.

Croatia reported that it blocked entry to 9,487 people at its borders in the first 8 months of the year. Despite credible reports during the year about illegal and violent pushbacks of migrants by Croatian police into Bosnia and Serbia, in breach of EU refugee and human rights law, Croatia faced no consequences from EU institutions. Croatia's president acknowledged in December 2018 on Swiss television that force is sometimes used, but later retracted her comments.

Despite the consistent recommendations to Croatia from international bodies to facilitate community-based support for all people with disabilities currently in institutions, Croatia persisted with plans to place adults with disabilities in foster care, publishing a draft law in December 2018. In January 2019, the Ministry of Social Policy indicated that 4,216 adults were placed in 1,481 foster care families.

In July 2019, Croatia ratified the Safe Schools Declaration pledging to refrain from the military use of schools in wars. According to the Ombudswoman for Children, Roma children were most deprived group in 2019, with limited access to services.

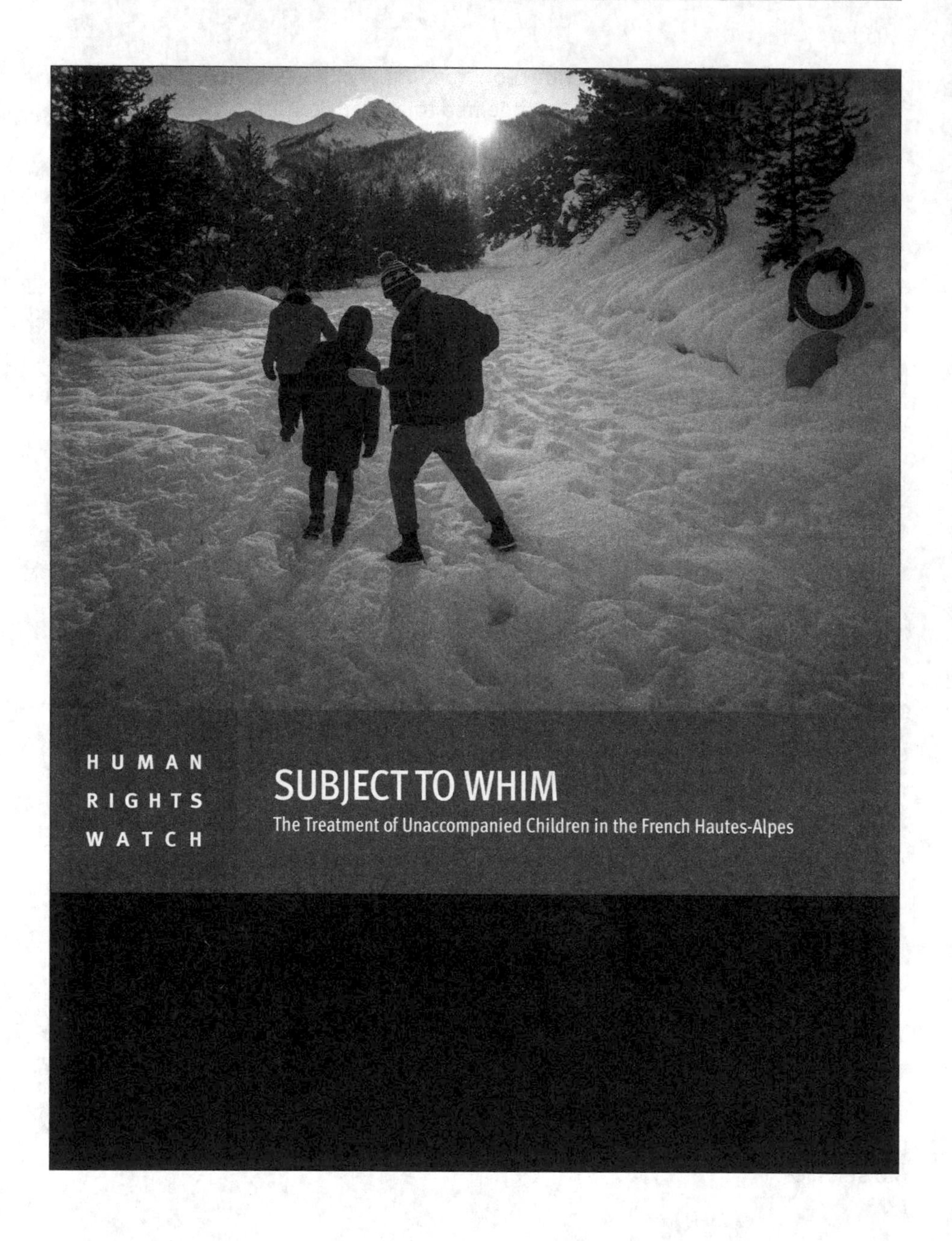
HUMAN
RIGHTS
WATCH
SUBJECT TO WHIM
The Treatment of Unaccompanied Children in the French Hautes-Alpes

In January, a Europe-wide universities-led Holocaust Remembrance project found historical revisionism in Croatia among the highest in the European Union.

During a year that saw several violent attacks on Croatian Serbs, Croatia's ombudswoman and civil society groups expressed concern about the climate of intolerance against minorities.

Between January and September 2019, Documenta, an NGO, registered 39 war crime cases against 59 defendants before courts in Croatia. In the same period, 15 people were convicted for war-related crimes, including one for sexual violence.

France

French police crowd control and anti-riot tactics, used during weekly demonstrations, injured thousands of people since the end of 2018. Those injured include peaceful demonstrators, high-school students, and journalists. There has been widespread criticism of police action, including by the United Nations and the French ombudsperson.

French authorities opened scores of investigations into excessive force allegations, but as of November, only eighteen had been passed to a judge. In November, the Paris prosecutor announced that two police officers will be prosecuted for violence, the first such cases. At time of writing no officers had been held to account.

France adopted a protest law in April that risks undermining the right to freedom of peaceful assembly. UN experts in February expressed concern about the law and already disproportionate restrictions on the right to protest in France.

French border police in the Alps summarily returned unaccompanied migrant children to Italy during the year, and some child protection authorities used flawed age assessment procedures on unaccompanied migrant children, depriving some of the protection and care to which they are entitled. These findings were confirmed by the ombudsman in an annual report on children's rights published in November.

The European Court of Human Rights ruled in February that France had subjected an unaccompanied child living in a makeshift camp in Calais to "degrading treatment" for failing to take steps to ensure he was identified as a child and given protection and care.

Aid workers and volunteers providing vital assistance to migrants were harassed by the police in Calais region and around the French-Italian border. Some faced trial and conviction for their humanitarian work.

In April, after a five-year investigation, the French ombudsman reported discriminatory and illegal orders at a specific police station in Paris, that targeted "black people and north Africans" in the surrounding area for identity checks and "homeless and Roma people" for systematic expulsion. French authorities gave no formal response.

In May, the National Human Rights Consultative Commission, an official body, published a report saying that in 2018, racist acts in France increased by 20 percent compared to 2017, with anti-Semitic acts increasing by more than 70 percent. The same report said that number of racist acts reported to the police decreased by 4 percent. The same month, SOS Homophobie, an NGO said it received 66 percent more reports of physical attacks on lesbian, gay, bisexual, and transgender (LGBT) people for 2018 compared to 2017.

In May, 17 humanitarian and human rights organizations denounced threats to press freedom after three French journalists were summoned by French intelligence services for investigating the use of French weapons by the Saudi-led coalition in the conflict in Yemen.

In September, the government announced measures to step up the fight against domestic violence, including steps to make it easier to report incidents and an increase in shelter spaces. It was criticized by civil society groups for not allocating enough resources to implement the plans. By November, 136 women had been killed in domestic violence in 2019.

In October, the National Assembly adopted a bill allowing lesbian couples and single women to access fertility treatments available only to heterosexual couples. It was before the Senate at time of writing.

Germany

Arrivals of asylum-seekers and migrants fell for a fourth year running. In the first 10 months of 2019, 122,225 asylum-seekers had been registered. By the end of June, 56,628 applications were pending.

Germany continued to play a leadership role in refugee resettlement in the EU. By October 30, Germany had accepted 229 refugees who had been rescued at sea. At time of writing, 13 municipalities had signed the "Safe Haven Cities" declaration, launched in April, indicating to the federal government that they were willing to accept resettled refugees rescued at sea.

A package of federal immigration and asylum law changes in June 2019, negatively impacted rights. NGOs criticized reductions in social benefits and the grounds for detaining migrants pending deportation, along with the continued use of prisons for immigration detention. Separate amendments to deportation law, which entered force in August, limited the ability of rejected asylum seekers who cannot be removed to work or study.

Attacks on refugees, asylum seekers and those providing them with assistance, remained a matter of concern. In the first half of 2019, attacks on refugees and asylum seekers, 60 attacks on refugee shelters, and 42 attacks against relief organizations and volunteers. Police authorities attributed the overwhelming majority of these attacks to perpetrators with a "right wing motivation."

The government disclosed in October that 12,500 "politically-motivated" criminal offences (a category that includes hate crimes) had been committed by members of far-right groups in the first eight months of the year.

Constitutional challenges were pending against laws in Bavaria that allow police to hold people in preventive custody for up to three months, in some instances without access to a lawyer, on the basis they could pose a danger to national security rather than for having committed a crime. During the year, legislators in at least four other German states proposed or passed similar worrying provisions.

Greece

Greece continued to host large numbers of asylum seekers while failing adequately to protect their rights.

In August, the UN Committee against Torture criticized the Greek government policy—linked to the EU-Turkey deal—of blocking asylum seekers who arrive on the Aegean islands from moving to the mainland.

Beginning in August, there was a sharp increase in the number of arrivals on the islands, leading to severe overcrowding and inhuman and degrading conditions in island camps.

At time of writing, 37,000 asylum seekers, the majority women and children, were on the islands, including more than 33,400 in camps designed to host a around 6,200.

Although authorities allowed more transfers during the year, the policy continued to trap thousands in overcrowded and abysmal conditions on the islands. This includes severe overcrowding, unsanitary, unhygienic conditions, and lack of basic services such as water and food. Medical care, trauma counseling, and psychosocial support remained inadequate with deteriorating mental health among asylum seekers, exacerbated by conditions of detention and uncertainty about the disposition of their cases.

Lack of adequate and secure facilities made physical and gender-based violence common in asylum camps. In its August report, the UN Torture Committee called on Greece to take effective measures to ensure that violence against refugee, asylum seeking, and migrant women is investigated, perpetrators are prosecuted, and victims are compensated.

In October, a new asylum law made it easier to detain asylum seekers for longer periods. It also reduced safeguards for asylum seekers, including by scrapping protections for vulnerable people.

The European Court of Human Rights ruled twice, in February and June, that Greece is in violation of its human rights obligations by detaining unaccompanied children in so-called protective custody in police station cells and detention centers. Despite the rulings, at time of writing 234 children were still detained in such premises, while hundreds more were in camps with adults or homeless due to authorities' failure to provide adequate shelter or foster care. The October asylum law failed to repeal the "protective custody" regime.

In March, a prosecutor launched an inquiry into allegations of pushbacks at the Greek-Turkish land border. Such pushbacks, including of Turkish asylum seekers, continued throughout the year. A 2018 similar investigation by the Greek ombudsman had yet to yield results.

In June, the government amended the criminal code to define rape as sex without consent, following widespread criticism of a draft bill that had failed to do so.

In a July report the ombudsman found that people with disabilities have limited access to public spaces, state services and transportation, face discrimination in the workplace, and have difficulties in accessing education. In a September review, the UN Committee on the Rights of Persons with Disabilities, criticized Greece's treatment of asylum seekers and refugees with disabilities. The Council of Europe Committee for the Prevention of Torture issued a report in February expressing concerns about inhuman and degrading treatment in psychiatric establishments and migrant detention centers

Hungary

Hungary's government continued its dismantling of democratic institutions and the rule of law.

In November, the government proposed changes to the administrative courts that would allow state institutions to appeal unfavourable administrative court decisions to the Constitutional Court, where a majority of the judges are close to the ruling party. This could affect issues like corruption, elections, and police conduct. The measures were before parliament at time of writing and expected to be adopted in December.

The move follows an unsuccessful attempt by the government to establish a new administrative court system overseen by the Ministry of Justice, adopted by the Hungarian parliament in December 2018, but scrapped in May 2019 after criticism from EU and Council of Europe's Venice Commission about the lack of checks and balances.

In June, the government renewed its attacks on academic freedom by introducing a law, approved by parliament, that increases state control over the Academy of Sciences, Hungary's largest and oldest academic institution. The law gives the government greater influence over scientific research and funding.

Hungarian authorities continued to limit the number of asylum seekers permitted to enter at border crossings to one or two asylum-seeking families per week, leaving thousands stranded in poor conditions in Serbia. According to UNHCR estimates, by early September, more than 300 people were detained in the two transit zones, including about 170 children. Pushbacks to Serbia remain a concern.

In February, the government resumed its policy of denying food to rejected asylum seekers in the transit zones on Hungary's border with Serbia. By August, the Hungarian Helsinki Committee, a civil society organization, had submitted emergency interventions on behalf of 27 food deprived asylum seekers to the European Court of Human Rights (ECtHR), which in all cases ordered the government to resume food distribution. The government complied with the orders in each case.

In July, the European Commission launched legal action against Hungary over the practice and referred to the EU Court of Justice the 2018 law criminalizing support to asylum seekers by non-governmental organizations. The Commission escalated the case in October. In October, the European Court of Human Rights ruled that the government's decision in 2015 to deny a journalist access to a refugee reception center violated media freedom.

In March, Fidesz was suspended from the European People's Party (EPP), the main centre-right European political family, for breaching the group's values concerning rule of law and fundamental rights but was allowed to remain part of the EPP group in the European Parliament. An internal investigation was ongoing at time of writing.

Media pluralism continued to decrease with more and more outlets espousing a pro-government line, either as a result of ownership by people close to the government or direct government influence. December 2018 saw the merger of nearly 500 media outlets into one conglomerate loyal to the government, seriously impeding media pluralism in the country. Pro-government media continued to smear critical journalists and media outlets.

The government has yet to ratify the Istanbul Convention, with a minister describing it in July as "political hysteria." There are no reliable statistics about domestic violence in the country.

Roma continued to face discrimination in housing, education, and public health care, according to the EU Fundamental Rights Agency.

Italy

There were at least 15 stand-offs at sea as Italian authorities denied permission to NGO ships to disembark people rescued at sea. In June, then-Interior Minister Matteo Salvini pushed through a government decree, converted to law by parliament in August, allowing Italy to deny NGOs authorization to enter territorial waters, ships to be seized and their owners fined. A new government, in place since September, indicated it would reform the decree.

By mid-November, 9,942 people reach Italy by sea, according to UNHCR, a 55 percent decrease compared to 2018.

Government decrees instituted in August an accelerated asylum procedure at the border and in October a list of 13 so-called safe countries of origin whose nationals now face a legal presumption they do not need protection.

Official statistics showed that asylum applications fell by over 50 percent compared to the previous year. In the first six months of the year, rejection rates hovered around 80 percent, significantly more than the 58 percent rejection rate in 2017. This is largely due to the abolition, in late 2018, of humanitarian protection permits.

In August, the UN High Commissioner for Human Rights (OHCHR) expressed serious concern over an increase in intolerance, racial and religious hatred and xenophobia, and the role of political leaders and members of government in allowing or encouraging these phenomena. The Italian NGO Lunaria reported a significant increase in violent racist crime in 2018: 126 incidents compared to 46 in 2017.

A law to combat gender-based violence, came into force in August. The law increases prison sentences for sexual crimes and domestic violence, criminalizes forced marriage, and requires prosecutors to meet within three days anyone who reports domestic or gender-based violence to police.

Netherlands

A controversial new law banning full-face coverings, including the niqab and burka worn by some Muslim women, on public transport, in hospitals, town halls, and educational institutions, entered force in August. There were complaints from public sector organizations that the law was unclear and from nongovernmental groups that it would have a discriminatory impact on Muslim women. Some local police forces and transport authorities said they would not prioritize enforcing the ban.

During the year the UN Human Rights Committee, the European Commission against Racism and Intolerance and the UN special rapporteur on freedom of religion and belief raised concerns about the discriminatory impact of legislation and public rhetoric on religious minorities, and Muslims in particular.

In May, the government proposed changes to the law on rape and sexual assault to introduce a requirement for consent, and to criminalize sexual harassment, to bring Dutch law into line with the Istanbul Convention. At time of writing no legislation had been introduced.

Dutch authorities continued to use their powers to remove Dutch citizenship from dual nationals suspected of traveling abroad to participate in terrorism. In April, however, the Council of State, the highest administrative court, annulled the decision to deprive two Dutch foreign fighters of citizenship, because the decision had been taken before the group they were believed to be affiliated with was proscribed. In November, a district court in the Hague ruled that the Dutch government should ensure the return of Dutch children, under the age of 12, of ISIS suspects, who remained in custody in northern Syria. The government announced that it would appeal the decision.

In April, the government told parliament it intended to simplify the process by which transgender adults could change their legal gender on their birth certificate, and to allow children aged 16 or under to apply to courts to have their gender registration changed, which is not currently permitted. No legislation had been introduced at time of writing.

In February, the government ended a policy in effect since 2012 allowing applications for permanent residency from children in asylum seeking families and unaccompanied undocumented children who had lived in the country for more than five years. It did, however, agree to consider applications of the 600-700 children in the Netherlands and eligible under the policy.

Poland

Government attacks on the country's judiciary continued in 2019.

Judges and prosecutors were subject to arbitrary disciplinary proceedings for standing up for the rule of law and speaking up against problematic judicial reforms, an interference with judicial independence. The Disciplinary Office, established in September 2018, brought disciplinary proceedings against judges and prosecutors. The European Commission in April initiated legal action against Poland for its disciplinary proceedings against judges.

In May, police arrested rights activist Elzbieta Podlesna over a picture of a religious icon with a rainbow halo on the grounds of offending religious feelings and confiscated her mobile phone, laptop, and memory cards. The investigation was ongoing at time of writing.

In June, Council of Europe Human Rights Commissioner, Dunja Mijatovic, raised concerns about dismissals, replacements, and demotions of judges and prosecutors, and called on Polish authorities to "ensure that disciplinary proceedings are not instrumentalised."

Judges and prosecutors were regularly discredited and smeared during the year by government officials and government aligned media.

In June, the EU Court of Justice ruled a 2018 Polish law that lowered the retirement age for the country's Supreme Court judges that would have forced out some of the judges, breached EU law. The government had already suspended the law in December 2018 pending the EU court ruling.

In November, the EU Court of Justice ruled in a case referred by the Polish courts that the new Disciplinary Chamber of the Polish Supreme Court can only be competent to rule on judges' retirement cases if its independence and impartiality is guaranteed.

An amendment to the penal code, approved by parliament would criminalize "promotion" or "approval" or sexual activity by minors, putting teachers and sex

No Woman
No Kraj
GIRLS
HUMAN
RIGHTS
WATCH
"The Breath of the Government on My Back"
Attacks on Women's Rights in Poland

educators at risk of imprisonment and limiting children's right to health information and care.

NGOs working on issues related to asylum and migration, women's rights, or lesbian, gay, bisexual, and transgender (LGBT) rights were often denied public funding.

During the year, LGBT people became the focus of government and ruling party homophobic attacks. In July, at least 30 cities and provinces in Poland declared "LGBT-free-zones," and Gazeta Polska, a pro-government newspaper, distributed "LGBT free zone" stickers in its publications. A Warsaw district court in July ordered the newspaper to immediately halt distribution of the stickers, pending the outcome of legal challenge by a rights activist.

Poland's Commissioner for Human Rights Adam Bodnar was the target of a smear campaign by pro-government media and public officials for defending the human rights of a murder suspect.

Pushbacks of asylum seekers, most from the Russian republic of Chechnya and Central Asia, to Belarus continued, with inconsistent application of a 2018 Polish court ruling to halt the practice.

In August, the United Nations Committee Against Racial Discrimination called on Poland to prevent hate speech in the media, and to take action against websites promoting racial hatred.

The UN Torture Committee in August called on Polish authorities to provide adequate protection for victims of domestic violence and to consider decriminalizing abortion.

Spain

National elections in April and again in November failed to give any party enough votes to form a government.

According to UNHCR, by mid-November 22,400 people had reached Spain by sea, a 62 percent decrease over the same period the previous year, the apparent result of intensified cooperation with Morocco. Land arrivals to Ceuta and Melilla, Spanish enclaves on the north African coast, were down by 23 percent over 2018.

HUMAN
RIGHTS
WATCH
NOTHING LEFT IN THE CUPBOARDS
Austerity, Welfare Cuts, and the Right to Food in the UK

In a March report, the International Organization for Migration (IOM) said almost half of 1,300 migrants and refugees in Spain interviewed in 2018 had experienced exploitation and abuse on their migration journey, the majority in Morocco.

In February, the UN Committee on the Rights of the Child said Spain's 2014 summary return of an unaccompanied Malian boy from Melilla to Morocco had violated his rights. Such summary returns continue and remain authorized by a controversial 2015 Spanish law. In October, a Ceuta judge closed on a technicality the case against 16 Guardia Civil agents in connection to the February 2014 deaths of 14 people at the border, little over a month after ordering their prosecution.

In June, the Supreme Court convicted five men for the gang rape of a woman in Pamplona in 2016, overruling a lower court's 2018 conviction of the men on lesser charges, and sentenced them to 15 years' imprisonment. In November, a Barcelona court convicted a different group of five men on lesser charges of abuse, rather than rape, because no violence or intimidation had been used because the 14-year-old victim was unconscious. The cases sparked protests and government pledges to examine possible changes to the criminal code. To date, no legal changes have been made.

In October, the Supreme Court convicted 9 pro-independence Catalan politicians and activists of sedition and sentenced them to between 9 and 13 years for nonviolent acts in connection with the 2017 referendum on independence, previously deemed illegal by Spanish courts. Four were convicted of misusing public funds. All were acquitted of rebellion. Three other politicians were convicted of and fined for public order offences. In June, the UN working group on arbitrary detention said the detention of three of the defendants during the trial violated their rights.

In May, the UN Committee on the Rights of Persons with disabilities expressed concern about institutionalization of people with disabilities; the use of restraints and risk of violence in institutions; forced sterilization and abortions imposed on women and girls with disabilities; and the failure to guarantee full legal capacity to all people with disabilities.

In May, the UN Human Rights Committee found Spanish authorities responsible for the 2007 torture of a Basque separatist and urged Spain for the fourth time since 2009 to abolish incommunicado detention to prevent torture and cruel treatment.

United Kingdom

The UK's planned exit from the EU (Brexit) strained democratic institutions and put human rights and the rule of law at risk.

In September, the government was forced by parliament to publish a key planning document outlining potential impacts of the UK leaving the EU without an agreement (known as "no-deal" Brexit). Its publication raised serious rights concerns including those related to access to adequate food and medicine, fuel shortages, interruptions to social care for older people and people with disabilities, possible public disorder, and the risk of increased dissident activity in Northern Ireland. The government accepted that a "no deal Brexit" would have the greatest impact on economically vulnerable and marginalized groups.

In September, the Supreme Court ruled unlawful the government's five-week suspension of parliament earlier the same month, leading to parliament's recall. The government was forced by law adopted by parliament in September to seek an extension to the UK's membership of the EU aimed at avoiding a no-deal Brexit. Government sources criticized the Supreme Court ruling and threatened to ignore the binding law requiring an extension request.

The extension was granted by the EU27, and the Brexit date at time of writing was the end of January 2020. Parliament was dissolved in November after opposition parties agreed to a December 2019 general election (which had yet to take place at time of writing).

In May, the UN special rapporteur on extreme poverty published a report on the disproportionate negative impact of austerity-motivated spending cuts, combined with social security restructuring, on the rights of women, children, older people, and people with disabilities living on low incomes.

Reliance on emergency food assistance grew. The country's largest food bank charity network, the Trussell Trust, reported distributing 1.6 million parcels containing a three-day emergency supply of food across the country. The Independ-

THE
WalterNewby
CENTRE
50+
Community
Centre
UNMET NEEDS
Improper Social Care Assessments for Older People in England
HUMAN
RIGHTS
WATCH
SAMUEL CENTRE
FOR SOCIAL
CONNECTEDNESS

HUMAN
RIGHTS
WATCH
NO ESCAPE FROM HELL
EU Policies Contribute to Abuse of Migrants in Libya

ent Food Aid Network reported that, at time of writing, at least 819 independent centers were also distributing food aid.

The UK continued to detain asylum seeking and migrant children.

In October legislation passed by the UK Parliament to decriminalize abortion and provide for marriage equality in Northern Ireland in 2020 came into force when the region's devolved government failed to reconvene having been suspended since January 2017.

More than two years after the deadly Grenfell Tower fire in London that killed 71, there has been little accountability for the deaths or the fire. In October, the findings of the first phase of the public inquiry into the fire were published, focusing on the day of the fire. A criminal investigation was ongoing at time of writing.

In February, a new counterterrorism law entered into force, including measures that criminalize viewing online content, overseas travel and support to terrorism and could result in human rights violations. UK authorities continued to exercise powers to strip citizenship from UK nationals suspected of terrorism-related activity.

In July, the government refused to establish a judicial inquiry into UK complicity in the CIA-led torture and secret detention. At time of writing, no one in the UK had been charged with a crime in connection with the abuses. In November, a media investigation found evidence of a cover up by UK authorities of alleged war crimes by UK forces in Iraq and Afghanistan.

EU Foreign Policy

During a year where international law, bodies and mechanisms came under increasing attack by powerful countries including the United States, Russia and China, the European Union remained a staunch defender of multilateralism and a rules-based global order, despite internal divisions and resistance from individual EU members that sometimes led to muted positions or displayed EU double standards.

The unanimity rule in EU foreign policy at times proved to be an insurmountable obstacle, yet creative solutions were occasionally found. For example, travel bans to the 26-states Schengen zone were imposed against Saudi officials deemed to be involved in the murder of journalist Jamal Khashoggi, and when 27 of the 28 EU member states delivered a critical statement on Israel rights violations at the UN Security Council, circumventing Hungary's last minute attempt to veto the effort.

The EU and its member states played an important role in the UN Human Rights Council, sponsoring and supporting the adoption of resolutions establishing or renewing commissions of inquiries, fact-finding missions or otherwise independent monitoring of human rights crises in countries as diverse as the Democratic Republic of the Congo, the Philippines, Myanmar, Venezuela, Burundi, Yemen, Syria, South Sudan, Belarus, and Cambodia.

Both before and after the 2019 May elections, the European Parliament (EP) played an important role both in its bilateral diplomacy with third countries and in pushing EU institutions and governments to take appropriate measures in reaction to human rights violations worldwide, distinguishing itself as arguably the most progressive EU body.

Among the most noteworthy examples were EP calls for targeted sanctions against Chinese officials responsible for the mass detention of Uyghurs and other Turkic Muslims in Xinjiang; the awarding of the prestigious Sakharov Prize to Uyghur scholar Ilham Tohti; an urgent resolution on Myanmar expressing support for innovative initiatives to pursue accountability for atrocity crimes against the Rohingya, such as the opening of a case on Myanmar's possible violation of the UN Genocide Convention before the International Court of Justice; and a call for a much-needed "profound and comprehensive review" of the EU's relations with Egypt in response to continued crackdown on dissent and grave rights abuses with impunity.

Despite an overall good record, the EP also sparked controversy including by giving the green light to EU trade treaties with Morocco that include occupied Western Sahara, and voting down a resolution which would have called on EU member states to resume search and rescue operations in the Mediterranean.

The externalization of migration remained one of the most concerning aspects of the EU's foreign policy, largely operated through an unaccountable trust fund mainly aimed at strengthening border control in countries across the Sahel, the Horn of Africa and in Northern Africa. The EU's handling of the migration file was increasingly used to rebut the EU's arguments during human rights dialogues with third countries, and placed authoritarian leaders such as Turkey's President Recep Tayyip Erdoğan and Egypt's President Abdel Fattah al-Sisi in positions to pressure EU institutions.

Human rights conditionality attached to trade preferences and customs free access to the EU's internal marked remained important tools for leverage. In February, the European Commission launched a procedure to suspend, in part or in full, Cambodia's trade preferences, following Hun Sen's reluctance to revert his crackdown the country's political opposition and basic human rights as laid down in international law.

Countries such as Myanmar, Bangladesh, and Sri Lanka remain under tight scrutiny and risk similar consequences. Meanwhile, the European Commission and Council speeded up the conclusion of a free trade agreement with Vietnam despite the intensification of Hanoi's serious human rights violations.

Responding to continued serious violations in among others Burundi, Venezuela, Syria, Myanmar, Iran, and eastern Ukraine, the EU maintained targeted punitive sanctions such as travel bans and asset freezes against individuals and entities deemed responsible. The EU also maintained embargoes on arms and/or equipment that can be used for internal repression in a number of countries including China, Myanmar, and Sudan.

In October, EU member states established their latest legal framework for targeted sanctions against individuals and entities responsible for abuses in Nicaragua, but at time of writing no one had been listed. EU member states continued their deliberations on the adoption of a "global EU human rights sanctions regime" that would allow the EU to target individuals and entities responsible for serious violations of international human rights and humanitarian law, without adopting country-specific sanction regimes.

Georgia

Political tensions and sustained protests over electoral reforms marked 2019 in Georgia. The government used excessive force to disperse a largely nonviolent protest in June, detaining and injuring scores, and pursuing largely one-sided accountability for it. To avoid further political crisis, the chairman of the parliament resigned and the Georgian Dream majority initially conceded to holding the 2020 parliamentary vote by a fully proportional election system, but later voted down the initiative, sparking further protests. Protesters demanded snap elections and changes to the existing mixed electoral system that disproportionately favors the ruling party.

Other areas of concern included lax labor regulations resulting in labor practices that undermine workers' safety, threats to media pluralism, unjustifiably harsh drug laws, and discrimination against lesbian, gay, bisexual, and transgender (LGBT) people.

Lack of Accountability for Law Enforcement Abuses

Impunity for abuse by law enforcement officials remained a persistent problem. Authorities twice postponed the launching of the State Inspector's Office, created in 2018 to investigate abuses committed by law enforcement and other public officials, citing lack of financing. It became operational on November 1.

By September, the Ombudsman's Office received 54 complaints of ill-treatment by prison staff or police and petitioned the prosecutor's office to launch investigations in 52 cases. None resulted in criminal prosecution.

On the night of June 20, riot police fired rubber bullets and used tear gas against thousands of protesters outside the parliament building in Tbilisi. The protest was sparked by the presence of a delegation from the Russian Duma in the parliament's plenary chamber, as part of the Inter-Parliamentary Assembly of Orthodoxy.

Some protesters repeatedly tried to break through the police cordon, grabbing and damaging some riot gear. Otherwise the crowd was largely nonviolent. While riot police showed restraint initially, around midnight, without prior warning, they opened fire on the crowd with tear gas and rubber bullets, chasing and arresting people who tried to gather.

Some 240 people, including 80 police officers and 32 journalists, sustained injuries and sought medical attention. Many civilians sustained rubber bullet injuries to the head, legs, and back; two people each lost an eye.

Police arrested hundreds, and courts sentenced 121 protesters to up to 15 days in jail on misdemeanor violations.

Authorities pursued largely one-sided accountability. They launched a mass rioting investigation, charging at least 19 protesters, 15 of whom remained in pretrial custody at time of writing. Opposition parliamentarian Nika Melia was released under house arrest. The prosecutor's office designated 67 police officers and only four civilians as victims, depriving many of the injured protesters the opportunity to review investigation files. Following civil society criticism, three more people received victim status in November.

Meanwhile, the prosecutor's office charged three police officers with exceeding their powers and assaulting a detained protester; courts released all three on bail. The Interior Ministry reprimanded 11 law enforcement officers for misconduct and sent two cases to the prosecutor's office. The prosecutor's office authorized the public defender to monitor the ongoing investigation into police conduct.

Labor Rights

According to the Georgian Trade Union Confederation, 36 workers died and 107 were injured in work-related accidents through October. Georgian labor law does not sufficiently regulate working hours, rest time, weekly breaks, and night work, and does not provide for government oversight of all labor conditions. Lax regulations and resulting labor practices that often prioritize production targets undermine workers' safety. For example, workers in some manganese mines work 12-hour shifts underground, including at night, for 15 straight days, resulting in exhaustion and increasing the likelihood of workplace accidents and injuries. In May, some 2,500 miners from some of these mines went on strike for 12 days, demanding better working conditions and a pay rise.

HUMAN
RIGHTS
WATCH
"No Year without Deaths"
A Decade of Deregulation Puts Georgian Miners at Risk

Authorities drafted legislative amendments to address some of the gaps in the law regarding overtime, time off, and other issues, and to strengthen the labor inspectorate. The changes had not been introduced for parliamentary debate at time of writing.

Freedom of Media

The European Court of Human Rights' July decision finding no breach of fair trial guarantees in the ownership dispute over Rustavi 2—Georgia's most-watched television station—shook Georgia's media landscape. As a result, ownership reverted to a former owner, Kibar Khalvashi, who claimed that he had been forced to sell the station in 2006 below market value. Rustavi 2's general director, Nika Gvaramia, alleged the lawsuit was orchestrated by the government to take over the station because it was seen as aligned with the opposition.

Khalvashi appointed a new director general, Paata Salia, who pledged not to interfere with the station's editorial policy. However, Salia soon dismissed the newsroom head and producers and hosts of political and entertainment talk shows, claiming they had conflicts of interest because of their public statements against the new owner. The move prompted almost the entire newsroom to quit, resulting in temporary suspension of news broadcasts.

In August, the prosecutor's office brought "abuse of power" charges against Gvaramia, claiming he had struck a sham deal in 2015 on commercial ad placement on the station, allegedly resulting in the loss of 7.2 million GEL (approximately US$ 2.5 million). A court ordered Gvaramia to post 40,000 GEL (approximately US$ 13,500) bail. Some civil society organizations saw the "accelerated manner of the investigation" as politically motivated, likely "aimed at persecuting opponents and critical media."

In September, Gvaramia founded a new pro-opposition broadcaster "Mtavari Arkhi" (Main Channel) and hired many of former Rustavi 2 anchors and journalists.

Authorities also brought charges against Avtandil Tsereteli, father of the founder of TV Pirveli, another independent and critical broadcaster. The prosecutor's office alleged that Tsereteli assisted former TBC Bank Board Chair Mamuka Khazaradze and his deputy in "legalization of illicit income" of US$ 17 million in

2008. Civil society groups criticized the move as another attempt at "exert[ing] pressure on the independent and critical broadcaster."

Drug Policy

Although the overall numbers of drug-related prosecutions continued to decline, authorities maintained harsh drug laws that can be used to prosecute people for mere consumption (except for marijuana) or possession of drugs for personal use. Drug-related felonies often result in long sentences, prohibitive fines, and deprivation of other rights, including the right to drive a vehicle or work in an array of professions.

Draft legislative reform that would introduce public health approaches to drug use and largely overhaul punitive practices remained stalled in parliament at time of writing.

Sexual Orientation and Gender Identity

Activists planned Georgia's first-ever Pride Week— including various social, political, and cultural events and a Pride March— for June 22. On May 31, the Interior Ministry issued a statement saying that the events could not be held outdoors, citing the risks to people involved in the events. In its June 14 statement, the Georgian Orthodox Church urged the authorities "not to allow" Tbilisi Pride, calling it "absolutely unacceptable." Two days later, homophobic groups led by ultra-conservative businessman Levan Vasadze held a rally, announcing the formation of vigilante patrols against Tbilisi Pride and gay people. Police launched an investigation into Vasadze's statements that had no outcome at time of writing.

The indoor Pride events took place. On July 8 around 40 activists and LGBT supporters held a pride march outside the Interior Ministry.

In November, ultra-nationalist hate groups and their supporters organized protests against the screening of a Swedish-Georgian gay love-themed film, "And Then We Danced," in Tbilisi and Batumi, harassing and at times attacking moviegoers. Police said they detained 27 people on misdemeanor, disobedience, and hooliganism charges, and one person faced criminal violence charge.

Key International Actors

In March, the European Union and Georgia met to assess progress in implementing the Association Agreement. The sides welcomed "structural reforms and underlined the importance of ongoing reforms." The EU also highlighted the importance of an inclusive political environment, free and independent media and respect for rule of law and judicial independence.

In April, following its visit to Georgia, the United Nations Working Group on Business and Human Rights expressed concern about the adequacy of the regulatory framework for labor inspections.

In a May joint statement, the UN, EU, United States, and Council of Europe (CoE) representations in Tbilisi called for an end to violence and discrimination against LGBTQI+ persons in Georgia.

CoE Human Rights Commissioner Dunja Mijatovic also urged authorities to take decisive measures to ensure safety of people organizing and participating in the Pride March and respect people's right to be protected from violence and hate speech.

The June joint statement to mark the 10-year anniversary of the US-Georgia strategic partnership highlighted "a resilient and pluralistic democracy, free and fair elections, an independent media, respect for human rights ... transparent and accountable governance, and vibrant civil society" as essential elements of Georgia's development.

In a June statement, the US embassy expressed concerns about "the context and timing" of criminal charges pressed against the TBC Bank founders. The EU embassy also called for the case to be handled "in a transparent manner."

In June, the Organization for Security and Co-operation in Europe's representative on freedom of the media, Harlem Désir, deplored violence against media workers during demonstrations in Tbilisi. He called on authorities to ensure the safety of journalists at all times, and promptly and effectively investigate all incidents.

In a November joint statement, the EU and US embassies in Georgia noted the "deep disappointment of a wide segment of Georgian society" over failed electoral reform and called for "calm and respectful dialogue" to find "an acceptable path forward."

In a resolution adopted during its March session, the United Nations Human Rights Council expressed concerns about the ongoing borderization along the administrative boundary line with Georgia's conflict regions of Abkhazia and South Ossetia, and called for the UN High Commissioner's access to the regions.

The International Criminal Court (ICC) continued its investigation into war crimes and crimes against humanity committed in connection with the August 2008 Russia-Georgia war over South Ossetia. In January, Georgia and the ICC entered into an agreement to permit persons convicted by the ICC in any of its cases to serve their sentences in Georgia, subject to further decisions by the court and the government in specific instances.

Guatemala

Guatemala's progress in prosecuting corruption and abuse in recent years is at risk after the government decided not to extend the mandate of the United Nations-backed International Commission against Impunity in Guatemala (CICIG). CICIG ceased operation in September 2019. At time of writing, the attorney general had not taken steps to safeguard the prosecution of more than 60 ongoing corruption cases, including those against more than a dozen current and former Congress members, former ministers, former President Otto Pérez Molina, and former Vice-President Roxana Baldetti.

In July, the Guatemalan and US governments signed an agreement that would establish Guatemala as a "safe third country." At time of writing, it was unclear how the agreement would be implemented.

Public Security, Corruption, and Criminal Justice

Violence and extortion by powerful criminal organizations remain serious problems in Guatemala. Gang-related violence is an important factor prompting people, including unaccompanied children and young adults, to leave the country.

In recent years, investigations by CICIG and the Attorney General's Office have exposed more than 60 corruption schemes, implicating officials in all three branches of government, and prompting the resignation and arrest of the country's then-president and vice-president in 2015.

However, Guatemala suffers from high levels of impunity, partly because criminal proceedings against powerful actors often suffer unreasonably long delays due to excessive use of motions by criminal defendants. Those delays are compounded by courts often failing to respect legally mandated timeframes and sometimes taking months to reschedule suspended hearings. Intimidation against judges and prosecutors and corruption within the justice system continue to be problems. As a result, trials have not yet started for most major corruption cases brought since 2015.

Accountability for Past Human Rights Violations

The limited progress that Guatemala made in recent years in judging crimes of the past seems to have come to a standstill.

In November 2018, a former special forces member was convicted for his role in the 1982 Dos Erres massacre, in which Guatemalan army special forces killed around 200 civilians as part of its counterinsurgency policy during the armed conflict. In 2011 and 2012, five others had been convicted for their roles in the massacre. However, 10 others remain at large and three high-level former officials, including former leader Efraín Ríos Montt, died before facing trial.

In June, in a case regarding sexual violence against 36 Maya Achí women in the 1980s, a pretrial judge dismissed proceedings against six former paramilitaries and ordered the immediate release of the defendants after she excluded key evidence from the case, including testimonies from victims and witnesses. At time of writing, plaintiffs' appeals against the decision remained pending, as did the request from the prosecutor to strip the judge of immunity and charge her with malfeasance and denial of justice.

The same judge had reached a similar decision in the CREOMPAZ case, involving enforced disappearances and sexual violence at a military base during Guatemala's internal armed conflict. The judge excluded 123 of the 152 victims from the case and excluded key military documents from the evidence. The prosecutors' appeals remained pending at time of writing.

In March 2019, Guatemalan Congress passed the second (of three required) approvals of a bill that would provide amnesty for genocide and other past atrocities, in clear violation of international human rights law. That same month, the Inter-American Court on Human Rights ordered Guatemala, in a binding ruling, to shelve the proposed legislation and in July 2019, Guatemala's Constitutional Court issued a similar ruling. However, at time of writing, that had not happened.

Violence Against Journalists

Journalists are targets of harassment and violence. In February 2018, the bodies of journalist Laurent Castillo and radio worker Luis de León were found bound and with gunshot wounds to the head. In June 2017, TV journalist Carlos Rodríguez survived a gunshot to the head. In June 2016, radio journalist Álvaro

Aceituno was killed, and in March 2015, journalists Danilo López and Federico Salazar were assassinated. In January 2017, investigations by CICIG and the Attorney General's Office implicated Congressman Julio Juárez from former government party FCN-Nación in the latter crime. In June, a pretrial judge ordered Juárez to stand trial. At time of writing, a trial date had not been set.

Children's Rights

In March 2017, 41 adolescent girls were killed in a fire in the Hogar Seguro government-run shelter. Fifty-six girls had been locked up for the night in a space that could safely hold only 11, without access to water or a restroom, following a protest against the poor living conditions and treatment received in the shelter—including reports of sexual violence stretching back years. After at least six hours in those conditions, one of the girls set a mattress on fire so police officers on guard would let them out—but the police waited nine minutes before opening the door. Three public officials were due to stand trial in February 2019 for involuntary manslaughter and breach of duty, among other charges, but because of delays, the trial had not yet started at time of writing.

Sexual and Reproductive Health

In August 2018 Guatemalan Congress approved a preliminary version of the "Life and Family Protection" bill. This bill would expand the criminalization of abortion, currently legal only when the life of a pregnant woman or girl is in danger, and could subject women who have miscarriages to prosecution. It would also raise the maximum sentence for abortion from 3 to 10 years and would make it a crime to engage in "the promotion of abortion," which could mean that the provision of sexual and reproductive information, counseling, or referrals might result in sentences of up to 10 years.

The bill also contains provisions that discriminate against lesbian, gay, bisexual, and transgender (LGBT) people. It defines marriage as a union between people who were a man and a woman according to their sex assigned at birth, thus excluding many transgender people in addition to prohibiting same-sex unions. The bill defines "sexual diversity" as "incompatible with the biological and genetic aspects of human beings." It also establishes that "freedom of conscience and expression" protect people from being "obliged to accept non-heterosexual conduct or practices as normal."

This provision could be interpreted to mean that people can be denied services on the basis of sexual orientation or gender identity, in violation of international human rights law. Guatemala does not have legislation specifically protecting the rights of LGBT people.

Incoming President Giammatei stated during the election campaign that he supported the bill. At time of writing, the bill still needed further legislative approvals before the president could sign it into law.

Key International Actors

Since its start in 2007, the UN-backed CICIG played a key role in assisting Guatemala's justice system in prosecuting violent crime. CICIG worked with the Attorney General's Office, the police, and other government agencies to investigate, prosecute, and dismantle criminal organizations operating in the country. It identified more than 60 criminal structures, presented more than 110 cases—in which over 680 people were involved—and presented 34 proposals for legal reforms to Guatemala's Congress. According to an April opinion poll, more than 70 percent of the population supported CICIG.

However, after CICIG and the attorney general presented a renewed request in August 2018 to strip President Jimmy Morales of his presidential immunity in order to investigate his role in illicit campaign financing, Morales announced, flanked by military and police officers, that he would not renew CICIG's mandate. As a result, CICIG ceased operation in September 2019.

At time of writing, Guatemala's Attorney General had not agreed to a plan to guarantee the permanence of the prosecutor's office in charge of the prosecution of CICIG's cases.

In July, after the Trump administration had threatened to apply tariffs on Guatemalan products and fees on remittances from migrants, Guatemalan and U.S. officials signed an agreement that would establish Guatemala as a "safe third country," requiring citizens of other countries who passed through Guatemala before filing a claim for asylum in the U.S., to apply for asylum in

Guatemala instead. At time of writing, it was unclear how the agreement would be implemented.

The US Congress approved US$615 million in assistance for 2018 for the Plan of the Alliance for Prosperity in the Northern Triangle, a five-year initiative announced in 2014 aimed at reducing incentives for people to migrate from Guatemala, El Salvador, and Honduras by curbing violence, strengthening governance, and increasing economic opportunity in those countries. However, in March, President Donald Trump announced that aid to Northern Triangle countries would be cut. This would significantly reduce, or end, programs on local economic development, violence prevention, and anti-corruption efforts.

In 2019, Guatemala endorsed the Safe Schools Declaration, an international commitment to protect education during armed conflict.

Guinea

As opposition and civil society in Guinea raised concerns over a proposed constitutional revision that could permit President Alpha Conde to run for a third term run in 2020, the government cracked down on freedoms of assembly and speech.

The government banned all but a handful of street demonstrators, and security forces arrested dozens of protesters and broke up demonstrations using tear gas and, at times, live ammunition. At least 17 people were allegedly killed by security forces during protests in October and November, and protesters killed at least one gendarme. Six civil society activists leading opposition to a new constitution were also arrested and imprisoned in October. Several journalists were arrested on defamation charges and briefly detained for coverage critical of the government.

The government made little progress in investigating dozens of alleged unlawful killings that have occurred during protests in the last decade, with the February 2019 conviction of a police captain the first time a security forces' member has been held accountable for the death of a demonstrator since Condé came to power in 2010. In November, the justice minister said the long-delayed trial of those responsible for the 2009 stadium massacre would be held not later than June 2020.

Freedom of Assembly

The government largely continued to enforce a July 2018 ban on street protests, citing threats to public security. Opponents to a new constitution were particularly targeted by protest bans, including three protesters arrested in Coyah in March, a dozen members of the Bloc Liberal party on April 5, seven protesters in Kindia—initially sentenced to three months but released on appeal—and 40 people arrested on June 13 in N'Zérékoré after an effort by security forces to break up an opposition protest led to intercommunal clashes. Those arrested in N'Zérékoré were detained until a June 20 trial, when 22 were convicted of public order offences

The crackdown on protests intensified in October as the government banned and then violently dispersed three days of anti-constitution protests on October 14-16. Nine civil society leaders were arrested on October 12 and six convicted on October 22 for organizing the protests and sentenced to between 6 and 12 months' imprisonment. Dozens of demonstrators were also arrested, detained for several days, and then released or fined.

The government finally authorized several anti-constitution protests beginning October 24, although disagreement over the route of a November 14 protest led to clashes between protesters and security forces. Five anti-constitution activists also detained in Kindia on November 14. Pro-government supporters organized a rival protest on October 31.

Security Force Abuses

At least 11 demonstrators were allegedly shot dead by the security forces during protests from October 14-16. Protesters killed a gendarme on October 14. Security forces allegedly shot dead 3 people during a November 4 funeral procession to commemorate October's protest deaths. Security forces allegedly shot dead 3 more protesters on November 7. A student protester was also reportedly killed by the security forces in Labé on May 31.

Demonstrators arrested during protests in May, June, October, and November accused the police and gendarmerie of stealing money, telephones, and other possessions.

In July, the National Assembly adopted a law on the use of force by the gendarmerie that could shield law enforcement from prosecution in cases of unlawful killing. The law requires that force only be exercised where necessary and proportionate but does not explicitly limit the use of firearms to imminent threats of death or serious injury.

Also in July, the National Assembly adopted an anti-terrorism law with several provisions that could threaten human rights, including prolonged detention in police custody and vague offenses for "apologizing for terrorism."

Justice for the 2009 Stadium Massacre

Ten years after security forces massacred over 150 peaceful opposition supporters, and raped dozens of women, at a stadium on September 28, 2009, those responsible have not been tried. Guinean judges have indicted 14 people over the massacre, including Moussa Dadis Camara, then-leader of the military junta that ruled Guinea in September 2009, and individuals who remain in positions of power such as Moussa Tiegboro Camara, who is in charge of fighting drug trafficking and organized crime. In August 2019, a steering committee, established in August 2018 to organize the trial, confirmed Conakry's Court of Appeal as the site for the trial. Justice Minister Mohammed Lamine Fofana stated in November that the trial would take place no later than June 2020.

Accountability for Past Crimes

With the exception of a handful of cases, impunity largely continued for past human rights abuses. There have been no trials for at least a dozen alleged killings of demonstrators by the security forces during protests in 2018, as well as for demonstrators killed in protests in 2019. There have similarly be no trials for the killing of protesters prior to and following the 2015 presidential elections and the 2013 parliamentary elections; for the 2012 killing of six men in the southeastern mining village of Zoghota; or the 2007 killing by security forces of some 130 unarmed demonstrators.

On February 4, 2019, a court convicted police captain Kaly Diallo for shooting dead a protester in August 2016. However, the case was marred by charges by rights groups of inadequate evidence. Despite dozens of alleged unlawful killings during demonstrations by the security forces since 2010, the case was the first conviction of a security force member for killing a protester.

In February 2019, a court sentenced a captain in an elite police unit to six years' imprisonment for the 2016 torture of a detainee that had been filmed on a cellphone and widely shared.

The trial of the former governor of Conakry, Sékou Resco Camara, and the former head of the army, Nouhou Thiam, for the 2010 torture of several opposition detainees, which began in April 2018, was repeatedly delayed.

Freedom of Expression

Threats to media freedoms, which have increased in the last several years, continued in 2019 with several journalists arrested and then released for coverage critical of the government.

Journalist Lansana Camara was arrested March 26 on defamation charges for accusing a government minister of corruption. He was released on bail on April 2. Mohammed Bangoura, head of an online news site, was arrested July 1 on defamation charges after his site published an op-ed by an opposition politician. Two executives from The Lynx media group were arrested April 19 and later released on bail for broadcasting an interview with a ruling party dissident.

An opposition politician, Faya Millimouno, was detained August 2 on defamation charges for accusing a government minister of participation in a 2000 rebellion. He was released on bail August 9.

Judiciary and Detention Conditions

The judiciary continued to face various shortcomings, including lack of adequate court rooms and other physical infrastructure, as well as insufficient personnel and resources to investigate and prosecute human rights violations and other crimes.

Guinean prisons and detention centers operate far below international standards, with severe overcrowding due to over-reliance on pretrial detention, weak case management, and the failure of the courts to sit regularly. The country's largest detention facility in Conakry remained overcrowded with poor sanitary conditions. In July 2019, a facility built for 300 housed 1492 detainees.

Forced Evictions

Between February and May 2019, the Guinean government forcibly evicted more than 20,000 people from neighborhoods in Conakry to provide land for government ministries, foreign embassies, businesses, and other public works. The government did not provide adequate notice to most of those evicted, or any alternative housing for demolished homes.

Natural Resources

Guinea's natural resources, notably bauxite and gold, were a major driver of economic growth. The bauxite sector continued to expand rapidly in the Boké and Boffa regions, leading to thousands of farmers losing their land to mining, often for inadequate compensation, and damaging vital water sources in the area.

The government began the displacement of approximately 16,000 people to make way for the Souapiti hydroelectric dam. Although the dam will potentially increase access to electricity in Guinea, villages displaced so far have received inadequate compensation for their land, and inadequate assistance obtaining alternative livelihoods.

Key International Actors

Following the October repression of protests against a new constitution, the United Nations, the Economic Community of West African States (ECOWAS), the European Union and the United States, along with several European states, issued statements reiterating the importance of freedom of assembly and expression.

The Office of the United Nations High Commissioner for Human Rights on October 25 condemned the use of excessive use of force by security forces and the arrest of protest organizers. The ambassador of Russia, which has significant financial investments in the bauxite sector, spoke openly in favor of a Condé third term in January, spurring criticism from Guinean civil society.

The office of the UN special representative on sexual violence in conflict and the Team of Experts on the Rule of Law/Sexual Violence in Conflict continued to support accountability for rapes and crimes committed during the 2009 stadium massacre. The International Criminal Court (ICC) also continued to play a positive role in promoting the September 28, 2009 investigation through its engagement with Guinean authorities.

Haiti

Political instability in 2019 continued to hinder the Haitian government's ability to meet the basic needs of its people, resolve long-standing human rights problems, and address humanitarian crises.

In July 2018, the government's announcement that it would eliminate subsidies, allowing fuel prices to increase by up to 50 percent, led to widespread protests and the worst civil unrest the country has seen in years. In February 2019, demonstrations escalated after the government declared a state of economic emergency, with opposition groups demanding President Jovenel Moïse's resignation amid allegations that he had mismanaged government funds designated for social programs. In September, anti-government protests grew in size and police responded in several cases with excessive force. At time of writing, Haiti was entering its 10th week of demonstrations and political clashes.

Corruption, vulnerability to natural disasters, resurgent gang violence, and disproportionate use of force by police against protesters remain major human rights concerns in Haiti.

Displacement

Haitians remain susceptible to displacement by natural disasters, including tropical storms and hurricanes. Over 140,000 households still need decent shelter more than three years after Hurricane Matthew caused, by various estimates, between 540 and 1,000 deaths. Nearly 9,000 more people were displaced in 2018, the majority due to housing destroyed by an earthquake in October.

As of January 2019, nearly 35,000 people, more than half of them women and children, lived in displacement camps formed after a 2010 earthquake. Authorities have not provided assistance to resettle them or return them to their places of origin.

Rights to Health, Water, and Food

The country's most vulnerable communities continue to face environmental risks, such as widespread deforestation, pollution from industry, and limited access to safe water and sanitation. Some 2.6 million Haitians—approximately a quarter of the country's population—live with food insecurity. Low rainfall chronically affects much of the country.

Since its introduction by UN peacekeepers in 2010, cholera has infected more than 820,000 people and claimed nearly 10,000 lives. However, intensified control efforts—including an ambitious vaccination campaign—have resulted in a significant decline in cases, from more than 41,000 suspected cases and 440 deaths in 2016 to just over 300 suspected cases and three deaths from January through April 2019.

Criminal Justice System

Haiti's prison system remains severely overcrowded, with many inmates living in inhumane conditions. Over 115 people died in Haitian prisons in 2018 and 19 died between March 1 and May 15, 2019. According to the former UN independent expert on Haiti, overcrowding is largely attributable to high numbers of arbitrary arrests and the country's large number of pretrial detainees. As of May 2019, Haitian prisons housed just over 11,000 detainees, 73 percent of whom were awaiting trial.

Illiteracy and Barriers to Education

Illiteracy is a major problem in Haiti. According to the UN Development Programme (UNDP), approximately one-half of all Haitians age 15 and older are illiterate. The quality of education is generally low, and 85 percent of schools are run by private entities that charge school fees that can be prohibitively expensive for low income families. Nearly 180,000 children and youth remain out of primary and secondary school throughout the country.

Abuses by Security Forces

According to an investigation by the UN Mission for Justice Support in Haiti (MINUJUSTH), during October 2018 demonstrations police officers were responsible for three summary executions and 47 cases of excessive force that injured 44 protesters and killed another three. The MINUJUSTH report also notes that, during November 2018 protests, 21 casualties, including 6 deaths, allegedly resulted from police use of excessive force. In February 2019, as police sought to remove barricades and control massive anti-government demonstrations, clashes broke out and at least 34 people were killed and over 100 injured. Twenty-three police officers were also injured.

Between September 16 and October 17, the National Human Rights Defense Network (RNDDH) reported that at least eight journalists were injured during protests. Among those injured was an Associated Press photojournalist shot in the jaw by a Haitian senator who opened fire near the Senate building, and a cameraman for Radio Sans Fin shot in the wrist as police fired into a crowd. In October a radio journalist covering the protests was found shot dead in his car.

In November, the UN High Commissioner on Human Rights released a statement on the unrest, attributing at least 19 of the 42 deaths in protests since mid-September to government security forces.

RNDDH reported that at least 71 people were killed during a November 2018 massacre in the neighborhood of La Saline. Reports by the UN and the Haitian police in June indicated the involvement of two former Haitian National Police officers and two senior government officials. In September, as protests intensified, both government officials were removed from their posts.

Accountability for Past Abuses

Accountability for past human rights abuses continues to be a challenge in Haiti. As of November, a re-opened investigation into crimes committed by former President Jean-Claude Duvalier's collaborators remained pending. Duvalier died in 2014, six months after the Port-of-Prince Court of Appeal ruled that the statute of limitations could not be applied to crimes against humanity and ordered that investigations against him should continue for crimes committed during his presidency (1971-1986). Allegations of violations include arbitrary detentions, torture, disappearances, summary executions, and forced exile.

Women's and Girls' Rights

Gender-based violence is a widespread problem. Haiti does not have specific legislation against domestic violence, sexual harassment, or other forms of violence targeted at women and girls. Rape was only explicitly criminalized in 2005, by ministerial decree.

There has been little progress toward passage of a criminal code reform submitted to parliament in April 2017 that would address some of these gaps in protection. The draft criminal code would also partially decriminalize abortion, which is currently prohibited in all circumstances, including in cases of sexual violence.

Among the survivors of the November 2018 La Saline massacre are 11 women and girls who were gang-raped and received no medical support or counselling.

Sexual Orientation and Gender Identity

Lesbian, gay, bisexual, and transgender (LGBT) people continue to suffer high levels of discrimination. In 2017, the Haitian Senate passed two anti-LGBT bills, which were under consideration by the Chamber of Deputies at time of writing.

One bill would regulate conditions for the issuance of the Certificat de Bonne Vie et Mœurs, a certificate of good standing required by many employers and universities as proof that a person has not committed a felony. The bill lists homosexuality, alongside child pornography, incest, and commercial sexual exploitation of children, as a reason to deny a citizen a certificate.

The other bill calls for a ban on same-sex marriage, as well as any public support or advocacy for LGBT rights. Should the ban become law, "the parties, co-parties and accomplices" of a same-sex marriage could be punished by three years in prison and a fine of about US$8,000.

Deportation and Statelessness for Dominicans of Haitian Descent

The precarious status of many Dominicans of Haitian descent and Haitian migrants working in the Dominican Republic remained a serious concern in 2019. At least 250,000 such individuals re-entered Haiti between 2015 and 2018 after Dominican officials began deportations pursuant to a controversial 2015 Plan for the Regularization of Foreigners in the Dominican Republic. Many deportations did not meet international standards and many people were swept up in arbitrary, summary deportations. Many others left the Dominican Republic under pressure or threat.

As of mid-2018, more than 200,000 Haitians in the Dominican Republic reportedly were living without valid paperwork, at risk of deportation. During the first six months of 2019 alone, an average of more than 10,000 Haitians were returned to their country each month.

Mining and Access to Information

In the past decade, foreign investors have pursued the development of Haiti's nascent mining sector. In 2017, the Haitian government presented a draft mining law to parliament. According to the Global Justice Clinic of New York University School of Law, the draft law is silent on the rights of individuals displaced by mining activities and grants insufficient time for adequate environmental review, restricting the government's ability to study the documentation thoroughly and limiting opportunity for public participation or comment.

In addition, it contains provisions that could render all company documents, including those about environmental and social impacts, confidential for 10 years, preventing affected communities from engaging in meaningful consultation about mining projects. The draft law was awaiting consideration by parliament at time of writing.

Key International Actors

MINUJUSTH, intended to help promote rule of law, police development, and human rights, was extended in April for a final six-month period. In October, the UN Security Council transitioned to a non-peacekeeping special political mission, the United Nations Integrated Office in Haiti (BINUH).

In 2016, the UN secretary-general apologized for the UN's role in the cholera outbreak and announced intensifying efforts to treat and eliminate cholera and the establishment of a trust fund to raise $400 million to provide "material assistance" to those most affected by the epidemic. As of November 2019, only $27.7 million had been pledged to the effort.

In October, victims of the cholera outbreak petitioned the US Supreme Court to review the case of LaVenture et al v. United Nations in an effort to challenge the UN's immunity in cholera lawsuits. The court decided not to hear the case.

In response to the UN's La Saline massacre report, UN Secretary-General António Guterres commented in July that "[t]he allegations of complicity by at least two police officers and a representative of the State call for authorities to act swiftly to bring to justice those who are responsible for the crimes."

In October 2018, a US federal judge issued a preliminary injunction temporarily blocking a decision by the Trump administration to terminate Temporary Protected Status (TPS) for Haitians effective July 2019. Termination would affect an estimated 60,000 Haitians who were permitted to stay in the US following the 2010 earthquake, including the parents of more than 27,000 children born to Haitians in the US under the program. In February 2019, the Trump administration announced that it would extend TPS for Haiti until January 2020.

In April, a second US federal judge issued a separate injunction blocking the administration's plan to end TPS. In an effort to comply with these injunctions, in November the US Department of Homeland Security announced it would extend TPS for Haitians through January 4, 2021.

In 2019, Haiti endorsed the Safe Schools Declaration, an international commitment to protect education during armed conflict.

Honduras

Violent crime is rampant in Honduras. Despite a recent downward trend, the murder rate remains among the highest in the world. Poverty, violence, and insecurity cause significant outflows of migrants and asylum-seekers. Human rights groups reported unjustified lethal force and other excessive use of force by security forces during a police and military crackdown on public protests between March and July. The crackdown left several people dead and many more injured. It was not clear how many of those killed or injured were victims of excessive force by authorities.

Journalists, environmental activists, and lesbian, gay, bisexual, and transgender (LGBT) individuals are vulnerable to violence. Efforts to reform public-security institutions have stalled. Marred by corruption and abuse, the judiciary and police remain largely ineffective. Impunity for crimes and human rights abuses is the norm.

The Mission to Support the Fight against Corruption and Impunity in Honduras (MACCIH), established in 2016 through an agreement between the government and the Organization of American States (OAS), has investigated a small number of cases involving corruption of senior officials. As of September, officials were debating whether to extend MACCIH's mandate, which was set to expire at the end of 2019. In November, the Honduran government and the Secretary General of the Organization of American States (OAS), installed an evaluation board to review the performance of MACCIH, prior to examining whether or not to extend its mandate.

Police Abuse and Corruption

In December 2018, the legislature approved a resolution to extend the mandate of a Special Commission for Police Reform Restructuring, charged with removing active members of the National Police who do not comply with their duties, through January 2022. As of June 2019, almost half of more than 13,500 police officers evaluated by the commission had been removed for acts committed during their tenure as officers. However, the commission has been criticized for its opacity and several of the almost 6,000 dismissed officers have been arrested by police for alleged criminal acts committed after their dismissal. This prompted the government in July to establish an elite police force tasked with monitoring the activities of dismissed police officers after they are purged from the institution.

In February, the National Anti-Corruption Council, an independent civil-society group, accused, before the Special Prosecution Unit Against Impunity for Corruption, former president Porfirio Lobo of misappropriating government funds during his presidency. In May, MACCIH announced that it was investigating Lobo for allegedly laundering drug money for his electoral campaign. Lobo denies the allegations.

In August, media reported that a court sentenced former First Lady Rosa Elena Bonilla, wife of ex-President Lobo, to 58 years in prison on corruption charges. It was the first conviction achieved by MACCIH.

In August, media reported that United States federal prosecutors had released documents implicating Honduran President Juan Orlando Hernández in a drug trafficking and money laundering conspiracy with his brother Juan Antonio Hernández. After a two-week trial in the US, in October, Hernández was convicted of drug conspiracy. He is set to be sentenced in January 2020. President Hernández, who has not been charged, has "categorically denied" the accusations.

Judicial Independence

Judges face interference from the executive branch and others, including private actors with connections to government. In August, the United Nations special rapporteur on the independence of judges and lawyers reported that four justices of the Constitutional Chamber of the Supreme Court were removed by Congress for political reasons and noted the lack of transparency in judicial appointments and lack of public scrutiny in the appointment of high officials.

Crackdown on Protests

Nationwide protests and strikes erupted in April over the approval of regulations to restructure the health and education systems. The regulations were repealed in April, but protests continued. More demonstrations followed over corruption allegations implicating President Hernández.

Local human rights organizations reported that the crackdown between March and July killed at least six people, wounded 80, and included 48 arbitrary detentions. The Office of the High Commissioner for Human Rights in Honduras (OACNUDH) and the Inter-American Commission on Human Rights (IACHR) expressed concern over reports that security forces fired live ammunition into demonstrations.

Freedom of Expression, Association, and Assembly

International press freedom organizations report that journalists continue to be targets of threats and violence, both by individuals and state agents.

The Honduran human rights ombudsman, CONADEH, reported that as of September 2019, 79 journalists had been killed since October 2001, and that 91 percent of those killings remained unpunished.

In March, gunmen in Nacaome killed Valle TV reporter Leonardo Gabriel Hernández in retaliation, police said, for Hernández's work exposing organized criminal groups. Three other journalists had been killed in 2019 as of November.

In May, a new penal code was adopted that maintained the crimes of defamation, libel, and slander, all of which have been used to prosecute journalists for "crimes against honor." In August, Congress announced that it would decriminalize those offenses, allowing only civil suits. As of November, Radio Globo director David Romero remained in prison, serving a 10-year sentence for defamation, according to the Honduran press freedom organization C-Libre. He was originally convicted in 2016, and the Supreme Court upheld the conviction in January.

Because of their vague and broad wording, other provisions of the new penal code could criminalize the lawful exercise of the rights to protest and assembly. This includes the crime of "public disturbances," vaguely defined to include "violence or serious intimidation [that] frightens a population or part of it." The code also uses overly broad language in defining the crimes of "illicit assembly," "demonstrations," and "terrorism." In July 2019, the IACHR and OHCRH expressed concern over these provisions and called for their review. In November, the legislature postponed the entry into force of the penal code, which was planned for November 2019, to May 2020.

Attacks on Lawyers, Human Rights Defenders, and Environmental Activists

The UN special rapporteur on the situation of human rights defenders calls Honduras one of the most dangerous countries in Latin America for human rights defenders.

In February, Salomón Matute and his son Juan Samael Matute, both Tolupan indigenous persons who belonged to the San Francisco Locomapa tribe and the Broad Movement for Dignity and Justice (MADJ), died of gunshot wounds despite "precautionary measures" granted by the IACHR in 2013 to ensure the government protected them.

In October, María Digna Montero, a member of the Honduran Black Fraternal Organization (OFRANEH) and a defender of the indigenous Garifuna land and culture, was shot and killed in her home in Colón by unknown individuals.

In November 2018, a court found seven men guilty of the 2016 murder of environmental and indigenous-rights activist Berta Cáceres. Those convicted included a former chief of security for Desarrollos Energéticos SA (DESA), the company building the Agua Zarca dam, against which Cáceres had been campaigning at the time of her assassination.

Local activists have criticized the official Mechanism for the Protection of Journalists, Human Rights Defenders and Operators of Justice, created in 2015, for lacking uniform criteria in awarding protection measures and for being ineffective.

Sexual Orientation and Gender Identity

Violence based on gender identity or sexual orientation is widespread in Honduras. Several United Nations agencies working in Honduras have noted that violence against LGBT individuals forces them into "internal displacement" or to flee in search of international protection. The Honduras government keeps no data on killings based on sexual orientation or gender identity, but the Lesbian Network Cattrachas reported that between January and August 2019, at least 26 LGBT people had been killed. In one case documented by Human Rights Watch in June 2019, a transgender woman was killed and mutilated near San Pedro Sula in an apparent hate crime.

HUMAN
RIGHTS
WATCH
LIFE OR DEATH CHOICES FOR
WOMEN LIVING UNDER HONDURAS'
ABORTION BAN
Women Tell Their Stories

In March, a new adoption law that prohibits same-sex couples from adopting children went into effect.

Women's Sexual and Reproductive Rights

Abortion is illegal in Honduras in all circumstances, including rape and incest, when a woman's life is in danger, and when the fetus will not survive outside the womb. Under the new criminal code, women and girls who terminate pregnancies can face prison sentences of up to six years. The law also sanctions abortion providers.

The government also bans emergency contraception, or the "morning after pill," which can prevent pregnancy after rape, unprotected sex, or a conceptive failure.

Children's Rights

In 2017, the Honduran Congress unanimously passed a bill making all child marriage of those below the age of 18 illegal. The new bill replaces legislation that previously allowed girls to marry at 16 with permission from family. UNICEF reports that a third of all Honduran girls marry before 18.

CONADEH's Internal Displacement Unit reports that the forced recruitment of children by gangs or criminal groups is the fifth most frequent reason that Hondurans became internally displaced in the first semester of 2019. UNICEF has reported that no reliable statistics exist concerning how many children have been recruited into these groups.

Prison Conditions

Inhumane conditions, including overcrowding, inadequate nutrition, and poor sanitation are endemic in Honduran prisons. A December 2018 study by the National Committee on the Prevention of Torture, Cruel, Inhuman or Degrading Treatment, an official body, reported that the country's prisons held 21,004 inmates, a figure double that of a decade earlier.

Migrants and Refugees

In January, a new migrant caravan started forming in San Pedro Sula, heading toward Mexico and the United States. Media reported that Honduran authorities obstructed and in some cases barred Hondurans from leaving the country by demanding identity documents, establishing checkpoints and blockades, and even teargassing the caravan. The IACHR expressed concern over the use of violence and other measures to prevent people from leaving the country, and urged Honduras to guarantee the migrants' rights, including the right to leave any country.

In September, Honduras and the US signed an "asylum cooperation agreement" that requires Honduras to receive asylum-seekers who are referred by the US. Under the agreement, Honduras cannot return or remove the migrants until their asylum cases are resolved by the US federal authorities.

Key International Actors

In March, the US State Department confirmed that it was halting aid to Guatemala, Honduras, and El Salvador, after President Donald Trump criticized Northern Triangle countries for their alleged lack of action in stopping the northbound caravans. In June, the US announced it was restoring some aid, but would halt new funding if countries failed to reduce migration to the United States. In October, the US announced the partial restoration of previously frozen foreign aid to Honduras, as well as to El Salvador and Guatemala, after all three countries entered into asylum cooperation agreements with the US.

In April, the IACHR brought a case against Honduras before the Inter-American Court of Human Rights concerning the extrajudicial execution of a transsexual woman and human rights defender in 2009, while a curfew was in force. The IACHR determined that the killing was prompted by prejudice toward her gender identity and expression. The court took into consideration the context of violence and discrimination against LGBT people in Honduras.

In May, the IACHR visited Honduras, as a follow up to its 2018 visit.

The UN special rapporteur on the independence of judges and lawyers visited Honduras in August 2019 and reported that "Honduras needs urgent Government action to strengthen national capacities to fight corruption and reinforce the independence of its judicial system."

In August, the UN Working Group on Business and Human Rights visited Honduras to assess how the government and the business sector discharge their responsibility to prevent, mitigate, and remedy human rights abuses and negative impacts linked to business activity. The preliminary report documents that access to, use, and control over land by businesses is a recurring issue at the roots of many social conflicts.

In October, the IACHR published its report on the human rights situation in Honduras following a visit to the country in 2018. The report identifies institutional and human rights deficiencies, and highlights how lack of access to justice "has led to a structural impunity that perpetuates serious human rights violations."

India

The Bharatiya Janata Party (BJP) won the May 2019 elections with a majority to return Prime Minister Narendra Modi for a second term. The Modi government continued its widespread practice of harassing and sometimes prosecuting outspoken human rights defenders, and journalists for criticizing government officials and policies.

In August, the government revoked the special constitutional status of Jammu and Kashmir and split the province into two separate federally governed territories. Before the announcement, the government deployed additional troops to the province, shut down the internet and phones, and placed thousands of people in preventive detention, prompting international condemnation.

The government failed to properly enforce Supreme Court directives to prevent and investigate mob attacks, often led by BJP supporters, on religious minorities and other vulnerable communities.

In the northeast state of Assam, a citizenship verification project excluded nearly two million people, mostly of Bengali ethnicity, many of them Muslim, putting them at risk of statelessness.

Jammu and Kashmir

On February 14, a suicide attack on a security forces convoy in Pulwama district killed over 40 Indian troops. The Pakistan-based militant group Jaish-e-Mohammad claimed responsibility. It led to military escalation between India and Pakistan. Following the attack, Kashmiri students and businessmen in other parts of India were harassed, beaten, and even forcibly evicted from rented housing and dorms by BJP supporters.

On August 5, before revoking the state's special autonomous status, the government imposed a security lockdown and deployed additional troops. Thousands of Kashmiris were detained without charge, including former chief ministers, political leaders, opposition activists, lawyers, and journalists. The internet and phones were shut down. The government said it was to prevent loss of life, but there were credible, serious allegations of beatings and torture by security forces.

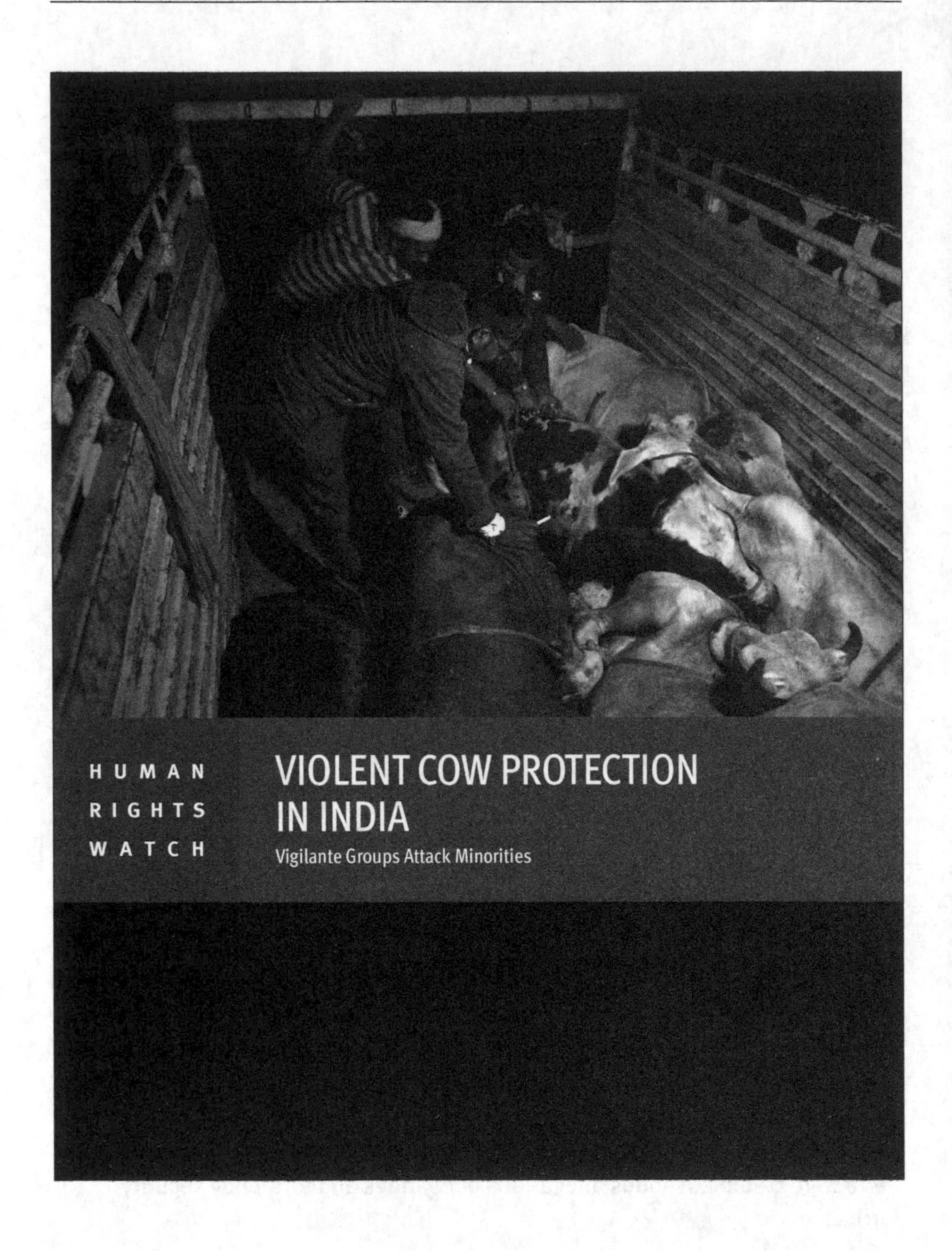
HUMAN
RIGHTS
WATCH
VIOLENT COW PROTECTION
IN INDIA
Vigilante Groups Attack Minorities

By November, even though some restrictions were lifted, hundreds remained in detention and mobile phone services and internet access was still limited. The government blocked opposition politicians, foreign diplomats, and international journalists from independent visits to Kashmir.

Violent protesters at times threatened those that failed to join shutdowns to counter government claims that the situation was normal. At least eight people were killed in attacks by militant groups.

Earlier, in July, the Office of the UN High Commissioner for Human Rights released an update on its 2018 report raising serious concerns about abuses by state security forces and armed groups in both Indian and Pakistani parts of Kashmir and said neither country had taken concrete steps to address concerns that the earlier report raised. The Indian government dismissed the report as a "false and motivated narrative" that ignored "the core issue of cross-border terrorism."

Impunity for Security Forces

Despite numerous independent recommendations, including by United Nations experts, the government did not review or repeal the Armed Forces (Special Powers) Act, which gives soldiers effective immunity from prosecution for serious human rights abuses. The law is in force in Kashmir and in several states in northeast India.

In Uttar Pradesh state, police continued to commit extrajudicial killings with impunity. As of June, at least 77 people had been killed and over 1,100 injured since the BJP state government took office in March 2017. In January, four UN rights experts raised concerns over the killings, and over police threats against those pressing for justice in these cases. A petition seeking a court-monitored independent investigation was pending in the Supreme Court at time of writing.

The killings highlighted continued lack of accountability for police abuses and the failure to enforce police reforms.

Dalits, Tribal Groups, and Religious Minorities

Mob violence against minorities, especially Muslims, by extremist Hindu groups affiliated with the ruling BJP continued throughout the year, amid rumors that they traded or killed cows for beef. Since May 2015, 50 people have been killed and over 250 people injured in such attacks. Muslims were also beaten and forced to chant Hindu slogans. Police failed to properly investigate the crimes, stalled investigations, ignored procedures, and filed criminal cases against witnesses to harass and intimidate them.

Dalits, formerly "Untouchables," faced violent attacks and discrimination. In September, the Supreme Court issued notices to authorities to examine caste-based exclusion at universities across India following a petition filed by mothers of two students—one Dalit and one from a tribal community—who committed suicide allegedly due to discrimination.

Nearly 2 million people from tribal communities and forest-dwellers remained at risk of forced displacement and loss of livelihoods after a February Supreme Court ruling to evict all those whose claims under the Forest Rights Act were rejected. Amid concerns over flaws in the claim process, the court stayed the eviction temporarily. In July, three UN human rights experts urged the government to conduct a transparent and independent review of the rejected claims, and evict only after it exhausted all options, ensuring redress and compensation.

Freedom of Expression and Privacy

Authorities used sedition and criminal defamation laws to stifle peaceful dissent. In October, police in Bihar state filed a case of sedition against 49 people, including well-known movie personalities, for writing an open letter to Prime Minister Narendra Modi expressing concerns over hate crimes and mob violence targeting minority communities. Following widespread condemnation, authorities closed the case within days.

Journalists were harassed, even detained, for their reporting or critical comments on social media, and faced increasing pressure to self-censor. In September, police in Uttar Pradesh filed a criminal case against a journalist for exposing mismanagement of the government's free meal scheme in government schools. In June, police arrested three journalists, accusing them of defaming the Uttar Pradesh state chief minister.

India continued to lead with the largest number of internet shutdowns globally as authorities resorted to blanket shutdowns either to prevent social unrest or to respond to an ongoing law and order problem. By November, there were 85 shutdowns, out of which 55 were in Jammu and Kashmir, according to Software Freedom Law Centre.

In July, the parliament passed amendments to the biometric identification project, Aadhaar Act, paving the way for its use by private parties. The amendments raised concerns over privacy and data protection and were made in the face of a September 2018 Supreme Court ruling restricting the use of Aadhaar for purposes other than to access government benefits and to file taxes.

In December 2018, the government proposed new Information Technology (Intermediary Guidelines) Rules that would greatly undermine rights to freedom of expression and privacy of users.

In October, the social media company WhatsApp, owned by Facebook, confirmed that 121 users in India were targeted by surveillance software owned by NSO, an Israeli firm, out of which at least 22 were human rights activists, journalists, academics, and civil rights lawyers. The government denied purchasing the software.

Civil Society and Freedom of Association

Authorities used the Foreign Contribution (Regulation) Act (FCRA) to harass outspoken rights groups and restrict their ability to obtain foreign funding. In June, authorities filed a criminal case against Lawyers Collective—a group that provides legal aid, advocates for the rights of marginalized groups, and campaigns to end discrimination against lesbian, gay, bisexual, transsexual, and queer (LGBTQ) people. In November, authorities sought the court's permission to arrest the organization's founders for custodial interrogation despite their cooperation in the investigation.

Nine prominent human rights activists, imprisoned in 2018 under a key counterterrorism law, the Unlawful Activities (Prevention) Act (UAPA), remained in jail, accused of being members of a banned Maoist organization and of inciting violent protests. In the same case, in September, authorities conducted a raid on the home of a Delhi University professor who has been vocal on the rights of persons with disabilities and against caste discrimination.

In August, the federal government passed amendments to the UAPA allowing individuals to be designated as terrorists despite concerns by rights groups over how the law already infringes on due process rights and has been misused to target religious minorities, critics of the government, and social activists. The amendments have been challenged in the Supreme Court as unconstitutional and the case was pending at time of writing.

Refugee and Citizenship Rights

In August, the government in Assam published the National Register of Citizens, aimed at identifying Indian citizens and lawful residents following repeated protests and violence over irregular migration of ethnic Bengalis from Bangladesh. The list excluded nearly two million people, many of them Muslims, including many who have lived in India for years, in some cases their entire lifetimes. There are serious allegations that the verification process was arbitrary and discriminatory, although those excluded from the list have the right to judicial appeal.

The Assam state government said it will build ten detention centers for those denied citizenship after appeal. In September, India's home minister declared that the National Register of Citizens will be implemented across the country and that the government will amend the citizenship laws to include all irregular migrants from neighboring countries apart from Muslims.

In 2019, the government deported eight Rohingya Muslims to Myanmar, a family of five members in January and a father and his two children in March, after deporting seven people in October 2018. In April, five UN human rights experts condemned the deportations saying they violated international law. They also raised concerns over indefinite detention of some Rohingya in India.

Women's Rights

High profile rape cases during the year, including against a BJP leader, highlighted how women seeking justice face significant barriers, including police refusal to register cases, victim blaming, intimidation and violence, and lack of witness protection. The accused leader was arrested in September after widespread condemnation, including on social media.

In April, a sexual harassment complaint against the sitting chief justice of the Supreme Court illustrated similar challenges. Other women who complained against powerful men also became vulnerable to criminal defamation cases.

Children's Rights

In August, the parliament amended the Protection of Children from Sexual Offences Act 2012, introducing the capital punishment for aggravated penetrative sexual assault of anyone under 18 years, and increased the penalty for other sexual offenses. This was despite concerns raised by child rights groups that it could lead to a decrease in police complaints because in nearly 95 percent of reported cases, the perpetrator is known to the victim, in positions of authority, or family members.

In November, following a petition by child rights activists, the Supreme Court sought a detailed report from the juvenile justice committee of the Jammu and Kashmir High Court on the alleged detention of children and other abuses during the lockdown imposed since August. The committee earlier submitted a police list of 144 detained children, the youngest being 9. Most, police said, were released, after warnings against participating in violent protests.

Disability Rights

Girls and women with disabilities continue to be at a heightened risk of abuse and face serious barriers in the justice system, despite legal provisions to safeguard their rights.

Thousands of people with psychosocial or intellectual disabilities languish in residential institutions, where they face overcrowding, lack of hygiene, and physical, verbal, and even sexual violence. Some people with psychosocial disabilities are even shackled—chained or locked up in small confined spaces—due to stigma associated with mental health conditions and lack of appropriate community-based support services.

Sexual Orientation and Gender Identity

The parliament passed the Transgender Persons (Protection of Rights) Bill. Rights groups criticized the law for failing to provide full protection and recognition to transgender people. The law is unclear on a transgender person's right to self-identify, which India's Supreme Court recognized in a landmark judgment in 2014. Its provisions are also contrary to international standards for legal gender recognition.

Key International Actors

The US Congress held two hearings that largely focused on Kashmir. Several lawmakers criticized India's actions in Kashmir, including political detentions and communications blockade, and raised concerns over other abuses including the citizenship verification process in Assam.

In August, the UN Security Council held a closed meeting on Jammu and Kashmir for the first time in decades. China, which called the meeting at Pakistan's behest, said members were concerned about human rights, and increasing India-Pakistan tensions. US President Donald Trump offered to mediate and resolve the dispute.

In September, the European Union raised the situation in Jammu and Kashmir at the UN Human Rights Council, encouraging India to lift remaining restrictions and to maintain the rights and fundamental freedoms of the affected population. The European Parliament also held a special debate on Kashmir, urging both India and Pakistan to respect their international human rights obligations.

Throughout the year, the UN special procedures issued several statements raising concerns over a slew of issues in India including extrajudicial killings, potential statelessness of millions in Assam, possible eviction of tribal communities and forest-dwellers, and communications blackout in Kashmir. In September, the UN Human Rights High Commissioner Michelle Bachelet expressed concerns over rights violations in Jammu and Kashmir.

Foreign Policy

Relations with Pakistan continued to deteriorate over the year. A militant attack in February targeting a security forces convoy in Kashmir led to retaliatory air strikes. In August, after India's decision to revoke special status for Jammu and Kashmir, Pakistan downgraded its diplomatic relations and expelled the Indian high commissioner. Pakistan, backed by China and several members of the Organization of Islamic Cooperation, also delivered a statement on rights violations in Kashmir at the UN Human Rights Council session in September. Despite a downward spiral in relations, in November, the two countries opened a visa-free border crossing for Indian pilgrims to visit a Sikh shrine in Pakistan.

India did not raise rights protections publicly during bilateral engagement with other neighbors including Bangladesh, Nepal, Sri Lanka, and Afghanistan. In August, India's foreign minister, during his visit to Bangladesh, expressed willingness to provide more assistance to displaced Rohingya in Bangladesh and toward development in Rakhine state in Myanmar. In response to concerns regarding the deportation of nearly 2 million people excluded from the citizenship verification project in Assam, the foreign minister told Bangladesh that it was India's internal matter.

In a sign of growing ties with the United Arab Emirates, Prime Minister Modi was awarded the country's highest civilian honor by the crown prince during his visit in August. India faced questions from a UN body and international rights groups for its alleged role in March 2018 for intercepting and deporting the 32-year-old daughter of the Dubai ruler who was trying to flee what she said were restrictions imposed by her family.

In July, India maintained its past position and abstained from voting at the UN Human Rights Council including on the renewal of the mandate for an independent expert on protecting LGBT people from violence and discrimination.

Indonesia

Indonesian President Joko "Jokowi" Widodo won re-election in April, securing 53 percent of the vote over his rival, Prabowo Subianto. In August, Jokowi announced that Indonesia will build a new national capital in East Kalimantan.

During his first term, Jokowi took only small and tentative steps to advance human rights. Religious and gender minorities continue to face harassment. Authorities arrest and prosecute people under the blasphemy law, and all cases that went to trials resulted in prison terms. Jokowi also did not press for investigation of gross human rights abuses in Indonesia's past.

In August, a racist attack against West Papuan students in Surabaya triggered an uprising in Papua and West Papua provinces. It prompted the Jokowi administration to send more than 6,000 troops to the two provinces. At least 53 people, both Papuans and migrants from other parts of Indonesia, were killed in the ensuing clashes. Indonesian authorities also shut down the internet there.

On September 17, the outgoing parliament passed a bill weakening Indonesia's Corruption Eradication Commission. It also planned to pass a new criminal code, which had provisions that would violate the rights of women, religious minorities, and lesbian, gay, bisexual, and transgender (LGBT) people, as well as freedom of speech and association. The Papua uprising and these rushed legislative amendments triggered the biggest nationwide protests in 20 years against Jokowi's ruling coalition, prompting Jokowi to have parliament delay voting on the draft criminal code and three other bills until 2020.

Freedom of Religion

In 2019, Indonesian authorities put three women on trial for alleged violations of the country's blasphemy law. In March, a Serang court sentenced Aisyah Tusalamah, who has a psychosocial disability, to five months' imprisonment for posting an allegedly blasphemous video. Police detained Suzethe Margareta, who has paranoid schizophrenia, for bringing her dog to a mosque in Bogor in June. In November, a court in South Sulawesi sentenced Eka Trisusanti Toding, an English teacher, to five months jail over her allegedly blasphemous comments on Facebook about Islam. In April, the Supreme Court rejected a Buddhist woman's appeal of a blasphemy verdict in Medan, North Sumatra. Meliana had complained about the decibel level of the call to prayer at a mosque in 2016 and was sentenced to one-and-a-half years in prison.

Ahmad Moshaddeq, 75, the founder of Millah Abraham—a new religion with a back-to-the-land movement—died inside a Jakarta prison in February while serving a five-year prison term for "blasphemy against Islam." More than 7,000 members of his community were forcibly evicted from their farm houses on Kalimantan island in 2016.

The draft criminal code seeks to expand Indonesia's blasphemy law from one to six articles to include offenses such as "persuading someone to be a nonbeliever."

Freedom of Expression and Association

In May, six people died and more than 200 were injured in Jakarta after supporters of Prabowo Subianto, who lost the presidential election, clashed with security forces and set fire to a police dormitory and vehicles. Prabowo initially refused to accept the April election result, filing a petition at the Constitutional Court, but he lost the lawsuit in May.

In September, Surabaya police issued an arrest warrant for Veronica Koman, an Indonesian human rights lawyer, alleging she was "spreading fake news and provoking unrest." Koman has shared videos on her Twitter account of the recent unrest in Papua.

In September, thousands of Indonesian students protested nationwide against the new law weakening the Corruption Eradication Commission and changes included in the draft criminal code. Their seven-point petition also demanded the government prosecute corporations involved in forest fires, stop militarization in West Papua, investigate past gross human rights abuses, and stop criminalizing activists. Two students were killed in Kendari, South East Sulawesi, and hundreds were injured.

In September 27, police arrested documentary filmmaker Dandhy Laksono after he posted a tweet about violence in Jayapura and Wamena, Papua. He was charged with violating the online hate speech law.

Women's and Girls' Rights

In September, parliament revised the 1974 marriage law, raising the minimum age of marriage for girls and boys with parental consent from 16 to 19, but retaining a clause that allows courts to authorize marriages of girls below 19, with no minimum age restriction. Around 14 percent of girls in Indonesia are married before age 18, and 1 percent marry before age 15.

The Jokowi government failed to stop abusive, unscientific "virginity tests" of women who apply to join the military, or to institute measures to curb female genital mutilation, which continues to be used in rites of passage in some areas. Parliament also failed to pass a draft bill on sexual violence.

Papua and West Papua

After video circulated of Indonesian militias racially abusing Papuan students in Surabaya on August 17 amid rumors that students there had damaged an Indonesian flag flying outside their dorm, Papuans demonstrated in at least 30 cities across Indonesia, including Jakarta. Rioting Papuans burned down the local parliament building in Manokwari, and prisons in Sorong, West Papua province, and Jayapura, Papua province.

In Deiyai on August 28, video footage posted on social media shows police shooting live ammunition into a crowd of Papuan protesters inside the Deiyai Regency office. Eight Papuans and one Indonesian soldier were killed, and 39 Papuans were injured. Police arrested 16 men, charging them with rioting.

On September 1, a mob joined by police and soldiers armed with machetes surrounded a Papuan student dorm in Jayapura, after which a Papuan student was stabbed to death and more than 20 were injured.

In total, Indonesian authorities have detained 22 people in Jakarta, Manokwari, Jayapura and Sorong in connection with raising the pro-Papuan independence Morning Star flag or speaking about "West Papua independence" in public.

On September 23-24, at least 43 people were killed in Wamena and more than 1,500 people were evacuated by air to Jayapura. After alleged racial taunts by a teacher, students marched to the local regent office and later burned it down.

Protesters also torched the business area, killing at least 24 settlers from other parts of Indonesia who dominate the economy there.

Sexual Orientation and Gender Identity

Indonesian authorities continued their assault on the basic rights of LGBT people. HIV rates among men who have sex with men (MSM) have increased five-fold since 2007 from 5 to 25 percent, and arbitrary and unlawful police raids on private LGBT gatherings in recent years, often assisted by militant Islamists, have effectively derailed public health outreach efforts to vulnerable populations.

Among the most controversial provisions of the draft criminal code is a provision that would punish extramarital sex by up to one year in jail. While the provision does not specifically mention same-sex conduct, same-sex relationships are not legally recognized in Indonesia and if passed it would effectively criminalize all same-sex conduct.

In March, a gay former policeman filed a lawsuit against the Central Java Police after he was dismissed in December 2018 for allegedly failing to protect the image of police as a force upholding "religious norms, codes of decency, and local values." Two courts rejected his legal challenge.

In November, Medan court in North Sumatra rejected a lawsuit from college students Widiya Hastuti and Yael Sinaga, the editor and publisher of Suara USU, a student newspaper, against North Sumatra University after the administration closed down the publication and dismissed the 17-person newsroom staff following the publication of a lesbian love story in March. Administrators claimed that the story was "promoting homosexuality."

Disability Rights

Despite a 1977 government ban on the practice, people with psychosocial disabilities continue to be shackled by family members, traditional healers, and staff in state institutions, in some cases for years. Due to prevalent stigma and inadequate support services, including mental health care, more than 57,000 Indonesians with psychosocial disabilities (mental health conditions) have been chained or locked in a confined space at least once in their lives.

"When We Lost the Forest, We Lost Everything"
Oil Palm Plantations and Rights Violations in Indonesia
HUMAN RIGHTS WATCH
Aliansi Masyarakat Adat Nusantara

In 2018-2019, the Indonesian government took important steps to uphold the rights of people with psychosocial disabilities. Several agencies—including the National Human Rights Commission, National Commission for Violence Against Women, National Commission for Child Protection, the Ombudsman, and the Witness and Victims Protection Agency—signed an agreement to monitor places where people with psychosocial disabilities have been shackled or detained. These include traditional faith healing centers, social care institutions, and mental health facilities.

Environmental Rights

In July, forest fires began to ravage Sumatra and Kalimantan islands, many of the fires deliberately lit to clear land for vast oil palm or paper pulp plantations. In late August, the fires burned many areas in 13 provinces; the provinces of Riau, Central Kalimantan, and West Kalimantan suffered the worst levels of air pollution. The Air Quality Index in some of those 13 provinces reached the maximum 500 level, affecting millions of people with respiratory problems (levels above 300 are so hazardous that everyone can experience effects). The police has charged five corporations and 218 individuals involved in the fires.

Consortium for Agrarian Reform, an Indonesian nongovernmental organization, documented more than 650 land-related conflicts affecting over 650,000 households in 2017, and about 410 conflicts affecting 87,568 households in 2018.

Indigenous People Rights

A patchwork of weak laws, poor government oversight, and failure of oil palm plantation and paper pulp companies to fulfill their human rights responsibilities have also affected Indigenous peoples' rights to their forests, livelihood, food, water, and culture, including in two cases documented in detail by Human Rights Watch in 2019.

In 2004, West Kalimantan, Iban villagers were pushed off their land by an oil palm company, PT Ledo Lestari, when bulldozers and other equipment rolled in to raze their land. A decade later, PT Ledo Lestari signed agreements with some families to relocate their homes a few kilometers into the plantation but did not provide any compensation for the loss of their indigenous forest and livelihoods derived from it. Their community is now located within the company's oil palm plantation, leaving them no land to grow food and sustain their livelihood. The forest has been largely destroyed, including plants they use for food and materials used to make mats and baskets they sell to supplement household revenue.

In Jambi, Sumatra, the company PT Sari Aditya Loka 1 did not adequately consult with an indigenous group, the Orang Rimba, who were forced off their land, and did not mitigate the harm after earlier legal reforms had introduced clear obligations to do so. The company has to date not organized any meaningful consultations nor reached agreement to provide remedies to the Orang Rimba displaced from their forests. Many Orang Rimba are now homeless, living in plastic tents without livelihood support, and in abject poverty.

Key International Actors

In January, Indonesia began its two-year term on the United Nations Security Council, choosing peacekeeping as the theme of its May presidency but mostly abstaining on sensitive issues, including the ongoing humanitarian and human rights crisis in Venezuela.

At the UN Human Rights Council in Geneva, and in the UN General Assembly's Third Committee in New York, Indonesia was among the Muslim-majority countries that did not sign a statement supporting China's policies in Xinjiang that ignored widespread repression of the region's Muslims. The Xinjiang issue has been a key test of whether members of the Organization of Islamic Conference (OIC), including Indonesia, will press an increasingly powerful China to end its systemic abuses against Muslims. The 57-country OIC has largely remained silent.

At time of writing, the Indonesian government had not set dates for a visit to Papua and West Papua by the UN high commissioner for human rights, despite President Jokowi's 2018 invitation to the commissioner. In August, the Pacific Islands Forum, a regional group, "strongly encouraged" Indonesia to finalize terms of the visit. In September, the high commissioner, Michelle Bachelet, noted she was "disturbed by escalating violence in the past two weeks in the Indonesian provinces of Papua and West Papua, and especially the deaths of some protestors and security forces personnel."

In August, Australia and Indonesia signed a free trade agreement. Prime Minister Scott Morrison witnessed the signing along with President Jokowi in Jakarta. Both countries are among the world's top 20 economies but not among each other's top 10 trading partners.

On June 23, leaders of the Association of Southeast Asian Nations (ASEAN), including Jokowi, met in Bangkok, but did not call on Myanmar to provide a path to citizenship for Rohingya Muslims, including some 730,000 who fled Rakhine State to escape an ethnic cleansing campaign organized by Myanmar's military in 2017 and who now live in Bangladesh or are seeking refuge in other ASEAN countries.

The European Union-Indonesia human rights dialogue took place in November in Brussels; the European Union raised concerns on some provisions in the draft criminal code, including the death penalty.

Iran

In 2019, Iran's judiciary dramatically increased the cost of peaceful dissent, sentencing dozens of human rights defenders to decades-long prison sentences. Repressive domestic security agencies, in particular the Islamic Revolutionary Guard Corps' (IRGC) Intelligence Organization, continue to suppress civil society activists, such as detained environmentalists, including through reported abuse and torture in detention. As broad United States sanctions impact the country's economy and Iranians' access to essential medicines, authorities maintain a tight grip over peaceful assembly, particularly labor-related protests.

Right to Peaceful Assembly and Free Expression

Iranian authorities brutally repressed nationwide protests that erupted after the increase of fuel prices on November 25. Video footage and eyewitness accounts that emerged after a near total government shutdown of the internet in the country show security forces directly targeting protesters who posed no threat to life. According to Amnesty International, as of December 4, at least 208 people had reportedly been killed in the protests, and a member of the parliament estimated that security forces had arrested about 7,000 people. As of December 4, the government has refused to announce the total number of deaths, and detainees remained at great risk of mistreatment.

Iran's judiciary and security agencies continue to use vaguely defined provisions in the penal code to arrest and prosecute activists for peaceful assembly and free expression.

On January 20, authorities arrested Ismael Bakhshi, a prominent labor activist, and Sepideh Gholian, a journalist and labor activist, after they alleged that they had been tortured when they were detained in the aftermath of sugarcane factory labor protests in November 2018. On September 7, rights groups reported that branch 26 of Tehran's revolutionary court had sentenced Bakhshi and Gholian to 14 years and 19 years and 6 months respectively for their peaceful activism. The court also sentenced Amir Amirgholi, Sanaz Allahyari, Asal Mohammadi, and Amir Hossein Mohammadifar, members of the editorial board of a labor-related online forum called Gam, who have also been detained since January, to 18 years each in prison on similar charges. If the verdicts are upheld, each of the six labor rights defenders will have to serve at least seven years of their prison sentence. In October, authorities temporarily released the labor activists until the court of appeal issues a verdict in their case.

On May 1, plainclothes police arrested at least 35 activists who had gathered in front of the Iranian parliament in a peaceful demonstration organized by independent labor organizations. Most were released on bail, but in August branch 28 of Tehran's revolutionary court sentenced Atefeh Rangriz, an activist, and Marizeh Amiri, a journalist, both of whom have been detained since May, to 11 years and 6 months in prison with 74 lashes and 10 years and 6 months in prison with 148 lashes, respectively. If the sentences are upheld, Rangriz and Amiri must serve at least seven-and-a-half and six years of their sentences in prison, respectively. In October, authorities released Rangiz and Amir temporarily until the court of appeal issues a verdict in their case.

On August 24, a lawyer reported that branch 15 of Tehran's revolutionary court had sentenced Kioomars Marzban, a 26-year-old satirist, to 23 years in prison on charges including "cooperating with an enemy state." Marzan has also been convicted of insulting authorities and sacred beliefs. If his sentence is upheld, he will serve 11 years.

In August, authorities also arrested at least 16 activists in Tehran and Mashhad who had called for resignation of Ayatollah Khamenei, Iran's supreme leader, in an open letter.

Death Penalty and Inhumane Punishment

According to rights groups, Iran had executed at least 227 people as of November 1, compared to 253 in 2017.

The decrease in the total number of executions over the past two years is largely due to a 2017 amendment to Iran's drug law that increased the requirements for imposing the death penalty for drug-related charges.

The judiciary also executed one person below the age 18 and at least 2 individuals who were sentenced to death for crimes they allegedly committed as children. Under Iran's current penal code, judges can use their discretion not to sentence to death individuals who committed their alleged crime as children.

However, several individuals who were retried under the penal code for crimes they allegedly committed as children have been sentenced to death again.

Iranian law considers acts such as "insulting the prophet," "apostasy," same-sex relations, adultery, and certain non-violent drug-related offenses as crimes punishable by death. The law also prescribes the inhumane punishment of flogging for more than 100 offenses, including the "disrupting public order" charge that has been used to sentence individuals for their participation in peaceful assemblies.

Human Rights Defenders and Civil Society Activists

Scores of human rights advocates, including Narges Mohammadi and Atena Daemi, remain behind bars for their peaceful activism.

On March 11, authorities sentenced Nasrin Sotoudeh, a prominent human rights lawyer, to 33 years in prison and 148 lashes for her peaceful activism, including defending women who protested compulsory hijab laws. On April 23, the court of appeal upheld the sentence. Sotoudeh, who has been detained since June 2018, will have to serve at least 12 years in prison.

Since January 2018, authorities have detained environmentalists Houman Jokar, Sam Rajabi, Taher Ghadirian, Morad Tahbaz, Amirhossein Khaleghi, Sepideh Kashani, Niloufar Bayani and Abdolreza Kouhpayeh, all members of a local biodiversity conservation group, on accusations of espionage. Another environmentalist arrested at the time, Kavous Seyed Emami, a Canadian-Iranian professor and environmentalist, died in detention in February 2018.

While Iranian authorities claimed that he committed suicide, they have not conducted an impartial investigation into his death and placed a travel ban on his wife, Maryam Mombeini, until October. During a trial session in February 2019, Niloufar Bayani stated in the courtroom that the detained environmentalists faced psychological torture and were coerced into making false confessions. Authorities have not publicly provided any evidence concerning any of the detained environmentalists' alleged crimes, while several senior Iranian government officials have said that they did not find any evidence to suggest that the detained activists are spies.

Due Process Rights and Fair Trial Standards

On March 7, Iranian leader Ayatollah Ali Khamenei appointed Ebrahim Raeesi, who served on a four-person committee that ordered the execution of several thousand political prisoners in 1988, to lead Iran's judicial branch. Iranian courts, and particularly the revolutionary courts, regularly fall far short of providing fair trials and use confessions likely obtained under torture as evidence in court. Authorities routinely restrict detainees' access to legal counsel, particularly during the investigation period.

Several individuals charged with national security crimes, as well as human rights defenders Arash Sadeghi and Saeed Shirzad, suffered from a lack of adequate access to medical care in detention.

The IRGC's Intelligence Organization continues to arrest Iranian dual and foreign nationals on vague charges such as "cooperating with a hostile state." At least a dozen of these individuals remain behind bars, deprived of due process, and are routinely subjected to pro-government media smear campaigns.

Women's Rights, Sexual Orientation, and Gender Identity

Iranian women face discrimination in personal status matters related to marriage, divorce, inheritance, and child custody. A married woman may not obtain a passport or travel outside the country without the written permission of her husband. Under the civil code, a husband is accorded the right to choose the place of living and can prevent his wife from having certain occupations if he deems them against "family values."

Iranian women, unlike men, cannot pass on their nationality to their foreign-born spouses or their children. However, after more than a decade of women's rights activism, on October 2, the Guardian Council, a body of 12 Islamic jurists, finally approved an amended law that the Iranian parliament had passed on March 13, that now allows Iranian women married to men with foreign nationality to request Iranian citizenship for their children under age 18. A child who has already turned 18 could directly request Iranian citizenship. The law, however, required the Intelligence Ministry and the Intelligence Organization of the Islamic Revolutionary Guard Corps (IRGC) to certify that there is no "security problem" before approving citizenship.

On June 26, the Supreme Court issued a unanimous opinion that obliged the state compensation fund to pay the difference in Diya, a compensation paid to a victim's family, between men and women in cases of death and bodily injuries.

Over the past two years, Iranian courts have handed down harsh sentences to dozens of women who protested compulsory hijab laws in Iran, as well as well-known human rights defenders, including Farhad Meysami and Reza Khandan, Sotoudeh's husband, who supported their efforts.

On July 31, branch 31 of Tehran's revolutionary court sentenced Yasman Ariani, her mother Monireh Arabshahi, and Mojgan Keshavarz, who were all arrested for protesting compulsory hijab laws, to 5 years for "assembly and collusion to act against national security," one year for "propaganda against the state," and 10 years for "encouraging and providing for [moral] corruption and prostitution." The court sentenced Keshavarz to an additional seven-and-a-half years for "insulting the sacred." If these sentences are upheld on appeal, each woman will serve at least 10 years of their sentence.

On August 27, the court sentenced Saba Kordafshari, a 22-year-old woman who was also arrested for protesting compulsory hijab, to 15 years in prison for "encouraging and providing for [moral] corruption and prostitution," seven-and-a-half years for "assembly and collusion to act against national security," and one-and-a-half years for "propaganda against the state." If the sentences are upheld, she will have to serve at least 15 years.

On September 2, Sahar Khodayari, a 29-year-old woman who was arrested in March when she tried to enter a stadium to watch a football game, set herself on fire in front of the court after she was threatened with a six-month imprisonment. Khodayari was reportedly charged with "wearing improper hijab" and "confrontation with the police." Her death sparked domestic and international outcry with activists as well as football players calling on the International Football Federation (FIFA) to pressure Iran to overturn the ban against women attending stadiums. On October 10, Iranian authorities allowed a limited number of seats for women—around 3,000 out of 85,000 in the stadium—for an international football match. Despite this important advance, the general ban on women attending Iran's national league games remains.

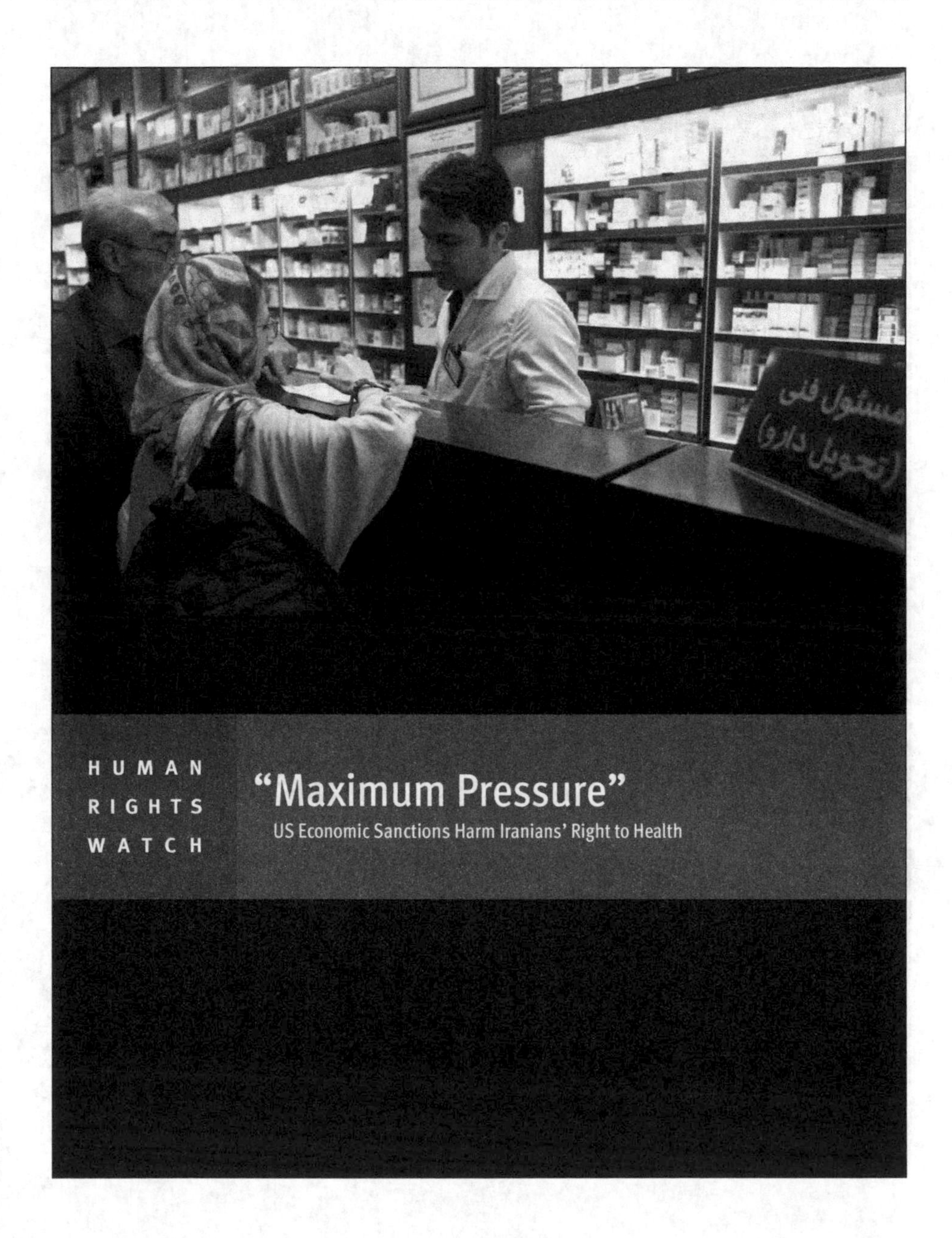
HUMAN
RIGHTS
WATCH
"Maximum Pressure"
US Economic Sanctions Harm Iranians' Right to Health

"Just Like Other Kids"
Lack of Access to Inclusive Quality Education for Children with Disabilities in Iran
HUMAN RIGHTS WATCH
Center for HUMAN RIGHTS in Iran

Iranian law allows girls to marry at 13 and boys at age 15, as well as at younger ages if authorized by a judge. Efforts by a number of parliamentarians to increase the minimum age of marriage have been blocked by the judicial parliamentary commission.

Iranian law vaguely defines what constitutes acts against morality, and authorities have long prosecuted hundreds of people for such acts, as well as for consensual extramarital sex.

Under Iranian law, same-sex conduct is punishable by flogging and, for men, the death penalty. Although Iran permits and subsidizes sex reassignment surgery for transgender people, no law prohibits discrimination against them.

Treatment of Minorities

Iranian law denies freedom of religion to Baha'is and discriminates against them. Authorities continue to arrest and prosecute members of the Baha'i faith on vague national security charges, and close down or suspend licenses for businesses owned by them. Iranian authorities also systematically refuse to allow Baha'is to register at public universities because of their faith.

The government also discriminates against other religious minorities, including Sunni Muslims, and restricts cultural and political activities among the country's Azeri, Kurdish, Arab, and Baluch ethnic minorities.

Disability Rights

People with disabilities face stigma, discrimination, and lack of accessibility when accessing social services, healthcare, and public transportation and may receive medical treatment, including electroshock therapy, without their informed consent. Local and national authorities have taken insufficient steps to address the situation.

During the 2018-2019 school year, only 150,000 out of an estimated 1.5 million children with disabilities of school age were enrolled in school, based on government figures, and more than half of them in special schools that segregated them from other students. Estimates put the total number of school-age children with disabilities in Iran at 1.5 million. One serious problem is a mandatory government medical test that deems some children with disabilities "uneducable" and excluded them from education all together. Other barriers include physical inaccessibility of school buildings, discriminatory attitudes of school staff, and lack of adequate training for teachers and school administrators in inclusive education methods.

Key International Actors

The United States has increasingly targeted Iran with broad economic sanctions. While the US government has built exemptions for humanitarian imports into its sanction regime, banking restrictions have drastically constrained the ability of Iranian entities to finance such humanitarian imports, including vital medicines and medical equipment, causing serious hardships for ordinary Iranians.

In February, European Union foreign ministers adopted conclusions reaffirming support for and commitment to the Joint Comprehensive Plan of Action over Iran's nuclear activities, and expressing concerns about the human rights situation in Iran. In April, the EU renewed for one year its targeted sanctions responding to human rights violations in Iran, which are in place since 2011.

In March and in September, the European Parliament adopted resolutions on the human rights situation in Iran, focusing on human rights defenders, women's rights, and the situation of dual nationals in Iran. The resolutions called for the release of arbitrarily detained activists, as well as an amendment to article 48 of the country's Criminal Procedure Law to ensure that all defendants have the right to be represented by a lawyer of their choice and to a fair trial.

Iraq

Security forces met protests in Baghdad and cities in southern Iraq in October and November with excessive force, killing hundreds. Other violations of freedom of assembly and expression and women's rights persisted, along with the right to water, health, and a healthy environment, and the government continued to use the death penalty extensively.

In response to the protests, Prime Minister Adil Abd Al-Mahdi resigned from office on November 29.

Excessive Force Against Protesters

Clashes with security forces left at least 350 protesters dead in protests in Baghdad and Iraq's southern cities from early October to December. In addition to live ammunition, in Baghdad security forces fired teargas cartridges, in some cases directly at protesters, killing at least 16. Security forces also used live ammunition in other cities.

Authorities arbitrarily detained protesters and released them later without charge, and others went missing. Security forces arrested some Iraqis simply for expressing support for the movement with Facebook messages.

Security forces threatened and fired at medics treating protesters.

The government repeatedly throttled the internet to prevent people from uploading and sharing photos and videos of the protests, and blocked messaging apps.

Justice for Worst ISIS Abuses

During 2019, the extremist group ISIS continued to carried out attacks, mostly killings of community leaders and targeting security forces. Some of the crimes perpetrated by ISIS since 2014 amounted to war crimes and may have amounted to crimes against humanity and genocide. Iraq failed to make war crimes and crimes against humanity specific offenses under Iraqi law.

A 2017 UN Security Council resolution created a UN investigative team to document serious crimes committed by ISIS in Iraq. In 2019, UNITAD assisted Iraqi au-

HUMAN
RIGHTS
WATCH
"Everyone Must Confess"
Abuses against Children Suspected of ISIS Affiliation in Iraq

thorities in exhuming at least 14 mass grave sites left by ISIS in Sinjar, as a first step towards gathering evidence and building cases against ISIS suspects.

An Iraqi law from 2009 created commissions to compensate Iraqis affected by terrorism, military operations, and military errors. Compensation commissions in areas that fell under ISIS control have received thousands of compensation requests but have not paid out many claims since 2014.

German judicial authorities continued efforts to investigate ISIS crimes in Syria and Iraq under the international law principle of universal jurisdiction.

Member states of the Global Coalition to Defeat ISIS continued discussions on accountability options for ISIS crimes, including the possibility of establishing a criminal tribunal in the region.

Arbitrary Detention, Due Process, and Fair Trial Violations

Iraqi forces arbitrarily detained ISIS suspects, many for months. According to witnesses and family members, security forces regularly detained suspects without any court order or arrest warrant, and often did not provide a reason for the arrest.

Authorities systematically violated the due process rights of ISIS suspects and other detainees, such as guarantees in Iraqi law that detainees see a judge within 24 hours, have access to a lawyer throughout interrogations, and have their families notified and able to communicate with them.

The counterterrorism court in Nineveh represents an exception, where Human Rights Watch observed improvements to trial proceedings in 2019. Judges at the court required a higher evidentiary standard to detain and prosecute suspects, minimizing the court's reliance on confessions alone, erroneous wanted lists, and unsubstantiated allegations.

Authorities prosecuted child suspects as young as 9 with ISIS affiliation in Baghdad-controlled areas and 11 in the Kurdistan region, younger than the minimum age of criminal responsibility under international law, and in violation of international standards that recognize children recruited by armed groups primarily as victims who should be rehabilitated and reintegrated into society.

Iraqi judges prosecuted ISIS suspects with the charge of ISIS affiliation, on the overbroad charge of Iraqi counterterrorism legislation. Trials were generally rushed, based on a defendant's confession, and did not involve victim participation. The Iraqi government and Kurdistan Regional Government (KRG) conducted thousands of trials of ISIS suspects without a strategy to prioritize the worst abuses.

Despite requests, the government failed to disclose which security and military structures have a legal mandate to detain people, and in which facilities.

Torture and Other Forms of Ill-Treatment

Throughout 2019 Human Rights Watch received reports of widespread use of torture, including of children, by Iraqi and KRG forces to extract confessions. One man had to have his arm amputated because of arterial damage caused by torture in custody.

A Human Rights Watch study of appeals court decisions in terrorism-related cases showed that in close to two dozen cases in 2018 and 2019 judges appeared to ignore torture allegations or to rely on uncorroborated confessions. Some of the torture allegations had been substantiated by forensic medical exams, and some of the confessions were apparently extracted by force. In each of these cases, the trial courts took the torture allegations seriously, found them credible, assessed the evidence, and acquitted the defendants. Despite this, on appeal, the Federal Court of Cassation appeared to ignore torture allegations or to rely on uncorroborated confessions and ordered a retrial.

Despite extensive evidence of torture in detention in Iraq, in 2019 the Syrian Democratic Forces (SDF) in northeast Syria transferred at least 900 Iraqi detainees with alleged links to ISIS to Iraq. In addition, US-led coalition and SDF forces transferred at least 47 non-Iraqi foreign males suspected of ISIS affiliation to Iraq for investigation in 2018 and early 2019, including at least 11 French nationals who have been sentenced to death. In at least 30 of the cases, US forces facilitated the transfer from SDF to Iraqi custody according to court documents, testimony from defendants, and other sources.

Two of the French citizens transferred from northeast Syria to Iraq and prosecuted in Baghdad for ISIS affiliation told the judge that Iraqi security forces tortured or coerced them into making a confession.

Authorities detained criminal suspects in overcrowded and in some cases inhumane conditions. A source within the penitentiary system shared with Human Rights Watch photos of overcrowded prison cells in Nineveh holding women and children on charges of ISIS affiliation in conditions so degrading that they amounted to ill-treatment.

Despite commitments by then-Prime Minister Haidar Abadi in September 2017 to investigate allegations of torture and extrajudicial killings, authorities apparently took no steps in 2019 to investigate these abuses.

Collective Punishment

Iraqi families perceived to have ISIS affiliation, usually because of family name, tribal affiliation, or area of origin, were often denied security clearances required to obtain identity cards and all other civil documentation. This restricted their freedom of movement, right to education, and right to work, as well as access to welfare benefits and birth and death certificates needed to inherit property or remarry. Denial of security clearances also blocked such families from making claims to the commissions established in 2009 to compensate Iraqis affected by terrorism, military operations, and military errors, and from bringing court cases or challenging seizure of property by security forces or local families.

Some families were able to obtain security clearance if they were willing to first appear before a judge to open a criminal complaint against their relative who was suspected of having joined ISIS in a process known as *tabriya*. After individuals opened the criminal complaint, the court issued them a document to present to security forces to obtain their security clearance. This mechanism was particularly effective in Anbar governorate, where most families with relatives suspected of ISIS affiliation that Human Rights Watch interviewed in 2019 had been able to obtain security clearance by through *tabriya*.

Forced returns and blocked returns of displaced persons persisted throughout 2019. In early July security forces launched screenings across camps for displaced people in Nineveh to determine their origins and possible links to ISIS.

HUMAN
RIGHTS
WATCH
BASRA IS THIRSTY
Iraq's Failure to Manage the Water Crisis

Over the next two months, authorities in Nineveh and Salah al-Din evicted hundreds of displaced people in camps outside of their governorate of origin, in some cases transporting them to their home communities despite families' serious security concerns.

At least 30,000 Iraqis who fled Iraq between 2014 and 2017, including some who followed ISIS as it retreated from Iraqi territory, were housed in and around al-Hol camp in northeast Syria. In 2019 the Iraqi government prepared to bring its nationals back and confine them in de facto detention camps because of perceived links to ISIS. The government discussed broader plans to detain families with perceived ISIS affiliation in a mass internment scheme but has yet to agree on such a plan.

In 2019, thousands of children without civil documentation because a relative was thought to have joined ISIS were prevented from enrolling in state schools, including schools inside camps for displaced people.

Lawyers and aid workers providing assistance to families with perceived ISIS affiliation reported that security forces threatened and in some instances detained them for providing these services.

Access to Water

For almost the past 30 years, authorities failed to provide people in southern Iraq, and particularly in Basra, with safe drinking water. Multiple government failures since the 1980s, including poor management of upstream sources, inadequate regulation of pollution and sewage, and chronic neglect and mismanagement of water infrastructure caused the quality of waterways to deteriorate. The shortages led to farmers' irrigation of land with polluted and saline water, degrading the soil and killing crops and livestock.

The degradation of Basra's water sources became a full-blown crisis in the summer of 2018, when at least 118,000 people were hospitalized due to symptoms doctors identified as related to water quality. Because of high rainfall and snowmelt in late 2018/early 2019, the health crisis did not recur in 2019, but authorities took no significant steps to address the causes of the health crisis. Authorities failed to make public any investigation into its specific causes or any action plan to deal with the roots of the crisis. This lack of action is particularly concerning given projected increases and lower rainfall due to climate change.

Women's Rights, Gender Identity, Sexual Orientation, Morality Laws

Human Rights Watch and other organizations documented a system of organized rape, sexual slavery, and forced marriage by ISIS forces of Yezidi women and girls from 2014 to 2017. However, no ISIS member in Iraq has been prosecuted or convicted for those specific crimes.

While the Kurdistan Region of Iraq has a 2011 law on domestic violence, women have few legal protections to shield them from domestic violence in Baghdad-controlled territory. Efforts in parliament to pass a draft law against domestic violence stalled throughout 2019. Iraq's criminal code, applicable in both Baghdad-controlled territory and the Kurdistan Region of Iraq, criminalizes physical assault but lacks any explicit mention of domestic violence. Instead, article 41(1) provides that a husband has a legal right to punish his wife, and parents can discipline their children within limits prescribed by law or custom and the penal code also provides for mitigated sentences for violent acts including murder for so-called "honorable motives" or if catching his wife or female relative in the act of adultery/sex outside of marriage.

While sexual assault is criminalized, article 398 provides that such charges be dropped if the assailant marries the victim. While no recent national studies on domestic violence have been carried out, women's rights organizations reported a high rate of domestic violence

Iraq's criminal code does not prohibit same-sex sexual relations, although article 394 makes it illegal to engage in extra-marital sex. Paragraph 401 of the penal code holds that any person who commits an "immodest act" in public can be put in prison for up to six months, a vague provision that could be used to target sexual and gender minorities, although such cases have not been documented.

Death Penalty

Iraq has long had one of the highest rates of executions in the world, alongside China, Iran, and Saudi Arabia. The judiciary continued to hand down death sentences to many of those convicted of ISIS affiliation under counterterrorism legislation and carried out executions without disclosing official numbers. In August 2019, authorities released Ministry of Justice data that showed 8022 detainees were on death row and the state had executed over 100 between January and August 2019.

In the Kurdistan Region of Iraq, the KRG implemented a de facto moratorium on the death penalty in 2008, banning it "except in very few cases which were considered essential," according to a KRG spokesperson.

The Iraqi criminal code prohibits the use of the death penalty against children.

Key International Actors

The US-led coalition against ISIS, including Australia, Belgium, Canada, Denmark, France, the Netherlands, and the United Kingdom, as well as Iranian and Turkish forces, continued to support Iraqi and KRG troops in military operations against ISIS. The coalition countries rarely made public the parameters or the exact recipients of their assistance in 2019.

Turkey increased its operations in northern Iraq against the armed Kurdistan Workers' Party (PKK). The PKK, an armed group outlawed but active in Turkey, has long maintained a presence in northern Iraq near the Turkish, Iranian, and Syrian borders. After unknown gunmen killed a Turkish diplomat in Erbil in July 2019, Turkey carried out airstrikes. As a result of the killing, the KRG imposed severe movement restrictions on Turkish residents of a camp in its territory who are seen as broadly sympathetic to the PKK.

Israel and Palestine

The Israeli government continued to enforce severe and discriminatory restrictions on Palestinians' human rights; restrict the movement of people and goods into and out of the Gaza Strip; and facilitate the transfer of Israeli citizens to settlements in the occupied West Bank, an illegal practice under international humanitarian law.

Israel's twelve-year closure of Gaza, exacerbated by Egyptian restrictions on its border with Gaza, limits access to educational, economic and other opportunities, medical care, clean water and electricity for the nearly 2 million Palestinians who live there. Eighty percent of Gaza's population depend on humanitarian aid.

Israeli forces stationed on the Israeli side of fences separating Gaza and Israel continued to fire live ammunition at demonstrators inside Gaza who posed no imminent threat to life, pursuant to open-fire orders from senior officials that contravene international human rights standards. According to the Palestinian rights group al-Mezan, Israeli forces killed 34 Palestinians and, according to Gaza's Health Ministry, injured 1,883 with live ammunition during these protests in 2019 as of October 31.

Fighting between Israel and Palestinian armed groups in Gaza involved unlawful attacks and civilian casualties. During a flare-up in early May, Israeli airstrikes killed 25 Palestinians, 13 of whom were civilians killed in strikes that appeared to contain no military objective or caused disproportionate civilian loss in violation of the laws of war, while Palestinian armed groups fired 690 unguided rockets towards Israeli population centers, war crimes, killing four Israeli and two Palestinian civilians.

During the first nine months of 2019, Israeli authorities approved plans for 5,995 housing units in West Bank settlements, excluding East Jerusalem, as compared to 5,618 in all of 2018, according to the Israeli group Peace Now. Israeli cabinet officials in September approved ex-post facto the outpost settlement of Mevo'ot Yericho in the Jordan Valley that had been illegal even under Israeli law, just days after Prime Minister Benjamin Netanyahu vowed to annex the Jordan Valley if re-elected.

Meanwhile, Israeli authorities destroyed 504 Palestinian homes and other structures in 2019 as November 11, the majority for lacking construction permits. Israel makes it nearly impossible for Palestinians to obtain such permits in East Jerusalem or in the 60 percent of the West Bank under its exclusive control (Area C). The demolitions displaced 642 people as of September 16, more than the total number of people displaced in 2018 (472), according to the UN Office of the Coordination of Humanitarian Affairs (OCHA). The Israeli rights group B'Tselem recorded more demolitions of Palestinian homes in East Jerusalem in 2019 than in any other year since at least 2004.

Both the Fatah-dominated Palestinian Authority (PA) in the West Bank and Hamas authorities in Gaza arrested opposition supporters and other critics and tortured some in their custody.

GAZA STRIP

Closure

Israel imposes sweeping restrictions on the movement of people and goods into and out of the Gaza Strip. A general travel ban excludes only what Israel calls "exceptional humanitarian cases," meaning mostly medical patients and their companions, as well as prominent businesspersons who can obtain permits. In the first nine months of 2019, the army denied or failed to respond in a timely manner to 34 percent of permit applications from Palestinians with scheduled medical appointments outside Gaza, according to the World Health Organization (WHO). The rejection or delay rate for applications for those injured in demonstrations along the fences separating Israel and Gaza is 82 percent.

During the first nine months of 2019, an average of about 462 Palestinians exited the Erez crossing into Israel each day, an increase from previous years, but a fraction of the daily average of more than 24,000 in September 2000, according to the Israeli rights group Gisha. Outgoing goods in the same period, mostly destined for the West Bank and Israel, averaged 252 truckloads per month, compared to the monthly average of 1,064 truckloads prior to the June 2007 tightening of the closure.

Families in Gaza on average received 12 hours of electricity a day in the first 10 months of 2019 according to OCHA, nearly doubling the 2018 average, thanks largely to additional fuel purchased by Qatar through Israeli vendors. The continuing shortfall, though, compromises Gaza's water supply and sewage treatment. As of mid-November, 46 percent of "essential" medicines were reported at zero stock at Gaza's Central Drug Store, according to WHO.

Between May and November 2019, Israel responded several times to the launching of rockets or incendiary balloons from Gaza into Israel by restricting access to Gaza's territorial waters for fishermen, closing Israeli crossings to Gaza, blocking the movement of people and goods, and slashing fuel imports to Gaza's power plant for days at a time. These measures amount to collective punishment in violation of international humanitarian law.

Israeli restrictions on the delivery of construction materials to Gaza, ostensibly to prevent their use for military purposes such as building tunnels, and a lack of funding have impeded reconstruction of homes damaged or destroyed during Israeli military operations. Over 12,000 Palestinians who lost their homes during the 2014 fighting between Israel and armed Palestinian groups remain displaced as of April, according to OCHA.

Egypt also restricts the movement of people and goods at its border with Gaza at Rafah. In the first eight months of 2019, an average of 12,026 Palestinians crossed monthly in both directions, a significant increase from previous years, but less than the average of 40,000 in the months before the military coup in Egypt in 2013.

Israeli Actions in Gaza

As of November 11, lethal force by Israeli forces resulted in the killing of 71 and injuring 11,453 Palestinians in Gaza, OCHA reported. An additional 33 were killed and 114 injured, according to al-Mezan, during escalated fighting between November 12 and 14. Many of the killings took place in the context of protests, when Israeli forces fired on people who approached or attempted to cross or damage fences between Gaza and Israel, using live ammunition in situations where lesser measures could have been used, in contravention of the international human rights law standard for policing situations that lethal force be used only as a last resort to prevent an imminent threat to life. The gunfire maimed many people, including 128 between the start of protests in March 2018 and September 2019 whose limbs had to be amputated.

Hamas and Palestinian Armed Groups' Actions in Gaza

Palestinian armed groups in Gaza fired 1,378 rockets towards Israel, as of November 19, according to the Meir Amit Intelligence and Terrorism Information Center.

Attacks by armed groups in Gaza have killed four Israeli civilians and injured more than 123 Israelis. Rockets that fell short killed a pregnant Palestinian mother of nine and a toddler in Gaza.

Hamas authorities continue to provide no information about two Israeli civilians with psychosocial disabilities, Avera Mangistu and Hisham al-Sayed, whom they have apparently held for more than four years after they entered Gaza, in violation of international law.

Hamas authorities held 1,885 Palestinians in detention as of April 23, according to figures it provided Human Rights Watch. Between January 2018 and March 2019, it detained 4,235 people, including 66 for social media posts or for allegedly violating broadly worded offenses such as "harming revolutionary unity" and "misuse of technology" used to punish peaceful dissent or opposition. According to the Palestinian statutory watchdog Independent Commission for Human Rights (ICHR), Hamas authorities detained more than 1,000 Palestinians during March 2019 demonstrations against the high cost of living.

Hamas authorities also said they received 47 complaints of arbitrary arrest and torture during this period, none of which resulted in criminal convictions for the alleged wrongdoer. The ICHR received 138 complaints of arbitrary arrest and 155 complaints of torture and ill-treatment against Hamas security forces, as of September 30.

Hamas authorities have carried out 25 executions since they took control in Gaza in June 2007 following trials that lacked appropriate due-process protections. Courts in Gaza have sentenced 128 people to death since June 2007, according to the nongovernmental Palestinian Center for Human Rights. There were no executions in 2019.

Laws in Gaza punish "unnatural intercourse" of a sexual nature, understood to include same-sex relationships, with up to 10 years in prison.

HUMAN
RIGHTS
WATCH
BORN WITHOUT CIVIL RIGHTS
Israel's Use of Draconian Military Orders to Repress Palestinians in the West Bank

WEST BANK

Israeli Actions in the West Bank

In the West Bank, including East Jerusalem, Israeli security forces killed 23 Palestinians and wounded at least 3,221, including those suspected of attacking Israelis, but also passersby and demonstrators, as of November 11. In many cases, video footage and witness accounts strongly suggest that Israeli forces used excessive force. As of November 11, attacks by Israeli settlers killed two Palestinians, injured 84, and damaged property in 234 incidents, according to OCHA.

Palestinians killed five Israelis and wounded at least 46 in the West Bank, as of September 17, according to OCHA.

Israelis largely failed to hold accountable security forces who used excessive force against Palestinians or settlers who attacked Palestinians and destroyed or damaged their homes and other property.

Settlements, Discriminatory Policies, Home Demolitions

Israel continued to provide security, infrastructure administrative services, housing, education, and medical care for more than 642,867 settlers residing in unlawful settlements in the West Bank, including East Jerusalem.

The difficulty in obtaining Israeli-issued building permits in East Jerusalem and Area C has driven Palestinians to construct housing and business structures that are at constant risk of demolition or confiscation by Israel on the grounds of being unauthorized. The UN considers 46 Palestinian communities at "high risk of forcible transfer." International law prohibits an occupying power from destroying property unless "absolutely necessary" for "military operations." On July 22, Israeli authorities demolished nine "unlicensed" residential buildings and one other structure, containing about 70 apartments, in the Jerusalem neighborhood of Sur Baher, on the stated grounds that they were too close to the separation barrier that Israel constructed, displacing 24 people. At time of writing, Israel had yet to demolish the Palestinian village of Khan al-Ahmar east of Jerusalem, despite a 2018 Supreme Court decision empowering it to do so.

Israeli authorities also continued their practice of demolishing the homes of families in retaliation for attacks on Israelis allegedly carried out by a family member, a violation of the international law prohibition on collective punishment.

Freedom of Movement

Israel maintained onerous restrictions on the movement of Palestinians in the West Bank. OCHA documented 705 permanent obstacles such as checkpoints across the West Bank in July. Israeli-imposed restrictions designed to keep Palestinians far from settlements forced them to take time-consuming detours and restricted their access to their own agricultural land.

The separation barrier, which Israel said it built for security reasons but 85 percent of which falls within the West Bank rather than along the Green Line separating Israeli from Palestinian territory, cuts off many Palestinians from their agricultural lands and isolates 11,000 Palestinians who live on the western side of the barrier but are not allowed to travel to Israel and must cross the barrier to access their own property and other services.

Arbitrary Detention and Detention of Children

As of October 31, according to Prison Services figures, Israeli authorities held 4,731 Palestinians in custody for "security" offenses, including 2,840 convicted prisoners, 1,061 pretrial detainees, and 460 in administrative detention based on secret evidence without charge or trial. Excluding Jerusalem residents, West Bank Palestinians were tried in military courts, including those charged with nonviolent speech or protest activity. Those courts have a near-100 percent conviction rate. Israel incarcerates many West Bank and Gaza Palestinian detainees and prisoners inside Israel, complicating family visits and violating the provisions of international humanitarian law that prohibit their transfer outside the occupied territory.

As of August 31, Israel was detaining 185 Palestinian children, many suspected of criminal offenses under military law, usually stone-throwing. Israel denied Palestinian children arrested and detained in the West Bank legal protections granted to Israeli children, including settlers, such as protections against nighttime arrests and interrogations without a guardian present. Israeli forces frequently used unnecessary force against children during arrest and physically abused them in custody.

Palestinian Authority's Actions in the West Bank

The PA held 1,134 people in detention as of April 21, according to figures it provided Human Rights Watch. Between January 2018 and March 2019, it detained 1,609 persons for insulting "higher authorities" and creating "sectarian strife," charges that in effect criminalize peaceful dissent, and 752 for social media posts. The PA also said it received 346 complaints of arbitrary arrest and mistreatment during this period, of which authorities found wrongdoing in 48 cases. Of these, 28 resulted in warnings or administrative sanctions and 20 were referred for prosecution, with only one conviction: an intelligence officer who received a 10-day sentence for assaulting demonstrators.

The ICHR received 213 complaints of arbitrary arrest, 140 complaints of people held without trial or charge pursuant to orders from a regional governor, and 138 complaints of torture and ill-treatment at the hands of PA security forces, as of September 30. In a meeting with Human Rights Watch in July, PA Prime Minister Mohammad Shtayyeh vowed that "no citizen would be detained for exercising their freedom of expression."

In August, the PA police spokesperson announced a ban on activities by the Palestinian lesbian, gay, bisexual, and transgender (LGBT) group Al-Qaws for Sexual & Gender Diversity in Palestinian society and vowed to prosecute its members. Police subsequently told rights groups that they disavowed the statement but have yet to publicly repudiate it.

The personal status law continues to discriminate against women, including in relation to marriage, divorce, custody, and guardianship of children and inheritance. Palestine has no comprehensive domestic violence law to prevent abuse and protect survivors. In September, authorities charged three family relatives in connection with the killing of 21-year-old Beit Sahour resident- Israa Ghrayeb in August, an apparent act of domestic violence.

ISRAEL

Israel held parliamentary elections in April 2019, but the Knesset dissolved itself in May after parties failed to form a majority-led government. Elections were held again in September, but at time of writing, parties had again not formed a government.

The Israeli Supreme Court is examining constitutional challenges to the Nation State Law adopted in 2018. The law, which has constitutional status, makes it a national priority to build homes for Jews but not others, and revokes the status of Arabic as an official language of Israel.

In November, Israel expelled a Human Rights Watch official, a decision that the Supreme Court upheld, on the asserted ground that the organization's call on businesses to stop operating in West Bank settlements constituted a boycott call and were thereby grounds for deportation under Israeli law. In October, Israeli authorities prevented a Palestinian staff member of Amnesty International from traveling out of the Occupied West Bank for undisclosed "security reasons." In August, Israeli authorities denied entry to US Congresswomen Ilhan Omar and Rashida Tlaib because of their support for boycotts of Israel.

The Israeli government continued the policy described by the Interior Minister at the time of making "miserable" the lives of the roughly 32,000 Eritrean and Sudanese asylum seekers present in the country who refused to depart. The government did so through restrictions on movement, work permits, and access to health care, and confiscation of a portion of their salaries.

Israeli law prohibits discrimination on the basis of sexual orientation and gender identity. However, same-sex marriage is not legal. In July, 23 Israeli couples held a mass wedding to campaign for marriage equality in the country.

Key International Actors

In March, the US recognized Israel's annexation of the Golan Heights, denying the reality of Israeli occupation and protections due the Syrian population there under international humanitarian law. The US has maintained and expanded aid cuts to the West Bank and Gaza, including to USAID projects. In November, the State Department announced that it no longer considers Israeli settlements to violate international humanitarian law "per se", putting the United States outside the international consensus on the issue.

The European Union criticized the demolitions in Sur Baher in Jerusalem in July and Netanyahu's promise in September to annex the Jordan Valley.

In April, the global tourism company Airbnb reversed its November 2018 pledge to remove listings from Israeli settlements in the West Bank from its website, pursuant to a settlement reached to lawsuits in Israel challenging its decision and following actions by several US states to penalize it under anti-boycott laws.

The prosecutor for the International Criminal Court continued her preliminary examination into the situation in Palestine to determine whether the criteria have been met to merit pursuing a formal investigation.

In July, the UN secretary-general reported that Israeli forces had killed 56 Palestinian children and injured 2,733 in 2018, but as in previous years, did not include Israel in his annual "list of shame" for grave violations against children in armed conflict.

The Office of UN High Commissioner for Human Rights had yet to fulfill its mandate, at time of writing, to transmit to the UN Human Rights Council a database of businesses that have enabled or profited from settlements more than two-and-a-half years after its initial scheduled release.

HUMAN
RIGHTS
WATCH
"A Really High Hurdle"
Japan's Abusive Transgender Legal Recognition Process

Japan

Japan is a prosperous liberal democracy with the third largest economy and a vibrant civil society. In July, the ruling Liberal Democratic Party (LDP) won a solid majority in an upper house election. However, the LDP and its allies failed to maintain a two-thirds majority needed to pursue Prime Minister Shinzo Abe's grand political goal of amending Japan's post-war pacifist constitution. In November, Abe became the longest-serving Japanese prime minister.

Japan's long overlooked "hostage" justice system, in which criminal suspects are held for long periods in harsh conditions to coerce a confession, received renewed attention after the high-profile arrest of former Renault and Nissan head Carlos Ghosn in November 2018 for alleged financial misconduct.

Japan has no law prohibiting racial, ethnic, or religious discrimination, or discrimination based on sexual orientation or gender identity. It accepts an extremely small number of refugees each year, mostly from Asia. Japan has no national human rights institutions.

Death Penalty

In December 2018, Japan executed two men on death row for crimes including murder and robbery. In August 2019, two more men were also executed for crimes involving murder and robbery. Anti-death penalty advocates have long raised concerns about death row inmates having inadequate access to legal counsel, being notified of their execution only on the day it takes place, and some being executed after their lawyers filed a request for retrial.

Disability Rights

In April, the Japanese parliament enacted legislation to compensate people forcibly sterilized under the Eugenic Protection Act between 1948 and 1996. Under the law, approximately 25,000 people were sterilized. In May, a district court in Sendai ruled that the plaintiff's constitutional right to pursue happiness, including reproductive rights, had been violated under the now-defunct act. The court, however, rejected compensation sought by the plaintiff, citing the 20-year statute of limitations.

In July, Prime Minister Abe offered the government's first official apology to families who had members who lived with leprosy and had suffered under the government's segregation policy between 1907 and 1996, after the government decided it would not appeal a district court ruling that ordered the state to pay compensation. In November, Japan's House of Councilors (Upper House) approved a law that will enable compensation for affected families.

Women's Rights

Protests erupted across Japan this year after a string of rape cases resulted in acquittals. Japan's rape law requires that prosecutors prove that violence or intimidation was involved, or that the victim was "incapable of resistance." In one case, a court acquitted a father accused of raping his 19-year-old daughter, although the court recognized that the sex was non-consensual and that he had been physically and sexually abusing the victim since she was younger.

Sexual Orientation and Gender Identity

In January, the Supreme Court ruled that the 2004 Gender Identity Disorder Special Cases Act— which requires that transgender people be sterilized to obtain documents reflecting their gender identity—as constitutional. The court stated that there is a "need to avoid abrupt changes in a society where the distinction of men and women have long been based on biological gender." However, the court also said that the law was constitutional only "at this time," and two justices of the four-judge bench recognized the need to reform Japan's law in their concurring opinion.

In February, various same-sex couples in different cities filed lawsuits against the government over the constitutionality of not recognizing same-sex marriage in the first legal challenge of its kind in Japan. In May, supplementary resolutions approved by parliament made it a requirement for the government to include the prevention of Sexual Orientation Gender Identity (SOGI) harassment and outing—exposing someone's LGBT identity without permission—into the upcoming guidelines for corporations dealing with harassment by superiors in the workplace. The draft guidelines the government revealed in October, however, failed to specify SOGI harassment as required by the Diet supplementary resolutions. The guidelines were still under discussion at time of writing.

Children's Rights

In June, Japan's parliament, the Diet, revised laws to ban corporal punishment against children by parents and other guardians. The law also started the review process to create mechanisms to protect children's rights following several fatal cases of abuse in the name of discipline.

Indigenous Rights

In April, the Diet passed a bill which for the first time recognized the Ainu as the indigenous people of Japan, as well as banning discrimination against them.

Refugees

Japan's asylum and refugee determination system remains strongly oriented against granting refugee status. In 2018, the Justice Ministry received 10,493 applications for refugee status, largely by people from Nepal, Sri Lanka, and Cambodia. The ministry recognized 42 people as refugees, while another 40 asylum seekers were classified as needing humanitarian assistance, allowing them to stay in Japan. In October, a group of lawyers submitted a claim to the UN Working Group on Arbitrary Detention against the government immigration detention practices, which do not require the necessity of detention and can stretch for years.

Migrant Workers

As Japan continues to experience a serious labor shortage, in April a revised immigration law went into effect, which allows more than 300,000 foreigners to receive work visas in sectors including farming, fishery, and nursing. Previously, Japan only accepted highly skilled foreign workers; blue-collar foreign workers were typically required to apply for visas as either interns or students.

Separately, the government continued the "Foreign Technical Intern Training Program," which binds workers to their sponsoring employers without the option of changing them, to recruit more foreign workers, many from Southeast Asia. The program has drawn criticism for human rights violations, including payment of sub-minimum wages, illegal overtime, forced return of whistleblowers to their home countries, and dangerous or unhygienic working conditions. In March, the

Justice Ministry said 171 "trainees" died between 2012 and 2017, 17 of them by suicide.

Labor Rights

In June, Japan voted in favor of the International Labour Organization's groundbreaking Convention on Violence and Harassment after parliament enacted legislation in May that requires corporations to implement measures to prevent power harassment as early as April 2020 for large businesses and April 2022 for medium-to-small businesses.

Freedom of Media and Expression

In August, after receiving a flood of complaints and death threats, organizers of a Japanese art exhibition in Aichi prefecture were forced to withdraw an art installation called the "Statue of a Girl of Peace," which symbolizes "comfort women" or women who were forced to work in Japan's World War II-era brothels. Many of the women were Korean. The issue has remained a flashpoint in Japan-Korean bilateral relations. The exhibition re-opened briefly for a few days before it officially ended in October.

Criminal Justice

Japan's long overlooked "hostage" justice system, in which criminal suspects are held for long periods in harsh conditions to coerce a confession, received renewed attention after the high-profile arrest of former Renault and Nissan head Carlos Ghosn in November 2018. While Ghosn was detained for 108 days and then another 21 days for financial misconduct allegations, he was granted bail quickly compared to other equivalent cases, apparently due to the international criticism.

In June, a 2016 law came into force that requires video and audio recording of interrogations to a small segment of criminal cases, such as serious cases to be tried by the lay judge system. However, Japanese criminal procedure law continues to allow suspects to be detained for up to 23 days prior to prosecution without the possibility of release on bail and prohibits lawyers from being present during interrogations.

Foreign Policy

Japan's official policy is to "contribute to the improvement of the world's human rights environment" through methods including the "UN's primary human rights forums and bilateral talks." In March, Japan contradicted this policy by suddenly dropping its long-standing leadership on the annual United Nations Human Rights Council resolution on North Korea.

In recent years, Japan has abstained from almost all Myanmar-related resolutions at UN forums, including those related to atrocities against the Rohingya.

Japan also did not address the collapse of democratic institutions and the sharply deteriorating human rights environment in Cambodia, where Prime Minister Hun Sen cracked down on opposition politicians, independent media, and political activists. Japan took the lead in drafting a weak resolution on Cambodia at the UN Human Rights Council in September.

Jordan

In 2019, protests against the Jordanian government's economic austerity policies increased, including a mass public teachers' protest and one-month strike beginning in September. The teachers demanded a 50 percent pay raise they said the government promised in 2014, but eventually agreed to a 35 to 75 percent raise depending on a teacher's rank. As protests grew, authorities stepped up arrests of political and anti-corruption activists.

In early May, Jordan reshuffled the heads of major security agencies, appointing Maj. Gen. Ahmed Hosni to lead the General Intelligence Department (GID), Jordan's main intelligence agency, and Salameh Hammad as Interior minister.

Jordan hosted over 657,000 Syrian refugees and over 90,000 refugees of other nationalities in 2019, but authorities have not allowed Syrians to enter Jordan to seek asylum since mid-2016 and took steps to prevent others from seeking asylum in 2019. In 2019, Jordanian authorities did not allow aid deliveries from Jordan to tens of thousands of Syrians at a remote camp along the border.

Freedom of Expression

Jordanian law criminalizes speech deemed critical of the king, foreign countries, government officials and institutions, Islam and Christianity, as well as defamatory speech.

Authorities detained over 30 political and anti-corruption activists in 2019 and filed charges against some that violated the right to free expression. Most of those detained were linked to a loose coalition of political activists across the country known as the *hirak* (movement). The charges filed against activists ranged from insulting the king ("lengthening the tongue against the king") to the vague charge of "undermining the political regime" and online slander.

Among the activists detained in 2019 was Sabri al-Masha'leh, a 31-year-old teacher from the town of Dhiban. Authorities arrested him in response to four Facebook posts he wrote in February, only one of which referred to the king by name. Prosecutors charged him with insulting the king, and in April Amman's Court of First Instance sentenced him to two years in prison. The court later reduced the sentence to one year, which al-Masha'leh is serving in Sawaqa Prison, south of Amman.

Authorities detained Ahmed Tabanja, 33, a human rights activist from the northern town of Irbid, on March 17, while he used his phone to broadcast over Facebook Live a protest by unemployed Jordanians in front of the royal court complex in Amman.

In late December 2018, authorities proposed amendments to Jordan's 2015 Electronic Crimes Law that would overly restrict freedom of expression by stipulating criminal penalties for posting "rumors" or "fake news" with "bad intentions" or engaging in "hate speech" online. The amendments maintain criminal penalties for online defamation but, in a positive move, would eliminate pretrial detention for this offense. Jordan's lower house of parliament rejected the draft amendments in February, and as of September they were under consideration in the upper house.

Freedom of Association and Assembly

In 2019, Prime Minister Omar al-Razzaz convened an inter-ministerial committee to overhaul the country's pre-approval process for local and international nongovernmental organizations (NGOs) operating in Jordan to receive funding from foreign sources. Local NGO leaders have long complained that the pre-approval process instituted in 2015 lacks transparency and can take months. In June, Jordan's central bank suddenly mandated that all money transfers from an international NGO's headquarters to its branch in Jordan require government pre-approval, but the government ordered the bank to reverse the decision on July 11.

Under the Public Gatherings Law amended in March 2011, Jordanians did not require government permission to hold public meetings or demonstrations, but organizations and venues continued to seek permission from the Interior Ministry or General Intelligence Department to host public meetings and events. In some cases in 2019, security authorities cancelled public events without explanation.

Refugees and Migrants

By late 2018, over 657,000 people from Syria had sought refuge in Jordan, according to the UN High Commissioner for Refugees (UNHCR). Over 85 percent of Syrians lived outside refugee camps. In 2019, Jordan did not permit Syrians to enter the country to seek asylum.

According to UNHCR, Jordan also hosted asylum seekers and refugees from other countries in 2019, including 67,500 Iraqis, 14,600 Yemenis, 6,100 Sudanese, and 1,700 from other countries. Beginning in January, Jordanian authorities prevented UNHCR from registering as asylum seekers individuals who officially entered the country for the purposes of medical treatment, study, tourism, or work, effectively barring non-Syrians from being recognized as refugees and leaving many without UNHCR documentation or access to services.

In 2019, authorities continued to implement the Jordan Compact, which aimed to improve the livelihoods of Syrian refugees by granting new legal work opportunities and improving the education sector. By August 2019, labor authorities had issued or renewed at least 153,535 work permits for Syrians since 2016. Most professions, however, remained closed to non-Jordanians, and many Syrians continued to work in the informal sector without labor protections.

In August, the Jordan office of the United Nations Relief and Works Agency for Palestine Refugees in the Near East (UNRWA) announced a budget shortfall of $151 million following the cancellation of all US funding to the agency in 2018. UNRWA warned that the funding gap would disrupt vital education, relief, and health services to the over 2 million Palestine refugees living in Jordan.

In 2019, Jordanian authorities did not allow aid deliveries from Jordan to tens of thousands of Syrians at Rukban, an unorganized camp along Jordan's border with Syria. Camp residents have been besieged by Syrian government-aligned forces since 2018 and face limited access to food, water, and medical assistance. In late August, a UN official said that the UN would help facilitate voluntary evacuations of camp residents to other parts of Syria, and that only 12,700 people remained in the camp.

Jordan hosted around 70,000 migrant domestic workers in 2019, mostly from the Philippines, Sri Lanka, and Indonesia. NGOs repeatedly referred domestic workers who had suffered multiple abuses to labor ministry investigators. Abuses included non-payment of wages, unsafe working conditions, long hours, document confiscation, and physical, verbal and sexual abuse.

Women's and Girls' Rights

Jordan's personal status code remains discriminatory, despite a 2010 amendment that widened women's access to divorce and child custody. Marriages between Muslim women and non-Muslim men are not recognized. In 2019, lawmakers rejected a proposed amendment to the personal status law that would have increased the minimum marriage age from 15 to 16, albeit without the exception that children between ages 16 and 18 could marry with court approval.

Article 9 of Jordan's nationality law does not allow Jordanian women married to non-Jordanian spouses to pass on their nationality to their spouse and children. In 2014, authorities issued a cabinet decision purporting to ease restrictions on non-citizen children of Jordanian women access to key economic and social rights, but the easing fell short of expectations. In 2019, as part of an overhaul of the country's labor law, authorities exempted non-citizen children of Jordanian women from work permit requirements, but many professions in Jordan remained closed to non-Jordanians.

Article 98 of Jordan's penal code, amended in 2017, states that the "fit of fury" defense does not apply to perpetrators of crimes "against women" who cannot receive mitigated sentences, but judges continued to impose mitigated sentences under article 99 if family members of victims did not support prosecutions of their male family members. Local media reported in July that 12 women in had been killed by family members in Jordan since the beginning of 2019.

Criminal Justice System

As of November, authorities had not carried out any executions in 2019, but Jordan's National Center for Human Rights (NCHR) reported that there were 151 people on death row by the end of 2018.

In July, security officials expelled over 200 members of the extended al-Shahin family from their home governorate of Madaba on the basis of a local practice known as *jalwa*, under which security authorities can temporary displace family members of accused murderers to deter potential revenge attacks. The abusive practice is a clear violation of Jordan's constitution, and in recent years the Interior Ministry sought to reintroduce the concept into law.

Local governors continued to use provisions of the Crime Prevention Law of 1954 to place individuals in administrative detention for up to one year, in circumvention of the Criminal Procedure Law. The NCHR reported that 37,683 persons were administratively detained in 2018, some for longer than one year, marking an increase of over 2,700 from the number of administrative detainees in 2017.

Key International Actors

Under the terms of a Memorandum of Understanding between the United States and Jordan signed in 2018, the US provided $1.275 billion in aid to Jordan in 2019. The US did not publicly criticize human rights violations in Jordan in 2019, except in annual reports.

The International Criminal Court (ICC) Appeals Chamber ruled on May 6, 2019 that Jordan had failed to meet its international legal obligations to arrest then-President Omar al-Bashir of Sudan, who is sought by the ICC for alleged crimes committed in Darfur, Sudan, during a 2017 visit. But the judges decided not to refer to Jordan's lack of cooperation to the court's assembly of members or the UN Security Council.

Jordan is a member of the Saudi/Emirati-led coalition fighting the Houthi forces in Yemen.

Kazakhstan

A leadership change in Kazakhstan in 2019 did not significantly improve respect for human rights. On March 19, Kazakh President Nursultan Nazarbaev resigned after 30 years in power, naming Senate speaker Kassym-Jomart Tokaev as interim president. In snap elections in June, Tokaev ran as the ruling party candidate and won in a vote marred by irregularities. The authorities responded to widespread peaceful protests around the elections with mass detentions. Kazakhstan continued to unfairly jail rights activist Max Bokaev, and intensified harassment of perceived or actual opposition members. Independent trade unions remained stymied by the government's ongoing failure to reform the 2014 Trade Union Law.

Elections

In snap presidential elections on June 9, Tokaev won with 70 percent of the vote. The Organization for Security and Co-operation in Europe (OSCE) said the vote was marred by "significant irregularities," including ballot stuffing. Thousands took to the street to contest the outcome.

Freedom of Assembly

There was a significant increase in protest activity in Kazakhstan in 2019. In the build-up to elections in June, authorities denied permits for peaceful protests, regularly broke up demonstrations, and detained participants of single-person pickets. One man was detained just for holding up a blank poster.

Between election day on June 9 and June 13, 4,000 people were detained nationwide for protesting the vote. Ryszard Komenda, reginal representative on Central Asia for the Office of the United Nations High Commissioner for Human Rights (OHCHR), called the government's actions "extremely regrettable," and urged it to respect freedom of assembly.

After the elections, President Tokaev signaled that he would relax constraints on freedom of assembly, specifically by reforming the country's restrictive protest law, although no legal changes have so far taken place. While some protests were allowed to go ahead without arrests or other interventions, protests against growing Chinese investment resulted in dozens of arrests, and more than 100 people were detained at demonstrations called for by banned opposition movement Democratic Choice of Kazakhstan in September. Kazakhstan's parliament passed a law in October creating additional legal penalties for parents accused of "involving" their children in protests.

Civil Society

A new youth movement called Wake Up, Kazakhstan was formed to advocate for constitutional reform. Members of the group and other youth activists complained of pressure from the authorities such as threats, limits on foreign travel, and increased surveillance, particularly on protest days. Despite this, the group was able to hold rallies in August and November without intervention.

Serikzhan Bilash, whose activism drew attention to the crackdown in China's Xinjiang region, pleaded guilty to spurious criminal charges of incitement in August. Bilash was banned from civic activism as a condition of his release. In February Bilash was fined $670 for leading a rights group called Atajurt that the authorities had refused to register.

Maks Bokaev, imprisoned for peacefully protesting proposed land code amendments in 2016, continued to serve a wrongful five-year sentence. In September, he was denied a request to be transferred to a prison closer to his home. Mukhtar Dzhakishev, former head of the atomic energy agency Kazatomprom, was denied parole in September despite international calls for his release. He has been serving a 14-year sentence since 2010.

Freedom of Expression

According to Adilsoz, a local media watchdog, there were 54 detentions, arrests, convictions, or limits on the freedom of journalists between January and September. There were eight attacks, including during a press conference in July hosted by a human rights group in which five journalists had equipment damaged or stolen. Radio Azattyq, the Kazakh-language service of Radio Free Europe/Radio Liberty, complained of repeated interference in its work, including attacks with pepper spray.

Telecoms providers stopped requiring users to download a technology that experts worried might allow authorities to sidestep encryption mechanisms and monitor conversations, after President Tokaev abandoned the measure in August.

In August, journalist Yaroslav Golyshkin, who was serving an eight year sentence since 2015 on charges of "blackmail," was pardoned by President Tokaev and released.

Arrest and Harassment of Perceived Opposition Members

Authorities increased harassment of perceived or actual Democratic Choice of Kazakhstan (DVK) supporters after the group was banned in 2018. As of March, at least nine people were convicted of involvement with DVK, several merely for reposting or sharing DVK materials online.

In Almaty, three women who were put into pretrial detention in July after participating in a rally DVK called for in May were convicted in November, but were sentenced to one year of "limited freedom," rather than prison.

Freedom of Religion

In the first half of 2019, authorities brought 106 administrative cases against individuals or religious communities, leading to fines or short-term bans on worship—an increase from the same period last year, according to the religious freedom watchdog Forum18.

In January, parliament recalled amendments to the country's religion law that would have significantly increased restrictions and sanctions on religious teaching, proselytizing, and publications.

Labor Rights

Authorities took no effective steps to restore freedom of association rights for independent trade unions in 2019. At a meeting in June, the International Labour Organization (ILO) criticized Kazakhstan for ongoing restrictions on union activities. The government said amendments to trade union legislation were submitted to parliament in July, but was not publicly available at time of writing.

HUMAN
RIGHTS
WATCH
"On the Margins"
Education for Children with Disabilities in Kazakhstan

Three activists—Nurbek Kushakbaev, Amin Eleusinov, and Larisa Kharkova—remained banned from leading trade unions. The Congress of Independent Trade Unions of Kazakhstan (now Congress of Free Trade Unions of Kazakhstan) continued to be denied registration. In July, a court sentenced trade union leader Erlan Baltabay to prison for seven years on charges of misappropriating union funds. Though he was released in August due to a presidential pardon, in October he was sentenced to five more months in prison for failing to pay a required fine.

Counterterrorism and Extremism

Kazakhstan repatriated 524 citizens—mostly women and children—who were detained in northern Syria as Islamic State (ISIS) suspects or relatives. Following a visit to Kazakhstan in May, the UN special rapporteur on human rights and counterterrorism praised the repatriations while emphasizing that deradicalization and reintegration programs for returnees, as well as trials for those accused of crimes, must comply with human rights. The special rapporteur also said Kazakhstan should amend overbroad laws on terrorism and extremism that target civil society or religious groups.

In August, a court sentenced eight men who participated in an online religious discussion group to five to eight years in prison for "propaganda of terrorism" and "inciting hatred," despite a reported lack of evidence that any of them promoted or had links to violent extremism.

Domestic Violence

Kazakhstan has no criminal statute against domestic violence, which remains widespread and under-reported. Services for survivors are inadequate and do not meet international standards. Police routinely fail to register complaints, adequately respond to domestic violence cases, and inform survivors of their rights to protection orders. In its fifth periodic review of Kazakhstan in October, the Committee on the Elimination of Discrimination against Women (CEDAW) expressed concerns about decriminalization of domestic violence and urged Kazakhstan to "restore full criminal responsibility" for these crimes.

Sexual Orientation and Gender Identity

In March, the UN Committee on Economic, Social and Cultural Rights expressed concern that Kazakhstan's constitution and laws do not explicitly prohibit discrimination on the basis of gender identity or sexual orientation, and called on Kazakhstan to adopt anti-discrimination legislation.

In May, a court backed the Almaty city Justice Ministry in its repeated decisions to deny registration to Feminita, a group that focuses on the rights of lesbian, bisexual, and queer women. That decision was upheld by an appeals court in September.

In a positive move, Kazakhstan's Supreme Court ruled in July that a man who filmed a lesbian couple kissing and distributed that video online had violated their privacy.

Disability Rights

Despite government promises, progress on inclusive education remained slow, with very low rates of enrollment of children with disabilities in mainstream public schools. Schools often deny children enrollment based on the results of a problematic mandatory medical-educational exam. Many schools fail to provide reasonable accommodations and support to children with disabilities who do attend. Many children with disabilities are isolated in segregated special schools or education at home. Over 2,000 children with disabilities live in closed state institutions, where they may face violence, neglect, physical restraint, and overmedication. Kazakhstan has no time-bound plan to close these institutions.

Torture

In several cases, police officers and prison officials were convicted and sentenced to prison on charges of torture. However, of 119 reports of torture registered by law enforcement agencies in the first half of 2019, only 13 had been sent to court.. In August, seven prison officials were arrested after videos leaked showing officers torturing inmates in the prison of Zarechnoe. President Tokaev ordered the general prosecutor to conduct a "detailed investigation," but human rights activists expressed concern in October after more than half of the plaintiffs withdrew their accusations against prison officers.

Asylum Seekers and Refugees

In October, two ethnic Kazakh citizens of China were detained after crossing the border between the two countries in eastern Kazakhstan. They said they were fleeing repressive measures—including arbitrary detentions and torture—by the Chinese authorities in Xinjiang. They are being held in pretrial detention in a remote city in eastern Kazakhstan, according to their lawyer.

Key International Actors

In March, the European Parliament adopted a resolution calling on Kazakhstan to end its broad violations of human rights, including the rights to freedom of expression, assembly, and religion. It also called for the freeing of unjustly imprisoned activists, including Max Bokaev. European Council President Donald Tusk said in a visit in May that he had spoken with Tokaev about reforms, including the improvement of rule of law and fundamental rights.

Following election irregularities reported by the OSCE monitoring mission, the United States called on Kazakhstan to respect citizens' human rights and "immediately release all those detained for taking part in peaceful protests regarding the election." The European Union similarly called on Kazakhstan's new government to address shortcomings observed during the vote. The EU separately criticized Kazakhstan for its failure to adopt amendments to the Trade Union Law, noting that its enhanced Partnership and Cooperation Agreement "includes commitments to effectively implement the ILO fundamental Conventions."

During the EU-Kazakhstan Human Rights Dialogue in November, the EU raised concerns about the ability of article 174 of Kazakhstan's Criminal Code—which outlaws national, interethnic, or religious incitement—to stifle freedom of expression. It also encouraged Kazakhstan's government to foster peaceful assembly and review existing legislation on trade unions.

Kenya

Lack of accountability for serious human rights violations by security forces, including extrajudicial killings and enforced disappearances, remain a major concern in Kenya, despite promises by President Uhuru Kenyatta to address key issues, including those that have in the past undermined Kenya's ability to hold peaceful elections. Kenyan authorities failed to investigate security forces abuses, including extrajudicial killings and enforced disappearances, and hold those responsible to account.

While senior government officials, including President Kenyatta, publicly promised to respect freedom of expression and media, the working environment for bloggers, journalists, and activists remains hostile as police threatened journalists and bloggers, and arrested and detained journalists and activists.

In Lamu, Kenyan security forces harassed and detained activists expressing rights concerns relating to the government's massive infrastructure development projects, accusing some as terrorists. Kenyan authorities also continued abusive evictions of people from the Maasai Mau forest.

In January, armed gunmen attacked DusitD2, a hotel west of downtown Nairobi, killing at least 24 people. Al-Shabab, the Islamist armed group based in neighboring Somalia, claimed responsibility for the attack.

Lack of Accountability for Serious Crimes

Despite documentation and investigations into the violence during the 2017/2018 elections, in which more than 100 were killed, the government has yet to bring charges against any security officers. A government inquest into the killings of nine-month-old baby Samantha Pendo in Kisumu and nine-year-old Stephanie Moraa in Nairobi found at least five senior police commanders and other government officials responsible for the abuses, but authorities had yet to hold anyone to account for the killings and other violations in the election period.

There was also no progress in investigating or holding anyone to account for the violence around the 2007/2008 elections in which 1,100 people were killed.

In 2015, President Kenyatta announced plans to establish a restorative Ksh10 billion fund (approximately US$100 million) for victims of rights abuses, including of the 2007/2008 post-election violence, but did not set up the fund until April and had yet to make any payouts at time of writing.

Kenya has yet to surrender three persons wanted by the International Criminal Court (ICC) on allegations of witness tampering in cases relating to the 2007/2008 election violence. Other ICC cases against Kenyatta, Deputy President William Ruto, and a former broadcaster Joshua arap Sang, collapsed amid witness tampering allegations and state non- cooperation.

Authorities have not investigated most of the reported extrajudicial killings in Nairobi's informal settlements. In 2018, the Independent Policing Oversight Authority (IPOA), a civilian police accountability institution, told media it was investigating 243 killings by police, but the institution appears overwhelmed by the sheer volume of the cases and undermined by the lack of cooperation police. The institution secured convictions against just three officers since it started working in 2012, media reported.

Abuses by Security Forces

In July 2019, Human Rights Watch found that police in Kenya killed no fewer than 21 men and boys in Nairobi's informal settlements, apparently with no justification, claiming they were criminals. Rights activists in those neighborhoods believe that, based on the cases they know about and those reported in the media, police have unlawfully killed many more in the past year. In October 2018, the Daily Nation reported that police killed at least 101 people in Nairobi and more than 180 people across Kenya in a nine-month period.

In February, Kenyan activist, Caroline Mwatha Ochieng, who worked alongside others in Nairobi to document police killings in informal settlements, died under unclear circumstances that police say are not linked to her work, as claimed by activists.

In November, a video circulated on social media showing police beating a student protester on a Nairobi university campus, prompting wide public condemnation of excessive use of force by police.

In December 2018, Human Rights Watch issued a report documenting a pattern of harassment, intimidation and other abuses of at least 35 environmental activists in Lamu over the past five years. Security forces in Lamu have broken up protests, restricted public meetings and threatened, arrested and prosecuted activists on various charges, including terrorism.

The activists were protesting potential environmental and health concerns related to projects associated with the Lamu Port-South Sudan-Ethiopia Transport corridor (LAPSSET) project. LAPSSET the largest infrastructure project planned in East Africa includes a port in Lamu, three international airports, a road and railway network, resort cities and a coal-fired power plant.

Abuses During Land Evictions

Authorities have carried out serious abuses while evicting communities from the Maasai Mau forest, who authorities say encroached forest land. Ongoing since 2014, the evictions were especially abusive in July and December 2018, when security officials beat people, torched homes and destroyed crops, leaving thousands stranded in the cold. Human Rights Watch found at least nine people, including two babies, died during the eviction and at least four people are still missing.

Authorities have not investigated these abuses, and in August announced plans to commence a second round of evictions of another group of people still living in the forest. Kenyan and international guidelines on evictions require authorities to issue adequate eviction notice, and compensate or resettle the evictees. Evictees and communities still residing in the Mau forest have challenged the legality of the 2018 evictions and seek to stop the second round of evictions.

Freedom of Expression and Media

The Media Council of Kenya reported that between May 2017 and April 2018, there were at least 94 incidents of abuses against journalists and bloggers in Kenya, the highest in a decade. In a number of those cases, police and, in some cases individuals linked to politicians, threatened and attacked activists and journalists on duty. Authorities failed to investigate or hold anyone to account for physical attacks, harassment, and intimidation against journalists.

Police disrupted and banned protests, arresting and detaining activists, contrary to constitutional guarantees to the right to protest or picket. On July 19, police tear-gassed and detained at least three activists who were protesting in Nairobi for peace in South Sudan. The three were later released without charge. On July 21, police arrested 12 human rights activists for holding a public meeting to discuss issues affecting a community school in Nairobi's Mathare neighborhood. They were later released without charge.

In March, government published a new bill, the Public Order (Amendment) Bill, 2019, seeking to amend an existing law to make organizers of public meetings or protests responsible for loss of property or life and to provide compensation to those affected by the protests. If adopted, the new law would restrict free assembly and expression, contrary to the constitution, which guarantees these rights.

Authorities tried to introduce administrative measures that restrict freedom expression and media. In May, Kenya Film Classification Board, a state regulatory agency, published new strict regulations and harsher sanctions relating to both filming and exhibition of films. The regulations were however withdrawn following a public outcry.

Sexual Orientation and Gender Identity

In May, the High Court upheld sections of the penal code that punish consensual same-sex relations with up to 14 years in prison. Three Kenya lesbian, gay, bisexual, and transgender (LGBT) activist groups have appealed the decision.

The Court of Appeal upheld two rulings that affirmed the rights of LGBT people, one pertaining to the right to freedom of association, and another allowing a transgender woman to change her name and remove the gender marker from her school-leaving certificate.

LGBT refugees and asylum seekers from neighboring countries faced attacks both in Kakuma refugee camp and in Nairobi neighborhoods. In June, police forcibly returned a group of LGBT asylum seekers from Nairobi to Kakuma, despite admissions from UNHCR that it could not ensure their safety in the camp. In response to advocacy from intersex activists, Kenya in August became the first country in Africa to include an intersex category in its census

Key International Actors

With its forces still deployed in Somalia and South Sudan, Kenya remains a key player, and continues counterterrorism efforts, in the region. However, in 2019, the tensions between Kenya and Somalia resulting from the dispute over maritime boundaries in the oil-rich Indian ocean—to be decided by the International Court of Justice—appeared to escalate. In February, Kenya, for the third time in seven years, threatened to shut down Daadab refugee camp by August for security reasons.

In May, Kenya denied at least three Somali lawmakers and a cabinet minister entry into the country on Somali passports, resulting in a diplomatic standoff between the two countries and adding to the ongoing mistrust and tensions. Somali leaders who presented non-Somali passports were however allowed into the country.

Kosovo

The European Union-sponsored normalization dialogue between Pristina and Belgrade stalled in November 2018 after Serbia blocked Kosovo from joining Interpol. In response, Kosovo imposed 100 percent import duties on all goods from Serbia and Bosnia and Herzegovina.

Progress towards accountability for serious war crimes committed during the 1998-1999 Kosovo war was slow. Prime Minister Ramush Haradinaj, who served as a commander in the Kosovo Liberation Army during the war, resigned in July following a summons for questioning by the special war crimes prosecutor in The Hague; Vetevendosje, the previous opposition party, won snap elections in October. Journalists faced threats and intimidation, and prosecutions of crimes against journalists are slow. Tensions between Serbs and Kosovo Albanians continued, particularly in the north. Roma, Ashkali, and Balkan Egyptian communities continued to face discrimination.

Accountability for War Crimes

The Hague-based Specialist Chambers and Prosecutor's Office trying serious war crimes committed during the 1998-1999 summoned three suspects during the year for questioning but had issued no indictments at time of writing. In July, the Hague Prosecutor's Office summoned Kosovo Prime Minister Ramush Haradinaj for questioning, prompting his resignation. Former senior Kosovo Liberation Army (KLA) fighters are expected to be indicted and stand trial.

In July, the Basic Court in Pristina remanded Goran Stanisic, a former member of the Yugoslav reserve forces, into custody for his alleged participation in forced displacement, robbery, intimidation, and involvement in the killing of dozens of civilian Albanians in Slovinje village in central Kosovo during an attack by Serbian forces in April 1999.

Also in July, the court in Prizren convicted former KLA unit commander Remzi Shala to 14 years in prison for the 1998 kidnapping of an ethnic Albanian who was later found dead.

In April, the Court of Appeals in Pristina upheld the six-and-a-half years prison sentence of former policeman Zoran Vukotic for torturing ethnic Albanian prisoners in the Mitrovica area, in northern Kosovo in May 1999. The court ordered his retrial for attacking fleeing civilians during the same time period.

In June, Kosovo's Special Prosecution Office charged Zoran Djokic, member of an organized criminal group of Serbs wearing military, paramilitary and police uniforms, with the killing of 33 Kosovo Albanians in Peja village in April 1999.

The Human Rights Review Panel, an independent body set up in 2009 to review allegations of human rights violations by staff of the now-concluded European Rule of Law Mission (EULEX), ruled in 13 cases between January and September. Twenty-four cases were pending before the panel at time of writing. Since its existence, the panel has registered 200 cases.

Accountability of International Institutions

The United Nations failed during the year to apologize and pay individual compensation to lead poison victims forced to live in camps run by the UN Interim Administration Mission in Kosovo (UNMIK) in northern Kosovo after the 1998-1999 war, as recommended by the Human Rights Advisory Panel (HRAP), an independent body set up in 2006 to examine complaints of abuses by UNMIK. Victims are displaced members of the Roma, Ashkali and Balkan Egyptian communities. By time of writing, one state had made a modest contribution to a voluntary trust fund established by UN Secretary-General Antonio Guterres in 2017 to benefit these communities (not specifically those affected by lead poisoning).

Treatment of Minorities

Roma, Ashkali, and Balkan Egyptians continued to have difficulties acquiring personal documents, affecting their ability to access health care, social assistance and education. No concrete progress was reported towards integration of the Roma, Ashkali, and Balkan Egyptian communities.

Inter-ethnic tensions continued during 2019 particularly in Kosovo's divided north. In July, Kosovo's Prosecutor's Office indicted former minister of local government administration Ivan Todosijevic of inciting and spreading hate, division and intolerance between nations, racial and ethnic communities. The indictment followed a statement three months earlier by Todosijevic in which he, in his position as minister, said that Kosovo Albanians fabricated claims of crimes against them during the 1998-1999 war while committing crimes against Serbs. He was subsequently fired by then-Prime Minister Haradinaj.

The police investigation into the January 2018 murder of Kosovo-Serb politician Oliver Ivanovic was broadened in May to include two new, unnamed suspects. In October, police arrested two suspects, including an ethnic Serb police officer. Two other suspects have been in custody since November 2018. Ivanovic was shot dead by unknown assailants outside his office in Mitrovica, northern Kosovo.

Kosovo police registered seven cases of incitement of religious, ethnic and racial hatred between January and August without providing more disaggregated data or information on other bias crimes.

Women's Rights

Despite some positive developments, domestic violence remained a problem in Kosovo with inadequate police response, few prosecutions and continued failure by judges to issue restraining orders against abusive partners.

In April, authorities launched a national unified database enabling monitoring and prosecution of domestic violence cases to ensure accountability by requiring relevant institutions to update the database with necessary information from central and local levels. The Constitutional Court ruled in February that the Kosovo Assembly could amend the Constitution to recognize the Council of Europe Convention on Preventing and Combating Violence and Domestic Violence (also known as the Istanbul Convention).

The 2018 application process for wartime survivors of sexual violence to be granted legal status as war victims and to seek financial compensation from authorities had limited reach. By June, around 800 survivors of sexual violence had applied, of which 145 had been approved and 102 rejected, and the remaining pending at time of writing. Approved victims receive 230 euros per month and may be eligible for health benefits for illnesses linked to violence suffered during the war. Women survivors are not automatically entitled to free primary or secondary health care, or free psychosocial assistance, unlike other civilian war victims.

Asylum Seekers and Displaced Persons

During the first ten months of the year, the United National High Commissioner for Refugees registered 115 voluntary returns of members of ethnic minorities to Kosovo, down from 153 during the same period in 2018.

The Kosovo Ministry of Internal Affairs registered 800 forced returns, mostly from Germany, to Kosovo between January and August. The Ministry of Internal Affairs reported that ethnic data was missing. Among those forcibly returned to Kosovo 189 were children. Returnees were provided limited assistance upon return.

Sexual Orientation and Gender Identity

Online hate speech against lesbian, gay, bisexual, and transgender (LGBT) rights activists remained a problem. Cel Kosovo, an LGBTI organization, registered 18 cases of threats and discrimination against members of the LGBT community, of which six were investigated by police at time of writing. Cel stated that LGBT activists had received more than 150 online death threats during the year. All were reported to police, but no cases were prosecuted. In April, a new criminal code entered into force, strengthening the protection for members of the LGBT community by adding to the definition of a "hate act" a crime committed against a person, group of persons, property or affinity with persons on grounds including sexual orientation and gender identity.

Freedom of Media

Threats and attacks against journalists continued while investigations and prosecutions were slow. Threats on social media platforms remained a widespread problem. Between January and September, the Association of Journalists of Kosovo registered 11 cases of threats and violence against journalists and media outlets, including four physical attacks and seven threats. Police were investigating four of the reported cases at time of writing.

In August, the ruling PDK (Democratic Party of Kosovo) issued a statement calling an online news outlet, *Gazeta Express*, "fake news," encouraging citizens to be doubtful of its reporting. The Association of Journalists of Kosovo had reported in May that PDK head Kadri Velesi put pressure on the editor-in-chief of *Gazeta Express*. Police were investigating at time of writing.

TV BESA reporter Gramos Zurnaxhio was attacked and received death threats in July while he was covering the demolition of a building complex in Prizren. The assailants were reportedly company workers and police were investigating at time of writing.

Key International Actors

European Council President Donald Tusk in April urged Kosovo authorities to improve relations with Serbia to ensure progress towards future EU membership but failed to stress human rights concerns with authorities.

In March, the UN special rapporteur on the implications for human rights of the environmentally sound management and disposal of hazardous substances and wastes reiterated his call on the UN to pay compensation to Roma families affected by lead poisoning in the UNMIK-run camp.

In June 2019, the special rapporteur addressed letters to the leaders of several organizations in the United Nations system, reiterating the need for the UN system as a whole to contribute to mobilizing the necessary resources to provide the victims their right to an effective remedy.

In May, the European Commission called for strengthening of rule of law institutions, noting that the judiciary remains vulnerable to political influence. The commission also noted that more financial resources and better coordination is needed to implement human rights frameworks. In November 2018, the European Parliament adopted a resolution calling on the UN "to swiftly deliver the necessary support to the victims.

Kuwait

Kuwaiti authorities continue to use provisions in the constitution, the national security law, and other legislation to restrict free speech, prosecute dissidents, and stifle political dissent.

Despite recent reforms, migrant workers do not have adequate legal protections, and remain vulnerable to abuse, forced labor, and deportation for minor infractions.

The Bidun, a community of stateless people who claim Kuwaiti nationality, continue to remain in legal limbo while the government addresses this longstanding issue largely through abuse and coercion.

Kuwait continues to allow Human Rights Watch access to the country, unlike many of its Gulf neighbors, and engaged in dialogue with the organization on a range of human rights issues during a 2019 visit by Human Rights Watch.

Migrant Workers

Two-thirds of Kuwait's population is comprised of migrant workers, who remain vulnerable to abuse despite recent reforms. In January 2018, the Philippines Department of Labor and Employment (DOLE) issued a temporary ban on Filipinos seeking to migrate to Kuwait for work, pending an investigation into the deaths of seven domestic workers in the country. In May 2018, both countries agreed on additional legal protections for Filipino workers in Kuwait, including the right for workers to retain their passport. Since then, local media reported at least one case, in May 2019, where an employer allegedly sexually assaulted and beat a Filipina domestic migrant worker to death.

In 2015, the National Assembly passed a law granting domestic workers the right to one day off per week, 30 days paid leave per year, a maximum 12-hour working day with rest, and an end-of-service benefit of one month's wage for every year worked at the end of the contract, among other rights. In 2016 and 2017, the Interior Ministry passed implementing regulations for the law, and mandated that employers must pay overtime compensation and established a minimum wage of KD60 (approximately US$197) for domestic workers. However, protections for domestic workers are still weaker than those in Kuwait's labor law. The domestic worker law fails to set out enforcement mechanisms and lacks mechanisms to sanction employers who confiscate passports or fail to provide adequate housing, food, and medical expenses, work breaks, or weekly rest days. Human Rights Watch found that migrant domestic workers are still subject to abuse and exploitation including excessively long working hours without rest or days off, forced confinement to the house, delayed or unpaid salaries, and physical and sexual abuse. Many domestic workers have not been able to claim their rights under the new law, in part because of the *kafala* system under which they cannot leave or change employers without their employer's consent. If they flee their employer, they can be arrested for "absconding."

Freedom of Expression

Kuwaiti authorities have invoked several provisions in the constitution, penal code, Printing and Publication Law, Misuse of Telephone Communications and Bugging Devices Law, Public Gatherings Law, and National Unity Law to prosecute journalists, politicians, and activists for criticizing the emir, the government, religion, and rulers of neighboring countries in blogs or on Twitter, Facebook, or other social media platforms.

In July 2018, Kuwait's Court of Cassation convicted 16 people and sentenced them to two to three-and-a-half years in prison with labor over storming parliament and calling for the country's prime minister to resign during a 2011 protest. On October 23, authorities arrested one of the convicts, Fahad Al Khannah, a former lawmaker, after he returned to Kuwait from Turkey. On November 5, he was released from detention with an Amiri pardon.

The Cybercrime Law, which went into effect in 2016, includes far-reaching restrictions on internet-based speech and activism, such as prison sentences, and fines for insulting religion, religious figures, and the emir. Human rights defenders, such as Abdulhakim Al-Fadhli, Hamed Jameel, Khalifa Al-Anezi, Karima Karam, Anwar Al-Roqi, and Aisha Al-Rasheed have been targeted with this law for their peaceful activities on the internet, especially those supporting Bidun rights.

Treatment of Minorities

The Bidun, a community of between 88,000 to 106,000 stateless people who claim Kuwaiti nationality, remain in legal limbo, dating back to the foundation of the Kuwaiti state in 1961.

Claiming that most of the Bidun moved to Kuwait from neighboring countries in search of a better livelihood and hid their other nationalities to claim Kuwaiti citizenship, the government refers to them as "illegal residents," resulting in obstacles to them obtaining civil documentation, consistently receiving social services, and interfering with their fundamental rights to health, education, and work, among others.

The Central System for the Remedy of Situations of Illegal Residents, the current administrative body in charge of Bidun affairs, since 2011 has started issuing temporary ID cards. However, the process of determining applicants' eligibility for services and whether they hold another nationality remains opaque. The ID cards issued to Bidun in recent years have often indicated that the cardholder possesses another nationality, such as Iraqi, Saudi, or Iranian citizenship, but it remains unclear how the Central System determines the individual's alleged nationality and what due process systems are available for Bidun to challenge the Central System's decision.

Article 12 of the 1979 Public Gatherings Law bars non-Kuwaitis from participating in public gatherings. In July, Kuwait's State Security agency arrested at least 14 activists from the Bidun community after they organized a peaceful sit-in at al-Hurriya Square in al-Jahra town, near Kuwait City, in response to the death of Ayed Hamad Moudath. Moudath, 20, died by suicide on July 7 after the government reportedly denied him civil documentation. More than a dozen jailed activists began a hunger strike on August 22 to protest violations against themselves and the Bidun community.

Terrorism and Security

In July, Kuwaiti authorities unlawfully returned eight Egyptian dissidents despite the serious risk of torture and persecution they face in Egypt, claiming Egyptian authorities sought them for crimes they allegedly committed in Egypt as members of the Muslim Brotherhood.

In May 2018, Kuwaiti authorities arrested and extrajudicially deported to Saudi Arabia dual Qatari-Saudi national Nawaf al-Rasheed, a poet and university student who lives in Qatar, on unclear grounds, ostensibly "under bilateral mutual security arrangements."

Women's Rights, Sexual Orientation, and Gender Identity

Kuwaiti personal status law, which applies to Sunni Muslims who make up the majority of Kuwaitis, discriminates against women. For example, some women require a male guardian to conclude their marriage contracts; women must apply to the courts for a divorce on limited grounds, unlike men who can unilaterally divorce their wives; and women can lose custody of their children if they remarry someone outside the former husband's family. Men can marry up to four wives, without the permission or knowledge of the other wife or wives. A man can prohibit his wife from working if it is deemed to negatively affect the family interests. The rules that apply to Shia Muslims also discriminate against women.

Kuwait has no laws on domestic violence and does not explicitly criminalize marital rape. A 2015 law creating family courts in each governorate set up a national center to "combat domestic violence," but requires the center to prioritize reconciliation over protection for domestic violence survivors. A draft domestic violence bill remained pending in parliament.

Under article 153 of the Kuwaiti penal code, a man who finds his mother, wife, sister, or daughter in the act of adultery (*zina*) and kills them is given a reduced sentence of either a small fine or a maximum three-year prison sentence. Under article 182, an abductor who uses force, threat, or deception with the intention to kill, harm, rape, prostitute, or extort a victim is spared any punishment if he marries the victim with her guardian's permission. Kuwaiti women married to non-Kuwaitis, cannot pass citizenship to their children or spouses, unlike Kuwaiti men.

Under the penal code, sexual relations outside marriage, including adultery and sex between unmarried persons, is criminalized, as are same-sex relations between men which are punishable by up to seven years in prison. Transgender people can face one year in prison, a 1,000 Kuwaiti dinar fine (US$3293), or both, under a 2007 penal code provision that prohibits "imitating the opposite sex in any way." Transgender people under this provision have been subjected to arbitrary arrests, degrading treatment, and torture while in police custody. Even cisgender people have been arrested under the law as the law fails to define what "imitating" the opposite sex means.

Key International Actors

Kuwait joined the Saudi-led coalition that began attacking Houthi forces in Yemen on March 26, 2015, with media reporting that Kuwait had deployed 15 aircraft. Kuwait has not responded to Human Rights Watch inquiries regarding what role, if any, it has played in unlawful attacks in Yemen.

Kyrgyzstan

Long-term human rights concerns persisted in Kyrgyzstan in 2019. A court upheld a life sentence for rights defender Azimjon Askarov in July, despite international calls for his release and changes to Kyrgyzstan's criminal code. While freedom of assembly was largely respected, use of overly broad and vague definitions of criminal acts such as "incitement" or "extremism" remained the norm.

A political standoff between President Sooronbai Jeenbekov and former President Almazbek Atambaev heated up in August when a raid to arrest Atambaev turned violent, killing one person and injuring 45, including journalists. In the wake of these events, the government seized Atambaev's assets, including office space and equipment belonging to the television station Aprel.

Despite the criminalization of domestic violence in January, measures to protect women remained inadequate and inconsistent. On March 14, President Jeenbekov signed a bill ratifying the Convention on the Rights of Persons with Disabilities (CRPD).

Access to Justice

Despite international calls for the release of rights defender Azimjon Askarov, a regional court upheld his life sentence in July. Askarov's lawyers have appealed his case, which they brought in light of changes to Kyrgyzstan's criminal code, to the Supreme Court. Members of civil society who have visited the 68-year-old Askarov say he has several health problems and no access to a doctor outside the prison where he's being held. In October, Askarov wrote an open letter complaining about prison conditions, including arbitrary use of solitary confinement and limitations of family visits. In a separate case, Askarov was named in a lawsuit for failing to pay "moral compensation" to the victims of his alleged crimes.

Victims continue to wait for justice nine years after June 2010 interethnic violence, which left hundreds killed and thousands of homes destroyed. Ethnic Uzbeks were disproportionately affected.

Civil Society

Civil society groups faced some ongoing pressure. In May, a meeting of the Coalition Against Torture—an alliance of 17 organizations—was broken up by men with cameras who identified themselves as a patriotic youth movement. In March, the Deputy Minister of the State Committee for National Security (GKNB) urged parliament to draft a law imposing greater restrictions on civil society, suggesting that Kyrgyzstan should have more control over international financing of nongovernmental organizations (NGOs). The GKNB later backed away from these comments. Chris Rickleton, an Agence-France Presse journalist, and Mihra Rittman, Human Rights Watch Central Asia Senior Researcher, remain banned from working in Kyrgyzstan.

In 2018, two reports by human rights organizations—including one about the 2010 interethnic violence—were included on a list of "extremist" material and banned by court order. The court also prohibited ADC Memorial, a Brussels-based organization and co-author of one of the reports, from operating in Kyrgyzstan. After the Supreme Court reversed that decision, a lower court returned the case to the prosecutor's office in January 2019. The reports are no longer banned in Kyrgyzstan.

Freedom of Expression

On August 7, special forces attempted to detain former President Almazbek Atambaev, who had resisted multiple prior summons by police, at his home outside Bishkek. Government forces engaged in a lengthy standoff with armed supporters of Atambaev, and only succeeded in arresting him on August 8. One commander was killed in the violence and at least 45 people were injured, including several journalists. Harlem Desir, the Organization for Security and Co-operation in Europe's (OSCE) representative for freedom of the media, expressed concerns about injured journalists, stating that "the safety of journalists who cover political events must be respected by all actors."

Aprel—a television station controlled by Atambaev—was taken off the air during the raid on August 7. When Atambaev was arrested and charged with inciting unrest, conspiracy to murder, and kidnapping among other crimes, the court ruled to freeze his assets, including Aprel's office space and equipment. On August 9, special forces forced employees to exit the Aprel office, leaving their equipment behind. In September, Aprel announced that it would continue broadcasting on social media platforms using donated equipment. OSCE Representative Desir, speaking of Aprel, said "media diversity should preserved even in difficult situations."

Kyrgyzstan media experts said defamation lawsuits continue to be a tool for politicians seeking to silence media outlets. Reporters without Borders noted little progress on reforming defamation legislation, leaving the door open to future lawsuits.

Statutes containing overly broad definitions of acts such as "incitement" continued to be used selectively against those who peacefully protested or expressed their political opinions. In March, a couple who held up posters condemning Russian President Vladimir Putin outside the Russian Embassy in Bishkek were detained and accused of "inciting national enmity," though charges were dropped in July. Similarly, a teacher was charged with "inciting interethnic discord" for anti-Russian comments on Facebook, but was acquitted in May.

Labor Rights

In October, Kyrgyzstan's parliament approved in a second reading amendments to a trade union law that would severely restrict independent union organizing. The amendments would grant the Federation of Trade Unions a monopoly over all federal-level union activity, and would force smaller unions to affiliate with the Federation, giving it a veto over their charters and other activities. The International Labour Organization and IndustriALL Global Union criticized the proposed law, which they said would restrict freedom of association and the right to organize. A third and final reading had not been scheduled at time of writing.

Terrorism and Counterterrorism

In January 2019, amendments to the criminal code made it no longer a crime to possess materials such as videos and pamphlets that the authorities classified as "extremist," unless they were for a purpose such as dissemination. Suspects who were previously convicted solely for possessing extremist materials were able to seek judicial review of their cases. Government officials told Human

Rights Watch in May that such cases would be reviewed and where appropriate, sentences canceled and people released. However, local human rights lawyers said that while some judges ordered a prisoner's release upon review, some were denied and remained in prison. Kyrgyzstan continues to employ an overly broad and vague definition of extremism that can capture non-violent behavior or content.

Kyrgyzstan announced steps toward repatriating some of the hundreds of citizens detained in Iraq as spouses and children of Islamic State (ISIS) suspects, and said it already had an agreement to return some 70 children from Iraq.

Violence Against Women and Girls

Kyrgyzstan adopted a strengthened Family Violence Law in 2017 and criminalized domestic violence in January 2019. However, authorities are not consistently enforcing protective measures for women and girls, including both the Family Violence Law and a 2016 law to curb child and forced marriage. Crucially, the government has not yet appointed a body overseeing implementation of domestic violence prevention measures, as required by law

In December 2018, a man was sentenced to 20 years in prison for kidnapping Burulai Turdaaly Kyzy and stabbing her to death in a police station, a case that sparked national outrage. In April, three police officers charged were sentenced on charges of negligence and fined in connection to the case.

Torture

Torture by law enforcement officials continues, impunity for which is the norm. According to government statistics sent to the anti-torture group Voice of Freedom, 171 allegations of torture were registered in the first half of 2019, though only one case had so far been sent to court. According to international and local groups, changes to Kyrgyzstan's criminal code in 2019 helped to strengthen protection against torture and increase punishments for perpetrators.

Sexual Orientation and Gender Identity

Lesbian, gay, bisexual, and transgender (LGBT) people continue to face ill-treatment, extortion, and discrimination by state and non-state actors. Activists organizing a March 8th parade for women's rights and equality said officials threatened to suspend the march if LGBT groups took part. Ultimately the march went forward, but organizers were threatened by the nationalist group Kyrk Choro (40 Warriors), who held a counter-protest. The event also provoked anti-LGBT rhetoric in parliament, where one member said LGBT people should be "not just cursed, but beaten." Other events hosted by LGBT groups have been targeted by nationalist groups who threaten and film participants without consent.

Key International Actors

In July, the European Union and Kyrgyzstan finalized the negotiations of an Enhanced Partnership and Cooperation Agreement that would foresee greater collaboration on political, security, and trade issues. EU High Representative Frederica Mogherini said she discussed the case of Azimjon Askarov, as well as broader judicial independence, with Kyrgyz leaders. In January, the European Parliament adopted a resolution to "express dissatisfaction" with Askarov's ongoing sentence and "request his immediate release," and pressed Kyrgyzstan to foster "a favorable environment for... the independent media" and to thoroughly investigate the 2010 interethnic violence. In their human rights dialogue with Kyrgyz representatives in May, EU officials stressed positive developments in media freedom but articulated concerns with regards to officials' comments about limiting NGO funding.

In response to the events surrounding the arrest of former President Atambaev, the head of the OSCE's parliamentary assembly urged Kyrgyz authorities to "exercise restraint" and to "continue strengthening democratic institutions and the rule of law" ahead of parliamentary elections in 2020.

A UN Working Group on Enforced or Involuntary Disappearances delegation praised Kyrgyzstan for making enforced disappearances a crime, as well as new mechanisms to notify relatives of those disappeared. The group also noted that issues remained, particularly with regards to investigating 17 cases of disappearances from the June 2010 interethnic violence.

HUMAN
RIGHTS
WATCH
"There is a Price to Pay"
The Criminalization of Peaceful Speech in Lebanon

Lebanon

The rights situation in Lebanon deteriorated in 2019, culminating in widespread anti-government protests that began on October 17. Security forces at times used excessive and unnecessary force against protesters and on several occasions failed to stop attacks on demonstrators.

Lebanese authorities have prosecuted individuals for peaceful speech, and security agencies interrogating these individuals have in some cases subjected them to abuse and detained them pretrial. Accountability for torture remains elusive, despite the passage of an anti-torture law.

Women still face discrimination under 15 separate religion-based personal status laws and both child marriage and marital rape remain legal. Unlike men, women cannot pass their citizenship to their children and foreign spouses.

Although Lebanon passed a law banning the open burning of waste, the practice is still widespread, endangering the health of residents.

There are approximately 1.5 million Syrian refugees in Lebanon; 73 percent lack legal status. Authorities forcibly deported over 2,500 refugees.

Freedom of Assembly and Freedom of Expression

Anti-government protests began on October 17 prompted by the announcement of new taxes. The protests quickly devolved into anger against the entire political establishment, whom protesters blame for corruption and the country's dire economic situation. Prime Minister Said Hariri resigned on October 29 in response to the mass protests.

On October 18, security forces fired tear gas and rubber bullets at thousands of largely peaceful protesters in downtown Beirut. Security forces on several occasions failed to stop attacks on peaceful demonstrators and occasionally used excessive force to disperse protesters and clear roadblocks by beating protesters with batons and rifle butts.

In 2019, authorities continued to detain and charge individuals for speech critical of government officials, especially in relation to corruption allegations, and religious institutions. Lawyers also used defamation laws to file complaints against individuals and publications expressing concern about the country's economic situation.

Security agencies, including the Internal Security Forces' cybercrimes bureau, have summoned activists for interrogation over peaceful speech, in some cases subjecting them to abuse, violating their privacy, detaining them pretrial, and compelling them to sign commitments to cease their criticisms.

Defaming or criticizing the Lebanese president or army is a criminal offense carrying penalties of up to two and three years in prison, respectively. The Lebanese penal code criminalizes libel and defamation, authorizing imprisonment of up to three months, and up to one year in the case of public officials.

Ill-Treatment and Torture

Despite parliament passing an anti-torture law in 2017, torture by security forces persists, judicial authorities continue to ignore the law's provisions, and accountability for torture remains elusive.

Judicial authorities failed to investigate torture allegations by Hassan al-Dika, arrested on drug-related charges, against members of the Internal Security Forces (ISF) prior to his death in custody on May 11.

Ziad Itani, a prominent actor falsely accused of spying for Israel, alleged that State Security officers tortured him in 2017. Despite his filing a lawsuit against his alleged torturers in November 2018, the judiciary has taken no substantive action on his case.

On March 7, Lebanon's Council of Ministers appointed the five members of the national preventative mechanism to monitor and investigate the use of torture, but it has still not allocated funding for the mechanism.

Military Courts

Lebanon continues to try civilians, including children, in military courts, in violation of their due process rights and international law.

On March 7, military courts sentenced two journalists to three months' imprisonment in absentia for allegedly insulting a security agency on Facebook. On appeal in April, the military court declared a lack of jurisdiction and referred the case back to the military prosecutor.

Women's Rights

Women, who have played a leading role in the protests that began on October 17, continue to face discrimination under 15 distinct religion-based personal status laws. Discrimination includes inequality in access to divorce, child custody, and inheritance and property rights. Unlike men, Lebanese women also cannot pass on their nationality to foreign husbands and children.

Lebanon has no minimum age for marriage, and some religious courts allow girls younger than 15 to marry. Parliament failed to take up draft bills that would set the age of marriage at 18.

In 2017, Lebanon's parliament repealed article 522, which had allowed rapists to escape prosecution by marrying the victim, but left a loophole with regard to offences relating to sex with children aged 15-17 and sex with virgin girls with promises of marriage.

A 2014 Law on the Protection of Women and Family from Domestic Violence established important protection measures and introduced policing and court reforms but failed to criminalize all forms of domestic violence, including marital rape.

Sexual Orientation and Gender Identity

Article 534 of the penal code punishes "any sexual intercourse contrary to the order of nature" with up to one year in prison. In March, the top military prosecutor acquitted four military personnel accused of sodomy and ruled that homosexuality is not a crime. This follows a district court of appeals' similar groundbreaking ruling in July 2018, and four judgments from lower courts declining to convict gay and transgender people under article 534 since 2007.

General Security banned entry to at least six individuals after they participated in a gender and sexuality conference in September 2018, which it attempted to shut down.

"Don't Punish Me for Who I Am"
Systemic Discrimination Against Transgender Women in Lebanon
HUMAN RIGHTS WATCH
MOSAIC
حلم
HELEM

Transgender women in Lebanon face systemic violence and discrimination in accessing basic services, including employment, health care, and housing.

Migrant Workers

An estimated 250,000 migrant domestic workers, primarily from Sri Lanka, Ethiopia, the Philippines, Nepal, and Bangladesh, are excluded from labor law protections.

The *kafala* (sponsorship) system subjects them to restrictive immigration rules under which they cannot leave or change employers without permission of their employer, placing them at risk of exploitation and abuse.

Civil society organizations documented frequent complaints of non-payment or delayed payment of wages, forced confinement, refusal to provide time off, and verbal and physical abuse. Migrant domestic workers seeking accountability for abuse face legal obstacles and inadequate investigations.

On May 5, migrant domestic workers organized a protest in Beirut demanding better working conditions and the abolishment of the *kafala* system.

A former minister of labor created a committee to reform Lebanon's labor law and "break" the *kafala* system, but no reforms have been announced yet.

Refugees

Nearly 1 million Syrian refugees are registered with the United Nations High Commissioner for Refugees (UNHCR) in Lebanon. The government estimates the true number of Syrians in the country to be 1.5 million.

Lebanon's residency policy makes it difficult for Syrians to maintain legal status, heightening risks of exploitation and abuse and restricting refugees' access to work, education, and healthcare. Seventy-three percent of Syrians in Lebanon now lack legal residency and risk detention for unlawful presence in the country.

The Higher Defense Council took several decisions that increased pressure on Syrian refugees in Lebanon, including the deportation of Syrians who enter Lebanon illegally, the demolition of refugee shelters, and a crackdown on Syrians working without authorization. On August 26, General Security said it deported 2,731 Syrians since May 21, placing them at risk of arbitrary detention and

HUMAN
RIGHTS
WATCH
"I Don't Want My Child
to Be Beaten"
Corporal Punishment in Lebanon's Schools

torture. These coercive measures come amid xenophobic rhetoric from leading politicians calling for the return of Syrian refugees.

General Security estimates that over 170,000 Syrians returned to their country from Lebanon between December 2017 and March 2019. Syrians said they are returning because of harsh policies and deteriorating conditions in Lebanon, not because they think Syria is safe.

According to the Lebanese Palestinian Dialogue Committee, there are approximately 174,000 Palestinian refugees living in Lebanon, where they continue to face restrictions, including on their right to work and own property. In addition, approximately 30,000 Palestinians from Syria have sought refuge in Lebanon.

Education

More than 300,000 school-age Syrian children were out of school during the 2017-2018 school year, largely due to parents' inability to pay for transport, child labor, school directors imposing arbitrary enrollment requirements, and lack of language support. As of mid-October 2019, Syrian students had not begun afternoon shifts at public schools. The Education Ministry blamed a shortfall in donor funding.

Children with disabilities are often denied admission to schools and for those who manage to enroll, most schools do not take reasonable steps to provide them with a quality education.

Although Lebanon has banned corporal punishment in schools, the ban is often disregarded, largely due to a lack of accountability for abusers.

Environment and Health

Despite the passage of a solid waste management law in 2018 banning the open burning of waste, municipalities still engage in the practice, posing health risks to residents, especially children and older persons. Open burning is more common in poor areas of the country.

On August 27, the cabinet endorsed the Environment Ministry's roadmap to create 25 sanitary landfills and three waste incinerators. However, the cabinet did not agree on how to tackle Beirut's looming trash crisis as both major landfills reach capacity.

Legacy of Past Conflicts and Wars

An estimated 17,000 Lebanese were kidnapped or "disappeared" during the 1975-1990 civil war. On November 12, 2018, parliament passed a landmark law creating an independent national commission to investigate the fate of the disappeared.

On August 29, the Justice Ministry nominated 10 individuals to serve on the committee. Their nominations must be approved by Cabinet.

Key International Actors

Syria, Iran, and Saudi Arabia maintain a strong influence on Lebanese politics through local allies.

Tensions between Hezbollah and Israel increased following the crash of two Israeli drones in Beirut's southern suburbs on August 25.

The international community has given Lebanon extensive, albeit insufficient, support to help it cope with the Syrian refugee crisis and to bolster security amid spillover violence.

Lebanese armed forces and police receive assistance from a range of international donors, including the United States, European Union, United Kingdom, France, and Saudi Arabia.

Libya

Governance in Libya remained divided between two feuding entities: the internationally recognized and Tripoli-based Government of National Accord (GNA); and their rivals in eastern Libya, the Interim Government, which is supported by the Libyan House of Representatives (HOR) and by the armed group known as the Libyan National Army (LNA).

Intermittent armed conflicts in most parts of the country since the end of the 2011 revolution that ousted Moammar Gaddafi have displaced more than 300,000 civilians.

Armed groups based in the west of the country and linked with the GNA fought off attempts by Gen. Khalifa Hiftar, the LNA commander, and his allies in the west, to capture the capital Tripoli, beginning in April and continuing at time of writing. The violence, which included attacks on civilian homes and infrastructure, killed more than 200 civilians as of early November.

Armed groups, some of them affiliated with the GNA or the Interim Government, carried out extrajudicial executions and abducted, tortured, and disappeared people.

Migrants and asylum seekers continued to go to Libya, including many hoping to reach Europe. While in Libya, they faced arbitrary and abusive detention by the GNA Interior Ministry and abusive conditions in facilities controlled by smuggler and traffickers.

Political Transition and Constitution

Clashes among armed groups in western Libya in January, Hiftar's assault on Tripoli in April, and intermittent fighting in the south deepened the political impasse and derailed the United Nations-brokered political process. Talks between the main conflict parties, Khalifa Hiftar, and Fayez Serraj, GNA prime minister, collapsed when Hiftar launched his offensive on Tripoli on April 4.

The High National Elections Commission was unable to organize a referendum on the draft constitution planned for January 2019 due to the prevailing insecurity, failure by the GNA to allocate funds to hold it, and the need for the House of

Representatives to modify the referendum law. At time of writing, no new date had been agreed on.

Armed Conflict and War Crimes

The UN Security Council established in Resolution 1970 (2011) individual targeted sanctions and an open-ended arms embargo on the supply of arms and military equipment to and from Libya. As of September, the UN said it had begun investigating over 40 cases of violations of the arms embargo. Ghassan Salame, head of the UN mission in Libya, said on September 25 that the country has become "possibly the largest drone war theatre in the world," with drones being deployed a total of 900 times by various parties to the conflict.

General Hiftar launched his attack to conquer Tripoli on April 4, supported by LNA units and armed groups, including the al-Kani militia from Tarhouna, his main ally in the west, against the GNA and affiliated armed groups from western Libya. As of November, the fighting, which is concentrated in the southern suburbs of Tripoli, had killed over 200 civilians, injured over 300, and displaced over 120,000. According to the United Nations Children' Fund, as of June, 21 schools were being used as shelters for displaced persons in and around Tripoli. The violence had led to the suspension of school for 122,088 children.

In July, an airstrike by the LNA on Tajoura Migrant Detention Centre east of Tripoli, resulted in the deaths of at least 44 migrants and more than 130 injured after two missiles landed in a hangar filled with detainees. The LNA initially claimed it had been targeting a weapons depot belonging to a Tripoli-based militia within the same compound as the migrant prison, but later denied involvement. Since the start of the fighting, the GNA failed to evacuate detention centers under its authority that are in proximity to the front lines and allegedly in proximity to where weapons were stocked, including Tajoura.

In August, the Red Crescent Society of Tarhouna transferred to Tripoli and Misrata the bodies of 12 detainees, including civilians and fighters, who had been held by the LNA-affiliated Kani militia from Tarhouna for an undisclosed period of time. According to the GNA Health Ministry, the bodies bore signs of torture and possible execution, and as of September, not all had been identified.

The LNA, or forces that support them, conducted air strikes in October that resulted in civilian casualties that appeared to be unlawful. On October 6, the LNA struck an equestrian club in Tripoli, injuring six children and killing several horses. The UN's investigation found there were no military assets or military infrastructure at the site. On October 14, an LNA airstrike apparently targeting a military compound killed three girls and wounded their mother and another sister in their home. According to the United Nations Children Fund (UNICEF), the fighting killed seven children within a span of two weeks in October.

As of July, the World Health Organization reported a total of 37 attacks on medical facilities during the Tripoli clashes, which killed 11 health workers and injured 33 health workers and patients.

The LNA struck Mitiga airport, currently the only functioning airport in Tripoli, on multiple occasions since the beginning of the war, claiming the airport was being used by the GNA-linked groups to import weapons. On September 1, an LNA aerial attack on Mitiga resulted in the injury of two crew members of a commercial airline. As of November, Mitiga was still shut and all flights were diverted to Misrata airport, 200 kilometers to the east.

In eastern Libya, the LNA in February took control of Derna, a city it had besieged for three years purportedly to drive out militants who were controlling the city. Residents reported that LNA-linked groups arbitrary detained and ill-treated residents and deliberately damaged homes, including by arson. According to local authorities who fled Derna after the LNA takeover, hundreds of Derna residents remained displaced, fearing reprisals if they returned.

On July 17, a member of the House of Representatives, Seham Sergewa, was abducted from her home in the eastern city of Benghazi and disappeared. Relatives and Benghazi residents with knowledge of the incident blamed an armed group with links to the LNA. Her husband was shot and injured during the incident and the family home looted and torched, according to relatives. Sergewa had publicly opposed the military assault by the LNA on the capital. At time of writing, there was no information on her whereabouts.

Three UN staff members were killed and two more injured on August 10, after a car exploded next to their convoy in Benghazi. As of November, the perpetrators remained unidentified.

In the south, clashes between LNA and a GNA-affiliated armed group known as the South Protection Force centered in Murzuq escalated in August, killing more than 100 people. On August 4 alone, more than 40 people were killed, including civilians, and more than 50 injured after the LNA reportedly conducted several airstrikes on a residential area in Murzuq. The LNA is trying to expel GNA-affiliates to expand its control in the south.

While the extremist group Islamic State (ISIS) no longer controls territory in Libya, its fighters carried out attacks in the eastern city of Derna and the southern city of Sebha, mostly against LNA fighters.

In September, the United States military said it conducted airstrikes on four different days within 10 days against ISIS targets in southern Libya, killing a total of 43 alleged militants. These strikes, the first conducted by the US military in 2019, were carried out by drones. The US said no civilians were killed in the strikes; this information could not be independently verified.

Judicial System and Detainees

Civilian and military courts operated at reduced capacity or not at all in in some parts of the country due to the insecurity and attacks by armed groups against judges, prosecutors, and lawyers. Prison authorities, often only nominally under the authority of one or the other of the rival governments, continued to hold thousands of detainees in long-term arbitrary detention without charges. Prisons in Libya are marked by overcrowding, bad living conditions, ill-treatment and lack of specialized services for women detained with their children.

Dozens of women and children, most of them foreign, remained held without charge in two prisons in Tripoli and Misrata and a facility for orphaned children run by the Red Crescent in Misrata. Authorities are holding them because they were family members of ISIS suspects. Thirty-seven Tunisian children, including six orphans, were among those held since December 2016. Prospects for their release remained dim because of the reluctance of their governments to repatriate them.

In June and July respectively, the GNA Justice Ministry released on health grounds two former Gaddafi prime ministers who a Tripoli criminal court had sentenced to death in 2015 in a flawed trial, Abuzeid Dorda and al-Baghdadi al-Mahmoudi.

International Criminal Court

Saif al-Islam Gaddafi, a son of Muammar Gaddafi, who was sentenced to death in absentia by a Libyan court in 2015, continued to be subject to an ICC arrest warrant for his alleged role in attacks on civilians, including peaceful demonstrators, during the country's 2011 uprising. At time of writing, his whereabouts remained unknown.

Two other Libyans continued to be subject to ICC arrest warrants: Al-Tuhamy Khaled, former head of the Internal Security Agency under Moammar Gaddafi, for war crimes and crimes against humanity committed in Libya between February and August 2011, and LNA commander Mahmoud El-Werfalli for the war crime of murder related to several incidents in and around Benghazi between June 2016 and January 2018.

Death Penalty

The death penalty is stipulated in over 30 articles in Libya's penal code, including for acts of speech and association. No death sentences have been carried out since 2010, although both military and civilian courts continued to pronounce them.

Internally Displaced Persons

The International Organization for Migration (IOM) estimated that 301,407 people were internally displaced in Libya as of July, almost all due to the security breakdown. The largest groups of IDPs were from Tripoli and the southern city of Sebha, and from Benghazi, where General Hiftar started a military campaign in 2014 purportedly to root out terrorism.

The displaced include most of the 48,000 former residents of the Libyan town of Tawergha, who in 2011 fled armed groups predominantly from Misrata who accused them of having committed serious crimes in a bid to support Gaddafi against those seeking his ouster. Tawerghans have not been able to return home despite reconciliation agreements with Misrata forces. Massive and deliberate destruction of the town and its infrastructure between 2011 and 2017 and scant public services have deterred them.

Freedom of Speech and Expression

Freelance Libyan photojournalist Mohamed Ben Khalifa was killed on January 19 after sustaining shrapnel wounds from indiscriminate shelling while covering clashes in Tripoli.

In May, unidentified fighters shot Hani Amara, a Libyan photojournalist for Reuters, in the thigh as he was covering the Tripoli clashes. On May 2, the LNA-allied al-Kani militia from Tarhouna, arrested Mohamed al- Qurj and Mohamed al- Shibani, two journalists with Libya Al-Ahrar TV, a private Libyan satellite channel that opposes the LNA, while they were reporting on the clashes in Tripoli. The militia released the two after 23 days.

Women's Rights and Sexual Orientation

Libyan law does not specifically criminalize domestic violence. Personal status laws discriminate against women with respect to marriage, divorce, and inheritance. The penal code allows for a reduced sentence for a man who kills or injures his wife or another female relative because he suspects her of extramarital sexual relations. Under the penal code, rapists can escape prosecution if they marry their victim.

The penal code prohibits all sexual acts outside marriage, including consensual same-sex relations, and punishes them with flogging and up to five years in prison.

Migrants, Refugees, and Asylum Seekers

As of October 31, the IOM recorded 9,648 arrivals to Italy of migrants who departed from Libya and 692 deaths in the central Mediterranean. Libyan coast guards intercepted and returned to Libyan shores 8,283people, including 374 children. According to IOM, 203 persons were missing at sea.

Migrants and asylum seekers who are captured at sea and returned to Libyan territory are placed in detention under the GNA Interior Ministry, where many suffer inhumane conditions including beatings, sexual violence, extortion, forced labor, and inadequate medical treatment, food and water. The Department for Combating Illegal Migration (DCIM), under the GNA Interior Ministry, manages the formal migrant detention centers, while smugglers and traffickers run informal ones.

According to the IOM, there were 655,144 migrants in Libya, including 85,891 in urban areas in Tripoli, as of October 31. That month, the IOM estimated that the 26 official detention centers in Libya were holding a total of 4,754 people.

The European Union has continued to provide training, equipment, and funds to Libyan coast guard forces to intercept boats both in Libyan coastal waters and international waters, and to return migrants and asylum seekers to Libyan territory where they are detained in inhuman and degrading conditions. The EU's aiding and abetting of Libyan coast guard forces appears motivated, in part, to reduce arrivals in Europe and to avoid triggering EU nonrefoulement obligations by outsourcing interdiction to Libyan coast guard forces.

Key International Actors

The United Arab Emirates, Egypt, Russia, and France played key roles in supporting the LNA and Turkey in supporting the GNA. Turkey reportedly supplied the GNA with armed drones that it used to strike LNA positions and armored vehicles. Egypt reportedly supplied the LNA with military equipment, and the United Arab Emirates (UAE) reportedly supported the LNA with armed drones that were used to strike positions of GNA-allied groups in Tripoli and Misrata. France gave political support to General Hiftar, and according to news reports Russia increased its support of Hiftar by providing hundreds of fighters, including snipers, through a Kremlin-linked private group.

The UN Security Council in June renewed the arms embargo on Libya. According to a confidential report of the UN Panel of Experts on Libya delivered to Security Council members on October 29 and leaked to the press, in 2019, the United Arab Emirates, Jordan, and Turkey "routinely and sometimes blatantly supplied weapons with little effort to disguise the source." According to news reports, Jordan provided training to LNA fighters; the UAE allegedly used attack aircraft on behalf of the LNA; and Turkey allegedly supplied the GNA forces with military material, including armored vehicles and drones. According to a news report, Sudan provided 1,000 fighters to support the LNA.

As of November, the Security Council had not yet taken measures against entities allegedly providing weapons to the warring parties.

Since the end of the 2011 revolution, the council has imposed individual targeted sanctions in the form of asset freezes and travel bans on only eight individuals, including two militia commanders and six more individuals in relation to alleged abuses of migrants and illicit trafficking and smuggling.

The European Council in March extended the mandate of Operation Sophia until September 30, then again for another six months until 31 March 2020. The operation involves airplanes, drones and ships deployed to capture and destroy vessels used by migrant smugglers or traffickers; training the Libyan Coastguard and Navy; and enforcing the UN arms embargo off the coast of Libya. The deployment of the operation's naval assets remains suspended.

In October, the United Nations General Assembly confirmed Libya's bid to join the UN Human Rights Council from 2020 to 2022.

Malaysia

Malaysia continued to make slow progress in 2019 in some areas of the governing Pakatan Harapan's reform agenda, such as lowering the voting age, strengthening parliamentary independence, and abolishing restrictions on protest marches. However, the government backed away from other commitments, including by withdrawing from the Rome Statute of the International Criminal Court (ICC) in April 2019, barely a month after filing its accession; retreating from a commitment to completely abolish the death penalty; and failing to carry out commitments to abolish or reform a range of abusive laws.

Freedom of Expression

The government has yet to fulfill its promise to abolish the much-abused sedition act. The law continues to be used, particularly against those voicing criticism of Malaysia's royalty. Some of those speaking critically about race and religion have also faced criminal investigations, including member of parliament Charles Santiago, who was one of five individuals called in for questioning in September after controversial Islamic preacher Zakir Naik filed a criminal defamation complaint against them. Santiago was questioned for criticizing Naik's claim that Malaysian Indians were more loyal to India's prime minister than to that of Malaysia. In March, Allister Cogia was sentenced to more than 10 years in prison for social media comments deemed insulting to Islam.

In October 2019, the lower house of parliament once again voted to repeal the Anti-Fake News Law passed during the waning months of the prior administration. Malaysia's Senate stymied efforts to repeal the law in 2018. Government promises to amend the Communications and Multimedia Act and the Official Secrets Act remain unfulfilled.

Criminal Justice System

In October 2018, the government announced its intention to abolish the death penalty and impose a moratorium on executions. In March, however, it announced that it would maintain the death penalty but would merely end the mandatory application of the punishment. Malaysia currently permits the death penalty for various crimes and makes the sentence mandatory for 11 offenses.

The government has yet to introduce legislation to abolish even the mandatory death penalty.

Malaysia continues to detain individuals without trial under restrictive laws. Twelve people, including two Democratic Action Party lawmakers, were detained under the Security Offenses (Special Measures) Act in October on allegations of supporting the now-defunct Liberation Tigers of Tamil Eelam (LTTE).

SOSMA allows for preventive detention of up to 28 days with no judicial review for a broadly defined range of "security offenses." Both the 1959 Prevention of Crime Act and the 2015 Prevention of Terrorism Act give government-appointed boards the authority to impose detention without trial for up to two years, renewable indefinitely, to order electronic monitoring, and to impose other significant restrictions on freedom of movement and association. No judicial review is permitted for these measures. The new government has committed to "abolish draconian provisions" in these laws, but has yet to do so.

Pakatan Harapan had also pledged to repeal the 2016 National Security Council Act, which gives broad emergency-like powers to a federal agency under the Prime Minister's Department. Instead of repealing it, the government introduced amendments via a bill that was submitted for first reading in April 2019, some of which increased the council's powers instead of curtailing them. The amendments had yet to pass at time of writing.

Police Abuse and Impunity

Police abuse of suspects in custody continues to be a serious problem, as does a lack of accountability for such offenses. The standard of care for those indent Police Complaints of Misconduct Commission. While tabling the bill is a positive step forward towards police accountability, some of the bill's provisions raise concern about the independence and authority of the proposed commission.

Refugees, Asylum Seekers, and Trafficking Victims

Malaysia has not yet fulfilled its commitment to ratify the 1951 Refugee Convention. Over 150,000 refugees and asylum seekers, most of whom come from Myanmar, are registered with the United Nations High Commission for Refugees (UNHCR) in Malaysia. Asylum seekers arrested by authorities are treated as "illegal migrants" and locked up in overcrowded and unsanitary immigration detention centers. The new government committed to improve the situation for refugees and asylum seekers, but they have no legal status and remain unable to work, travel, or enrol in government schools.

Malaysia deported asylum seekers from Egypt, Thailand, and Turkey in 2019, violating customary international law.

In January, the government announced the formation of a Royal Commission of Inquiry (RCI) to investigate mass graves found in remote jungle camps on the Thai-Malaysian border in 2015. The RCI held hearings in May and June, but had not issued a public report at time of writing. To date, no Malaysians have been held responsible for their role in the deaths of over 100 ethnic Rohingya trafficking victims whose bodies were found in the camps. The 12 police officers initially charged in the case were released in March 2017.

Freedom of Assembly and Association

In March, the police called in for questioning at least nine organizers and speakers of the Women's March held in observance of International Women's Day after a public backlash against the visible presence of lesbian, gay, bisexual, and transgender (LGBT) activists and their allies in the march. The organizers were investigated for sedition and violation of the Public Peaceful Assembly Act, but ultimately no charges were filed against them.

In July, parliament passed amendments to the Peaceful Assembly Act, reducing the notice period from 10 to 7 days and removing the restriction on protests in which participants march from one place to another. However, the law still permits criminal prosecution of those organizing or participating in peaceful assemblies. While the amended law authorizes the police to impose a non-criminal financial penalty rather than formally prosecuting a violator, exercise of that option would require the public prosecutor's written consent.

Freedom of Religion

Malaysia restricts the rights of followers of any branches of Islam other than Sunni, with those following Shia or other branches subject to arrest for deviancy. In September, the Selangor Islamic Religious Department (JAIS) instructed mosques in the state to deliver a sermon describing Shia Muslim beliefs and practices as “deviant,” “heinous,” “nonsense,” and “nauseating.” On September 6, JAIS arrested 23 Shia, including children, for practicing their religion, while another eight Shia were arrested at a private event in Johor on September 9.

In August, the High Court dismissed a challenge by Sisters in Islam, a civil society group working to promote the rights of Muslim women, to a fatwa issued against it in 2014. The broadly worded fatwa declares that Sisters in Islam and “any individuals, organizations and institutions holding on to liberalism and religious pluralism” are deviant from Islamic teachings.

Sexual Orientation and Gender Identity

Discrimination against LGBT people remains pervasive in Malaysia. Federal law punishes “carnal knowledge against the order of nature” with up to 20 years in prison and mandatory whipping. Numerous state Sharia laws prohibit both same-sex relations and non-normative gender expression, resulting in frequent arrests of transgender people. Government officials, including Prime Minister Mahathir Mohamad, have made statements expressing lack of support for the LGBT community. In June 2019, Mahathir said that the discussion of LGBT rights was being promoted by “Western countries” and was “unsuitable” for Malaysia.

Three transgender women were killed between November 2018 and January 2019. No one has been convicted in any of the killings. Eight men have been charged in the brutal beating of a transgender woman in Negeri Sembilan in August 2018. The victim suffered broken ribs, a ruptured spleen, and head injuries. The case remained pending at time of writing.

In March 2019, the minister for religious affairs, Mujahid Yusof Rawa, called the participation of LGBT people at a march for International Women’s Day an “abuse of democratic space.” The backlash against participants was vocal and severe, with some reporting harassment on social media, including threats of violence.

In August 2019, Malaysian authorities censored gay scenes from the Elton John biopic, “Rocketman,” sparking condemnation by art critics.

Child Marriage

Malaysia permits child marriage under both civil and Islamic law. Girls age 16 and older can marry with permission of their state's chief minister. For Muslims, most state Islamic laws set a minimum age of 16 for girls and 18 for boys, but permit marriages below those ages, with no apparent minimum, with the permission of a Sharia court. While the government announced in August that it has put in place stricter guidelines for the granting of permission for children to marry, it has not ended the practice.

Key International Actors

The Malaysian government has continued to speak out strongly about Myanmar's mistreatment of the Rohingya Muslims. The government has been unwilling, however, to openly criticize China's treatment of Uyghurs and other Turkic Muslims in Xinjiang, with Prime Minister Mahathir saying that doing so "would not achieve anything." China is Malaysia's largest trading partner, and Mahathir has said he is committed to strengthening ties between the two countries. Malaysia showed it is willing to buck Association of Southeast Asian Nations (ASEAN) norms in November when it permitted Sam Rainsy, exiled Cambodian opposition leader, to visit Kuala Lumpur despite strenuous objections from Phnom Penh.

Maldives

Although the Maldives took some steps in 2019 to address longstanding human rights concerns, in November the government shut down the most prominent human rights organization in the country in response to complaints from religious leaders that it had insulted Islam. Extremist groups continued to pose a threat to human rights defenders and activists whom they accused of being "too secular," and to exert influence over the police courts, and other government institutions.

In its 2018 electoral victory, the Maldives Democratic Party (MDP) ousted the abusive authoritarian government of President Abdulla Yameen. Ibrahim Mohamed Solih took office as president and vowed to implement an ambitious reform agenda that included strengthening judicial independence, restoring fundamental rights, and investigating abuses that had taken place under the Yameen administration. His party won a majority in April 2019 parliamentary elections, enhancing the government's capacity to undertake human rights reforms.

Attacks on Human Rights Defenders

The Maldivian Democracy Network (MDN), a leading human rights organization, and its staff faced threats for a 2015 report on radicalization, published during the previous Yameen government, which Islamist groups claimed included language insulting Islam. Although MDN issued an apology for causing unintended offense and removed the report from its website, Islamist groups issued threats on social media against MDN staff and other rights groups and activists. The government detained two men for making death threats against the MDN founder, Shahindha Ismail. On November 5, the government yielded to pressure from Islamist groups and political opposition figures, including former president Yameen, and ordered the dissolution of MDN.

Accountability for Past Abuses

In November 2018, the Solih government established the Commission on Deaths and Disappearances to investigate past attacks on activists and journalists. Cases included the 2014 abduction of Ahmed Rilwan, who had criticized Islamist gangs and exposed government corruption, and Yameen Rasheed, a blogger and activist who was stabbed to death in April 2017. In January, the commission chair, former Attorney General Husnu Al Suood, stated that extremist Islamist gangs had influence over police and criminal courts, and colluded to protect perpetrators and "fix" the outcome of trials.

On September 1, the commission issued a draft report accusing a local extremist group with ties to Al-Qaeda of Rilwan's murder. On November 17, the commission reported that local extremists had also murdered a former MP, Dr. Afrasheem Ali, in 2012. In both cases, the commission implicated police and politicians in shielding the perpetrators from prosecution. The trial of six suspects accused of killing Yameen Rasheed was delayed repeatedly.

In a separate case, the commission recommended charges against prison officials over the death of a prisoner who had not received needed medical care in November 2016.

Torture, Mistreatment, and Prison Conditions

In April, a government-established prison audit commission issued a report detailing corruption, systemic abuse and mistreatment throughout detention facilities in the Maldives. The commissioner of prisons, Abdulla Munaz, declared a Malé prison annex used for older and sick inmates "unfit for humans" after an inspection, and closed it. The home minister established a committee to oversee prison reform, reduce overcrowding, and implement the audit commission's recommendations.

In June, prison guards beat and pepper-sprayed inmates at Maafushi Prison after a prisoner attacked an off-duty guard. Prisoners alleged that wounded inmates were left without medical care for extended periods. Home Minister Imran Abdulla acknowledged that guards had used what he termed "excessive force" and vowed to end torture in prisons.

A video showing police officers beating an unarmed man went viral on social media in July, prompting the police commissioner to suspend the officers involved and promise an investigation, saying the "culture of police brutality needs to go." The Human Rights Commission of the Maldives (HRCM) also launched an investigation.

Freedom of Expression and Human Rights Defenders

Gangs that endorse a violent Islamist ideology, including some linked to prominent politicians, continued to threaten human rights defenders, journalists, and civil society groups. The targets included individuals who promoted freedom of expression and religion, published material deemed offensive to Islam, or backed the rights of lesbian, gay, bisexual, and transgender (LGBT) people. Human rights activists reported that they were targeted by online outlets Vaguthu Online, Siru Arts, and Murtad Watch ("Apostate Watch"), and threatened with violence.

On January 23, unidentified assailants vandalized Mandhu College after its chairman, Ibrahim Ismail, criticized clerics who had voiced support for a magistrate who had sentenced a woman to stoning. Islamist groups also accused Ismail of blasphemy and threatened him on social media.

On September 11, police arrested a man who had received death threats online and charged him with insulting Islam. The Maldives penal code criminalizes "criticism of Islam in a public medium." Police investigated the threats but made no arrests.

After the September 2018 elections, parliament repealed the Anti-Defamation and Freedom of Expression Act, which the previous government had used to levy heavy fines against media that published content critical of the president.

Women's Rights

In a historic vote on September 3, the parliament confirmed former judges Dr. Azmiralda Zahir and Aisha Shujune Mohamed as the first female justices of the Maldives Supreme Court. Some clerics had opposed the appointments. Women are severely underrepresented in the Maldives' judiciary, parliament, and local governing bodies. The Judicial Service Commission launched an investigation into sexual harassment in courts after a string of recent complaints against members of the judiciary.

On January 7, 2019, a magistrate in Naifuri, an island in northern Maldives, sentenced a 25-year-old woman to death by stoning on charges of adultery. The Maldives Supreme Court overturned the verdict the following day, prompting extremists to denounce the ruling and threaten human rights activists who had criticized the stoning verdict.

Gender-based violence is endemic in the Maldives. Maldivian women routinely face harassment in public, most of which goes unreported. On March 8, International Women's Day, activists organized an "Occupy *Reygandu*" ("Occupy the Night") gathering in Malé and two southern cities to highlight the need for safe public spaces. Another protest, "Occupy *SaiHotaa,*" focused on women's harassment-free access to restaurants.

Sexual Orientation and Gender Identity

The Maldivian penal code criminalizes adult, consensual same-sex sexual conduct; punishment can include imprisonment of up to eight years and 100 lashes, although this is not often applied. Extremist groups in the Maldives have used social media to harass and threaten those who promote the rights of LGBT people.

Key International Actors

During a visit in June, the United Nations special rapporteur for cultural rights, Karima Bennoune, urged the government to "grab the chance offered by a moment of reform" to combat extremism and ensure the rights of all to take part in cultural life without discrimination. UN Special Rapporteur on Torture Nils Melzer conducted his first official visit to the Maldives in November.

The Maldives' major donors and allies welcomed President Solih's pledges to implement democratic reforms and restore fundamental rights. The European Union, which had threatened sanctions against members of the Yameen administration in 2018, congratulated the Maldives on its return to "the path of democracy." The European Union also provided assistance to the Maldives to strengthen judicial reform and address climate change.

Indian Prime Minister Narendra Modi made a state visit to the Maldives in June, during which he and President Solih signed a range of trade and development agreements, including a memorandum on information-sharing between the Indian navy and the Maldives.

Although Solih had criticized the scale of debt for projects China had financed in the Maldives under the previous administration, his government signed new loan agreements, stating that China remains "an important bilateral development partner."

Mali

Mali's human rights situation deteriorated in 2019 as hundreds of civilians were killed in numerous incidents by ethnic self-defense groups, most for their perceived support of Islamist groups, and attacks by armed Islamists intensified in northern and central parts of the country. These groups, allied to Al-Qaeda and the Islamic State, targeted Malian security services, peacekeepers, international forces, and increasingly, civilians. Malian security forces subjected numerous suspects to severe mistreatment and several died in custody or were forcibly disappeared.

The worsening security situation in the country provoked a political crisis and led to delays in the constitutional review process and parliamentary elections. The peace process envisioned to end the 2012-2013 crisis in the north made scant progress, including on disarmament and the restoration of state authority.

Over 85,000 civilians fled their homes as a result of violence in 2019. Humanitarian agencies were attacked, largely by bandits, undermining their ability to deliver aid. Rampant banditry continued to undermine livelihoods, and protests against the government over corruption continued.

Little progress was made toward providing justice for victims of abuses, and rule-of-law institutions remained weak. A new justice minister improved detention conditions and pledged to prioritize the fight against impunity. The military justice system made some progress in investigating dozens of past extrajudicial killings by their forces.

Atrocities against civilians and the deteriorating security situation in the Sahel, garnered significant attention from Mali's international partners, notably the United Nations, France, Germany, the European Union, and the United States. These actors regularly denounced atrocities through public statements but were inconsistent in their calls for accountability.

Communal Violence

During 2019, at least 400 civilians were killed in incidents of communal violence in central and northern Mali. The violence pitted ethnically aligned self-defense groups against mainly ethnic Peuhl or Fulani communities accused of supporting Islamist armed groups.

The most lethal attacks in central Mali were perpetrated by Dogon militiamen including the worst single atrocity in Mali's recent history as at least 150 civilians were massacred on March 23 in Ogossagou village; a January 1 attack on Koulogon village killed 37 civilians, and June attacks in Bologo and Saran villages left over 20 dead. After the Ogossagou massacre, the government pledged but failed to disarm and dissolve the implicated militia. Peuhl militiamen were implicated in the June 9 massacre of 35 Dogon civilians in Sobane-da village.

Scores of farmers, herders and traders were killed by different ethnic militias in reprisal killings as they tended their fields or animals and went to market, provoking widespread displacement and a hunger crisis.

Abuses by Islamist Armed Groups

Attacks by armed Islamists allied to Al-Qaeda, and to a lesser extent the Islamist State affiliate in the Sahel, killed over 150 civilians, as well as scores of government forces and at least 16 United Nations Multidimensional Integrated Stabilization Mission in Mali (MINUSMA) peacekeepers, including the January 20 attack on the Aguelhok UN base that killed 11 Chadian peacekeepers.

Armed Islamists massacred numerous civilians, including in Menaka region and at least 38 in Yoro and Gangafani II villages near the Burkina Faso border. In several instances, they removed men from public transportation vehicles and killed them, including around the towns of Sévaré and Bandiagara.

Over 50 civilians were killed by improvised explosive devices planted on roadways, especially in central Mali. On September 3, an explosion killed 14 bus passengers near Dallah, and a June attack near Yoro killed 11. Armed Islamists planted explosives in the bodies of security force members, and in February a civilian's body, which exploded during his burial, killing 17.

Armed Islamists continued to threaten, and sometimes kill local leaders deemed government collaborators and beat those engaged in cultural practices they had forbidden. They also imposed their version of Sharia (Islamic law) via courts that did not adhere to fair trial standards.

Abuses by State Security Forces

Since late 2018, numerous men detained by the security forces during counterterrorism operations were subjected to enforced disappearance, five were allegedly executed or died in custody, and dozens more were subjected to severe mistreatment in detention. Numerous men accused of terrorism-related offenses were detained by the national intelligence agency in unauthorized detention facilities and without respect for due process.

Military investigations into the alleged extrajudicial killing of almost 50 suspects in Diourra, Boulikessi and Nantaka in 2018 progressed but at time of writing no soldier had been prosecuted.

Progress in the professionalization of the security forces was evident in the increased presence of military police responsible for ensuring discipline during military operations and increased patrols to protect civilians.

Children's Rights

Over 150 children were killed during communal violence, by explosive devices or in crossfire. The UN Children's Fund (UNICEF) reported 99 cases of recruitment and use of children by armed groups in the first six months of 2019, more than double those reported the previous year. Over 900 schools remained closed and 270,000 children were denied the right to education because of insecurity and displacement.

Judicial and Human Rights Legal Framework

The Malian judiciary remained plagued by neglect and mismanagement, and many posts in northern and central Mali were abandoned due to insecurity. Hundreds of detainees were held in extended pretrial detention due to the courts' inability to adequately process cases.

Justice Minister Malick Coulibaly, appointed in May, took concrete steps to improve prison conditions and vowed to improve access to justice and make progress on atrocity cases.

In July, the parliament passed a law of "national understanding," which civil society groups contended could lead to impunity for some serious human rights violations.

The mandate of the Specialized Judicial Unit against Terrorism and Transnational Organized Crime (Specialized Judicial Unit), created by law in 2013, was in July expanded to include international human rights crimes.

In October, the government extended for one year the state of emergency, first declared in 2015. The state of emergency gives security services additional authority and restricts public gatherings.

Accountability for Abuses

There was scant progress on delivering justice for atrocities committed since 2012-2013, however several investigations were opened by local courts and the Specialized Judicial Unit, including into the Ogossagou massacre. Local groups said the government was reluctant to question or charge militia leaders credibly implicated in massacres, favoring short-term reconciliation efforts envisioned to mitigate communal tension.

In contrast, the Specialized Unit was actively investigating over 200 terrorism-related cases and in 2018, completed 10 trials.

Human Rights and Truth and Reconciliation Mechanisms

The National Commission for Human Rights (CNDH) investigated some abuses, issued several communiques, visited detention centers, and set up a program to provide legal support to the indigent.

The Truth, Justice and Reconciliation Commission, established in 2014 to investigate crimes and root causes of violence since 1960, has taken over 14,000 victim and witness statements, but its credibility was weakened by the inclusion of armed group members and exclusion of victims' representatives. Public hearings were scheduled to begin in December.

Key International Actors

France and the US led on military matters, the EU on training and security sector reform, and the UN on rule of law and political stability.

The G5 Sahel multinational counterterrorism military force, created in 2017, comprising forces from Mali, Mauritania, Burkina Faso, Niger, and Chad, did not become fully operational as a result of insufficient financial support and equipment.

In September, the Economic Community of West African States (ECOWAS), pledged US$1 billion to help support G5 Sahel and national militaries in countering terrorism from 2020- 2024.

Operation Barkhane, the 4,500-member French regional counterterrorism force, conducted numerous operations in Mali. The EU Training Mission in Mali (EUTM) and EU Capacity Building Mission (EUCAP), continued to train and advise Mali's security forces.

In August, the UN Security Council renewed for one year the mandate of the Mali Sanctions Committee Panel of Experts and imposed an asset freeze and travel ban against those individuals and entities who obstruct the 2015 peace accord and commit human rights abuses. In July, the Council put five men—two businessmen, two armed Islamists, and a parliamentarian—on the sanction list.

MINUSMA meaningfully supported the government, including in atrocity investigations, and community reconciliation efforts, and increased patrolling. However, its robust civilian protection mandate was challenged due to persistent attacks against peacekeepers and lack of equipment.

The International Commission of Inquiry, established in 2018 by the UN secretary-general as provided by the 2015 peace accord, investigated serious violations of international human rights and humanitarian law between 2012 and January 2018.

In June, the UN Security Council renewed and strengthened MINUSMA's mandate by including the deteriorating security situation in Mali's center as a second strategic priority.

The 13,000-strong force was also tasked with increasing efforts to protect civilians and support efforts to bring perpetrators to justice.

The UN independent expert on Mali visited the country in February and issued several statements on the importance of addressing impunity. During its March session, the UN Human Rights Council decided to continue the mandate of the decided to continue the mandate of the independent expert for another year.

The International Criminal Court (ICC) continued investigation into alleged war crimes committed in Mali, opened in 2013, and in March, the ICC Registrar visited Mali. However, it had not yet sought arrest warrants for any individuals at time of writing.

Mauritania

Former Defense Minister Mohamed Ould Ghazouani won presidential elections in June, succeeding two-term incumbent Mohamed Ould Abdel Aziz. Abdel Aziz, who came to power in 2008 following a coup, did not run in 2019. In an effort to crush protests over the first-round victory by Ghazouani, whom Abdel Aziz backed, authorities detained without charge pro-opposition leaders and arrested dozens of opposition activists, releasing most but sentencing others to prison terms. Authorities also suspended mobile and fixed-line internet service the day after the elections for 10 days.

Authorities used laws on criminal defamation, the spread of "false information," and blasphemy to prosecute and jail human rights defenders, activists, bloggers, and political dissidents.

Slavery has not been eliminated despite multiple laws banning it and specialized courts to prosecute those who subject people to slavery.

Freedom of Expression

Prosecutors use repressive legislation that includes criminal defamation and broad definitions of terrorism and "inciting racial hatred" to censor and prosecute critics for nonviolent speech. An anti-discrimination law adopted in 2017 states in Article 10, "Whoever encourages an incendiary discourse against the official rite of the Islamic Republic of Mauritania shall be punished by one to five years in prison."

On February 1, authorities dropped charges and released activist Abdallahi Salem Ould Yali, jailed in January 2018 on charges of incitement to violence and racial hatred under the penal code, counterterrorism law, and cybercrime law. Yali was arrested for WhatsApp messages in which he called on Haratines, the ethnic group to which he belongs, to resist discrimination and demand their rights.

Authorities on March 22 arrested two bloggers, Abderrahmane Weddady and Cheikh Ould Jiddou, for Facebook posts criticizing corruption and accused them of knowingly spreading false information about Mauritanian funds allegedly frozen in the United Arab Emirates. The two are known to criticize Mauritania's leaders, including alleging wrongdoing by then-former President Mohamed Ould Abdel Aziz. Authorities granted pretrial release to Wedaddy and Ould Jiddou on June 3 but confiscated their travel documents. No trial date had been set at time of writing.

The government severed mobile internet service for 10 days on June 23, one day after the presidential elections. While fixed-line internet service was still available in some offices and businesses, most Mauritanians could not access it because they rely on their phones for internet access. Authorities justified the shutdown as necessary for security.

On July 29, authorities freed blogger Mohamed Cheikh Ould Mkhaitir who had been held in a blasphemy case for five-and-a-half years. Authorities arrested him in January 2014 for denouncing what he said was the misuse of Islam to justify caste discrimination in Mauritania. A court initially sentenced him to death for blasphemy. An appeals court revised the sentence to two years in prison, which he had already served. But instead of releasing him, authorities held him in solitary and arbitrary detention for another 21 months, ostensibly for his own protection, then transferred him directly out of the country. At time of writing he was seeking asylum in France.

In October, students demonstrated regularly in Nouakchott against a 2018 rule that prevented students who had reached the age of 25 from enrolling for the first time in public universities, a rule that seemed to affect low-income students disproportionately. Police dispersed the protests, apparently using excessive force, on several occasions. On November 6, the government suspended the discriminatory rule for the academic year 2019/2020.

Freedom of Association

The restrictive 1964 Law of Associations requires associations to obtain formal permission to operate legally and gives the Ministry of Interior far-reaching powers to refuse such permission on vague grounds such as “anti-national propaganda” or exercising “an unwelcome influence on the minds of the people.”

The ministry has withheld recognition from several associations that campaign on controversial issues, such as the Initiative for the Resurgence of the Abolitionist Movement (IRA) and “Hands Off My Nationality,” which accuses the government of discriminating against blacks in the national civil registration process. Members of the IRA, including its leader Biram Dah Abeid, have been subject to arrests and harassment.

Human Rights Watch representatives conducted research in Mauritania in 2019 without obstacles but were unable to meet with high level government officials. Nouakchott airport officials in March 2019 barred a delegation of Amnesty International from entering the country citing lack of "authorization."

Freedom of Movement

Mauritanian authorities in October granted a passport to Mohamedou Ould Slahi, three years after he returned to his native Mauritania, after he spent more than 14 years in arbitrary detention in Jordan, Afghanistan, and the US-run Guantanamo detention center. Mohamedou says he requires medical care related to his long detention that is unavailable in Mauritania.

Political Opposition

In the aftermath of the June 22, 2019 presidential election and ensuing protests, some of which resulted in clashes with security forces, Mauritanian authorities temporarily detained pro-opposition public figures and dozens of opposition activists who denounced the official results as fraudulent.

The Interior Ministry announced on June 25 that security forces had arrested 100 protesters. Authorities have released some of them but others remain held on charges such as taking part in unauthorized demonstrations, damaging public property, and disturbing the peace. Courts sentenced at least 13 of the protesters to six months in prison. In November, authorities released all remaining people held in conjunction with election protests.

Authorities arrested Samba Thiam, an opposition political activist working with an opposition candidate and founder of the unrecognized political party Progressive Forces for Change, on June 25, three days after the presidential election. They released him without charge on July 3. Thiam said authorities required him to sign a pledge to cease activities and speech "promoting violence and extreme views," both of which he denied doing.

Authorities on June 26 also arrested journalist Seidi Moussa Camara, who writes critically of authorities, but released him without charge on July 3. Camara is an ally of the anti-slavery group Initiative for the Resurgence of the Abolitionist Movement (IRA), whose leader, Biram Dah Abeid, came in second in the election.

On July 3, security agents arrested journalist Ahmedou Ould Wedia from Mauritania's Al-Mourabitoun television channel. He was questioned by a prosecutor and released without charge on July 15. Wedia is reportedly close to the opposition party Tawassoul, whose candidate came in third in the elections.

Slavery

Mauritania abolished slavery in 1981, the world's last country to do so, and criminalized it in 2007. The Global Slavery Index, which measures forced labour and forced marriage, estimates that there are 90,000 living in "modern slavery" in Mauritania, or 2.4 percent of the population. Three special courts that prosecute slavery-related crimes have tried a handful of cases since their creation under a 2015 law. According to the 2019 US State Department Trafficking in Persons Report, Mauritania investigated four cases, prosecuted one alleged trafficker, but did not convict any. Nine appeals cases remained pending at the anti-slavery court.

Death Penalty

Mauritania's laws impose the death penalty for a range of offenses, including, under certain conditions, blasphemy, adultery, and homosexuality. A de facto moratorium remains in effect on capital punishment and on corporal punishments that are inspired by Islamic Sharia law and found in the penal code

Women's Rights

The 2017 law on reproductive health recognizes it as a right, even as Mauritania maintained its ban on abortion. The country's general code on children's protection criminalizes female genital mutilation (FGM); however, according to the United Nations it is still prevalent, particularly in rural communities.

Mauritanian law does not adequately define the crime of rape and other forms of sexual assault, although a draft law on gender-based violence, which contains more specific definitions, was pending before parliament. The criminalization of consensual adult sexual relations outside marriage likely deters girls and women from reporting assaults, because they can find themselves charged if the judiciary views the sexual act in question as consensual.

Mauritania's laws on divorce, child custody, and inheritance discriminate against women.

Sexual Orientation

Article 308 prohibits homosexual conduct between Muslim adults and punishes it with death for males. There were no publicly known cases of persons in detention for homosexuality and no one was sentenced to death in 2019 for homosexual conduct.

Key International Actors

Mauritania is a member of the G5 Sahel, an alliance of five countries headquartered in Nouakchott that cooperate on security, including counterterrorism. As of January 1, 2019, Mauritania lost trade preference benefits from the US under the African Growth and Opportunity Act (AGOA) as "Mauritania has made insufficient progress toward combating forced labor, in particular the scourge of hereditary slavery.... [and] continues to restrict the ability of civil society to work freely to address anti-slavery issues."

On October 17, 2019, the UN General Assembly confirmed Mauritania's bid to join as a member the UN Human Rights Council for 2020-2022.

Mexico

Human rights violations committed by security forces—including torture, enforced disappearances, and abuses against migrants—have continued under the administration of President Andrés Manuel López Obrador, who took office in December 2018. Impunity remains the norm. President López Obrador created the National Guard, made up largely of military personnel, and ordered its deployment to control irregular immigration. Laws enacted in 2017 could help address the problems of torture and disappearances, but implementation lags.

In February, a well-respected human rights defender was appointed to head the National Search Commission (CNB) and charged with coordinating the nationwide search for disappeared persons.

Abuses against migrants, attacks on independent journalists and human rights defenders, and limitations to accessing sexual and reproductive rights remain serious concerns.

Criminal Justice System

The criminal justice system routinely fails to provide justice to victims of violent crimes and human rights violations, despite a 2013 law intended to ensure them justice, protection, and reparations. In a 2018 report, the special rapporteur on human rights defenders declared that about 98 percent of crimes committed in Mexico remained unsolved. Causes of failure include corruption, inadequate training and resources, and complicity of prosecutors and public defenders with criminals and abusive officials. In November 2019, the United Nations Human Rights Committee expressed its concern for "recurrent" impunity in relation to grave human rights violations, and highlighted the "grave" shortcomings in investigations and prosecutions for these cases.

Military Abuses and Impunity

Mexico has relied heavily on the military to fight drug-related violence and organized crime, leading to widespread human rights violations by military personnel. Between December 2012 and January 2018, the National Human Rights

Commission (CNDH) received more than 4,600 complaints regarding alleged military abuses. From January to July 2019, it received 241 such complaints.

In 2014, Congress reformed the Code of Military Justice to require that abuses committed by members of the military against civilians be prosecuted in civilian, not military, courts. However, the pursuit of justice for these violations remains elusive. In November 2019, the UN Human Rights Committee highlighted its concern about the 2016 reforms to the Military Code of Criminal Procedures and the Code of Military Justice that provided military prosecutors and judges with ample faculties to search dwellings and intervene in private communications without a warrant.

In November 2018, the Supreme Court struck down the Interior Security Law because it "[normalized] the use of the armed forces in public security issues," which the court ruled was unconstitutional and violated Mexico's international obligations.

However, that same month, President López Obrador announced the creation of the National Guard to replace the federal police in public security operations and "temporarily" collaborate in public security tasks in states and municipalities. Inaugurated in June, it is comprised largely of military troops and led by an army general who retired from active duty in August. The law regulating the National Guard allows its members to take part in criminal investigations and undertake intelligence activities with "preventive" purposes.

Torture

Torture is widely practiced in Mexico to obtain confessions and extract information. It is most frequently applied between when victims are detained, often arbitrarily, and when they are handed to civilian prosecutors—a time when they are often held incommunicado at military bases or illegal detention sites. Confessions obtained through torture are used as evidence at criminal trials.

In 2016, Mexico's national statistics office (INEGI) surveyed more than 64,000 people incarcerated in 338 Mexican prisons countrywide. Almost two out of three (64 percent) reported some type of physical violence at the time of arrest, including electric shocks, choking, and smothering. Between 2013 and 2018, 2,751 persons deprived of liberty died in federal and state prisons, according to data obtained by the UN Committee Against Torture.

From December 2012 through January 2018, the Attorney General's Office opened more than 9,000 investigations into torture. According to the office, its department of forensic specialists participated in 1,903 alleged torture cases in 2019, and CNDH received 84 torture complaints between January and September 2019. In its 2019 review of Mexico, the UN Committee Against Torture highlighted that out of 3,214 Mexican torture complaints made in 2016 alone, only eight resulted in an arrest and trial. The Committee against Torture expressed concern at reports that courts routinely fail to investigate torture allegations, placing the burden of proof on victims.

Investigations suffer from serious shortcomings. In 2018, the Mexican Office of the OHCHR published an investigation that stated it had found "solid grounds" to conclude that at least 34 detainees had been tortured during the investigation of the 2014 disappearance of 43 students from Ayotzinapa. In June 2019, local media circulated a video in which one of the 34 detainees is seen bound, blindfolded, and subjected to asphyxiation, electric shocks, and beatings during interrogation by public officials. In September, a main suspect in the Ayotzinapa disappearances was acquitted due to irregularities and human rights violations, including torture, during the investigations. At time of writing, 77 persons had been acquitted in the case, based on similar grounds.

The 2017 Law to Investigate, Prevent, and Sanction Torture aimed to curb torture and exclude from judicial proceedings testimony obtained through torture, but implementation has been slow. The National Mechanism to Prevent Torture (MNPT), which is linked to the CNDH, reported in 2018 that less than half of Mexican states had adopted similar legislation, as national law requires. As of November 2019, the Attorney General's Office had yet to fulfill the law's requirement that it have infrastructure for a national torture registry in place by December 2017.

Enforced Disappearances

Since 2006, enforced disappearances by security forces have been a widespread problem. Criminal organizations have also been responsible for many disappearances.

Prosecutors and police routinely neglect to take basic investigative steps to identify those responsible for enforced disappearances, often telling the missing people's families to investigate on their own. By January 2019, the Attorney General's Office had opened 975 investigations into allegations of enforced disappearances and had pressed charges in only 12 cases. By September 2019, the office's specialized unit on kidnappings reported having only one open investigation into disappearances committed by non-state agents. In November, the UN Human Rights Committee highlighted its concern for "alarming" impunity in cases of disappearances, including those where organized crime and authorities were allegedly colluded.

The 2017 law on disappearances established a single nationwide definition for the crime and mandated the creation of entities to facilitate the investigation and prosecution of disappearances. These include the CNB created to coordinate search efforts in the field, and the National Search System (SNB), established to coordinate state institutions involved in the search for the disappeared.

In August, Karla Quintana, the National Search Commissioner, head of the CNB, stated that the whereabouts of 40,000 people who had gone missing remained unknown. In November, the commissioner announced the creation of a new national registry for disappeared persons. Authorities noted that the official number of missing persons will likely increase after the establishment of the new registry. According to official numbers, by August, 4,874 bodies had been found in 3,024 clandestine graves nationwide between 2006 and 2019.

As of September, the SNB was not yet fully operational. A Standardized Protocol for the Search of Disappeared and Missing Persons, which the law mandated be in place by April 2018, had likewise failed to materialize. By September, seven out of 32 had failed to establish local search commissions or offices as the law directs. In May, the National Search Commissioner announced the beginning of the process towards a regional search plan in Northeast Mexico, and the federal government established a subsidy to provide funds to local search commissions.

Victims' families have repeatedly denounced serious shortcomings regarding the identification and storage of bodies. Government officials conceded that more than 26,000 bodies remain unidentified. In August, the National Search Commissioner reported the creation of a national forensic assessment to address obstacles to identifying and storing bodies. The same month, following demands by families, the government announced the creation of an Extraordinary Mechanism of Forensic Identification to identify bodies.

Extrajudicial Killings

In November 2019, the UN Human Rights Committee expressed its concern for reports of extrajudicial killings in Mexico, and the frequent impunity in these cases.

In September 2019, eight civilians were allegedly victims of extrajudicial executions by state police in Tamaulipas in Northern Mexico. At time of writing, authorities had issued arrest warrants against seven state police officers for the crimes of murder, abuse of authority, breaking and entry, and giving false reports to authorities. By October, authorities were still investigating.

There is no reliable information about the number of extrajudicial executions. Most homicides are never prosecuted. Government authorities only register the number of homicides, not their context. Although the Defense Ministry has said it stopped registering the numbers of civilians it killed as of 2014, civil society organizations said in 2019 that declarations made by the minister indicated that the information exists, but that the ministry has refused to release it and has not provided a substantiated explanation.

Attacks on Journalists and Human Rights Defenders

Journalists, particularly those who report on crime or criticize officials, often face harassment and attacks by both government authorities and criminal groups. Following a country visit in April, the UN high commissioner for human rights described the situation of human rights defenders and journalists as "alarming." The CNDH reported 148 journalists killed between 2000 and 2018, and 21 disappeared between 2005 and 2018. From January to July 2019, seven journalists were killed.

Authorities routinely fail to investigate crimes against journalists adequately, often preemptively ruling out their profession as a motive. Since its creation in 2010, the federal Special Prosecutor's Office to investigate crimes against journalists has opened more than 1,000 investigations. Between 2010 and December 2018, the Special Prosecutor's Office brought 186 charges for crimes against journalists, only 16.3 percent of those received out of all received complaints. During the same period, it obtained 10 convictions. In the face of such uninvestigated violence, many journalists self-censor.

Human rights defenders in Mexico are often subjected to intimidation, criminalization, and violence. Between January and July, at least 13 human rights defenders had been killed, an increase from past years, according to OHCHR. As with journalists, violence against human rights defenders is rarely investigated or prosecuted.

In 2012, the federal government established the National Protection Mechanism to issue and coordinate implementing protective measures for journalists and human rights defenders under threat. Between October 2012 and March 2019, 800 journalists and defenders requested protection measures; 678 such requests were granted. In July, OHCHR expressed concern for the mechanism's lack of sufficient resources, lack of clear procedures and problems in effectively coordinating protective measures.

Women's and Girls' Rights

In 2018, the UN Committee on the Elimination of All Forms of Discrimination Against Women (CEDAW) expressed concern for persistent patterns of "generalized" violence against women, including sexual violence. Despite this, Mexican laws do not adequately protect women and girls against domestic and sexual violence. Some provisions, including those that make the severity of punishments for some sexual offenses contingent upon the "chastity" of the victim, contradict international standards.

In August, the Supreme Court ruled that rape victims need not file a criminal complaint to access abortion services, and that health providers did not have to verify that a crime was committed to perform the abortion.

In October 2019, the decriminalization of abortion in the southern state of Oaxaca entered into force. In September, local lawmakers legalized abortion regardless of the cause until week 12 of pregnancy, making it the second state in the country to adopt such legislation, together with Mexico City.

Women and girls continue to face alarming rates of gender-based violence. According to official data, during January through July 2019 nationwide, there were 540 femicides—defined by Mexican law as depriving a woman of her life based on her gender. By April 2018, an official registry had recorded 9,522 women and girls as missing.

Migrants and Asylum Seekers

Migrants traveling through Mexico are frequently endure abuses and human rights violations. In some cases, government authorities have been alleged to have been involved. From January to September 2019, the CNDH received 599 complaints of abuses against migrants, most of which were made against members of the federal police.

In January 2019, the Trump administration began returning asylum seekers to Mexico while their claims are pending under the Migrant Protection Protocols. At time of writing, over 40,000 asylum seekers had been returned, many to dangerous and unlivable conditions in Mexico, with significant barriers to obtaining legal representation and a fair hearing. They included asylum seekers with disabilities or other chronic health conditions, despite initial guidance that no one with "known physical/mental health issues" would be in the program.

In June, the United States government threatened to impose tariffs on Mexican products unless Mexico accepted a significant increase in returns of asylum seekers to Mexico to wait for the court proceedings in the US and stopped migrants en route to the US border. In response, the López Obrador administration announced it would deploy 6,000 members of the new National Guard to control irregular migration, a decision that effectively militarized Mexico's borders.

In June, the CNDH issued protective measures for a shelter in the northern Mexican states of Sonora and Coahuila, after National Guard members attempted to enter, in violation of Mexican law, to examine migrants' immigration status.

As of September, government-run migrant holding centers were overcrowded, with detained migrants experiencing inhumane leading to inhumane conditions, including extreme heat, bug infestations, lack of access to basic hygiene, limited medical services, and poor quality food.

With the support of the UN High Commissioner for Refugees, Mexico's refugee agency granted refugee status to nearly 5,000 individuals from Venezuela, Honduras, El Salvador, and Guatemala in 2018, an increase of 75 percent compared with 2017. The agency extended complementary protection, a status offering safeguard against deportation for vulnerable individuals who do not qualify for recognition as refugees, to an additional 2,200 persons in 2018, compared with 1,265 in 2017. In the first eight months of 2019, Mexico's refugee agency said it had recognized 3,173 refugees and granted complementary protection to an additional 702 people from these four countries.

Sexual Orientation and Gender Identity

Mexico City and 18 additional Mexican states have legalized same-sex marriage. In other states, same-sex couples must file a constitutional challenge (*amparo*) to be allowed to marry. A 2015 Supreme Court decision holding that the sole legal definition of marriage is between a man and a woman violates the constitution. In May, the Supreme Court ruled that a same-sex couple from Aguascalientes should be allowed to register their child, protecting the best interest of the child, and upholding the principles of equality and non- discrimination.

In July, in response to a case filed by five transgender people in Querétaro, a federal judge ruled that trans people should be able to change their names and gender markers on birth certificates through a simple administrative process before the state Civil Registry. It found that legislation requiring trans people to seek individual court rulings to change their birth certificates was discriminatory and overly burdensome. The ruling makes Querétaro the eighth of Mexico's 32 jurisdictions to establish an administrative path to legal gender recognition for trans people.

Disability Rights

In its 2014 concluding observations on Mexico, the UN Committee on the Rights of Persons with Disabilities found that despite new laws and programs protecting the rights of people with disabilities, serious gaps remained, including in access to justice, legal standing, and the right to vote; access to buildings, transportation, and public spaces; violence against women; and education. As of November, President Lopez Obrador had not appointed a chair of the National

Council on People with Disabilities (CONADIS), the high-level body coordinating efforts to implement disability rights at the federal level and with state authorities.

In March, the Supreme Court ruled that limiting the legal capacity of a complainant, a man with an intellectual disability, was discriminatory. However, this judgment only protects the rights of the complainant—and not other people with disabilities—to, for example, decide to marry or sign contracts.

Key International Actors

In March, the UN Human Rights Council adopted a report on Mexico, as part of its Universal Periodic Review (UPR) mechanism. Mexico accepted 262 of the 264 recommendations it received, including one to establish an independent mechanism against impunity to investigate "atrocity crimes" and human rights violations. Other recommendations accepted by Mexico include creating an independent and autonomous Attorney General's Office, and combating impunity and corruption.

In April, UN High Commissioner for Human Rights Michelle Bachelet visited Mexico and signed two agreements: one to provide "technical assistance" to the controversial National Guard, and another to collaborate with a presidential commission working on the Ayotzinapa disappearances. She noted the need to create a new civil police force capable of combatting organized crime and drug trafficking while respecting human rights. She also addressed the "crosscutting" nature of impunity, her concern for sexual torture of women deprived of liberty, and violence against journalists and human rights defenders.

In May, the UN Committee against Torture concluded its seventh periodic review of Mexico. It expressed concern regarding the lack of adoption of the National Program on Torture and the use of the army in public security operations, given reports of soldiers committing grave human rights.

The UN Committee on the Elimination of Racial Discrimination (CERD) indicated in August that Mexico had failed to adopt sufficient measures to counter historic and structural discrimination against indigenous peoples and Afro-Mexicans. It highlighted that indigenous and Afro-Mexican human rights defenders are subjected to violence, threats, and attacks on their lives, as well as criminalization of their activities. The CERD claimed Mexico's migration policies at times failed to protect migrants and asylum seekers, including children.

In August, the government announced it would accept the jurisdiction of the UN Committee on Enforced Disappearance to process individual complaints, and invite the committee to carry out a country visit in 2020.

In November, the UN Human Rights Committee reported that Mexico faced high rates of violence motivated by gender identity or orientation, including killings. The committee emphasized its concern for high rates of unsafe abortions and obstacles in accessing abortions in rape cases, in violation of Mexican law. It called on the state to avoid a militarized approach to law enforcement and form the National Guard as a civilian institution.

Since 2007, the United States has allocated nearly US$2.9 billion in aid via the Mérida Initiative to help Mexico combat organized crime. President López Obrador declared in May that his government would reject the initiative and seek reorientation of cooperation to contribute to development in Mexico's Southeast and Central American countries.

Morocco

While there remained some space to criticize the government in Morocco—provided that any harsh criticism avoided the monarchy and other "red lines"—authorities continued to selectively target, prosecute, jail, and harass critics, and enforce various repressive laws, notably pertaining to individual liberties.

Freedom of Assembly, Police Violence, and the Criminal Justice System

On April 6, an appeals court in Casablanca confirmed the first-instance verdicts against Hirak protest leaders in the Rif region of Morocco, who were sentenced on June 2018 to up to 20 years in prison, largely based on statements that they said were made under police torture.

The Hirak, a protest movement in the Rif region that started in 2016, staged several largely peaceful mass protests for better socioeconomic conditions until a police crackdown in May 2017 led to the arrest of more than 450 activists, including about 50 leaders who underwent a mass trial in Casablanca that lasted more than a year.

Since the confirmation of the verdicts, the Hirak leaders have been held in various prisons in Morocco. Several staged hunger strikes in protest of what they called political trials.

The Code of Penal Procedure gives a defendant the right to contact a lawyer after 24 hours in police custody, extendable to 36 hours. But detainees do not have the right to a have a lawyer present when police interrogate or present them with their statements for signature.

Freedom of Association

On April 16, an appeals court in Casablanca confirmed the dissolution of Racines, a cultural association, four months after a court of first instance ordered it. The decision was taken after the governor of Casablanca petitioned a tribunal to act against the group for "organizing an activity including interviews interspersed with clear offenses towards institutions." The basis for this complaint was that in August 2018 Racines offered its Casablanca office as a venue for recording a YouTube-based talk show in which guests criticized King Mohammed VI's speeches and policies.

Authorities frequently impeded events organized by local chapters of the Moroccan Association for Human Rights (AMDH) by denying access to planned venues. On at least five occasions in 2019, including in Azrou, Tiznit, and Benslimane, authorities blocked the entrance of community centers and other meeting rooms where AMDH events were programmed.

According to AMDH, as of September 2019, authorities had refused to process the administrative formalities of 62 of its 99 local branches, impeding their ability to carry out functions like opening new bank accounts or renting space.

Freedom of Expression

The Press and Publications Code, adopted by parliament in July 2016, eliminates prison sentences for speech-related offenses. Meanwhile, the penal code maintains prison as a punishment for a variety of nonviolent speech offenses, including for "causing harm" to Islam, the monarchy, and "inciting against" Morocco's "territorial integrity," a reference to its claim to Western Sahara.

On September 30, a court in Rabat convicted and sentenced Hajar Raissouni, a 28-year-old journalist, to one year in prison for having an abortion and sex outside marriage after police arrested her on August 31. A prosecutor publicly disclosed deeply personal details about her sexual and reproductive life, and a judge refused to provisionally release her pending trial.

The court sentenced Raissouni's fiancé, Rifaat al-Amin, to one year in prison. The doctor accused of performing Raissouni's abortion received a two-year prison sentence, while a medical assistant and an office assistant both received suspended sentences for taking part in the procedure. All the individuals denied the charges. Raissouni, Al-Amin, and the doctor were freed on October 16 after receiving a royal pardon. The case was possibly motivated by Raissouni being a journalist at *Akhbar Al Yaoum*, a daily newspaper that authorities have targeted repeatedly for its independent reporting and commentary, and her being a relative of high-profile dissidents.

On April 6, an appeals court upheld the three-year prison sentence pronounced against journalist Hamid El Mahdaoui for failing to report a security threat. The verdict was based on a phone call El Mahdaoui received in May 2017 from a man who said he intended to create armed strife in Morocco. The court did not accept the journalist's defense that he had concluded the declarations of the caller, whom he did not know, were idle chatter that did not warrant alerting the authorities. Authorities have a long history of targeting El Mahdaoui, a government critic.

On February 11, an appeals court in Tetouan sentenced Soufian al-Nguad, 29, to one year in prison for "incitement to insurrection," after he posted comments on Facebook encouraging people to march in protest against the death of Hayat Belkacem. In September 2018, coastguards killed the 20-year old Moroccan woman while firing on a boat that was apparently crossing the strait of Gibraltar to bring migrants clandestinely to Europe. A first-instance court sentenced al-Nguad to two years in prison. Though authorities pledged to investigate Belkacem's killing, their findings had not been publicly disclosed at time of writing.

Western Sahara

The United Nations-sponsored process of negotiations between Morocco and the Polisario Front on self-determination for the Western Sahara, most of which is under de facto Moroccan control, remained stalled, after the resignation in May of Horst Kohler, the envoy of the UN secretary-general. Kohler had not been replaced at time of writing. Morocco proposes a measure of autonomy under its rule but rejects a referendum on independence.

Moroccan authorities systematically prevent gatherings in the Western Sahara supporting Sahrawi self-determination, obstruct the work of some local human rights nongovernmental organizations (NGOs), including by blocking their legal registration, and on occasion beat activists and journalists in their custody and on the streets.

In 2019, 23 Sahrawi men remained in prison after they were convicted in unfair trials in 2013 and 2017 for the killing of 11 security force members, during clashes that erupted after authorities forcibly dismantled a large protest encampment in Gdeim Izik, Western Sahara, in 2010. Both courts relied almost entirely on their confessions to police to convict them, without seriously investigating claims that the defendants had signed their confessions under torture without being permitted to read them.

Authorities allowed Claude Mangin, an activist for Sahrawi rights and the French wife of prisoner Naama Asfari, a member of the "Gdeim Izik" group, to enter Morocco in February for the first time in 30 months to visit him. However, they prevented her from re-entering Morocco in July.

On July 8, a court in El Ayoun, Western Sahara, sentenced Nezha Khalidi, a member of Equipe Media, a collective of media activists who favor self-determination for Western Sahara, to a fine for exercising journalism without official credentials. Police arrested her while she was live-streaming a street scene and denouncing Moroccan "oppression."

Refugees

The government has yet to approve a draft of Morocco's first law on the right to asylum. As of June 2019, the ministry of foreign affairs had granted, or started the administrative process for granting refugee cards, along with special residency permits and work authorizations to 803 persons, most of them sub-Saharan Africans, whom the UN High Commissioner for Refugees (UNHCR) had recognized. All of the 6,244 refugees recognized by the UNHCR since 2007 have access to public education and health services and most of them have regular residency permits and work authorizations, according to the UNHCR representation in Morocco.

Women's and Girls' Rights

The Family Code discriminates against women with regard to inheritance and procedures to obtain divorce. The code sets 18 as a minimum age of marriage but allows judges to grant "exemptions" to marry minor girls aged 15 to 18, at the request of their family. In 2018, 40,000 such exemptions were granted, amounting to almost 20 percent of marriages recorded during the year, in what Justice Minister Mohamed Aujjar called "an alarming increase."

A law on violence against women criminalizes some forms of domestic violence and establishes preventive measures, but does not set out duties of police, prosecutors, and investigative judges in domestic violence cases, or fund women's shelters.

Morocco criminalizes abortion, thus endangering women's human rights including to life, health, freedom from cruel, inhuman, and degrading treatment, and privacy. According to the Moroccan Association to Combat Clandestine Abortions, between 600 and 800 abortions a day take place on average in Morocco, with about two-thirds of them by licensed doctors.

Domestic Workers

A law that took effect in 2018 provides domestic workers with labor protections, including mandatory labor contracts, mandatory days off, minimum age, minimum wage, and maximum working hours guarantees. It imposes fines on employers who violate the law, and prison sentences for some repeat offenders. However, the government did not engage in any noticeable communication efforts to make sure the general public, including domestic workers and employers are aware of the existence of the law.

Right to Private Life, Sexual Orientation, and Gender Identity

In a report released in June, the office of the General Prosecutor stated that 7,721 adults were prosecuted for having non-transactional sexual relations outside of marriage in 2018. The number includes 3,048 who were charged with adultery, 170 with same-sex relations, and all of the rest for sex between unmarried persons.

In Morocco, consensual sex between adults who are not married to one another is punishable by up to one year in prison. Article 489 of the penal code stipulates prison terms of six months to three years for "lewd or unnatural acts with an individual of the same sex."

Key International Actors

In an attempt to comply with European Court of Justice rulings stating that trade agreements between European Union countries and Morocco can only apply to Western Sahara with "the consent of its people," the European Commission and parliament conducted consultations with some elements of the population of Western Sahara. The Polisario Front refused to take part in the consultations.

In January and in February, claiming to have taken "all reasonable and feasible measures" in order to ascertain the concerned people's consent, the EU Council and the European Parliament approved trade agreements with Morocco, which allow for the exploitation of Western Sahara's agricultural and fisheries resources. In April, the Polisario announced legal actions against these decisions before the European Court of Justice.

Mozambique

In August, Mozambique President Filipe Nyusi and the leader of the country's main opposition party Renamo, Ossufo Momade, signed a new peace agreement pledging to end years of violence and pave the way for elections in October. A month later, the country received Pope Francis, whose presence was aimed at strengthening the peace agreement. Despite the deal, the election campaign was marred by political violence targeting mainly opposition supporters.

During 2019, the spate of attacks by a suspected Islamist armed group increased in the northern province of Cabo Delgado. Soldiers deployed to the region to fight the armed groups were implicated in acts of intimidation, arbitrarily arrests, and ill-treatment of detainees. Journalists and activists continued to face intimidation and harassment, and there has been lack of accountability for past crimes.

Election Violence

The country's sixth general election was marred by violence and politically motivated attacks. In October, an election observer, Anastancio Matavele was shot dead in broad daylight allegedly by five members of the police elite force. The incident happened a week before election day, in Gaza province, where Human Rights Watch had documented serious abuses and incidents of violence since the start of the election campaign on August 31, including violations of the right to peaceful assembly and arbitrary arrests of opposition candidates.

In its assessment of the election, the Electoral Commission expressed concern over "growing cases of destruction of propaganda material, violation of freedom of assembly and physical attacks," and that in two weeks of campaigning, 14 people died and 29 people were detained.

Also, vehicles moving around in Manica and Sofala provinces, near Gorongosa, were attacked on different occasions by armed men believed to be part of a dissident group of Renamo guerrillas who rejected the August peace agreement. The leader of the group claimed responsibility for two of the attacks, and threatened to continue if the election campaign was not suspended.

Violations and Attacks in the North

Attacks by a suspected Islamist armed group, locally known as both Al-Sunna wa Jama'a and Al-Shabab, continued in the northern province of Cabo Delgado, with armed groups changing their tactics. In addition to beheading people and burning houses, the group became implicated in kidnapping of women, as well as attacks on public transport and killing of military personnel. The extremist group Islamic State (ISIS) claimed responsibility for at least two of the attacks; however, the extent of ISIS involvement, if any, is unclear. The attacks began in October 2017 on police stations in Mocimboa da Praia district, then spread to other districts in the northern part of Cabo Delgado, notably in Macomia, Palma and Nangade. The violence also affected the electoral process, with government imposing restrictions to campaign parades in northern Cabo Delgado.

Impunity for Past Crimes

Impunity for serious abuses by state security forces and Renamo persisted, and parliament in July approved a broad amnesty law that exempted Renamo members from prosecution for crimes committed between 2014 and 2016. During this time, both government security and defense force and Renamo armed men were involved in sporadic fighting that led to serious human rights abuses, including enforced disappearances, torture, killings, and destruction of private property, documented in Human Rights Watch's 2018 report "The Next One to Die."

Freedom of Expression and Assembly

During 2019, crackdown on rights to freedom of expression and peaceful assembly continued. In January, the police surrounded the Maputo office of the Centre for Public Integrity (CIP), an independent civil society organization, after the organization launched a campaign against the repayment of illegal loans amounting to about US$2.2 billion. Police also ordered people to remove campaign t-shirts and stop distributing them. In March, authorities disrupted a march organized by a local primary school to mark the city's annual carnival. Days later, the mayor of Maputo rejected plans for Mozambique's leading women's rights group, Forum Mulher, to march against domestic violence on International Women's Day.

HUMAN
RIGHTS
WATCH
"From Cradle to Grave"
Discrimination and Barriers to Education for Persons with Albinism in Tete Province, Mozambique

Freedom of Media

State security forces intimidated, detained, and prosecuted journalists covering the fight against an Islamist armed group in the northern province of Cabo Delgado. The government barred media organizations and journalists from visiting the province, while the army and police detained journalists who managed to get there. In January, police from Macomia district arrested, without a warrant, journalists Amade Abubacar and Germano Daniel Adriano while they were interviewing villagers who had fled their homes due to intensified attacks. Abubacar was held in pretrial detention for nearly 100 days, including 12 days in incommunicado military detention. A month earlier, soldiers detained an academic, a journalist, and a driver in Mocimboa da Praia district after they interviewed residents of Chitolo village.

Women's and Girls' Rights

In March, tropical cyclone Idai hit near the coastal city of Beira, bringing heavy rains that left entire villages in Manica, Sofala, and Zambezia provinces submerged as floodwaters rose. Tens of thousands of people were displaced and, according to the United Nations, over 1.85 million people, most of them women and children, needed urgent assistance. Victims, residents, and aid workers told Human Rights Watch that local community leaders coerced women into engaging in sex in exchange for aid.

There has been some significant progress in the rights of Mozambican women and girls. In December 2018, the Mozambican Ministry of Education revoked a 2003 decree banning pregnant girls and adolescent mothers from attending day classes and ordered them to only attend night classes. In July, Mozambique's national assembly took an important step toward ending the country's high rate of child marriage by unanimously adopting a law that prohibits marriage of children younger than 18 years old, without exception.

Disability Rights

Although the reports of attacks and abductions of people with albinism have declined since 2015, many families of children with albinism still live in fear, some keeping their children out of school. In 2019, Human Rights Watch also found that children living with albinism in Tete province face discrimination, stigma, and rejection at school, in the community, and at times by their own families. They struggle to overcome barriers such as threats of attacks, bullying, and lack of reasonable adjustments in the classroom, which violate their right to education.

Sexual Orientation and Gender Identity

Four years since the decriminalization of homosexuality in Mozambique, and despite a November 2017 court decision that declared unconstitutional a law with vague "morality" provisions that had been used to justify denying registration to lesbian, gay, bisexual, and transgender (LGBT) groups, the government has still not registered the country's largest LGBT group, Lambda.

The UN Human Rights Council has appealed on several occasions to the government to register nongovernmental organizations that work on issues of sexual orientation and gender identity. Despite authorities showing some tolerance for same-sex relations and gender nonconformity, LGBT people continue to experience discrimination at work and mistreatment by family members.

Key International Actors

Switzerland was instrumental in brokering the August 2019 Mozambique peace agreement, with Swiss diplomats playing a major role as mediators. In August, the chairperson of the African Union Commission hailed the amnesty signed that month as a vital milestone in ending the Mozambican conflict. In June, Mozambique hosted for the first time the US-Africa Business Summit. While the meeting was important for promoting investment in the country, its agenda did not include discussions about the links between business, insecurity, and human rights in the areas being considered by investors.

Pope Francis visited Mozambique in September. He met with youth from different religions, as well as political and civic leaders, encouraging them to consolidate the peace accord. In September, the European Union, which deployed 32 long-term election observers for the general elections, expressed concern over the violence and political harassment during campaign. After the elections, the EU said its observers mission identified some irregularities and malpractices on election day and during the results management process, including ballot-box stuffing, multiple voting, intentional invalidation of votes for the opposition, and altering of polling station results with fraudulent addition of extra votes.

Myanmar

The government of Myanmar in 2019 continued to defy international calls to seriously investigate human rights violations against ethnic minorities in Shan, Kachin, Karen, and Rakhine States. A United Nations-mandated Fact-Finding Mission (FFM) found sufficient evidence to call for the investigation of senior military officials for crimes against humanity and genocide against ethnic Rohingya Muslims. The government has been unwilling to address the root causes of the crises, including systematic persecution and violence, statelessness, and continued military impunity.

In August 2019, the FFM called on Myanmar's security forces to stop using sexual and gender-based violence, including rape and gang rape, against women, children and transgender people, to terrorize and punish ethnic minorities. The military has used sexual violence to devastate communities and deter women and girls from returning to their homes.

De facto leader Aung San Suu Kyi and her civilian government have repeatedly refused to cooperate meaningfully with UN rights investigators' pursuit of accountability for rights violations. The government has not granted visas for independent UN investigators including Special Rapporteur Yanghee Lee and the members of the UN FFM, and limited access to the country by staff of the Office of the UN High Commissioner for Human Rights.

Rohingya Under Threat

More than two years after the Myanmar military's campaign of ethnic cleansing in northern Rakhine State, over 900,000 Rohingya refugees remain in overcrowded camps in Cox's Bazar in Bangladesh, now the largest concentration of encamped refugees in the world.

The FFM's final report in September 2019 found that the 600,000 Rohingya remaining in Rakhine State were still the target of a government campaign to eradicate their identity, and were living under "threat of genocide." The report found the laws, policies, and practices that underpin the government's persecution of the Rohingya—and which serve as causal factors for the killings, rapes and gang rapes, torture, and forced displacement by the military and other government authorities—remain in place.

In July 2019, a delegation of senior Myanmar officials arrived in Cox's Bazar to promote refugee repatriation. The delegation pressured refugees to enter a digitized National Verification Card (NVC) process but would not guarantee they would be granted citizenship. The government has made no efforts to amend the discriminatory 1982 Citizenship Law that effectively stripped Rohingya of their citizenship rights. Refugees who want to return are required to sign up for the NVC, which identifies them as foreigners in Myanmar, making them vulnerable to discrimination and restrictions on their rights.

On August 22, Bangladesh and Myanmar made a second attempt to return refugees to Myanmar. Unlike the first attempt to return refugees in November 2018, Bangladesh this time agreed to consult with the UN refugee agency, asking UNHCR to assess the intentions of the 3,450 refugees Myanmar said were eligible to return, selected from a list of 22,000 names shared by Bangladesh. Once again, Bangladeshi officials, UN staff, and journalists waited for refugees to appear for voluntary return to Myanmar, but none did.

UNHCR has stated that conditions in Myanmar are not currently conductive for voluntary returns of refugees in dignity and safety. Facilities that resemble detention camps, surrounded by barbed-wire perimeter fences and security outposts, have been built to receive and house returning refugees from Bangladesh. Satellite images of the Hla Poe Khaung Transit Centre show it was built on top of razed Rohingya villages.

The approximately 128,000 Rohingya and Kaman Muslims confined to closed internally displaced people (IDP) camps in central Rakhine State have little freedom of movement and limited access to important health, education, and other humanitarian services. In addition, there are security concerns for refugees returning to Rakhine State due to hostilities between the Myanmar military and the insurgent Arakan Army.

Ethnic Conflicts and Forced Displacement

Fighting between the Myanmar military and ethnic armed groups intensified in 2019. The government regularly barred rights monitors and journalists from con-

HUMAN
RIGHTS
WATCH
"Give Us a Baby
and We'll Let You Go"
Trafficking of Kachin "Brides" from Myanmar to China

flict areas and denied access to UN and international humanitarian agencies seeking to provide food, medicine, and other important aid.

Starting in November 2018, fighting increased between the Arakan Army and government security forces in Rakhine and Chin States. The government ordered an internet blackout that began on June 21 across eight townships in Rakhine State and Paletwa township in Chin State, making it very difficult to verify reports of attacks on civilians and arbitrary detention, torture, and deaths in military custody. The internet ban was lifted from Chin State and four townships in Rakhine State on September 1, leaving Ponnangyn, Mrauk-U, Kyauktaw, and Minbya still under blackout.

The UN Office for the Coordination of Humanitarian Affairs (OCHA) estimates at least 33,000 ethnic Rakhine remain displaced due to fighting, including 3,300 children out of 9,000 IDPs in northern Rakhine State. The figure is contested; the UN special rapporteur stated as many as 65,000 were displaced. A lack of food security, access to shelter and basic humanitarian services, and inability to access to livelihoods remain major problems for Rakhine civilians.

Civilians continued to be targeted during hostilities in northern Burma. Northern Shan State witnessed renewed fighting where 17 civilians were killed and 27 injured in the first few weeks of fighting, many of them women and children, according to the UN. Fighting broke out on August 15 after insurgent Northern Alliance forces, minus the Kachin Independence Army, carried out coordinated attacks on military targets and civilian structures. The Myanmar military quickly counterattacked. Fighting is affecting civilians in at least five townships in northern Shan State, with civilians killed by shelling and in crossfire.

The fighting caused the displacement of an estimated 8,000 people who sought shelter in schools, monasteries, and churches. By the end of September, approximately 2,000 remained displaced.

In Kachin State, the United Nations Children's Fund, UNICEF, reported an estimated 6,385 IDPs had returned to their areas of origin. However, more than 97,000 remained displaced, some for many years already, in 136 IDP camps, or camp-like settings throughout the state. Just over 40 percent of those IDPs were in camps in areas controlled by Kachin armed groups. Humanitarian assistance was barred from reaching those areas outside the government-controlled areas. In addition to fighting, return by IDPs to their original areas was hampered by landmines and unexploded ordinance.

Trafficking of women and girls remains a serious problem in Kachin and northern Shan States as revealed in Human Rights Watch's report "'Give Us a Baby and We'll Let You Go': Trafficking of Kachin 'Brides' from Myanmar to China." IDPs face economic desperation from displacement by conflict, inability to pursue viable livelihoods by farming, and little access to other forms of employment.

Women are often breadwinners, and the eldest daughters face cultural expectations that they will help provide for their families. Young women and girls are being lured into China from IDP camps and villages near the porous border, on false promises of gainful employment and then sold to Chinese families for forced marriage. Neither the Myanmar nor the Chinese governments have taken necessary steps to prevent trafficking, recover victims, bring perpetrators to justice, and assist survivors.

Freedom of Expression and Repressive Laws

Freedom of expression declined sharply in Myanmar in 2019. More than 250 people faced lawsuits under various rights-restricting laws.

In May, Reuters journalists Wa Lone and Kyaw Soe Oo were released from prison on a presidential amnesty after serving eight months of a seven-year prison sentence under the colonial-era Official Secrets Act. The pair had reported on a military massacre of Rohingya in Rakhine State's Inn Din village and police arrested them in December 2017. The politically motivated nature of the trial became clear when the court convicted them, despite a police officer testifying on the stand that arresting officers had been ordered to entrap the two journalists.

Prosecutions for criminal defamation continued under article 66(d) of the 2013

Telecommunications Act, frequently used as a tool to restrict freedom of expression online and curtail criticism of members of parliament, the government and military. Athan, a local group, reported that about 45 percent of all charges against media or journalists were filed under article 66(d). More than 250 people have faced criminal law suits in 2019 under various laws restricting freedom of expression. Authorities also used the Unlawful Associations Act and criminal defamation provisions under section 500 of the Myanmar Penal Code against journalists and critics.

HUMAN
RIGHTS
WATCH
DASHED HOPES
The Criminalization of Peaceful Expression in Myanmar

At time of writing, 11 lawsuits encompassing 50 persons had been filed in 2019 under penal code articles 505(a), barring criticism of the military, and 505(b), prompting "fear or alarm to the public ... whereby any person may be induced to commit an offence against the state or against the public tranquility."

On August 29, the prominent filmmaker, Min Htin Ko Ko Gyi, was sentenced to one year in prison with hard labor under article 505(a) of the penal code for criticizing the military on Facebook. Despite suffering from liver cancer and being visibly unwell during his trial, Min Htin Ko Ko Gyi was repeatedly denied bail to seek medical care outside prison.

In April and May, seven members of a traditional theater group were arrested for their satirical performance deemed critical of the military. On October 30, five members were sentenced under article 505(a) of the penal code to one year each. On November 18, Kay Khine Tun, Zayar Lwin, Paing Ye Thu, Paing Phyo Min, and Zaw Lin Htut received an added one-year sentence by a different court, also under 505(a) charges. Su Yadanar Myint will serve one year while Nyein Chan Soe was acquitted. All seven defendants face additional charges under section 66(d) for "defaming" the military, which brings a maximum prison sentence of two years.

Article 8(f) of the Law Protecting the Privacy and Security of Citizens also contributed to the rise in defamation charges against ordinary citizens. There were 78 cases against individuals at time of writing, which aimed to limit online speech and criticism of the government. The law also enables third-party complaints to be filed against an individual.

Protesters were often targeted under the Peaceful Assembly and Peaceful Procession Law, which requires organizers to seek approval from authorities 48 hours prior to holding an event. Two Kachin activists, Paulu and Seng Nu Pan, were sentenced in September to 15 days in jail, for a street performance marking the eight-year anniversary of the end of a 17-year ceasefire in Kachin State. Paulu received an additional three months in jail for contempt of court, after presenting the presiding judge with a set of broken scales symbolizing the broken justice system.

Farmers across the country also faced difficulties with repressive laws. In March, the Vacant, Fallow and Virgin Lands Management Law came into effect, requiring anyone occupying land classified as "vacant, fallow, or virgin" to apply for permits. Failure to apply and continuing to use the affected land could mean up to two years in prison. In September, eight farmers were sentenced to two years for farming land in the Irrawaddy Division that local government sold to a private company.

Article 377 of the colonial-era penal code criminalizes adult consensual same-sex conduct.

Key International Actors

On November 11, Gambia brought a case against Myanmar before the International Court of Justice for its atrocities against the Rohingya as violating the Convention on the Prevention and Punishment of the Crime of Genocide. Gambia's filing marked the first time that a country without any direct connection to the crimes relied on its membership in the Genocide Convention to bring a case before the world court.

On November 13 in Argentina, Rohingya and Latin American human rights organizations used the principle of universal jurisdiction to file a criminal case against Myanmar's top military and civilian leaders, including Aung San Suu Kyi, for crimes committed in Rakhine State. This avenue is available for crimes so serious that all states have an interest in addressing them.

The International Criminal Court (ICC) on November 14 also confirmed it would begin investigations into alleged crime against humanity, namely deportation, other inhumane acts, and persecution committed against Rohingya in Myanmar since October 2016. The court in 2018 confirmed its jurisdiction over the crime of deportation, which was completed in Bangladesh, an ICC member country, as well as other related crimes.

In July, the United States imposed travel bans against key military leaders, including commander in chief Gen. Min Aung Hlaing, for their role in the persecution of the Rohingya. His second-in-command, Gen. Soe Win, and two other senior officials were also subjected to travel bans. In September, a bill was passed by the US House of Representatives by a huge majority to strengthen sanctions against Myanmar's military leaders.

The UN-mandated FFM ended its mission in September, handing over evidence of serious crimes committed by Myanmar's armed forces against the Rohingya,

Kachin, Shan, and Karen ethnic minorities to the newly operational Independent Investigative Mechanism for Myanmar (IIMM).

The UN Human Rights Council mandated the IIMM to follow up from the FFM, and collect and preserve evidence of serious crimes to facilitate and expedite fair and independent criminal proceedings

Released on August 5, the FFM investigative report on military-owned businesses in the Myanmar Economic Corporation and Union of Myanmar Economic Holdings holding companies, found at least 14 foreign firms have partnerships with military enterprises, and at least 44 have other commercial ties. The report found these military businesses generate revenue strengthened the military and provided financial support for its operations that violated international human rights and humanitarian law.

The Independent Commission of Enquiry (ICOE), established by the Myanmar government in July 2018, operates without transparency, lending further weight to concerns about its credibility to investigate allegations of grave abuses against the Rohingya. Governments such as those of the United Kingdom and Japan continue to support the ICOE despite profound concerns about its independence, impartiality, and working methods.

The European Parliament passed a resolution on September 19 calling for the imposition of a comprehensive arms embargo on Myanmar and referral of the situation of Myanmar to the ICC. The resolution called on EU members to support efforts aimed at holding Myanmar to account for violations of the UN Genocide Convention before the International Court of Justice.

Despite strong findings pointing to Myanmar's security forces' responsibility for atrocities against the Rohingya, the UN Security Council remains paralyzed, making impossible the referral of Myanmar to the ICC and the imposition of sanctions on military and government officials implicated in grave abuses against the Rohingya.

In May, the report of an independent inquiry into UN involvement in Myanmar was published, finding "systemic and structural failures," which undermined the UN response to the crisis.

Nepal

After taking office in 2018, the government of Prime Minister K.P. Oli signaled its intention to amend its laws to ensure accountability for the serious crimes committed by individuals on all sides during the 10-year Maoist insurgency, which ended in 2006. However, after consultations with various groups, the process again became deadlocked, as authorities continued to favor impunity for perpetrators—both security forces and members of the ruling Nepal Communist Party—over justice for victims.

Despite a two-thirds' parliamentary majority, the Oli government made little progress in implementing the federal structure created under the 2015 constitution, including devolving some powers over justice and policing.

In 2019, the government proposed new laws curtailing free expression and limiting the powers of the National Human Rights Commission.

The government has outlawed several practices harmful to women and girls in recent years. However, weak enforcement along with remaining gaps in laws on sexual violence and gender discrimination continue to leave women, particularly ethnic minorities, at high risk of abuse.

Transitional Justice

The Oli government proposed amendments in the law relating to transitional justice, but they did not meet international standards that could ensure those most responsible for the worst crimes committed during the conflict come to trial. Instead, the current government, like its predecessors, continued to resist amending the transitional justice legislation to abide by a landmark 2015 Supreme Court ruling, which struck down key components of the current law, such as provisions that would allow amnesties even for perpetrators of war crimes and crimes against humanity.

A commitment to transitional justice was included in the 2006 Comprehensive Peace Agreement, but it was not until 2015 that a Truth and Reconciliation Commission (TRC) and a Commission of Investigation on Enforced Disappeared Persons (CIEDP) were finally established. Despite being previously extended, the terms of members of both commissions expired in spring 2019. The TRC had registered 58,052 complaints of abuses, including allegations against senior figures, while the CIEDP had registered over 3,200 cases of people who remain "disappeared" over 10 years since the conflict ended. However, neither commission had completed a single investigation before the commissioners' mandates expired.

Victims' groups objected to the stalled system for appointing new commissioners, which appeared designed to ensure that selected candidates are acceptable to political leaders and the army. Victims' groups also demanded that the transitional justice law be amended before the commissions resume work, and that they be consulted on strengthening the process, demands which the government has so far resisted.

Freedom of Expression

Attacks increased against journalists and against the freedom of expression of ordinary citizens online. Critical voices were subjected to intimidation by ruling party supporters. Police used the Electronic Transactions Act, which is supposedly designed to address online fraud, to arrest journalists and bloggers, including those reporting on corruption, and even a comedian who upset a movie director with a negative review.

The government presented three pieces of new legislation that further seriously erode freedom of expression. The Media Council Bill establishes a new, government-controlled media council, with the power to impose sanctions, including fines and loss of accreditation, on journalists, editors, and publishers if, for example, they are deemed to have harmed the "image or prestige" of an individual. The new Information Technology Bill is even more draconian than the Electronic Transactions Act it replaces, creating new offences so broadly defined they could plausibly be interpreted to included much online expression, and imposing custodial penalties for those who are convicted. Finally, the Mass Communications Bill duplicated similar provisions, with further penalties, for loosely defined acts of expression.

Human Rights Defenders

The government proposed a new law that undermined the independence of the National Human Rights Commission by giving the attorney general powers to decide which cases it brings before the courts, and by removing its right to maintain regional offices.

The Home Ministry prepared draft legislation that will give the government powers to monitor and control the activity of all domestic and international organizations in Nepal. Human rights defenders feared that these powers will be used to harass activists, and to deny access to external funding for human rights work.

Women's and Girls' Rights

The government has outlawed a number of harmful practices including chhaupadi (menstrual seclusion), dowry, witchcraft allegations, and child marriage. However, enforcement remains weak, and these deeply entrenched practices continue.

Legal gaps and lack of political will continue to mar accountability for sexual violence, especially for victims from minority communities. A statute of limitations of one year on rape and sexual violence allegations prevents many cases from being brought to justice.

Despite numerous protests, the government failed to adopt policies to protect and provide justice for women and girls, especially those from minority communities, who faced rape and sexual violence. Instead, numerous cases are mishandled by authorities, including that of a 15-year-old Dalit girl from Mahottari, in southeast Nepal, whose rape and murder at the end on 2018 the police refused to register during 2019.

There is no comprehensive legislation banning gender discrimination. Article 11 of the 2015 Constitution of Nepal confers a fundamentally inferior legal status on women, by preventing them from passing citizenship to their children according to the same terms as Nepali men.

In November 2018, the United Nations Committee on the Elimination of Discrimination Against Women recommended that Nepal endorse the Safe Schools Declaration, an international commitment to protect education during armed conflict. At time of writing, it had yet to do so.

Treatment of Minorities

Caste and ethnic minorities remained more vulnerable than others to abuses, including excessive use of force by police, and torture in police custody. Crimes, such as sexual violence, against members of minority communities often go unreported and uninvestigated. In a case brought to the United Nations Human Rights Committee by a member of an indigenous group who had suffered forced labor and torture, the Committee found that Nepal must remove obstacles to victims seeking justice.

Survivors of natural disasters, such as seasonal flooding, who disproportionately belong to minority communities, were often not provided with adequate relief, such as basic shelter. Four years after the 2015 earthquake, which destroyed nearly 1 million homes, many survivors still live in temporary shelter.

The government's Public Service Commission sought to undermine constitutional guarantees of quotas for minority communities in civil service jobs, by defying hiring procedures.

The government also failed during the year to publish the report of the Lal Commission, which investigated deadly violence between members of minority communities and the police in 2015.

Disability Rights

Despite progress in law and policy, tens of thousands of children with disabilities remain out of school, or are segregated at school in different classrooms from other students.

Key International Actors

In 2015, India was widely seen as backing a blockade of trade goods across Nepal's southern border. Since then, Nepal has attempted to reset its relations with India with discussions that include existing treaties, trade and transit, and border management. Despite its role in brokering the 2006 peace agreement, India failed to call for proper transitional justice.

Meanwhile, Nepal in 2019 strengthened investment and trading ties with China, including participation in China's "Belt and Road" Initiative. As a result, restrictions on free assembly and expression rights of the Tibetan community continued, under political pressure from China.

In 2017, Nepal was elected to the United Nations Human Rights Council for a three-year term.

Members of the international community, including diplomatic missions in Kathmandu, UN special rapporteurs, and others, continued to warn the government that if a transitional justice process that meets international standards is denied within Nepal, perpetrators of war crimes and crimes against humanity may be subject to prosecution abroad under the principal of universal jurisdiction.

Nicaragua

Since taking office in 2007, the government of Nicaraguan President Daniel Ortega has dismantled nearly all institutional checks on presidential power. Stacked with his supporters, the Electoral Council has barred opposition political parties and removed opposition lawmakers. The Supreme Court of Justice has upheld Electoral Council decisions undermining political rights and allowing Ortega to circumvent a constitutional prohibition on re-election and run for a second term.

Ortega's Sandinista Party secured a 79 percent majority in Congress in 2016, enabling it to fast-track institutional reforms that gave the president direct personal control over the police and army, allowed him to legislate by decree, and run for re-election indefinitely.

A brutal crackdown by National Police, the sole government law enforcement body in Nicaragua, and armed pro-government groups in 2018 left 300 dead, over 2,000 injured, and hundreds arbitrarily arrested and prosecuted. Since dissipation of the protests, the Ortega government has brought hundreds of criminal cases against protesters and critics, but as of September had only opened four investigations into allegations of misconduct by the National Police.

Other persistent problems in Nicaragua include severe restrictions on freedom of expression and association, political discrimination against state workers who support the opposition, and stringent abortion laws that leave no options for rape victims.

Crackdown on Dissent

In April 2018, massive anti-government protests broke out countrywide. The National Police, in coordination with armed pro-government groups, brutally repressed protesters, resulting in 328 deaths and more than 2,000 people injured. As the crackdown intensified, some individuals responded violently and official figures show that 22 police officers died in the context of the demonstrations between April and September 2018.

Hundreds of protesters were arbitrarily arrested and detained, many for several months. As of February 2019, the Inter-American Commission on Human Rights

(IACHR) documented at least 777 people arrested during the crackdown. Many were subject to torture and other ill-treatment, including electric shocks, severe beatings, fingernail removal, asphyxiation, and rape.

Prosecutions of detainees were marred by serious violations of due process and other fundamental rights. Many detainees were held incommunicado, subjected to closed-door trials, and denied the right to confer privately with their defense lawyers. Many were charged with "inciting terrorism" using Nicaragua's overly broad counterterrorism law or other serious crimes, despite what the Office of the High Commissioner of Human Rights (OHCHR) found to be often insufficient or contradictory evidence.

In February 2019, the government and the opposition resumed stalled negotiations. However, pro-government elements continued to suppress protesters violently. In March, an alleged member of the Sandinista Party shot at demonstrators, injuring three. In June, pro-government mobs beat and threw stones at Catholic churchgoers gathering in memory of 15-year-old Sandor Dolmus, an altar boy shot in the chest during protests a year earlier. Police also arrested, and subsequently released, over 100 people in the context of new protests in March.

From mid-March to mid-June, the Ortega administration released, mostly under restrictive regimes such as house arrest, 492 people detained in the context of the protests. The IACHR estimated that about 130 people remained in prison as of October.

In mid-June, a broad amnesty for crimes committed in the context of the anti-government protests came into force. All of those released under restrictive measures were then granted amnesty, the OHCHR reported. Although the amnesty excluded certain crimes, it risks being used to shield from prosecution officers responsible for serious abuses, given the lack of judicial independence. The OHCHR reported in September that authorities had prosecuted only individuals involved in protests or critical of the government, except for one case involving a man convicted of murdering a Brazilian student during the unrest in July 2018, who was later released under the amnesty law. The OHCHR also said in September that the Attorney General's office had opened investigations into four complaints of alleged abuse by police forces against detainees; one complaint was dismissed for lacking credibility and the other three had not advanced at the time of writing. President Ortega has promoted top officials implicated in abuses.

Human Rights Defenders

Human rights defenders and other critics of the government's human rights record have continued to be the targets of death threats, intimidation, online defamation campaigns, harassment, surveillance, and assault. In some cases, human rights defenders were arrested and detained through processes marred by due process violations.

In November and December 2018, Congress stripped nine nongovernmental organizations (NGOs) of their legal registration, effectively forcing them to close.

The IACHR has noted an increase in harassment, attacks, and threats against human rights defenders since protests broke out in 2018. In August 2019, a pro-government mob attacked and robbed Aura Alarcón, an attorney who defended protesters, at a bus station in Managua. Alarcón said policemen watched without intervening. Also in August, prominent human rights defender and leader of Nicaragua's workers party, Freddy Navas, was detained and questioned by police upon his return to Nicaragua from Costa Rica. He was accused of financing a march in Costa Rica and had his personal belongings confiscated.

In September, the commander in chief of the Nicaraguan Army, Julio César Avilés Castillo, accused NGOs of being coup-plotters who have violated the laws of the republic.

Freedom of Expression

The Ortega regime restricts freedom of expression for journalists and media outlets through threats, insults, physical attacks, detentions, arbitrary searches of documents, and forced closures.

In December 2018, the National Police raided the offices of news outlet Confidencial, confiscated materials, and occupied the headquarters. Also in December, police raided the studio of news channel 100% Noticias and detained, on terrorism charges, Miguel Mora, the channel's owner, and Lucía Pineda, its chief press officer. The two were held without due process, in conditions that included solitary confinement, for five months. They were freed under the amnesty law in June 2019.

Nongovernmental organizations (NGOs) estimate that over 100 journalists have fled Nicaragua since April 2018.

Since the outlawing of anti-government demonstrations in September 2018, the National Police have denied eight requests for protest permits.

Political Discrimination

During the crackdown, Nicaraguan Health Ministry authorities fired at least 400 doctors, nurses, and other health workers from several public hospitals in apparent retaliation for participation in protests or expression of disagreement with government policy. Forty professors from the National University of Nicaragua accused of supporting or taking part in anti-government demonstrations were also fired in August 2018. The IACHR found that authorities threatened public officials with dismissal if they did not participate in pro-government demonstrations.

Nicaraguan Asylum Seekers

More than 88,000 Nicaraguans have fled their country since the crackdown began, the IACHR reports. In April, the United Nations High Commissioner for Refugees (UNHCR) reported that the number of Nicaraguans applying for asylum in neighboring Costa Rica had about doubled, to 29,500, from 15,584 in October 2018. Another 26,000 were waiting to have their claims processed.

While most fleeing Nicaraguans have gone to Costa Rica, thousands more have gone to Mexico, Panama, and the United States.

Women and Girls' Sexual and Reproductive Rights

Nicaragua has, since 2006, prohibited abortion in all circumstances, even if a pregnancy is life-threatening or the result of rape or incest. Women and girls who have abortions face prison terms as long as two years. Medical professionals who perform abortions face sentences of one to six years. The abortion ban forces women and girls facing unwanted pregnancies to have clandestine abortions, risking their health and lives.

Key International Actors

The continuing human rights abuses in Nicaragua have been met with strong regional and international condemnation.

In March, the UN Human Rights Council adopted its first resolution on Nicaragua with cross-regional support, condemning abuses and urging Ortega's government to resume cooperation with international human rights bodies and negotiations with the opposition. In May, Nicaragua underwent its Universal Periodic Review (UPR) at the council, during which 90 delegations submitted recommendations for improving human rights standards in Nicaragua.

In June, the Organization of American States (OAS) General Assembly passed a resolution proposed by the OAS Permanent Council Working Group on Nicaragua that opens the door to evaluation of Nicaragua's compliance with the 2001 Inter-American Democratic Charter. The resolution urges the Nicaraguan government to take a series of steps to resume negotiations with the opposition and restore access for international rights-monitoring mechanisms. It instructed the Permanent Council to appoint a commission to undertake diplomatic efforts toward solving the crisis and to produce a report within 75 days. However, in September, the Ortega government barred the appointed commission from entering the country. Last year, the regime expelled IACHR Special Monitoring Mechanism for Nicaragua (MESENI) and the IACHR-appointed Interdisciplinary Group of Independent Experts (GIEI).

In September, UN High Commissioner for Human Rights Michelle Bachelet released a comprehensive report on the human rights record of Nicaragua from August 2018 to July 2019. The report recommended that Nicaragua guarantee freedoms for civil society, reinstate NGOs and media outlets, pursue investigations, prosecute individuals accused of human rights abuses in the context of the protests, and end arbitrary arrests, among other measures.

Since protests began, the US Treasury Department has imposed targeted sanctions against nine Nicaraguan officials responsible for abuses or corruption. Five were sanctioned in 2018 pursuant to Executive Order 13851 and the Global Magnitsky Act of 2016, which allows for sanctions against violators of human rights. Four were sanctioned in June pursuant to the Nicaraguan Human Rights and Corruption Act of December 2018. In June, Canada also imposed targeted sanctions against key Nicaraguan officials.

In October, the European Union adopted a sanctions framework for Nicaragua, which provides a legal mechanism for imposing targeted sanctions, including travel bans and asset freezes against top Nicaraguan officials responsible for abuse.

Nigeria

Despite claims by federal authorities of increased security measures, an atmosphere of insecurity persisted across Nigeria in 2019. In May, President Muhammadu Buhari began his second four year term following general elections marred by political violence which killed at least 11 people.

The northeast Boko Haram conflict entered its tenth year, with renewed fighting between security forces and Boko Haram factions killing an estimated 640 civilians in 2019 alone. An estimated 27,000 people, including 37 aid workers, have been killed since the onset of the conflict in 2009,according to the United Nations Office for Coordination of Humanitarian Affairs (UNOCHA), 37 aid workers.

The military's decision in August to gather troops from countryside outposts into 'super camps' in the northeast impeded humanitarian access and left communities vulnerable to attacks. In the northeast, at least 223,000 people are without security while 100,000 have been cut off from humanitarian access as a result of the military's departure. Humanitarian actors have no access to an estimated 823,000 people, according to UNOCHA.

Elsewhere in the country, there were widespread kidnapping, banditry and recurring cycles of deadly violence between herdsmen and farmers.

The clampdown on peaceful protests, arrest and detention of activists, and media repression signified a renewed intolerance of free speech and dissent by Nigerian authorities.

China joined the rank of key international actors including the United Nations, United States and the United Kingdom providing support for the Nigerian government's northeast counter insurgency measures.

Abuses by Boko Haram

Boko Haram killed at least 405 children and abducted at least 105 during 2018 and the group continued lethal attacks on civilians including suicide bombings and abductions. In January, at least 60 people were killed when Boko Haram fighters overran Rann, Borno state.

HUMAN
RIGHTS
WATCH
"They Didn't Know
if I Was Alive or Dead"
Military Detention of Children for Suspected Boko Haram
Involvement in Northeast Nigeria

In February, just days before national elections, eight people were killed in a suicide bomb attack by suspected insurgents in Borno capital city, Maiduguri. Kashim Shettim, then-governor of the state survived an attack that killed at least three people while on a campaign tour to Gamboru Ngala, near the Cameroon border. A similar attack in September on the new state governor, Babagana Umaru Zulim killed four in Konduga, near Maiduguri. In June, triple suicide bombings in the same town killed some 30 and injured another 40. In July, at least 65 people were killed after Boko Haram fighters opened fire on a group of men attending a funeral in Nganzai, Borno state.

In July, Boko Haram fighters killed one and abducted six staff of the international aid group, Action Against Hunger. One of the abducted workers remained missing at time of writing.

Boko Haram maintained control of some villages near Lake Chad, northern Borno State . The splinter faction of the group known as the Islamic West Africa Province (ISWAP) overran dozens of army bases, killing dozens of soldiers since January.

Authorities continued to detain thousands of alleged Boko Haram members without trial in overcrowded military barracks in the northeast. In October, the authorities released 25 children held as Boko Haram suspects from Giwa barracks in Borno state after Human Rights Watch reported that children are being held in degrading and inhuman conditions in Giwa barracks. Nigerian authorities detained at least 418 children in 2018 for their or their parents' alleged association with Boko Haram.

Conduct of Security Forces

There was little progress on accountability for security forces abuses. Neither the report of the Presidential Judicial Panel set up in August 2017 to investigate the military's compliance with human rights obligations, allegations of war crimes, and other abuses nor that of a Presidential Panel of Inquiry set up in 2018 to investigate abuses by the Police Special Anti-Robbery Squad (SARS) have been made public.

In March, the spokesperson for the Independent National Electoral Commission (INEC), Festus Okoye, accused soldiers of intimidation and unlawful arrest of election officials in Rivers State governorship elections. The Nigerian Army immediately announced the creation of a committee to investigate those allegations within two weeks, but was yet to publish a report at time of writing.

Security forces continued the crackdown on members of the Shia Islamic Movement of Nigeria (IMN) protesting the detention of their leader Sheikh Ibrahim El Zakzaky and his wife Ibraheema since December 2015, despite court orders for their release. In July, Nigerian police fired at the group's procession in Abuja, Nigeria's federal capital, killing 11. A journalist and a police officer were also killed in the violence, while dozens of IMN members were wounded or arrested.

In April, about 65 women were arrested in Abuja by a task force comprising officers from the city's environment and social development agency and local police during raids on night clubs. Women's rights groups took to the streets to protest the raids and the allegations by some arrested women that policemen sexually abused, exploited and extorted them in custody. Twenty-nine women pleaded guilty to prostitution charges and were ordered to pay a fine of three thousand naira (about US$8.50) each.

Intercommunal Violence

Clashes between herders and farming communities continued in the Middle Belt, while other parts of the country faced general insecurity, including banditry and kidnappings for ransom. In February, clashes and reprisal attacks between the Fulani and Adara communities in Kajuru, Kaduna state killed more than 130 people.

In July, the federal government buckled under the weight of heavy widespread criticism and suspended the Ruga Settlements program under which special grazing zones and settlements were established for herdsmen across the country. Critics cited, among other flaws, lack of consultation with communities in proposed grazing zones.

In Zamfara state, incessant banditry attacks and kidnappings persisted despite the deployment of military troops in 2018 to tackle insecurity in the state. According to credible media reports, over 200 people were killed in the state by suspected bandits in the first 100 days of 2019.

HUMAN
RIGHTS
WATCH
"You Pray for Death"
Trafficking of Women and Girls in Nigeria

The Abuja-Kaduna highway, a major route out of Abuja to the northwest of the country became notorious for bandit attacks and kidnappings. The inspector general of police, Mohammed Adamu said in April that 1,071 people were killed in criminal attacks and 685 kidnapped across the country in the first quarter of 2019 alone.

Public Sector Corruption

The Economic and Financial Crimes Commission (EFCC) recorded some progress in the trial of corruption cases.

The supreme court affirmed in March, forfeiture orders granted by federal high courts in Lagos under the Advanced Fee Fraud Act and other Fraud related offences Act, of US$8.4 million and 2.4 billion naira [$66.6 million] allegedly traced by EFCC to Patience Jonathan, wife of former President Goodluck Jonathan.

In June, a Jigawa state high court sentenced Auwal Jibrin, a deputy director with INEC, to six years imprisonment, for unlawful enrichment and gratification, while another INEC official in the state Garba Ismaila received a seven-year jail term on the same charges.

A federal high court in July ordered the interim forfeiture to the government, of jewelry valued at an estimated $40 million recovered by the EFCC from the Abuja home of former petroleum minister Decani Alison-Madueke. The agency had in April secured a similar interim forfeiture order against the former minister's alleged property in Port Harcourt. The court found that the property was "reasonably suspected to be proceeds of unlawful activity."

Sexual Orientation and Gender Identity

Nigerian laws, policies and political discourse continued to reinforce intolerance same-sex relations and gender nonconformity throughout 2019. Nigerian law criminalizes same-sex conduct as well as public show of same-sex amorous relationships, same-sex marriages, and the registration of gay clubs, societies, and organizations. In January, Lagos state police spokesperson Dolapo Badmos, through her private Instagram account warned gay people to leave Nigeria or risk prosecution under the Same Sex Marriage Prohibition Act.

A Sharia (Islamic law) court in Kano in January fined 11 women charged under the state's Immoral Acts law for allegedly planning a same-sex wedding. The victims were arrested in December, 2018 by local religious police, known as Hisbah.

Freedom of Expression, Media, and Association

Armed soldiers raided offices of *Daily Trust* newspapers in January, temporarily detaining staff for allegedly publishing classified military information.

In June, the Nigerian Broadcasting Commission (NBC) suspended the licenses of the African Independent Television (AIT) and Raypower Radio station for allegedly airing inflammatory and inciting programs against the government and broadcasting uncensored and unedited social media content. Shortly afterwards, the Department of State Security Services (DSS) declared a crackdown on social media users for posting materials described as threatening to the country's peace and stability.

On August 3, DSS operatives arrested Omoyele Sowore, a 2019 presidential candidate and publisher of New York-based Nigerian news website, Sahara Reporters, accusing him of planning an insurrection aimed at a forceful takeover of government through his calls for nationwide protests tagged 'Revolution Now.' A federal high court in Abuja approved Sowore's detention under the anti-terrorism law, for a renewable 45-day period, on August 8. Sowore was charged with treason, cybercrime, and money laundering offenses in September and was granted bail pending trial in October, under stringent terms.

The terms were later changed by the court, which issued an order for his release on November 6 after his lawyers satisfied the conditions. The DSS did not comply with the order for his release despite civil society protests. He remained in detention at time of writing.

Police clamped down on the "Revolution Now" protests across the country and the government said Amnesty International's Nigeria office was on its security watch for allegedly tweeting a message by the protest organizers.

Following police violence during IMN protests in Abuja, the Nigerian government proscribed the Muslim Shia group, after a court ruled on July 26, that group's activities amounted to "acts of terrorism and illegality."

HUMAN
RIGHTS
WATCH
NIGERIA:
PEOPLE WITH MENTAL HEALTH
CONDITIONS CHAINED, ABUSED
Ban Chaining; Provide Mental Health Services
November 2019

Key International Actors

Forty UN agencies and international humanitarian organizations, including United Nations High Commissioner for Refugees and United Nations Development Programme launched in January, the 2019 Nigeria Regional Refugee Response Plan (RRRP) with an appeal for $135 million to provide aid to civilians displaced by the Boko Haram insurgency in the Lake Chad Basin region.

In January, the Chinese government pledged 50 million Yaun ($5.5 million) for the purchase of military equipment to support the Nigerian government's counterinsurgency plans.

In August, UN Special Rapporteur on Extrajudicial, Summary and Arbitrary Executions, Agnes Callamard visited Nigeria to examine violations of the right to life by state and non-state actors. She highlighted in a statement, growing insecurity and widespread failure by authorities to hold perpetrators accountable.

International actors, notably the UN, US, and UK continued to support the Nigerian government's effort to tackle security challenges and provide humanitarian aid to vulnerable communities but failed to publicly condemn government security forces abuses. UK Foreign Secretary Jeremy Hunt visited northeast Nigeria in May, to reaffirm UK's commitment to supporting Nigeria and its neighbors in the fight against Boko Haram. The UK provided over £200 million (approx. $259 million) in aid to Nigeria, of which about £100m was allocated to the north-east for security and humanitarian support, including training and capacity building for government forces deployed in the northeast.

The UK and US raised concerns during Nigeria's 2018 Universal Peer Review about lack of progress on accountability for rights violations by security forces.

Foreign Policy

Nigeria was appointed to the Working Group on Communications for the UN Commission on the Status of Women, in March. On June 4, Tijjani Muhammad-Bande, Nigeria's permanent representative to the UN was elected to a one-year term as president of the UN General Assembly's 74th session starting September 2019.

In June, Nigeria a member of the UN Human Rights Council since 2017, voted against a resolution to extend the mandate of the Independent Expert on Sexual Orientation and Gender Identity, and abstained from the resolution to extend the mandate of the Special Rapporteur on Eritrea.

President Buhari reiterated his support to the International Criminal Court (ICC), urging developed countries to "take the ICC more seriously in order to strengthen democracy and the rule of law" during the visit of Judge Chile Eboe-Osuji, president of the ICC, to Nigeria in June. The Office of the Prosecutor of the ICC continued its preliminary examination relating to the situation in Nigeria in 2019.

North Korea

North Korea remains one of the most repressive countries in the world. Kim Jong Un, the third leader of the Kim dynasty, continues to serve as head of government and the ruling Workers' Party of Korea, using threats of execution, arbitrary punishment of crimes, and detention and forced labor to maintain fearful obedience. Kim also continues to tightly restrict travel out of the country and communication with the outside world.

The government does not tolerate any dissent. It bans independent media, civil society, and trade unions, and systematically denies basic rights, including freedom of expression, assembly, association, and religion. It systematically extracts forced, unpaid labor from its citizens to build infrastructure and public implement projects. The government also fails to protect or promote the rights of numerous at-risk groups, including women, children, and people with disabilities.

In 2019, Kim Jong Un continued the diplomatic engagement efforts he started in 2018, and met with Chinese President Xi Jinping, South Korean President Moon Jae-in, US President Donald Trump, Vietnamese President Nguyen Phu Trong, and Russian President Vladimir Putin.

Flouting the International Human Rights System

North Korea has ratified many important international human rights treaties, yet is known for ignoring their requirements. While it topically engaged with some international human rights mechanisms, there was little evidence of real progress on the ground.

A 2014 United Nations Commission of Inquiry (COI) report on human rights in the Democratic People's Republic of Korea (DPRK, North Korea) concluded the government committed crimes against humanity, including extermination, murder, enslavement, torture, imprisonment, rape, and other forms of sexual violence, and forced abortion. It recommended the UN Security Council refer the situation to the International Criminal Court. The North Korean government continues to deny its findings and refuses to cooperate with the Office of the High Commissioner for Human Rights in Seoul or with Tomas Ojea Quintana, UN special rapporteur on the situation of human rights in North Korea.

On December 17, 2018, the UN General Assembly adopted a resolution without a vote condemning human rights in the North Korea. On March 22, 2019, the UN Human Rights Council (HRC) adopted without a vote a resolution emphasizing the advancement of accountability mechanisms to ensure eventual prosecution of North Korean officials responsible for crimes against humanity. As recommended by the COI and mandated by subsequent HRC resolutions, the UN High Commissioner for Human Rights continues to gather evidence of human rights abuses and crimes against humanity committed by the government.

On May 9, 2019 the North Korean government underwent a Universal Periodic Review (UPR), the HRC's peer-review process that considers each UN member state's human rights record every four-and-a-half years. Out of 262 recommendations made by 87 states, North Korea accepted 132 recommendations, mostly concerning joining other international instruments, treaty bodies, developing more laws, the rights of children, women, people with disabilities, food, health, education, justice, movement, religion, expression, water and sanitation.

Refugees and Asylum Seekers

In 2019, Kim Jong Un's government continued to try to stop people from leaving North Korea without permission, by jamming Chinese mobile phone services at the border, targeting for arrest those communicating with people outside the country or trying to leave, and publicizing punishments imposed on persons caught escaping.

Networks that facilitate North Koreans' escape to safe third countries report more Chinese government limits on their efforts, including an increase in random checks on roads, new technologies including electronic IDs, and other strict controls. They also report that North Korea continues to prevent people from leaving and to pressure the Chinese government to track down North Koreans and return them. In 2011, before the rise of Kim Jong Un, 2,706 North Koreans arrived in South Korea; only 1,137 arrived in 2018 and only 771 between January and September 2019.

The Ministry of People's Security considers defection to be a crime of "treachery against the nation." North Koreans forcibly returned by China face abuses that the UN Commission of Inquiry has condemned as crimes against humanity. Depending on the authorities' assessments of what returnees did while in China, those returned can be sent to short-term detention facilities (*rodong danryeondae*), long term ordinary prisons (*kyohwaso*), or to North Korea's horrific political prison camp system (*kwanliso*).

Since it is near certainty that such punishments await those who are returned, North Koreans fleeing into China should be protected under international law as *refugees sur place*. But the government of China continues to fail to meet its obligations to protect refugees as a state party to the 1951 Refugee Convention and its 1967 protocol. The government continues to send back North Koreans and deny permission to UN refugee agency officials to travel to border areas where North Koreans are present. On November 7, the South Korean government deported two North Korean fishermen to face murder charges in North Korea.

Forced Labor

The North Korean government systematically requires forced, uncompensated labor from most of its population—including workers at state-owned enterprises or deployed overseas, women, children, and prisoners—to control its people and sustain its economy. A significant majority of North Koreans must perform unpaid labor, often called "portrayals of loyalty" at some point in their lives.

Ordinary North Korean workers are not free to choose their own job. The government assigns jobs to both men and unmarried women from cities and rural areas. In theory, they are entitled to a salary, but in many cases, these enterprises do not compensate them, forcing them to find other jobs to survive while paying bribes not to go to their officially assigned workplace. Failing to show up for work without permission is a crime punishable by three to six months in labor training camps (*rodong dallyeondae*).

The government also compels many North Koreans to join paramilitary labor brigades (*dolgyeokdae*), that the ruling party controls and operates, and work primarily on buildings and infrastructure projects. Prisoners in political prisons (*kwanliso*), ordinary prison camps (*kyohwaso*), and short-term detention facilities also face back-breaking forced labor in dangerous conditions, sometimes in winter weather without proper clothing.

North Korea is one of the only seven UN members states that has not joined the International Labour Organization (ILO) and during the UPR review, the government did not accept recommendations that it should join.

At-Risk Groups

North Korea uses *songbun*, a socio-political classification system created at the country's founding, that groups people into varying classes including "loyal," "wavering," or "hostile," discriminating against lower classed persons in areas including employment, residence, and schooling. Pervasive corruption allows some maneuvering around the strictures of the *songbun* system, with government officials accepting bribes to allow exceptions to *songbun* rules, expedite or provide permissions, provide access to certain market activities, or avoid possible punishments.

Women in North Korea suffer widespread gender-based abuses in addition to the abuses suffered by the population in general. In detention facilities, security personnel have subjected women to rape and other sexual violence. Human traffickers and brokers, often linked to government actors, subject women to sexual exploitation and sexual slavery in China, including through forced marriage. Women face high levels of discrimination and sexual harassment and assault in the workplace, and constant exposure to government-endorsed stereotyped gender roles. State authorities engage in abuses against women and systematically fail to offer protection or justice to women and girls experiencing abuses.

Key International Actors

China is the most influential international actor in North Korea. Most of North Korea's energy supplies come from China and it is the country's largest trading partner. China's President Xi Jinping met twice with Kim, in January and June.

South Korea's current Moon administration has not adopted a clear policy on North Korean human rights issues. The North Korean Human Rights Act, which came into effect in September 2016, specifically requires the government to implement the recommendations of the COI report, assist North Koreans who escaped their country, and research and publish status reports on human rights in North Korea. To date, however, South Korea has still not created a North Korea Human Rights Foundation, mandated by the law, to fund further investigations and action on rights abuses.

Moon met with Kim and President Trump in an impromptu summit on June 30, 2019 but did not publicly raise human rights issues during the session. On November 14, in the UN General Assembly's Third Committee, the South Korean government withdrew its name from a list of more than 40 co-sponsors of a resolution condemning human rights abuses in North Korea, which they had co-sponsored annually since 2008.

Japan continues to demand the return of 12 Japanese citizens whom North Korea abducted in the 1970s and 1980s. Some Japanese civil society groups insist the number of abductees is much higher.

The United States government continues to impose human rights-related sanctions on North Korea, including targeted sanctions on government entities, as well as on Kim Jong Un and on several other top officials. On December 10, 2018, the Treasury Department added three senior North Korean officials to its sanctions list, and the State Department released a report on serious human rights abuses and censorship in North Korea. President Trump met twice with Kim in 2019, in February and June, but discussions were reportedly entirely limited to weapons proliferation issues.

From 2014 to 2017, the US government led efforts at the UN Security Council every December to put North Korea's egregious human rights violations on its formal agenda as a threat to international peace and security. But in December 2018, the Security Council failed to hold such discussion because of lack of support among council members and the Trump administration's focus on nuclear talks with Pyongyang. A 2019 Security Council session on North Korea's human rights situation was scheduled for December 10.

HUMAN
RIGHTS
WATCH
"No Room to Bargain"
Unfair and Abusive Labor Practices in Pakistan

Pakistan

Although Prime Minister Imran Khan pledged to make social justice a priority after taking office in July 2018, his administration has increased restrictions on media, the political opposition, and nongovernmental organizations (NGOs).

Scores of civilians were killed in attacks by the Pakistani Taliban, Al Qaeda, and other armed groups. Members of extremist groups, government officials, and politicians threatened the media and carried out violent attacks on journalists.

Women, religious minorities, and transgender people continued to face violence, discrimination, and persecution, with authorities often failing to provide adequate protection or hold perpetrators accountable.

The government cracked down on members and supporters of political parties. Several opposition leaders, including former heads of state and cabinet ministers, were arrested over corruption allegations. Members of the Pashtun Tahhaffuz Movement (PTM) held protests demanding accountability for extrajudicial killings and enforced disappearances.

In May, Aasia Bibi, a Christian woman who had spent eight years on death row for blasphemy, was released and allowed to rejoin her family in Canada. The Pakistan Supreme Court had acquitted Aasia in October 2018, but she had remained in custody due to nationwide protests by religious groups.

Freedom of Expression and Attacks on Civil Society

Pakistan's media operated in a climate of fear that impeded coverage of abuses by both government security forces and extremist armed groups. On June 16, Muhammad Bilal Khan, a freelance journalist who ran a popular YouTube channel covering politics, was stabbed to death in Islamabad. In response to such threats and attacks, journalists increasingly practice self-censorship.

Media outlets came under pressure from authorities against criticizing the government. In some cases, regulatory agencies blocked cable operators from broadcasting networks that aired critical programs. GEO TV, a private television channel, was forced off the air or had its audience's access restricted as punishment for editorials criticizing the government.

On July 9, the Pakistan Electronic Media Regulatory Authority (PEMRA) blocked three television news channels—Capital TV, 24 News HD and Abbtakk News Network—after they broadcast speeches of opposition leaders. The Pakistan Broadcasters Association, a private industry association, claimed that the channels were taken off air without giving them a reason or a hearing. On July 1, PEMRA terminated a live interview with former President Asif Ali Zardari on GEO TV shortly after it began.

On February 9, the Federal Investigating Agency arrested Rizwan-ur-Rehman Razi, a journalist and television host in Lahore, for social media posts that allegedly "defamed state institutions" in violation of Pakistan's cybercrimes law. Razi was subsequently released. In May, the authorities arrested a journalist, Gohar Wazir, for reporting on protests by minority Pashtuns.

Human Rights Watch received several credible reports of intimidation, harassment, and surveillance of various NGOs by government authorities. The government used the "Regulation of INGOs in Pakistan" policy to impede the registration and functioning of international humanitarian and human rights groups.

In May, authorities registered a criminal case for inciting violence and defaming state institutions against Gulalai Ismail, a women's rights activist and Pashtun leader, following protests against the rape and murder of a 10-year-old girl in Islamabad. After months in hiding, Ismail fled to the US, where she sought asylum.

Freedom of Religion and Belief

The Pakistani government did not amend or repeal blasphemy law provisions that provide a pretext for violence against religious minorities, as well as arbitrary arrests and prosecution. Hundreds have been arrested over blasphemy allegations, most of them members of religious minorities. The death penalty is mandatory for blasphemy, and 40 people remained on death row at time of writing.

In April, a tailor in Taxila, Punjab, was arrested after local traders and religious leaders accused him of blasphemy. In May, riots erupted in Mirpurkhas, Sindh, after a Hindu veterinary doctor was accused of blasphemy for allegedly providing medicines wrapped in paper printed with Islamic verses.

The provisions of Pakistan's penal code, which perpetuate discrimination against the Ahmadis, a religious minority, remain unchanged. In August, the district administration in Lahore sealed an Ahmadiyya prayer center after the local clerics objected to Ahmadis being allowed to pray openly.

Women's and Children's Rights

While numerous cases of violence against women and girls highlighted the difficulty survivors face getting justice, authorities succeeded in enforcing some key reforms.

In August, in an important enforcement of laws to prosecute so-called "honor killings," the parents of Qandeel Baloch, a Pakistani social media celebrity who was murdered by her brothers in July 2016, were denied their request to "pardon" the perpetrators. After Qandeel's murder, the parliament passed a law closing the pardon loophole used by families to protect perpetrators. However, very few cases of honor killings were prosecuted.

In July, the Supreme Court of Pakistan held that in cases of acid attacks, a mercy petition filed by the victim forgiving the perpetrator cannot be allowed because it constitutes "extreme cruelty."

The Sindh provincial cabinet approved a new law in August providing the right of women agricultural workers to have a written contract, minimum wage, welfare benefits, and gender parity in wages. The law marked the first time that Pakistan recognized the right of women agricultural workers to unionize

In August, the national assembly's standing committee on law and justice rejected a bill proposing to fix the minimum age of marriage of girls at 18. Early marriage remains a serious problem, with 21 percent of girls in Pakistan marrying before the age of 18, according to UNICEF A number of women and girls were trafficked to China and sold as "brides."

Over 5 million primary-school-age children are out of school, most of them girls, for reasons including lack of schools in their areas, child marriage, and gender discrimination.

Child sexual abuse remains common. According to the organization Sahil, more than 10 cases of child sexual abuse are reported daily across Pakistan.

Terrorism, Counterterrorism, and Law Enforcement Abuses

The Tehrik-Taliban Pakistan (TTP), Al Qaeda, and their affiliates carried out suicide bombings and other indiscriminate attacks against security personnel that caused hundreds of civilian deaths and injuries during the year. They also carried out unlawful attacks targeting civilians.

On April 12, 20 people were killed, and 48 injured in an improvised explosive device attack in a market in Quetta, Balochistan, targeting the Hazara community. On July 21, nine people including six policemen were killed in two attacks in Dera Ismail Khan district, Khyber-Pakhtunkhwa. The TTP claimed responsibility for all the attacks.

On April 18, unidentified assailants forced 14 passengers to disembark from a passenger bus on the Makran Coastal Highway and then executed them. On May 12, after militants attacked a hotel in Gwadar, Balochistan, killing 5 people, the Balochistan Liberation Army (BLA) claimed responsibility.

Pakistani law enforcement agencies were responsible for human rights violations including detention without charge and extrajudicial killings. Pakistan failed to enact a law criminalizing torture despite Pakistan's obligation to do so under the Convention against Torture.

On January 19, the police in Sahiwal district, Punjab killed four members of a single family including a teenage girl in an operation police claimed was targeting a militant leader. However, witness accounts suggest that the police fired indiscriminately at the family's car. The police officials involved were arrested and face murder charges.

On September 1, Saluhddin Ayubi in Rahim Yar Khan district, Punjab was arrested for robbing a cash machine and soon died in custody. His family claimed Ayubi, who had a mental health condition, had been tortured to death by the police. A forensic report subsequently corroborated the torture claims.

In August, the Punjab anti-corruption department accused police officers in Lahore of keeping suspects in a secret detention cell and torturing them. Punjab police ordered an inquiry.

In May, three people were killed and several others injured in violence between Pashtun activists and the army in North Waziristan. Each accused the other of initiating the clash at a military checkpoint at Khar Kamar.

Death Penalty

Pakistan has more than 4,600 prisoners on death row, one of the world's largest populations facing execution. At least 511 individuals have been executed since Pakistan lifted the moratorium on death penalty in December 2014. Those on death row are often from the most marginalized sections of society.

In June 2019, Pakistan's Supreme Court halted the execution of Ghulam Abbas, a prisoner with a psychosocial disability who had spent more than 13 years on death row.

Sexual Orientation and Gender Identity

According to local groups, at least 65 transgender women have been killed in Khyber Pakhtunkhwa province since 2015. In January, a transgender woman was killed in Karak, Khyber Pakhtunkhwa after being attacked on her way back from a music concert. In July, police in Sahiwal district, Punjab, found the bodies of two transgender women who had been tortured to death. In August, Honey, a transgender woman, was shot and killed in Manshera district, Khyber Pakhtunkhwa. Activists allege that authorities had not brought perpetrators to account.

Parliament passed a comprehensive transgender rights bill in 2018. However, Pakistan's penal code criminalizes same-sex sexual conduct, placing men who have sex with men and transgender women at risk of police abuse, and other violence and discrimination.

Attacks on Health Workers

The TTP and other Islamist militant groups carried out violent attacks on healthcare workers involved in providing grassroots services and polio immunization.

A spate of attacks in April resulted in the government temporarily suspending the polio immunization campaign throughout the country. On April 23 and April 24, police officers protecting polio workers were gunned down in Khyber Pakhtukhwa. On April 30, two unidentified assailants killed a female polio worker in Chaman, Balochistan. The vaccination campaign resumed after the government launched an awareness campaign and asked social media platforms to remove anti-vaccine content.

Key International Actors

Prime Minister Khan visited the United States, the country's largest development and military donor, in July, during which he pledged to facilitate the Afghan peace process.

Pakistan and China deepened extensive economic and political ties in 2019, and work continued on the China-Pakistan Economic Corridor, a project consisting of construction of roads, railways, and energy pipelines. In July, Pakistan along with more than a dozen Muslim majority countries signed a letter supporting China's policies in Xinjiang that ignored widespread repression of the region's Muslims.

In May, Pakistan and the International Monetary Fund (IMF) agreed on a US$6 billion bailout package for Pakistan.

In June, the European Union and Pakistan announced their 2019 Strategic Engagement plan, which includes cooperation on human rights. In January, the European Union's High Representative Federica Mogherini welcomed the release of Aasia Bibi, calling on Pakistani authorities to ensure her safety and that of her family.

Historically tense relations between Pakistan and India deteriorated further following a February suicide bomb attack on a convoy of security vehicles in Pulwama in Jammu and Kashmir. Pakistan-based Islamist militant group Jaish-e-Mohammed claimed responsibility for the attack.

In September, following the Indian government's decision to revoke the constitutional autonomy of Jammu and Kashmir state, and arrest Kashmiri leaders and cut off phones and the internet, Pakistan downgraded its diplomatic relations, expelled the Indian high commissioner, and sought international intervention with a Security Council discussion. The Security Council held a closed-door discussion on the issue at the request of Pakistan and the backing of China. It also attempted to get support for a resolution on Kashmir at the UN Human Rights Council. When this did not materialize, Pakistan, backed by China and many states of the Organization of Islamic Cooperation, instead delivered a joint statement.

Papua New Guinea

In 2019, lack of accountability for police violence persisted in Papua New Guinea (PNG), and weak enforcement of laws criminalizing corruption and violence against women and children continued to foster a culture of impunity and lawlessness. Although a resource-rich country, almost 40 percent of its population lives in poverty, which, together with poor health care, barriers to education, corruption, and economic mismanagement, stunts PNG's progress.

PNG imposes the death penalty for serious crimes such as murder, treason and rape amongst others, although authorities have not carried out any executions since 1954.

Peter O'Neill resigned as prime minister in May, amid weeks of political instability fueled by key party defections over his handling of the PNG LNG gas project and dissatisfaction over failure to protect the interests of landowners. PNG's new prime minister, James Marape, has committed to fixing a myriad of problems in the country, although progress remains slow.

Women's and Girls' Rights

Domestic violence affects more than two-thirds of women in Papua New Guinea. In March 2019, more than 200 domestic violence and sexual violence cases were reported in Lae and Port Moresby, where over 23 murders alone were attributed to domestic violence.

In July, six people were killed in an ambush in Menima village and in retaliation for their deaths, days later gunmen killed eight women and five children in a brutal massacre in the Hela Province. Newly appointed Prime Minister James Marape condemned the killings, calling for the death penalty against perpetrators, although no one had been arrested at time of writing.

Sorcery-related violence continued to endanger the lives of women and girls, although there were no new reported incidents during 2019 at time of writing. In June, six men in New Ireland were sentenced to eight years in jail for torturing three women in 2015, claiming they had practiced sorcery. This followed a 2018 sentence, where eight men were sentenced to death and 88 were imprisoned for life for sorcery-related killings.

Children's Rights

According to a report by international nongovernmental organizations (NGOs) released in July, 75 percent of children surveyed across 30 communities in Bougainville, an autonomous island region, and Morobe province had experienced violence at home.

PNG has an underfunded health system and children are particularly vulnerable to disease. An estimated one in thirteen children die each year from preventable diseases, and large numbers of children experienced malnutrition resulting in stunted growth.

School attendance rates for children have improved, however the United Nations Children's Fund, UNICEF, estimates that a quarter of primary and secondary school-aged children do not attend school, especially girls. Only 50 percent of girls enrolled in primary school make the transition to secondary school.

Police Abuse

Despite the establishment of a police task force in 2018 to investigate unlawful conduct by police officers in Port Moresby, police violence continues, especially targeting those suspected of crimes. In November, a video emerged on social media of police viciously beating three men in Port Moresby. Two police officers were charged and suspended following the release of the video.

Media reports state that between September 2018 and January 2019, 133 police have been investigated and 42 arrested, yet convictions remain rare outside Port Moresby. In the same time period, PNG courts convicted and imprisoned 15 police officers in the country's capital for a range of offences including brutality, aiding prison escapees, and domestic violence.

At time of writing, no police officers had been prosecuted for killing 17 prison escapees in 2017 and four prison escapees from Buimo prison in Lae in 2018. Police officers who killed eight student protesters in Port Moresby in 2016 have also not been held accountable.

In March, the Australian Broadcasting Corporation (ABC)reported 50 complaints by the community of Alotau in the Milne Bay Province against police for brutality.

In July, the National Court in Kimbe sentenced three officers to 20 years in prison for killing a person while they were drunk on duty.

Corruption

Corruption is widespread. In June, Prime Minister Marape announced a commission of inquiry into a A$1.2 billion (US$823.4 million) loan entered into by the former government from the Australian branch of Swiss bank UBS. In December 2018, an ombudsman report into the scandal named nine individuals, including the current prime minister, as failing to comply with proper processes and procedures including findings of potential breaches of multiple acts of parliament and the PNG constitution. In October, police filed an arrest warrant for former prime minister, Peter O'Neill, but it was later withdrawn during a legal battle regarding the validity of the warrant.

In July, PNG police charged a former forestry minister with misappropriating A$944,331 (US$648,000) which was set aside for health workers' houses.

Asylum Seekers and Refugees

At time of writing, about 262 refugees and asylum seekers remain in Papua New Guinea, transferred there by the Australian government since 2013. In 2019, the government shut down refugee and asylum seeker facilities on Manus Island and transferred refugees to other facilities in Port Moresby. About 50 "failed" asylum seekers, mostly from Iran, are detained in the Bomana Immigration Center, held virtually incommunicado and denied access to lawyers and their families. Refugee advocates reported that detainees at the Bomana Immigration Centre have no access to phones or the internet, unless they have agreed to assisted "voluntary" return.

Medical facilities on Papua New Guinea have been unable to cope with the complex medical needs of asylum seekers and refugees. Since the re-election of the Australian Coalition government in May, there have been dozens of suicide attempts and acts of self-harm by refugees and asylum seekers.

In June, the UN High Commissioner for Refugees concluded that the mental health crisis cannot be appropriately addressed in PNG and that those with mental health conditions should be transferred back to Australia as a matter of urgency. At time of writing, the Australian government was attempting to repeal a law to facilitate transfers of refugees and asylum seekers requiring medical treatment from offshore locations to Australia.

Land Rights

PNG is rich in natural resources, but the unequal distribution of revenue from mining causes friction as landholders reap little benefit and bear the brunt of environmental degradation, exploitation and economic harm from extractive activities. The Marape government has warned foreign companies, especially mining companies, that they must pay appropriate taxes and royalties to landowners. In multiple cases, landowners have reported being mistreated by foreign companies.

The lease for the Porgera mine by Barrick Gold, a Canadian gold mining company, and Zijin, a Chinese gold mining company, was set to expire in August 2019. That same month, Barrick's CEO met with local landowners, who raised concerns about the social, economic, and environmental impacts of the mine. The mine will continue to operate while negotiations are underway.

Disability Rights

Despite the existence of a national disability policy, people with disabilities are often unable to participate in community life, attend school, or work because of lack of accessibility, stigma, and other barriers. Access to mental health services is limited, and many people with psychosocial disabilities and their families often consider traditional healers to be their only option.

In 2018, the National Executive Committee directed various government bodies to draft a Disability Bill to address barriers that people with a disability face and to protect their rights. The bill is currently undergoing consultation with key stakeholders.

Sexual Orientation and Gender Identity

Same-sex relations are punishable by up to 14 years' imprisonment in PNG's criminal code. While there is little information on actual convictions, the law is sometimes used as a pretext by officials and employers to harass or extort money from gay and lesbian people in PNG, including gay refugees.

Key International Actors

Australia is the biggest provider of aid and investment to PNG, but China is increasingly playing a larger role, especially in infrastructure projects such as roads and schools. However, there are plans to invest in other projects, such as building a A$400 million (US$270 million) Chinatown in Port Moresby. At the end of 2018, PNG owed almost 24 percent of the country's total external debt of approximately A$588 million (US$402 million) to China.

PNG is currently seeking international assistance to refinance A$12 billion (US$8.2 billion) in national debt. In August, the Marape government requested that A$607.5 million (US$416.9 million) of Australia's aid budget to the country be redirected to its treasury department, which Australia refused. Prime Minister Marape also suggested that China open a free trade agreement with PNG, and that it assist in refinancing PNG's debt.

In November, at time of writing, a referendum was called to decide whether Bougainville will remain a part of Papua New Guinea, or whether it will become a separate country. The result of the referendum is non-binding and there are risks of violence if the population votes for independence and the PNG government refuses to accept the outcome of that referendum.

Peru

Judicial investigations into grave human rights abuses committed during the 20-year armed conflict that ended in 2000 remain slow and limited. Violence against women, abuses by security forces, and threats to freedom of expression are also major concerns.

Former President Alberto Fujimori returned to prison in January 2019, after a Supreme Court judge annulled a "humanitarian pardon" that had allowed for his release in December 2017. Fujimori was sentenced in 2009 to 25 years in prison for killings, enforced disappearances, and kidnappings.

Since 2018, Peru has been rocked by a series of corruption scandals involving all living former presidents since 2001, as well as members of the judiciary and the National Magistrate Council.

In response to the crisis, President Martín Vizcarra has, since July 2018, sought a series of political, justice, and anti-corruption reforms. A referendum in December 2018 approved a single-term limit for congressmen, new financing rules for political parties, and changes to the Magistrate's Council. Other reforms, including gender parity for congressional elections, have also been approved.

Confronting Past Abuses

Efforts to prosecute grave human rights abuses committed during the armed conflict have had mixed results.

Peru's Truth and Reconciliation Commission estimated that almost 70,000 people died or were subject to enforced disappearance during the country's armed conflict between 1980 and 2000. Many were victims of atrocities by the Shining Path and other insurgent groups; some were victims of human rights violations by state agents.

Authorities have made slow progress in prosecuting abuses committed by government forces during the armed conflict. As of September 2019, courts had issued rulings in 86 cases related to abuses committed during the armed conflict, Peruvian human rights groups reported, including 44 convictions.

In December 2017, then-President Pedro Pablo Kuczynski granted former President Fujimori a "humanitarian pardon," based on claims of illness, but in October 2018, a Supreme Court judge overturned the pardon. Fujimori returned to prison in January 2019. In February, the Special Criminal Chamber of the Supreme Court upheld the decision.

In November 2018, Fujimori was charged for his alleged role in forced sterilizations of mostly poor and indigenous women during his presidency. The case was pending at time of writing. More than 5,000 victims of forced sterilizations committed between 1995 and 2001 had registered in a government registry, at time of writing.

Also at time of writing, Former President Ollanta Humala continued to face criminal investigations for his alleged role in atrocities and cover-up of egregious human rights violations committed at the Madre Mía military base, in the Alto Huallaga region, during Peru's armed conflict.

Courts have made very little progress in addressing abuses, including extrajudicial killings, enforced disappearances, and torture, committed during the earlier administrations of Fernando Belaúnde (1980-1985) and Alan García (1985-1990). In October 2018, the National Criminal Chamber declared Gen. Daniel Urresti not guilty of the 1988 murder of journalist Hugo Bustíos. But in April 2019, the Supreme Court annulled the decision and ordered a new trial, arguing that the chamber failed to evaluate properly the evidence. In August 2019, 13 soldiers were indicted in connection with rapes of nine women committed between 1984 and 1995 in the districts of Manta and Vilca.

In 2018, President Vizcarra passed a decree establishing a genetic profile bank to help in the search for the disappeared.

Police Abuse

Security forces have used excessive force when responding to occasional violent protests over mining and other large-scale development projects, according to the Ombudsman's Office and local rights groups. According to the Ombudsman's Office, 57 civilians have died in the context of protests since 2013. Such killings have significantly declined since 2016.

In 2015, then-President Humala issued Decree 1186 that limited the use of force by police. However, Law 30151, passed in 2014, grants legal immunity to police who kill in "fulfilment of their duty." The law may make it impossible to hold accountable police officers who use lethal force unlawfully.

In July 2019, a Congressional commission passed a "Police Protection" bill that could seriously aggravate the risk of police abuse. The bill, pending at time of writing, would abrogate the requirement included in Decree 1186 that policemen should use force in ways proportionate to risks to life and physical integrity. It would also bar judges from sending police officers to pretrial detention.

Freedom of Expression

Threats to freedom of expression continue to be a concern in Peru, with some journalists facing criminal prosecution for their work.

In late 2018, the archbishop of the northern region of Piura sued journalists Paola Ugaz and Pedro Salinas for defamation after they published a series of stories on sexual abuse by members of the Sodalitium Christianae Vitae, a Catholic society. In April 2019, Salinas received a one-year suspended prison sentence, 120 days of community service, and a fine of approximately US$24,000 dollars. By August 2019, the archbishop withdrew his complaints against Salinas and Ugaz, the cases were closed, and Salinas's conviction was revoked. But by then, a former manager of a real estate company mentioned in the stories had filed a new suit against Ugaz in connection with the same publications.

Women's and Girls' Rights

Gender-based violence is a significant problem in Peru. The Ministry of Women reported that 149 women were victims of "femicides" (defined in Peru as the killing of a woman in certain contexts, including domestic violence) in 2018, and 99 were victims from January through July 2019. In July 2019, a court in Lima sentenced Adriano Pozo to 11 years in prison for the attempted femicide of activist Arlette Contreras, but declared him not guilty of attempted rape. The case had prompted massive rallies, in 2015, against gender-based violence.

Women and girls in Peru have a right to access abortions only in cases of risk to their health or life. In July 2019, a Lima court dismissed a lawsuit filed in 2014 by an NGO seeking to abrogate a protocol that establishes what constitutes risk to health or life and have such decisions rest instead with individual doctors.

In 2019, a judge in Lima overturned a 2009 Constitutional Court ruling that had banned the free distribution of emergency contraception pills in the country.

In August, President Vizcarra signed a law establishing gender parity in congressional elections. The law requires that 40 percent of congressional candidates be female by 2021, 45 percent by 2026, and 50 percent by 2031.

Sexual Orientation and Gender Identity

Same-sex couples in Peru are not allowed to marry or engage in civil unions. In August, a judge ordered the civil registry to recognize the marriage of a same-sex Peruvian couple who had wed in the United States. An appeal was pending at time of writing.

In November 2018 and January 2019, lawmakers introduced bills aimed at eliminating so-called "gender ideology" from public policy. The bills would exclude use of the concept of gender (which proponents of the bill consider ideologized) from domestic legislation, including sexual education in school.

Human Rights Defenders and Community Leaders

Human rights defenders, and environmental activists, as well as other community leaders, have been killed, and threatened in recent years in Peru.

In January 2019, Wilbelder Vegas Torres, an indigenous leader and environmental defender, was assassinated in a district in the northern region of Piura. Villagers told reporters that Vegas had received threats linked to his opposition to illegal mining operations in the San Sebastián de Suyo communal lands.

In April, authorities found the burned body of British environmental activist Paul McAuley in Belén, a district in the Amazonian region of Loreto.

Also in April, the Ministry of Justice approved a protocol establishing measures to protect at-risk human rights defenders and their relatives.

Refugees, Asylum Seekers, and Migrants

More than 280,000 Venezuelans are seeking asylum in Peru, the largest number of registered Venezuelan asylum seekers in any country.

More than 800,000 Venezuelans live in Peru. In January 2018, President Kuczynski authorized a year-long temporary residency permit for those who arrived before December 31, 2018, and who requested it before June 30, 2019. But in August 2018, the government restricted the permit to those who arrived before October 31, 2018, and requested it by December 31, 2018. Those who hold the permit—more than 486,000 at time of writing—are allowed to work, enroll their children in school, and access health care.

In October 2018, a judge annulled a passport requirement for entry, instated that August. The requirement would have effectively closed the door to many Venezuelan exiles, as obtaining a passport in Venezuela is extremely difficult. In June 2019, however, the government passed a resolution requiring all Venezuelan migrants to apply for a humanitarian visa at a Peruvian consulate before entering. A lawsuit filed against the resolution by a coalition of nongovernmental organizations was pending at time of writing.

Key International Actors

In July, the Inter-American Commission on Human Rights (IACHR) and the Organization of American States' special rapporteur on economic, social, cultural and environmental rights expressed concern over repeated instances of oil spills in the Peruvian Amazon, which, they said, harmed the rights of indigenous populations.

In 2017, Peru hosted a meeting at which foreign affairs ministers of 12 nations signed the Lima Declaration—a statement that condemns the rupture of democratic order and the systematic violation of human rights in Venezuela. This coalition of governments—called the "Lima Group" since then—has led efforts to address the human rights crisis in Venezuela.

In September 2018, Peru and five other countries referred the situation in Venezuela to the International Criminal Court prosecutor. In January 2019, Peru recognized Juan Guaidó, president of the National Assembly, as interim president of Venezuela.

As a member of the UN Human Rights Council, Peru has supported resolutions to spotlight human rights abuses, including in the Philippines, Syria, Myanmar, Iran, and Venezuela.

Philippines

Three years after President Rodrigo Duterte took office in June 2016, his "war on drugs" has killed thousands of people largely from impoverished urban areas. Extrajudicial killings by police and their agents have continued on a regular basis, spreading from the capital region, Metro Manila, into other cities and provinces. The impact of the "drug war" includes not only loss of life but damage to the livelihoods, education, and the mental health of surviving family members.

In July 2019, the United Nations Human Rights Council adopted a resolution asking the Office of the High Commissioner for Human Rights to submit a report in June 2020 on the human rights situation in the Philippines, bringing to bear international pressure for accountability. The Duterte administration responded by ordering the suspension of all negotiations for financial assistance from the 18 countries that endorsed the resolution.

State security forces and government-backed paramilitaries continue to harass, threaten, arbitrarily arrest, and in some instances attack and kill political activists, environmentalists, community leaders, and journalists.

General elections in May 2019 solidified Duterte's power base as more politicians allied themselves with his ruling party. Duterte's former aide, Christopher Go, and his former police chief, Ronaldo dela Rosa, who initially spearheaded the "drug war," were among those elected to the Senate. Dela Rosa was named to head the Senate committee charged with investigating police matters and the "drug war."

"War Against Drugs"

The government's "drug war" continued in 2019, with new cases appearing in the media daily. The modus operandi for the killings involved police raiding homes to apprehend alleged drug dealers or users, who instead of being taken into custody would be reported dead, with the police claiming self-defense. Human Rights Watch has documented the police planting weapons near suspects bodies to justify their lethal use of force.

The Philippine National Police reported that 5,526 suspects were killed in police operations from July 1, 2016, to June 30, 2019. However, this number does not include the thousands more whom unidentified gunmen killed in cases that the police do not seriously investigate, pushing the death toll to as high as 27,000 according to estimates by domestic human rights groups. Research by Human Rights Watch and credible media outlets such as Rappler and Reuters indicate that these vigilante-style killings were perpetrated by police officers themselves or by killers linked to the authorities.

Previously concentrated in Metro Manila, an increasing number of the killings are now being carried out in other urban areas, notably Cebu CIty in the central Philippines and Bulacan province just north of Manila. Human Rights Watch also found "drug war" killings in many other cities and towns in 2019.

Of these thousands of cases, only one case has resulted in the conviction of police officers. In November 2018, three police officers were sentenced to up to 40 years in prison for the murder of 17-year-old Kian delos Santos. CCTV footage showed the police officers taking the teenager into a back alley where he was later found dead. The police claimed in September 2019 that 103 police officers were facing criminal charges in court for their role in "drug war" killings, fewer than half of those implicated.

President Duterte continued to endorse the anti-drug campaign, warning in a September 25 speech that, "if you go into drugs . I will kill you." He added: "Even with the United Nations listening, I will kill you, period."

Killing of Political Activists, Community Leaders, Human Rights Defenders

The extrajudicial killing by security forces and their agents of political activists, environmentalists, and human rights defenders continued, most notably on the central Philippine island of Negros. According to a Rappler tally, there were 116 killings on Negros from July 1, 2016, to August 27, 2019. While some cases may be drug-related, most victims were activist farmers and farmer group leaders, reflecting the violent land conflict that has wracked the island for decades. The killings on Negros spiked in July, when 14 land activists were fatally shot in a single week.

Similar killings occurred in other parts of the country. On July 2, unidentified gunmen shot labor organizer and political activist Dennis Sequeña at a workers' meeting in Cavite. On July 7, a church activist, a provincial politician, and a businessman were killed in separate attacks by unidentified gunmen on motorcycles. The previous month, four—Neptali Morada, Nonoy Palma, Ryan Hubilla, and Nelly Bagasala—were killed in different attacks in less than 48 hours. In September, Global Witness reported that the murder of environmentalists had increased under the Duterte administration, and that the Philippines in 2018 became the most dangerous country in the world for land and environmental activists.

Human Rights Watch and other rights groups have linked many of these killings to members of the military, police, or security force-backed militias. Few of the killings of activists over the years have been seriously investigated, and few have resulted in convictions.

Attacks on Civil Society

The Duterte administration has not relented in its campaign against members of civil society. On July 18, for example, police filed sedition complaints against Vice President Leni Robredo and 35 other people, including priests and bishops, political opposition members, and human rights lawyers and activists whom it claimed had participated in a plot to oust Duterte. The respondents all denied the charge.

Also in July, Duterte's national security adviser, Hermogenes Esperon, filed perjury charges against religious and activist groups for allegedly lying in their petition seeking judicial protection from state security forces. The petitioners alleged that they were being targeted by the military. They also asserted that Esperon's complaint constituted retaliation to silence them. Senator Leila de Lima, a main critic of Duterte who initiated an investigation into the "drug war" killings in 2016, has been held in police detention since February 2017, facing fabricated drug charges.

Meanwhile, the government has continued its campaign of "red tagging" activists by accusing them of being members or sympathizers of the communist New People's Army. Over the years such allegations have often been followed by lethal attacks.

Freedom of Media

Political attacks against journalists intensified in 2019, beginning with the arrest on two occasions of Maria Ressa, executive editor of Rappler, a news website, which has published extensively on the “drug war.” Ressa faced baseless cases of tax evasion and libel, while Rappler received official scrutiny for alleged funding by foreigners.

One journalist had been killed as of November: news anchor Eduardo Dizon of Kidapawan City in Mindanao, who was shot dead on July 10. At least one other, Brandon Lee, suffered serious injuries from an attack by a gunman in August in the northern Philippines.

Other members of the press were subjected to red-baiting and threats, notably Cong Corrales, associate editor of the Mindanao *Gold Star Daily*, and Froilan Gallardo, a senior correspondent for MindaNews. The country’s intelligence service in September “red-tagged” journalist Sonia Soto, manager of a radio station in Pampanga province, accusing her being having links to communist groups.

Children’s Rights

The government’s brutal “drug war” has devastated the lives of countless children and their families. Human Rights Watch research in the past year shows that the killing of breadwinners has resulted in psycho-social trauma and economic hardships for affected families, with many children having to stop going to school and begin working. Some of these children are bullied in schools and in their communities; many are driven to extreme poverty that forces them live in the streets. The government has done little to address these consequences of its “drug war.”

Apart from being direct victims of the “drug war” itself – several children have been killed by stray bullets during anti-drug raids. An initiative started in February in Congress to lower the age of criminal responsibility from the current 15 to 12, with some even proposing it be lowered to 9, could result in more and younger children being locked up in ill-maintained detention facilities.

In a positive move, Congress in February approved a new law protecting children during armed conflict. It appears to be the world’s first law explicitly criminalizing the military occupation of schools. However, at time of writing the Duterte administration had not yet endorsed the Safe Schools Declaration, an international commitment to protect education during conflict.

Sexual Orientation and Gender Identity

The Philippine Congress failed in 2019 to pass pending legislation prohibiting discrimination based on sexual orientation and gender identity in employment, education, health care, housing, and other domains. It also has not passed legislation recognizing same-sex partnerships and extending benefits to same-sex couples.

Death Penalty

Allies of President Duterte in both houses of Congress pushed for the reimposition of the death penalty, especially for drug crimes. In September, Congress conducted hearings on numerous bills that seek to amend existing laws to include capital punishment. In the Senate, where previous death penalty bills have foundered, Senator Manny Pacquiao led the campaign to resuscitate the measure, with the help of newly elected senators who ran under Duterte's party banner.

Key International Actors

The United States remains the key economic and security ally of the Philippines, although there have been growing concerns in Washington about the Duterte administration's increasingly cozy relationship with China.

On July 11, 2019, the UN Human Rights Council adopted a resolution sponsored by Iceland, despite efforts by the Philippines to block the resolution, including through an extensive misinformation campaign and wide-reaching diplomatic pressure. The resolution requested the Office of the High Commissioner for Human Rights (OHCHR) to present a report on the human rights situation in the Philippines. The passage of this ground-breaking resolution marked the first time the Philippines was the subject of such a measure from the Human Rights Council. In September, the OHCHR began soliciting inputs from member states, civil society, and the UN system for the report, due in June 2020.

In retaliation, the Duterte government in late August issued a memorandum ordering agencies of the Philippine government not to accept financial assistance from the 18 countries that voted in favor of the resolution. The memorandum "suspended all new talks and deals for foreign loans and grants" from the countries, due to "the administration's strong rejection of the resolution of the UN Human Rights Council."

The prosecutor of the International Criminal Court continued to conduct a preliminary examination of alleged crimes in the Philippines since July 1, 2016— despite the Philippines' withdrawal from the Rome Statute, which took effect in March. The Office of the Prosecutor confirmed its jurisdiction over crimes committed while the Philippines was still an ICC member.

Qatar

In November, Qatar entered the third and last year of its technical cooperation program with the International Labour Organization (ILO) aimed at extensively reforming migrant workers' conditions including by replacing the kafala (sponsorship) system, which gives employers extensive powers over migrant workers, with a new contractual system.

However, the kafala system remains in place and continues to facilitate the abuse and exploitation of the country's migrant workforce. Families from the Ghufran clan remain stateless and deprived of key human rights 20 years after the government stripped them of their citizenship.

Qatari laws continue to discriminate against women and lesbian, gay, bisexual, and transgender (LGBT) individuals. Throughout 2019, the diplomatic crisis persisted between Qatar on one side and Saudi Arabia, Bahrain, Egypt, and the United Arab Emirates (UAE) on the other, over Qatar's alleged support of terrorism and ties with Iran, impacting the rights of Qataris and other Gulf and Egyptian nationals too.

Migrant Workers

Qatar has a migrant labor force of over 2 million people, who comprise approximately 95 percent of its total labor force. Approximately 1 million workers are employed in construction while another 100,000 are domestic workers. The kafala system governing the employment of migrant workers gives employers excessive control over them, including the power to prevent them from changing jobs, escaping abusive labor situations, and, for some workers, leaving the country.

In October 2017, the International Trade Union Confederation announced Qatar's agreement with the International Labour Organization (ILO) to substantially reform the current kafala system, institute a nondiscriminatory minimum wage, improve payment of wages, and end document confiscation and the need for an exit permit for most workers wanting to leave the country. The agreement called for stepped-up efforts to prevent forced labor, enhance labor inspections and occupational safety and health protocols—including by developing a heat mitiga-tion strategy—and refine the contractual system to improve labor recruitment procedures.

Since then, the government has introduced several reforms. They include in 2017 setting a temporary minimum wage, introducing a law for domestic workers, and setting up new dispute resolution committees; in 2018 establishing a workers' support and insurance fund, and ending the requirement for most workers to get their employer's permission to leave the country; and in 2019 mandating the establishment of joining labor committees at companies employing more than 30 workers for collective bargaining, and disseminating enhanced guidelines on heat stress aimed at employers and workers.

While positive, these reforms have not gone far enough, and implementation has been uneven. The 2017 domestic workers law is poorly enforced and does not meet international standards. The workers' support and insurance fund, introduced in October 2018 to make sure workers receive wages when companies fail to pay, is not yet operating. Authorities are failing to enforce bans on passport confiscations and workers' paying recruitment fees. Most importantly, the kafala system by and large remains in place. The partial reform of the exit permit system does not apply to domestic workers, government employees, and up to 5 percent of any company's workforce who still need their employer's permission to leave the country. While others no longer need an exit permit, they may not be able to leave if their passports are confiscated.

The heat stress guidelines are also not comprehensive or obligatory for employers and do not come with any enforcement mechanisms. In 2019, Qatar continued to enforce a demonstrably rudimentary midday summer working hours ban. Moreover, for six years, Qatar has not made public meaningful data on migrant worker deaths that would allow an assessment of the extent to which heat stress is a factor. However, new medical research published in July 2019 concluded that heatstroke is a likely cause of cardiovascular fatalities among migrant workers in Qatar.

Qatar's labor law does not guarantee migrant workers the right to strike and to free association. In August 2019, despite a ban on migrant workers striking, thousands of workers employed by at least three different companies went on strike to protest poor working conditions, unpaid and delayed wages, and threats of reduced wages.

On October 16, 2019, the ILO announced that Qatar's Council of Ministers endorsed new legislation that would allow workers to change employers without employer consent, and a new law to establish a non-discriminatory minimum wage. The legislation, which still requires approval by Qatar's Shura (Advisory) Council and sign-off by the Emir, is expected to come into force by January 2020. According to the statement, a ministerial decree by the minister of interior was also signed, removing exit permit requirements for all workers, except military personnel.

Women's Rights

Qatar allows men to pass citizenship to their spouses and children, whereas children of Qatari women and non-citizen men can only apply for citizenship under narrow conditions, which discriminates against Qatari women married to foreigners, and their children and spouses.

In September 2018, Qatar passed a permanent residency law that for the first time provides that children of Qatari women married to non-Qatari men, among others, can apply for permanent residency allowing them to receive government health and educational services, to invest in the economy, and own real estate. However, the law falls short of granting women equal rights to men in conferring nationality to their children and spouses.

The concept of male guardianship is incorporated into Qatari law and regulations and undermines women's right to make autonomous decisions about marriage and travel. Qatar's personal status law also discriminates against women in marriage, divorce, child custody, and inheritance. The law provides that women can only marry if a male guardian approves; men have a unilateral right to divorce while women must apply to the courts for divorce on limited grounds; and a wife is responsible for looking after the household and obeying her husband. Under inheritance provisions, female siblings receive half the amount their brothers get. Single women under 25 years of age must obtain their guardian's permission to travel outside Qatar. While married women at any age can travel abroad without permission, men can petition a court to prohibit their wives' travel. A wife can be deemed disobedient, and thus lose her husband's financial support, if she travels despite his objection.

Qatar has no law on domestic violence and only has an article in the family law forbidding husbands from hurting their wives physically or morally, and general provisions on assault.

Refugee Rights

In September 2018, Qatar's Emir signed into law the Gulf region's first asylum law. The law demonstrates Qatar's intention to refugee rights but falls short of its international obligations, particularly with regard to its restrictions on freedom of movement and expression. Qatar is not a signatory to the 1951 Refugee Convention and its 1967 Protocol.

In April 2019, Qatar introduced two ministerial decrees determining the categories of individuals who have the right to obtain asylum and laying out the benefits and rights afforded to asylees. However, the committee authorized to determine asylum claims is yet to be established, meaning the law is not yet in operation. Throughout 2019, the Interior Ministry's search and follow up department repeatedly threatened two individuals with deportation without cause and despite both individuals' stated desire to seek asylum under the new law.

Statelessness

Qatar's decision to arbitrarily strip families from the Ghufran clan of their citizenship starting in 1996 has left some members still stateless 20 years later and deprived them of key human rights. In 2019, Qatar made no commitments to rectify their status.

Stateless members of the Ghufran clan are deprived of their rights to work, access to health care, education, marriage and starting a family, owning property, and freedom of movement. Without valid identity documents, they face restrictions accessing basic services, including opening bank accounts and acquiring drivers' licenses, and are at risk of arbitrary detention. Those living in Qatar are also denied a range of government benefits afforded to Qatari citizens, including state jobs, food and energy subsidies, and free health care.

Qatar is not party to the 1954 or the 1961 UN Statelessness Conventions. Its laws on nationality say nothing about revoking citizenship when that would leave the person stateless.

Sexual Orientation and Morality Laws

Qatar's penal code criminalizes sodomy, punishing same-sex relations with imprisonment for one to three years. Individuals convicted of *zina* (sex outside of marriage) can be sentenced to prison. In addition to imprisonment, Muslims can be sentenced to flogging (if unmarried) or the death penalty (if married). Women are disproportionately impacted as pregnancy serves as evidence of extramarital sex and women who report rape can find themselves prosecuted for consensual sex instead.

Under Article 296 of the penal code, "[l]eading, instigating or seducing a male anyhow for sodomy or dissipation" and "[i]nducing or seducing a male or a female anyhow to commit illegal or immoral actions" is punishable by up to three years. The law does not penalize the person who is "instigated" or "enticed." It is unclear whether this law is intended to prohibit all same-sex acts between men, and whether only one partner is considered legally liable.

Section 47 of the 1979 Press and Publications Law bans publication of "any printed matter that is deemed contrary to the ethics, violates the morals or harms the dignity of the people or their personal freedoms." Throughout 2018, private publishing partners in Qatar, including the partner of the *New York Times*, censored numerous articles that touched on LGBT topics, in line with the country's anti-LGBT laws.

Key International Actors

In June 2019, the crisis pitting Saudi Arabia, Bahrain, United Arab Emirates, and Egypt against Qatar entered its third year. Travel between these countries and Qatar remains restricted, and the land border with Saudi Arabia remains closed. Qataris can only visit relatives in Saudi Arabia, Bahrain, and the UAE if they obtain those governments' permission explaining the "humanitarian" reason for their trip. In UAE and Bahrain, speech critical of their governments' isolation of Qatar or expressing sympathy for Qatar is prosecuted as a crime.

Qatar and the United States signed a number of bilateral agreements, including on civil aviation, counterterrorism, and cybersecurity. In January 2019, US Secretary of State Mike Pompeo signed a memorandum of understanding with Qatar regarding the expansion and renovation of al-Udeid Air Base, the largest US military base in the region.

Russia

The human rights situation in Russia continued to deteriorate in 2019. With few exceptions, authorities responded to rising civic activism with bans, repressive laws, and showcase prosecutions. Record numbers of people protested the groundless exclusion of opposition candidates from a local election in Moscow, and authorities responded with an overwhelming show of force, detentions, and rushed criminal prosecutions. The heightened repression spurred a widespread public "freedom for political prisoners" campaign, which led authorities to release several people from jail.

Officials' disregard for public concerns about the environmental and health impacts of waste management projects sparked widespread protests, and the authorities routinely harassed and prosecuted environmental activists.

The government introduced new restrictions to online speech and adopted a law that could allow it to isolate the Russian segment of the internet.

The "foreign agents" law continued to suffocate nongovernmental organizations (NGOs), while authorities unleashed an intimidation campaign against individuals for allegedly defying the law banning "undesirable" foreign organizations.

Torture and Cruel and Degrading Treatment

Torture and other ill-treatment remained widespread; especially in pretrial detention and prisons. The trial continued against Yaroslavl prison staff arrested for beating an inmate in 2018. In August, authorities promised an investigation into reports that inmates are ill-treated to coerce confessions in designated cells in St. Petersburg's pretrial jail. In September, a court delivered the first-ever verdict against a former Federal Security Service (FSB) officer for torturing a suspect.

However, authorities often deny that ill-treatment takes place and refuse to prosecute those responsible for it. Human rights defenders documented numerous cases of failure to ensure justice for survivors.

Election Protests

In mid-July, disqualification of viable opposition candidates—many of them allies of opposition politician Alexei Navalny—from the September Moscow City Council elections sparked sustained, unauthorized, but peaceful protests. Police used excessive force against peaceful protesters, dozens of whom sustained injuries, and arrested record numbers of demonstrators and random bystanders.

Apparently aiming to discourage further protests, authorities opened several major criminal investigations. By November, 23 people were arrested on unfounded charges of "mass rioting" and/or assaulting police. Five were sentenced, for assault, to two-to-three-and-a-half years in prison, one of whom was released in September, following a vigorous public campaign.

An appeals court issued him a one-year suspended sentence. Seven were released and their cases closed. Eleven remained in jail or under house arrest, including Yegor Zhukov, whose charges were changed to "inciting extremism online." Aidar Gubaidulin was put on an international wanted list after he fled Russia, fearing imprisonment. One activist, Konstantin Kotov, received a four-year prison sentence merely for repeated participation in unsanctioned demonstrations. Courts issued warnings to two couples who brought their children to the protests, after the prosecutor's office sought to have them stripped of their parental rights. One man received five years' imprisonment for a tweet that was interpreted as threatening law enforcement officers' children.

Authorities opened a criminal investigation into election interference targeting opposition figures excluded from the ballot, and unregistered independent candidates served consecutive temporary arrest sentences. Civil lawsuits seek to hold protest leaders responsible for alleged damages, for millions of rubles, related to unsanctioned protests. A money-laundering investigation opened in August targeted the Anti-Corruption Fund (FBK)—an organization led by Navalny. Nationwide raids of the organization's premises and freezing of its activists' bank accounts followed the September vote.

Police in Ulan-Ude used excessive force and carried out arbitrary detentions to break up peaceful, election-related protests triggered by, among other things, the victory of the ruling party's mayoral candidate. Approximately 20 were detained; two were fined, two received short jail sentences, and the rest were released without charge. One of the protest leaders sustained a concussion and a fractured vertebra after police detention. Police opened a criminal investigation into assaulting a police officer for spraying pepper gas that the activists claimed the police used against them. In October, the activist was sentenced to a fine.

Freedom of Association

Authorities continued their large-scale smear campaign against NGOs.

A law adopted in October 2018 banned organizations designated as "foreign agents" from providing anti-corruption evaluations of draft legal acts.

Since December 2018, the Justice Ministry added 12 organizations to its list of "foreign agents," including three human rights organizations, a group working on HIV/AIDS prevention, and FBK.

Authorities continued to fine organizations and their leaders for violating the "foreign agents" law, including failing to include "foreign agent" disclaimers on their social media posts and other publications. Fines and other pressures forced several more groups to close, including one that supported people with diabetes.

In November, the Supreme Court ruled to shut down Movement for Human Rights, one of the country's oldest human rights groups.

Authorities launched the first-ever criminal investigations for involvement in "undesirable organizations," targeting four activists of the pro-democracy Open Russia movement. In September, Yana Antonova's case went to trial. Another activist, Anastasiya Shevchenko, remained under house arrest since January. Both face up to six years in prison, if convicted. Dozens of others were interrogated or fined, for actions ranging from social media posts about Open Russia to holding placards with the movement's yellow and black colors.

In October, authorities conducted en masse house searches and blocked bank accounts of several activists they suspect of having ties with FBK.

In November, Russian authorities banned as undesirable the Czech humanitarian organization "People in Need."

Freedom of Expression

In December 2018, President Vladimir Putin signed into law amendments decriminalizing first-time incitement to hatred offenses. Russian authorities often misuse incitement to hatred offences to stifle legitimate protected speech.

Russian authorities continued to use repressive legislation to stifle critical and independent voices online and offline.

In an emerging trend, authorities restricted artistic freedom by canceling numerous rap and pop music performances under the pretext of protecting children from the promotion of drugs, suicide, and homosexuality.

The government continued to curtail internet freedom. Google's transparency report showed that the total volume of content that the Russian government has requested it to block on YouTube and its other platforms spiked in 2018.

In May, Putin signed a law enabling Russian authorities to partially or fully block access to the internet in Russia, without judicial oversight, in the event of as yet undefined security threats. The law, which partially came into force in November, and at time of writing was due fully in force in January 2020, envisages the creation of a national domain system, providing the government with centralized control of the country's internet traffic that would enhance its capacity to conduct fine-grain censorship of internet traffic.

Courts issued crippling fines to NGOs and independent media. A massive fine in late 2018 against *The New Times* magazine, known for its critical coverage of government policies, was for alleged failure to report foreign funding. In October 2018, a court ordered Transparency International Russia to pay a million rubles (US$15,200) in libel damages to the co-manager of Putin's 2018 electoral campaign. The same month, an NGO working on drug policy was fined for promoting drug use over an article on how certain drug users can reduce health risks. All three avoided closure by raising money for fines through crowdfunding.

Cases against at least 45 people were opened and courts already issued 23 fines for insulting the authorities, under a March 2019 law that bans dissemination of "fake news" or expressing "blatant disrespect" for the state.

In February, authorities opened a criminal terrorism propaganda investigation against a journalist, Svetlana Prokopyeva, for remarking in a broadcast about a suicide bombing that some government policies might be radicalizing youth. The news outlets that published her comment were also fined.

In May, two veteran reporters with *Kommersant*, a highly respected news outlet, were pressured into resigning in retaliation for a news story, prompting the entire politics desk to quit. Ivan Golunov, a journalist with the independent outlet *Meduza* was arrested on bogus drug charges because of his investigative work on high-level corruption. After massive local and international campaigns, authorities released Golunov, dropped the charges, and sacked two high-level police officials. An investigation is ongoing into the attempt to fabricate the case against Golunov.

In November, the Russian parliament passed a new bill enabling authorities to expand the status of "foreign agents" to private persons, including bloggers and independent journalists.

Freedom of Religion

Russian authorities continued to persecute minority religious groups groundlessly designated as "extremist" under Russia's overly broad counter-extremism law despite no evidence that they espoused or committed violence.

In February, a court in Oryol sentenced Dennis Christensen, a Jehovah's Witness and a Danish citizen, to six years' imprisonment on extremism charges. In November, a court in Tomsk handed down the same sentence to another Jehovah's Witness, Sergei Klimov. At least 285 Jehovah's Witnesses have been convicted or were facing trial or under investigation in Russia in 2019. Forty-six are in pretrial custody.

Authorities prosecuted on extremism charges members of certain Islamic groups that have no history of incitement or violence. In October 2019, at least two followers of the late Turkish theologian Said Nursi, branded extremist and banned in 2008, continued to serve three-to-eight-year sentences. Four were released in 2019; one of them, Yevgeniy Kim, was stripped of his Russian citizenship after serving almost four years and remained in detention pending deportation since April 2019. Trials on extremism charges were pending against two others.

Human Rights Defenders

In March, a court in Chechnya sentenced Oyub Titiev, Grozny director of Human Rights Centre Memorial, to four years on bogus drug charges. In June, Titiev was paroled, after 17 months behind bars.

Several human rights lawyers and activists were targeted in Krasnodar region. Human rights lawyer Mikhail Benyash was sentenced to a fine for assaulting a police officer. The charges against Benyash were brought after he was arrested in 2018, held in incommunicado detention, and beaten. In November 2018, unknown perpetrators torched the car of Benyash's lawyer, Lyudmila Aleksandrova, who also represents victims in cases against law enforcement agencies. In September, police in Sochi raided the home of human rights defender Semyon Simonov, breaking his door, and confiscating his and his wife's electronics and documentation pertaining to his work.

In August, police and security services raided and searched the Moscow and Nazran offices of Russian Justice Initiative, an NGO that has won several hundred cases against Russia at the European Court of Human Rights. In Moscow, authorities did not show a search warrant. Authorities in Nazran said the search stemmed from an investigation into alleged foreign funding of unsanctioned protests.

2019 marked 10 years since the murder of Natalia Estemirova, a human rights defender in Chechnya. Russian authorities have not carried out an effective investigation.

Environmental Defenders

Throughout the year, people across Russia protested, trying to prevent the construction or expansion of landfills, waste incineration plants, and waste processing plants that they believed would jeopardize their rights to health and a healthy environment.

In Arkhangelsk region, private security guards used violence against protesters who seek to block the illegal construction, in swampy woodlands, of what would be the largest landfill in Europe. In March, police criminally charged three activists with vigilantism for trying to stop the actions of a private subcontractor who was using an excavator to threaten activists, injuring one. But authorities refused to prosecute the private actors responsible for this and private security, for violence against protesters.

Local authorities also harassed protest leaders and grassroots activists who objected to projects to "export" Moscow's garbage to their regions. Two activists, Vyacheslav Yegorov in Kolomna, in Moscow region, and Andrey Borovikov in Arkhangelsk, were indicted for repeated violations of public assembly rules and may face up to five years in prison for peacefully protesting. Borovikov was sentenced to a fine. Yegorov's trial was pending at time of writing. Authorities in Kolomna and Arkhangelsk repeatedly denied permits for peaceful protests in the center of these cities, relegating them to the outskirts.

In June, Alexandra Koroleva, leader of Ecodefense!, an environmental group, fled Russia after authorities opened five criminal cases against her in one day for failing to pay "foreign agent" fines, threatening her with imprisonment.

Another group, Environmental Watch for the Northern Caucasus and its head, Andrey Rudomakha, were targeted several times for associating with the Open Russia movement. In April, the organization was fined for posting blogs on Open Russia's website. In April and July, police raided the group's premises, and during the latter, they beat and pepper sprayed Rudomakha. Both times, police confiscated electronics and documentation, paralyzing the organization's work.

In January, Greenpeace Russia learned that an investigation into the 2016 beatings of its staff was closed without anyone being held responsible. The investigation into the severe beating of Rudomakha in 2017 remained stalled. Both incidents took place in Krasnodar.

North Caucasus

In July, the independent newspaper Novaya Gazeta, Memorial and Committee Against Torture, two Russian prominent human rights groups published findings of their joint investigation of the extrajudicial execution of 27 Chechnya residents by local authorities in January 2017. There have been no effective investigations into the allegations.

Mass protests against the border demarcation between Ingushetia and Chechnya resumed in March. The protest was authorized on March 26, but the following day protesters were forcibly dispersed. Some physically resisted police.

Thirty-three people, including the protest's leaders, were arrested on charges of violence against police. In July, police arrested a former editor of Fortanga, an online media outlet, who had reported on the protests, on drug possession charges. The journalist alleged that security officials planted the drugs and tortured him to force a confession.

In June, authorities in Dagestan arrested Abdulmumin Gadzhiev on bogus terrorism charges in apparent retaliation for his journalism work for the independent newspaper *Chernovik*. If convicted, Gadzhiev could face up to 20 years' imprisonment.

Sexual Orientation and Gender Identity

In December 2018 and January 2019, police in Chechnya carried out a new round of unlawful detentions, beatings, and humiliation of men they presumed to be gay or bisexual. No one was held accountable for this or for Chechnya's 2017 anti-gay purge. Russian LGBT Network, an NGO, estimated that 20 men were held. All were believed to have been released. In May 2019, unknown individuals broke into the St. Petersburg apartment of a volunteer with the Russian LGBT Network and threatened her and the organization's emergency program coordinator.

In June, a same-sex Russian couple with two adopted children had to flee the country after being targeted by authorities. Russian law bans adoptions for same-sex couples. Authorities charged the case workers assigned to the family with inadequate performance of duties, a criminal offense.

In November, authorities opened a criminal case into alleged sexual assault of children over a YouTube video of children talking to a gay man about his life.

Gender-Based Violence

Domestic violence remained pervasive but under-reported, and services for survivors inadequate. In July, Russia's ombudsperson publicly reiterated her support for a law on domestic violence. In October, parliament held its first preliminary debate on the bill.

In July, the European Court of Human Rights (ECtHR) issued its first ruling on a domestic violence case in Russia. The court ordered the authorities to pay the applicant 20,000 euros in damages and recognized the Russian authorities' "reluctance to acknowledge" the gravity of domestic violence.

Racial Discrimination and Minority Rights

Police continued racially profiling people of non-Slavic appearance, often subjecting them to arbitrary detention, and extortion.

National censuses showed a continuing fall, in some cases drastic, in the number of speakers of minority languages. Council of Europe (CoE) experts on national minorities found that policies continue to reinforce dominance of Russian without effective support for minority languages.

In November, authorities ordered the closure of the Center for Assistance to Native Peoples of the North on a bureaucratic pretext.

Russia and Ukraine (see also Ukraine chapter)

The Russian government continued to provide political and material support to armed groups in eastern Ukraine but took no measures to rein in their abuses, including arbitrary detention and ill-treatment of detainees. De facto authorities in Crimea continued to harass Crimean Tatars. Since 2015, Russian authorities have prosecuted at least 63 Crimean Tatars on trumped-up terrorism charges and handed down up to 17- year sentences.

In September, Russia released 35 people, including Crimean filmmaker Oleg Sentsov, who was serving 20 years on bogus terrorism charges, as part of a prisoner exchange with Ukraine.

Russia and Syria (see also Syria chapter)

Russia continued to play a key military role alongside the Syrian government in offensives on anti-government-held areas, participating in indiscriminate attacks hitting schools, hospitals, and civilian infrastructure.

Starting in April, the Syrian-Russian offensive to regain control of Idlib province, which included the use of internationally prohibited weapons, killed over one thousand civilians and displaced more than 600 thousand. Russia remains the biggest weapons supplier to the Syrian government.

Russia continued to use its diplomatic power at the UN Security Council and elsewhere to block accountability for Syrian crimes. Russian officials urged countries to launch reconstruction efforts in order to facilitate the return of refugees but failed to address key obstacles to return.

On September 19, Russia cast its 13th veto on Syria since the start of the conflict to block a Security Council resolution demanding a truce in the northwest because it did not include an exemption for military offensives against groups Russia and the Damascus government consider to be terrorist organizations.

Key International Actors

In January and February, the Council of Europe commissioner for human rights and the EU diplomatic service (EEAS) called on Russian authorities to investigate the persecution of LGBT people in Chechnya.

In June, the CoE Parliamentary Assembly (PACE) ratified the credentials of the Russian delegation, which fully resumed its work at PACE after losing its voting rights in 2014 over the occupation of Crimea. In return, PACE called on Russia to cooperate with the investigation into the downing of Malaysia Airlines flight MH17 in Ukraine and ending LGBT rights violations.

In July, the ECtHR found that Russia had to pay 42,500 euros in damages to three LGBT rights groups for refusing their registration.

In August, the ECtHR ruled against Russia over the 2009 death of Sergei Magnitsky in remand prison, finding, among other things, that Russia violated his right to life.

In July, the European Parliament adopted a resolution on Russia condemning persecution against environmental activists and the situation of Ukrainian political prisoners. The EEAS criticized Russia for the detention of protesters in Moscow, the detention of Ukrainian citizens, and abuses against Crimean Tatars.

At the March session of the UN Human Rights Council, the UK delivered a joint statement on behalf of more than 30 countries, condemning "renewed persecution of LGBTI persons in Chechnya."

At his press conference with Putin before their August meeting, French President Emmanuel Macron said police use of force at the Moscow protests was not in line with international standards.

Rwanda

The ruling Rwandan Patriotic Front (RPF) continued to exert total control over political space in Rwanda in 2019. President Paul Kagame and other senior government officials, regularly threatened those who criticize the government or the RPF. Several opposition members and one journalist disappeared or were found dead in mysterious circumstances. Although the Rwandan Investigation Bureau (RIB) said they launched investigations into the cases, they rarely shared their findings. In October, security forces reportedly killed 19 people alleged to have been involved in an attack in Musanze District.

Arbitrary detention, ill-treatment, and torture in official and unofficial detention facilities continued, according to credible sources. Human Rights Watch continued to document the illegal detention and ill-treatment of street children in Kigali.

Political Repression

After years of threats, intimidation, mysterious deaths, and high profile, politically motivated trials, few opposition parties remain active or make public comments on government policies.

In 2019, three members of the unregistered Forces Démocratiques Unifiées (FDU)-Inkingi opposition party were reported missing or found dead. In September, Syldio Dusabumuremyi, the party's national coordinator was stabbed to death. At the time, the RIB announced it had two men in custody. Eugène Ndereyimana, also a member of FDU-Inkingi, was reported missing on July 15, after he failed to arrive for a meeting in Nyagatare, in Rwanda's Eastern Province.

Anselme Mutuyimana, an assistant to FDU-Inkingi's then-leader, Victoire Ingabire, was found dead in March with signs of strangulation. The RIB said it had launched investigations into the cases.

Boniface Twagirimana, the party's deputy leader, who "disappeared" from his prison cell in Mpanga, southern Rwanda, in October 2018 was missing at time of writing.

In November, Victoire Ingabire announced the creation of a new party, Development and Liberty for All (Développement et Liberté pour tous or Dalfa Umurinzi), and told media the party would campaign to open political space and would focus on development.

Freedom of Expression

State interference and intimidation have forced many civil society actors and journalists to stop working on sensitive political or human rights issues. Most print and broadcast media continued to be heavily dominated by pro-government views. Independent civil society organizations are very weak, and few document and expose human rights violations by state agents.

Constantin Tuyishimire, a journalist with TV1 Rwanda who covers northern Rwanda, was reported missing in July while he was supposed to be on a reporting trip to Gicumbi District. Authorities said they believed he had probably fled to Uganda due to unpaid debts, although people close to him could not confirm this.

The BBC Kinyarwanda service remained suspended, as it has been since 2014.

Sexual Orientation and Gender Identity

Rwanda is one of the only countries in East Africa that does not criminalize consensual same-sex relations. When gospel singer Albert Nabonibo came out as gay in August 2019, the then-foreign affairs minister publicly expressed support for him.

Repression Abroad

In September, South Africa's National Prosecution Authority issued arrest warrants for two Rwandans accused of murdering Rwandan critic Col. Patrick Karegeya, who was found dead in his hotel room in Johannesburg on January 1, 2014. During an inquest into Karegeya's murder, which began on January 16 in Johannesburg, a head magistrate asked why no arrests had been made even though the names and passport numbers of four suspects were known to police. South Africa's special investigative unit said in written testimony that Karegeya's murder and attacks on Rwanda's former army chief of staff Gen. Kayumba Nyamwasa "were directly linked to the involvement of the Rwandan government."

In October, a *Financial Times* investigation revealed that Rwandan authorities had used Israeli software developed by the NSO Group to spy on political dissidents and critics living abroad. The spyware targeted individuals through WhatsApp calls and allowed hackers to access personal data on the phone, such as messages and location.

Arbitrary Detention, Ill-Treatment, and Torture

Although lack of access to the country and detention centers to conduct research posed challenges to documenting violations, reports continued that prison guards used threats, beatings, and intimidation against detainees, including to extract confessions.

Illegal Detention in Gikondo Transit Center

The detention continued of street vendors, sex workers, street children, and other poor people at Gikondo transit center, an unofficial detention center where individuals exhibiting "deviant behaviours" are sent as part of a rehabilitation process.

Detention at Gikondo is arbitrary and conditions are harsh and inhumane. Police or others, acting on the orders or with police assent, often ill-treat and beat detainees. Children are detained in deplorable and degrading conditions. Authorities often do not provide basic necessities, such as a regular supply and reasonable quantities of food and clean water for detainees, who are often held in cramped conditions. Detainees sometimes sleep on the bare floor.

The Rwandan Parliament adopted a law on rehabilitation services in March 2017. An April 2018 ministerial order on transit centers established that a person who "exhibits deviant behaviors" can be admitted, and defines these as behavior such as prostitution, drug use, begging, vagrancy, informal street vending, or any other deviant behavior that is harmful to the public.

Rights of Refugees

In February, the National Commission for Human Rights published the findings of its investigation into the February 2018 killing of at least 12 people, when police fired live ammunition on refugees from the Democratic Republic of Congo.

They were protesting outside the United Nations High Commissioner for Refugees (UNHCR) office in Karongi District, Western Province.

The report concluded that the police "had used all peaceful and less harmful means to contain the situation" and that eventually "live ammunition was used as the last resort after [a] violent and organized attack was launched by a group of demonstrators against police." The commission's report contradicted independent accounts, including by Human Rights Watch, that Rwandan police used excessive force.

Rwandan police arrested over 60 refugees between February and May 2018 and charged them with participating in illegal demonstrations, violence against public authorities, rebellion, and disobeying law enforcement. Some were also charged with "spreading false information with intent to create a hostile international opinion against the Rwandan state." Human Rights Watch learned that between October 2018 and September 2019, 35 refugees were sentenced to between 3 months to 15 years; 22 were released, and at least 4 others were still on trial at time of writing.

Most of the refugees, ethnic Banyamulenge from neighboring Democratic Republic of Congo, have been in Rwanda since 1996.

The Government of Rwanda, UNHCR, and the African Union signed an agreement in September to set up a transit mechanism to evacuate refugees out of Libya. Rwanda has agreed to receive and provide protection to refugees and asylum-seekers who are currently being held in detention centres in Libya, where they face abuses and insecurity. Under the agreement, they will be transferred to Rwanda on a voluntary basis. In September and October, 189 people, predominantly from the Horn of Africa, were evacuated to Rwanda. UNHCR has committed to pursuing solutions for the evacuees.

Justice for the Genocide

Twenty-five years after the 1994 genocide, a significant number of people responsible for the genocide, including former high-level government officials and other key figures, have been brought to justice.

In recent years, the Rwandan government has requested extradition treaties with dozens of countries in an attempt to try remaining genocide suspects in Rwanda.

In 2018, it ratified treaties with Ethiopia, Malawi, and Zambia. And on January 28, genocide-suspect Vincent Murekezi was extradited to Rwanda from Malawi "courtesy of a prisoner exchange agreement" where he had been convicted of fraud-related offenses.

In March 2019, Dutch police arrested a Rwandan man suspected of being involved in the genocide, after a request for extradition by Rwandan authorities. According to a local media report published in August 2019, Rwandan judicial authorities have sent out over 1,000 extradition requests for genocide suspects.

In November, the trial began in a Belgian court of genocide-suspect Fabien Neretse, charged with 13 counts of murder and accused of causing an "incalculable" number of additional deaths.

Key International Actors

The European Union's 2018 human rights report, published in May 2019, concluded that there were "continued reports of serious violations of civil and political rights." In a France 24 interview in June, President Kagame dismissed the report as "ridiculous," brushing aside questions about critics being killed, physically attacked, jailed, silenced, or forced into exile ahead of the 2017 presidential election.

Rwanda remains a prominent player on the international stage. Former Foreign Affairs Minister Louise Mushikiwabo is the current secretary general of the International Organization of La Francophonie, an international institution which promotes the spread of French language and values. In February, Kagame was elected president of the East African Community, a six-nation intergovernmental organization in the Great Lakes region. Rwanda is set to host the Commonwealth Heads of Government Meeting in June 2020.

Saudi Arabia

Saudi Arabia faced unprecedented international criticism in 2019 for its human rights record, including the failure to provide full accountability for the murder of Saudi journalist Jamal Khashoggi by Saudi agents in October 2018, as well as the country's dismal treatment of Saudi dissidents and human rights activists.

Amid the criticism, Saudi authorities announced landmark reforms for Saudi women that, if fully implemented, represent a significant step forward including allowing Saudi women to obtain passports and travel abroad without the approval of a male relative for the first time. However, discrimination remains in other areas, and women's rights activists remain detained, on trial, or silenced for their activism.

Through 2019, the Saudi-led coalition continued a military campaign against the Houthi rebel group in Yemen that has included scores of unlawful airstrikes that have killed and wounded thousands of civilians.

Yemen Airstrikes and Blockade

As the leader of the coalition that began military operations against Houthi forces in Yemen on March 26, 2015, Saudi Arabia has committed numerous violations of international humanitarian law. As of June, at least 7,292 civilians had been killed and 11,630 wounded, according to the Office of the United Nations High Commissioner for Human Rights (OHCHR), although the actual civilian casualty count is likely much higher. The majority of these casualties were a result of coalition airstrikes.

Since March 2015, Human Rights Watch has documented numerous unlawful attacks by the coalition that have hit homes, markets, hospitals, schools, and mosques. Some of these attacks may amount to war crimes. Saudi commanders face possible criminal liability for war crimes as a matter of command responsibility. Human Rights Watch documented five deadly attacks carried out by coalition naval forces on Yemeni fishing boats since 2018 that killed at least 47 Yemeni fishermen, including seven children, as well as the coalition's detention of more than 100 others, some of whom say they were tortured in custody in Saudi Arabia.

HUMAN
RIGHTS
WATCH
THE HIGH COST OF CHANGE
Repression Under Saudi Crown Prince Tarnishes Reforms

The conflict exacerbated an existing humanitarian crisis. The Saudi-led coalition has imposed an aerial and naval blockade since March 2015 and restricted the flow of life-saving goods and the ability for Yemenis to travel into and out of the country to varying degrees throughout the war. (See also Yemen chapter).

Freedom of Expression, Association, and Belief

Saudi authorities in 2019 continued to repress dissidents, human rights activists, and independent clerics.

In March, Saudi Arabia opened individual trials of prominent Saudi women before the Riyadh Criminal Court and dismissed all allegations that the women faced torture or ill-treatment in detention. Most of the women faced charges that were solely related to peaceful human rights work, including promoting women's rights and calling for an end to Saudi Arabia's discriminatory male guardianship system.

Prosecutors also accused the women of sharing information about women's rights in Saudi Arabia with journalists based in Saudi Arabia, diplomats, and international human rights organizations, including Human Rights Watch and Amnesty International, deeming such contacts a criminal offense. On June 27, Saudi authorities opened a separate trial of prominent human rights activists Nassima al-Sadah and Samar Badawi before the Specialized Criminal Court in Riyadh, but by November the charges against them were not public. Authorities allowed for the "temporary release" of most of the women activists in March and May pending the outcome of their trials, but as of November the trials appeared to be on hold and four—Loujain al-Hathloul, Samar Badawi, Nassima al-Sadah, and Nouf Abdulaziz—remained in detention.

Saudi prosecutors in 2019 continued to seek the death penalty against detainees on charges that related to nothing more than peaceful activism and dissent. By November, those on trial facing the death penalty included prominent cleric Salman al-Awda, whose charges were connected to his alleged ties with the Muslim Brotherhood and public support for imprisoned dissidents, as well as Hassan Farhan al-Maliki on vague charges relating to the expression of his peaceful religious ideas.

Over a dozen prominent activists convicted on charges arising from their peaceful activities were serving long prison sentences. Prominent activist Waleed Abu al-Khair continued to serve a 15-year sentence that the Specialized Criminal Court imposed on him after convicting al-Khair in 2014 on charges stemming solely from his peaceful criticism in media interviews and on social media of human rights abuses.

With few exceptions Saudi Arabia does not tolerate public worship by adherents of religions other than Islam and systematically discriminates against Muslim religious minorities, notably Twelver Shia and Ismailis, including in public education, the justice system, religious freedom, and employment.
Government-affiliated religious authorities continued to disparage Shia and Sufi interpretations, versions, and understandings of Islam in public statements, documents, and school textbooks.

Saudi Arabia has no written laws concerning sexual orientation or gender identity, but judges use principles of uncodified Islamic law to sanction people suspected of committing sexual relations outside marriage, including adultery, extramarital, and homosexual sex. If individuals are engaging in such relationships online, judges and prosecutors utilize vague provisions of the country's anti-cybercrime law that criminalize online activity impinging on "public order, religious values, public morals, and privacy."

Criminal Justice

Saudi Arabia applies Sharia (Islamic law) as its national law. There is no formal penal code, but the government has passed some laws and regulations that subject certain broadly defined offenses to criminal penalties. In the absence of a written penal code or narrowly-worded regulations, however, judges and prosecutors can convict people on a wide range of offenses under broad, catch-all charges such as "breaking allegiance with the ruler" or "trying to distort the reputation of the kingdom." Detainees, including children, commonly face systematic violations of due process and fair trial rights, including arbitrary arrest.

On April 23, 2019, Saudi Arabia carried out a mass execution of 37 men in various parts of the country. At least 33 were from the country's minority Shia community who had been convicted following unfair trials for various alleged crimes, including protest-related offenses, espionage, and terrorism.

Judges routinely sentence defendants to floggings of hundreds of lashes. Children can be tried for capital crimes and sentenced as adults if they show physical signs of puberty.

One of those executed on April 23, Abdulkareem al-Hawaj, committed his offenses and was arrested when he was a child. As of September 2019, Ali al-Nimr, Dawoud al-Marhoun, Abdullah al-Zaher, and others remained on death row for allegedly committing protest-related crimes while they were children. Saudi judges based the capital convictions primarily on confessions that the defendants retracted in court and said had been coerced under torture, allegations the courts did not investigate.

According to Interior Ministry statements, Saudi Arabia executed 179 persons between January and mid-November, mostly for murder and drug crimes. Eighty-one of those executed were convicted for non-violent drug crimes. Executions are carried out by firing squad or beheading, sometimes in public.

Women's and Girls' Rights

In late July, Saudi Arabia's Council of Ministers promulgated landmark amendments to the three laws that will begin to dismantle the country's discriminatory male guardianship system.

The changes to the Travel Documents Law permit "anyone holding Saudi nationality" to obtain a Saudi passport, allowing women over 21 to obtain their own passports without their male guardian's permission for the first time. In mid-August, Saudi authorities announced further changes to regulations allowing women over 21 to travel abroad freely without permission from their male guardian.

The reforms also included important advances for women on civil status issues, whereby a woman can now register her children's births with the civil status office, which was previously restricted to fathers or paternal relatives, as well as inform the office of a death, marriage, or divorce. The changes allow women, along with their husbands, to be considered a "head of household" with respect to their children, which should improve Saudi women's ability to conduct government business on their children's behalf.

Finally, changes to the Labor Law clarified that a "worker" can be female as well as male and introduced a new protection against discrimination in employment on the basis of sex, disability, or age. This major advance should make it illegal for private employers to demand that potential female employees obtain approval of their male guardian to work.

Despite the changes, Saudi women still must obtain a male guardian's approval to get married, leave prison, or obtain certain healthcare. Women also continue to face discrimination in relation to marriage, family, divorce, and decisions relating to children (e.g. child custody). Men can still file cases against daughters, wives, or female relatives under their guardianship for "disobedience," which can lead to forcible return to their male guardian's home or imprisonment. Women's rights activists who fought for these important changes remain in jail or on trial for their peaceful advocacy.

Migrant Workers

Millions of migrant workers fill mostly manual, clerical, and service jobs in Saudi Arabia, though government efforts to nationalize the workforce in addition to the imposition of a monthly tax on foreign workers' dependents in mid-2017 and increasing exclusions of migrants from certain employment sectors led to an exodus of at least 1.1 million migrant workers between January 2017 and September 2018.

Some migrant workers suffer abuses and exploitation, sometimes amounting to conditions of forced labor. The kafala (visa sponsorship) system ties migrant workers' residency permits to "sponsoring" employers, whose written consent is required for workers to change employers or leave the country under normal circumstances. Some employers confiscate passports, withhold wages, and force migrants to work against their will. Saudi Arabia also imposes an exit visa requirement, forcing migrant workers to obtain permission from their employer to leave the country. Workers who leave their employer without their consent can be charged with "absconding" and face imprisonment and deportation.

In November 2017, Saudi Arabia launched a campaign to detain foreigners found in violation of existing labor, residency, or border security laws, including those without valid residency or work permits, or those found working for an employer other than their legal sponsor. On September 21, 2019, authorities announced that the campaign had netted over 3.8 million arrests, including for over 3 million residency law violations and over 595,000 labor law violations.

The campaign had referred over 962,000 individuals for deportation. The International Organization for Migration (IOM) estimates as many as 500,000 Ethiopians were in Saudi Arabia when the deportation campaign began. About 260,000 Ethiopians, an average of 10,000 per month, were deported from Saudi Arabia to Ethiopia between May 2017 and March 2019, according to the IOM, and deportations have continued.

Saudi Arabia is not party to the 1951 Refugee Convention and does not have an asylum system under which people fearing persecution in their home country can seek protection, leading to a real risk of deporting them to harm.

Migrant domestic workers, predominantly women, faced a range of abuses including overwork, forced confinement, non-payment of wages, food deprivation, and psychological, physical, and sexual abuse for which there was little redress.

Key International Actors

As a party to the armed conflict in Yemen, the US provided logistical and intelligence support to Saudi-led coalition forces. In July, the US Congress voted to block an $8.1 billion sale of precision-guided bombs and related components to Saudi Arabia but failed to override President Donald Trump's veto.

On June 20, a UK appeals court ruled that the UK government's refusal to consider Saudi Arabia's laws-of-war violations in Yemen before licensing arms sales was unlawful. The UK government appealed but agreed to suspend new arms sales to Saudi Arabia until the UK government makes a new lawful decision on arms licenses or obtains a new court order. Three months after the court ruling, the UK apologized for a couple of arms sales to Saudi Arabia despite a court ruling that led the UK to stop issuing licenses.

In February, the European Parliament adopted a resolution calling on Saudi Arabia to immediately and unconditionally release women's rights defenders and other dissidents. The resolution also called for an EU-wide ban on export of surveillance systems, reiterated that arms sales to Saudi Arabia contravene the EU's common position on arms exports, and called for "restricted measures against Saudi Arabia in response to breaches of human rights, including asset freezes and visa bans." The European Union released statements in October and November calling for accountability for the murder of Jamal Khashoggi, but had not yet at time of writing publicly called for the release of 2015 Sakharov Prize laureate Raif Badawi.

At the UN Human Rights Council in March, Iceland delivered the first ever joint statement on Saudi human rights abuses on behalf of 36 countries, calling on Saudi Arabia to release human rights defenders detained for exercising their fundamental freedoms, and condemning "in the strongest possible terms" the killing of Jamal Khashoggi. This was followed by a further joint statement at the Human Rights Council's September session, highlighting serious human rights violations in Saudi Arabia, calling on Saudi authorities to ensure truth and accountability for the murder of Khashoggi, and for an end to impunity for torture and extrajudicial killings.

In July, UN Secretary-General Antonio Guterres released his annual "list of shame" for violations against children in armed conflict. This list included many of Yemen's warring parties—the Houthis, Al-Qaeda in the Arabian Peninsula, pro-government militias, and Security Belt forces. However, the secretary-general placed the Saudi-led coalition on a special list for countries that put in place "measures to improve child protection," even though the number of child casualties attributed to the coalition was higher than the previous year.

The secretary-general also resisted calls from human rights organizations to launch an investigation into Khashoggi's murder, eliciting criticism from UN special rapporteur for extrajudicial killings, Agnes Callamard. Callamard conducted her own investigation and determined that a further criminal investigation should look into possible responsibility of senior Saudi leaders, including the crown prince.

Serbia

There was little improvement in human rights protection in Serbia in 2019. War crimes prosecutions in domestic courts were slow and lacked necessary political support. The asylum system remained flawed, with low recognition rates. The situation for journalists remained precarious, with attacks and threats for reporting on sensitive issues. The European Union-mediated Belgrade-Pristina dialogue stalemate continued.

Migrants, including Asylum Seekers, and Long-Term Displaced Persons

Between January and the end of August, Serbia registered 6,156 persons who submitted their intent to seek asylum, compared to 4,715 during the same period in 2018. Pakistanis comprised the largest national group in 2019, followed by Afghans and Bangladeshis. Only 161 people actually filed for asylum during the same period.

By the end of August, the United Nation refugee agency UNHCR estimated that there were approximately 5,420 asylum seekers and migrants in Serbia. Many left Serbia for Bosnia and Herzegovina, aiming to reach an EU Schengen country via Croatia. Most asylum seekers and migrants are housed in 16 government-run reception centers across Serbia.

The asylum system remained flawed with low recognition rates compared to EU averages and long delays before decisions are made. Between January and August, Serbia granted refugee status to only 14 asylum seekers and subsidiary protection to 15. Over the past decade, Serbia has only granted refugee status to a total of 69 people and subsidiary protection to 89.

By end of July, 437 unaccompanied children were registered with Serbian authorities, the majority from Afghanistan, compared to 257 during the same period in 2018. Serbia still lacks formal age assessment procedures for unaccompanied children, putting older children at risk of being treated as adults instead of receiving special protection. Only three institutions exist for unaccompanied children, with a total of 40 places. Two government approved institutions managed by nongovernmental organizations have capacity to host an additional 30. Remaining unaccompanied children stay in open asylum centers, often with unrelated adults, making them vulnerable to abuse.

There was little progress towards durable solutions for refugees and internally displaced persons from the Balkan wars living in Serbia. According to the Serbian commissioner for refugees and migration, as of July, there were 26,520 such refugees in Serbia, most from Croatia, and 199,584 internally displaced people, most from Kosovo.

Freedom of Media

Serbian journalists continued to face attacks and threats. Pro-government media outlets frequently smear independent outlets and journalists, describing them as "traitors" and "foreign mercenaries." Media plurality was compromised by majority of media being aligned with the ruling party.

Between January and late July, the Independent Journalists' Association of Serbia (NUNS) registered 27 incidents of violence, threats, or intimidation against journalists, including eight physical attacks and 19 threats. Serbia dropped from 76th to 90th place on the Reporters Without Borders' World Press Freedom Index list out of 180 countries.

In July, Zana Cimili, a Kosovo journalist working at TV N1 received anonymous death threats on social media, saying that the person had "a life-long desire to kill an Albanian, even an Albanian child." A person was arrested the following day and the investigation was ongoing at time of writing.

Slobodan Georgiev, Serbia editor for the Balkan Investigative Reporting Network's (BIRN), received threats in April after a video that labels him and other independent journalists and outlets traitors circulated on Twitter, allegedly by a government official. Organization for Security and Co-operation in Europe representative for media freedom, Harlem Desir, condemned the video, stating that portraying journalists as traitors can endanger their safety.

A commission established to investigate the murders of three prominent journalists made some progress. In April, the High Court in Belgrade sentenced former state security officials Radomir Markovic and Milan Radonjic to 30 years in prison, and Ratko Romic and Miroslav Kurak to 20 years in prison for organizing and participating in the lethal shooting in 1999 in Belgrade of Slavko Curuvija, the former owner of the newspaper Dnevni Telegraf and weekly magazine Exropljanin. The murders of Dada Vujasinovic, in 1994, and Milan Pantic, in 2001, remained unsolved.

Accountability for War Crimes

Progress on war crimes prosecutions was slow and lacked political will, adequate resources and strong witnesses support mechanisms. The low numbers of high ranking officials prosecuted and convicted by courts remained a problem.

By August, the Belgrade Appeals Court had convicted five lower ranking officials of war crimes, while the first instance court had rendered two convictions and three acquittals. At time of writing, 56 individuals were under investigation for war crimes, and 20 cases were pending before Serbian courts. Since the establishment of the War Crimes Prosecutor Office in 2003, 133 judgments have been issued, of which 83 were convictions and 50 acquittals.

In September, the Belgrade High Court sentenced a former member of the Special Operations Unit, an elite Serbian unit, to eight years' imprisonment for the June 1992 war-time rape of a Bosnian woman in Brcko.

In June, the Belgrade High Court convicted eight former members of the Serbian police, the Yugoslav People's Army, and paramilitary units of killing 28 civilians in the Croatian village Lovas in 1991 and sentenced them to a total of 47 years in prison.

The Belgrade High Court in April sentenced an ex-soldier in the Bosnian Serb Army to four years in prison for the 1992 killing of a Bosniak civilian and for the attempted murder of two other civilians the same year.

Also in April, the Belgrade High Court sentenced ex-Yugoslav Army officer Rajko Kozlina to 15 years in prison for the murders of at least 31 Kosovo Albanian civilians in the village of Trnje in March 1999 but acquitted Kozlina's superior, Pavle Gavrilovic. The court argued that it could not be proven that Gavrilovic had given an order that "there should be no survivors."

The Belgrade High Court held hearings during the year in the trial of eight Bosnian Serb former police officers charged with the killing in a warehouse in Kravica village of more than 1,300 Bosniak civilians from Srebrenica in July 1995.

Chief Prosecutor Serge Brammertz at the Mechanism for International Criminal Tribunals (MICT) expressed concern in July to the UN Security Council that in Serbia, and other former Yugoslav countries, convicted war criminals are considered heroes and glorified by politicians, with widespread denial by public officials of war crimes. He called on Serbia and neighboring countries to support the regional cooperation process to hold war criminals to account.

Members of the US Congress in February urged President Aleksandar Vucic to take action to resolve the 1999 murders of three Albanian-American Bytiqi brothers after they were detained by Serbian police. In May, Vucic told the Serbian parliament that there is no evidence of who committed the murders. In July, Congress's House of Foreign Affairs Committee passed a resolution urging Serbia to hold responsible people to account for the three killings.

Sexual Orientation and Gender Identity

Attacks and threats of lesbian, gay, bisexual, transgender, and intersex (LGBTI) people and activists remained a concern. Serbian LGBTI rights organization DA SE ZNA!, between January and mid-August, recorded 24 incidents against LGBTI people, including 17 physical attacks, and five threats. Investigations are often slow and prosecutions rare.

The September Pride parade in Belgrade took place under heavy policy protection and without major incidents.

Disability Rights

Serbia did not adopt a comprehensive plan to move people with disabilities out of institutions and into community based living. Children with disabilities do not have access to inclusive education

Key International Actors

In August, the US, UK, France, Germany, and Italy called on Belgrade and Pristina to stop thwarting the European Union-mediated dialogue, stalled since 2018.

In its May 2019 report on Serbia's accession negotiations, the European Commission stressed that the lack of progress in the area of freedom of expression and media freedom was a serious concern and called on authorities to step up efforts to investigate attacks and threats against journalists. The Commission also called on Serbia to increase measures to protect the rights of LGBTI persons, persons with disabilities, persons with HIV/AIDS and other vulnerable individuals.

The US government in October appointed Richard Grenell, the US ambassador to Germany, as special envoy for the ongoing Serbia-Kosovo negotiations. A separate US special representative for the Balkans was appointed in August.

The UN special rapporteur on torture and other cruel and inhuman or degrading treatment or punishment in his January 2019 report expressed grave concerns about arbitrary detention and the use of torture and ill-treatment during police interrogations and called on Serbia to adopt the regulations, instructions and training to ensure a modernized forensic, non-coercive investigation methodology. He also called on authorities to introduce independent and effective complaints and investigation mechanisms.

The UN Committee on the Elimination of Discrimination Against Women (CEDAW) in its February 2019 Concluding Observations raised concerns about the lack of effective investigations of cases of gender-based violence against women, the discrepancy between the number of criminal charges and convictions, and that the majority of those convicted receive suspended sentences. CEDAW urged Serbia to ensure that cases of violence against women are properly investigated and perpetrators prosecuted.

In May, Council of Europe Human Rights Commissioner Dunja Mijatovic called on Serbian lawmakers not to pass the law that enables life sentence without parole, and reminded Serbia about its obligations under the European Convention of Human Rights.

Singapore

Singapore's restrictions on speech tightened in 2019 with the passage of the overly broad Protection Against Online Falsehoods and Manipulation Act. Authorities continued to use existing laws to penalize peaceful expression and protest, with activists, lawyers, and online media facing prosecution, civil defamation suits, and threats of contempt of court charges.

Freedom of Expression and Peaceful Assembly

Freedom of speech in Singapore is restricted through the use of broadly worded criminal laws and the use of civil lawsuits and regulatory restrictions. In April 2019, activist Jolovan Wham and opposition politician John Tan were sentenced to pay fines of S$5,000 (approximately US$3,620) each for "scandalizing the judiciary" on social media. Wham was convicted for posting on Facebook that "Malaysia's judges are more independent than Singapore's for cases with political implications." Tan's conviction was for commenting on his Facebook page that Wham's prosecution "only confirms that what [Wham] said is true."

Terry Xu, editor of The Online Citizen, one of the few alternative news sites in Singapore, is facing both criminal and civil defamation charges for material published on the platform. In December 2018, he was charged with criminal defamation for publishing a letter criticizing a Facebook post by a lawmaker and alleging corruption in the upper echelons of the Singapore government. Although The Online Citizen took down the letter two weeks later after an order from the government Info-communications Media Development Authority (IMDA), both Xu and the author of the letter were charged with criminal defamation. If convicted, they face up to two years in prison.

In September 2019, Prime Minister Lee Hsien Loong sued Xu for civil defamation after The Online Citizen published claims made against Lee by his siblings about the disposition of the home of Lee Kwan Yew. While at time of writing Lee had not sued those who made the statements cited in the article, he was seeking to recover damages and costs from Xu.

In May, the Singapore Parliament passed the Protection of Online Falsehoods and Manipulation Act, a sweeping piece of legislation that permits a single government minister to declare that information posted online is "false," and order the "correction" or removal of such content where, in their view, doing so is in the public interest. The law applies to digital content that is accessible in Singapore regardless of where the content was posted and to platforms such as WhatsApp and Signal. It includes criminal penalties for failure to comply with such orders.

The government maintains strict restrictions on the right to peaceful assembly through the Public Order Act, requiring a police permit for any "cause-related" assembly if it is held in a public place, or in a private venue if members of the general public are invited.

The definition of what is treated as an assembly is extremely broad and those who fail to obtain the required permits face criminal charges. Jolovan Wham was convicted in January 2019 of violating the Public Order Act by permitting Joshua Wong, a citizen of Hong Kong, to participate in an indoor conference via Skype without first obtaining a police permit. He was sentenced to 16 days in jail or a fine of S$3,200 (approximately US$2,357). In January 2019, three United Nations experts issued a statement raising concern about the conviction and calling for amendment of the Public Order Act. In October 2019, the High Court dismissed Wham's appeal of his conviction.

Wham was also facing charges for organizing a peaceful protest on a train and a candlelight vigil for a condemned prisoner, and was being investigated for violating the Public Order Act by taking a photograph of himself outside a courthouse while holding a sign calling for the criminal defamation charges against Terry Xu to be dropped.

Criminal Justice System

Singapore retains the death penalty, which is mandated for many drug offenses and certain other crimes. However, under provisions introduced in 2012, judges have some discretion to bypass the mandatory penalty and sentence low-level offenders to life in prison and caning. There is little transparency on the timing of executions, which often take place with short notice. While the number of those executed in 2019 is uncertain, a Malaysian man was executed in March despite pending petitions for clemency and 10 individuals were notified in July that their petitions for clemency had been rejected.

Those speaking out against the death penalty in Singapore have faced repercussions. In July, the Singapore Attorney-General's Chambers sent a letter to the court accusing a Malaysian lawyer seeking clemency for a Malaysian man on death row of making "scandalous allegations against Singapore and its legal system." In August, the Attorney General's Chambers filed a complaint with the Law Society accusing lawyer M. Ravi of conduct unbecoming of a lawyer and asking the Law Society to take action against him for statements made in connection with his defense of an inmate on death row.

Corporal punishment is common in Singapore. For medically fit males ages 16 to 50, caning is mandatory as an additional punishment for a range of crimes, including drug trafficking, violent crimes (such as armed robbery), and even immigration offenses such as overstaying a visa by more than 90 days.

Sexual Orientation and Gender Identity

The rights of lesbian, gay, bisexual, and transgender (LGBT) people in Singapore are severely restricted. Sexual relations between two male persons remains a criminal offense under criminal code section 377A and there are no legal protections against discrimination based on sexual orientation or gender identity. Three court challenges to the constitutionality of section 377A were pending before the Singapore courts at time of writing.

The Media Development Authority effectively prohibits all positive depictions of LGBT lives on television or radio. In July 2019, Singapore Polytechnic withdrew an invitation to a local DJ, Joshua Simon, to give a TED talk after he refused to delete references to his sexuality from the presentation.

Migrant Workers and Labor Exploitation

Foreign migrant workers are subject to labor rights abuses and exploitation through debts owed to recruitment agents, non-payment of wages, restrictions on movement, confiscation of passports, and sometimes physical and sexual abuse. Foreign women employed as domestic workers are particularly vulnerable to abuse.

Work permits of migrant workers in Singapore are tied to a particular employer, leaving them vulnerable to exploitation. Foreign domestic workers, who are covered by the Employment of Foreign Manpower Act rather than the Employment Act, are effectively excluded from many key labor protections, such as limits on daily work hours and mandatory days off. Labor laws also discriminate against foreign workers by barring them from organizing and registering a union or serving as union leaders without explicit government permission.

In June, Singapore was one of only six countries to abstain from a new International Labour Organization convention protecting against violence and discrimination in the workplace.

Key International Actors

Singapore is a regional hub for international business and maintains good political and economic relations with both China and the United States, which considers it a key security ally.

While the European Parliament passed a resolution in February raising concerns about the country's treatment of its LGBT population and ongoing restrictions on freedom of expression and assembly, few countries publicly criticized Singapore's poor human rights record, focusing their priorities instead on trade and business.

Somalia

Ongoing armed conflict, insecurity, lack of state protection, and recurring humanitarian crises exposed Somali civilians to serious abuse. There are an estimated 2.6 million internally displaced people (IDPs), many living unassisted and vulnerable to abuse.

The United Nations Assistance Mission in Somalia (UNSOM) recorded a total of 1,1154 civilian casualties by mid-November. Sixty-seven percent of this figure is due to indiscriminate and targeted attacks, the majority improvised explosive devices (IEDs) attacks, by the Islamist armed group Al-Shabab. Inter-clan and intra-security force violence, often over control of land and revenge killings, led to civilian deaths, injuries, and displacement, as did sporadic military operations, including airstrikes, against Al-Shabab by Somali government forces, African Union Mission in Somalia (AMISOM) troops, and other foreign forces.

Federal and regional authorities, particularly in Somaliland, continued to restrict free expression and media freedoms, including by harassing and arbitrarily detaining journalists and perceived critics, and temporarily shutting down media outlets.

Relations between the federal government and the federal member states deteriorated, diverting attention from needed reforms and on occasion resulting in abuses.

In January, when Somalia became a member of the UN Human Rights Council, the federal government expelled the UN head in Somalia, Nicholas Haysom, pointing to a letter in which he had raised human rights concerns around government actions in Baidoa. The government has yet to endorse the list of nominees for the country's first independent National Human Rights Commission. The government appointed individuals implicated in serious human rights abuses to high-level positions. Positively, Somalia ratified the UN Convention on the Rights of Persons with Disabilities and produced its first report for the Committee on the Rights of the Child.

Abuses by Government and Allied Forces

Somali government forces responded to a handful of largely peaceful demonstrations with lethal force. In May, security forces killed at least one child as students peacefully protested in Beletweyn, following a government decision to postpone exams.

In December 2018, during the run-up to regional presidential elections in Baidoa, Ethiopian forces arrested Mukhtar Robow, a former Al-Shabab leader who ran for the regional presidency, sparking protests. Security forces, notably police forces, responded with lethal force, killing at least 15 protesters and injuring many others between December 13 and 15, according to the UN. Amnesty International documented the killing of a member of parliament and a child on December 14. Dozens were arbitrarily arrested, reportedly including children.

Dozens of government and security officials as well as former electoral delegates and clan elders who had been involved in the 2016 electoral process, were assassinated; Al-Shabab claimed responsibility for some of the killings.

Military courts continue to try defendants in a broad range of cases, including for terrorism-related offenses, in proceedings that violate fair trial standards. According to media reports and the UN, between December 31, 2018, and early November, 2019, the government had carried out at least 16 executions, all for alleged terrorism-related offenses.

Al-Shabab Abuses

Al-Shabab executed after unfair trials individuals it accused of working or spying for the government and foreign forces, with media reporting an uptick in executions mid-year; and extorted "taxes" through threats.

Al-Shabab conducted targeted and indiscriminate attacks against civilians and civilian infrastructure using improvised explosive devices (IEDs), suicide bombings, and shelling, as well as assassinations, particularly in Mogadishu and Lower Shabelle, which resulted in over 750 civilian deaths and injuries, according to the UN.

Abuses against Children

All Somali parties to the conflict commited serious abuses against children, including killings, maiming, and the recruitment and use of child soldiers.

In 2018, the UN documented more cases of children recruited and used as soldiers in Somalia than in any other country in the world. This trend continued in 2019 as Al-Shabab pursued an aggressive child recruitment campaign with retaliation against communities refusing to hand over children.

Somali federal and regional authorities unlawfully detained children simply for alleged ties to Al-Shabab and at times prosecuted in military courts, children for terrorism-related offenses. The government failed to put in place juvenile justice measures, notably for children accused of Al-Shabab-related crimes.

Sexual Violence

Internally displaced women and girls remain at particular risk of sexual and gender-based violence by armed men and civilians.

The UN documented over 100 incidents of sexual violence against girls. The cases of two girls who were gang raped by civilians and died received significant public attention. Aisha Ilyas Adan, 12, went missing on February 24, and her body was discovered the next day near her home in North Galkayo, Puntland. According to multiple media reports, Aisha was raped, mutilated, and strangled to death. Three men were sentenced to death under Puntland's 2016 Sexual Offences Act, which includes death penalty sentences for "aggravated" cases of rape. Human Rights Watch opposes the death penalty in all cases.

The Somali penal code, currently being revised, classifies sexual violence as an "offence against modesty and sexual honor" rather than as a violation of bodily integrity; it also punishes same-sex intercourse. The federal Sexual Offences Bill has been submitted before parliament, but had yet to be debated at time of writing.

Freedom of Expression and Association

The federal government, regional authorities, notably in Puntland and Jubaland, and Al-Shabab continued to intimidate, harass and attack journalists. While Somali authorities seldom investigate cases of killings or attacks on journalists, a Somali media organization reported that the military court in Mogadishu in absentia sentenced to five years a police officer for the July 2018 killing of cameraman Abdirizak Kasim Iman.

Two journalists, Mohamed Sahal Omar and Somali-Canadian Hodan Nalayeh, were killed in a July 12 Al-Shabab attack on a hotel in the southern port city of Kismayo.

In September and October, authorities in Puntland repeatedly harassed journalists at Daljir Radio after the station reported on alleged arbitrary arrests and mistreatment of detainees, including the alleged death in custody of one detainee as a result of mistreatment, by Puntland security forces.

In late May, the police detained for three days Ali Adan Munim, reporter at the private Goobjoog media outlet, citing Facebook posts in which Ali criticized National Intelligence and Security Agency (NISA) treatment of detainees and had said he had obtained copies of national exams. He was accused of insulting public officials, disrupting government work, and spreading propaganda.

Displacement and Access to Humanitarian Assistance

The humanitarian crisis in the country continued due to the ongoing conflict, violence, and increasingly frequent drought. The UN explicitly linked the humanitarian situation to climate change, among other factors. It declared that 2.1 million Somalis face acute food insecurity, as of late September, many of them children and internally displaced.

The UN and Norwegian Refugee Council also reported that over 300,000 people had been newly displaced as of September. These individuals faced serious abuses, including sexual violence, forced evictions, and limited access to basic needs such as food and water. According to humanitarian agencies, over 173,255 people had been evicted, most forcibly, by August 2019, primarily in Mogadishu.

Humanitarian agencies face serious access challenges due to insecurity, targeted attacks on aid workers, generalized violence, and restrictions imposed by parties to the conflict. Al-Shabab continues to prohibit many nongovernmental organizations and all UN agencies from working in areas under its control, blockading some government-controlled towns.

Somaliland

The Somaliland government severely restricted reporting and free expression on issues deemed controversial or overly critical of the authorities.

There was a significant number of arbitrary arrests of journalists and temporary closure of media outlets. On February 10, the regional court in Hargeisa suspended the *Foore* newspaper for one year and fined the editor, Abdirashid Abdiwahab Ibrahim, 3 million Somaliland shillings (US$300). The newspaper was accused of spreading misinformation after it reported on the building of a new presidential palace in Hargeisa. The ban on *Foore* was lifted in August.

The government also arbitrarily arrested perceived government critics. On January 12, poet Abdirahman Ibrahim Adan (known as "Abdirahman Abees") was arbitrarily arrested and charged with "insulting the police" after he highlighted various due process abuses in Somaliland. He was acquitted and released on February 25.

Key International Actors

International support and attention focused on building Somalia's security sector, improving relations between federal and state authorities, and regional electoral processes. Attention to ensuring accountability for abuses remained minimal.

Following the December 2018 police violence in Baidoa, key international partners—the European Union, the United Kingdom and Germany—temporarily suspended support to police in the South West State.

After the Somali government expelled special representative of the secretary-general Haysom, the UN suspended its monthly reporting on human rights issues.

The US military increasingly conducted airstrikes in Somalia and joint military operations against Al-Shabab. Media and NGOs documented several civilian casualties. In April, AFRICOM acknowledged two civilian casualties in an April 2018 strike, citing internal reporting errors.

In August, six UN Security Council member states blocked a bid by Kenya to impose additional counterterrorism sanctions on Al-Shabab that could have jeopardized the delivery of humanitarian aid.

International donors supported the establishment of a new civilian court and prison complex in Mogadishu. At time of writing, the court's mandate remained unclear, and no juvenile facilities set up.

The competition between UAE and Qatar over political and economic dominance in Somalia continued to exacerbate intra-Somalia tensions, both between Mogadishu and federal states, and with Somaliland.

South Africa

On May 8, Matamela Cyril Ramaphosa was elected to a five-year term as president after serving briefly in the same role following the resignation of Jacob Zuma in February 2018. The election saw the lowest voter turnout in history, as many South Africans expressed frustration over growing inequality, high unemployment, and corruption.

Economic insecurity, among other factors, led to xenophobic violence against African foreign nationals and their businesses in March 2019, when hundreds of foreign nationals in Durban sought shelter at police stations or other places, as their homes, trucks, and other belongings were looted or destroyed. The same day the attacks began, on March 25, the South African government launched a National Action Plan to combat Racism, Racial Discrimination, Xenophobia and Related Intolerance.

Former President Jacob Zuma appeared before the Commission of Inquiry into Allegations of State Capture, Corruption and Fraud in the Public Sector including Organs of State in July. The commission, led by Deputy Chief Justice Raymond Zondo, was established by Ramaphosa in August 2018 in response to allegations that the former president had entered into an agreement in which companies owned by the Gupta family were awarded lucrative government contracts and influence in exchange for employing Zuma's family members and financial compensation. At time of writing, Zuma had not been charged or convicted for these crimes.

Xenophobic Attacks on Foreign Nationals

From March 25 to April 2, 2019, violence by South Africans against foreign nationals erupted in the eastern eThekwini municipality, one of South Africa's most heavily populated areas, which includes the city of Durban and surrounding towns. Police did not make any arrest following the looting and destruction of foreign-owned homes and businesses, during which some foreign nationals were killed and several others seriously injured.

More than 200 people—mostly foreign truck drivers—have been killed in South Africa since March 2018, based on research by the Road Freight Association, which represents road freight service providers. Groups of people claiming to be South African truck drivers have thrown gasoline bombs at trucks and shot at, stoned, stabbed, and harassed foreign truck drivers to force them out of the trucking industry. Many foreign truck drivers have lost their jobs, despite having valid work permits, or have been unable to return to work due to injuries or damage to their trucks. Some of the attackers claimed affiliation to the All Truck Drivers Foundation (ATDF), an association of local truck drivers.

Police Minister Bheki Cele said in June the police had arrested 91 alleged attackers; however, they were only charged with minor traffic offenses, and the minister did not describe any clear steps police would take to stop the violence and protect truck drivers and cargo.

In September, sporadic violence targeting African foreign nationals and their businesses broke out in parts of Durban, Pretoria, Johannesburg City and surrounding areas of Germiston, Thokoza, Katlehong, Alberton, Alexandra, and Malvern. The attacks left 12 people dead, thousands displaced, and businesses wantonly looted. More than 600 people were arrested on various charges related to public violence and looting, malicious damage to property, and grievous bodily harm. The arrests took place amid concerns that, as with previous waves of xenophobic violence, prosecutions will fail if police investigations are not thorough. On September 3, President Ramaphosa posted a video message on Twitter in which he condemned the violence in the strongest terms and called for the attacks to stop immediately.

On March 25, the government launched a National Action Plan to combat xenophobia, racism, and discrimination, marking an important step toward addressing the widespread human rights abuses arising from xenophobic and gender-based violence and discrimination that continue to plague South Africa.

The five-year plan, developed in consultation with civil society, aims to raise public awareness about anti-racism and equality measures, improve access to justice and better protection for victims, and increase anti-discrimination efforts to help achieve greater equality and justice.

But the Action Plan fails to address a key challenge fueling the problem: the lack of accountability for xenophobic crimes. Virtually no one has been convicted for past outbreaks of xenophobic violence, including the attacks in 2019, the Dur-

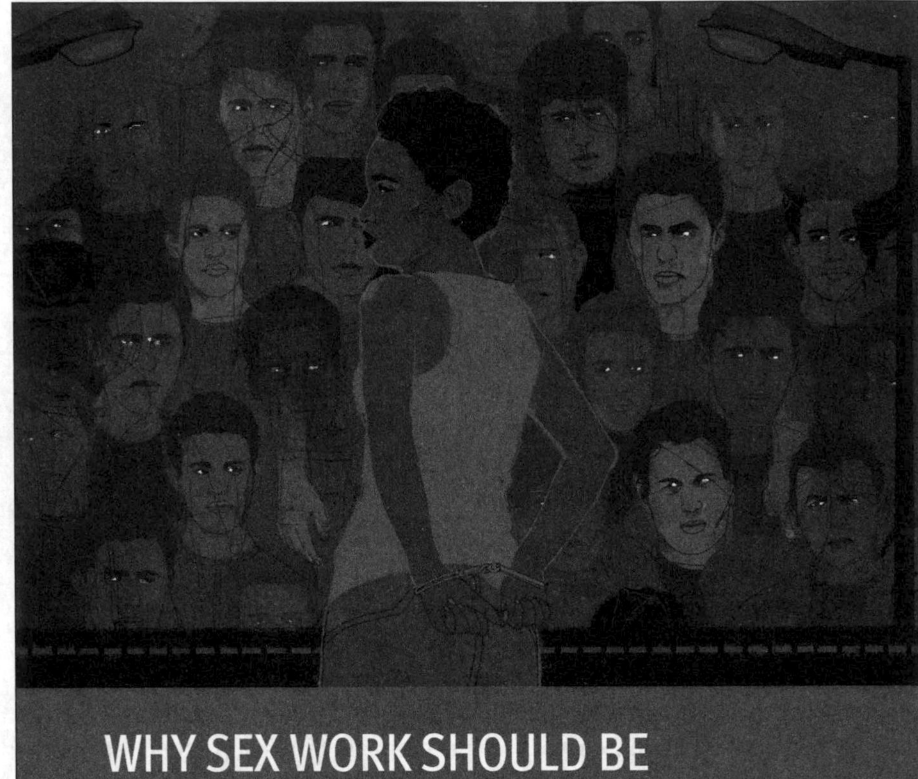

WHY SEX WORK SHOULD BE DECRIMINALISED IN SOUTH AFRICA

ban violence of April 2015 that displaced thousands of foreign nationals, and the 2008 attacks on foreigners, which resulted in the deaths of more than 60 people across the country.

Disability Rights

In February, Ramaphosa acknowledged that South Africa has "not achieved nearly enough" regarding the rights of people with disabilities. The ruling African National Congress's (ANC) 2019 election manifesto stated the party's commitment to including "the needs of people with disability in all government programmes." It acknowledged that the education, training, and health systems need "radical improvements."

South Africa continues to expand its parallel, special education system for people with disabilities and those deemed to have ongoing learning barriers, preventing them from learning in an inclusive general school system. Human Rights Watch and expert groups' research shows that social workers and education officials refer children to special schools in many cases after a long and tedious process of referrals and assessments. Such referrals often prevent children's entry into inclusive, mainstream education. This limits their access to a full cycle of basic education, to which they are entitled by law. Many children are in special schools that segregate them and do not support their holistic development or cognitive skills.

The lack of reliable enrollment data specifically about children with disabilities significantly affects South Africa's ability to ensure that it can guarantee high-quality, inclusive primary and secondary education for people with disabilities. South Africa's laws do not automatically guarantee the right to free education, but most children who attend public schools do not pay school fees. By contrast, most children who attend public special schools are charged fees, and many children with disabilities attending mainstream schools are also charged additional fees.

Women's Rights

In March 2019, Ramaphosa said his government was looking into decriminalizing sex work, which has been illegal in South Africa since at least the early

"We Know Our Lives Are in Danger"

Environment of Fear in South Africa's Mining-Affected Communities

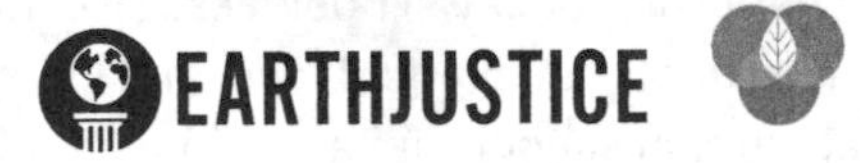

1900s. South African laws also prohibit other aspects of sex work, including running or owning a brothel, living off the earnings of "prostitution," and enticing a woman into "prostitution."

Criminalization has undermined sex workers' access to justice for crimes committed against them and exposed them to unchecked abuse and exploitation by law enforcement officials, including police officers. And although the Department of Health's National Strategic Plan on HIV for Sex Workers is grounded in respect for the human rights of sex workers, criminalization hinders sex workers' efforts to access health care, including HIV prevention, treatment, care, and support.

Nationwide protests took place in September following the killings of multiple women and many instances of gender-based violence. The violence spurred an #AmINext movement where women on social media called out their alleged abusers. Protesters called for a national emergency and expressed anger over the government's failure to better protect women. According to the Women's Minister, Maite Nkoana-Mashabane, more than 30 women were killed by their spouses in August alone.

In response to the protests, the ANC vowed to amend the Sexual Offences Act and Domestic Violence Act in order to ensure harsher punishments for offenders, as well as other reforms, including making the National Register for Sex Offenders (NRSO) public.

In September, the Equality Court ruled that a trans woman detained in a male prison, Jade September, had the right to express her gender identity while in prison. This meant that, as a woman transgender inmate, she could express her gender identity while incarcerated in an all-male prison, including the right to wear her hair long; wear make-up; wear female clothing and be addressed by officials using female pronouns.

Environmental Defenders

During 2019 there was no progress in identifying or arresting those responsible for the murder of Sikhosiphi Rhadebe, a Xolobeni community activist killed in 2016. His family said the investigation into his murder had stalled. Community activism against the harmful impact of mining, like Rhadebe's, has often been met with harassment, intimidation, and violence.

Community and environmental rights activists have faced harassment for demanding their rights to health and a healthy environment. South Africa is one of the world's biggest coal producers, and a leading producer of a wide range of metals. The serious environmental, health, and social impacts of mining, coupled with a lack of transparency, accountability, and consultation, have increased public opposition to mining projects.

Foreign Policy

South Africa, as a non-permanent member of the United Nations Security Council for 2019-2020, played a leading role in addressing the situation in Sudan, advocating for the UN to adhere to the decisions made by the African Union Peace and Security Council in an effort to stem abuses against civilians. Sweeping political changes in Sudan also led South Africa to push for a responsible and flexible drawdown of the UN peacekeeping force in Darfur, UNAMID, in opposition to China and Russia's position to keep UNAMID's exit on schedule. In May, an informal Security Council discussion on Cameroon's humanitarian situation was met with strong opposition from South Africa, as well as the other two African members of the council. South Africa also opposed a Security Council discussion on Venezuela in January.

Following the outbreak of xenophobic violence in September, South Africa's diplomatic relations with other African nations, notably Nigeria, became strained. Nigeria repatriated over 600 of its citizens living in South Africa following the attacks. Following reprisal attacks in Nigeria, the South African government on September 5 temporarily shut down its embassy in Abuja, Nigeria.

South Africa held the World Economic Forum on Africa in Cape Town in September but Malawi, Rwanda, and the Democratic Republic of Congo did not attend due to the xenophobic attacks against their citizens in South Africa.

On October 29, 2019, the South Africa Parliament revived the International Crimes Bill whose purpose is to withdraw the country from the International Criminal Court.

South Korea

The Republic of Korea (South Korea) is a democracy that has appropriate protections in place for most political, civil, and socio-economic rights. However, discrimination can be severe against at-risk groups, including women, lesbian, gay, bisexual, and transgender (LGBT) persons, and racial and ethnic minorities like refugees and migrants, and companies lack legal obligations to respect human rights. The government also maintains unreasonable restrictions on freedom of expression, association, and assembly.

Women's Rights

Discrimination against women is widespread in South Korea. Gender-based stereotypes concerning the role of women in the family and society are common—including widespread social stigma and discrimination against unmarried mothers—and are often unchallenged or even encouraged by the government.

A relatively small proportion of women occupy decision-making positions in the business, political, and public sectors, and there is a 35 percent wage gap between men and women. *The Economist* magazine's "Glass Ceiling Index," which evaluates women's higher education, women in managerial positions, and number of female members in parliament, gives South Korea the lowest rank among countries that belong to the Organization for Economic Co-operation and Development (OECD).

In positive developments, however, on April 11, South Korea's Constitutional Court overturned the country's strict abortion laws, which criminalized the procedure in most cases, and ordered the National Assembly to rewrite laws governing the procedure by the end of 2020.

The #MeToo movement also continued to gain ground in 2019, reaching political elites and entertainment stars. On January 23, Ahn Tae-gun, a former senior prosecutor, was sentenced for two years for sexually harassing Seo Ji-hyun, a junior colleague who publicly accused him in 2018 and helped fuel the nascent #MeToo movement in the country. On February 1, the Seoul High Court sentenced Ahn Hee-jung, a prominent politician in South Chungcheong province who had been considered a possible presidential candidate, to three-and-a-half years in prison for raping his former secretary, Kim Ji-eun.

The government is struggling with a growing problem with digital sex crimes—non-consensual online sharing of intimate images, including secretly filming using hidden cameras (known as *molka*). On March 18, Jung Joon-young, a K-pop star, was arrested after admitting to secretly filming himself having sex with at least 10 women and sharing the videos with friends on a group chat. On March 23, two men were arrested for streaming the "intimate private activities" of at least 1,600 motel guests across the country from hidden cameras in 30 motels in 10 cities. Government data released in 2019 showed that victims reported about 6,800 *molka* cases to police in 2018 but only a third were referred for trial, and fewer than one in ten trials led to prison sentences.

Sexual Orientation and Gender Identity

The growing LGBT movement in South Korean continues to trigger increased resistance by conservative Christian anti-LGBT groups. In June, Seoul's 20th Pride Parade saw record participation with around 70,000 people, but mushrooming LGBT events outside the capital still face local resistance. In August, the 3rd Busan Queer Culture Festival was forced to cancel its rally because the local district office denied them permission for road use. In August, at the 2nd Incheon Queer Cultural Festival, police recruited around 3,000 officers to protect a few hundred people from the LGBTQ community, nongovernmental organizations, and embassies, who were surrounded by thousands of mostly Christian anti-LGBT protesters.

The Constitutional Court is currently reviewing the 1962 Military Criminal Act (Article 92-6), which punishes sexual acts between soldiers with up to two years in prison under a "disgraceful conduct" clause, regardless of consent and whether they have sex in or outside of military facilities.

Refugees

South Korea is one of the few countries in Asia to be a party to the 1951 UN Refugee Convention and its 1967 Protocol. However, it continues to reject almost all non-North Korean asylum seekers entering the country. (North Koreans are granted automatic citizenship and are not processed as ordinary asylum seekers).

Of the 16, 173 people who sought asylum in 2018 and who were not from North Korea, the government finished reviewing 3,879 cases, and granted only 144 refugee status. In some cases, the government issued humanitarian visas to allow continued stay in the country, but in most instances, applicants were rejected outright.

Of over 500 Yemeni refugees who arrived at the South Korean island of Jeju in 2018, only two were granted asylum, in December 2018, while 412 others received temporary humanitarian status and 56 were ordered to leave.

Policy on North Korean Human Rights

President Moon Jae-in's administration has still not clearly enunciated its policy on North Korean human rights issues in the context of its new diplomatic opening with Pyongyang.

South Korea has yet to fully implement the North Korean Human Rights Law that came into effect in September 2016, which requires Seoul to implement the recommendations of the COI report, assist North Koreans who escaped their country and South Korean nationals detained in North Korea, and research and publish status reports on human rights conditions in North Korea.

It failed to establish the North Korea Human Rights Foundation, designed to support research on North Korea's rights situation and fund groups working on North Korean rights issues. The foundation is also supposed to help the government develop a strategy to promote rights in the North. The government also failed to appoint an ambassador at large on North Korean human rights, vacant since September 2017.

On November 7, the South Korean government deported two North Korean fishermen to face murder charges in North Korea. On November 14, in the UN General Assembly's third committee, the South Korean government decided to withdraw its name from a list of more than co-sponsorship from a resolution condemning human rights abuses in North Korea, which they had been supporting since 2008.

Freedom of Expression

Although South Korea has a free press and a lively civil society, successive South Korean governments and large corporations have at various times used draconian criminal defamation laws, the national security law, and restrictive interpretations of other laws, which are still in place, to create a chilling effect that limits critical scrutiny of the government and corporations.

Criminal defamation law allows for up to seven years' imprisonment and a fine. The law focuses solely on whether what was said or written was in the public interest and does not allow for truth as a complete defense. The National Security Law criminalizes any dissemination of anything that the government classifies as North Korean "propaganda." (The two Koreas are technically still at war, as the Korean War ended with only a ceasefire in 1953). The law imposes significant restrictions on the freedom of South Koreans to create and join political associations by imposing severe criminal penalties on anyone who joins, praises or induces others to join an "anti-government organization," a term not clearly defined in law.

Worker's Rights

South Korea joined the International Labour Organization (ILO) in 1991 but has not ratified 4 of the ILO's 8 core conventions. In September, the South Korean Cabinet approved a motion for parliamentary approval to ratify the ILO conventions on freedom of association (Convention 87), the right to organize and collectively bargain (Convention 98), and the prohibition of forced labor (Convention 29). It also proposed three bills reforming labor union laws, including one allowing the creation unions for public servants and teachers.

South Korean companies have an absence of legal obligations to conduct due diligence into human rights abuses in the entities they control, including those in their supply chains (subcontractors, suppliers, franchisees, etc.).

Key International Actors

South Korea has a mutual defense treaty and close bilateral relations with the United States, yet the country's continued economic growth remains highly dependent on close trading relationships with many other countries around the world, including Japan and China—which together account for approximately one-quarter of South Korea's exports.

On June 30, President Moon and US President Donald Trump met with North Korean leader Kim Jong Un in an impromptu summit in which neither publicly raised human rights; and the resumption of working level nuclear talks was announced. In October, North Korea's government said that current non-proliferation talks with the US had collapsed.

The relationship between South Korea and Japan has been important in mobilizing strong international attention to North Korea's human rights record. However, it worsened in 2019, mainly because South Korea's Supreme Court, in October and November 2018, ordered two Japanese companies to compensate 14 victims of forced labor during the Second World War. Japan believes the matter was settled under a 1965 treaty.

In August, in direct response to the case, Japan moved to restrict exports of important high-tech material to South Korea. In response, South Korea abruptly broke off its intelligence sharing arrangement with Japan, leading to criticism from the United States and complicating ongoing cooperation between the three countries, including on addressing human rights issues in North Korea.

South Sudan

In 2019, fighting between the two main warring parties declined following the signing of the "revitalized" peace agreement in September 2018. However, amid delays implementing the peace deal, sporadic fighting continued between the army and rebel groups that were not part of the agreement.

Armed actors committed serious abuses including indiscriminate attacks against civilians including aid workers, unlawful killings, beatings, arbitrary detentions, torture, sexual violence, looting and destruction of property. Some of the abuses may constitute war crimes or crimes against humanity. All sides restricted access to United Nations, ceasefire monitors, and aid workers.

Since the conflict started in December 2013, more than 4 million people have fled their homes, with 2.1 million taking refuge in neighboring countries. Close to 200,000 people are living in six UN "protection of civilians" sites across the country. Seven million people require humanitarian assistance, most of whom faced acute food shortages.

Parties extended the formation of a transitional government of national unity twice—first in May by 6 months, then in November by 100 days—due to delays in implementation of key tasks including security arrangements and determination of states and their boundaries. The government would be led by President Salva Kiir with Riek Machar as first vice president and four additional vice presidents and would govern for a 36-month transitional period.

The government continued to restrict media and civil society and arbitrarily detain journalists, perceived critics and opponents including rights activists.

There was no progress in establishing a hybrid court, comprising South Sudanese and other African judges and prosecutors, envisioned in the 2015 and 2018 peace agreements to try grave crimes committed since December 2013.

Attacks on Civilians

Sporadic fighting continued in parts of central and eastern Equatoria between the government's army, the rebel Sudan People's Liberation Movement/Army-in-Opposition (SPLM/A-IO) under Dr. Machar and non-signatories to the September 2018 peace agreement, notably the National Salvation Front, NAS.

During counter-insurgency operations in Yei River state in December and January 2019, government forces attacked villages, killed, raped, and destroyed and looted property. NAS soldiers were also responsible for unlawful attacks on aid workers and civilians and restricted the movement of the general populace.

The UN peacekeeping mission (UNMISS) documented at least 104 civilian killings, 187 abductions, and 35 others wounded in the 30 attacks between September 2018 and April in Central Equatoria by various armed groups.

People with disabilities and older people were at heightened risk during attacks and faced challenges accessing humanitarian assistance. The 2019 Security Council, in a resolution renewing UNMISS' mandate, expressed for the first time "serious concern about the dire situation of persons with disabilities in South Sudan," including abandonment, violence, and lack of access to basic services.

Arbitrary Detentions and Enforced Disappearances

The National Security Service (NSS) harassed, arrested, and detained activists, journalists, and perceived dissidents, and imposed restrictions on nongovernmental organizations (NGOs). Detainees are held in squalid conditions and largely denied access to family, lawyers, and medical care.

In May, a high court sentenced six men to prison terms of between 2 and 13 years on charges of terrorism, sabotage, and treason stemming from the October 7 uprising at the NSS main detention facility in Juba. The men had been detained by the NSS in 2017 and 2018 without charge for close to a year. Among them was prominent economist and activist, Peter Biar Ajak, detained without charge since July 2018. Ajak was sentenced to a 2-year jail term on trumped up charges of disturbing the peace for speaking to foreign press.

Between June and November, military intelligence detained at least four youth from Lakes without charge or trial in the Giyada military barracks for criticizing the director of MI.

South Sudanese and Kenyan officials denied knowledge of the whereabouts of the two forcibly disappeared men, lawyer Dong Samuel Luak and opposition member Aggrey Ezbon Idri, who were abducted in Nairobi in January 2017 and last seen at the NSS headquarters in Juba. In April, the UN Panel of Experts concluded that it is "highly probable" that the two men were executed at the NSS training facility in Luri on the outskirts of Juba on January 30, 2017. In July, two human rights groups filed a petition at the East African court of Justice suing Kenya and South Sudan for the enforced disappearance of the two men.

Freedom of Expression, Association

In March, the South Sudan Media Authority, an oversight mechanism, suspended UN's Radio Miraya, citing its failure to comply with media regulations. The UN, stating its agreement with South Sudanese authorities to operate in the country, has continued to broadcast without license. The ministry of information continued to block access to online media websites Radio Tamazuj and Sudan Tribune and blogs Nyamilepedia and Paanluel Wel since 2017.

In May, the minister for information, Michael Makuei Lueth, warned against protests, in response to calls by the Red Card Movement, a diaspora youth group, for public anti-government demonstrations. Government security forces closed public spaces and protests did not take place. The government, with support from Kenyan authorities, conducted a campaign of cross-border harassment, intimidation, and threats against movement members.

Authorities harassed, arrested, and detained at least 16 journalists between January and September. On July 17, newspaper editor, Michael Christopher was detained in connection to an opinion article he wrote in support of protests in Sudan in January. He was released on August 26 without charge.

On October 31, authorities revoked press credentials and expelled Sam Mednick, a freelance journalist for the Associated Press, in response to an article she wrote. A French journalist Bastein Renouill, on assignment with France24 was arrested and deported on November 4.

South Sudan's laws criminalize consensual same-sex relations, and make it an offence for "any male person who dresses or is attired in the fashion of a woman in a public place".

Legislative Developments

In April, the National Constitutional Amendment Committee (NCAC) presented draft amendments to the minister of justice and constitutional affairs draft, to reform the country's security organs—including the army—as required by the peace agreement. The National Security Service amendment bill, finalized in July, was also pending at time of writing. However, the bill retains NSS powers of detention and arrest without warrant, in violation of international norms.

In November, the minister presented to the national legislative assembly a bill incorporating the 2018 "revitalized" agreement into the existing transitional constitution-the agreement has supremacy over the constitution.

Children and Armed Conflict

Government forces and rebel groups continued to forcibly recruit children. The UN secretary-general's 2019 report on children in armed conflict documented how 25 children in 2018 were forced into armed groups, with 7 killed or maimed and 7 raped. Meanwhile authorities released over 950 children from an armed group in Yambio between February 2018 and August 2018. In February 2019, 119 children were released from an armed group.

Justice and Accountability

South Sudan did not make progress in establishing the African Union-South Sudanese hybrid court envisioned in the peace agreement. It has yet to sign the memorandum of understanding with the AU or promulgate legislation to establish the court.

In April, the government hired Gainful Solutions Inc., a US-based lobby group to "reverse current sanctions and further block potential sanctions" and "delay and ultimately block establishment of the hybrid court..." Following public criticism, the terms of the contract were later revised to exclude blocking of the hybrid court.

The US in December 2018 sanctioned Gregory Vasily, Israel Ziv, Obaw William Olawo, and three firms they control for their role in fueling the conflict.

Appeals stalled in the case of the Terrain hotel attack on the outskirts of Juba, in which soldiers raped and sexually assaulted at least five aid workers and murdered a journalist in July 2016. A court sentenced 10 soldiers to prison terms of 7 years to life imprisonment for the crimes in 2018. As the court case file disappeared, the court could not hear appeals by both victims and those convicted.

In September, a special court to address non-conflict related sexual and gender-based violence crimes was launched and operationalized.

Key International Actors

In March, the UN Security Council renewed the mandate of UNMISS for another year, and the UN Human Rights Council renewed the mandate of the Commission on Human Rights in South Sudan for another year. The commission presented its report documenting continuing human rights violations, including rape and sexual violence, finding they may amount to war crimes.

The UN Panel of Experts on South Sudan in an April report found that neighboring states likely violated the terms of the UN arms embargo imposed on South Sudan in 2018, including by not providing inspection reports as required, making it impossible for the panel to ascertain whether any new weapons were imported. In July, the UN Security Council voted to renew the UN arms embargo by a year, and extended an asset freeze and global travel ban for eight South Sudanese nationals for their role in the conflict.

In October, the US sanctioned businessmen Ashraf Seed Ahmed Al-Cardinal and Kur Ajing Ater and five companies controlled by Al-Cardinal for their involvement in bribery, kickbacks, and procurement fraud with senior government officials.

The Intergovernmental Authority on Development (IGAD) and the African Union continued to play a key role in mediating the conflict.

In November, president Museveni of Uganda, president of Sudan's Transitional Sovereign Council, Abdal-Fatah Al-Burhan, and Kenya's special envoy on South Sudan, Kalonzo Musyoka, facilitated talks between South Sudanese parties in Kampala, Uganda, where they agreed to the extension of the pre-transitional period by 100 days.

Sri Lanka

On April 21, Easter Sunday, Islamist suicide bombers attacked churches and hotels in Colombo and two other cities, killing over 250 women, men, and children and injuring hundreds more. For the following four months, the government imposed a state of emergency. Hundreds were detained without charge under the Prevention of Terrorism Act. Anti-Muslim mobs, sometimes linked to nationalist politicians, and incited by extremist Buddhist monks, attacked Muslim property. Mainstream and social media vilified Sri Lankan Muslims and asylum-seekers, putting them at risk of assault.

In November, Gotabaya Rajapaksa was elected president. As defence secretary in the administration of his brother, Mahinda Rajapaksa from 2005-2015, he was accused of numerous crimes, including attacks on journalists and activists, and implicated in alleged war crimes and crimes against humanity.

In May, ethnic Tamil victims' groups marked 10 years since the end of the war between the government and the Liberation Tigers of Tamil Eelam, with protests and vigils against the government's failure to address conflict-related violations and provide redress.

In August, President Maithripala Sirisena appointed Maj. Gen. Shavendra Silva as army chief, a move described by United Nations experts as an "affront to victims." During the last months of fighting in 2009, he led a military division implicated in numerous war crimes.

President Sirisena announced in June he would end a 43-year unofficial moratorium on the death penalty and resume executions.

Despite agreeing to protect lesbian, gay, bisexual, and transgender (LGBT) people from discrimination, the government did not revoke sections 365 and 365A of the penal code, which criminalize same-sex conduct.

Transitional Justice and Security Sector Reform

In March, Sri Lanka supported a consensus resolution of the UN Human Rights Council, requesting that the government "implement fully" the measures set out in a previous resolution of 2015, and encouraging "the adoption of a time-bound implementation strategy." This included a number of commitments to justice and accountability for violations committed during the 26-year civil war, through an office of missing persons, an office for reparations, and by setting up an independent accountability mechanism including international investigators, prosecutors, and judges.

Despite important initial developments after the 2015 resolution—including lifting severe restrictions on freedom of speech and association, holding consultations, releasing some civilian land held by the military, and re-establishing an independent government human rights commission—progress has slowed considerably.

Commissioners were appointed to the Office for Reparations in April. The Office on Missing Persons (OMP) began work in 2018, recording over 14,000 cases, but made little progress in discovering their whereabouts. Relatives of the forcibly disappeared protested against the OMP, questioning its authority and independence.

In July, a court acquitted, due to "lack of evidence," all 13 policemen accused in the 2006 shooting of five Tamil students in Trincomalee in a case known as "Trinco Five." The execution-style killing of 17 aid workers in 2006 in Muttur, and the murder of journalist Lasantha Wickrematunge in Colombo in 2009, both of which implicated government security forces, have not resulted in any arrests.

Police identified 14 suspects in the abduction and murder of at least 11 young Tamil men between 2008 and 2009. All of the suspects were naval officers, including the former navy commander, Adm. Wasantha Karannagoda.

Other commitments not met by the government include security sector reform and repealing the draconian Prevention of Terrorism Act (PTA). A Counter Terrorism Act (CTA) to replace the PTA was drafted, but it also contains provisions that would facilitate abuse.

Treatment of Minorities

In the aftermath of the Easter Sunday bombings, anti-Muslim mobs killed one person and caused extensive damage to homes and businesses. About 1,100 Muslim refugees and asylum seekers, including members of the persecuted Ahmadiyya religious community from Pakistan, were subjected to harassment and threats, forcing them to take shelter in crowded and unsanitary temporary refuges.

Despite previous targeting of Muslims, such as in Kandy district in 2018, the government did not adequately protect vulnerable communities, prosecute attackers, or confront virulent anti-Muslim hate speech.

In May, President Sirisena pardoned Gnanasara Thero, a prominent monk and leader of a militant anti-Muslim organization, who was serving a jail sentence for contempt of court.

Tamils, particularly in the Northern Province, continued to face harassment and intrusive surveillance.

Human Rights Defenders

Activists and civil society members, particularly in the north and east of the country, were increasingly subjected to surveillance and harassment. The UN special rapporteur on freedom of peaceful assembly and association, Clément Nyaletsossi Voulé, reported undue rights constraints.

Some families of people forcibly disappeared during the war reported intimidation by soldiers. The army also disrupted Tamil memorial events. In May, families of the disappeared from Ampara were at a remembrance ceremony when soldiers arrived and destroyed or removed banners and decorations, and threatened to arrest the participants.

Voulé reported concerns that, particularly in the north and the east, associations proposing to work on subjects including LGBTI rights, disappearances, land rights, and post-conflict reconciliation, were denied registration, and were subject to surveillance and intimidation. Activists said that these problems increased after the Easter Sunday attacks.

Women's and Girls' Rights

The government agreed to revise the 1951 Muslim Marriage and Divorce Act. Activists said the amended law should make 18 the minimum age of marriage, without exception, and that women should not have to obtain a guardian's permission to get married. They also called for a removal of the exemption of penalties for rape of married Muslim girls above the age of 12, and demanded reform in the operation of Qazi courts, which currently have no female judges.

Following the Easter Sunday bombings, the government issued orders forbidding face coverings, especially the veils worn by some Muslim women. Following this order, Muslim women including those wearing other forms of dress, such as headscarves and abayas, faced harassment at work and in public places, and some were denied access to public services such as schools, hospitals, and universities.

Death Penalty

President Sirisena's decision to resume executions of persons sentenced to death was a major setback. The Supreme Court stayed the execution of four prisoners convicted of drug offenses.

Key International Actors

The UN High Commissioner for Human Rights strongly criticized the government's failure to implement its human rights commitments, and warned that "continuing impunity risks fueling communal or inter-ethnic violence, and instability." Following the appointment of Gen. Silva as army chief, the UN suspended the use of non-essential Sri Lankan troops as peacekeepers.

The core group presenting the UN Human Rights Council resolution (Canada, Germany, North Macedonia, Montenegro, and the United Kingdom) called on the Sri Lanka government to set a clear timeline to meet its commitments, which it said were essential for "national healing, stability and prosperity."

Sri Lanka has military and security cooperation with the United States, India, and European governments, although the US warned this would be curtailed following Gen. Silva's appointment. Sri Lankan trade with the EU under the GSP+ scheme, links better market access to human rights and labor standards. However, the EU, like other foreign partners, has been muted in its response to Sri Lankan rights abuses.

Sri Lanka is a participant in China's "Belt and Road" Initiative, although there are concerns about the debt burden this is creating, for instance in relation to southern Hambantota Port, control of which has been granted to China for 99 years.

Sudan

Following months of protests, Sudan's president for 30 years, Omar al-Bashir, was ousted in April and replaced by a military council. Following negotiations between the military leaders and opposition groups, a transitional government led by a "sovereign council" composed of military and civilian members replaced the military council in August.

The periods of protests both before and after al-Bashir's ouster was marked by serious human rights violations against protesters, starting December 2018. Government security forces routinely used live ammunition against unarmed protesters, detained activists and political opponents, censored media and blocked access to the internet. After April 11, Rapid Support Forces (RSF)—the paramilitary force known for attacks on civilians in Darfur since 2013—continued the crackdowns. The bloodiest was their attack on the protesters' sit-in in Khartoum on June 3.

Conflicts in Darfur, Southern Kordofan, and Blue Nile continued at low levels, and restrictions on humanitarian aid access persisted. In Darfur, government forces attacked villages in Jebel Mara. The African Union/United Nations mission in Darfur (UNAMID) temporarily halted withdrawal plans in June, in view of national political changes and news that the RSF occupied bases the mission handed over to the government. In May, the ruling military council issued a decree stating that all UNAMID bases be handed over to the RSF, in contravention of United Nations rules and procedures.

The agreement to form the transitional government included setting up a national independent investigation into events of June 3. The agreement also called for accountability for all past abuses under the al-Bashir government. Although women played an important role in the protests, women's rights groups expressed disappointment that few women were included in a transitional government. The government has yet to cooperate with the International Criminal Court (ICC) in respect of cases against al-Bashir and four other men on charges of genocide, crimes against humanity and war crimes committed in Darfur.

HUMAN
RIGHTS
WATCH
"They Were Shouting *'Kill Them'*"
Sudan's Violent Crackdown on Protesters in Khartoum

Crackdowns on Protesters

Sudanese took to the streets in towns across the country in December to protest price hikes and demanded President Omar al-Bashir step down. Government security forces responded with lethal violence, shooting live ammunition at unarmed protesters, beating and arresting hundreds and killing scores of people between December and April. Security forces chased protesters into hospitals and shot tear gas into operating rooms, impeding the provision of medical care to wounded protesters. At least one doctor was killed and several others arrested for providing medical services.

President al-Bashir declared a state of emergency on February 22, banning protests and authorizing "emergency courts" to try violators in speedy trials. Many protesters were detained, tried summarily, and imprisoned or fined, without due process protections.

On April 11, defense minister and first vice president, Awad Ibn Ouf, announced the arrest of al-Bashir. On April 12, Lt. Gen. Abdel Fatah al-Burhan, former commander of the army's ground forces, took over and formed the Transitional Military Council (TMC), appointing Lt. Gen. Mohamed Hamdan Dagalo "Hemedti," RSF commander, as his deputy.

Despite the TMC's promises to protect the protesters' camp near military headquarters, security forces continued to use live ammunition against unarmed protesters calling for transition to civilian rule.

On June 3, government forces led by the RSF shot live bullets at protesters, beat them with sticks and batons, rounded up hundreds and subjected them to various forms of humiliation, including beating, rape and sexual assaults. They also attacked hospitals and clinics and prevented wounded protesters from receiving needed medical help. An estimated 120 were killed and hundreds wounded; some bodies were dumped into the river Nile and an unknown number of people were reported missing.

The TMC spokesperson denied government forces attacked protesters and claimed their operation was limited to criminal activity in an area near the sit-in. He later said the dispersal was planned, but that mistakes were made. The attorney-general launched an investigation into the violence and recommended charges be brought against eight soldiers including for crimes against humanity.

On June 30, the anniversary of al-Bashir's assumption of power, RSF soldiers opened fire on protesters calling for justice for June 3 victims, as they crossed a bridge linking Khartoum and Omdurman, killing eight. Another three bodies were found the next day in Omdurman covered with banners used in protests, with blood stains on their bodies and a megaphone near where the bodies were found. The father of one victim said he believed his son died from torture.

On July 29, RSF soldiers shot at high school students in al-Obeid, North Kordofan protesting price hikes and poor transportation services killing five of them, according to media reports. On August 1, RSF soldiers reportedly killed four more protesters in Omdurman. TMC immediately denounced the violence, admitting that nine RSF soldiers were involved in the shootings in Omdurman and el-Obeid and that those responsible had been dismissed from service and referred for prosecution.

Arbitrary Detentions, Torture

In response to the protests starting in December, National Intelligence and Security Service (NISS) officials arrested and rounded up protesters, opposition members, and activists. Security agents subjected detainees to abuses while in detention including beatings, inhumane conditions in a facility known as "the refrigerator," and insults and beatings during interrogations. Many detainees were not allowed family visitation or access to lawyers. Women released from detention told Human Rights Watch they were beaten and sexually harassed and threatened with rape.

Dozens of students from Darfur arrested in mid-December were rounded up in their dormitories, severely beaten and forced to make televised "confessions" of having links to the Sudan Liberation Movement/Army, a Darfur rebel group led by Abdelwahid al-Nur. They were later released without charges.

On February 3, Ahmed al-Khair, a teacher in East Sudan, died while in NISS custody. Witnesses and his family found signs of torture on his body, according to media. Authorities later charged 40 NISS agents in connection with the killing.

Sudan has failed to investigate other allegations of torture by national security officials and has yet to ratify the Convention Against Torture, which it signed in 1986. In violation of international human rights law, it retains the death penalty and corporal punishment for numerous crimes, including consensual same-sex conduct.

Freedom of Media

Since protests started in December 2018, authorities imposed even more restrictions on media, seized and confiscated newspapers, arrested journalists covering protests, shut down their offices, and blocked access to the internet.

Nine journalists were briefly arrested on December 26 by the NISS while gathered outside the headquarters of the independent Sudanese newspaper *Al-Tayar* in protest against harassment of the media. Many other journalists were arrested while covering protests or during journalists strikes. In late December, authorities restricted access to social media for several days.

On December 25, authorities blocked London-based al-Araby TV journalists from covering the protests and deported them. On January 22, authorities revoked permits of reporters working with Al Jazeera, al-Arabiya and Anadolu news agency.

On February 22, NISS officials arrested the editor-in-chief of *Al-Tayar*, after he appeared on TV criticizing al-Bashir's emergency declaration. He was released on March 30 without charge.

After al-Bashir's ouster, authorities allowed media coverage of protests for several weeks, but on May 31, they shut down Al Jazeera offices. Authorities sought to suppress information about the June 3 violence by restricting media access to the country, by cutting off completely cutting internet access on June 10 for over a month.

Conflict and Abuses in Darfur, Southern Kordofan, and Blue Nile

In January, Sudan declared an open-ended unilateral ceasefire in Darfur and the other conflict zones. However, government forces, including the RSF, reportedly continued to attack sites in the Jebel Mara, destroying dozens of villages between July 2018 and February 2019, according to reports.

UNAMID halted plans to further downsize and exit Sudan by 2020, in view of the formation of transitional government after al-Bashir ousting and the occupation and use of the mission's bases by RSF soldiers. Authorities continued to limit peacekeepers and aid groups' access to displaced people and conflict-affected areas.

Eight years into the armed conflict in Southern Kordofan and Blue Nile, the government and armed opposition failed to agree on modalities for supplying life-saving aid to civilians in need. However, negotiations between the government and all armed groups resumed in Juba in September leading to new agreement on access.

Refugees and Migrants

Sudan hosts about 1.1 million refugees and migrants from the region, mostly South Sudanese (more than 858,000 as of September). Authorities also reported an increase of Eritrean refugees, estimating that half of these new arrivals migrate to other countries, making them vulnerable to human trafficking and smuggling. Hundreds of thousands of Sudanese refugees from Darfur, Southern Kordofan and Blue Nile live in camps in Chad, South Sudan and Ethiopia.

Key International Actors

Hours after the June 3 crackdown, the African Union condemned the violence and called for an "immediate and transparent investigation" into the events, to hold those responsible to account. On June 6, the AU suspended Sudan's membership, but lifted the suspension in September.

The US, United Kingdom, and Norway, troika members, condemned the attacks on protesters and blamed the TMC for ordering it. The US, which lifted economic sanctions on Sudan in 2017, has promised to revise its Sudan policy with a view to supporting the transitional government.

The EU also condemned the June 3 violence against protests and in late July suspended projects related to migration and border control, which are part of the EU-Horn of Africa Migration Route Initiative, known as "Khartoum Process." The program had prompted fears that EU was supporting the RSF to carry out-migration control.

The UN secretary-general, following the establishment of the transitional government in August, called for the lifting of all economic and financial sanctions imposed on Sudan, as well as the country's removal from the US list of state sponsors of terrorism.

In September, the UN Human Rights Council adopted a resolution to continue the work of the Independent Expert on human rights in Sudan for another year. The resolution also supported the establishment of a country office of the Office of the High Commissioner for Human Rights in Khartoum, Sudan's capital.

In October, the UN Security Council adopted a resolution extending UNAMID's mandate for one year and tasking UN secretary-general along with AU chairperson to submit options for a post-UNAMID follow up presence based on needs and views of Sudan government after March. The mission will maintain its protection of civilians and human rights-monitoring functions through the end of its mandate.

The TMC declined to hand al-Bashir over to the ICC but try him in Sudan in on corruption and money laundering charges. The UN Security Council failed to press Sudan to cooperate with the ICC for the surrender of the al-Bashir and four other fugitives sought on alleged Darfur crimes, despite having referred the situation to the ICC in 2005. The ICC first announced charges in 2007.

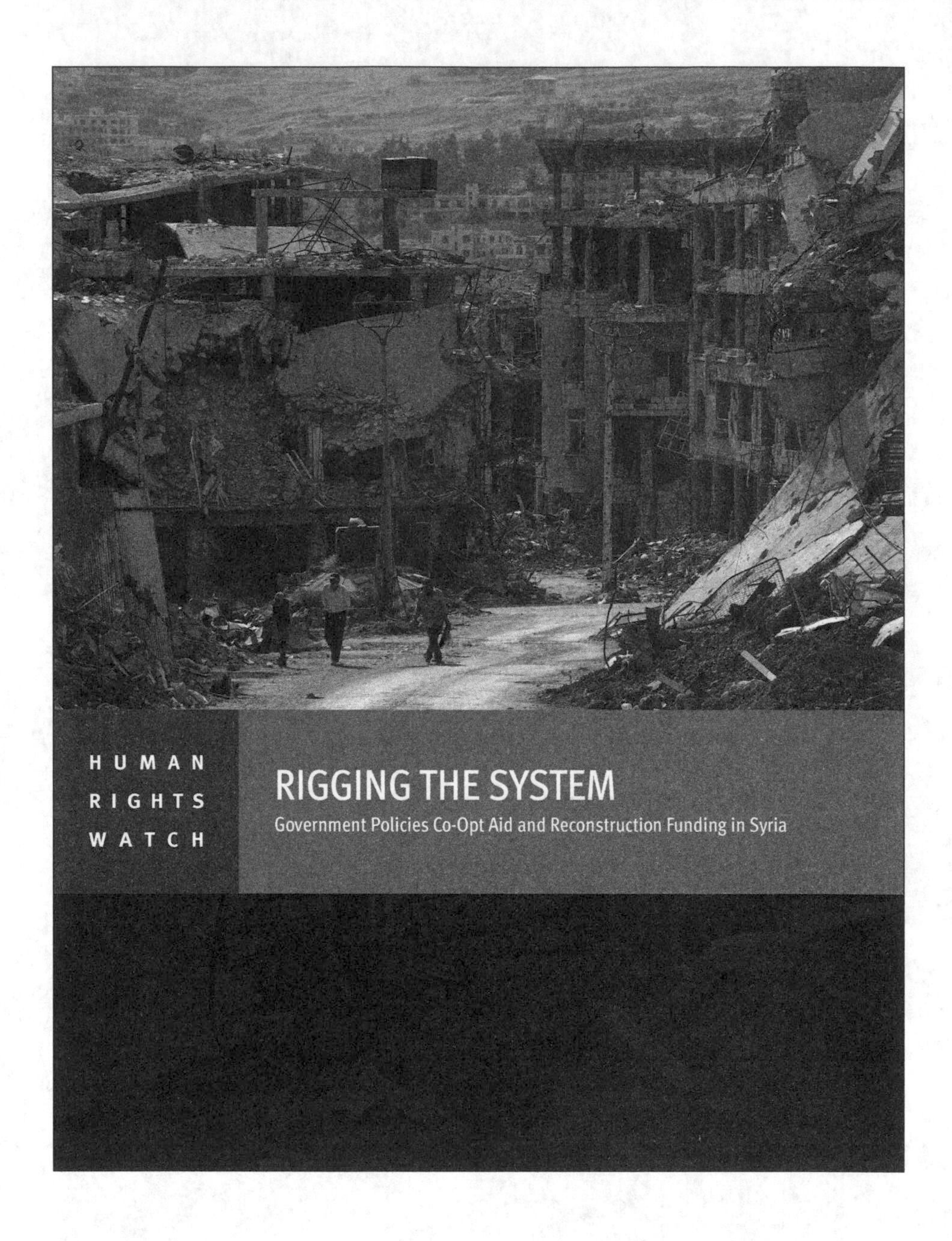
HUMAN
RIGHTS
WATCH
RIGGING THE SYSTEM
Government Policies Co-Opt Aid and Reconstruction Funding in Syria

Syria

Events in Syria of 2019 reinforced the conclusion that the atrocities and rights violations that have characterized the conflict continued to be the rule, not the exception.

The Syrian-Russian military alliance in April re-launched military operations against Idlib, the last anti-government foothold, with indiscriminate attacks and prohibited weapons. Areas recaptured by the government saw property confiscations, widescale demolitions of homes, and arbitrary detentions. Those who "reconciled" with the government continue to suffer abuses at the hands for government forces.

The UN Office for the Coordination of Humanitarian Affairs (OCHA) projected that 11.7 million people in Syria would require humanitarian and protection assistance in 2019. Instead of securing funding to address the population's vital needs, the Syrian government developed a legal and policy framework to co-opt humanitarian and reconstruction funding to advance its own interests. Aid groups, United Nations agencies, and donors participating in abusive reconstruction efforts, or allowing aid diversion without due diligence, risked complicity with the government's human rights violations.

Non-state armed groups opposing the government also committed serious abuses, leading arbitrary arrest campaigns in areas they control and launching indiscriminate ground attacks on populated residential areas in government-held territory.

In northeast Syria, the number of civilians killed and the degree of destruction as a result of the US-led coalition and its local ally, the Syrian Democratic Forces, suggested a degree of destruction and loss of life in areas held by the extremist group Islamic State (ISIS) that indicate a failure to take all necessary precautions to protect civilians.

The fate of thousands kidnapped by ISIS remained unknown, with no steps taken by Kurdish authorities, the US-led coalition, or the Syrian government to determine their fate. Despite the international focus on those detained and disappeared by the Syrian government, including by the special envoy and the Security Council, little progress was made.

Violations by the Syrian-Russian Military Alliance

The Syrian-Russian military alliance launched hundreds of daily attacks since late April 2019 to re-take areas in northwest Syria from anti-government groups. Using tactics reminiscent of the alliance's takeover of Aleppo and Ghouta, Syrian and Russian forces used internationally banned cluster munitions, incendiary weapons, and explosive weapons with wide-area effect including improvised "barrel bombs" against schools, homes, and hospitals, destroying key towns in the area and killing over 1000 civilians, including more than 300 children. In mid-August, the Syrian-Russian military alliance killed 20 civilians in a strike on a displacement compound located in the town of Hass, Idlib. The attack was unlawful and amounted to a war crime.

Those forces destroyed or rendered inoperable over 50 health facilities. Russia and Syria targeted hospitals using coordinates these facilities had shared with Russia through a United Nations deconfliction mechanism, according to Physicians for Human Rights and other humanitarian groups. On August 1, the United Nations announced that UN Secretary-General Antonio Guterres would launch an investigation into hospital attacks in Syria.

According to the United Nations, northwest Syria is home to 3 million civilians, at least half of whom have been displaced at least once. Civilians in these areas effectively had nowhere to go, lacking resources to relocate, unable to cross into Turkey, and fearing persecution if they relocated to government-held areas.

Property Rights, Humanitarian Aid, and Reconstruction Funding

The Syrian government enforced a legal and policy framework that enables it to co-opt millions of dollars of international funding earmarked for humanitarian aid and reconstruction. The government restricted humanitarian organizations' access to communities that needed or allegedly received aid, selectively approved aid projects to punish civilians in anti-government held areas, and required that humanitarian groups partner with security-vetted local actors. Based on past incidents, there is a continuing risk that aid be siphoned through the abusive state apparatus to punish civilian populations it perceived as opponents and reward those it perceived as loyal.

The government arbitrarily designated hundreds of people from areas formerly held by anti-government groups as terrorists and froze their assets, in line with Decree 63 and the 2012 Counterterrorism Law, which authorities often used to criminalize the work of human rights activists and humanitarian workers. The measures have far-reaching impact on families and relatives, even if they had not been designated as terrorists.

Abuses by Non-State Armed Groups

Hay'et Tahrir al-Sham (HTS), Jaysh al-Izza (JAI), and affiliated groups launched indiscriminate attacks on civilian areas under government control. These attacks have led to scores of civilian casualties and may have amounted to war crimes, according to the Independent International Commission of Inquiry on Syria (COI).

Despite its territorial retreat, ISIS led several insurgencies throughout Deir Ezzor, and prevented civilians from fleeing the violence, including by punishing them and placing landmines to deter them from escaping.

Security conditions in areas surrounding Afrin, which has been controlled by the Syrian National Army, a coalition of Turkey-backed Free Syrian Army (FSA) factions, deteriorated considerably. Those factions have committed war crimes, according to the COI, targeting civilians, taking hostages, planting car bombs, conducting arbitrary arrests, extortion, torture, and enforcing a rigid dress code for women and girls.

Arbitrary Detention and Enforced Disappearances

In areas retaken from the anti-government groups, including Eastern Ghouta, Daraa and southern Damascus, Syrian security forces arrested hundreds of activists, former opposition leaders and their family members, although they had all signed reconciliation agreements with authorities guaranteeing that they would not be arrested.

Tens of thousands of persons have been detained or disappeared since 2011, the vast majority by government forces. Thousands died in Syrian government custody from torture and horrific detention conditions. In 2019, the government updated the records of hundreds thought to be disappeared or dead, but none of their families have received their loved ones' remains or additional information from authorities.

Hay'et Tahrir al-Sham (HTS), an al-Qaeda affiliate predominantly active in Idlib, arbitrarily arrested numerous residents in areas under its control. In January 2019, Human Rights Watch documented 11 arrests; in six of the cases, individuals were apparently tortured. Local rights groups have gathered files or evidence on hundreds of other cases.

ISIS seized thousands of individuals, including activists, humanitarian workers, and journalists, whose fate remained unknown, according to local human rights monitors and families of those kidnapped. Neither the Kurdish-led Syrian Democratic Forces (SDF), the Syrian government nor the US-led international coalition have created mechanisms to handle families' queries.

In May 2019, Human Rights Watch was among eight Syrian civil society and international human rights organizations that called on UN Security Council member states to urgently address the widespread arbitrary detentions, kidnapping, torture and other-ill treatment, and enforced disappearances of tens of thousands of Syrians at the hands of the Syrian government, armed anti-government groups, and ISIS.

Violations by Turkey and Turkish-Backed Forces

On October 9, following an announcement by the United States administration of the withdrawal of its forces from Syria, Turkey invaded northeast Syria. Non-state actors backed by Turkey, including the Syrian National Army, mobilized in support of the offensive, dubbed "Operation Peace Spring." Kurdish authorities, in response, struck a deal with Damascus, allowing Syrian forces to deploy and retake control of multiple towns across the Syrian-Turkish border.

Reports have surfaced of Turkish-backed factions committing a host of violations, including summary killings of Kurdish forces, political activists, and emergency responders, and looting and confiscation of property.

On October 26, the Turkish foreign minister announced that Turkey "will not tolerate even the least violation of human rights violations." Reports from local and international monitoring groups, however, have documented several indiscriminate attacks by Turkey on civilians and civilian objects in northeast Syria.

Violations by US-Backed Forces and the US-Led Coalition

The Battle of Baghuz in February 2019 brought about the territorial demise of ISIS. The battle was marked by intense US-led coalition air attacks and ground artillery shelling by the SDF. Human Rights Watch identified more than 630 major damage sites and widescale destruction of buildings throughout the town as the last battle commenced, when a large number of civilians were present in those areas. The UK-based monitoring group Airwars estimated that at least 416 civilians died in US-led coalition airstrikes between January and June 2019.

The coalition did not thoroughly investigate the attacks that killed civilians. It made one condolence payment to a family in January 2019, but it did not create a program for compensation or other assistance to civilians harmed by coalition operations. The US Defense Department attributed the lack of payments to "practical limitations" and "limited US presence, which reduces the situational awareness required to make ex gratia payments."

Witnesses who managed to flee the last remaining enclaves controlled by ISIS—in part by paying smugglers hefty sums—described harrowing humanitarian conditions and relentless attacks in areas where they lived. ISIS punished those who had even considered leaving and deployed mines along escape routes to deter attempts.

While the Turkish invasion of northeast Syria has reduced the areas under the control of Kurdish-led authorities, at time of writing the Kurdish-led Autonomous Administration for Northeast Syria remained in control of most of the 110,000 ISIS suspects and family members. They included 62,000 Syrians and Iraqis, and more than 11,000 non-Iraqi foreign women and children related to ISIS suspects, who were being held in al-Hol desert camp in appalling and sometimes deadly conditions. Insufficient resources and restrictions on humanitarian access have contributed to deteriorating camp conditions.

Most countries have refused to repatriate their citizens, including women or children, or have only brought home small numbers of orphans. Countries including France, the United Kingdom, and the Netherlands cited logistical and security challenges to repatriating citizens. However, Kazakhstan, Uzbekistan, and Tajikistan together repatriated more than 756 nationals with links to ISIS, most of them women and children. Foreign ISIS suspects arrested in Syria, notably

French ones, were transferred to Iraq despite torture, flawed trials and death penalty. The UN special rapporteur on extrajudicial executions rebuked France for its alleged involvement in the transfers of its nationals sentenced to death in Iraq.

Displacement Crisis

Military operations have displaced more than 600,000 individuals in Idlib and Hama and at least 180,000 individuals in northeast Syria, according to UN OCHA.

The Turkish-Syrian border remained sealed and Turkish border guards routinely pushed back asylum seekers, including with live ammunition, killing dozens since January 2019, according to the Syrian Observatory of Human Rights.

Around 18,000 individuals left al-Rukban camp near the Syrian-Jordanian border for government-held areas. Humanitarian aid restrictions imposed by the government and Jordan's refusal to allow Rukban residents to seek asylum in Jordan or provide cross-border aid meant that camp residents faced serious risk of starvation and disease, as well as threat of attack. Those who returned to government-held areas ended up in displacement centers. While the UN and Syrian Arab Red Crescent provided services at these displacement camps and at the crossing points, reports surfaced of detentions and ill-treatment of evacuees who returned to government-held areas.

Syrian refugees in neighboring countries faced pressure from host countries to return to Syria, despite serious safety concerns and lack of transparency around conditions in areas held by the government. UNHCR records indicate that more than 40,000 refugees had returned as of June 2019.

In Turkey, more than 3.6 million Syrian refugees, including half-a-million in Istanbul alone, received temporary protection. In 2019, however, Turkish authorities detained and forcibly returned many Syrians after making them sign "voluntary return" forms. Many ended up in Idlib and areas under the control of Hay'et Tahrir al-Sham, where they were either arrested by that group or caught in the Syrian-Russian military offensive.

Turkey also proposed the creation of a buffer zone in northeast Syria, where it intends to move at least 1 million Syrians currently in Turkey. If such a zone is created, it would not necessarily guarantee the protection of civilians, and would include a number of human rights concerns.

Lebanon, which hosts around 1.5 million Syrian refugees, relentlessly promoted returns and took active steps to curb the inflow of refugees starting in April. General Security, the agency responsible for the country's border control, said it deported 2,731 Syrians between May 21 and August 28, 2019, following its May 13 decision to deport all Syrians who entered Lebanon irregularly after April 24, and directly handed them to the Syrian authorities. At least three of those deported were detained by Syrian authorities upon their return.

UN Security Council and General Assembly

In response to attacks by the Syrian-Russian military alliance on health and other humanitarian facilities in Idlib and northern Hama, and pressure from UN member states and human rights groups, UN Secretary-General Antonio Guterres launched an investigation into hospital attacks in Syria. At time of writing, he had not committed to making the findings public.

On August 7, the United Nations Security Council held its first briefing on the issue of those detained and missing in Syria.

On September 19, Russia cast its 13th veto to block a Security Council resolution demanding a truce in northwest Syria because it did not include exemption for military offensives against groups Russia and Syria consider to be terrorist organizations.

The International Impartial and Independent Mechanism (IIIM), an evidence-gathering body established by the UN General Assembly in December 2016, continued to gather and preserve evidence for future criminal prosecutions.

Key International Actors

Despite the appointment of a new UN special envoy to Syria, Geir Pederson, UN-led political negotiations remained at a virtual standstill.

Russia, Turkey, and Iran continue to wield influence in Syria, with Russia spearheading efforts to politically legitimize the Syrian government, and encourage the return of refugees and the provision of funding for reconstruction. April saw the collapse Russian-Turkish agreement that had established a ceasefire in Idlib in September 2018.

The United States conducted airstrikes against ISIS in northeast Syria, as part of the US-led coalition, and provided financial and logistical support to the Syrian Democratic Forces. On October 6, US President Donald Trump abruptly announced the withdrawal of US troops from northern Syria, paving the way for Turkey's military push against Kurdish-led forces.

The US-led coalition struck in August what it claimed was an al-Qaeda entity in Idlib. On October 27, a US military operation in Idlib resulted in the death of Abu Bakr al-Baghdadi, ISIS' leader. Israel also reportedly conducted several air strikes on government-held areas in January and August.

The European Union hosted its third Brussels conference on Syria in March, focusing on the return of refugees and reconstruction. In September 2019, there were reports that Hungary planned to upgrade its diplomatic ties with Syria, breaking European consensus. Both the EU and the US renewed and expanded sanctions on the Syrian government.

Following years of preparation, the Syrian Constitutional Committee met on October 30 under the auspices of the United Nations in Geneva, Switzerland. The committee consists of 150 delegates tasked with reforming the country's constitution.

Tajikistan

Tajikistan's dire human rights situation worsened further in 2019. Authorities continued a crackdown on government critics, jailing opposition activists, journalists, and even social media users perceived to be disloyal for lengthy prison terms. Freedom of expression and religion are severely restricted, nongovernmental organizations (NGOs) are subjected to intimidation, and the internet is heavily censored. Authorities harassed relatives of peaceful dissidents abroad and used politically motivated extradition requests made via INTERPOL, the international police organization, to forcibly return political opponents from abroad.

Prison Conditions and Torture

Prison conditions are abysmal, with regular reports of torture. In November 2018 and May, two prison riots in Khujand and Vahdat, respectively, resulted in the deaths of at least 50 prisoners and five prison guards in circumstances which remain unclear. Authorities announced that it was necessary to use lethal force to put down apparently violent uprisings within the prisons. In both cases, dozens of prisoners were killed, which raised legitimate concerns about use of disproportionate or excessive force and unjustified resort to lethal force.

Another 14 prisoners died of poisoning on July 7, allegedly as the result of eating tainted bread while being transported on a truck from prisons in Khujand and Istaravshan to prisons in Dushanbe, Norak, and Yovon.

During a prison visit on March 9, imprisoned political activist and deputy head of the banned Islamic Renaissance Party of Tajikistan (IRPT) Mahmadali Hayit showed his wife, Savrinisso Jurabekova, injuries on his forehead and stomach that he said were caused by beatings from prison officials to punish him for refusing to record videos denouncing Tajik opposition figures abroad. Jurabekova said that her husband said he was not getting adequate medical care, and fears he may die in prison as a result of constant beatings.

Harassment of Dissidents Abroad

In December 2018, IRPT activist Naimjon Samiev was forcibly disappeared in Grozny, Chechnya, and was returned to Tajikistan, where he was sentenced to 15 years in prison on politically motivated charges.

In February 2019, Tajik and Russian officials arbitrarily detained and forcibly returned to Tajikistan Sharofiddin Gadoev, 33, a peaceful opposition activist who was visiting Moscow from his home in the Netherlands. Russian and Tajik authorities used physical force to detain him in Moscow and forced him onto a plane, beating him in Moscow and on the flight to Tajikistan. While he was held in Tajikistan, the government published choreographed videos designed to show that he "voluntarily" returned to Tajikistan. Gadoev and his relatives said the statements were made under duress. The activist was returned in March 2019 to the Netherlands following an international campaign.

In May 2019, Russian authorities arrested IRPT member Amrullo Magzumov at Vnukovo airport in Moscow at the request of the Tajik authorities. Two days later, he was forcibly returned to Tajikistan without trial.

In September 2019, Belarusian border guards detained IRPT member and independent journalist Farhod Odinaev, 42, under a Tajik extradition request after he attempted to cross the Belarus-Lithuania border on his way to attend a human rights conference in Warsaw, Poland. In November, Belarus authorities rejected Tajikistan's request for Odinaev's extradition.

Dissidents' Families

Authorities regularly harass the Tajikistan-based relatives of peaceful dissidents who live abroad. Activists based in France, Germany, and Poland told Human Rights Watch that their relatives are regularly visited by security services who pressured them to denounce them and provide information on their whereabouts or activities and threatened them with imprisonment if their relatives continue their peaceful opposition work.

In June, Europe-based journalist Humayra Bakhtiyar, 33, told Human Rights Watch that authorities were harassing her family in Dushanbe in order to pressure her to return to Tajikistan. She said police had recently called her 57-year-old father, Bakhtiyar Muminov, to come for a talk on June 12, her birthday, despite her father having suffered a heart attack that required surgery in April. Police told Muminov to convince his daughter to return to Tajikistan or he would lose his job as a schoolteacher, as he had "no moral right to teach children if he was unable to raise his own daughter properly." Police placed a call to Bakhtiyar and had her father repeat their questions into the phone. They later threated to arrest Muminov.

Freedom of Expression

Authorities regularly block access to a wide spectrum of internet news and social media sites, including YouTube, Facebook, and *Radio Ozodi*, the Tajik service of Radio Free Europe/Radio Liberty. They also cut access to mobile and messaging services when critical statements about the president, his family, or the government appear online. Over 25 journalists have been forced in recent years to leave the country and to live in exile.

Journalists are frequently the subject of attacks. According to the National Association of Independent Media of Tajikistan, it receives at least 10 reports each month from journalists regarding threats and restrictions on access to information while conducting their work.

Radio Ozodi came under intense pressure in October after the Tajik foreign ministry refused to extend the accreditation of 18 reporters and staff. Following a meeting in November between the president of Radio Free Europe Jamie Fly and Tajik president Emomali Rahmon, the Tajik president's office said rumors of the closure of *Radio Ozodi* were "false."

In July, Russian officials blocked the website of Asia-Plus, Tajikistan's leading independent news agency. Later, in August, the agency's web addresses based in Tajikistan were taken offline globally when unknown persons changed technical settings in the systems of the internet service provider. Asia-Plus, whose journalists in the past have been harassed by security services and whose website has been subjected to politically motivated blocking, moved its website to a domain hosted outside of Tajikistan. Authorities have also repeatedly denied them and other independent channels, such as the Penjiken-based *Orionnur*, a license to broadcast television programming.

МИЛИТСИЯ
HUMAN
RIGHTS
WATCH
“Violence With Every Step”
Weak State Response to Domestic Violence in Tajikistan

Freedom of Religion or Belief

In January, Radio Ozodi reported that officials in Dushanbe denied passports to over a dozen men unless they shaved their beards. President Rahmon has repeatedly urged Tajiks to not wear beards or hijab, and in recent years police and security services have fingerprinted and forced as many as 13,000 Tajik men to shave their beards.

In February, police arrested Shamil Khakimov, a Jehovah's Witness based in Khujand, and seized a number of books, including copies of the Bible, which the authorities have classified as extremist literature. In August, Khakimov was placed on trial on charges of "inciting religious hatred." Tajikistan banned Jehovah's Witnesses in 2007.

Domestic Violence

The government has made important efforts to combat domestic violence but survivors, lawyers, and service providers reported that the 2013 domestic violence law remains largely unimplemented. Domestic violence and marital rape are not specifically criminalized. Police often refuse to register complaints of domestic violence, fail to investigate complaints, or issue and enforce protection orders. A lack of services for survivors, including immediate and longer-term shelters, leave women without clear pathways to escape abuse.

In November 2018, the United Nations Committee on the Elimination of Discrimination against Women (CEDAW) expressed concern that domestic violence is "widespread but underreported," and that there is "systemic impunity for perpetrators ... as illustrated by the low number of prosecutions and convictions" and no systematic monitoring of gender-based violence.

Key International Actors

In July, the UN Human Rights Committee (HRC) issued Concluding Observations on Tajikistan's rights record, voicing concern over a wide spectrum of abuses, including politically-motivated imprisonment, torture, restrictions on lawyers, pressure on NGOs, domestic violence, and reports that suspected lesbian, gay, bisexual, and transgender (LGBT) people were being identified and their names placed on a state registry.

In July, the UN Working Group on Enforced or Involuntary Disappearances (WGEID) visited Tajikistan. The working group expressed concern that the existence of mass graves and the fate of thousands of persons unaccounted for in connection with Tajikistan's 1992-1997 civil war remain a "virtually unaddressed issue" and that more should be done "to deal with issues related to truth, justice, reparation and memory in relation to the serious human rights violations." The working group also pointed to a "number of recent and previous cases of Tajik individuals, reportedly political opponents who were residing abroad and were forcibly returned to Tajikistan. In some cases, these individuals have appeared in detention in Tajikistan after short periods of disappearance, while in a few instances their whereabouts are still unknown."

In June, the UN Working Group on Arbitrary Detention issued an opinion finding the detention of Tajik human rights lawyer, Buzurgmehr Yorov, to be a violation of international law and called for his release. The UN concluded that the charges against Yorov were baseless and that the government's motivation was to punish him for his representation of the political opposition. Earlier rulings by the UN working group and the UN Human Rights Committee called for the release of imprisoned opposition figures Mahmadali Hayit and Zayd Saidov.

In June, Organization for Security and Co-operation Media Freedom Representative Harlem Désir called on Dushanbe to reinstate *Radio Ozodi* journalist Barotali Nazarov's withdrawn press accreditation and to issue accreditation to his colleagues. He also called on authorities to investigate reports of intimidation of the family of journalist Humayra Bakhtiyar, who left Tajikistan in 2016.

In December 2018, the embassies of France, Germany, the United Kingdom, the United States, and the European Union urged the government to protect freedom of speech and media, particularly relating to the blocking of websites. At an event to mark World Press Freedom Day in May, US Ambassador John Pommersheim, former British Ambassador Hugh Philpott, and EU delegation political officer Nils Jansons renewed calls for open internet access and freedom of expression in Tajikistan.

In June, the EU and Tajikistan held the 7th Cooperation Committee meeting in Dushanbe, part of a series of meetings with high-level EU representatives. The EU emphasized freedom of expression and other fundamental freedoms, and called on the Tajik government to provide greater space for civil society.

Tanzania

Tanzania's human rights record continued to deteriorate under President John Magufuli, who was elected into office in 2015. The government lifted some restrictions on the publication of independent statistics, but continued to restrict media and critics of the government, deregister civil society groups, arrest journalists, restrict civic space, and undermine the rights of women and of children.

Freedom of Expression and Media

The Tanzanian government cracked down on media and civil society groups and individuals critical of the government. In February, the Ministry of Information, Culture, Arts and Sports suspended *The Citizen* newspaper for seven days for violating the Media Services Act, accusing the newspaper of publishing two biased articles. One was about United States lawmaker Bob Menendez raising concerns about "the gradual downward spiral of respect for civil liberties in Tanzania," and another reported that the Tanzania shilling was falling against the US dollar.

On April 25, authorities at the Julius Nyerere International Airport in Dar es Salaam detained and eventually deported Wairagala Wakabi, director of the Ugandan-based Collaboration on International ICT Policy in East and Southern Africa (CIPESA), as he was on his way to receive a human rights award.

On July 29, 2019, six plainclothes policemen arrested high-profile investigative journalist Erick Kabendera at his home in Dar es Salaam. He was later charged with non-bailable offenses related to money laundering, tax evasion, and leading organized crime. Kabendera had written for several international publications critiquing Tanzanian politics, including *The East African, The Guardian* and *The Times of London*.

On August 22, police detained Joseph Gandye, a journalist with Watetezi TV, in Dar es Salaam following a police summons. Gandye, had published an investigative piece on police brutality in Mafinga in Iringa in central Tanzania on August 9. On August 23, police released Gandye without having charged him.

In 2018, parliament passed the Electronic and Postal Communications (Online Content Regulations) giving the Tanzania Communications Regulatory Authority (TCRA) wide discretionary powers to license blogs, websites, and other online

THE CITIZEN
Makonda threatened TV staff with blackmail, jail
Acacia Sh8.8 trillion merger talks collapse
HUMAN RIGHTS WATCH
"As Long as I am Quiet, I am Safe"
Threats to Independent Media and Civil Society in Tanzania

content. In January, the High Court in Mtwara quashed an application by the civil society organizations Legal and Human Rights Centre (LHRC), trustees of the Media Council of Tanzania, and the Tanzania Human Rights Defenders Coalition, challenging the regulations.

At the close of 2018, Bob Chacha Wangwe appealed his 2017 conviction for publication of false information under the Cybercrimes Act for critiquing on Facebook the conduct of elections in Zanzibar in 2015. A Dar es Salaam court sentenced him to 18 months' imprisonment or a fine of 5 million Tanzania shillings (US$2,175). In March, the High Court of Tanzania in Dar es Salaam upheld Bob Chacha Wangwe's appeal against his conviction, citing lack of evidence.

Legislative Reforms

In June, parliament amended the Statistics Act of 2015, which previously made it a crime to publish statistics not approved by the National Bureau of Statistics (NBS). The amended law removed the criminal offense of publishing independent statistical information and provided that every person has a right to collect and disseminate such information, including those different from the NBS's.

In March, the East African Court of Justice held that the Media Services Act of 2016 violated protocols of the EAC treaty and called on the Tanzanian government to amend it to be in line with the treaty. Following this, the government expressed willingness to have a dialogue with media sector stakeholders on media laws but had not amended the law.

Government Opponents and Other Critics

The government has continued to restrict the political opposition. In January, Parliament passed amendments to the 2002 Political Parties Act, which granted broad powers to the Registrar of Political Parties to demand information from political parties, to suspend individual members of political parties, and required institutions or individuals to get approval from the Registrar to conduct civic education, or face criminal sanctions including imprisonment or fines.

Nine leaders of the main opposition party, Chama Cha Demokrasia na Maendeleo (Chadema), are currently facing charges for sedition, incitement to violence, and holding an "illegal rally" in February 2018. On March 7, the High Court ordered that Chadema politicians Freeman Mbowe and Esther Matiko, who had been jailed since November 23, 2018, for failing to appear for a court hearing, be released and have their bail reinstated.

In May, armed men abducted Mdude Nyagali, a high-profile dissident and opposition activist, as he left work in Mbozi in western Tanzania on the evening of May 5, according to a statement from Chadema party. Nyagali was found on May 9, at Inyala, about 150 kilometers away from Mbozi, seriously injured and unable to speak.

Sexual Orientation and Gender Identity

Tanzania's Sexual Offenses Special Provisions Act of 1998 makes consensual adult same-sex conduct punishable by up to life imprisonment. The government has shut down drop-in centers serving lesbian, gay, bisexual, and transgender (LGBT) people and other key populations and has banned distribution of water-based lubricant, an HIV prevention tool.

Although President Magufuli pledged in a November 17 meeting with senior World Bank officials that Tanzania would not "pursue any discriminatory actions related to harassment and/or arrest of individuals, based on their sexual orientation," arrests on the grounds of alleged sexual orientation continued to take place.

In April, the government banned CHESA, a health and rights organization serving LGBT communities, along with Kazi Busara na Hekima (KBH Sisters), and AHA Development Organisation in Tanzania, based on claims that they violated Tanzanian law, ethics, and culture. In September, the deputy home affairs minister called on police to arrest people who "promote homosexuality." The government has not yet followed through on a pledge to international donors to formally ban forced anal examinations, a discredited method of "testing" for signs of same-sex intercourse.

Children's Rights

In 2017, President Magufuli banned pregnant girls and young mothers from attending school. Police have arrested pregnant schoolgirls and their families to force them to reveal the identity of the men or boys who had impregnated them while schools have subjected girls to forced pregnancy tests. In June, Tanzanian civil society organizations filed a complaint before the African Committee of Experts on the Rights and Welfare of the Child, seeking to have this policy annulled. Following discussions between the government and the World Bank on a loan for secondary education, the government committed to finding ways for pregnant girls to return to school.

In August, Tanzania's government banned teachers in the lower grades of primary school from entering classrooms with canes.

In October, Tanzania's Court of Appeal upheld a 2016 High Court ruling directing the government to raise the legal age of marriage to 18 years for both girls and boys. Tanzania's Marriage Act of 1971 had set the minimum marriage age for girls at 15 with parental consent, and 18 for boys, and permitted the marriage of 14-year-old children when a court is satisfied that there is the existence of special, but unspecified, circumstances.

Women's Rights

In September 2018, President Magufuli denounced family planning, asking women to give up using contraception. Two weeks later, the government suspended radio, and television spots encouraging family planning. In March, the Ministry of Health, Community Development, Gender, Elderly and Children wrote to all heads of 18 institutions responsible for family planning in Tanzania, directing them to resume radio and television advertisements.

Disability Rights

In response to ritual killings and amputations of people with albinism, especially children, the Tanzanian government established "temporary holding shelters," or boarding schools for children with albinism. While the shelters may have contributed to a decline in the number of physical attacks, they have serious negative impacts on children with albinism. They isolate them from their families and communities and exclude them from inclusive education in mainstream schools.

Refugees

Between September 2017 and October 31, 2019, 78,380 Burundian refugees returned home from Tanzania under a voluntary repatriation agreement involving Tanzania, Burundi, and the United Nations High Commissioner for Refugees (UNHCR). In March 2018, Tanzania and Burundi set a goal of voluntarily repatriating 2,000 Burundians a week under the agreement.

In August 2019, Tanzanian and Burundian authorities announced a plan to send all 183,000 Burundian refugees living in three camps in Kigoma, northwestern Tanzania, back to Burundi by the end of 2019. Between August and October, Tanzanian officials also made threatening public statements, closed down a refugee camp market, and repeatedly changed administrative requirements for aid organizations operating in the camps.

On October 15, Tanzanian authorities unlawfully coerced more than 200 unregistered asylum seekers into returning to Burundi by threatening to withhold their legal status in Tanzania.

Key International Actors

The East African Court of Justice remains an instrumental institution on human rights in Tanzania, making key legal decisions on the treatment of individuals as well as the running of institutions.

In November 2018, the World Bank withheld $300 million (£232 million) of a $500 million loan to Tanzania, citing the ban on pregnant schoolgirls. In September, the World Bank approved a $450 million loan for food consumption and livelihoods, education, and health care in Tanzania, acknowledging the amendment of the Statistics Act and the government's commitment to facilitate all girls to complete their education.

In August, the US Embassy in Dar es Salaam and the British High Commission expressed concern about due process and lengthy pretrial detention following the arrest of journalist Erick Kabendera.

Thailand

The general election on March 24, 2019, was held under severe restrictions on civil and political rights. Prime Minister Gen. Prayut Chan-ocha started his second term in July showing the same disregard for human rights that characterized the previous five years of military rule. Impunity for human rights violations continued unabated.

Legacy of Military Rule and Impunity for Human Rights Violations

As the chief of the National Council for Peace and Order (NCPO) junta, Prayut wielded power from 2014 to 2019 that was unhindered by oversight or accountability. While the NCPO disbanded after the new government took office in July, the constitution protects junta members and anyone acting on the junta's orders from ever being held accountable for human rights violations committed during military rule. No redress is available for victims of those rights violations. The government still has not repealed all of the rights-violating NCPO orders.

Censorship and Restrictions on Free Expression

Outspoken media outlets and reporters faced intimidation and punishment for commentaries critical of the junta. In September, political commentator Chalermchai Yodmalai was fired from the radio program "101 News Angle" on FM101 Radio for alleging corruption at the National Defense College and criticizing military procurement. In March, prominent news anchor Orawan Choodee was removed from the political debate program "Election War 19" on the state-controlled MCOT Channel 9 after she asked questions critical of Prayut and the NCPO junta.

In February, the National Broadcasting and Telecommunications Commission forced Voice TV off the air for 15 days, accusing the station of providing airtime to opposition politicians to criticize the junta. Before the general election on March 24, stories about Thailand on major international news networks including CNN, Al Jazeera, and the BBC were cut off for many days on the main cable television service provider, TrueVisions.

HUMAN
RIGHTS
WATCH
"To Speak Out is Dangerous"
The Criminalization of Peaceful Expression in Thailand

On October 3, Belgian journalist Kris Janssens was detained for about five hours by Thai immigration officers and told not to pursue his investigative story about the string of violent attacks against pro-democracy activists in Thailand.

Even though the junta's ban on a public assembly was lifted in December 2018, at least 130 pro-democracy activists in Bangkok and other provinces faced illegal assembly charges during the year 2019 under the Public Assembly Act, and in some cases sedition, for peacefully holding rallies and posting Facebook commentaries calling on the junta to fulfill its promise to promptly hold the general election and immediately lift restrictions on freedom of speech, assembly, and association. In July, Bangkok's Dusit District Court convicted Phayao Akkahad of illegal assembly related to a street performance she staged in December 2018 to demand justice for the death of her daughter during the 2010 political confrontations.

The junta used the Computer-Related Crime Act to make criticism a criminal offense. In April, pro-democracy activist Anurak Jeantawanich was charged with cybercrime for his Facebook commentaries accusing the NCPO of manipulating the general election to allow Prayut to hold onto power. In February, authorities charged Thanathorn Juangroongruangkit and other two leaders of the Future Forward Party with cybercrimes over their Facebook commentaries alleging the junta bribed opposition politicians to join Prayut's side in the general election.

In October, the military brought a sedition complaint against opposition leaders, academics, and human rights activists, accusing that their seminar about the restive southern border provinces contained distorted information that could lead to chaos, public disobedience, or even unrest in the country. If found guilty, they face up to seven years in prison.

In three instances in June, Thai officials pressured activists, including a foreign satirist, a well-known comedian, and high school students to retract or apologize for videos or photos on social media deemed to ridicule military rule.

In July, famous singer and prominent pro-democracy activist Tanat Thanawatcharanont was released from prison by royal pardon after having served more than five years on *lese majeste* (insulting the monarchy) charges. At time of writing, there were at least 25 people in detention after being convicted of *lese majeste* or still awaiting trial. While Thai authorities avoided using the draconian article

112 of the penal code since 2018, they have prosecuted critics of the monarchy using other legal provisions. In X, the government arrested at least 20 members of the anti-monarchy Organization for Thai Federation and charged them with various crimes including sedition, cybercrime, illegal assembly, and criminal association.

Military Detention, Torture, and Military Courts

Under the civilian government, the military continues to arrest and interrogate people for a wide range of offenses related to national security and detain them without access to lawyers.

Torture has long been a problem in Thailand, but the penal code still does not recognize torture as a criminal offense. Between 2016 and 2018, the National Human Rights Commission of Thailand received more than 100 torture allegations from the deep south provinces of Pattani, Yala, and Narathiwat, where the military routinely uses a combination of the Martial Law Act and the Emergency Decree on Public Administration in a State of Emergency to detain and interrogate suspects for up to 37 days without charge or access to legal counsel. On August 25, Abdulloh Esormusor, an ethnic Malay Muslim rubber farmer who was accused of involving in the insurgency, died after falling comatose in military custody. However, the military continued to summarily dismiss allegations that soldiers tortured or otherwise ill-treated detainees.

Over the past five years, the junta put more than 1,800 civilians on trial before military tribunals. On July 9, Prayut issued NCPO Chief Order 9/2019 providing offenses under the NCPO orders must be prosecuted in civilian courts.

Enforced Disappearances

The United Nations Working Group on Enforced or Involuntary Disappearances has recorded 82 cases of enforced disappearance in Thailand since 1980, including prominent Muslim lawyer Somchai Neelapaijit.

In recent years, dissidents who fled persecution in Thailand have faced enforced disappearance in neighboring countries. At least two Thai exiles in Laos, Wuthipong Kachathamakul and Itthipol Sukpaen, were forcibly disappeared in 2016 and 2017 respectively. In 2018, Surachai Danwattananusorn, Chatchan

Boonphawal, and Kraidet Lueler were abducted and murdered in Laos. In May, authorities in Vietnam repatriated Chucheep Chivasut, Siam Theerawut, and Kritsana Thapthai to Thailand and the three men have since disappeared.

Thailand signed the International Convention for the Protection of All Persons from Enforced Disappearance in January 2012 but never ratified the treaty. The penal code still does not recognize enforced disappearance as a criminal offense.

Thai authorities engage in practices that facilitate enforced disappearances, such as the use of secret detention by anti-narcotics units, and secret military detention of national security suspects and suspected insurgents in the southern border provinces.

Lack of Accountability for 2010 Violence

Despite evidence showing that soldiers were responsible for most casualties during the 2010 political confrontations with the United Front for Democracy Against Dictatorship (the "Red Shirts") that left at least 90 dead and more than 2,000 injured, no military personnel or officials from the government of former Prime Minister Abhisit Vejjajiva have been charged for killing or wounding demonstrators or bystanders.

Human Rights Defenders

The government has not met its obligation to ensure human rights defenders can carry out their work in a safe and enabling environment. Against the backdrop of a string of brutal attacks in 2019 targeting prominent pro-democracy activists Sirawith Seritiwat, Anurak Jeantawanich, and Ekachai Hongkangwan, the government has done little to better protect them. The government has not seriously investigated these attacks and instead told activists and dissidents to give up political activity if they wanted state protection.

On August 5, prominent environmentalist Eakachai Itsaratha was abducted in Phatthalung province by assailants affiliated with local politicians, who threatened him to stop opposing a rock quarry project planned for the province.

On November 11, the Central Criminal Court for Corruption Cases approved arrest warrants for Chaiwat Limlikit-aksorn and three other forestry officials in connection with the abduction and murder of the prominent ethnic Karen human rights defender Porlajee Rakchongcharoen, known widely as "Billy," in April 2014. However, the killings of more than 30 human rights defenders and civil society activists since 2001, including land rights activist Den Khamlae, remained unresolved. Military cover-up and shoddy police work hampered the efforts to prosecute soldiers who shot dead teenage ethnic Lahu activist Chaiyaphum Pasae at a checkpoint in March 2017 in Chiang Mai province.

Despite entreaties from civil society advocates, the government did not take concrete action to end strategic lawsuits against public participation (SLAPP) used by government agencies and private companies to intimidate and silence those rights activists and advocates.

The government has not revamped the National Human Rights Commission of Thailand, even after the resignation of two prominent human rights advocates Angkhana Neelapaijit and Tuenjai Deetes meant the commission has not had a quorum since July. The Global Alliance of National Human Rights Institutions rates the commission as substandard because of its selection process for commissioners and its lack of political independence.

Violence and Abuses in the Southern Border Provinces

Since January 2004, Barisan Revolusi Nasional (BRN) insurgents have committed numerous laws-of-war violations. Around 90 percent of the more than 7,000 people killed in the armed conflict in Thailand's southern border provinces have been civilians. Insurgents expanded their operations by carrying out multiple arson and bomb attacks in Bangkok and Nonthaburi province on August 1 and 2. During the Muslim holiday of Ramadan, insurgents committed at least 21 attacks on civilians in Songkhla, Pattani, Yala, and Narathiwat provinces.

The government has not prosecuted members of its security forces responsible for torture and unlawful killings of ethnic Malay Muslims. In many cases, authorities provided financial compensation to the victims or their families in exchange for their agreement not to speak out or file criminal cases against officials.

Refugees, Asylum Seekers, and Migrant Workers

Thailand is not a party to the 1951 Refugee Convention or its 1967 protocol. Thai authorities continued to treat asylum seekers, including those recognized as refugees by the UN High Commissioner for Refugees, as illegal migrants subject to arrest and deportation.

Under immense domestic and international pressure, Thai authorities released Saudi teenager Rahaf Mohammed al-Qunun and Bahraini football player Hakeem Al-Araibi in January and February respectively after attempting to return them to face likely persecution in their home countries.

In January, outspoken Vietnamese dissident Truong Duy Nhat was abducted by Vietnamese officials with Thai assistance in Pathum Thani after he applied for refugee status with the UNHCR. Thai authorities have failed to investigate the apparent enforced disappearance of Od Sayavong, a refugee from Laos and prominent critic of the Lao government, who was last seen at his house in Bangkok on August 26.

The government refused to let the UNHCR conduct refugee status determinations for Lao Hmong, ethnic Rohingya and Uighurs, and other people from Myanmar and North Korea held in indefinite immigration detention.

Migrant workers from Myanmar, Cambodia, Laos, and Vietnam who report abuses face retaliation by recruitment agents, traffickers, employers, and corrupt police and other officials. Thammakaset Company Limited continued to pursue retaliatory prosecution of migrant workers, human rights activists, and journalists involved in reporting on abusive labor conditions at its chicken farm in Lopburi province.

Despite government-instituted reforms in the fishing industry, many migrant workers still face forced labor, remain in debt bondage to recruiters, cannot change employers, and receive sub-minimum wages that paid months late.

In October, the United States government suspended US$1.3 billion in trade preferences for Thailand because of its failure to adequately provide internationally recognized worker rights, such as protection for freedom of association and collective bargaining. This suspension will take effect in April 2020.

Gender Inequality

While Thailand enacted the Gender Equality Act in 2015, implementation remains problematic due to broad exceptions allowing noncompliance for religious principles or for purposes of national security. Lack of access to remedies also remains a critical issue.

The Ministry of Justice presented a draft civil partnership law, the Life Partners Act, to a public hearing in August. If enacted, the draft law would be an important step towards recognizing the fundamental dignity of same-sex couples and providing them with important legal protections. The current draft, however, still needs improvements to comply with international standards on equality and non-discrimination.

Key International Actors

The United States, European Union, Australia, Japan, and many other countries have increasingly moved toward normalization of relations and increased trade with Thailand, even though the March 24 election fell short of being free and fair. Diplomats have spoken out, but have not taken substantive action, about government-appointed and controlled Election Commission of Thailand's post-election actions to rejigger results and disqualify opposition politicians. Renewed close relations between the US and Thai militaries, including resumption of weapons sales, sent the message that the US disregarded the Thai military's dismal record on rights abuses.

Most of the communications by the UN Human Rights Council's special procedures to the Thai government regarding civil and political rights in Thailand under military rule remained unanswered.

Tunisia

In 2019, Tunisia witnessed its second legislative and presidential elections since adopting a new constitution in 2014. During the campaign, candidates focused on debating reforms to the economy and government social programs and devoted less attention to individual liberties and addressing past human rights violations.

First-time candidates shook up the electoral races, and legislative and judicial measures that seemed designed to undermine the most prominent among them cast a shadow over the integrity of the process.

The death in office in July of President Beji Caid-Essebsi highlighted the dangers of the continuous absence of the constitutional court, since that constitutionally-mandated institution could have addressed conflicts that arose in interpretations of the constitution over situations when a president is unable to fulfill his functions. The constitutional court's absence also undermined rights protections, because it was not there to rule on the constitutionality of repressive laws.

A state of emergency remained in effect throughout the year, renewed by President Essebsi and then by interim President Mohamed Ennaceur.

Implementation of the Constitution

Parliament failed again in electing its allotted quota of Constitutional Court members, impeding the election and nomination of the rest of the members by the Supreme Magistrate Council and the president of the republic, respectively.

The absence of the court translated into the continuing application of repressive legislation, such as laws criminalizing speech, without the chance of appealing their constitutionality. Parliament amended the electoral law a few months prior to elections in a way that seemed designed to exclude specific presidential and legislative candidates through measures applied retroactively. A constitutional court, if it existed, would likely have subjected the electoral law amendments to constitutional scrutiny. In any event, the law did not take effect because the president of the republic did not sign it.

Parliament has also failed to elect members of several other constitutional authorities, such as the Human Rights Commission and the Commission on Corruption and Good Governance.

Freedom of Expression, Association, Assembly, and Conscience

Tunisian authorities continued to prosecute peaceful expression on the basis of repressive articles in the penal code and other codes, despite adopting, in November 2011, Decree Law 115 on freedom of the press that liberalizes the legal framework applicable to written media. The ongoing prosecutions affected whistleblowers and would-be whistleblowers.

On May 28, police arrested Yacine Hamdouni at his home in Tunis. They brought him to the Anti-Crime Police Brigade in Gorjani and interrogated him about two Facebook posts from May 2019. In those posts, he accused a senior security official of corruptly using an official car for private purposes. On June 6, a Tunis First Instance court convicted Hamdouni of defamation, dissemination of "false information," accusing officials of wrongdoing without providing proof, and "harming others via public telecommunication networks," and sentenced him to one year in prison, reduced to six months on appeal.

Authorities also undermined freedom of conscience by using a vague provision of the penal code on "publicly offending morality" to convict café owner Imed Zaghouani on May 29, 2019, for keeping his café in Kairouan open during Ramadan fasting hours. Zaghouani spent 10 days in jail before a court sentenced him to a suspended term of one month in prison and a fine of 300 dinars (US$100).

The National Registry of Organizations law, adopted in 2018, requires new and existing associations to comply with new registration procedures, as part of Tunisia's response to the International Financial Action Task Force (FATF) 2017 report, which called Tunisia deficient in combating money laundering and terrorism financing. Some Tunisian associations expressed concern that this new requirement represents a step backward from the liberal 2011 law on associations, which enabled associations to register through a simple declarative act.

Transitional Justice

Tunisia adopted legislation in 2013 to address crimes of the past, which included the creation of a Truth and Dignity Commission. The commission was mandated to investigate all serious human rights violations from 1955 to 2013 and is designed to provide accountability for torture, forced disappearances, and other abuses of the past. During the years it operated, from 2013 to 2018, the commission received more than 62,000 complaints and held confidential hearings for more than 50,000 of these.

On March 26, the commission published its five-volume report analyzing and exposing the senior officials and state institutions responsible for systematic human rights abuses over five decades. The commission outlined the role of former presidents Habib Bourguiba and Zine el-Abidine Ben Ali and others in torture, arbitrary detention, and numerous other abuses. The commission documented abuses not only against political opponents but against their families, including sexual assaults of the wives and daughters of opposition members. The commission named President Caid Essebsi, who died later in 2019, as complicit in torture when serving as the interior minister for Bourguiba, from 1965 and 1969.

The law also tasked the commission with referring cases of torture, forced disappearance, and other serious abuses to 13 specialized chambers created within ordinary courts to try those responsible for grave human rights violations committed since 1955. By the end of the commission's mandate, it had transferred to the specialized courts173 cases of human rights violations, including cases of torture, enforced disappearances, and arbitrary detentions.

The specialized courts opened 38 trials around the country, involving 541 victims and 687 accused. In at least 13 trials, the defendants did not attend; in 16 others, only their lawyers appeared. The first case before a specialized court involved the forced disappearance of Kamel Matmati, an Islamist activist whom the police arrested in 1991. It opened in Gabes on March 29, 2018, and was continuing at time of writing

Counterterrorism and Detention

The state of emergency declared by President Essebsi in 2015 and repeatedly renewed after a number of attacks by armed extremists remained in effect at time of writing. Essebi first declared the state of emergency after a suicide attack in 2015 on a bus, claimed by the extremist group Islamic State (ISIS), killed 12 presidential guards. The emergency decree empowers authorities to ban strikes or demonstrations deemed to threaten "public order." Under the decree, authorities have placed hundreds of Tunisians under house arrest.

The government eased conditions of house arrests in 2018. But many who remained under house arrest were also banned from travel under a procedure called "S17," which the state can impose on any person who is presumably suspected of intending to join an armed group abroad. The procedure allows restrictions on movement both abroad and inside Tunisia. A person placed under the S17 procedure risks lengthy questioning whenever they are stopped at a routine police check.

Interior Minister Hicham Fourati declared on February 7 that he could not provide the exact number of citizens placed under the S17 procedure. He also stated that more than 800 citizens contested the procedure in court, 51 of them winning their challenges.

Violence in police stations or prisons is still present; Tunisian nongovernmental organizations (NGOs) reported tens of cases of alleged torture in 2018. A case of suspicious death took place in Bouhajla, a small town in the region of Kairouan. Police detained peddler Abderrazek Selmi, 58, on June 8, following a dispute with officers. Doctors at a Kairouan hospital pronounced Selmi dead later that day and informed the general prosecutor that Selmi's death was suspicious, citing injuries to his face and body. Authorities had not released an autopsy report at time of writing, and no charge had been filed in connection with his death.

About 200 children and 100 women Tunisians who are ISIS suspects or family members of ISIS suspects remained trapped without charge in squalid conditions in Libya and Syria. Authorities rebuffed demands by Tunisian family members to bring them home.

Women's Rights

In 2018, the presidentially appointed Commission on Individual Freedoms and Equality recommended, among other things, equality between men and women in inheritance.

In November 2018, the presidency of the republic submitted a bill to parliament that would provide equality in inheritance. The bill did not advance in 2019.

Sexual Orientation and Gender Identity

Despite accepting a recommendation during its Universal Periodic Review at the UN Human Rights Council in May 2017 to end the discredited police practice of administering anal testing to "prove" homosexuality, the government has not yet taken steps to carry out this pledge. Authorities have continued to prosecute and imprison presumed gay men under article 230 of the penal code, which provides up to three years in prison for "sodomy."

The government has also continued to harass Shams, an NGO supporting sexual and gender minorities. On February 20, the government appealed a 2016 court decision affirming Shams's status as a legally registered NGO. The government argued that Shams' objective, as stated in its bylaws, to defend sexual minorities, contravenes "Tunisian society's Islamic values, which reject homosexuality and prohibit such alien behavior." It further argued that Tunisian law, which criminalizes homosexual acts in article 230 of the penal code, prohibits the establishment and activities of an association that purports to defend such practices. On May 20, the government lost the appeal.

In July, Tunisia voted at the UN Human Rights Council in favor of renewing the mandate of the independent expert on protection against violence and discrimination based on sexual orientation and gender identity.

Key International Actors

The United Nations special rapporteur on freedom of religion or belief presented the report of his 2018 visit to Tunisia to the Human Rights Council on March 1. The report included recommendations related calling to ensure the Baha'i community's ability to "to secure legal personality to enable them to manifest their faith," and decriminalizing consensual same-sex relations.

The United Nations special rapporteur on freedom of assembly and association presented the report of his 2018 visit to Tunisia to the Human Rights Council on June 25. The report recommended reforms to the state of emergency bill, to ensure that it respects freedoms guaranteed by the constitution, and to revise the law on the National Registry of Organizations to exempt associations from its registration requirements.

Turkey

Turkey has been experiencing a deepening human rights crisis over the past four years with a dramatic erosion of its rule of law and democracy framework. While the consolidation of President Recep Tayyip Erdoğan's unchecked power continued, local elections on March 31, 2019, saw his Justice and Development Party allied with the far right lose in major cities including Istanbul and Ankara, despite winning 51 percent of votes nationwide. Opposition candidate Ekrem İmamoğlu massively increased his narrow win in Istanbul in a June 23 rerun of the election controversially authorized by the Higher Election Board without legitimate grounds.

Executive control and political influence over the judiciary in Turkey has led to courts systematically accepting bogus indictments, detaining and convicting without compelling evidence of criminal activity individuals and groups the Erdoğan government regards as political opponents. Among these are journalists, opposition politicians, and activists and human rights defenders. The largest group was people alleged to have links with the movement run by US-based Sunni cleric Fethullah Gülen, whom the government accuses of masterminding the July 2016 coup attempt.

On October 9, after the US withdrawal of troops from the region, Turkey invaded territory in northeast Syria, assisted by Syrian non-state actors. Turkey cited its main aim as removing the Kurdish forces and administration that controlled the area on the grounds of their close link to the armed Kurdistan Workers' Party (PKK) with which Turkey had been engaged in a decades' long conflict (see Syria chapter).

After the State of Emergency

Restrictive powers and practices ending in July 2018 have set back Turkey's human rights record.

Terrorism charges continued to be widely misused in the third year after the coup attempt. As of July 2019, Ministry of Justice figures stated that 69,259 people were on trial and 155,560 people still under criminal investigation on terrorism charges in cases linked to the Gülen movement, which Turkey's government

HUMAN
RIGHTS
WATCH
LAWYERS ON TRIAL
Abusive Prosecutions and Erosion of Fair Trial Rights in Turkey
Tehlikedeki Avukatlar

terms the Fethullahist Terrorist Organization (FETÖ) and deems a terrorist organization. Of those, 29,487 were held in prison either on remand or following conviction. An estimated 8,500 people—including elected politicians and journalists—are held in prison on remand or following conviction for alleged links with the outlawed Kurdistan Workers' Party (PKK/KCK) and many more on trial but at liberty, although official figures could not be obtained.

Severe restrictions on the right to assembly in Turkey have followed provincial governors being granted extra powers in July 2018 to restrict movement and assemblies in their provinces citing vague public order and security concerns. This has disproportionately affected demonstrations in or concerning the mainly Kurdish southeast and assemblies by lesbian, gay, bisexual or transgender (LGBT) groups throughout the country.

As of October 25, 2019, the commission, established in 2017 to review the mass dismissals of public officials under the state of emergency, had issued decisions in 92,000 cases (with 8,100 reinstated in their jobs or similar measures of redress) and with another 34,200 cases to review. Appeals proceed slowly through two Ankara administrative courts.

Trials continued of military personnel and others for involvement in the July 2016 coup attempt in which 250 people died. As of July, 3,611 defendants were convicted and 2,608 acquitted, according to Ministry of Justice figures. The Court of Cassation began to uphold verdicts in some cases and many appeals are pending.

The Erdoğan presidency's judicial reform amendment package adopted by parliament in October amended various laws, but was too generalized and vague to offer hopes of genuine measures to address the deep and pervasive deficiencies of Turkey's justice system.

Freedom of Expression, Association, and Assembly

An estimated 119 journalists and media workers at time of writing are in pretrial detention or serving sentences for offenses such as "spreading terrorist propaganda" and "membership of a terrorist organization." Hundreds more are on trial though not in prison. Most media, including television, conforms to the Erdogan presidency's political line.

Despite a top Court of Cassation ruling to quash the convictions of 13 journalists and executives from the daily *Cumhuriyet* newspaper, at their November retrial the Istanbul lower court defied the top court by once again convicting them of "aiding and abetting terrorist organizations." The Istanbul court meted out the same prison sentences it gave at their first trial ranging from nearly four years to over eight years, but this time aquitted journalist Kadri Gürsel. All men are at liberty after spending prolonged periods in prison. They are appealing against the convictions.

After being convicted and sentenced to ten years and six months prison for "aiding and abetting a terrorist organization," at his retrial in November the writer Ahmet Altan was first released from over three years of pretrial detention and then one week later rearrested after an Istanbul court reversed the decision. The entire process against Altan has been arbitrary and demonstrates heavy political interference by the executive.

Journalists working for Kurdish media in Turkey continue to be disproportionately targeted and there are severe restrictions on critical reporting from the southeast of the country.

An August regulation binds regular internet broadcasting to Turkey's official media regulation authority, the Radio and Television Supreme Board (RTÜK), and means that news broadcasts via YouTube, platforms such as Netflix, social media broadcasting via Periscope and other platforms, will all be subjected to the inspection and RTÜK sanctions such as suspension of content if deemed to violate Turkey's laws. Internet broadcasters must obtain licenses to broadcast in Turkey even if operating from abroad and violation of laws may result in their suspension. Rights groups have concerns that the new regulation may result in further censorship of online news and other content.

Authorities continue to block websites and order the removal of online content while thousands of people in Turkey face criminal investigations, prosecutions, and convictions for their social media posts. There has been a dramatic rise in the number of prosecutions and convictions on charges of "insulting the president" since Erdoğan's first election as president in 2014. Wikipedia remains blocked in Turkey since April 2017.

In July, the Constitutional Court ruled that the rights of academics who signed a January 2016 petition had been violated. Cases opened against 822 academics had resulted in hundreds of convictions for "spreading terrorist propaganda" for criticizing the government's military operations in the southeast and calling for a peace process. The Constitutional Court ruling has led to the acquittal of the academics.

An Istanbul court convicted the Istanbul chair of the Republican People's Party (CHP), Canan Kaftancıoğlu, on charges including insulting the president, to a nine-year eight-month prison sentence for social media posts dating from 2012-17. The conviction was under appeal at time of writing but if upheld could result in her being barred from political activity and jailed. The case against Kaftancıoğlu is part of a pattern of harassment of opposition politicians.

Human Rights Defenders

The targeting of human rights defenders increased with the June opening of a trial against businessman and civic leader Osman Kavala. Kavala has been held in pretrial detention since November 2017. Along with 15 others engaged in peaceful activism and the arts, he is charged with organizing and financing the 2013 Gezi Park mass protests in Istanbul. Presenting no evidence of criminal activity, the indictment against the 16 also smears US-based philanthropist George Soros and states that he masterminded the Gezi protests. Rights defender Yiğit Aksakoğlu, detained since November 2018, was released at the June hearing. The trial was continuing at time of writing.

The trial of nine prominent rights defenders from Turkey and two foreign nationals continued. All were detained and charged in 2017 with terrorism offenses. Among them are Amnesty International Turkey honorary chair Taner Kılıç, who spent over a year in detention, and former director İdil Eser.

Prosecutions and convictions of lawyers, including some focused on human rights, stood out as exemplifying the abusive use of terrorism charges. In March an Istanbul court convicted Ankara lawyer Selcuk Kozağaçlı, chair of the shuttered Contemporary Lawyers Association, on charges of membership of an armed organization to a prison sentence of over 11 years, along with 11 other lawyers. Their cases were under appeal at time of writing.

There has been no effective investigation to date into the fatal shooting on November 28, 2015 of human rights lawyer Tahir Elçi.

In April, an Ankara court lifted the Ankara governor's blanket ban in effect since November 2017 on public events by lesbian, gay, bisexual and transgender (LGBT) rights groups. However, bans on events in the city and in other cities around Turkey continue on a systematic basis demonstrating a repressive approach on LGBT rights. The Istanbul annual Pride march was banned for the fifth year, and other pride marches in cities such as Antalya and Izmir were also banned.

Police used teargas to disperse women's rights activists attending the Istanbul International Women's Day demonstration on March 8 to protest the endemic problem of violence against women in Turkey.

Torture and Ill-Treatment in Custody, Abductions

A rise in allegations of torture, ill-treatment and cruel and inhuman or degrading treatment in police custody and prison over the past four years has set back Turkey's earlier progress in this area. Those targeted include Kurds, leftists, and alleged followers of Fethullah Gülen. Prosecutors do not conduct meaningful investigations into such allegations and there is a pervasive culture of impunity for members of the security forces and public officials implicated.

The European Committee for the Prevention of Torture (CPT) has conducted two visits to detention places in Turkey since the coup attempt, one in May 2019, though the Turkish government has not given permission for reports from either visit to be published.

There were abductions of six men in February and one in August in circumstances that amount to possible enforced disappearances by state agents, with six surfacing in police custody months later and then remanded to pretrial detention but restricted from seeing lawyers sent by the families.

Turkish authorities continued to seek the extradition of alleged Gülen supporters, many of them teachers, from countries around the world. Countries that complied with Turkey's requests bypassed legal procedures and judicial review. Those illegally extradited in this way were detained and prosecuted on return to Turkey.

Kurdish Conflict and Crackdown on Opposition

Sporadic armed clashes between the military and the armed Kurdistan Workers' Party (PKK) in the southeast continued through 2019, mainly in rural areas. Once again Erdoğan's government has refused to draw a distinction between the PKK and the democratically elected Peoples' Democratic Party (HDP) which won 11.9 percent of the national vote in the most recent parliamentary elections.

In August, the Interior Ministry removed from office the HDP mayors of Diyarbakır, Van and Mardin greater municipalities, newly elected by the majority of votes in the March 31 local elections, accusing them of links with terrorism on the basis of ongoing criminal investigations and prosecutions. In place of the voters' chosen mayors, the Interior Ministry appointed provincial governors as "trustees" to run the municipalities and dissolved the local council, thus suspending local democracy in each city. In the following months, the removal of other elected HDP mayors in districts in the region continued with 24 removed at the time of writing and 14, including Diyarbakir Mayor Adnan Selçuk Mızraklı, jailed pending investigation and trial.

Cases against HDP politicians provide the starkest evidence that authorities bring criminal prosecution and use detention in bad faith and for poltical purposes. Turkey failed to comply with a 2018 ECtHR ruling ordering the release of former HDP co-chair Selahattin Demirtaş and appealed to the Court's Grand Chamber. Three days after the September Grand Chamber hearing, President Erdoğan stated that he would not let Demirtaş or his co-chair Figen Yüksekdağ out of prison. The ECtHR is expected to give its ruling in the first half of 2020.

Refugees and Migrants

Turkey hosts the world's largest number of refugees, around 3.7 million from Syria. Turkey also hosts asylum seekers from Afghanistan, Iraq and other countries. The Istanbul governor announced in July that Syrians and others not registered in Istanbul would be transferred to other provinces. The Turkish authorities unlawfully deported some Syrians from Istanbul and other provinces to Syria, including after coercing some of them through violence, verbal threats and the threat of indefinite detention into signing voluntary return forms. The border with Syria remains closed to new asylum seekers. President Erdoğan has repeatedly stated that Syrians in Turkey should be resettled in a safe zone in northeast Syria.

Key International Actors

Turkey's political relationship with the European Union and EU member states remains limited though it maintains its stated aim is to accede to the EU. The EU recognized the negative climate in Turkey in various statements, and in its May progress report. It condemned Turkey's military incursion into northeast Syria, while prioritizing its focus on its migration deal with Turkey. In June, the EU Council noted that "Turkey has been moving further away from the European Union."

US-Turkish relations have declined further over Turkey's acquisition in 2019 of Russian S-400 missiles, an unprecedented development for a NATO member state. Tensions remain over other aspects such Turkey's October military incursion into northeast Syria; Turkey's abusive prosecution of three US consular staff who are Turkish nationals, one of whom remained detained; and the presence on US soil of Fethullah Gülen.

The ECtHR ruled in April that former member of the constitutional court Alpaslan Altan had been wrongfully deprived of his liberty because there was a lack of reasonable suspicion to justify his initial arrest after the July 2016 coup attempt. In a September decision relevant to many prisoners held far from their families, the European Court found that transfer to distant prisons constituted a violation of the right to respect for private and family life.

Turkmenistan

The Turkmen government's dire human rights record saw no improvements in 2019. Turkmenistan remains an isolated and repressive country under the authoritarian rule of President Gurbanguly Berdymukhamedov and his associates.

Turkmenistan's economic crisis continued in 2019. The government abandoned subsidies on water, gas, and electricity. Emigration from the regions most affected by the crisis continued, but authorities attempt to bar people from traveling abroad to seek work.

The government brutally punishes all unauthorized forms of religious and political expression. Access to information is tightly controlled by the state. No independent human rights monitoring groups are allowed. Dozens of forcibly disappeared are presumably held in Turkmen prisons.

Freedom of Media and Information

There is a total absence of media freedom in Turkmenistan. The state controls all print and electronic media. Foreign media outlets have almost no access to the country. The government retaliates against local stringers for foreign outlets.

The state continues to limit and tightly control internet access. In January, Radio Free Europe/Radio Liberty (RFE/RL) reported that the government allegedly uses imported, privately developed surveillance equipment to track and block websites, identify people which use services to bypass blocks, intercept phone calls, and block mobile messengers.

RFE/RL and the Turkmen Initiative for Human Rights (TIHR), an exile group, reported that in January the government started blocking all Virtual Private Networks (VPN) services. According to an exile-run news website, Turkmen.news, by the end of July most VPN servers were not accessible.

In March, the border control authorities, without explanation, barred Soltan Achilova, an independent journalist, from boarding a flight to attend a conference abroad. On August 20, the Security Ministry informed her that she may travel abroad.

On March 23, Saparmamed Nepeskuliev, a freelance contributor to Turkmen.news and RFE/RL left Turkmenistan. Prior to his departure, he wrote on his Facebook page that since his 2018 release from prison, plainclothes security service agents openly followed him wherever he went and surveilled him at home.

Civil Society

Independent groups cannot openly carry out human rights work inside Turkmenistan. Operating a nongovernmental organization without registration is punishable by a fine, short-term detention, and confiscation of property. Registration requiriments remain burdensome. Civil society activists are constantly threatened by authorities.

On September 6, labor rights activist Gaspar Matalaev was released from prison, after fully serving a three-year prison sentence on unfounded fraud charges in retaliation for monitoring state-sponsored forced labor in the cotton harvest.

An activist for Baloch minority rights, Mansur Mingelov, convicted in 2012 on bogus narcotics and other charges continued to serve his 22-year sentence.

In June, Turkmenistan's ombudsperson, Yazdursun Gurbannazarova, published the second annual report on the institution's work. She received 985 complaints, the majority of them on housing issues and disagreement with a wide range of court decisions. Sixteen were resolved. Gurbannazarova also reported that she received 150 complaints of civil and political rights violations, three of which were resolved.

Freedom of Movement

People whom the government considers disloyal, including the families of dissidents and prisoners, are arbitrarily banned from foreign travel by the authorities. In April, the United Nations Human Rights Committee communicated a complaint to the Turkmen government regarding the case of the Ruzimatov family, relatives of a former official in exile. Authorities have banned Rashid Ruzimatov and his wife, Irina Kabaeva, from traveling abroad since 2003, and his son Rakhim since 2014.

Authorities continued to bar citizens from the most economically distressed regions from leaving Turkmenistan and to pressure people to persuade their relatives living abroad to return.

Memorial, an independent Russian human rights group, reported that since 2018, Turkmen authorities have been banning a dual Russian-Turkmen citizen, Stanislav Chubchik (Osipov), from leaving the country. Chubchik left Turkmenistan in 2014, and returned to visit family on March 5, 2018. The next day the migration service barred him from leaving the country for five years on bogus grounds. Police and unidentified people repeatedly harassed and intimidated Chubchik in Ashgabad in 2018 and 2019.

Housing and Property Rights

In March, TIHR reported that Ashgabat authorities announced plans to expropriate and demolish 75 private homes. According to RFE/RL, in July, homeowners of dozens of private houses near Ashabat International Airport also received demolition notifications. Authorities informed homeowners that they would provide apartments as compensation if they have relevant documents, but provided no information about the terms of compensation.

For more than two years, owners of homes demolished in 2015 and 2016 and who made down payments to the state on new homes, continued to rent interim dwellings while construction of their new houses remained unfinished. The government provided low-interest mortgages but no compensation for the demolished homes or the temporary accommodation because homeowners supposedly lacked resident permits or other ownership documents for their demolished homes.

Freedom of Religion

Turkmenistan forbids unregistered congregations and religious groups. Religious literature is censored by authorities. The state harshly punishes unauthorized religious activity.

Turkmenistan offers no alternative military service and objectors face persecution. An independent religious freedom group Forum 18 reported that at least six objectors were jailed, three others remain in prison. All seven are Jehovah's Witnesses.

On February 13, a 55-year-old Jehovah's Witness adherent Bahram Hemdemov, was released after serving four years in Seydi Labor Camp on charges of "incitement of religious hatred" for hosting a worship meeting.

Political Prisoners, Enforced Disappearances, and Torture

Torture and ill-treatment remain integral to Turkmenistan's prison system. It is impossible to determine the exact number of political prisoners as the justice system of Turkmenistan completely lacks transparency. The government does not disclose information, in sensitive cases trials are closed, and independent monitoring is not possible as it puts monitors at risk of reprisals.

In March, Turkmen authorities released dissident Gulgeldy Annaniyazov after 11 years in prison but sent him for a five-year term to "a designated place of living," or forced internal exile, which they claimed was part of his initial sentence. His family visited him there in March.

Dozens of prisoners remained forcibly disappeared or held incommunicado, in complete isolation from family, lawyers, and the rest of the world, some for almost 17 years. Families do not have official information about their fate and whereabouts. According to an international campaign dedicated to ending enforced disappearances in Turkmenistan, Prove They Are Alive, about 121 people remain forcibly disappeared. Many of them are believed to be held in Ovadandepe prison, known for torture, long-term incommunicado detentions, inhumane conditions, and holding political prisoners.

In June, Turkmen.news reported that security officials repeatedly summoned and threatened a sister of Begench Beknazarov after she attempted to visit or send him a parcel. Bekhazarov was sentenced in 2005 presumably, for alleged involvement in the 2002 alleged coup attempt. His fate and whereabouts remain unknown.

Authorities released Seyran Mamedov after he had served 12 years in prison and three in forced internal exile for allegedly helping the suspected 2002 coup plotters leave Turkmenistan.

In July, Eziz Khudaiberdiev died in a prison hospital. He was one of 10 men serving a 23-year sentence, following a closed 2017 trial, on multiple trumped-up charges, including inciting religious hatred, and for being affiliated with the Fethullah Gülen movement. In 2019, information became available that one of his co-defendendants, Akmyrat Soyunov, died in October 2018. He was also serving a 23-year prison term.

Sexual Orientation and Gender Identity

Under Turkmen law same-sex conduct between men is criminalized and punishable by a maximum two-year prison sentence.

Key International Actors

The United States State Department continued to classify Turkmenistan as a "country of particular concern" under the International Religious Freedom Act of 1998. Citing "important national interest," it also announced a waiver of any sanctions that could accompany the designation. The State Department gave Turkmenistan the lowest possible ranking in the 2019 US Trafficking in Person (TIP) report as the country failed to meet minimum standards to address human trafficking for the fourth year in a row. On May 22, five US senators in a letter to President Berdymukhamedov called for Annaniyazov's release.

On March 29, the UN Human Rights Committee found the detention of three Jehovah's Witnesses conscientious objectors to have violated their rights under the International Covenant on Civil and Political Rights.

During its annual human rights dialogue with Turkmenistan in May, the European Union raised a range of concerns. It urged Turkmenistan to grant the International Committee of the Red Cross full and unhindered access to places of detention. The EU noted that the government had not extended visit invitations to the UN special rapporteur on torture, to the UN Working Group on Arbitrary Detention, or to the UN Working Group on Enforced Disappearances. In July, the EU announced an agreement to open a delegation in Ashgabat. In September, an EU statement at the Organization for Security and Co-Operation in Europe expressed concern about enforced disappearances in Turkmenistan's prisons and urged the Turkmen government to address it.

On February 7, the European Bank for Reconstruction and Development cancelled a loan for offshore oil development. According to Crude Accountability, an independent environmental and human rights organization, the projected loan lacked a comprehensive social and environmental impact assessment.

United Arab Emirates

Despite declaring 2019 the "Year of Tolerance," United Arab Emirates rulers showed no tolerance for any manner of peaceful dissent. Ahmed Mansoor, an award-winning human rights activist sentenced to 10-years in prison solely for exercising his right to free expression, went on hunger strike to protest his prison conditions and unjust conviction. Activists who had completed their sentences as long as three years ago continued to be detained without a clear legal basis.

The UAE announced in June the withdrawal of most of its ground troops from the Saudi-led military operations in Yemen, but UAE-backed Yemeni troops continued to commit abuses there.

Freedom of Expression

In March 2019, Ahmed Mansoor, a leading Emirati human rights defender, began a month-long hunger strike to protest his unjust conviction and awful prison conditions. The UAE in 2017 detained Mansoor on speech-related charges that included using social media to "publish false information that harms national unity." Authorities held him in an unknown location for more than a year with no access to a lawyer before sentencing him in May 2018 to 10 years in prison. On December 31, 2018, the UAE's Federal Supreme Court upheld Mansoor's sentence.

Prominent academic Nasser bin-Ghaith remained in prison, serving 10 years on charges stemming from criticism of UAE and Egyptian authorities. Bin-Ghaith, who was in poor health and denied adequate medical care in al-Razeen prison, initiated a months-long hunger strike in November 2018, his third reported hunger strike since April 2017.

In July 2019, British academic Matthew Hedges lodged a complaint against Emirati authorities with the United Nations Working Group on Arbitrary Detention and the UN high commissioner for human rights. After his May 2018 arrest, authorities detained him in solitary confinement where Hedges alleged he was mistreated. On November 21, 2018, the Abu Dhabi Federal Court of Appeal sentenced him to life in prison on spying charges. The UAE pardoned him five days later, following an international outcry.

As of November 2019, UAE authorities continued to hold two Emiratis, Khalifa al-Rabea and Ahmed al Mulla, who completed their sentences on state security charges between one and three years ago. They had been convicted on the basis of their ties to al-Islah, a legally registered Islamist political movement that the UAE banned in 2014 as "terrorist." Authorities arbitrarily kept them behind bars for "counselling," according to Emirati activists. On August 5, 2019, the UAE president pardoned three other activists also held beyond the completion of their sentences, saying they had "returned to the correct path." Emirati news organizations shared a video of Osama al-Najjar, Badr al-Buhairi, and Othman al-Shehhi publicly denouncing al-Islah.

Detainee Abuse and Fair Trial Violations

Especially in cases related to state security, individuals were at serious risk of arbitrary and incommunicado detention, torture, and ill-treatment, prolonged solitary confinement, and denial of access to legal assistance. Forced confessions were used as evidence in trial proceedings, and prisoners complained of dismal conditions and inadequate medical care.

In 2017, a UAE court convicted Alia Abdel Nour of terrorism in a 2017 case marred by allegations of torture and serious due process violations. Suffering from cancer, she was denied regular family visits, and after her transfer to a hospital in November 2016, authorities shackled her hands and feet to her hospital bed for extended periods. Despite her failing health, authorities ignored repeated calls by international rights groups, European parliamentarians, United Nations experts, and family members to release her on humanitarian grounds. Abdel Nour died in detention on May 4, 2019.

On February 13, 2019, eight Lebanese nationals detained for more than a year without charge first appeared in court in a terrorism trial on charges of links to Hezbollah in Lebanon. Their trial was marred with allegations of ill-treatment and forced confessions. Family members said they were held in prolonged solitary confinement and denied access to their families and legal counsel, and were unable to review the evidence against them. On May 15, 2019, a UAE court sentenced one to life in prison, two to 10-year sentences, and acquitted five.

Throughout 2019, UAE prison authorities denied non-national detainees living with HIV regular and uninterrupted access to life-saving antiretroviral treatment in flagrant violation of the right to health. In at least two UAE prisons, detainees living with HIV were also segregated from the rest of the prison population and faced stigma and systemic discrimination.

Unlawful Yemen Attacks and Detainee Abuse

In 2019, despite announcing the withdrawal of most of its ground troops in June, the UAE remained part of the Saudi-led military operations in Yemen and restated its intention to maintain a presence in Aden and southern governorates, and its support for certain Yemeni forces.

A United Nations report released on September 3, 2019 by the Group of Eminent Experts on Yemen, appointed by the UN High Commissioner for Human Rights, said UAE-backed forces and armed groups committed grave abuses including enforced disappearances, arbitrary arrests and detention, and torture and other ill-treatment, including rape and other forms of sexual violence. The report also stated that during 2018 and continuing into 2019, UAE and UAE-backed forces have used threats and intimidation to prevent journalists in Aden who were critical of UAE of accessing areas under their control.

Migrant Workers

Foreign nationals accounted for more than 80 percent of the UAE's population, according to 2015 International Labour Organization figures.

The kafala (visa-sponsorship) system continued to tie migrant workers visas to their employers. Those who leave their employers without permission faced punishment for "absconding," including fines, prison, and deportation. Many low-paid migrant workers remain acutely vulnerable to forced labor.

The UAE's labor law excluded from its protections domestic workers, who faced a range of abuses, including unpaid wages, house confinement, workdays up to 21 hours, and physical and sexual assault by employers. Domestic workers faced legal and practical obstacles to redress. While a 2017 law on domestic workers does guarantee some labor rights, it is weaker than the labor law and falls short of international standards.

Women's Rights

Discrimination on the basis of sex and gender is not included in the definition of discrimination in the UAE's 2015 anti-discrimination law.

Some provisions of Federal Law No. 28 of 2005 regulating personal status matters discriminate against women. For a woman to marry, her male guardian must conclude her marriage contract; men can unilaterally divorce their wives, whereas a woman must apply for a court order to obtain a divorce; a woman can lose her right to maintenance if, for example, she refuses to have sexual relations with her husband without a lawful excuse; and the law obliges women to "obey" their husbands. A woman may be considered disobedient if she decides to work without her husband's consent.

Following amendments in 2016, the UAE's penal code no longer explicitly permits domestic violence. However, there is no law criminalizing domestic violence. Marital rape is also not a crime.

Sexual Orientation and Gender Identity

Article 356 of the federal penal code criminalizes (but does not define) "indecent assault" and provides for a minimum sentence of one year in prison. UAE courts use this article to convict and sentence people for same-sex relations as well as consensual heterosexual relations outside marriage. Women are disproportionately impacted as pregnancy serves as evidence of extramarital sex and women who report rape can find themselves prosecuted for consensual sex instead. The UAE's penal code punishes "any male disguised in a female apparel and enters in this disguise a place reserved for women or where entry is forbidden, at that time, for other than women" with one year's imprisonment, a fine of up to 10,000 dirhams (US$2,723), or both. In practice, transgender women have been arrested under this law even in mixed-gender spaces.

Different emirates in the UAE have laws that criminalize same-sex sexual relations. In Abu Dhabi, "unnatural sex with another person" can be punished with up to 14 years in prison. Article 177 of Dubai's penal code punishes consensual sodomy by imprisonment of up to 10 years.

Key International Actors

In January, Denmark announced it would no longer export arms to the UAE. In February, investigations by CNN and Amnesty International found that the UAE was supplying various militias in Yemen with US and European manufactured weapons. In July 2019, a congressional effort in the United States to block the sale of billions of dollars' worth of weapons to the UAE and Saudi Arabia failed after President Donald Trump vetoed the resolutions. Between January and June, the German government approved $26.1 million worth of defense exports to the UAE.

In 2019, the UAE authorities invested in a "soft power" strategy aimed at painting the country as a progressive, tolerant, and rights-respecting nation. In February, in response to an invitation by Sheikh Mohammed bin Zayed Al Nahyan, crown prince of Abu Dhabi, Pope Francis visited the UAE, delivered a public mass, met privately with the crown prince, and attended an interfaith summit. The Pope did not publicly address UAE abuses, and there is no indication that he raised human rights concerns privately.

Uganda

Violations of freedom of association, assembly, and expression continued in 2019 as authorities introduced new regulations restricting online activities and stifling independent media. The government arrested its political opponents and blocked political and student rallies. These restrictions on expression and assembly, arbitrary detentions and prosecutions of outspoken critics, and the government's failure to ensure accountability for past abuses, do not bode well for the 2021 general elections.

Freedom of Expression

The Ugandan government continued to undermine freedom of expression by imposing new regulations on bloggers and website owners. In 2019, the government introduced new regulations requiring online operators to apply for authorization to host blogs and websites or risk being shut down. Government also censored media outlets, and arbitrarily detained outspoken critics of the president.

In April, the UCC directed 13 radio and television stations to suspend their staff, accusing them of airing programs that were "unbalanced, sensational and often give undue prominence to specific individuals," after they aired news reports covering opposition politician Robert Kyagulanyi, also known as Bobi Wine. In the same month, police switched off three radio stations in Kabale, Jinja, and Mubende as they hosted prominent opposition leader Kizza Besigye.

In July, media reported that operatives in civilian clothes bundled Joseph Kabuleta, a pastor and government critic, into a police vehicle without registration plates in Kampala. Police said Kabuleta was arrested because of his Facebook posts describing President Yoweri Museveni as a "a Gambler, Thief and Liar." After his release, Kabuleta said police ill-treated him by throwing water on him while filming him.

In August, a court convicted and sentenced academic and activist, Stella Nyanzi, to 18 months' imprisonment for "cyber harassment" under the Computer Misuse Act for a poem she published on Facebook in 2018 criticizing President Museveni. The court ruled that the poem violated prohibitions on "obscene, lewd, lascivious or indecent" content.

Freedom of Assembly

In April, security officers arrested Kyagulanyi while on the way to address a press conference on issues of "police brutality, injustice and abuse of authority." A week later, he was charged with disobedience of statutory duty for leading a protest in July 2018 against a tax on social media use that the government imposed.

In August, Kyagulanyi faced additional charges for inciting violence and with intent to "alarm, annoy or ridicule" the president, stemming from 2018 when Kyagulanyi and 33 other people were arrested and charged with treason on allegations that they threw stones at the president's car during an election campaign rally in Arua in Northern Uganda. Kyagulanyi and the others alleged that security forces tortured them in detention.

On May 30, the Constitutional Court declared unconstitutional Section 36 of the Police Act, which allowed police to use unlimited force when dispersing crowds and gatherings with no liability for deaths or injuries. The decision signals the need for reform of other laws that allow police and other security forces to arrest and disperse crowds without limits on the use of force or firearms.

The police used the 2013 Public Order Management Act (POMA) to block, restrict, and disperse peaceful assemblies and demonstrations by opposition groups, often with excessive force. In April, police blocked rallies in support of Kizza Besigye, a leader in the opposition Forum for Democratic Change (FDC), in the Northern Ugandan town of Lira and in Kasese, in the west. In September, police blocked a rally in Mbale, in the east, and arrested arrested FDC President Patrick Oboi Amuriat and three others. On November 4, police blocked FDC from holding a press conference in Kampala, and arrested Beisgye before releasing him on bond later that day.

In October, police and military forces cracked down on student protests at Makerere University in Kampala, firing teargas into student residences, raiding dormitories, beating and arresting students, detaining dozens for days without charge.

Electoral Reforms

Several reforms have been proposed to the laws governing elections and political parties in the build-up to elections in 2021. In July, the attorney-general tabled several proposals including barring candidates from running as independents after participating in party primaries and preventing independent presidential candidates from forming alliances with political parties. Opposition lawmakers said the reforms targeted Kyagulanyi, who said he would run for president in 2021 as an independent candidate.

In April, the Supreme Court upheld the Constitutional Court's ruling supporting parliament's 2017 approval of the removal of a 75 year age limit for presidential candidates from the Ugandan constitution. The ruling National Resistance Movement party announced in March that President Museveni, 74, would be its candidate for "2021 and beyond."

Lack of Accountability for Torture, Killings

In 2018, the director for public prosecutions ordered the police to investigate allegations that security operatives tortured Kyagulanyi and 33 others in Arua in August 2018. To date, police have made no public announcements regarding the progress or conclusion of the investigations and have made no arrests in connection with the allegations.

In August, the speaker of parliament, Rebecca Kadaga, directed parliament's Human Rights Committee to investigate claims of the existence of safe houses kept by the Internal Security Organisation (ISO) to illegally detain and torture people. This comes after police redesignated Nalufenya detention facility in Jinja, Eastern Uganda, as a standard police station in 2018. Nalufenya had been a notorious place of torture and long-term detention without trial.

In September, the Treasury's Office of Foreign Assets Control in the United States designated former police chief Kale Kayihura for gross human rights violations and corruption through his role as former inspector general of police. While head of police, Kayihura oversaw the Flying Squad Unit and the Nalufenya Special Investigations Center.

Migrants and Refugees

In March, the minister of disaster preparedness and refugees, Hilary Onek, told refugees from Rwanda and Burundi to consider returning home because their countries were politically stable, despite reports by the United Nations High Commissioner for Refugees that conditions were not yet favourable for their return.

Children's Rights

In July, government officials and police violently and arbitrarily rounded up over 600 children and young adults in Kampala as part of an exercise by local authorities to remove and resettle homeless street children. Witnesses said police used sticks and batons to beat these children as they forced them into vehicles. Ugandan authorities have carried out similarly operations in the past.

Sexual Orientation and Gender Identity

Crackdowns on lesbian, gay, bisexual, transgender, and intersex activists continued and same-sex relations remained illegal in Uganda. In May , police shut down celebrations marking the International Day Against Homophobia, Biphobia, Intersexism, and Transphobia event in Kampala, accusing the nongovernmental organization Sexual Minorities Uganda of planning an illegal gathering , forcing the organization to move the event to a private residence.

In October, Brian Wasswa, a young gay man who worked as a paralegal with the Human Rights Awareness and Promotion Forum and as an HIV peer educator with TASO, an HIV/AIDS NGO, was beaten to death with a hoe at his home in Jinja. The following week, Ethics and Integrity Minister Simon Lokodo announced government plans to reintroduce an anti-homosexuality bill in parliament, under which people convicted for consensual same-sex acts would face the death penalty. The government later announced that it had no plans to reintroduce the law.

Prosecutions for Serious Crimes

In 2019, the case of Dominic Ongwen, alleged former Lord's Resistance Army (LRA) commander charged with 70 counts of war crimes and crimes against humanity, continued at the International Criminal Court (ICC). In October, the court announced that closing statements in this case would commence on March 10, 2020. Two ICC warrants remain outstanding for the arrest of LRA leader Joseph Kony LRA leader and Vincent Otti, who is presumed dead.

The International Crimes Division (ICD) of Uganda's High Court continued the trial of alleged former LRA commander Thomas Kwoyelo—in custody since his capture in the Democratic Republic of Congo in 2009—on charges of war crimes and crimes against humanity. The trial has had numerous delays. In September, the ICD confirmed charges of terrorism, murder, attempted murder, aggravated robbery against Jamil Mukulu, alleged leader of the rebel Allied Democratic Forces (ADF), and 37 others.

Key International Actors

In August, Japan, the United Kingdom, and Germany suspended direct funding of Uganda's refugee programme because the government failed to punish government and aid officials who colluded in the fraudulent inflation of the refugee population according to the UN's 2018 audit report, which revealed gross mismanagement of funds meant for refugees.

In May, the European Union Delegation, the Heads of Mission of Austria, Belgium, Denmark, France, Germany, Ireland, Italy, the Netherlands, Sweden and UK and the Heads of Mission of Iceland, Japan, Norway, Republic of Korea and United States issued a joint statement regarding freedom of expression and assembly in Uganda, citing in particular the UCC's April 30 decision to suspend senior staff of 13 radio and television stations on allegations of breaching minimum broadcasting standards. They also expressed concerns over the excessive use of force by police against peaceful protesters and political opposition.

Ukraine

Hostilities in eastern Ukraine entered their sixth year and continued to put civilians' lives and well-being at risk, even as absolute numbers of civilian casualties dropped. Former comedian Volodymyr Zelensky won the presidential election in May. Snap parliamentary elections in July delivered his party, Servant of the People, a single-party parliamentary majority, for the first time since Ukraine's independence. After taking office, Zelensky demonstrated commitment to carrying out anti-corruption reform and ending the armed conflict with Russia.

In 2019, environment for media in Ukraine remained unsafe. Violence by far-right groups continued.

In September, Russia and Ukraine exchanged a total of 70 prisoners. Eleven prisoners held by Russia on politically motivated charges, including Oleg Sentsov, Edem Bekirov, Pavlo Hryb, Olexander Kolchenko, Roman Sushenko, and 24 Ukrainian sailors Russia captured in the Kerch strait in 2018, were part of the swap.

In November, Ukraine became the 100th country to endorse the Safe Schools Declaration, an international political commitment to make schools safe during times of war.

Armed Conflict

2019 saw a significant decrease in civilian casualties. The leading causes were shelling by artillery and mortars, fire from light weapons, landmines, and explosive remnants of war.

Between January and May 2019, attacks on schools on both sides of the contact line tripled compared with the same period in 2018. Throughout six years of conflict, 147 children were killed.

The government continued discriminatory policies requiring people living in Russian proxy-held areas to register as internally displaced and regularly travel to, and maintain residence in, governmental areas in order to access social benefits. This continued to create hardship for many older people in accessing their pensions; those unable to regularly cross due to health or mobility issues could not access their pensions at all. In December 2018, the Supreme Court found residency verifications for pensioners to be unconstitutional. In May 2019, it found that requiring pensioners to register as displaced put additional burden on access to pensions.

Limited access to basic facilities and emergency medical help remained a problem at some crossing points. Between January and April 2019, at least 19 people, mostly older persons, died from health complications while crossing the line of contact.

In positive developments, in March authorities annulled expiration dates for electronic passes required to travel across the contact line. In August, authorities provided an electric cart to drive older people and people with disabilities crossing the pedestrian- only Stanytsia Luhanska checkpoint. In November, they completed much-needed repairs to the destroyed bridge at this crossing point, which will reduce some of the hazards of crossing.

Russia-backed armed groups continued to hold pro-Ukraine bloggers and journalists Stanyslav Aseev and Oleh Halaziuk on dubious charges. In August, separatists in Luhansk region sentenced student Sergei Rusinov to six years in jail for "terrorism" for his pro-Ukraine social media posts.

Rule of Law, Judicial Reform

Justice for crimes committed during the 2014 Maidan protests and violence in Odesa remained largely unaddressed. In August, the Prosecutor General's Office ordered the dissolution of units within its Special Investigative Department tasked with investigating Maidan-related abuses and, in November, transferred all ongoing cases to another investigative body, the State Bureau of Investigations. The move was done without a clear handover procedure, resulting in the effective suspension of all ongoing investigations. Activists and lawyers raised alarm about the possible collapse of all Maidan-related investigations and the loss of work that has already been done on those cases.

In June, Andrii Kozlov was dismissed from the High Qualification Commission of Judges, after he publicly criticized his colleagues' attempts to falsify the voting procedure to protect from dismissal a judge who was involved in persecuting Euromaidan activists.

In July, President Zelensky proposed expanding the lustration law to cover people who served in public office between February 23, 2014 and his inauguration. The current lustration law bans broad categories of people who worked in official positions under pre-2014 governments from holding certain government positions.

Two September developments marked significant progress towards fulfilling Zelensky's election promise to combat corruption: parliament voted to cancel immunity for lawmakers, and Ukraine's High Anti-Corruption Court finally became operational. In November, Zelensky signed a law on whistleblowers, providing protection and offering financial remuneration to those willing to report on corruption.

Freedom of Religion

In January, the head of the global Orthodox Church granted independence to the newly formed Orthodox Church of Ukraine, separating it completely from the Russian Orthodox Church. A number of congregations transitioned to the new church, sometimes accompanied by violence involving supporters of both churches and, in some cases, local authorities. In several reported cases involving intimidation and threats against members and clergy of the Ukrainian Orthodox Church, the police did not respond and in some cases, contributed to it. The Ukrainian Security Service (SBU) carried out dozens of raids at priests' residences and churches aligned with the Russian Orthodox Church.

In "separatist"-controlled areas, reported incidents of violence and intimidation against the Orthodox Church of Ukraine included searches of churches' premises and priests' homes and confiscation of property.

Freedom of Expression, Attacks on Journalists

Independent media remained under pressure. The Institute of Mass Information, a media watchdog, documented at least 11 cases of journalists beaten or injured and one killed, between January and July 2019. It also reported dozens of cases of journalists receiving threats and facing obstruction, in some cases by authorities, including damaged equipment and restricted access to officials and events.

In June, investigative journalist Vadym Komarov died from severe head injuries he sustained in a May attack by an unidentified assailant. In previous years he had been threatened and attacked. Investigators linked the attack to his journalism. The investigation was ongoing at time of writing.

In June, a court sentenced to prison five men who planned and carried out the 2018 acid attack on anti-corruption activist Kateryna Handziuk, who died from the wounds she sustained. At time of writing, the organizers who ordered the attack had yet to be indicted.

In August, a court released Russian journalist Kyrill Vyshinskiy, editor of a Russian state wire service, held since May 2018 on dubious treason charges, from pretrial custody. In September, Vishinsky went to Russia as part of the prisoner swap.

In August, a court upheld a defamation claim by Ukrainian far-right nationalist group, C14, against the independent internet television station Hromadske.TV after the outlet referred to C14 as a "neo-Nazi" group. At time of writing the decision was under appeal.

In April, the Ukrainian parliament adopted a law requiring that Ukrainian language be used in most aspects of public life. The law raised concerns about sufficient guarantees for the protection and use of minority languages.

Crimea

Throughout the year, Russian authorities in occupied Crimea continued to harass Crimean Tatars, prosecuting dozens on trumped-up terrorism charges.

In March alone, Russian authorities arrested 24 men, most of whom were active in Crimean Solidarity, a legal and social support group for families of those arrested for political reasons. All were charged with association with Hizb ut-Tahrir, a pan-Islamist movement that is proscribed in Russia as a "terrorist" organization but is legal in Ukraine. None were accused in relation to any act of violence. Russian security agents tortured or ill-treated at least four. In June, authorities arrested eight men in Crimea on similar charges.

In June, the European Court of Human Rights ordered Russian authorities to immediately hospitalize Edem Bekirov, a gravely ill Crimean Tatar activist in pretrial detention since December 2018. Russia defied the request and released Bekirov only in August. In September, Bekirov returned to Kyiv as part of the prisoner exchange.

In December 2018, Russia's Justice Ministry requested that the Crimean Bar Association expel human rights lawyer Emil Kurbedinov because of his alleged involvement in "extremist activities." Earlier in December, Kurbedinov was sentenced to five days in jail for a 2013 social media post about a Hizb ut-Tahrir meeting in Crimea.

Hate Crimes

Members of groups advocating hate and discrimination continued putting ethnic minorities, lesbian, gay, bisexual, and transgender (LGBT) people and rights activists at risk. In some cases, law enforcement's efforts in countering such violence improved as compared to previous years and helped to prevent far-right attacks, including during public events. In others, police responses were largely ineffective.

Police successfully prevented violent attacks against participants in women's rights rallies held on March 8 in seven Ukrainian cities.

The Equality March, held in Kyiv in June, was Ukraine's largest-ever pride event, drawing 8,000 participants. It was mostly peaceful and well-protected by police.

In April, far-right activists in Kyiv disrupted the European Lesbian Conference by trying to break through security cordons and spraying tear gas.

In April, police in Dnipro raided a gay club, forcing customers to lay on the floor for hours, using homophobic slurs, and filming. Two people were injured.

Key International Actors

The Organization for Security and Co-operation in Europe (OSCE) and the Council of Europe's Parliamentary Assembly (PACE) found the presidential election competitive and featuring a high turnout. Its observation mission noted that the campaign for July parliamentary elections respected fundamental freedoms but was marred by "widespread malpractice and the misuse of political finance."

At its annual Human Rights Dialogue, held in Kyiv in March, Ukraine and the European Union discussed ways to protect the rights of internally displaced persons (IDPs), including de-linking of pension payments from IDP status. Other topics included the rights of LGBT persons and ethnic, linguistic, religious, and national minorities, the need to investigate attacks against civil society and the media, as well as the need to take into account the Venice Commission opinion on the draft law on the use of state language.

At the EU-Ukraine summit in July, the EU condemned Russian measures entitling Ukrainian citizens of the areas under control of Russia-proxies to apply for Russian citizenship in a simplified manner. The EU leaders also agreed on the importance of accelerating Ukraine's reform efforts to combat corruption.

A resolution on Ukraine adopted at the 41st session of the United Nations Human Rights Council (HRC) recognized the need for ongoing reporting on human rights issues and invited the High Commissioner for Human Rights to continue to update the HRC. In its September report, the UN Office of the High Commissioner for Human Rights welcomed the decline in civilian casualties and called attention to the impact of the conflict on people living along both sides of the contact line and the lack of protection for media and civil society. The UN called on Ukraine to "reduce the impact on civilians" and to "prevent, stop and condemn all acts of violence" against media professionals and activists.

Following an April-May visit to Ukraine, the UN independent expert on protection against violence and discrimination based on sexual orientation and gender identity expressed concern over the use of violence and promotion of hatred against LGBT people by far-right groups.

The OSCE media freedom representative made several statements expressing concern about freedom of expression, condemning the killing of journalist Vadim Komarov and criticizing the court ruling fining Hromadske TV.

In June, the Joint Investigative Team, which has been carrying out the criminal inquiry into the downing of flight MH17 in July 2014, announced that the Public Prosecution Service of the Netherlands will prosecute four suspects for downing the plane. The trial will take place in the district court of the Hague in 2020.

In 2016, Ukraine's parliament amended article 124 of the constitution, removing a constitutional barrier to ratification of the Rome Statute as of June 2019.

Although Ukraine is not a member of the International Criminal Court (ICC), it accepted the court's jurisdiction over alleged crimes committed on its territory since November 2013. The ICC prosecutor's preliminary examination as to whether it should open an investigation into abuses committed during the armed conflict is merited remained ongoing.

United States

In 2019, the United States continued to move backwards on rights. The Trump administration rolled out inhumane immigration policies and promoted false narratives that perpetuate racism and discrimination; did not do nearly enough to address mass incarceration; undermined the rights of women and lesbian, gay, bisexual, and transgender (LGBT) people; further weakened the ability of Americans to obtain adequate health care; and deregulated industries that put people's health and safety at risk.

In its foreign policy, the Trump administration made little use of its diminishing leverage to promote human rights abroad; continued to undermine multilateral institutions; and flouted international human rights and humanitarian law as it partnered with abusive governments—though it did sanction some individuals and governments for committing human rights abuses.

Criminal Legal System

The US continues to have the highest reported criminal incarceration rate in the world, with 2.2 million people in jails and prisons and another 4.5 million on probation and parole as of 2017, the latest year for which Bureau of Justice Statistics figures were available at time of writing. The figures show a slight decrease in the number of people incarcerated from 2016 to 2017 and a 10 percent decrease from a decade earlier.

This decrease can be partly attributed to greater recognition among policy makers and the public of unfairness in the US criminal legal system and the harm caused, which has spurned many state-level reforms. Still, in several states incarceration rose, as did the incarceration rate for women, which grew by 750 percent from 1980 to 2017.

On the federal level, following enactment of the First Step Act at the end of 2018, more than 3,000 people were released from prison in July, earlier than they would have been without the legislation. Though hailed as a major bipartisan criminal reform initiative, the law left many concerns unaddressed and affected only a small number of those held in the federal criminal system, which itself accounts for only about 10 percent of the total number of people incarcerated in the United States.

Stark racial disparities still exist in the prison population. While the overall imprisonment rate was down, among black women it was nearly twice as high as among white women and the imprisonment rate for black men was almost six times the rate for white men. For younger black men, the disparity was even larger.

The death penalty is allowed in 29 states. According to the Death Penalty Information Center, 20 people in seven states had been executed in 2019 by the middle of November— all in the south and mid-west of the country. There were eight executions in Texas; three in Alabama and Georgia; two in Florida and Tennessee; and one each in Missouri and South Dakota. The Trump administration announced a resumption of federal executions in July after 16 years without them, but a federal court blocked the resumption in November. In California, which has over 730 prisoners on death row, the governor imposed a moratorium on executions, and in New Hampshire, the legislature repealed its death penalty statute.

Poor people accused of crimes continue to be jailed because courts require money bail as a condition of release, forcing people not convicted of any crime to stay behind bars for long periods of time awaiting trial and resulting in coerced guilty pleas. A movement to eliminate money bail is growing but many states are replacing it with risk assessment tools that could entrench discrimination while failing to lower pretrial rates of incarceration. New York enacted pretrial reform measures in April that are expected to dramatically reduce the number of people who can be detained pretrial using money bail and improve due process for the remainder. The measures, which take effect in January 2020, do not mandate the use of risk assessment tools.

Laws banning individuals with criminal convictions from voting continue to exist throughout the US. In 2018 voters in Florida approved a measure restoring the right to vote to 1.4 million residents with felony convictions, but in July the state enacted a law requiring those affected to pay all financial obligations, including excessive fines and fees, before this right is restored.

Children in the Criminal and Juvenile Justice Systems

On any given day, approximately 50,000 children are held in confinement. In the juvenile justice system, 2,200 youth are imprisoned for "status" offenses—non-criminal acts that are considered violations of the law only because the individuals in question are under 18 years old.

Additionally, all 50 states continue to prosecute children in adult criminal courts. According to the Citizens Committee for Children, roughly 32,000 children under 18 are admitted annually to adult jails. The Sentencing Project reports there are approximately 1,300 people serving life without parole sentences (LWOP) for crimes committed below age 18. Oregon passed a law eliminating the use of juvenile LWOP. In all, 22 states and the District of Columbia now prohibit juvenile life without parole.

Racial disparities persist at every stage of a person's contact with the law, leaving children of color disproportionately represented in juvenile justice systems across the country; in 37 states, rates of incarceration were higher for black children than for white, according to The Sentencing Project.

Racial Justice and Policing

Stark inequalities in wealth exist throughout the United States, and poverty intersects with crime, which is used to justify more aggressive policing in poor, often minority, communities. Rather than address problems of poverty—including homelessness, mental health, and gang involvement—with services, support, and economic development, many US jurisdictions simply add more police and effectively "criminalize" poor communities, a vicious circle that fuels high rates of incarceration.

Government tracking of police violence continues to be incomplete. According to the Washington Post, police reportedly shot and killed 783 people in the US in 2019 as of mid-November, a reduction from the previous year. Of those killed whose race is known, 20 percent were black even though blacks make up 13 percent of the population. Racial disparities in police use of force, arrests, citations, and traffic stops continue to exist.

09/16/2016 19:43:56
WA L
11047@GID
Tulsa Police Department
HUMAN
RIGHTS
WATCH
"Get on the Ground!"
Policing, Poverty, and Racial Inequality in Tulsa, Oklahoma

Human Rights Watch documented substantial racial disparities in policing in a case study of the city of Tulsa, Oklahoma. Black residents consistently reported experiences of abusive policing.

Recognition grew in 2019 that current racial disparities in policing, criminal justice, and other aspects of American life cannot be understood without reference to slavery and its continuing impact on society. Congress held an historic hearing on Juneteenth, a day honoring the abolition of slavery in the US, to discuss possible ways to account for these harms, including reparations and more investment in black communities to address continued inequality and discrimination.

Poverty and Inequality

In September, the Census Bureau released a study showing that income inequality in the US had hit the highest level in five decades. About 40 million people live in poverty, many of them members of households with at least one wage earner making at or near the federal minimum wage of $7.25 per hour.

The Trump administration continued to take actions to restrict access to health care, targeting changes to the Medicaid program, private insurance subsidies, and other key elements of the Affordable Care Act that will result in greater inequities in access to care and health outcomes. Many states with federal support have imposed work requirements, drug testing, and other barriers to Medicaid eligibility for low-income individuals.

Court-mandated fines and fees disproportionately impact the poor and communities of color. When a person cannot afford them, they can face arrest warrants, extended sentences, and incarceration, often putting them further in debt. Many local jurisdictions fund themselves by imposing such fees, even for minor violations such as jaywalking—a practice that incentivizes over-policing and aggressive prosecution.

The Trump administration continued to undermine consumer protections against predatory lenders and abusive debt collectors, whose unregulated services can trap families in poverty. The Consumer Financial Protection Bureau, delayed implementation of a rule regulating payday and other small lenders that often carry exorbitant interest rates. Another proposed rule threatens to weaken protections from false, deceptive, and misleading practices by debt collectors.

Rights of Non-Citizens

The US government in 2019 continued to disregard its obligations to asylum seekers under international law, leaving many refugees without effective protection. In January, the administration began returning asylum seekers to Mexico while their claims are pending under the Migrant Protection Protocols, known as the "Remain in Mexico" program.

At time of writing, over 55,000 asylum seekers had been returned to often dangerous and unlivable conditions in Mexico, with significant barriers to obtaining legal representation and a fair hearing. This included asylum seekers with disabilities or other chronic health conditions despite initial guidance that no one with "known physical/mental health issues" would be placed in the program. In the city of Ciudad Juárez, Human Rights Watch documented the cases of six such individuals, four of them children.

In July, the administration announced an interim rule to bar asylum eligibility for individuals who travel through a third country and attempt to enter the US without having applied for protection in that country. This would essentially bar all but Mexicans from applying for asylum at the US southern border.

The US continued to limit the number of asylum seekers accepted at southern ports of entry, leading some to risk their lives attempting to cross illegally.

In July, the administration also announced a new rule making people anywhere in the country who cannot prove at least two-years' presence in the US subject to fast-track deportations, which have returned asylum seekers and refugees to harm.

Migrant children coming to the US-Mexico border were held in inhumane conditions in jail-like Border Patrol facilities without contact with family members, regular access to showers, clean clothes, toothbrushes, proper beds, or medical care, for weeks at a time. Children as young as two or three were held in these facilities without adult caregivers. Families and adults were also held in dangerously overcrowded facilities for longer than the 72-hour legal limit.

HUMAN
RIGHTS
WATCH
"We Can't Help You Here"
US Returns of Asylum Seekers to Mexico

US officials continued to regularly separate migrant children from adult relatives, including from parents in some cases. A government watchdog agency found children separated from parents have experienced severe trauma. Despite this, the Trump administration announced a new regulation that would allow children and their families to be detained indefinitely and thereby risk severe trauma.

Three migrant children died in 2019 shortly after entering the US, following the deaths of three children in 2018, the first deaths of children in US immigration custody in a decade. At least seven adults died in the custody of US Customs and Border Protection (CBP); six adults died in the custody of US Immigration and Customs Enforcement (ICE). Deaths in detention have previously been linked to poor medical care in US detention facilities.

The number of immigrants in ICE custody reached a record high of 55,000 people per day, even as new governmental reports revealed egregious violations of governmental detention standards. Several detainees on hunger strike were force-fed using a process that is inherently cruel, inhuman, and degrading.

In August, the administration released a rule that could allow the federal government to deny permanent residency ("green cards") to immigrants who use Medicaid, food stamps, housing vouchers, or other forms of public assistance, generating fear among non-citizens in need of these services from accessing them.

The Trump administration repeatedly threatened mass raids, stoking fear in immigrant communities. In August, US immigration authorities arrested 680 people in raids on food processing plants in Mississippi, the largest workplace raid in the US in over a decade. Immigrant workers in the meat and poultry industry experience serious workplace abuses but fear of deportation prevents many from speaking out. The US continued to deport long-term residents without appropriate consideration of their family and community ties, or their fears of harm if returned to their home countries.

Despite these ongoing abuses, Congress continued to authorize the administration's requests for additional funding for immigration agencies with insufficient requirements for standards, oversight, and transparency.

Environmental Rights

The Trump administration has continued to weaken or repeal dozens of rules that protect the environment and public health. In July, the Environmental Protection Agency (EPA) decided not to ban chlorpyrifos, a neurotoxic pesticide that, according to studies funded by the agency, has been linked to developmental delay in children.

Also in July, the EPA proposed significantly rolling back regulations governing coal ash, a highly toxic byproduct of coal combustion that constitutes the second largest waste stream in the US. The rule change increases the risk of air and water pollution and poses a serious health risk.

In September, the Trump administration repealed a major clean water regulation that had placed limits on polluting chemicals that could be used near streams, wetlands, and other bodies of water.

Also in September, the Trump administration announced it would revoke California's authority to set auto emissions rules that are stricter than federal standards, prompting California and nearly two dozen other states to sue.

These moves were part of a wide-ranging attack on efforts to fight climate change and reduce regulation of industries, increasing health and safety risks.

Older People's Rights

Nursing homes across the US routinely give antipsychotic drugs to residents with dementia to control their behavior, often without adequate consent. This abusive practice remains widespread and can amount to cruel, inhuman, or degrading treatment yet the Centers for Medicare and Medicaid Services (CMS) has proposed further deregulation of such institutions.

Women's and Girls' Rights

The current patchwork of healthcare coverage across states leaves many women and girls uninsured and creates an environment in which women die at higher rates than they do in comparably wealthy countries from preventable maternal and gynecological cancer-related deaths.

30
HUMAN
RIGHTS
WATCH
"When We're Dead and Buried,
Our Bones Will Keep Hurting"
Workers' Rights Under Threat in US Meat and Poultry Plants

Human Rights Watch has documented how Alabama's failure to expand Medicaid eligibility, along with a mix of other policies and practices, has led to a high rate of preventable cervical cancer deaths that disproportionately impacts black women in the state. Alabama, along with Texas, has the lowest Medicaid eligibility levels in the nation and is seeking a waiver to make eligibility even more difficult.

A Trump administration "gag" rule went into effect in August barring doctors receiving federal family planning (Title X) funds from giving women information on the full range of pregnancy options available to them. The rule led Planned Parenthood, which provides pregnancy and women's health services to more than 1.5 million low-income women each year, to withdraw from the Title X program.

This rule compounds the harm of another Trump administration rule that permits employers to opt out of providing contraceptive coverage in their employee health insurance plans by claiming religious or moral objections to Affordable Care Act requirements. A federal judge in November blocked another proposed rule that would dramatically expand the ability of healthcare providers to turn away patients based on religious or moral objections, including women seeking reproductive health services.

A few states took steps to proactively protect or expand protections for women's health, but the trend in most states was towards increasingly extreme abortion bans. Alabama passed a draconian law criminalizing abortion and attempted abortion with no exception for victims of sexual violence. In October, a lower court issued a preliminary injunction to prevent the law from taking effect.

Delaware and New Jersey banned all marriage before age 18, and several states were considering bans, but child marriage remained legal in some form in 48 states.

Sexual Orientation and Gender Identity

In January , the Supreme Court permitted a Trump administration ban on transgender service in the military to take effect as litigation proceeds. The Department of Health and Human Services in May proposed a rule that would narrow how it defines sex discrimination, permitting insurers and health care providers to discriminate against transgender patients. At time of writing, at least 22 transgender people had been killed in the US in 2019.

The House of Representatives voted to reauthorize the Violence Against Women Act, which includes provisions for LGBT survivors of violence. The House also passed the Equality Act, which would expressly prohibit discrimination based on sexual orientation and gender identity under various federal civil rights laws. The Senate did not vote on either bill.

Protections for LGBT individuals at the state level are uneven. At time of writing, only 20 states had laws expressly banning discrimination based on both sexual orientation and gender identity in employment, housing, and public accommodations.

Surveillance and Data Protection

The US lacks comprehensive national data protection laws, including laws that prevent law enforcement from obtaining unnecessary and disproportionate access to personal data. Through the unacknowledged practice of "parallel construction," the subject of a 2018 Human Rights Watch report, the government has been able to use data from secret surveillance programs in criminal investigations, and then reconstruct that evidence through other means, without disclosing the secret monitoring to judges or defendants. This deprives litigants of the chance to challenge potentially unlawful surveillance, and makes surveillance especially difficult for courts to review in the US.

In August, the Trump administration asked Congress to renew section 215 of the USA Patriot Act, which has enabled the National Security Agency (NSA) to gather, store, and search hundreds of millions of US telephone records in violation of human rights. The then-director of national intelligence (DNI) admitted in a letter to Congress that the NSA had suspended this program due to longstanding legal and technical difficulties and had deleted the data it had previously stored. Nevertheless, the DNI argued that Congress should keep this massive surveillance provision on the books for future use. The law was due to expire in December 2019 in the absence of congressional action.

Freedom of Expression

President Trump continued to attack news media outlets throughout 2019, characterizing them as, among other things, "the enemy of the people" and "degenerate[s]." These attacks not only erode public trust in the media, but also increase the threat of violence against journalists and other media workers.

The public release of a criminal indictment of Julian Assange, creator of WikiLeaks, for alleged violations of the Espionage Act prompted widespread concern among journalists that the government could begin prosecuting media outlets that publish classified information—even if release of the information is in the public interest. Such prosecutions would hinder media freedom and impede the public's right to receive information.

A leaked government document showed that CBP had made a list of journalists, activists, and others addressing immigration issues near the country's southern border; some of these individuals said they were subjected to extra questioning by officials when crossing the border, potentially discouraging activities protected by the right to free expression.

National Security

Men espousing white supremacist, anti-Semitic, and misogynist views continued to carry out mass shootings in 2019. In El Paso, Texas, a man allegedly killed 22 people and injured 27 others after posting a racist text online. In California, a man allegedly killed a woman and wounded three other congregants at a synagogue. In Dayton, Ohio, a man who reportedly had a history of threatening behavior toward women killed nine people and injured 27 more.

The ability of the shooters to obtain military-style weapons to carry out these killings fueled growing public support for stronger federal laws restricting some access to guns.

Despite a rise in white supremacist attacks over the past decade, particularly since 2016, and evidence that some perpetrators are part of a growing transnational white supremacist movement, US law enforcement agencies have devoted far fewer resources to preventing such attacks than to the threat of attacks inspired by extreme interpretations of Islam. In September, the Department of Homeland Security added white supremacist violence to its list of priority threats for the first time since the list was formed after the attacks of September 11, 2001.

The US continues to indefinitely detain 31 men without charge at Guantanamo Bay, all of whom have been imprisoned for well over a decade, some since 2002. The prosecutions continue of seven men on terrorism-related charges, including five on charges connected to the September 11, 2001 attacks, before Guantanamo's military commissions, which do not meet international fair trial standards and have been plagued by procedural problems and years of delays. Two men convicted before the commissions are also at Guantanamo, one serving a life sentence and the other awaiting sentencing.

Foreign Policy

In 2019, President Trump continued to praise authoritarian leaders and refrain from raising human rights concerns publicly in bilateral meetings. He met with North Korean leader Kim Jong Un in February, and again in June along with South Korean President Moon Jae-in. He hosted Egyptian President Abdel Fattah al-Sisi at the White House in April and met with him again on the sidelines of the Group of 7 (G7) summit in August, reportedly referring to him as his "favorite dictator." In May, Trump described Hungarian Prime Minister Viktor Orban, then visiting the White House, as doing a "tremendous job." In September, Trump met with Indian Prime Minister Narendra Modi in Houston, and in November hosted Turkish President Recep Tayyip Erdogan, focusing his public comments on praise of their policies rather than these governments' worsening human rights records.

The Trump administration repeatedly condemned certain Chinese government abuses, particularly violations of religious freedom and the rights of ethnic minorities, and in October added the Xinjiang Public Security Bureau, other government agencies, and eight Chinese technology firms, including iFlytek and Hikvision, to a sanctions list. But these steps were undermined by Trump's many positive remarks about President Xi Jinpeng's leadership.

In April, the ICC prosecutor confirmed that the United States had revoked her visa in connection with her inquiry into possible war crimes by US forces in Afghanistan.

The State Department's annual human rights country reports, released in March, once again excluded analysis of women's reproductive rights, including information on preventable maternal mortality and access to contraception.

In March, President Trump signed a proclamation recognizing the Israeli-occupied Golan Heights as part of the state of Israel, disregarding the protections due to the residents of the Golan Heights under international humanitarian law. In November, the State Department announced that it no longer considers Israeli settlements to violate international humanitarian law "per se", putting the United States outside the international consensus on the issue.

In April, the US threatened to veto a UN Security Council resolution on sexual violence in armed conflict because it mentioned women's reproductive health services. Because the US refused to accept any language that recognized that victims of rape in war should have access to sexual and reproductive health services, the resolution was ultimately adopted without it.

In June, the Trump administration leveraged the threat of tariffs against Mexican goods to pressure Mexico to commit to an unprecedented increase in immigration enforcement and to accept non-Mexican asylum seekers back from the United States under an abusive returns program. The Trump administration also reached agreements to send asylum seekers to Honduras, El Salvador, and Guatemala, despite these countries' precarious security conditions and inadequate protection systems. In September, the US government announced it would cap the annual number of refugees admitted at 18,000—by far its lowest ceiling in four decades.

In a rebuke to the Trump administration's inaction on Saudi Arabia's human rights abuses, the Senate in June voted to block the administration's use of emergency authority to complete several arms sales, worth more than $8 billion, to Saudi Arabia, the United Arab Emirates, and other countries. However, Trump vetoed the resolution and the arms sales were allowed to move forward.

The United States has continued to impose visa restrictions and asset freezes on perpetrators of grave human rights violations and corruption. In July, the State Department imposed visa bans on several senior foreign military commanders for their involvement in gross human rights abuses, in particular Myanmar's ethnic cleansing campaign against Rohingya Muslims.

Also in July, Secretary of State Mike Pompeo announced the formation of a Commission on Unalienable Rights to provide "an informed review of the role of human rights in American foreign policy." Many of the commissioners have public records opposing key internationally recognized human rights, including on reproductive freedom and LGBT rights.

Following the 2018 US cancellation of the Joint Comprehensive Plan of Action, as the nuclear deal with Iran was known, the US reimposed broad sanctions on Iran and penalties for companies transacting with Iran. In April the US designated Iran's Islamic Revolutionary Guard Corps (IRGC) as a Foreign Terrorist Organization, and in September the US sanctioned the Central Bank of Iran for supporting IRGC, among others. In October, Human Rights Watch documented the severe harm these sanctions are causing to Iranians needing health care and medicine.

The State Department failed to release a long-promised second review of Trump administration's Mexico City Policy, or "global gag rule," which blocks federal funding for nongovernmental organizations operating outside the US that provide abortion counseling or referrals, or advocate to decriminalize abortion or expand services. In March, Pompeo announced that the rule would be interpreted more strictly against what are mostly small, grassroots foreign organizations.

The US continued targeted killings of terrorist suspects in countries including Yemen and Somalia, many with armed drones. It also carried out large-scale military operations against non-state armed groups including the Taliban in Afghanistan and the Islamic State (ISIS) in Iraq and Syria. In May, the Department of Defense reported that in 2018, 120 civilians were killed and approximately 65 civilians injured during US military operations in Iraq, Syria, Afghanistan, and Somalia, and no civilian casualties from US operations in Yemen or Libya. Independent tracking organizations published civilian casualty estimates related to US operations in Afghanistan, Iraq, Syria, Somalia, Yemen, and Libya that far exceed those of the Defense Department. The US did not publicly report on any casualties from lethal operations by the Central Intelligence Agency.

Throughout the year, the US engaged in negotiations with Taliban leaders on the terms for a US troop withdrawal based on Taliban pledges not to allow any armed group to carry out attacks on the US from Afghanistan. However, Trump called off US negotiations on September 7, leaving further talks in limbo.

US airstrikes in Afghanistan reached record levels, with over 8,000 bombs and missiles dropped on Afghanistan between January and September, killing and injuring over 800 civilians, at least 250 of them children. An estimated 14,000 US troops remained in Afghanistan, including US special forces involved in combat operations. CIA-backed Afghan paramilitary units outside the regular chain of command have committed extrajudicial executions and enforced disappearances.

Uzbekistan

Three years since Uzbekistan's President Shavkat Mirziyoyev assumed the presidency, he has taken some concrete steps to improve the country's human rights record. In August, ordering the closure of the notorious Jaslyk prison, long a symbol of torture and imprisonment of government critics, Mirziyoyev fulfilled a key demand of United Nations human rights bodies. In May, breaking with decades of censorship of the internet, authorities lifted a ban on several critical websites.

At the same time, the government remains authoritarian. Thousands of people, mainly peaceful religious believers, remain in prison on false charges. The security services retain vast powers to detain perceived critics, and there is no genuine political pluralism.

Political Prisoners and Lack of Rehabilitation

Since September 2016, authorities have released more than 50 people imprisoned on politically motivated charges, including rights activists, journalists, and opposition activists.

Prison authorities have also reportedly released hundreds of independent Muslims, who practice Islam outside strict state controls, but this is impossible to verify. Since late 2017, authorities claim to have removed over 20,000 citizens from security services' "blacklists," which allowed authorities to regularly summon for questioning those suspected of extremism and restrict their movements.

While the releases raised hopes for reform, authorities have not provided former prisoners with avenues for legal redress, including overturning unjust convictions, or access to adequate medical treatment, even though many remain in terrible health due to their ordeal.

Some released activists, such as opposition figure Samandar Kukanov and rights defender Chuyan Mamatkulov, have challenged their unjust convictions in court. While Mamatkulov has succeeded in obtaining a new trial, in July the Supreme Court rejected Kukanov's effort to quash the conviction, ruling that "all charges in the case ... had been proven."

Criminal Justice, Torture

Despite a 2018 decree that reduced their powers, Uzbekistan's security services continued to wield enormous power. They used treason (article 157) and other charges to detain so-called enemies of the state.

One example are the charges brought against retired Uzbek diplomat Kadyr Yusupov, 67, who served as Uzbekistan's head of mission to the Organization for Security and Co-operation in Europe (OSCE), among other positions, until his retirement in 2009. In December 2018, Yusupov was admitted to hospital with serious injuries following an apparent suicide attempt. Security services detained him straight from his hospital bed in Tashkent on treason charges. He has been held at a Tashkent pretrial detention facility ever since.

Yusupov's relatives told Human Rights Watch that during the first four months of his detention, officers psychologically tortured him, threatening that if he did not admit guilt, they would rape him with a rubber baton, rape his wife and daughter, and arrest his two sons. Yusupov's trial began in Tashkent in June. As with several ongoing cases concerning charges of treason, it is closed to the public.

Andrei Kubatin, a professor of Turkic studies, has been imprisoned since December 2017 on fabricated treason charges and was tortured in detention. His crime was allegedly sharing publicly available, historical documents with a Turkish cultural attaché. Kubatin's case, around which numerous international scholars have rallied, shows that despite efforts by President Mirziyoyev to rein in the security services, they continue to play an outsize role. Kubatin was released in late September and fully exonerated, with charges against him dropped.

Thousands of others, most of them peaceful religious believers, are jailed on extremism and other political charges. They include Akrom Malikov and Rustam Abdumannapov, scholars; Mirsobir Hamidkariev, a film producer; Aramais Avakyan, a fisherman; Vladimir Kaloshin, a journalist; Ruhiddin Fahriddinov (Fahrutdinov), an independent religious cleric; and Ravshan Kosimov, Viktor Shin, and Alisher Achildiev, soldiers.

Freedom of Media, Civil Society

Freedom of speech has improved and on several occasions President Mirziyoyev has urged media not to hold back in addressing urgent social issues, but free speech remains restricted. In December 2018, the government restored access to YouTube and Facebook, which had been periodically blocked. In May, the government unblocked at least 11 websites that had been inaccessible for over a decade, including Eurasianet, Fergana News, Human Rights Watch, and the BBC's Uzbek service. In the past two years, Eurasianet, Voice of America, and the BBC's correspondents have all received accreditation. However, *Ozodlik*, the Uzbek service of Radio Free Europe/Radio Liberty (RFE/RL), remains inaccessible and unable to operate.

The OSCE's special representative on media freedom, Harlem Desir, welcomed the move to unblock and provide accreditation to some news outlets, but said authorities should unblock *Ozodlik* and all other inaccessible sites.

In 2018 and 2019, the Justice Ministry announced new regulations on nongovernmental organizations (NGOs), ostensibly designed to relax registration procedures and control over these groups' activities. One positive move eliminated the rule that NGOs could keep funds in only two state-approved banks. But the government has yet to overturn a restrictive 2015 law requiring NGOs to receive advanced permission to conduct virtually any activity. NGOs said this provision has a chilling effect on their work and infringes on freedom of expression and association.

The ministry has yet to register any new human rights organizations and on three occasions rejected the application by released rights defenders, Azam Farmonov, Agzam Turgunov, and Dilmurod Saidov, to register an NGO called Restoration of Justice. The group would focus on criminal justice reform and legal rehabilitation for people who have been wrongfully imprisoned.

Barriers to NGO registration also affect international organizations. While Human Rights Watch has been able to freely visit the country and conduct research since August 2017, it remains unable to register due to a 2011 Supreme Court decision.

Sexual Orientation and Gender Identity

Alongside Turkmenistan, Uzbekistan is one of only two post-Soviet states where consensual sexual relations between men are still criminalized, carrying a prison sentence of one to three years (article 120).

Hate crimes against lesbian, gay, bisexual, and transgender (LGBT) people, especially beatings and torture of men perceived to be gay, occur with regularity and are often recorded and posted online. In August, an Istanbul-based LGBT activist, Shohruh Salimov, along with others, sent a public appeal to President Mirziyoyev asking him to scrap article 120 and protect the lives of LGBT people. Instead of investigating the attacks, police visited his relatives' home and threatened to arrest him. LGBT activists told Human Rights Watch they constantly fear arrest and being disowned by family and friends.

Property Rights

In 2019, there was rising public anger over hastily conducted mass demolitions across the country, which have been carried out as a campaign of urban renewal and beautification. International human rights law requires that any process of expropriation or government acquiring of an individual's property be subject to due process and appropriate and adequate compensation. Expropriation should never be arbitrary nor place an undue burden upon individuals. The government's campaign led some residents to take desperate measures.

On July 20, following several other isolated incidents of self-immolation by disaffected residents faced with forced eviction, the owner of a workshop set for demolition in the village of Yakkabog in Uzbekistan's southeastern Qashqadaryo province doused the deputy district head, Mansur Tuymaev, with gasoline, setting him on fire when he arrived to supervise the demolition of the building. *Ozodlik* reported that anger against Tuymaev and demolitions conducted with little to no compensation or notice had been seething for months in the community.

In July, more than 1,000 people demanding compensation for their demolished homes blocked a road in northwestern Khorezm province to fend off attempts by police and soldiers to disperse them. Uzbekistan's constitution and other laws guarantee the right to private property, protect against arbitrary interference with this right, and even guarantee government support in obtaining housing. International human rights law protects against arbitrary interference with the home and property, and also protects the right to housing.

Forced Labor

Forced labor in the cotton sector remained widespread, despite efforts by authorities to enforce an earlier public decree prohibiting forced mobilization of public sector workers.

Civil society groups such as the Uzbek-German Forum for Human Rights documented many examples of forced labor during the autumn 2019 harvest. In November, it reported that public sector employees from across the country, with the exception of those in larger cities, had complained of having to pick cotton or pay for someone to do it in their place.

Key International Actors

In September, the UN special rapporteur on the independence of judges and lawyers, Diego García-Sayán, visited Uzbekistan. During his visit, while he noted and welcomed steps to improve judicial independence and rule of law, he concluded "substantial threats against judicial independence and the rule of law remain," including broad powers that prosecutors retain in criminal proceedings, which limit the independence of judges to decide cases autonomously and in accordance with his or her conscience.

In July, the US State Department's trafficking-in-persons report kept Uzbekistan in its place on the "Tier II watch list," citing the government's efforts to combat forced and child labor in the country's cotton sector.

The US State Department upgraded Uzbekistan's ranking in its annual International Religious Freedom report, removing it from the list of "countries of particular concern"— states which commit serial violations of religious freedom—and placed it on a watchlist. The State Department made this designation despite the views of the Commission on International Religious Freedom, a US congressional advisory body, that recommended Uzbekistan stay on the list.

In a March report, the European Parliament called on the European Union to closely monitor Uzbekistan's political reforms and urged Tashkent to create a "genuinely independent parliament resulting from a genuinely competitive election" and to take steps aimed at "protecting human rights, gender equality and freedom of the media." The report came after Brussels open talks with Tashkent on a Comprehensive Enhanced Partnership and Cooperation Agreement (EPCA) with Uzbekistan, which would upgrade existing trade arrangements and other areas of cooperation.

VENEZUELA'S HUMANITARIAN EMERGENCY
Large-Scale UN Response Needed to Address Health and Food Crises
HUMAN RIGHTS WATCH
JOHNS HOPKINS
BLOOMBERG SCHOOL of PUBLIC HEALTH

Venezuela

In early January 2019, Juan Guaidó, the National Assembly president, asked Venezuelans to mobilize in support of restoring constitutional order in the country. On January 23, hundreds of thousands poured into the streets. During the protest, Guaidó claimed that he was taking power as interim president of Venezuela and said that he would call for free and fair elections. More than 50 countries have since expressed support for Guaidó. The country remained at a political impasse at time of writing.

No independent government institutions remain today in Venezuela to act as a check on executive power. A series of measures by the Maduro and Chávez administrations stacked the courts with judges who make no pretense of independence. The government has been repressing dissent through often-violent crackdowns on street protests, jailing opponents, and prosecuting civilians in military courts. It has also stripped power from the opposition-led legislature. In September, the UN Human Rights Council adopted a resolution creating the first international investigative mechanism into atrocities committed in Venezuela.

Severe shortages of medicines, medical supplies, and food leave many Venezuelans unable to feed their families adequately or access essential healthcare. The massive exodus of Venezuelans fleeing repression and shortages is the largest migration crisis in recent Latin American history.

Other persistent concerns include brutal policing practices, poor prison conditions, impunity for human rights violations, and harassment by government officials of human rights defenders and independent media outlets.

Refugee Crisis

The United Nations High Commissioner for Refugees reported that, as of November, approximately 4.5 million of an estimated 32 million Venezuelans had fled their country since 2014. Many more not reported by authorities have also left.

The causes of the exodus include simultaneous political, economic, human rights, and humanitarian crises. In addition to those qualifying for refugee status based on fear of being persecuted, many are unable or unwilling to return because of the humanitarian emergency they face at home, which includes difficulty accessing food, medicines, and medical treatment.

Many Venezuelans in other countries remain in an irregular situation, which severely undermines their ability to obtain work permits, send their children to school, and access health care. This makes them vulnerable to exploitation and abuse and means they need humanitarian assistance.

Persecution of Political Opponents

The Venezuelan government has jailed political opponents and disqualified them from running for office. In November, Venezuelan prisons and intelligence headquarters held nearly 400 political prisoners, according to the Penal Forum, a Venezuelan network of pro-bono criminal defense lawyers.

In April, opposition leader Leopoldo López, who was serving a 13-year sentence under house arrest on unsubstantiated charges of inciting violence during a demonstration in Caracas in 2014, was released by his guards so he could participate in an attempted military uprising. After the uprising failed, he sought refuge at the Spanish embassy in Caracas, where he remained at time of writing.

In May, intelligence agents detained Edgar Zambrano, the National Assembly vice president, for his alleged participation in the April military uprising. His lawyers were not allowed to be present when he was brought before a judge, and he remained without contact with his family for over a month. He was accused of treason but was conditionally released in September. A total of 13 opposition legislators fled the country, and four were living in foreign embassies in Caracas at time of writing.

Venezuelan intelligence and security forces have detained and tortured military personnel accused of plotting against the government. Authorities have also detained and tortured the family members of some suspects to determine their whereabouts. Some detainees were tortured to force them to provide information about alleged conspiracies.

Crackdown on Protest Activity

In two crackdowns in 2014 and 2017, Venezuelan security forces and armed pro-government groups called "colectivos" attacked demonstrations—some attended by tens of thousands of protesters. Security force personnel shot demonstrators at point-blank range with riot-control munitions, brutally beat people who offered no resistance, and staged violent raids on apartment buildings. Security forces have committed serious abuses against detainees that in some cases amount to torture—including severe beatings, electric shocks, asphyxiation, and sexual abuse.

In 2019, security forces responded with violence to protests in support of Guaidó, firing pellets or live ammunition at close range against demonstrators. Hundreds were detained and dozens killed in several incidents in January and May.

The Penal Forum counts more than 15,000 people arrested since 2014 in connection with protests, including demonstrators, bystanders, and people taken from their homes without warrants. Around 8,900 had been conditionally released as of November, but they remained subject to criminal prosecution. More than 840 civilians have been prosecuted by military courts, in violation of international law.

Many others arrested in connection with the protests or political activism remain under house arrest or in detention, awaiting trial. Others have been forced into exile.

Alleged Extrajudicial Killings

Police and security forces have killed nearly 18,000 people in Venezuela in instances of alleged "resistance to authority" since 2016. Interior Minister Néstor Reverol reported in December 2017 that there were 5,995 such cases in 2016 and 4,998 in 2017. Venezuelan security forces killed nearly 7,000 people in incidents they claimed were cases of "resistance to authority" in 2018 and the first five months of 2019, according to official figures cited by the UN Office of the High Commissioner for Human Rights (OHCHR).

Nobody has yet compiled detailed information as to how many of these killings by security forces have been extrajudicial executions, but OHCHR concluded that "many" may constitute extrajudicial killings. Human Rights Watch documented several such killings in 2019.

Between 2015 and 2017, Venezuelan security forces swept through low-income communities during what was known as the "Operation to Liberate and Protect the People" (Operación de Liberación y Protección del Pueblo, OLP). Participating security forces included the Bolivarian National Guard, the Bolivarian National Police (PNB), the Bolivarian National Intelligence Service (SEBIN), the Scientific, Penal, and Criminal Investigative Police (CICPC), and state police.

These raids resulted in widespread allegations of violations such as extrajudicial killings, mass arbitrary detentions, mistreatment of detainees, forced evictions, destruction of homes, and arbitrary deportations. In November 2017, Venezuela's then-attorney general said security forces had killed more than 500 people during OLP raids. Government officials repeatedly said the OLP victims were armed criminals who had died during "confrontations." In many cases, witnesses or families of victims challenged these claims. In several cases, victims were last seen alive in police custody.

FAES, a special police force created in 2017 to combat drug trafficking and criminal organizations, replaced the OLPs in security operations. FAES officials have committed egregious violations, including killings and torture, with impunity in low-income communities that no longer support Nicolás Maduro. OHCHR reported that "authorities may be using FAES and other security forces as an instrument to instill fear in the population and to maintain social control."

Impunity for Abuses

Venezuelan authorities reported that, as of June 2019, 44 people were detained and 33 arrest warrants were issued for people allegedly responsible for killings during demonstrations in 2017 and 2019. Authorities claim five FAES agents were convicted of attempted murder and other crimes for events occurred in 2018, and that another 388 FAES agents were under investigation for alleged crimes committed in 2017 and 2019.

Impunity for human rights abuses, however, remains the norm. OHCHR reported in July 2019 that factors contributing to impunity include "lack of cooperation by security and armed forces with investigations," "the tampering with crime scenes" by security forces, and de facto immunity of senior officials, and lack of judicial independence.

Judicial Independence

Since former President Hugo Chávez and his supporters in the National Assembly conducted a political takeover of the Supreme Court in 2004, the judiciary stopped functioning as an independent branch of government. Members of the Supreme Court have openly rejected the principle of separation of powers and have consistently upheld abusive policies and practices.

In July, the Supreme Court ruled in favor of Judge María Lourdes Afiuni but did not lift all conditions for her release. Afiuni spent a year in jail and several under house arrest, after she was arbitrarily prosecuted starting in 2009 when she released a government critic on conditional liberty, following a recommendation by the UN Working Group on Arbitrary Detention. A lower court had granted her conditional liberty in 2013.

Humanitarian Emergency

Venezuelans are facing severe shortages of medicine, medical supplies, and food, seriously undermining their rights to health and food. In 2017, the Venezuelan health minister released official data indicating that during 2016 maternal mortality had increased 65 percent, and infant mortality 30 percent. Days later, the health minister was fired. The government has not since published epidemiological bulletins.

Venezuela's health system is in utter collapse, with the re-emergence and spread of vaccine-preventable diseases previously declared eliminated, such as measles and diphtheria, and increases in outbreaks of infectious diseases such as malaria and tuberculosis. Research by Venezuelan organizations and universities documents high levels of food insecurity and child malnutrition among Venezuelans.

Constituent Assembly

In 2017, President Maduro convened a "Constituent Assembly" by presidential decree, despite a constitutional requirement that a public referendum be held before any effort to rewrite the Constitution. The assembly is made up exclusively of government supporters chosen through an election that Smartmatic, a British company hired by the government to verify the results, said had produced results whose accuracy it could not guarantee. The Constituent Assembly has, in practice, replaced the opposition-led National Assembly as the country's legislative branch. In 2019, it lifted the parliamentary immunity of several opposition legislators and extended its mandate until December 2020.

Freedom of Expression

For more than a decade, the government has expanded and abused its power to regulate media and reduce the number of dissenting media outlets. The government can suspend or revoke licenses to private media if "convenient for the interests of the nation," arbitrarily suspend websites for the vaguely defined offense of "incitement," and criminalize expression of "disrespect" for high government officials. While a few newspapers, websites, and radio stations criticize the government, fear of reprisals has made self-censorship a serious problem.

During the attempted military uprising in April, Venezuelan authorities took CNN and BBC off cable TV and shut down Radio Caracas Radio. Leading Venezuelan media freedom groups reported death threats and attacks on journalists covering demonstrations, including beatings and pellets fired at them at close range.

In November 2017, the Constituent Assembly adopted a Law Against Hatred that includes vague language undermining free speech. It forbids political parties that "promote fascism, hatred, and intolerance," and imposes prison sentences of up to 20 years on those who publish "messages of intolerance and hatred" in media or social media. In 2018, prosecutors charged several people with these crimes, including Jesús Medina, the only Venezuelan journalist held in a Venezuelan prison at time of writing. Medina was detained by intelligence agents when he was working on an investigative project at a Caracas hospital.

Human Rights Defenders

Government measures to restrict international funding of nongovernmental organizations—combined with unsubstantiated accusations by government officials and supporters that human rights defenders seek to undermine Venezuelan democracy—create a hostile environment that limits the ability of civil society groups to promote human rights.

In 2010, the Supreme Court ruled that individuals or organizations receiving foreign funding can be prosecuted for treason. That year, the National Assembly enacted legislation blocking organizations that "defend political rights" or "monitor the performance of public bodies" from receiving international assistance.

In September, Diosdado Cabello, the head of the Constituent Assembly, said the assembly would adopt and implement a law to "severely sanction NGOs and people who are receiving money from the Imperialism to conspire against our country."

Political Discrimination

People who supported referenda on Chávez's and Maduro's presidencies have been fired from government jobs. A government program that distributes food and basic goods at government-capped prices has been credibly accused by Venezuelan citizens and nongovernmental groups of discriminating against government critics.

Prison Conditions

Corruption, weak security, deteriorating infrastructure, overcrowding, insufficient staffing, and poorly trained guards allow armed gangs to exercise effective control over inmate populations. Excessive use of pretrial detention contributes to overcrowding.

Key International Actors

In June, Michelle Bachelet, the UN high commissioner for human rights, visited Caracas. After her two-day visit, a small team from her office remained in Caracas to monitor the human rights situation. In July, her office released a scathing report concluding that Venezuelan authorities had failed to hold accountable perpetrators of egregious violations, including killings, excessive use of force, arbitrary arrests, and torture. The report also highlights the impact that food and medicine shortages have had on Venezuelans' rights to food and health.

In 2018, International Criminal Court (ICC) Prosecutor Fatou Bensouda announced a preliminary examination to analyze whether, since at least 2017, crimes occurring within the court's jurisdiction have taken place, including allegations of use of excessive force against demonstrators and detention of thousands of individuals, a number of whom are alleged to have suffered serious abuse in detention. Six countries—all ICC member countries—subsequently requested an ICC investigation, and three other countries have since expressed support for the states' referral.

Many South American governments have made considerable efforts to welcome Venezuelans. In 2019, however, several countries, including Chile, Peru, and Ecuador, imposed requirements that they first obtain visas, requirements that in practice severely limit Venezuelans' access to these countries. Venezuelans in some instances have faced xenophobic harassment abroad, including in parts of Colombia, Ecuador, Caribbean countries, and northern Brazil.

The Lima Group—consisting of at least 10 Latin American governments and Canada—continue to monitor the situation in Venezuela. In September, the UN Human Rights Council adopted a resolution proposed by Lima Group members to create an independent Fact Finding Mission to investigate allegations of atrocities committed in Venezuela, including extrajudicial killings, disappearances, and torture since 2014. The resolution also anticipates creation of a commission of inquiry if Venezuela fails to cooperate with the Office of the UN High Commissioner for Human Rights. The fact-finding mission will deliver its report to the Human Rights Council at its September 2020 session.

A second resolution was presented by Iran on Venezuela's behalf, and emphasizes "cooperation and technical assistance," while expressing concern at "the imposition of extraterritorial unilateral coercive measures." This resolution calls on the government of Venezuela to fully implement the recommendations in the High Commissioner's report, to allow access to UN experts, and to provide the Office of the High Commissioner with unlimited access to all regions and detention centers.

The High Commissioner's office also announced the signing of a memorandum of understanding with Venezuela, with a view to creation of a country office, although at the time it was issued many details had not yet been agreed.

The United States, Canada, the European Union, and Switzerland have imposed targeted sanctions on more than 100 Venezuelan officials implicated in human rights abuses and corruption. The sanctions include asset freezes and the cancellation of visas. In July, the EU reiterated its readiness to expand its targeted sanctions should negotiations not lead to concrete results. The European Parliament also called for additional sanctions against state authorities responsible for human rights violations and repression. Argentina, Brazil, and Peru have also prohibited more than 300 Venezuelan officials from entering their countries.

Since 2017, the United States has imposed financial sanctions, including a ban on dealings in new stocks and bonds issued by the Venezuelan government and its state oil company. Despite language excluding transactions to purchase food and medicines, these sanctions could exacerbate the already dire humanitarian situation in Venezuela due to the risk of over-compliance.

In April 2019, the UN Security Council held a formal session on Venezuela's humanitarian emergency. During the session, Human Rights Watch and Johns Hopkins Bloomberg School of Public Health presented a report concluding that severe medicine and food shortages within Venezuela, together with the spread of disease across the country's borders, has created a complex humanitarian emergency that requires a full-scale response by the United Nations.

Immediately following the meeting, after months of quiet diplomacy, UN Secretary-General António Guterres tweeted that 7 million Venezuelans were in need of humanitarian assistance. UN agencies operating in Venezuela assembled a humanitarian needs overview calling for US$233 million in assistance over during six months. As of November, it had not been fully funded or implemented.

An effort by Norway to mediate between Venezuelan authorities and the opposition, which consisted of several meetings in Norway and Barbados during 2019, had not led to concrete results at time of writing. A Contact Group composed of Costa Rica, Mexico, Uruguay, and several European governments met with Venezuelan authorities on several occasions in 2019 to push for free and fair elections in Venezuela.

As a member of the UN Human Rights Council, Venezuela has regularly voted to prevent scrutiny of human rights violations, opposing resolutions spotlighting abuses in countries including Syria, Belarus, Burundi, and Iran. In October, Venezuela was narrowly elected by the UN General Assembly to serve on the Human Rights Council for the 2020-2022 term, notwithstanding its declared intention to refuse to cooperate with the council's fact-finding mission, in violation of its membership obligations.

The Venezuelan government withdrew from the American Convention on Human Rights in 2013, leaving citizens and residents unable to request intervention by the Inter-American Court of Human Rights when local remedies for abuses are ineffective or unavailable. The Inter-American Commission on Human Rights continues to monitor Venezuela, applying the American Declaration of Rights and Duties of Man, which is not subject to states' ratification.

Venezuela is one of the dwindling number of countries in Latin America that has not signed the Safe Schools Declaration. In 2019, there were reports of members of the Bolivarian National Guard and members of armed pro-government groups using schools for military exercises, which affected students' access to education.

Vietnam

Vietnam did little to improve its abysmal human rights record in 2019. The government continues to restrict all basic civil and political rights, including freedom of expression, association, assembly, and the rights to freely practice beliefs and religion. It prohibits the formation and operation of any organization or group deemed threatening to the Communist Party's monopoly of power.

Authorities block accesses to websites and request that social media and/or telecommunications companies remove contents deemed to be politically sensitive. Those who criticize the one party regime face police intimidation, harassment, restricted movement, physical assault, detention, and arrest and imprisonment. Police detain political detainees for months without access to legal counsel and subject them to abusive interrogations. Party-controlled courts sentence bloggers and activists on bogus national security charges. In 2019, authorities convicted at least 25 people in politically motivated cases.

In January, Vietnam presented an inaccurate picture of its human rights record during its Universal Periodic Review (UPR) at the United Nations Human Rights Council in Geneva. The government implausibly claimed that it had fully implemented 159, and partially implemented a further 16, of the 182 recommendations accepted at its previous Universal Periodic Review (UPR) in 2014.

In October, Vietnam endorsed the Safe Schools Declaration, an international political commitment to protect education during armed conflict.

Freedom of Expression, Opinion, and Speech

Vietnamese rights bloggers face regular harassment and intimidation. Officials often arrest political critics for their posts on the internet. In 2019, Vietnam put on trial at least 14 people and sentenced them to between five and nine years in prison for "making, storing, disseminating or propagandizing information, materials and products that aim to oppose the State of the Socialist Republic of Vietnam."

Activists and bloggers face frequent physical assaults by officials or thugs who appear to work in coordination with authorities and enjoy impunity. In January, unidentified men abducted and hooded an anti-corruption campaigner, Ha Van

Nam, drove him around in a van while beating him, and then left him outside a hospital with two broken ribs. In June, rights activist Truong Minh Huong was attacked by four men in civilian clothes after meeting with families of several political prisoners. He suffered a broken rib.

In July, a group of rights activists was attacked in Nghe An province while traveling to a local prison to show support for political prisoners there on hunger strike protesting mistreatment. As the activists approached the prison, a large group of plainclothes men attacked them with sticks and helmets, broke their phones, and robbed them. Many were injured, including prominent blogger Huynh Ngoc Chenh and his wife, human rights activist Nguyen Thuy Hanh.

Police routinely place activists under house arrest or briefly detain them to prevent them from participating in meetings and protests or attending the trials of fellow activists. In March 2019, security agents prevented several writers and poets from leaving their houses to attend an award event organized by Van Viet, a literary group operating without government approval. In May, police blocked and prevented friends and colleagues trying to visit blogger Nguyen Huu Vinh, who just completed his five-year prison term. In May, security agents stopped former political prisoners Le Cong Dinh and Pham Ba Hai, and Cao Dai religious activist Hua Phi, from leaving their houses to meet with US diplomats prior to the 2019 US-Vietnam Human Rights Dialogue. In May, 44 activists and bloggers signed a public letter denouncing violations of their right to freedom of movement.

Police have also prevented rights campaigners from traveling abroad, sometimes citing vague national security reasons. In March, police barred political prisoner Nguyen Bac Truyen's wife, Bui Kim Phuong, from leaving Vietnam for Singapore. In June, pro-environment activist Cao Vinh Thinh was prohibited from leaving Vietnam for Thailand.

Freedom of Media and Access to Information

The Vietnamese government continues to prohibit independent or privately owned media outlets from operating. It exerts strict control over radio and television stations and printed publications. Criminal penalties apply to those who disseminate materials deemed to oppose the government, threaten national security, or promote "reactionary" ideas. Authorities block access to websites, frequently shut blogs, and require internet service providers to remove content or social media accounts deemed politically unacceptable.

Vietnam's problematic cybersecurity law went into effect in January 2019. The overly broad and vague law gives authorities wide discretion to censor free expression and requires service providers to take down content that authorities consider offensive within 24 hours of receiving the request.

In August, Minister of Information and Communications Nguyen Manh Hung claimed that Facebook had complied with "70 to 75 percent" of the government's requests to restrict content, up from "about 30 percent" previously. Among the materials Facebook removed, according to the ministry, were "more than 200 links to articles with content opposing the Party and the State."

The minister also claimed that Google complies with "80 to 85 percent" of its requests to restrict content on YouTube and other Google services, up from "60 percent" previously. The ministry did not disclose the sources of these figures or legal bases for these requests. The ministry said it has asked Facebook to limit some live-streaming capabilities and to "pre-censor" online content and remove ads "that spread fake news related to political issues upon request from the government."

Facebook told Human Rights Watch that its standards relating to takedowns and geographic blocking of content "are global." The process for taking down or blocking content, Facebook said in a written communication, is the "same in Vietnam as it is around the world." Reported content is first reviewed against the company's Community Standards; if it passes muster, Facebook says it will then assess whether the government request is legally valid under local law and international human rights law.

In May, a court in Dong Nai sentenced two Facebook users, Vu Thi Dung and Nguyen Thi Ngoc Suong, to six years and five years' imprisonment respectively, for reading and listening to materials on Facebook and distributing leaflets calling on people to protest against China and state oppression. They were charged with possessing materials "that aim to oppose the State of the Socialist Republic of Vietnam" under penal code article 117. Authorities convicted and sentenced rights activists Nguyen Ngoc Anh to six years in prison in June and Nguyen Nang Tinh to 11 years in prison in November, both for their posts on Facebook.

Freedom of Association and Assembly

Vietnam continues to prohibit independent labor unions, human rights organizations, and political parties. Organizers trying to establish unions or workers' groups face harassment, intimidation, and retaliation. In February, labor activist Nguyen Hoang Quoc Hung completed his nine-year prison term for helping to organize a strike in Tra Vinh province in 2010. Police immediately placed him under intrusive surveillance.

Under domestic and international pressure, the National Assembly passed a resolution in June to ratify International Labor Convention 98 on collective bargaining and the right to organize.

Authorities require approval for public gatherings, and systematically refuse permission for meetings, marches, or public gatherings they deem to be politically unacceptable.

Freedom of Religion

The government restricts religious practice through legislation, registration requirements, and surveillance. Religious groups are required to get approval from and register with the government, and operate under government-controlled management boards.

While authorities allow many government-affiliated churches and pagodas to hold worship services, they ban religious activities that they arbitrarily deem to be contrary to the "national interest," "public order," or "national unity," including many ordinary types of religious functions. Police monitor, harass, and sometimes violently crack down on religious groups operating outside government-controlled institutions. Unrecognized religious groups, including Cao Dai, Hoa Hao, Christian, and Buddhist groups, face constant surveillance, harassment, and intimidation. Followers of independent religious group are subject to public criticism, forced renunciation of faith, detention, interrogation, torture, and imprisonment.

In March, a court in Gia Lai province put Ksor Ruk on trial for following an unrecognized Dega Protestant sect and sentenced him to 10 years in prison. Ksor Ruk served a six-year prison sentence between 2005-2011 for the same violation. In August, Rah Lan Hip was convicted by the same court to seven years in prison, also for being involved with Dega Protestantism. In April 2019, police in Dien Bien province reported that they had successfully convinced "163 households including 1,006 people to have renounced an evil religion called 'Gie Sua.'" In May 2019, the United States Commission on International Religious Freedom published its report in which Vietnam is listed as a "Country of Particular Concern."

Key International Actors

China remains the most influential power on Vietnam. Maritime disputes continue to complicate the bilateral relationship of these Communist Party governments with similar repressive approaches to human rights. In July and August, China's survey ship Haiyang Dizhi 8 entered waters near Vanguard Bank, which caused protests in Hanoi. Vietnam appeared to benefit from the trade war between the United States and China. During the first eight months of 2019, China rose to become the largest direct investor in Vietnam.

Vietnam's relationship with the European Union improved significantly. In June, the EU and Vietnam signed the European-Vietnam Free Trade Agreement which will significantly boost trade between the two once ratified by both sides. Over the year, the EU raised concerns over convictions and imprisonment of several rights activists. In June, several members of the European Parliament wrote a letter urging the EU to press the Vietnamese government to improve its rights record.

The United States continues to expand ties with Vietnam. US Navy ships made several ports of call, and Vietnamese officers took part in US-led training, including in the United States. In February, President Donald Trump chose Vietnam as location for a summit with North Korean leader Kim Jong-un. In August, two senior US Air Force generals made a formal visit to the country, among other visits by US military officers as part of bilateral or regional events.

Australia's bilateral relationship with Vietnam continued to grow. In August 2019, Prime Minister Scott Morrison visited Hanoi, but failed to address human rights concerns publicly during his visit. Australia's concerns about Hanoi's human rights violations are relegated to an annual bilateral human rights dialogue, without any promising signs from Hanoi.

As the most important bilateral donor to Vietnam, Japan continues to remain silent on Vietnam's long history of rights repression. In May, Minister of Defense Takeshi Iwaya visited Vietnam to boost national defense cooperation between the two countries. In July, Prime Minister Shinzo Abe welcomed Prime Minister Nguyen Xuan Phuc in Tokyo. Human Rights Watch learned that human rights issues were not discussed in either meeting.

Yemen

The armed conflict in Yemen has resulted in the largest humanitarian crisis in the world; parties to the conflict have killed and injured thousands of Yemeni civilians. According to the Yemen Data Project, more than 17,500 civilians were killed and injured since 2015, and a quarter of all civilians killed in air raids were women and children. More than 20 million people in Yemen are experiencing food insecurity; 10 million of them are at risk of famine.

Since March 2015, Saudi Arabia and the United Arab Emirates (UAE) have led a coalition of states in Yemen against Houthi forces that, in alliance with former Yemeni President Ali Abdullah Saleh, took over Yemen's capital, Sanaa, in September 2014.

Over the past year, these alliances have fractured. Houthi forces, which still control much of northern and central Yemen, killed Saleh after clashes in December 2017. In southern Yemen, Saudi Arabia and the UAE have backed rival Yemeni groups—the Saudi-supported Yemeni government led by President Abdu Rabbu Mansour Hadi and the UAE-backed Southern Transitional Council (STC).

In August 2019, clashes occurred between Yemeni government and STC forces, with the UAE carrying out airstrikes in support of the STC. Across the country, civilians suffer from a lack of basic services, a spiraling economic crisis, abusive local security forces, and broken governance, health, education, and judicial systems.

Yemen's economy, already fragile prior to the conflict, has been gravely affected. Hundreds of thousands of families no longer have a steady source of income, and many public servants have not received a regular salary in several years. The country's broken economy has worsened the humanitarian crisis.

Coalition and Houthi forces have harassed, threatened, and attacked Yemeni activists and journalists. Houthi forces, government-affiliated forces, and the UAE and UAE-backed Yemeni forces have arbitrarily detained and forcibly disappeared scores of people. Houthi forces have taken hostages.

Since March 2015, the coalition has conducted numerous indiscriminate and disproportionate airstrikes killing thousands of civilians and hitting civilian structures in violation of the laws of war, using munitions sold by the United

States, United Kingdom, and others. Houthi forces have used banned antipersonnel landmines, recruited children, and fired artillery indiscriminately into cities such as Taizz, killing and wounding civilians, and launched indiscriminate ballistic missiles into Saudi Arabia.

Unlawful Airstrikes

Human Rights Watch has documented at least 90 apparently unlawful Saudi-led coalition airstrikes, including deadly attacks on Yemeni fishing boats that have killed dozens and appeared to be deliberate attacks on civilians and civilian objects in violation of the laws of war. At time of writing, according to the Yemen Data Project, the Saudi-led coalition has conducted more than 20,100 airstrikes on Yemen since the war began, an average of 12 attacks a day. The coalition has bombed hospitals, school buses, markets, mosques, farms, bridges, factories, and detention centers.

In August 2019, the Saudi-led coalition carried out multiple airstrikes on a Houthi detention center, killing and wounding at least 200 people. The attack was the single deadliest attack since the war began in 2015. Human Rights Watch has documented at least five deadly attacks by Saudi-led coalition naval forces on Yemeni fishing boats since 2018, killing at least 47 Yemeni fishermen, including seven children.

Indiscriminate Artillery Attacks

Houthi forces have repeatedly fired artillery indiscriminately into Yemeni cities such as Taizz and Hodeida, as well as launched indiscriminate ballistic missiles into Saudi Arabia, including Riyadh's international airport. Some of these attacks may amount to war crimes.

Children and Armed Conflict

Since September 2014, all parties to the conflict have used child soldiers under 18, including some under the age of 15, according to a 2019 UN Group of Eminent International and Regional Experts on Yemen report in 2019. According to the secretary general, out of 3,034 children recruited throughout the war in Yemen, 1,940—64 percent—were recruited by the Houthis.

In July, the UN secretary-general released his annual "list of shame" for violations against children in armed conflict during 2018. The list detailed that 729 children were killed or injured by Saudi-led coalition, 398 children were killed or injured by the Houthis, and the Yemeni government's forces were responsible for 58 child casualties.

Although the secretary-general listed the Saudi Arabia-led coalition in Yemen, he once again included the coalition in a category of parties taking steps to improve, despite overwhelming evidence that coalition forces killed and harmed children on a large scale in 2018.

Landmines

Houthi-planted landmines across Yemen continue to harm civilians and their livelihoods. Houthi forces have been using antipersonnel mines, improvised explosive devices (IED), and anti-vehicle mines along the western coast of Yemen, resulting in hundreds of civilian deaths and injuries. The landmines have also impeded aid workers' abilities to reach vulnerable communities. Landmine use has been documented in six governorates in Yemen since 2015. Since January 2018, at least 140 civilians, including 19 children, have been killed by landmines in just the Hodeidah and Taizz governorates.

Landmines emplaced in farmland, villages, wells, and roads prevent civilians from going about their daily life, especially farmers whose crops and clean water supply are affected. Demining efforts suffer from poor coordination, misinformation, and inadequate training, and do not comply with International Mine Action Standards (IMAS).

Arbitrary Detentions, Torture, and Enforced Disappearances

Houthi forces, the Yemeni government, the UAE, Saudi Arabia, and different UAE and Saudi-backed Yemeni armed groups have arbitrarily detained people, including children, abused detainees and held them in poor conditions, and abducted or forcibly disappeared people perceived to be political opponents or security threats.

The UN Group of Eminent Experts on Yemen found that UAE and UAE-backed forces practiced arbitrary detention and torture, including sexual violence, in detention facilities they controlled. The detainees subjected to abuse included suspected members of the Islamic State and Al-Qaeda in the Arabian Peninsula, according to investigative media and Human Rights campaigners' reports.

Since late 2014, Human Rights Watch has documented dozens of cases of the Houthis carrying out arbitrary and abusive detention, as well as enforced disappearances. Houthi officials have also used torture and other ill-treatment. Former detainees described Houthi officers beating them with iron rods and rifles and being hung from walls with their arms shackled behind them.

Mothers, sisters, and daughters of abducted men have demonstrated in front of prisons across major Yemeni cities, searching for their kidnapped sons, fathers, brothers, and other male relatives, organized under a group named "Mothers of Abductees Association." The association reported that there are 3,478 disappearance cases, at least 128 of those kidnapped have been killed.

Attacks on Civil Society

Houthis continue to harass and prosecute without legal basis academics, students, politicians, journalists and minority groups, including members of the Baha'i faith.

Blocking and Impeding Humanitarian Access

The Saudi-led coalition's restrictions on imports have worsened the dire humanitarian situation. The coalition has delayed and diverted fuel tankers, closed critical ports, and stopped goods from entering Houthi-controlled seaports. Fuel needed to power generators to hospitals and pump water to homes has also been blocked. Since May 2017, journalists and international human rights organizations, including Human Rights Watch have been facing restrictions by the Saudi-led coalition in using UN flights to areas of Yemen under Houthi control. The coalition has kept Sanaa International Airport closed since August 2016.

The Houthis have continued to impose severe movement restrictions, including the flow of aid, into Yemen's third largest city, Taizz, which has had a devastating impact on the local residents. Since 2015, the fight for control of Taizz between the Houthis and other armed groups has led to indiscriminate shelling and attacks against civilian areas.

The UN has accused the Houthis of stealing UN food aid in some areas controlled by the Houthi-authorities, and it promised to investigate corruption in its own agencies in the Yemen aid effort.

Violence against Women

Prior to the conflict, women in Yemen faced severe discrimination in law and practice. Warring parties' actions have exacerbated discrimination and violence against women and girls. Parties to the conflict have accused women of prostitution, promiscuity, and immorality using derogatory terms as part of their public threats and harassment against opponents. This increases risks of domestic violence, dissuades women and girls from movement outside the home, and seriously inhibits their participation in the economic and political spheres.

There is no minimum age of marriage and child marriage, which was prevalent in Yemen before the conflict. The practice has increased according to UNICEF.

Women, like men, have also faced torture and sexual violence during detention, according to the September report by the UN Group of Eminent International and Regional Experts, which verified 12 cases of sexual violence on five women, six men and a 17-year-old boy. Victims of sexual violence in Yemen are highly stigmatized, meaning vast underreporting is likely. Violence against women has increased 63 percent since the conflict escalated, according to the United Nations Population Fund.

Abuse of Migrants

Due to its position between the Gulf of Aden and the Red Sea, Yemen has been a key transit location for African migrants seeking employment opportunities in Saudi Arabia. In August, Human Rights Watch documented a network of smugglers, traffickers, and authorities in Yemen that kidnap, detain and beat Ethiopian migrants and extort them or their families for money upon their arrival.

Migrants who manage to elude capture and detention by Yemeni smugglers find their lives at increased risk as they travel through areas of active fighting in Yemen. Migrants' journeys are often delayed due to clashes between Houthi forces and groups aligned with the coalition. The Houthis and forces aligned with the Yemeni government have also detained, abused, and deported migrants.

About 260,000 Ethiopians, an average of 10,000 per month, were deported from Saudi Arabia to Ethiopia between May 2017 and March 2019, according to the IOM, and deportations have continued.

Of the estimated 500,000 Ethiopian migrants who were in Saudi Arabia when deportation campaigns began in 2017, it is likely that most of them passed through Yemen and faced the hardships documented by Human Rights Watch.

Accountability

Arms sales to the warring parties continue from Western countries such as the US, France, Canada, and others who risk complicity in war crimes and the humanitarian crisis in Yemen. In September, a UN Group of Eminent Experts on Yemen stated that "The parties to the conflict in Yemen are responsible for an array of human rights violations and violations of international humanitarian law. Some of these violations are likely to amount to war crimes."

The UN Group of Eminent Experts in September stated that several world powers, including the US, the UK, and France, may be complicit in war crimes in Yemen through arms sales and intelligence support given to the Saudi-led coalition.

The parties have failed to acknowledge any responsibility for violations and refuse to take any meaningful steps to remedy the situations in which they occur. This has resulted in a pervasive lack of accountability, which heightens disregard for the protection of the Yemeni population and foments a climate of impunity.

Despite mounting evidence of violations of international law by the parties to the conflict, efforts toward accountability have been inadequate. However, on June 20, 2019, the UK government agreed to suspend arms sales to Saudi Arabia after the UK Court of Appeal in London ruled that the government's refusal to consider Saudi Arabia's laws-of-war violations in Yemen before licensing arms sales was unlawful. The ruling requires the UK government to reconsider its decision on arms sales to Saudi Arabia. The UK is appealing the court decision.

Despite multiple congressional efforts in the US to end US arms sales to Saudi Arabia that could be used unlawfully in Yemen, President Donald Trump used his veto power to block such efforts and continued his support to Saudi Arabia, American's largest weapons buyer. France is under pressure to stop its arms sales to members of the Saudi-led coalition after a surge in its sales to Saudi Arabia.

A positive step was the extension of the mandate of war crimes investigators in Yemen by the UN Human Rights Council in September after the group found evidence of grave violations by all sides in the conflict.

Key International Actors

The UN-brokered peace talks between the Houthis and the Yemeni government in Sweden in December 2018 achieved a cessation of hostilities in the coastal towns of Hodeida, Salif, and Ras 'Issa. The Stockholm Agreement did not cover other ground fighting and the new military fronts. The US, the UK and other states that support Saudi Arabia and the United Arab Emirate militarily have also consistently been supporting the UN talks.

To date, the UN Security Council has used its sanctions regime against just one side, the Houthis, despite the fact that the Saudi-led coalition has committed numerous war crimes, according to research by the UN Group of Eminent Experts and groups like Human Rights Watch.

The murder of Saudi journalist Jamal Khashoggi in October 2018 galvanized international scrutiny of Saudi Arabia's international law violations in Yemen and other states' potential complicity in abuses through arms sales. Norway, Finland, the Netherlands and Germany reviewed or suspended their arms sales to members of the Saudi-led coalition. Other countries, notably the US, Canada, France and Australia are still supplying weapons or military equipment.

Zimbabwe

Despite President Emerson Mnangagwa repeatedly voicing his commitments to human rights reforms, Zimbabwe remained highly intolerant of basic rights, peaceful dissent, and free expression in 2019. During nationwide protests in mid-January, following the president's sudden announcement of a fuel price increase, security forces responded with lethal force, killing at least 17 people, raping at least 17 women, shooting and injuring 81 people, and arresting over 1,000 suspected protesters during door-to-door raids. In the months that followed, several civil society activists, political opposition leaders, and other critics of the government were arbitrarily arrested, abducted, beaten, or tortured. Little to no efforts were made to bring those responsible for the abuses to justice.

On September 6, Zimbabwe's long-time former ruler, Robert Mugabe, died in Singapore. Despite his 37 years in power having been marked by widespread human rights violations and the ruining of the country's economy, Mugabe was never held to account for his corrupt and abusive rule.

Freedom of Expression and Assembly

During nationwide protests against worsening economic conditions, security forces killed 14 men and 3 women between January 14 and February 5. Fourteen of the victims died from gunfire, while three died from injuries sustained following severe beatings. Most of those killed were from Epworth, Chitungwiza, and the Mbare and Warren Park suburbs of Harare, the capital. Security forces appeared to take advantage of the general unrest during the protests and crackdown to commit rape and other serious abuses. On January 15, the government instructed internet service providers to shut down access to social media and the internet. Access was restored on January 21.

Following the protests, security forces rounded up and detained hundreds of people, many of whom were brought before courts on charges of public violence and criminal nuisance.

The Zimbabwe Human Rights Commission investigated the protests and their aftermath and concluded in a report published in September that armed and uniformed members of the Zimbabwe National Army and the Zimbabwe Republic Police systematically tortured suspected protesters.

Following the protests, security forces intensified a crackdown on supporters of the opposition Movement for Democratic Change Alliance (MDCA), union leaders involved in organizing the protests, and civil society activists. Zimbabwe authorities frequently used section 22 of the Criminal Law (Codification and Reform) Act provision on "subverting a constitutional government" to prosecute those suspected of organizing protests. During 2019, several people were charged with "subverting a constitutional government." This includes seven activists arrested between May 20 and 27 at the Robert Mugabe International Airport in Harare on their return from a workshop on peaceful resistance and civil disobedience in the Maldives, hosted by the Centre for Applied Nonviolent Action and Strategies.

On September 14, as reported by the Zimbabwe Hospital Doctors Association, three unidentified men abducted Dr. Peter Magombeyi, a government employee and leader of the doctors' union that had organized a series of protests to demand better salaries for government doctors. Prior to his abduction, according to his family and colleagues who spoke to Human Rights Watch, Magombeyi received a text message from a local mobile number threatening him with disappearance. Zimbabwe's health minister, Obadiah Moyo, confirmed on September 16 that Magombeyi was missing and claimed to have activated all state security ministries to secure his whereabouts. After four days of torture and harassment, Magombeyi's abductors dumped him outside Harare.

The Mnangagwa administration made some efforts to amend or repeal repressive laws, including the Public Order and Security Act (POSA). The Maintenance of Peace and Order Bill (MOPO) was presented in parliament to replace the POSA, but the proposed new legislation potentially violates international human rights norms and standards, and is too similar to the POSA it seeks to replace. Under the MOPO bill, the exercise of the right to peaceful assembly is not fully guaranteed, as law enforcement agencies are still given broad regulatory discretion and powers.

Women's and Girls' Rights, Sexual Orientation, and Gender Identity

During 2019, Zimbabwe's Parliament debated a marriage bill, first introduced in January 2017, which is seen as a long-awaited chance for parliament to reconcile the country's marriage laws with its constitution. The proposed marriage law, which parliament has yet to finalize at time of writing, seeks to outlaw child marriage, but it does not adequately protect women's property at divorce. Without legal protection, many women could be left homeless or without a means of income after their marriage ends or if their husband dies.

Current laws on marriage and divorce do not conform to the country's constitution, which provides that spouses have equal rights and responsibilities.

The Matrimonial Causes Act technically allows for equitable distribution of property between spouses at divorce, considering direct and indirect contributions, such as raising children and caring for the family and household. But in practice, provisions of this law have not been fully applied and many women lose their property when a marriage ends or the husband dies, while men and their families keep everything.

Three years after Zimbabwe's Constitutional Court declared child marriage unconstitutional and set 18 as the minimum marriage age, the government has not put structures in place to implement the court's decision and ensure that girls under 18 are not forced into marriage. Zimbabwe's 2013 Constitution states that "no person may be compelled to enter marriage against their will" and requires authorities to ensure that children are not pledged into marriage, but the government has yet to amend or repeal all other existing marriage laws that still allow child marriage.

Section 73 of the Criminal Law (Codification and Reform) Act, 2004 punishes consensual same-sex conduct between men with up to one year in prison or a fine or both. This restrictive legislation contributes to stigma and discrimination against lesbian, gay, bisexual, and transgender (LGBT) people.

Right to Health

In September 2019, the Harare deputy mayor announced that the Harare City Council had shut down its main water treatment plant, known as Morton Jaffray, due to shortages of imported water treatment chemicals and low water levels at Lake Chivero. This exposed millions of Harare residents to the risk of waterborne diseases like cholera, which have ravaged the city in the past. The conditions that contributed to the spread of cholera during the latest outbreak in September 2018, and another outbreak a decade earlier, continued in 2019, namely: little access to potable water, inadequate sanitation services, and limited information on water quality.

Key International Actors

On March 4, US President Donald Trump extended sanctions against the Mnangagwa administration by one year, arguing that the new government's policies continued to pose an "unusual and extraordinary" threat to US foreign policy. Zimbabwe's immediate neighbors in the Southern African Development Community (SADC), including South Africa, supported the Mnangagwa administration and appeared to believe that the Zimbabwe economy is not performing well because of sanctions.

At the 39th SADC Summit held from August 17 to 18 in Tanzania, the summit elected President Mnangagwa as chairperson of the Organ on Politics, Defence and Security Cooperation. The SADC summit "noted the adverse impact on the economy of Zimbabwe and the region at large, of prolonged economic sanctions imposed on Zimbabwe, and expressed solidarity with Zimbabwe, and called for the immediate lifting of the sanctions to facilitate socio-economic recovery in the country."

Following a decision at the SADC summit, SADC member states on October 25 undertook various activities, including protests, to collectively voice their disapproval of the sanctions until the sanctions against Zimbabwe are lifted. The so-called sanctions are targeted sanctions on individual Zimbabweans, most of whom are government officials, and not economic sanctions that could affect the broader population, as the government has often suggested. The SADC leaders, however, failed to publicly address Zimbabwe's failure to respect human rights, good governance, and the rule of law, key pillars essential for the country's sustainable socio-economic recovery.

The United Nations special rapporteur on the rights to freedom of peaceful assembly and of association, Clément Nyaletsossi Voule, visited Zimbabwe in September and outlined a slew of "extremely disturbing" abuses by Zimbabwe's security forces in his preliminary findings, describing "reports of excessive, disproportionate and lethal use of force against protestors, through the use of tear gas, batons and live ammunition." Voule urged the government to thoroughly investigate the incidents and prosecute those responsible.

On October 1, the US Customs and Border Protection issued a ban on artisanal rough-cut diamonds from Zimbabwe's Marange diamond fields due to evidence of forced labor. US law prohibits importation of goods made with forced labor.